D1295182

Accounting for Economic Events

Accounting Publications of Scholars Book Co.

ROBERT R. STERLING, EDITOR

Accounting for Economic Events

Edgar O. Edwards, Ph.D.
Henry Gardiner Symonds Professor

Philip W. Bell, Ph.D.
William Alexander Kirkland Professor

L. Todd Johnson, Ph.D., C.P.A.
Associate Professor

Jesse H. Jones Graduate School of Administration
Rice University

Scholars Book Co.
4431 Mt. Vernon
Houston, Texas 77006

Library of Congress Cataloging in Publication Data

Edwards, Edgar O
    Accounting for economic events.

    Includes index.
    1. Accounting. I. Bell, Philip W., joint author.
II. Johnson, L. Todd, 1942–   joint author.
III. Title.
HF5635.E24   657   79-22971
ISBN 0-914348-28-0

Contents

PREFACE

ACCOUNTING FOR ECONOMIC EVENTS is designed for an introductory course in the principles of financial accounting as we believe such a course should be taught in a good undergraduate business school program or liberal arts economics curriculum. The book may also be useful for the type of "crash" introductory accounting course often given in the first year of graduate business or law school.

The book has been designed to convey the fundamentals of accounting practice but at the same time to raise for the student basic issues relating to the purposes and methodology of accounting so that these can be considered as the student proceeds. Hence, questions are raised throughout the book—especially in its later chapters—about the nature of current events to be recorded, the distinction between operating and holding activities, the use of accounting data to evaluate both internal and external decisions, and the adjustment of accounting data for specific price changes and for changes in the value of the monetary unit which is accounting's measuring rod.

The issues are important to the nonaccountant who will often be called upon to interpret accounting data during the course of his employment or for personal reasons. For the budding accountant, these issues will be focuses of much discussion in the years ahead, both within and outside the accounting profession. An early, rather than a later, exposure to them should strengthen the learning process and encourage an understanding of accounting purposes and functions as opposed to the unquestioning assimilation of "accepted principles."

The book is intended for a one-semester course. The material in it can be treated in three parts. Chapters 1-4 introduce accounting and the principles and practice of double-entry theory and, in an abbreviated fashion, run through the "accounting cycle" from initial journal entries to finished statements. Chapters 5-10 extend the student's thinking into critical problem areas—inventories and the cost of goods sold, plant assets and depreciation, long-run creditor and owner equities; pull this material together in worksheets to obtain finished position, income, and funds statements; and discuss the problems encountered in the consolidation of accounts.

As we move through these first ten chapters, questions are raised about limitations of traditional accounting principles and practice, but for the most part we stay within the realm of traditional practice. In particular, we keep to historical costs—we assume that there are no individual price changes to affect the accounts for a firm, nor any changes in the general price level. These matters are dealt with in Chapters 11–13, which concentrate on our approach to current value accounting and contrast it with the approaches of others.

We have prepared a solutions manual to the discussion questions and to the longer problem sets appearing at the end of each chapter. The manual is available free of charge to any teacher using or considering using the book. We would welcome in return comments, criticisms, and suggestions about the book and the manual.

We owe a debt of gratitude to many, many students—particularly to Bell's students at Haverford College, Lincoln University, Fisk University, the University of California at Santa Cruz, and Rice University, but also to Johnson's and Professor Robert R. Sterling's students at Rice. Their questions and complaints over the years of using a cumbersome typed manuscript forced us in part to make revisions that we believe have substantially improved the content. We are also much indebted to William Mackey, who assisted with an earlier draft, and to Howard Armitage, who at different stages made perceptive suggestions on the organization and content of Chapters 11–13. Mrs. Nora Quiocho of the Department of Accounting at Rice shouldered most of the burden of typing the final manuscript with amazing serenity and good cheer—she is a real friend. Many others too numerous to identify have also assisted at earlier stages. We are indebted to them and also to Mrs. J. C. Casey for her editorial work. Finally, each of us would like to express a special note of appreciation to our families who have actively supported us throughout the long gestation period of this book.

Edgar O. Edwards
Philip W. Bell
L. Todd Johnson
Houston, Texas

5 December 1978

CHAPTER 1

THE NATURE AND USES OF ACCOUNTING

ACCOUNTING PLAYS a pervasive part in our everyday lives. Most of us have checking accounts, charge accounts, expense accounts, and Social Security accounts. We are asked to account for our time and to maintain financial records for income tax purposes. Our daily newspapers feature stories of record sales, high earnings, large losses, and major bankruptcies. Whether we explicitly recognize it or not, accounting is an omnipresent element of our contemporary society.

WHAT IS ACCOUNTING?

The term *accounting* is derived from *account*. Recourse to any standard dictionary tells us that account is both a noun and a verb. As a noun, it is generally defined as a record of pecuniary transactions, an enumeration, an explanatory statement, or a recital of facts. As a verb, it means to keep records, especially of money, to give explanation, or to impute. The dictionary further defines accounting as the keeping and auditing of financial records. Hence, account and accounting have to do with the recording and keeping of facts, generally in terms of money, as a means and a basis for explanation.

Several organizations of accountants have attempted to define accounting. The American Institute of Certified Public Accountants (AICPA), the leading organization of practicing professional accountants in the United States, has stated that:

> Accounting is a service activity. Its function is to provide quantitative information, primarily financial in nature, about economic entities that is intended to be useful in making

1

economic decisions—in making reasoned choices among
alternative courses of action. Accounting includes several
branches, for example, financial accounting, managerial accounting, and governmental accounting.[1]

A similar definition has been proffered by the American Accounting
Association (AAA), an organization composed largely of accounting
professors and instructors. The Association's Committee to Prepare
a Statement of Basic Accounting Theory defined accounting as:

. . . the process of identifying, measuring, and communicating economic information to permit informed judgments and
decisions by users of the information. The concept of economics referred to in the preceding sentence holds that economics is concerned with any situation in which a choice must
be made involving scarce resources. The term "measurement"
includes the choice of an accounting method, as last-in,
first-out to measure inventory or deferral of federal income
taxes to measure income.[2]

Taken together, these two definitions provide a somewhat clearer
understanding of the nature of accounting than does a standard
dictionary or either of the two taken singly:

Accounting is the *measurement*—usually in monetary
terms—of *economic events* which pertain to *economic entities*
and which are relevant to the *informational needs of parties
who make and evaluate economic decisions with respect to those
economic entities,* parties to whom such measurements are
periodically communicated.

Because this definition is capable of being disaggregated into segments
corresponding to the italicized words and phrases, it will form the
core of our subsequent discussion. An understanding of these key
elements is essential before our skeletal outline of what accounting
is can become operational.

Measurement

In general usage, "measurement" has to do with quantifying the
dimensions of something, often in order to compare it with something

1. American Institute of Certified Public Accountants, *Statement of the Accounting
Principles Board No. 4: Basic Concepts and Accounting Principles Underlying Financial
Statements of Business Enterprises* (New York: AICPA, 1970), p. 17.
2. American Accounting Association, *A Statement of Basic Accounting Theory* (Evanston,
Illinois: AAA, 1966), p. 1.

else. Clearly in such an exercise the dimensions used must be applicable to the thing that is being quantified. You cannot measure the area of rectangular site A by multiplying its length by the width of rectangular site B. Nor can you measure the portion of land site A which has been cleared at time $(t + 1)$ by multiplying the length of land site A cleared at time $(t + 1)$ by the width of land site A that was cleared at time t. Second, a *unit* of measurement must be chosen, even if it is an arbitrary one, which is applicable to what is being measured, and it must be a unit that is generally understood if the results of measurement are to be communicated successfully to others. Pounds or grams cannot be used to measure area nor, in the United States, can hectares be used effectively, for this is not a unit that is generally employed in this country. Third, where comparisions are to be made, both of the above conditions must apply to each element (separately) being compared, and the unit applied to each element in the comparison must be the *same identical unit;* if two different units are employed, they must be such that one can be readily translated into the other. It would not be true to say that it was 48 degrees warmer today than yesterday at noon because it was 20 degrees (centigrade) yesterday and 68 degrees (Fahrenheit) today. The unit of measure was different on the two days, although both units were in "degrees." Since F = 32 + 1.8C, where F is temperature in degrees Fahrenheit and C is temperature in degrees centigrade, the temperature was in fact the same yesterday and today. Finally, the unit of measurement should transport over time without change.

In accounting measurement, the dimensions involved are normally price (p) and quantity (q), the one multiplied by the other to yield value. Ingots of steel and tons of coal cannot be added to obtain any meaningful total, but their values can be. The dollar is the accepted unit of value in the United States, for it is a generally understood unit. But prices in dollars and values in dollars produce special problems in the measurement exercise because individual prices are constantly changing, and the value of a dollar itself, in terms of the dollar's command over goods in general, is constantly changing because of changes in the general price level in the economy. Thus, in following our first rule of measurement above, in measuring dollar values *at a moment of time,* we use both the p and the q applicable to that moment of time. The value of a stock of inventory on December 31, 19X6, is the quantity we have on that date times the price existing in the market on that date, not the quantity on that date times the price existing on January 1, 19X6 (nor the price on that date times some earlier and, hence, now irrelevant quantity). In comparing values on two different dates, we must use the p's and q's appropriate for each date, just as in our land-clearing example above. The dimensions used in the measurement exercise must be appropriate for what is being measured—in this case, the p and q appropriate for the value on date 1 and the p and q appropriate for the value on date 2, respectively.

Further, in employing the dollar as our basic unit of measurement, over time we run into the problem that while our basic unit being used for comparisons looks the same—is the same piece of paper—it is clearly changing in terms of its command over goods ($100 in 1975 dollars was not worth as much as $100 in 1960 dollars). Forty-eight dollars held by an individual in 1975 might just buy the same basket of goods as $20 in 1960. It is like comparing 68°F today with 20°C yesterday. The temperature is actually the same today as yesterday, and the individual's wealth in this example, in *real terms,* was the same in 1975 as it was in 1960. In this sense the dollar, or any other monetary unit, does not travel well.

The fact that individual prices of particular goods change over time, so that the *current price* may differ sharply from the *historical (original purchase) price,* and the fact that the dollar itself changes in value over time, because of changes in the *general price level,* afford great difficulties for the process of measurement in accounting. We will treat these difficulties at some length in the last three chapters of this book. The difficulties necessitate, we feel, a fundamental recasting of the measurement which currently underlies basic accounting reports. Overcoming the difficulties, however, does not necessitate any fundamental change in ordinary, everyday accounting processes and techniques. Indeed, we shall argue that all "economic events" pertaining to "economic entities" must be recorded and kept in terms of traditional historical costs (e.g., in terms of prices and dollar values paid at time of purchase and sale) and that these records then must be adjusted or amended periodically to meet the difficulties posed above if the data are to meet the "informational needs of parties who make and evaluate economic decisions with respect to the economic entities involved." Before amending the measurement process of what goes on daily, we must thoroughly understand the process itself, and so the first ten chapters of the book will concentrate on this. In these chapters we will develop the accounting framework on the assumption—unless specifically noted—that prices do not change in the economy. Then, in Chapters 11–13 we will show how these results must be amended periodically if accounting data are to take account of the fact that prices *do* change in the economy all the time.

Economic Events

An *event* is an occurrence, something that happens. When the adjective *economic* is added, the occurrence is one concerning wealth or financial well-being. Thus, an economic event is an occurrence which alters wealth by changing its total or by modifying its composition in some manner.

Many economic events are signalled by *transactions,* the exchange of one item for another, as, for example, buying production materials for cash or obtaining cash in exchange for a note. Some may occur, however, in the absence of transactions, as, for example, losses following an earthquake, an increase in wages payable as payday approaches, or an increase in the value of land owned by the firm. We shall find that comprehensive conventional accounting records include nearly all (nontrivial) transactions, presumably because they are "objective" or "verifiable" events representing arms'-length changes between independent parties having opposing interests. Events not marked by transactions are less faithfully recorded, presumably because the changes in values involved are more difficult to verify. In the examples given above, the earthquake damage and the wages payable would typically be recorded but not the increase in value of land. Trivial economic events, such as the exchange of a $5 bill for five $1 bills, are not recorded on the grounds that the cost of doing so exceeds any informational benefits that can be realized.

Economic Entities

In lay usage, *entity* generally refers to a "thing"; but in the lexicon of accountants it has a more precise meaning, referring to either an individual or an organization. To be sure, not all individuals and organizations are accounted for; therefore, the adjective *economic* is appended. An informal neighborhood bridge club, for example, may very well be regarded as an organization—therefore, an entity—but it is probably not engaged in economic or financial activities and, accordingly, would not be subject to accountability. On the other hand, individuals and organizations engaged in economic activities would qualify as *economic entities.* Accounting for individual people as economic units should be self-evident, but organizations may not always be so obvious.

The difficulty in dealing with organizations stems at least in part from the fact that economic entities need not be legal entities. A corporation is a legal entity—a "legal being"—but a proprietorship (a business owned by one person) is not. Under the law, the proprietor's

personal properties and activities are inextricably commingled with those
of his or her business. By contrast, a corporation's affairs are legally
considered to be separate and distinct from those of its owners; in
effect, a corporation is a "person" in the eyes of the law. Thus, in
the case of the corporation, the legal and economic entities could be
one and the same, whereas the proprietorship could be regarded as
an economic entity for accounting purposes but not as a legal entity.

The matter is further complicated by the fact that an economic entity
may be divided into components (which are themselves economic entities)
or combined with other economic units to form larger units. To illustrate,
a corporation might be divided into divisions or departments, each
of which could be accounted for separately. For other purposes, the
corporation itself might be combined with other corporations into a
"family" of companies, as would be the case when the corporations
are under common ownership by another organization or an individual.
Taken even a step further, all businesses might be combined into the
business sector of the national economy. The possible aggregations
and disaggregations are almost limitless.

For our purposes, *an economic entity is any center of economic activity
having particular purposes or goals.* Because a given center of economic
activity may have multiple purposes or goals, it may be subdivided
into components or combined into larger units that correspond with
each particular purpose. And it may sometimes still be useful to divide
or combine even if all parts of the resultant entity have a single purpose
or goal. These purposes or goals are determined by the recipients
or *users* of accounting information, to whom we have referred as the
"parties who make and evaluate economic decisions." Thus, the delineation of an economic entity is a function of the user's particular
informational needs, just as this factor governs the nature of the
economic event to be recorded and reported on. Accordingly, the
identification of the users of accounting data is essential to the definitions
of both economic events and economic entities.

Users

It is probably no overstatement to say that virtually everyone is a
user of accounting information at one time or another. The widely
diverse array of individuals has spawned a similar assortment of
organizations designed to fulfill human wants and needs. Indeed,
organizations have no reason for existence other than for the fulfillment
of human desires.

For accounting purposes, a simplistic dichotomy is made of human behavior—that which is primarily oriented toward the making of a profit and that which is not primarily profit-motivated. This distinction leads to a similar dichotomy of organizations: (1) profit-oriented and (2) nonprofit. Business organizations—proprietorships, partnerships, corporations, and certain ventures—comprise the profit-oriented sector while all other types of organizations make up the nonprofit group. The latter, for example, might include individuals, the local YMCA, the United Fund, a church or religious group, a municipality, or the federal government.

Users of business accounting. Those who use accounting measurements of economic events pertaining to business interests are primarily motivated by having either direct or indirect economic interests in the business firm. Obviously, this group would include investors, both creditors and owners, who have committed their capital to the enterprise in the expectation (or hope) of receiving a return on their capital. Management certainly must use accounting information in order to make decisions as to the future course of the firm and to control its present activities. Employees, suppliers, customers, and taxing authorities, too, use accounting data regarding the firm in order to assess their various economic relationships with the business.

Others may be said to have an indirect economic interest in the firm. Some individuals and organizations with indirect interests provide an array of services for these who have actual or potential direct interests in the firm. Financial analysts and the stock exchanges are concerned with the allocation of capital in the business sector so as to achieve maximum welfare for investors. Trade associations seek information which will advance the cause of the industries they represent as well as their member firms. Labor unions, working on behalf of their members who are employees, seek to obtain the most favorable terms in contract negotiations with the firm. Others seek information on the firm in order to assess the social benefits and social costs involved in its operations. Regulatory agencies of the government, for example, are (or should be) concerned with the well-being of the public at large and are engaged in rate-setting, the enforcement of antitrust legislation, consumer protection, product safety, environmental problems and pollution, conservation, and the like.

Users of nonbusiness accounting. Accounting for persons and organizations not seeking to earn a profit encompasses a wide array, from the individual or family merely trying to live within its income all the way to the federal government. The great variety of "private associations" in the United States, which de Tocqueville noted in the 1830s, is even more conspicuous today, and their funding—from the local American Legion post or community action group to the American Medical Association or League of Women Voters—must be accounted for in some manner so as to fulfill the informational needs of members of the organization. This diversity of entities and users in the nonprofit category naturally requires both variety and flexibility in the accounting frameworks employed.

The accounting for nonprofit entities is concerned largely with the control of resources entrusted to them. Many of these organizations are sustained by tax-exempt contributions (as with the Red Cross and YWCA) or tax revenues (as with governmental units at the local, state, and national levels) and purport to serve the public interest. Many people have a legitimate interest—sometimes recognized, sometimes not—in the affairs of such organizations. Voters, parents, students, and taxpayers, for instance, may all be interested in the expenditure of school board funds; taxpayers as well as direct contributors to tax-exempt organizations will be interested in such organizations because the tax-exempt status makes taxpayers indirect contributors. Such organizations must be responsive to the needs of all of these groups in their reporting. But while there are these special types of problems related to accounting for particular types of nonprofit institutions, problems which are different from those related to accounting for business enterprises, the *basic principles* of accounting—double-entry theory, cash versus accrual accounting, accounting for inventories and long-term assets, accounting for short- and long-term liabilities, even problems of consolidation of accounts, and most certainly current value accounting (in effect, the substance of this book)—all apply to problems of nonprofit institutions as well as profit institutions. Nonprofit institutions are just as concerned as profit institutions with their "wealth" position at a moment in time; and while they are more concerned with the way revenue is spent rather than with maximizing the difference between revenues and expenses, they are just as concerned as business with minimizing expenses in the course of achieving their own objectives.

Periodic Communication

The communication of accounting measurements to users is the final step in the process of accounting. Once the economic entities to be accounted for have been defined in terms of user needs and the economic events associated with those entities have also been reduced to those relevant to users, then communication must occur to facilitate the making and evaluation of economic decisions.

Since much accounting data are recorded daily, communication theoretically could be just as frequent, and to some extent it is. Managers and administrators of economic entities typically need information on a daily or at least weekly basis in order to operate the organization. But many users, especially those not intimately involved with the day-to-day activities of the organization, have less persistent informational requirements because the decisions they must make and evaluate transpire with less frequency. Moreover, users internal to the entity are generally able to specify precisely the data they need as informational inputs whereas those external to the firm typically cannot. As a consequence, internal users can avoid being bombarded by data on a daily basis by asking only for that which is germane to their needs. External users, not in a position to make such specifications, would likely be inundated were accounting measurements provided to them on a daily basis. Some compromise is clearly mandated with respect to data transmittals to outside parties.

In an attempt to resolve this issue, accountants have adopted the periodicity concept; for accounting purposes, the continuum of events of economic entities is divided into time periods for communication purposes. Thus, accounting measurements are aggregated at the end of a period and disseminated to users in the form of accounting reports, more formally known as *financial statements.* These financial statements purport to contain information regarding the entity's activities during the period and its status at the close of the period. The time period most commonly selected for reports to external users is a year, although quarterly (three-month) reports are becoming increasingly available. It should be noted that the selection of the year as the basic accounting period does not necessarily mandate the use of a calendar year ending on December 31. Any other twelve-month period may be selected and these are known as *fiscal years.* Many governmental units, for example, have fiscal years extending from July 1 to the subsequent June 30. Firms that have a seasonal pattern of activity will often select a fiscal year that closes during the slack season when the accounting staff is not deeply involved with on-going activities.

Some Basic Concepts and Conventions of Business Accounting

Up to this point, our discussion has revolved around a generalized accounting model which would be equally applicable to profit-oriented and nonprofit entities. From this point on we will focus upon profit-

oriented entities—business firms—to the exclusion of nonprofit entities.
We do so because, compared to the accounting for nonprofit entities,
business accounting:

1. is more highly developed in both theory and practice;
2. lends itself more readily to uniform treatment, thereby facilitating comparisons between entities and over time;
3. is more widely used as a source of economic information;
4. contains the major unsolved problems in accounting theory as well as in practical applications; and
5. provides most of the basic concepts needed for, and readily transferable to, nonprofit entities.

If the more complex form of (profit-oriented) accounting is mastered,
then adjustment to less complicated types (such as nonprofit) should
be relatively easy.

When we turn our attention exclusively to the problems of accounting
for profit-oriented entities, our generalized model must become somewhat more specific. In particular, we must augment our list of accounting
concepts explained earlier as applicable to all entities by adding to
it certain concepts which are peculiar to accounting for businesses.

The Income Concept

Central to the activities of business entities (as opposed to other entities)
is the intent to make profits. Hence, accountants seek to measure profit
(or loss) as a "gauge" of success. When used comparatively (both within
and among firms and over time), this gauge and the information
underlying it serve as the basis for the evaluation of past decisions
and the making of new ones by parties both internal and external
to the business entity itself. Thus, the notion of a profit and its
attendant measurement lie at the core of business accounting.

Profit or income (accountants usually prefer the latter term, leaving
the former to economists) is generally regarded as "a change in material
welfare." For an individual, this translates into the change in that person's
wealth that would have occurred over a period had his or her consumption been nil (i.e., income is consumption plus saving). Income for
the business firm can be regarded as that part of the change in its
wealth that follows from its business activities. Hence, income for the
firm can be determined by analyzing changes in *either* its wealth *or*
its business activities. Accountants typically utilize the latter approach;
therefore, the concepts we now discuss are essential to the definition
of income as it is determined through an examination of business
activities.

The Matching Concept: Two Approaches

In order to measure the success or failure of business activities, utilizing the criterion of profit, accountants have adopted the concept of matching *efforts* with *accomplishments*. Business activities include the purchase of inputs (labor and material, for example), their transformation into saleable outputs (products or services), and the sale of some or all of the outputs available for sale. The acquisition of inputs and their transformation entail *costs* to the firm, which are the firm's *efforts;* its *accomplishments* are ultimately measured by its total *revenues.* For a short-lived firm, say, a Christmas tree buying-and-selling venture, *income* over the firm's lifetime can be defined as revenues minus costs (assuming that whatever is left unsold at the end of the venture has no value). The definition of income is not so clear, however, if we attempt to define it for any period shorter than the entire life of the Christmas tree venture. But that is precisely the task that the accountant must address. What are the difficulties and the choices?

Consider that, in a short time period, costs may be incurred (the purchase, transportation, and "flocking" of Christmas trees) without any sales being made. Can it be said that the firm has accomplished nothing (i.e., that no revenue has been generated)? Clearly the firm, being income-oriented, buys inputs because it thinks that they have a value in its possession equal to or greater than the cost entailed. Similarly, the firm may believe that the process of transformation (transportation to the sales lot, flocking) adds value more rapidly to the original inputs than would be indicated by the costs of transformation alone. Indeed, during that process and at its end, the firm may see that market values of its outputs at various stages of completion exceed the cumulative costs incurred, yet the firm may choose to retain the outputs for what it thinks will be a larger income upon later sale. Viewed in this manner, the generation of income can be considered as a process which is as continuous as the transformation process itself. The event of sale in this view would simply confirm the incomes or accomplishments already recorded as the production process proceeded. Under this approach, which we will term the "market value approach," income is considered to be generated as market values of outputs grow over and above the costs incurred to produce them. Therefore, income for any period is defined as increases in value occurring during the period minus the costs incurred during the period. This approach is appealing and realistic in many respects, but the means of measuring increases in value may be precarious and ambiguous. The measurement may entail accepting subjective judgments by the firm's management or having values defined by rejected opportunities. These considerations have led accountants to insist on what is regarded as more "objective" measures of value as a basis for determining and recognizing income, namely, *revenue realization.*

Under the revenue realization approach, income is recognized—regardless of one's view of how it is generated—as the firm's outputs are converted into cash form (or near-cash form) by means of sale. Income for any period is defined as revenues realized during the period minus the expenses incurred to produce those revenues. Although determining precisely when realization occurs can be troublesome, the critical problem with this approach is to define expenses. This is done by identifying those costs, whenever incurred, that have been embodied in the outputs sold to produce the revenues. Only those costs are classified as expenses. Hence, expenses are those costs that are matched to the realized revenues they are thought to have generated. Costs incurred to produce outputs that remain unsold at the end of the period are "stored" until the period in which they are finally sold, at which time they, too, will become expenses and be matched against the revenues realized. Stored costs are termed "unexpired costs" until they are matched with revenues when they become expenses, or "expired costs." However, in order to assign certain costs to match revenues of the period (leaving the remaining costs to attach to outputs unsold at the end of the period), accountants are forced to adopt schemes for cost allocation. Because allocations of some types of costs cannot be made by reference to objective events in the market place, some cost allocations must usually be arbitrary in character. Thus, the processes of both devising such allocation schemes and selecting one for application in a particular instance necessarily entail *subjective* judgments on the part of the accountant and/or management. It is not at all clear, therefore, that the revenue realization approach to the matching concept is indeed more objective than the market value approach.

For a comparison of the two approaches to matching and their attendant impact upon income, see Table 1-1. Note that both the accomplishments and efforts that are to be matched against one another, while containing certain common elements (in particular, R and C), each have unique elements as well (ΔM and ΔC). Thus, the two incomes that emerge from the matchings are likely to differ from one another in any given period, the difference being as follows:

Market Value Income $-$ Revenue Realization Income $=$ Difference

$$[(R + \Delta M) - C] \quad - \quad [R - (C - \Delta C_u)] \quad = \text{Difference}$$

By rearranging terms, we have:

$$[(R - C) + \Delta M] - [(R - C) + \Delta C_u] = \Delta M - \Delta C_u.$$

TABLE 1-1

*COMPARISONS OF TWO APPROACHES OF MATCHING
EFFORTS WITH ACCOMPLISHMENTS*

	Market Value Approach	Revenue Realization Approach
Accomplishments:		
Market value of outputs converted to cash (or near-cash form) by means of sale during period	R	R
Plus: Excess of market values of inputs and outputs held at end of period over those at beginning of period	ΔM	
Total Accomplishments	$R + \Delta M$	R
Minus Efforts:		
Costs incurred during period for inputs	C	C
Minus: Excess of unexpired costs of inputs and outputs held at end of period over those at beginning of period		ΔC_u
Total Efforts	C	$C - \Delta C_u$
Equal Income	$(R + \Delta M) - C$	$R - (C - \Delta C_u)$

The two incomes are therefore identical to each other except for the prices attached to inputs and outputs held at the beginning and end of the period; in one case, the prices of inputs and outputs are measured by reference to market prices, while in the other case they are measured on the basis of unexpired costs.

Over the lifetime of the business entity, the sums of the periodic incomes of each of the two approaches will be equal to one another. Although this may initially appear counter-intuitive, upon further reflection the equality should be more obvious. When we consider income over the life of the entity, we need consider only the R's and C's; the ΔM's and ΔC_u's can be ignored. At the beginning of the first period of the firm's life and again at the end of the last period, the firm holds neither inputs nor outputs; thus, no items exist to be priced at all.

Consider the Christmas tree buying-and-selling venture referred to earlier. At the beginning of the venture's life, the firm has no trees, no flocking materials, nothing. At the end of its life, either it will have no trees on hand or else the trees on hand will be worthless (i.e., market price = unexpired cost = zero). Thus, under *either* approach to matching, income will consist *only* of R's and C's. It is when we attempt to measure income for a period shorter than the venture's entire life that some trees (flocked and unflocked), flocking materials, and so forth, would be on hand. These inputs and outputs would then have to be priced but by different methods, market price or unexpired cost. Only in extremely rare circumstances would market prices equal unexpired costs; therefore, the incomes would likely differ under each of the two approaches.

Accountants have opted for the revenue realization approach to the matching concept on the basis of its supposed objectivity. In the accounting literature, most discussions of the application of the matching concept are therefore concerned with (1) the determination of the "critical event" at which revenues are thought to be realized, and (2) the allocation of costs as between expired (expenses) and unexpired (assets). We discuss the revenue realization problem in the next section; the problem of cost allocation pervades most chapters in this book.

The Revenue Realization Convention

In order for costs to be allocated between expired and unexpired, revenues must first be defined. This is done in terms of *realization*. In a strict sense, realization means the conversion of outputs into cash, but accountants have broadened its interpretation to include conversion to near-cash as well. To determine when a revenue is realized (and thus recorded in the accounting records of the entity), accountants have posited two general tests that must be satisfied before a revenue can be recognized in the accounting records of a business entity.

The first test is: *The provision of goods and/or services to customers must be substantially complete before revenue may be recognized.* In essence, this test precludes the anticipation of profit from the sale of goods as yet undelivered or the provision of services as yet unperformed. Otherwise, profits which may never materialize could be recorded prematurely.

The second test is: *In order to be recognized, revenue must be measurable with a reasonable degree of objectivity and certainty.* Without applying this test, it is thought that numerous *ex post* adjustments and corrections of the accounting records would be necessitated. This lack of precision would, of course, carry over to the costs that are allocated as expenses to be matched against the revenues recorded. It is feared that such imprecisions might reach such a magnitude that financial statements might be viewed as unreliable and, hence, rendered suspect.

Taken together, these two caveats effectively delimit the recognition of revenue to the *point of sale.* At that time, provision of goods and/or services is usually complete and virtually all important uncertainties will have been resolved (all or most related costs will have been incurred and the amount of revenue—the sales price—will have been fixed, especially if the sale was made for cash) by the process of arm's-length bargaining between independent parties (the buyer and seller). To be sure, there are exceptions to this general rule wherein revenues are recognized either prior or subsequent to the point of sale, but these exceptions must meet both of the tests outlined. And they are just that—exceptions—for far and away the vast preponderance of revenues are recognized at the point of sale. In the last three chapters, we shall raise questions about continued adherence to this concept, but until then we will abide by it as does, for the most part, the conventional theory and practice of accounting.

The Money Convention

We have already noted that the purchasing power of money may change over time and that money as a unit of measurement may vary in real value, making intertemporal comparisons difficult. Nevertheless, the accountant does use money as the unit of measurement and keeps records as though the real value of money were constant over time. This *money convention* does not deny that money changes in value but does state that it is not a proper function of accounting to account for changes in the value of the monetary unit itself. The argument is that *precise* measurement of such changes is not possible.

The Going Concern Convention

The final item indigenous to business accounting is that of the *going concern convention,* otherwise known as the *continuity convention.* Under this convention, it is assumed that, *lacking evidence to the contrary, the business entity has an indefinite life; continuance rather than imminent liquidation is the reasonable expectation.*

Continuity is a demonstrated fact of life, particularly when the business entity being accounted for is a large, publicly-held corporation. Many of these behemoths continue to exist (and, indeed, flourish and expand) long after their founders, investors, managers, and accountants have passed on and while other firms have wasted away, failed, or been absorbed by the more successful. The financial statements of all business entities, while prepared in accordance with the continuity convention, should disclose to users information for assessing prospects of success or failure. In fact, certain ratios drawn from traditional financial statements prepared in accordance with the going concern convention have been found to be rather accurate predictors of insolvency and bankruptcy. In addition, if profit (or lack thereof) is a gauge of efficiency, those firms less efficient than others should be readily apparent to users of financial statements, even if those statements employ the convention of continuity.

For now, we will reserve our judgment as to whether or not the continuity or going concern convention is essential to business accounting. We can say that it appears to be harmless at least, provided that users are cognizant of its existence—not an unreasonable prerequisite for what the law terms "the reasonably prudent man," especially one dealing in financial matters.

BUSINESS ACCOUNTING MODELS AND SYSTEMS

The concepts and conventions just discussed underlie the accounting for all business firms as the preceding concepts underlie accounting in general, be it for profit-oriented or nonprofit entities. Our focus was upon accounting *models,* the generalized accounting model for all entities and the specific accounting model common to all business entities.

When we turn our attention to a particular entity, such as Exxon or General Motors, we then focus upon a particular application of the overall model. Such applications are known as accounting *systems,* which are unique unto themselves just as each entity is itself unique. One accounting system may be quite similar to another, but that is merely a reflection that the two entities—being perhaps in the same industry—are also quite similar. The design of a system of accounts is clearly a fundamental task which can be accomplished only after careful consideration of the needs of the users and the resources available for the development and implementation of the system. The system which is ultimately established must be flexible and subject to redesign whenever the nature of information demanded is altered. A rigid and outmoded system will frustrate the efforts of the most conscientious accountant. Business accounting systems may be subclassified by: (1) the type of business involved, (2) the form of business organization, and (3) the size of the entity.

Type of business conducted. The subclassification by type of business is a more common distinction. Businesses may be divided into three groups: trading, manufacturing, and servicing (including banking and finance). Accounting techniques will vary substantially among these three types of enterprises and within each subclassification as well.

For firms in retail or wholesale trade, accounting is largely concerned with the purchase and resale of finished goods. Characteristically, plant and equipment are negligible in comparison to merchandise inventories (a building and its counters, perhaps, but these may be rented) and, except for very large enterprises, cost accounting will normally not be an important aspect of the accounting system of the business.

Of the three types of business accounting, manufacturing accounting is the most complex. Inventories for manufacturing firms include raw materials and goods in process as well as finished goods; buildings, machinery, and equipment are likely to be important parts of the business, a fact which leads to special accounting problems with respect to making allowances for their wear and tear; and cost and pricing problems are much more difficult than in wholesaling or retailing.

Some firms may conduct a highly integrated set of business activities extending from raw material production through its transformation into finished products and, hence, to the final retail sale of those products through its own trading outlets. The accounting system appropriate to such vertically integrated firms is unusually complex because effective control requires a high degree of coordination and effective evaluation requires the identification of suitable prices at which components are transferred from one segment of the enterprise to another. Conglomerates, which embrace many kinds of often unrelated business activities, raise accounting problems at the center that are largely financial in nature, operating control often being delegated to activity-related subsidiaries.

Accounting problems with respect to banks, insurance companies, investment houses, finance companies, and the like, are more nearly comparable with those of trading establishments than manufacturing concerns. Financial enterprises trade in claims to goods, rather than in goods themselves as is the case in retailing and wholesaling. Nevertheless, since claims may mature after varying lengths of time and are subject to different kinds of risks, the accounting problems of valuation and income determination are often more complex and substantially different in nature from those typical in retailing and wholesaling.

Form of business organization. Business accounting systems also may vary markedly according to the form of business organization adopted.

The problems involved in accounting for intricacies of stock transactions of a corporation are not encountered in the sole proprietorship or partnership. On the other hand, the definition of income and its division among owners may be much more complicated in the partnership than in the corporation.

Size of concern. Finally, the accounting system of a small concern may be quite different from that of a large one. The distinctions here relate almost entirely to the complexity of bookkeeping and/or data processing techniques and the volume of records required. Thus, computerized data processing is more common among large firms than it is among small ones.

Accounting as applied in these different types of business firms involves differences in techniques but not in general principles. Most of the differences will be touched upon in various sections of this book; the principles of accounting which are developed, however, are generally applicable to all types of business accounting problems.

USES OF ACCOUNTING INTERNAL TO THE FIRM

We have already touched upon the topic of users of accounting data earlier in this chapter as part of a more general discussion of the nature of accounting. Before concluding our introduction to business accounting, it is appropriate for us to reconsider and expand upon our earlier brief discussion by examining the uses of business accounting data with greater specificity.

The demand for data. The need for information of the type collected by the business firm derives largely from the change and uncertainty which characterize our economy. If it were known that tomorrow would be the same as today, the need for many kinds of information, such as the effects of changing prices on sales volume or estimates of alternative production costs or profit, would either be eliminated or reduced to one measurement which would suffice for all time. Most of the economic problems which give rise to the many demands for the uses of accounting data collected and interpreted on a continuing basis would be nonexistent. Decision making and control, two of the major functions of management, take on their full significance only under the pressure of uncertain change.

Uncertainty, at the same time that it multiplies the uses of accounting information, complicates accounting processes and imposes severe li-mitations on the accuracy of accounting results. The large size, continuous existence, and varied operations of the present-day business corporation magnify these difficulties. Accounting must provide management with the essential data for evaluating past decisions, for the making of new decisions, for the routine control of day-to-day operations, and for discovering and correcting honest errors and dishonest behavior—all this for organizations of astonishing complexity. And, of course, managers must thoroughly understand the data and the accounting procedures used to collect and report the data if they are to be able to make good use of the data. Further, these data are essential for accounting reports to· the owners of the business, a group which in most large corporations is distinct from management in both composition and interest.

The evaluation of past decisions. The evaluation of past decisions is necessary for several reasons. It is a means for determining success or failure. It also enables management to compare the results achieved by its firm with the results achieved by similar firms so that the degree of success or failure can be analyzed. Perhaps more important, management can isolate its past mistakes and take steps to correct them and to reduce the risk of their repetition. Prices that have been set too high can be lowered; an attempt to introduce a new product can be discontinued or the nature of the attempt altered; an organization of production which has proved efficient in one plant may be applied to another. Thus, the evaluation of past decisions not only indicates success or failure but is an essential part of the learning process of a successful management team.

Decision making. Accounting, in conjunction with statistics, economics, and engineering, must also provide data for the making of new decisions. Drawing on past experience and forecasting techniques, estimates of sales volume, selling prices, and production costs of new products must be prepared not only for one selling or production method but for several alternatives. If a new plant is contemplated, the accountants must gather data regarding freight rates, materials prices, labor supply, and so forth, at alternate locations; the accountant, with engineering assistance, must estimate the efficiencies of plants of different sizes; with the statistician the accountant must estimate sales potential over time and in different market areas.

Other types of decisions require the same careful preparation of data. The number of people to employ, the granting of a wage increase, the use of a different material in production, or a change in advertising policy will involve the accountant in one way or another. The accounting staff is a principal source of data upon which such decisions are based.

Control. An accounting system properly conceived and carefully maintained is also a necessary tool for management control. The proper inventory to carry, the provision of checks and double-checks for theft and errors, and the determination of departmental or product efficiency all involve the accountant who must provide management with pertinent data. A firm may incur losses because its inventory is too large or because of petty pilfering. Its earnings may be reduced because the profit on one item obscures losses on others.

USES OF ACCOUNTING EXTERNAL TO THE FIRM

While accounting data were at one time considered to be confidential and limited primarily to management with occasional morsels tossed to owners and creditors, the rise of the large corporation has stimulated political, social, and economic interest in business activities. The development of stock exchanges gave an early impetus to accurate, detailed reporting, but professional and governmental groups have since assumed key positions in developing the extensive disclosure of business accounting data which exists today.

The Evolution of Accounting Principles

While internal users of accounting data are able to specify the types of information they need and to obtain such data in the form of "customized" reports, the same is not true for external users. Instead, they must be satisfied with general purpose financial statements that are expected to fulfill a multiplicity of needs, regardless of the relationships the external user has with the firm (stockholder, creditor, employee, and so forth). Such general purpose financial statements are founded upon "generally accepted accounting principles," the body of concepts, assumptions, conventions, postulates, axioms, and standards that accountants employ in developing financial information.

A principle is regarded as "generally accepted" when it has "substantial authoritative support." This support may be from different sources. First, because accounting has developed historically as a pragmatic art, support may be based on *precedents*—what other accountants have done in identical or analogous situations in the past. In this sense, substantial authoritative support is much like the "common law" which has evolved over the years on a case-by-case basis. However, precedents often are in conflict with one another. One accountant may have treated in one fashion an identical situation which another accountant treated differently.

To rectify this dilemma, professional accounting organizations have developed a body of rules governing financial reporting in a manner similar to the development of "statutory law." During this century, the organization playing the predominant role in the United States has been the American Institute of Certified Public Accountants (AICPA). Since 1939, its Committee on Accounting Procedure has issued more than 50 "bulletins" concerning the treatment of particular accounting problems. In 1960, the Institute replaced the Committee on Accounting Procedure with the Accounting Principles Board (APB) which, until its demise in 1973, issued more than 30 "opinions" on accounting matters. Finally, in response to criticism of the APB, the AICPA and other concerned organizations established the Financial Accounting Standards Board (FASB) to promulgate "standards" of financial reporting. The collection of bulletins, opinions, and standards issued by the FASB and its predecessors constitutes in large part the "statutory law" of accounting.[3] Other "statutory laws" of accounting may be found in the pronouncements of the various government agencies—particularly the Securities and Exchange Commission (SEC)—as we will discuss shortly.

Substantial authoritative support for generally accepted accounting principles may also be found in the accounting literature as a whole. This includes textbooks, monographs, research studies, and journal articles authored by academics and practitioners. A consensus of opinion among writers—particularly those regarded as eminent authorities in the field—may constitute sufficient authoritative support for an accounting principle to be "generally accepted," particularly when the "common law" and "statutory law" of accounting are silent as to the issue in question.

Thus, the development of generally accepted accounting principles has been central to the standardization of accounting data and financial reports. The process is an on-going one because the collection is incomplete and in many cases internally inconsistent. Compared to its professional counterparts, such as law and medicine, accounting is in a comparatively virgin state, and much work remains to be done before it attains maturity.

The Influence of Government on Accounting Principles

Certain kinds of firms are of sufficient public interest to warrant a measure of government control over their operations. In order to

---

3. See, for example, *AICPA Professional Standards—Accounting—Current Text* (Chicago: Commerce Clearing House, published annually).

facilitate this control and to report its effects to the people, the government requires detailed periodic reports from various utilities such as gas; electricity; rail, truck, and air transportation; and communication.

Of the government agencies to which companies must submit periodic reports, the Securities and Exchange Commission is one of the most important. The SEC was established in 1934 in order to enforce legislation under the Securities Act of 1933 and the Securities Exchange Act of 1934 requiring the full and open disclosure of information by companies whose securities are listed on stock exchanges or who plan to sell any issues of securities to the general public. Periodically, these companies must file detailed financial reports to the commission, reports which become public information. The SEC has been empowered by Congress to prescribe the accounting principles to be followed in such reports; thus, the SEC has a direct role in the formulation of generally accepted accounting principles. Any material differences between the reports filed with the commission and those disseminated to stockholders must be both disclosed and reconciled in the stockholder reports. Because the disclosures must be made public in one form or another anyway, the accounting principles adopted by the SEC for use in its filings have a far greater impact upon financial reporting in general than might initially be supposed.

Besides the Securities and Exchange Commission, there is a myriad of other government agencies concerned with the financial affairs of companies. The Federal Trade Commission, in actively enforcing the antitrust laws, gathers quantities of information and publishes much of it (periodically or in the form of special reports). The Federal Environmental Protection Agency may require special data on reports relevant to its work. The data which these and other agencies gather serve not only to inform the public but also to provide the essential information upon which regulation is based. The Internal Revenue Service requires standardized data from business corporations in connection with the payment of corporate income taxes. While these are not made public, there is little doubt that the existence of the information in the firm has encouraged its publication and that standardization for tax purposes has enhanced the comparability of published accounting reports as well.

By-Product Beneficiaries

The widespread reporting of accounting information has proved a boon to many groups in the economy. Many of these are, at least on some counts, in opposition to the firm which originated the data, for example, labor unions, competitive firms, suppliers or customers of the firm, and prospective new firms or unions.

To the labor union, access to financial information about the firm with which the union is dealing is necessary if it is to promote the best bargain for its members. Other firms may find, in the profitability of their competitor, a clue to the efficiency of their operations or, in the amount spent on research, a hint that their own research programs are out of step.

Suppliers and customers, while often on cordial terms with the firm being dealt with, are also vigilant for any chance to increase or decrease prices as the case may be or to adjust volume. Having information about each other at least ensures that bargaining is done with substantial, if not full, knowledge.

The publication of accounting data puts prospective new firms in a better position to weigh the chances of making a successful entry. If firms in an industry are generally reporting large profits, firms will be tempted to enter, expand supply, and reduce profits for all, with the benefit accruing to society in the form of lower prices and perhaps more efficient production. If reported profits are low, some prospective new firms may be discouraged from entering, saving society the agony of bankruptcies and poorly-allocated resources.

Those who in some ways profit most from the reporting of accounting data are the researchers and analysts whose tasks include developing knowledge in all of the social sciences; advising on policy matters at national, state, and local levels; and guiding individuals and groups who deal in the securities issued by business firms, thus aiding in the allocation of capital funds. These are the private groups with presumably social interests that we spoke of earlier.

Sociologists, who are interested in understanding the ways in which groups of people develop and interact, are benefited by detailed data on a type of organization to which a large majority of working people belong. The accounting reports of state and local governments and their subdivisions provide excellent data for the urban sociologist.

The political scientist clearly derives greatest benefit from the reports of political entities and their subdivisions, but any study of the role of pressure groups must be concerned with their financial strength. Further, the role of government in economic life is a major one and the functions involved can be carried out intelligently only with the aid of comprehensive financial information on business entities.

The interests of these social scientists in accounting data is largely conditioned, however, by the extent to which their fields impinge upon economics. Perhaps 75 to 80 per cent of the micro-economic and macro-economic data with which economists work are derived from data supplied by private firms. At the micro-economic level, economists are concerned with and need relevant data from firms to analyze empirical questions such as the following: What size firm is the most efficient? What rate of growth in the size of firms is consistent with a policy of maintaining competition in an industry? What degree of concentration of power in an industry limits competition? What market practices are conducive or not conducive to competition? How do labor costs in industry X compare in the United States and Japan? All of these questions, and many more, bear upon the efficiency of resource allocation in an economy—how to get the most social benefits from a given amount of economic resources.

At the macro-economic level, the great bulk of the various social accounts collected and made available by government depends almost exclusively on data supplied by private business firms. An input-output table is simply an aggregation, with some consolidation, of data on costs (inputs) and revenues (outputs) of private business firms. The structure of the economy, as well as changes in structure over time, can then be analyzed. Linear programming techniques can be combined with input-output analysis to examine efficiency and plan for growth. The repercussions of a strike in a major industry on users of its output and on suppliers of its inputs or the effects of a movement from a war to a peace economy can be analyzed with an input-output table. Further consolidation of an input-output table yields national income and product accounts used for, among other things, analysis of growth problems, stability (full employment without inflation), and equity in income distribution. A considerable portion of the data that enter a country's balance of payments accounts originates as data of private business firms, particularly that involving direct investment. To analyze the effects of that investment on, say, a country's balance of payments necessitates again a thorough understanding of business accounting data. The analysis of money flows, which enhances our understanding of exchange in an economy, is heavily dependent on economic information originating in business firms.

Any contribution economists can make to a better or smoother functioning of the economy is, therefore, heavily dependent on the quality of the data supplied by private business firms (and economists' or other social scientists' understanding of the weaknesses and strengths of such data, i.e., their understanding of accounting principles and practices).

The accumulation of accounting data is not costless. If a firm's private benefits derived from using the data exceed its private costs in generating the data, there is no problem—the data will presumably be collected. To protect private investors, the Securities and Exchange Commission may, we feel legitimately, call for some data even if private costs exceed benefits to the firm as seen by the firm. On a broader scale, the government, in its capacity as overseer and regulator of the public interest, may do likewise where such demands for data are approved by the legislative and judicial process. If *social benefits* exceed *private costs*, the data should be collected and published. Who is going to pay for the difference may be a legitimate issue. But there are relatively few cases where more and better knowledge has hurt a society.

DISCUSSION QUESTIONS

1. The Random House dictionary defines "measurement" as "the act or process of ascertaining the extent, dimensions, quantity, etc., of something, especially by comparison with a standard."[4]
   a. What differences do you see in the phenomena accountants seek to measure and the phenomena (1) physicists and (2) political scientists seek to measure?
   b. What problems do accountants encounter in defining the p's and q's with which they deal so that they are comparable among entities and/or over time?
   c. What problems are confronted in defining a set of generally accepted accounting principles either as a distillation of experience or as a set of deductions from agreed premises?
   d. What problems can you identify if an improved set of accounting principles were to be adopted by some but not all business entities?
2. The chapter seems to suggest that the central purpose of accounting should be to supply information to meet "legitimate user needs." Consider Eastern Airlines.
   a. What kinds of information do you think might be needed by each of the following with respect to Eastern Airlines:
      (1) a bank loan officer considering a short-term loan to Eastern;
      (2) a (potential or actual) Eastern shareholder;
      (3) American Airlines, which is considering submitting an application to the Civil Aeronautics Board (CAB) for permission to fly a domestic route on which Eastern at present has a monopoly;

---

4. *The Random House Dictionary of the English Language,* College Edition (1968), s.v. "measurement."

(4) the CAB, which regulates both routes and fares on all domestic flights;

(5) a trade union representing some Eastern employees;

(6) an economist studying the degree of competitiveness and its implications with respect to the efficient allocation of resources in the airline industry.

b. Can the needs of these various external users be met by data related only to the present and past, or do they necessitate forecasts of the future; if the latter, whose forecasts? External users often want "reliable" data related to an (uncertain) future, but any attempt to provide such data inevitably involves *subjective* predictions and violates the *objectivity principle* of accounting. "Objectivity is satisfied if and only if the *same* set of data for a particular set of events is arrived at by two accountants working independently. If the objectivity principle were accepted as a condition governing provision of data to external users, this would seem to limit such data to those related to the present and past (and necessitate one common set of principles to be used in arriving at those data). Can data limited to the present and past be useful to the external users listed in (a) above; if so, how?

c. How do the needs for information of external users considered in (a) and (b) compare with the needs of Eastern's management for data?

(1) Consider the question of future forecasts. The SEC at one point considered making mandatory the publication of management's budgets and plans for the future, based on subjective forecasts. The SEC then retreated to a position where publication of such data is to be voluntary, as determined by management. Few firms do in fact publish such data. If available only to management, management has an interest in making its forecasts as accurate and reliable as possible (i.e., there is nothing to be gained by management fooling itself). Can the same be said were such forecasts to be made public (i.e., be made available to external users)?

(2) Consider, second, the relative needs and "rights" of internal and external users with respect to the *quantity* of information supplied. Management certainly needs data on the relative profitability of different divisions, related to different lines of activity—Chevrolet cars versus GMC transit buses, appliances, and so forth. Various external users, including shareholders, suppliers, customers, trade unions, *and competitors* (e.g., American Airlines in the Eastern case above) would also

like this information. It is not in *management's* interests to divulge such detailed breakdowns of operations. Economists would argue that it is in *society's* interests, in general, that such information be supplied to outsiders so that there is appropriate information provided to investors and resources can be allocated efficiently in the economy (i.e., the efficient allocation of resources in a competitive market economy necessitates disclosure of the fullest possible amount of information). What do you think, and what position do you think an individual certified public accountant and/or the accounting profession as a whole would take on this issue?

(3) If the firm is considered to be the appropriate entity on which to report to external users, does the multi-product firm gain an informational advantage over a single-product firm with which it competes? Why? Consider means by which such inequities might be resolved.

3. "If financial statements only had to be prepared twice—at the time a venture is started and at the time it liquidates—almost all of the interesting problems in accounting would evaporate. Significant problems arise only because of the period convention—the convention that stipulates that reports must be prepared at least yearly." Discuss.

4. a. A small wheat farmer produces 50,000 bushels of wheat during the year, incurring wage costs (including wages for self and family) of $60,000 and rental costs on the land of $30,000. He has sold 40,000 bushels at $2.20 per bushel and expects to be able to sell the remaining 10,000 bushels at the same price, although at year-end the price has dropped (he believes temporarily) to $2.00 a bushel and he is temporarily withholding the 10,000 bushels from the market. He has received cash amounting to $66,000 on 30,000 bushels sold and is owed for the other 10,000 bushels by established traders who have always made good on their contracts before. What would be the farmer's income as owner of the business for the year if the matching concept is employed and revenues are recognized on the basis of:

(1) realized and expected sale value?
(2) realized sale value only?
(3) realized sale value and liquidation value?
(4) realized cash receipts?

Which revenue recognition do you think is most appropriate? Why? What is the basic thinking that underlies the matching concept as employed in this problem?

b. Early in the new year, the farmer sells his remaining 10,000 bushels for $2.10 a bushel without incurring any additional costs and decides to discontinue the business. What income is produced by the business in year 2 according to each of the four revenue options listed in 4-a?

c. What is the total income produced by the business over the two years according to each of the four revenue options?

5. Curt Nance owns several business ventures. His largest venture is incorporated, with significant bonds outstanding and shares of stock owned solely by Nance. Other ventures are sole proprietorships, and some of them also involve creditor equities (i.e., borrowed capital). What is the appropriate accounting entity (or entities) to be "accounted for" from the viewpoint of:

a. creditors (bondholders) of the incorporated venture?

b. creditors in one of his sole proprietorships?

c. Curt Nance?

d. the Internal Revenue Service?

CHAPTER 2

THE BASIC THEORY OF DOUBLE-ENTRY ACCOUNTING

BUSINESS ACCOUNTING seeks to measure in various ways the effects of relevant events on the well-being of the business entity and its owners. While these effects are measured as they occur, the results are communicated to users of the data in the form of financial statements which are prepared periodically—at least annually but often quarterly or monthly. There are three principal financial statements: (1) the *position statement,* also known as the *statement of financial condition* or *balance sheet;* (2) the *income statement,* sometimes termed the *profit and loss statement* or *statement of earnings;* and (3) the *statement of changes in financial position,* also referred to as the *funds statement.* The position statement is a report of conditions at a moment in time, conditions which existed and were measured as of a specific date. It reports *stocks* at a moment in time and, as such, is analogous to a snapshot. In contrast, the income statement and the statement of changes in financial position both report *flows* over a period of time and are analogous to a movie. The income statement is concerned with those flows related to the business entity's profit-oriented activities whereas the statement of changes in financial position reports those flows stemming from the firm's major investment and financing transactions. For pedagogical purposes, we will not treat the statement of changes in financial position in depth until Chapter 9, concentrating our attention instead on the income and position statements.

There is—and it is fundamental to basic accounting theory—a vital link between the income statement for a period (the "movie") and position statements for the beginning and end of that period (two "snapshots"). The income statement explains how the profit-oriented

business activities of a firm have added to (or subtracted from) the
wealth of the firm as this was shown in the position statement prepared
for the beginning of the period. Of course, two position statements,
one for the beginning and one for the end of the period, will also
disclose the change in wealth. Such a *comparative position statement* will
do this, however, without explanation of how the change arose; it will
show only the form the change has taken. This chapter will suggest
how these fundamental statements are put together—the accounting
principles involved, evolving around the fundamental equation in
accounting—and the important interrelationships and fundamental
check that exists between the income and comparative position statements. Then in Chapter 3 we will discuss, elaborate upon, and modify
the basic concepts involved.

THE FUNDAMENTAL EQUATION

As an individual you may own certain things: some clothing, a bicycle
or automobile, and some cash or a bank deposit. At the same time
you may be owed a small amount of money by a friend or relative—you
have a claim on someone else. These are your *assets*—what you own
and what is owed to you. At the same time you may owe some money
to an individual or a bank. What you owe to others are *liabilities* for
you. The difference between what you own or is owed to you and
what you owe to others is (in financial terms) your *ownership*. Ownership
is the interest in your assets attributable to you as an owner. You
may legally own your car, but if a bank has a claim on it, your ownership
share in the car is the *residual* of the value of the car minus the claim
of the bank. (In Chapter 3 we shall define assets, liabilities, and ownership
with greater rigor; for now, these definitions will suffice.) Your financial
position today may be expressed by a basic equation fundamental to
all accounting:

$$\text{Assets} - \text{Liabilities} = \text{Ownership}$$

or

$$A - L = O.$$

This is an *ownership* or *proprietary* view of financial position.

We can look at your position in a somewhat different way. Your
assets (clothing, car, cash) must have been financed either by borrowing
(liabilities) or by contributions from yourself (from earned income, gifts,
or simply finding $10 on a street corner), i.e.,

$$\text{Assets} = \text{Liabilities} + \text{Ownership}$$

or

$$A = L + O.$$

Now we are looking at your assets—what you own or is owed to you—and how they were financed—the sources being creditor (L) or owner (O) contributions, the sum of liabilities plus ownership being termed *equities*. Whereas assets are resources, equities are the means of financing those resources and represent claims against the assets on the part of creditors and (the residual amount) yourself. The equation could be thought of simply as:

$$\text{Assets} = \text{Equities}.$$

For a business firm, this represents an *entity* view of financial position.

It is central to accounting, whether for an individual or a business enterprise, that this basic equation, in one or another of its forms, must hold at any moment in time. Hence, any event that changes the firm's total assets must also change its total equities and the two changes (Δ's) must be equal:

$$\Delta \text{ Assets} = \Delta \text{ Equities}.$$

Of course, some events may affect assets or equities in offsetting ways. Suppose, for example, that you use $100 of your cash to acquire a painting; the increase ($\uparrow$) in your asset, "paintings," is exactly offset by the decrease ($\downarrow$) in your asset, "cash." We can depict the effect of this event as follows:

$100
(Paintings) $\uparrow$

Δ Assets = Δ Equities

$100
(Cash) $\downarrow$

In the balance of this chapter we will employ the form of this equation that focuses attention on ownership. Toward the end of Chapter 3 we will introduce the entity view once again. Until then our analysis of events will be conducted using the equation:

$$\Delta A - \Delta L = \Delta O$$

This implies that any change, say, in the value of certain assets held by the individual or firm, must be matched by equal and offsetting changes in other assets, or in liabilities or ownership, in such a way that the equation remains in balance. Some combination of equal and offsetting changes lies at the heart of the principle of *double-entry accounting*. The double-entry approach to measurement underlies the whole process of record-keeping for economic entities; an understanding of its operation is essential for the analysis of the more substantive accounting issues considered in later chapters of this book. Let us see how the approach works as we use this equation to analyze the establishment of a new business entity and its performance over its first year of operations.

THE ESTABLISHMENT OF A NEW BUSINESS ENTITY

Let us suppose that an individual decides to start a business to sell logs for firewood. He forms a corporation which issues common stock, evidence of ownership, at $50 a share. He buys 100 shares himself for $5,000, and other investors buy another 100 shares. By virtue of the exchange of stock for cash, the initiating individual, or entrepreneur, and the other investors have become the firm's owners. Before this transaction took place, the firm had zero assets and equities, but afterwards it has $10,000 of each. In terms of the fundamental equation, the change in the firm's financial position is as follows:

$$\begin{array}{ccc} \$10,000 & \uparrow \qquad \uparrow & \$10,000 \\ \text{(Cash)} & & \text{(Common Stock)} \\ & \Delta A - \Delta L = \Delta O & \end{array} \qquad (2.1)$$

As suggested above, the transaction is conceived as having a *dual* or two-sided nature. The increase in assets was one aspect of the transaction, and the increase in ownership was the other. As we shall see, there is a dual aspect to every transaction affecting the business firm, which involves *two (or more) equal and offsetting changes* in our fundamental equation so that it *always remains in balance*. This is the heart of double-entry accounting, which has formed the basis of keeping accounts ever since early Renaissance times in Italy.

Now our initiating entrepreneur decides that the firm must raise more capital to get started. A small plot of land is needed for storage and distribution, a truck is needed to haul the logs from forest areas where they are being cut, and some inventory of logs to sell is needed. Our entrepreneur manages to buy the needed plot of land, worth $8,000, for $2,000 of the firm's own cash and $6,000 cash supplied to the seller by a local bank in exchange for a mortgage agreement wherein our company would repay the debt in five equal annual installments of $1,200 per year, each payable at year's end together with interest at eight per cent on this amount owing throughout this year. The transaction involving the purchase of the land affects our fundamental equation as follows:

$$
\begin{array}{c}
\$8,000 \uparrow \qquad \uparrow \$6,000 \\
\text{(Land)} \quad\quad\quad \text{(Mortgage Payable)} \\
\Delta A - \Delta L = \Delta O \\
\$2,000 \downarrow \\
\text{(Cash)}
\end{array}
\qquad (2.2)
$$

Again, of course, there are equal and opposite changes in the basic equation representing the firm's position at a moment of time, so that the equation remains in balance in accordance with double-entry theory. (For purposes of simplicity we will assume that all transactions involved in setting up the business occur on December 31, 19X8.) The land is now one of the firm's resources, something it owns. But its value is largely offset by a long-term liability that the firm owes. The bank is now a creditor to the firm and has first claim on one of the firm's assets (the land) should the firm go bankrupt. As can be seen, the interest of owners in the business has not been changed by this event.

Next our entrepreneur buys a used truck for $4,000 cash. This is simply an exchange of one asset (cash) for another (a truck), and changes in our fundamental equation would be as follows:

$$
\begin{array}{c}
\$4,000 \uparrow \\
\text{(Truck)} \\
\Delta A - \Delta L = \Delta O \\
\$4,000 \downarrow \\
\text{(Cash)}
\end{array}
\qquad (2.3)
$$

Finally, $3,000 worth of logs (50 cords at $60 a cord) are purchased from a logging firm on account, i.e., on credit, with an understanding that these accounts payable will be repaid when the logs are sold. We have:

$$
\begin{array}{c}
\$3,000 \uparrow \qquad \uparrow \$3,000 \\
\text{(Merchandise} \qquad \text{(Accounts} \\
\text{Inventory)} \qquad \text{Payable)} \\
\Delta A - \Delta L = \Delta O
\end{array}
\qquad (2.4)
$$

The logging firm, then, like the bank supplying mortgage money, is a creditor who has helped to finance our firm's assets. The Burnwell Firelogs Company, ready for business, has a position statement at the end of the day on December 31, 19X8, as shown in Table 2-1.

TABLE 2-1

BURNWELL FIRELOGS, INC.

POSITION STATEMENT

As of December 31, 19X8

ASSETS:		
Cash		$ 4,000
Merchandise Inventory		3,000
Truck		4,000
Land		8,000
Total Assets		$19,000
LIABILITIES:		
Accounts Payable	$ 3,000	
Mortgage Payable	6,000	
Total Liabilities		$ 9,000
STOCKHOLDERS' EQUITY:		
Common Stock	$10,000	
Total Stockholders' Equity		$10,000

BURNWELL'S FIRST YEAR OF OPERATIONS

While clearly the Burnwell Firelogs Company would keep individual records of each and every transaction engaged in during the year (we will discuss how such records are kept in Chapter 4), we will aggregate all transactions for the year in order to simplify our example. Let us look first at the pure trading aspects of Burnwell's operations. These are the principal activities of the business that are being conducted in search of a profit or, from the owners' point of view, an increase in the wealth of the owners. The details of these activities will be reported in the firm's income statement for the year in question. The change in the wealth of owners as a result of the business activities of the firm, *ownership income*, will be determined from the following equation:

Ownership Income = Revenues − Expenses

$$\Delta O = R - E$$

When this equation is combined with the equation detailing changes in financial position, we have two ways to determine the change in ownership that has taken place over the period as a result of business activity, namely:

$$\Delta A - \Delta L = \Delta O = R - E$$

A caveat is in order, however. Clearly, ownership can change in the absence of income if (1) owners increase their direct investment in the firm (for example, the firm sells more stock) or (2) the owners withdraw assets from the firm (for example, the firm pays cash dividends to the owners). Hence, this dual equation assumes that there are no direct investments and disinvestments, and it is in this form that we shall use it to analyze Burnwell's business activities for the year.

Burnwell sells 450 cords of wood at $80 a cord over the year, 250 cords for cash (250 × $80 = $20,000) and 200 cords on account (200 × $80 = $16,000). If the goods sold had cost Burnwell nothing, there would be no other changes in assets or liabilities as a result of this aggregate transaction. If revenues (sales) are viewed in this fashion, i.e., disassociated from expenses, and the fundamental equation is to remain in balance, ownership must be increased by the amount of sales, in this case by $36,000. We know, however, that there are expenses to be matched against these revenues before the ultimate change in ownership can be determined. Therefore, it makes sense to set up *temporary ownership accounts* in which we can collect information on profit-oriented business activities until we can determine precisely the direction and amount by which they will affect the ownership claims on the firm. These temporary accounts are those designated R and E, the former representing apparent increases in ownership, the latter representing apparent decreases in ownership. In the case of sales of $36,000, therefore, we record as follows:

$$\$20,000 \text{ (Cash)} \quad \$16,000 \text{ (Accounts Receivable)} \qquad \$36,000 \text{ (Sales)}$$

$$\Delta A - \Delta L = \Delta O = R - E \qquad (2.5)$$

In order to make these sales, of course, Burnwell had to purchase more inventories of logs. Suppose it purchased over the year on account 550 cords of wood at the (unchanged) price of $60 a cord (550 × $60 = $33,000). Looking at this aggregate transaction alone, Burnwell is clearly exchanging a liability for an asset, as with our original purchase, i.e., we have:

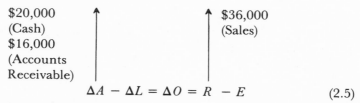

$$\$33,000 \text{ (Merchandise Inventory)} \qquad \$33,000 \text{ (Accounts Payable)}$$

$$\Delta A - \Delta L = \Delta O = R - E. \qquad (2.6)$$

Such are the pure purchase and sale transactions. We come now to the key accounting exercise, hinted at in the discussion of the matching convention in Chapter 1, of allocating asset costs to those which have "expired" during the year, and are thus expenses, and those which should remain on our books because they are still assets of the firm. The cost of goods available for sale during the year, an amount which is equal to our beginning inventory (BI) plus purchases (P), must be allocated either to the cost of goods sold $(COGS)$ or to the cost of goods still on hand, Burnwell's ending inventory (EI). In our case this is easy, for we kept a *perpetual inventory*, i.e., a record of the number and cost of each cord of wood sold (450 cords × \$60 = \$27,000). We should have, as a residual, an ending inventory of 150 cords × \$60 = \$9,000, as shown below:

Beginning Inventory (BI)	50 × \$60 = \$ 3,000
+ Purchases (P)	550 × 60 = 33,000
= Cost of Goods Available for Sale $(COGAFS)$	600 × \$60 = \$36,000
− Cost of Goods Sold $(COGS)$	450 × 60 = 27,000
= Ending Inventory (EI)	150 × \$60 = \$ 9,000

As we shall see in Chapter 5, if we did not keep track of individual items sold, we could compute the cost of goods sold as a residual by physically counting and valuing the inventory at the end of the year, following what is called a *periodic inventory system*. The cost of goods sold formula would be:

$$BI + P - EI = COGS$$

In either case, \$27,000 of the \$36,000 of merchandise acquired during the year has been disposed of, becoming now the cost of goods sold:

$$\Delta A - \Delta L = \Delta O = R - E$$

$27,000
(Cost of Goods Sold Expense)

\$27,000
(Merchandise
Inventory)

(2.7)

We could have compressed (2.5) and (2.7) by matching the cost of goods sold directly to sales at the time sales were made to obtain the gross trading profit and disposed with the recording of revenues and expenses as at the top of page 37; but we would then have lost the data essential for construction of the income statement.

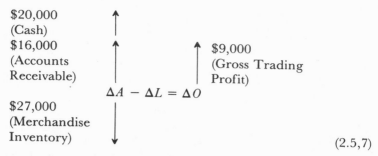

$$\Delta A - \Delta L = \Delta O$$

(2.5,7)

Burnwell had other expenses which must be matched against revenues. Salaries (in cash) paid out to our part-owner/manager over the year amounted to $6,000, and the firm made cash outlays of $3,000 to advertise in the local newspaper; i.e., we have:

$6,000 (Cash) $\Delta A - \Delta L = \Delta O = R - E$ ↑ $6,000 (Salaries Expense)

(2.8)

$3,000 (Cash) $\Delta A - \Delta L = \Delta O = R - E$ ↑ $3,000 (Advertising Expense)

(2.9)

Gasoline, repair, and other miscellaneous expenses, all paid in cash, amounted to $2,000, i.e.,

$2,000 (Cash) $\Delta A - \Delta L = \Delta O = R - E$ ↑ $2,000 (Miscellaneous Expenses)

(2.10)

These are some but not all of the events which affected the profits (or losses) of the firm during the year. In the meanwhile, other events took place which had no direct effect on profits. By the end of the year, $12,000 of the cumulative total of $16,000 in accounts receivable had been cancelled through cash payments to the firm, and the firm, in turn, had paid off in cash $26,000 of the $36,000 in accounts payable that had accumulated during the year. The effect of these aggregate transactions on our fundamental equation, and accounts, was:

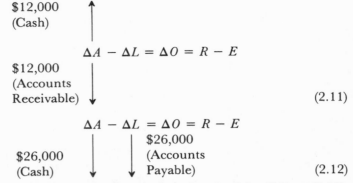

$$\$12,000 \atop (\text{Cash})$$

$$\Delta A - \Delta L = \Delta 0 = R - E$$

$$\$12,000 \atop (\text{Accounts Receivable})$$ $\qquad$ (2.11)

$$\Delta A - \Delta L = \Delta 0 = R - E$$

$$\$26,000 \atop (\text{Cash})$$ $\qquad$ $$\$26,000 \atop (\text{Accounts Payable})$$ $\qquad$ (2.12)

Now if we add all the cash transactions involved in (2.5) – (2.12), given a beginning cash balance of $4,000, it is evident that Burnwell got into a cash bind at some point during the year, i.e.,

Beginning balance	+$ 4,000
(2.5)	+ 20,000
(2.8)	− 6,000
(2.9)	− 3,000
(2.10)	− 2,000
(2.11)	+ 12,000
(2.12)	− 26,000
	−$ 1,000

The company realized its cash problem in time and borrowed $8,000 from its local bank at mid-year in exchange for a note payable in one year's time at ten per cent annual interest, interest to be payable semi-annually. This transaction's effect on the fundamental equation at the time the cash was received was:

$$\$8,000 \atop (\text{Cash})$$ $\qquad$ $$\$8,000 \atop (\text{Note Payable})$$

$$\Delta A - \Delta L = \Delta 0 = R - E.$$ $\qquad$ (2.13)

The mortgage outstanding involved repayment of one-fifth of the principal at the end of the year ($1,200). The repayment of principal on the mortgage at year-end affects our equation as follows:

$$\Delta A - \Delta L = \Delta 0 = R - E.$$

$$\$1,200 \atop (\text{Cash})$$ $\qquad$ $$\$1,200 \atop (\text{Mortgage Payable})$$ $\qquad$ (2.14)

Interest on the mortgage, eight per cent of $6,000, amounted to $480 and was paid in cash at the end of the year. This, from the point of view of the owners of the business, was an expense of business activities conducted during the year:

$$\begin{array}{c} \uparrow \$480 \\ | \text{ (Interest Expense)} \\ \Delta A \; - \; \Delta L \; = \; \Delta O \; = \; R \; - \; E \end{array}$$

$480
(Cash) ↓

(2.15)

In addition, interest for six months had to be paid at year-end on the short-term bank loan, and this amounted to $400 $[1/2 \times .10 (\$8,000)]$:

$$\begin{array}{c} \uparrow \$400 \\ | \text{ (Interest Expense)} \\ \Delta A \; - \; \Delta L \; = \; \Delta O \; = \; R \; - \; E \end{array}$$

$400
(Cash) ↓

(2.16)

The company has not yet accounted for all the economic events which have affected the financial position of the enterprise during the year. Salaries of $1,000 are owed our partial owner-manager at year-end. Not to include this as part of salaries expense would clearly understate expenses for the year. A liability exists on the part of the company. We have

$$\begin{array}{cc} \uparrow \$1,000 & \uparrow \$1,000 \\ | \text{ (Salaries} & | \text{ (Salaries} \\ | \text{ Payable)} & | \text{ Expense)} \\ \multicolumn{2}{c}{\Delta A \; - \; \Delta L \; = \; \Delta O \; = \; R \; - \; E} \end{array}$$

(2.17)

Further, Burnwell's truck has been partly "used up" over the year; its decline in value represents both wear-and-tear and aging. Without going into some of the complicating factors involved in arriving at an appropriate estimate of this depreciation (to be discussed at some length in Chapter 6 and elsewhere), let us just say that Burnwell predicts the life of the truck to be four years, after which it will be worth nothing, and assumes that the $4,000 truck will decline in value by $1,000 a year. This amount represents, in the view of management, an appropriate estimate of the expiration of the value of the asset each year. The truck has been used in earning revenues and has declined in value as a result of this use; depreciation is clearly a matching expense. But because the decline in value is an estimate, it makes sense to show the estimated decline in value separately from the value of the truck as shown in the firm's records. Hence, the decline in value is shown as an "allowance for depreciation" to recognize the expiration of asset value. We then represent the economic event of depreciation as it affects our fundamental equation as follows:

$$\Delta A - \Delta L = \Delta O = R - E \qquad (2.18)$$

↑ $1,000 (Depreciation Expense)

$1,000 (Allowance for Depreciation) ↓

The "allowance for depreciation" account is a contra-asset account to be deducted from the asset account "truck" (which stays at $4,000 in the accounts) in order to provide a figure for its net (depreciated) value, $3,000.

There could be many other adjustments that might have to be made at the end of the year—for example, to take account of taxes due but unpaid or expenses that might have been prepaid but not yet used up, such as prepaid insurance or advertising; but we will assume that now we have taken account of all relevant economic events affecting the financial position of Burnwell during the year. Let us see what our double-entry system yields.

THE COMPARATIVE POSITION STATEMENT, THE INCOME STATEMENT, AND THE FUNDAMENTAL CHECK

In Table 2-2 we list Burnwell's assets, liabilities, and residual (owner-ship) equity at the beginning of the year in the first (left-hand) column. In the middle section of the table we list all the changes in these items that occurred during the year as given by the changes in our fundamental equation (2.5)–(2.18). Given our double-entry system which always keeps our fundamental equation in balance, our ending assets must also equal ending equities, which of course proves to be the case. A simplified comparative statement of position is shown in Table 2-3. (In finished accounting statements, and indeed in general, negative figures are indicated by putting parentheses around them, as with the retained earnings figure.)

The change in owners' equity and the change in retained earnings, as shown in Tables 2-2 and 2-3, consist simply of all the changes in ownership equity as analyzed in equations (2.5)–(2.18). Burnwell's income statement is put together in such a way as to explain the change in ownership equity as shown by the change in retained earnings depicted on the comparative position statement. In Chapter 3 we shall suggest various issues involved in how such a statement should be put together to be more meaningful (and, indeed, issues involved in the organization and treatment of the comparative position statement as well). In Table

TABLE 2-2

Effect of Events of the Year 19X9 on Position Statement Items
of Burnwell Firelogs, Inc.

	Beginning Balance		Change During Year	Ending Balance	
Cash		$ 4,000	$+\$20,000_5, -6,000_8,$ $-3,000_9, -2,000_{10},$ $+12,000_{11},$ $-26,000_{12},$ $+8,000_{13}, -1,200_{14},$ $-480_{15}, -400_{16}$		$ 4,920
Accounts Receivable		-0-	$+\$16,000_5, -12,000_{11}$		4,000
Merchandise Inventory		3,000	$+\$33,000_6, -27,000_7$		9,000
Truck	$4,000			$4,000	
Less: Allowance for Depreciation	-0-	4,000	$-\$1,000_{18}$	$-1,000	3,000
Land		8,000			8,000
Total Assets		$19,000			$28,920
Accounts Payable		$ 3,000	$+\$33,000_6, -26,000_{12}$		$10,000
Salaries Payable		-0-	$+\$1,000_{17}$		1,000
Notes Payable		-0-	$+\$8,000_{13}$		8,000
Mortgage Payable		6,000	$-\$1,200_{14}$		4,800
Total Liabilities		$ 9,000			$23,800
Common Stock		10,000			10,000
Revenues			$\$36,000_5$		
Less: Expenses			$-\$27,000_7, -6,000_8,$ $-3,000_9, -2,000_{10},$ $-480_{15}, -400_{16},$ $-1,000_{17}, -1,000_{18}$		
Equals: Change in Ownership					$-4,880
Total Ownership		$10,000			$ 5,120

TABLE 2-3

BURNWELL FIRELOGS, INC.
COMPARATIVE POSITION STATEMENT
As of December 31, 19X8 and December 31, 19X9

	December 31, 19X8[1]		December 31, 19X9[1]	
ASSETS:				
Cash		$ 4,000		$ 4,920
Accounts Receivable		-0-		4,000
Merchandise Inventory		3,000		9,000
Truck	$4,000		$4,000	
Less: Allowance for				
Depreciation	-0-	4,000	1,000	3,000
Land		8,000 $19,000		8,000 $28,920
LIABILITIES:				
Accounts Payable		$ 3,000		$10,000
Salaries Payable		-0-		1,000
Note Payable		-0-		8,000
Mortgage Payable		6,000 $ 9,000		4,800 $23,800
STOCKHOLDERS' EQUITY:				
Common Stock		$10,000		$10,000
Retained Earnings				
(Deficit)		-0- $10,000		(4,880) $ 5,120

1. In formal position statements, end-of-the-year data are put on the left, beginning-of-the-year data on the right. The data are reversed here to be consistent with Table 2-2.

TABLE 2-4

BURNWELL FIRELOGS, INC.
INCOME STATEMENT
For the Year Ended December 31, 19X9

REVENUES:		
Sales		$36,000
EXPENSES:		
Cost of Goods Sold	$27,000	
Salaries	7,000	
Advertising	3,000	
Depreciation	1,000	
Interest	880	
Miscellaneous	2,000	40,880
INCOME (LOSS) TO OWNERS AND		
INCREASE (DECREASE) IN RETAINED		
EARNINGS		($4,880)

2-4 we simply list the change in retained earnings as given at the bottom of the middle section of Table 2-2 in one possible way.

The "fundamental check" mentioned earlier is that changes in ownership equity as reported on the income statement must equal changes in ownership equity as reported on the comparative position statement. If dividends were declared, both changes would be after dividends—a distribution of income to stockholders (whether paid in cash or simply accepted by the firm as a liability to be paid later). The double-entry system of accounting, wherein every relevant economic event affecting the economic entity has a dual aspect and is recorded in such a way as to leave the fundamental equation always in balance, should provide, inevitably, for consistency between the change in ownership equity in the enterprise as shown in the comparative position statement and income to owners (the increase or decrease in ownership equity) as shown on the income statement. We have:

$$
\left.
\begin{array}{rl}
\text{Revenues} & (R) \\
- \text{ Expenses} & (E) \\ \hline
= \text{ Income} & (Y) \\
- \text{ Dividends} & (D) \\
\Delta A - \Delta L = \Delta O
\end{array}
\right\}
\begin{array}{l}
\text{Income} \\
\text{Statement}
\end{array}
$$

Change in assets minus change in liabilities equals change in ownership equity

Comparative Position Statement

In the example we have used, the check works out as follows:

$$
\begin{array}{rr}
R & \$36,000 \\
-E & -40,880 \\ \hline
Y & -\$4,880 \\
-D & - \quad \text{-0-} \\ \hline
\end{array}
$$

$$
\begin{array}{ccccc}
\Delta A & - & \Delta L & = & \Delta O \\
\$9,920 & - & \$14,800 & = & -\$4,880
\end{array}
$$

BURNWELL'S OPERATIONS IN ITS FIRST YEAR: INCOME, GROWTH, AND LIQUIDITY CONSIDERATIONS

The Burnwell Company ends its first year of operations showing a growth in overall assets (from $19,000 to $28,920) and a growth in its cash balances (from $4,000 to $4,920). To many, one or both of these developments might suggest success. Indeed, one frequently hears of the merits of expanding assets to generate a favorable cash flow. On the other hand, Burnwell has reported a net loss to owners of $4,880 on its income statement. And if we take note of the changes which have occurred in its "net liquid assets" (cash and accounts receivable less accounts, salaries, and notes payable—see Chapter 3), we find that these have declined over the period by $11,080, from +$1,000 to −$10,080. How *do* we judge success or failure of a business enterprise?

Overall growth in assets and liquidity considerations are relevant factors in judging a firm's overall performance; but they are only partial considerations (and, we would argue, *supplementary* considerations) to income, which is the key or essential element. Certainly neither growth nor greater liquidity can be thought of as a substitute for the generation of income in measuring success. Both growth and greater liquidity can be obtained simply by exchanging appropriate liabilities (or new ownership equity) for appropriate assets. It is the increase in assets over and above the increase in liabilities, independent of new contributions of ownership capital, that must be considered the most crucial aspect of success, for the ability to grow and/or maintain or increase liquidity to a large extent depends on the generation of income. Nevertheless, these considerations—and, in particular, liquidity—are indeed relevant in judging the firm's position and performance, and it behooves us to consider them at this early juncture in concluding our preliminary view of accounting for the performance of the firm.

First, consider briefly growth or decline in assets. The changes shown by Burnwell's comparative position statement may be depicted as shown in Figure 2-1. The growth in assets of $9,920 has been financed entirely by new creditor equities (all short-term), and this growth in liabilities has exceeded the growth in assets by the amount of the firm's loss, $4,880. One cannot say out of hand that this situation is unhealthy— perhaps everyone recognized that Burnwell would have to incur losses in its first year or two in starting up but that future profit prospects were bright. Certainly the bank felt secure enough to lend Burnwell money. Nor is there anything inherently wrong with a firm growing largely through issuance of new liabilities, even involving a growth in liabilities relative to owner equities; as we shall see in later chapters, this is known as "trading on the equity"—wherein the return earned by the use of creditors' funds by the firm (hopefully) exceeds the cost of borrowing these funds with a resultant beneficial effect to owners. But in general a healthier situation than Burnwell's would be one in which *both* liabilities and ownership equity financed the increase in assets, the latter as a result, at least in part, of reinvestment of positive

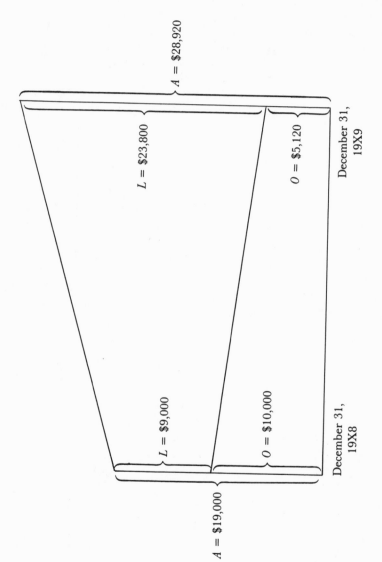

$A = \$28,920$

$L = \$23,800$

$O = \$5,120$

December 31, 19X9

$L = \$9,000$

$O = \$10,000$

December 31, 19X8

$A = \$19,000$

Figure 2-1

ownership income, i.e., we would have a situation such as that depicted
in Figure 2-2A. Even the situation depicted in Figure 2-2B might be
preferable to that depicted for Burnwell's actual operations above. We
have not exhausted the combination of changes in assets, liabilities,
and ownership equity that could occur over a year. Suffice it to say
at this point that the *way* in which these components of the position
statement change is one of the ingredients that one takes into account
in judging the overall performance of the firm.

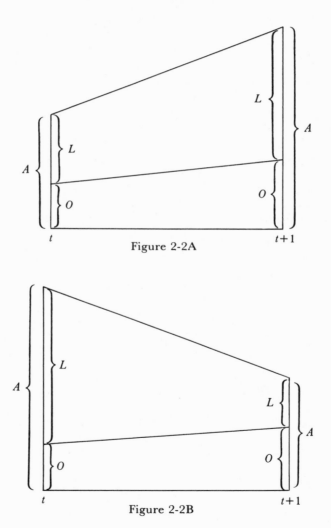

Figure 2-2A

Figure 2-2B

Another important ingredient—in addition to asset growth and the generation of income—involves liquidity considerations. Changes in these conditions are usually provided in a third type of statement depicting those economic events of the period which affect liquidity of the business entity, known as a "funds statement." A business firm may well generate income over a period but not have any increase in cash or liquid funds (defined loosely at this point as "net liquid assets" as above) to show for it. A stockholder may well ask: "You generated income. Where is it? Why am I not receiving dividends?" The generation of ownership income does not mean that a firm necessarily has increased cash or liquid funds to show for it, nor can the incurring of a loss be equated to a decrease of cash or liquid funds. The two phenomena are only dependent in part; they reflect different decisions, events, and considerations, as well as reflecting some decisions, events, and considerations that are common to both.

Table 2-5 shows why Burnwell's loss for the year is not balanced by an equal decrease in its cash balances. Sales of $36,000 generated only $32,000 in cash; there were sales of $20,000 directly for cash and $16,000 for accounts receivable, of which only $12,000 were turned into cash during the year. Cost of goods sold were $27,000, all on account, but only $26,000 of accounts payable were paid off in cash during the year. Similarly only $6,000 of the $7,000 in salaries expenses were paid in cash, the remaining $1,000 being equaled by wages payable. Advertising, interest, and miscellaneous expenses were all in cash, but, of course, no cash was involved in allowing for depreciation expense. Therefore, the revenues and expenses, taken alone, required cash outlays of $5,880 in excess of receipts. A check of other transactions treated individually above will show that only two involved cash: the payment of $1,200 principal on the mortgage and the receipt of $8,000 cash in exchange for the note payable. *Total* cash receipts, therefore, exceeded total cash expenditures by $920. As shown on our comparative position statement, cash balances increased between beginning and end of year from $4,000 to $4,920. There was a loss of $4,880 but a net increase in cash balances of $1,920. There is absolutely no reason for the two to be equal.

It is but a short step, along the same route, to reach a statement of "sources and uses of funds" for the Burnwell Company for 19X9, as shown in Table 2-6. We define "funds" here (to be considered further in Chapter 9) as cash and accounts receivable less accounts, wages, and notes payable—what we shall call "net current monetary assets" in our next chapter. We must then consider the effect of revenue and expense items and any other transactions as they give rise to an

TABLE 2-5
BURNWELL FIRELOGS, INC.
RECONCILIATION OF INCOME FLOWS AND CASH FLOWS
For the Year Ended December 31, 19X9

	Income		Revenues Not Collected During Period	Expenses Not Paid During Period	Cash	
	Revenues	Expenses			Receipts	Disbursements
Sales	$36,000		$4,000		$32,000	
Cost of Goods Sold		$27,000		$1,000		$26,000
Salaries		7,000		1,000		6,000
Advertising		3,000				3,000
Depreciation		1,000		1,000		
Miscellaneous		2,000				2,000
Interest		880				880
	$36,000	$40,880	$4,000	$3,000	$32,000	$37,880
Loss	4,880					
	$40,880	$40,880				
Other Cash Items:						
Mortgage Payable						1,200
Note Payable					8,000	
Total Cash					$40,000	$39,080
Increase in Cash						920
					$40,000	$40,000

TABLE 2-6
BURNWELL FIRELOGS, INC.
RECONCILIATION OF INCOME FLOWS AND FUNDS FLOWS
For the Year Ended December 31, 19X9

	Income		Not Increasing Funds	Not Decreasing Funds	Funds	
	Revenues	Expenses			Sources	Uses
Sales	$36,000				$36,000	
Cost of Goods Sold		$27,000				$27,000
Wages		7,000				7,000
Advertising		3,000				3,000
Depreciation		1,000		$1,000		
Miscellaneous		2,000				2,000
Interest		880				880
	$36,000	$40,880	-0-	$1,000	$36,000	$39,880
Loss	4,880					
	$40,880	$40,880				
Other Fund Items:						
Mortgage Payable						1,200
Merchandise Inventory						6,000
Total Funds					$36,000	$47,080
Decrease in Funds					11,080	
					$47,080	$47,080

increase or decrease in funds (the items identified taken together) rather than cash alone.

Viewed in this way, all $36,000 of sales gave rise to (were a source of) funds—$32,000 worth were sold in exchange, directly or indirectly, for cash while the other $4,000 worth were equaled by increases in accounts receivable. All of the cost of goods sold was paid for by funds—$26,000 in cash (that amount being used to pay off accounts payable during the year) and the remaining $1,000 offset by an increase in accounts payable (the remaining $6,000 of that increase going toward increasing inventories—see below). Similarly the salaries expense was met by using funds, $6,000 in cash and $1,000 in newly created salaries payable (a *decrease* in a fund asset and an *increase* in a fund liability are both *reductions* in funds). Depreciation expense involved neither cash nor any other liquid asset or liability. Perusing our other transactions again, we can see that only four involved the use of funds: the $1,200 repayment of principal on the mortgage payable, the $6,000 (accounts payable) which financed the increase in inventories, and the two cash payments of interest to the bank. No net change in funds was involved in the mid-year borrowing from the bank; one type of fund, a note payable, was exchanged for another type of fund, cash. Table 2-6 shows, then, that uses of funds exceeded sources of funds by $11,080, which is shown to be the net change in cash plus accounts receivable minus accounts, salaries, and notes payable on our comparative position statement in Table 2-3.

A firm may be much more interested in changes which occur in its funds position over a year than in those which occur in its cash position. We have associated funds loosely with "net liquid assets." Presumably non-cash funds can fairly readily be turned into cash, and cash is needed to meet non-cash fund liabilities. But further discussion of such matters necessitates more careful consideration of the nature of funds and other assets and liabilities which leads us to the next chapter.

DISCUSSION QUESTIONS

1. The following arguments were overheard in a discussion among some beginning students in accounting:

   "There is no special 'logic' to double-entry accounting. It is simply an archaic concept handed down from Renaissance times that accountants pay lip-service to today but do not really use in communicating information to management and the public."

" 'Double-entry theory' in accounting is absolutely *fundamental* to any understanding of the subject. It is a 'principle' in accounting that, unlike many other 'generally accepted accounting principles,' *all* accountants agree with and adhere to. There is simply no other way to approach the subject."

"While 'double-entry theory' is a *useful* concept in accounting, it is not a *fundamental* concept. Accounting records could readily be kept without reference to it, and accounting reports would be the same as they are today. It is a *convenient* but not a *necessary* concept for understanding accounting."

"A 'single-entry system' in accounting, which simply kept track of all assets and liabilities and changes in all assets and liabilities, would measure 'position' at a moment of time and 'income' over time every bit as well as the more complicated 'double-entry system.' So why complicate matters?"

Comment on each of the opinions expressed. Where do *you* stand? What do *you* think about the relevance and importance of "double entry theory" to an understanding of accounting?

2. At a cocktail party, a local small businessman—the proprietor of a variety store—made the following argument to a CPA friend of his:

"I studied accounting back at business school just as everyone else who majored in business. But when I got out into the real world, it became obvious to me that financial statements were of little or no use to me in managing my business. What I need to know is what *actually* happened during the period and how well off I am at the end of the period. Financial statements, based as they are on such things as the going concern convention and employing various arbitrary allocation schemes such as depreciation, don't tell me what I want to know. So instead of relying on them, I just look at my cash flows during the period. I record revenues when I receive cash and expenses when I pay cash. If revenues exceed expenses, then I have more cash at the end of the period and I'm that much better off. Besides, what good is "net income" if you can't spend it? Since I measure mine in cash terms, all my income can be spent. Finally, being on a cash basis makes my accounting records easier to keep *and* understand and they are completely accurate."

Discuss.

3. Fill in dollar amounts for the blanks represented by (1)–(7) in the following accounting reports of position and income of the PDQ company over three periods:

		Period 1		Period 2	Period 3
		Beginning	End	End	End
(A)	Assets	$25,000	$31,000	$35,000	$36,000
(L)	Liabilities	10,000	(2)	9,000	(6)
(O)	Ownership	(1)	(3)	(5)	24,000
(CC)	Newly Contributed Ownership Capital	$ 5,000		(4)	$ 3,000
(R)	Revenues	36,000		$31,000	(7)
(E)	Expenses	27,000		26,000	29,000
(D)	Dividends	4,000		4,000	2,000

Write down the two equations you have used in working out this problem, using the symbols listed on the left. What, exactly, is the "fundamental check" in accounting reports on income and comparative position?

4. Which of the four amounts
   Beginning Inventory
   Ending Inventory
   Purchases
   Cost of Goods Sold
   must be computed as a residual at the end of the period under (a) a perpetual inventory system, (b) a periodic inventory system?

5. Burnwell made an outlay of "funds" (net liquid assets) when it purchased its truck. No outlay of "funds" was involved when "depreciation" was computed at the end of the first year. Why, then, is the former *not* considered an "expense," while the latter *is* considered an "expense"? When is an "expenditure" (of funds) considered an "expense" and when is it not considered an "expense"?

6. The term "cost" has been defined by the Committee on Terminology of the American Institute of Certified Public Accountants in *Accounting Terminology Bulletin No. 4: Cost, Expense, and Loss* (New York: AICPA, 1975) as follows:

Cost is the amount, measured in money, of cash expended or other property transferred, capital stock issued, services performed, or a liability incurred, in consideration of goods or services received or to be received.

An accountant, then, tends to define "cost" in terms of what must be given up to acquire a good or service. An expenditure is a cost by this definition, whereas an expense is an "expired cost"—a cost which cannot contribute to the production of future revenues. When economists talk about costs, they generally mean expenses. Are the following "unexpired costs," "expired costs" (expenses), or neither by accountants' terminology?

a. Purchase of inventory which is sold.
b. Purchase of inventory which is not yet sold.
c. Payment of an account payable.
d. Payment of interest on a note payable.
e. Payment for a machine to be used in production.
f. Depreciation on the machine.
g. Payment of dividends.
h. Payment of next month's rent.

7.   "The primary function of depreciation is to *spread* the *original acquisition cost* of the asset, allocating to different periods the proportion of its original cost which was 'used up' in those periods."

"No, the primary function of depreciation is to measure the change in current market value of the asset as a result of use or aging."

"You are both wrong. The primary function of depreciation is to retain 'funds' in the business sufficient to *replace* the asset when it is 'used up'."

These three very different views will loom large in discussions later on in this book. What are your preliminary thoughts at this point?

PROBLEMS

2-1. *J. K. Lesser, Inc.*

On January 1, 19X1, J. K. Lesser began preparations for opening a new retail clothing store to be known as J. K. Lesser, Inc. During January, he engaged in the following transactions:

(1) Deposited $12,000 of his own money in a checking account at the First National Bank in the name of J. K. Lesser, Inc.

(2) Paid $300 to the state as fees for filing articles of incorporation. Related to this, he also paid $1,000 to E. Z. Munie, a lawyer, for her services rendered in connection with filing the papers of incorporation.

(3) Paid a printer $600 for printing articles of incorporation for J. K. Lesser, Inc.

(4) Issued all 1,000 common stock certificates to himself.

(5) Signed, in the name of the corporation, a three-year lease (from January, 19X1 through December, 19X3) on a store building. The lease called for monthly rental of $700 to be paid on the first day of each month. Rent for the first and last month was paid in advance at the date of signing the lease (January 1), in addition to a damage deposit equal to one month's rent.

(6) Paid utility deposits of $500. The deposits must be left with the utilities company so long as its services are used.

(7) Purchased store equipment (counters, display cases, cash registers, and so on) from a defunct retailer for $3,200.

(8) Purchased merchandise for $4,100 on credit from a wholesaler, H. I. Marchup.

(9) Hired a salesperson, Carmen Schmidt, on January 16. She is to begin work immediately to help prepare the store for its February 1 grand opening (checking in merchandise, stocking shelves, and so on). Her salary will be $650 per month, payable on the 15th and on the last day of the month.

(10) Placed an order for a two-page advertisement in *The Star-Dispatch* to announce the grand opening. The ad will run consecutively for three days, commencing on January 29 and will cost $800, to be payable on February 10. (The advertisement ran as scheduled.)

(11) Received, on January 31, utility bill of $120 for January.

(12) Paid Carmen Schmidt her salary for the second half of January.

INSTRUCTIONS:

(a) Using the equation $A - L = O$ or $A = L + O$, indicate by the use of arrows the impact of each of the foregoing on the firm's financial position. Put amounts next to the arrows as in the text.

(b) Prepare a position statement as of the end of the day on January 31, 19X1.

2-2. Poor Richard's Almanac

Richard Sweet decided that the small but growing town of Slippery Rock, Montana, was reaching the stage where a good stationery and office supplies store was needed and could be profitable. He engaged in the following transactions during October and November in preparation for the grand opening on December 1, 19X3.

(1) Borrowed $6,000 in his name from the local bank on October 1, 19X3. This money went into his own personal checking account. The note bore interest of nine per cent per annum, payable monthly; the October and November interest payments were made by Sweet at the end of each month. Sweet will use the borrowed money plus that already in his checking account to finance the store's establishment. All money spent by Sweet for the store will be regarded as an investment by him in the business entity.

(2) Hired a lawyer with whom he consulted on real estate, possible incorporation, tax matters, and other "starting up" problems. Sweet paid the lawyer $1,250 on November 1 and owed $450 on November 30, 19X3.

(3) Rented a store as of November 1 for one year at $1,500 a month, paying the first and last month's rent on that date. Rent for subsequent months is due on the last day of the preceding month and the December rent was paid from the store's checking account on November 30.

(4) Purchased a three-year comprehensive fire, theft, and liability insurance policy for $9,000, effective November 1. Coverage for a year was paid in advance, with two further installments to be paid on November 1, 19X4 and November 1, 19X5, if the policy continued.

(5) Purchased merchandise during early November, $4,000 for cash and $5,000 on account from suppliers.

(6) Established a new checking account at the local bank on November 25 in the name of "Poor Richard's Almanac" by transferring $4,000 from his personal account.

(7) Hired an assistant on November 15 to help in setting up the store. She was paid $750 with a check from the store's account as a half-month's wages on November 30.

(8) Arranged for a half-page advertisement announcing the gala opening of the store to appear in the local newspaper on December 1. The bill had not been paid as of November 30.

INSTRUCTIONS:

(a) Using either the equation $A - L = 0$ or $A = L + 0$, indicate with arrows the impact of each of the foregoing on the firm's financial position. Put amounts next to the arrows as in the text.

(b) Prepare a position statement as of November 30, 19X3.

2-3. Birchfield Beer Company

Late on the evening of June 30, 19X5 a reel of computer tape, part of Birchfield Beer Company's accounting records, was accidentally erased. As chief accountant, you have been asked to prepare Birchfield's position statement as of that date using the following information:

(1) The bank statement asked for by Birchfield shows a balance of $25,640 as of June 30, 19X5. Comparison with the company's check register indicates that checks still outstanding amount to $7,250, including one check *over a year old* to a former supplier in the amount of $150.

(2) An examination of Birchfield's customer accounts reveals a total of $36,000 in uncollected invoices. Among those invoices is one for $1,200 to Clarke Company, a firm that has recently been declared a bankrupt.

(3) A physical count indicates 24,000 cases of beer on hand in the warehouse on July 1. Each case cost $3.50.

(4) A cancelled check for $40,000 dated January 1, 19X5 is found; this check was issued in connection with the purchase of land to be used as a site for a new warehouse. A warehouse was constructed on this site and completed in late June. This construction was entirely financed by a long-term mortgage. The Deed of Trust related to this mortgage was found in Birchfield's safe deposit box and indicated that the mortgage amounted to $90,000.

(5) Birchfield is being sued for $10,000 by A. Knutt, a former employee. The firm's attorney is uncertain as to what the outcome of the suit will be.

(6) An examination of invoices from suppliers reveals a total of $12,500 unpaid as of June 30, 19X5.

(7) Birchfield's payroll amounts to $13,000 per month. The payroll is paid on the first of the month for the previous month's work.

(8) Birchfield's stock book indicates that 20,000 shares of common stock were issued at a price of $5 per share on January 1, 19X4, the date the company commenced business. The firm had an income of $30,000 during its first year and no dividends were paid.

INSTRUCTIONS:

Prepare Birchfield's position statement as of June 30, 19X5.

2-4. Morty's Mortuary

The president of Morty's Mortuary went to his reward unexpectedly on October 31, 19X8. You have been asked to prepare a final position statement for the firm as of that date. The following information is all that you can obtain:

(1) The inventory of caskets and supplies on hand October 31 cost $84,000.
(2) The bank balance on October 31, according to the company's check register, amounted to $21,175. Comparison with a subsequent bank statement indicates that two checks totalling $310 were issued prior to October 31 but were not recorded in the check register. The statement also indicates a service charge of $5 for the month of October.
(3) The mortuary has contracts outstanding with 20 individuals to provide them with funeral services when needed. Each individual has paid $5,000 as consideration for the contracts. These funds have been invested in a variety of short- and long-term bills, notes, and bonds.
(4) Examination of cancelled checks from prior years reveals that the land and funeral parlor were purchased six years ago for $15,000 and $50,000, respectively. At that time, the funeral parlor was expected to have a useful service life of 15 years.
(5) Unpaid bills on hand as of October 31 total to $19,300.
(6) The mortgage company has written to advise that the principal balance due on the funeral parlor is $26,000.
(7) A three-year insurance policy on the building is found. This policy, costing $10,800, covers the calendar years of 19X7, 19X8, and 19X9.
(8) The company's stock book indicates that 5,000 shares of common stock were issued to Morty for $50,000 cash when he started the business six years ago.
(9) Since commencing operations, the company's ownership income has amounted to $125,000; during this time, the company has paid cash dividends of $66,240.

INSTRUCTIONS:
Prepare a position statement as of October 31, 19X8.

2-5. *Sweets-N-Treats, Inc.*

The controller of Sweets-N-Treats, Inc. has disappeared and it is time to prepare the monthly income statement as of September 30, 19X5. You have been asked to help and upon investigation ascertain the following facts about operations in September.

(1) An inventory is taken at the end of every month. There were 12,000 lbs. of candy in the store on August 31, 19X5 and 15,000 lbs. on September 30, 19X5.

(2) Examination of invoices indicates that 21,000 lbs. of candy were purchased during the month of September. The candy is purchased from a supplier for $.75/lb.
(3) The sales price of the candy is $1.25/lb. and all sales are for cash.
(4) Rent for the building is $1,000 per month plus one per cent of sales.
(5) There are two employees who are each paid $800 per month and a manager who is paid $1,000 per month.
(6) You discover a sales ticket prepared by the controller for 2,000 lbs. of candy paid for in cash on 9/20/X5. The candy will not be delivered to the purchaser until 10/5/X5.
(7) Miscellaneous expenses for September totaled $600.
(8) One thousand shares were sold for $5.00 each when the firm was incorporated. No additional shares of stock have been sold and no dividends have been paid.

INSTRUCTIONS:

(a) Draw up an income statement for the month of September 19X5 for Sweets-N-Treats, Inc.
(b) Assuming that all of Sweets-N-Treats' transactions are strictly for cash and that you ascertain from the firm's bank and cash register that cash on hand on September 30, 19X5 is $7,400 (the departed controller has taken all records on the store's cash position with him), make up a comparative position statement for August 31/September 30, 19X5.
(c) What is the relationship between income for September and the change in retained earnings from beginning to end of month as shown on the comparative position statement? Explain succinctly the nature of the "fundamental check" between income statement for a period and the comparative position statement for the beginning and end of the period.

2-6. Schaeffer, Inc.

On January 1, 19X1, A. and B. Schaeffer organize a new corporation to be known as Schaeffer, Inc. The following transactions occur during the month of January:

(1) A. Schaeffer invests $5,000 cash for 250 shares of stock. B. Schaeffer invests land worth $5,000 and a building worth $15,000 for 1,000 shares.
(2) Legal fees relating to securing the corporate charter are paid in cash, $500.

(3) Utilities deposits in the amount of $200 are paid. The deposits must be left with the utilities company so long as its services are used.

(4) A three-year insurance policy on the building is acquired for $900. The policy is to go into effect on February 1.

(5) On January 1, store equipment is purchased for $5,000 including delivery and installation. A down payment of $1,000 is made and a $4,000 6 per cent note is given for the balance. The note is payable in ten equal monthly installments beginning on February 1, 19X1.

(6) The initial merchandise inventory of $10,000 is purchased on account from J. Widemargin, a local wholesaler.

(7) Various carpenters and painters are paid $2,000 for remodeling the store building.

(8) $20,000 is borrowed on January 1 from the bank on a 5-year 6 per cent note.

(9) The first month's interest on the bank note ($100) is paid, and the accounts are adjusted to record the accrual of a month's interest ($20) on the equipment note, due February 1.

(10) Schaeffer, Inc. enters into a contract which grants the company exclusive local selling rights for a national brand of merchandise. Schaeffer pays $7,500 under the contract, including $5,000 for merchandise.

(11) Sales for the first month are $2,000 cash and $10,000 on account. Cost of merchandise sold is $8,000.

(12) Selling expenses, including salesmen's wages, total $1,500 and are paid in cash.

(13) Administrative expenses amount to $1,200 and are paid in cash.

(14) Payments on account to J. Widemargin total $9,000.

(15) Depreciation for January was $150 on the building (including improvements) and $100 on the equipment.

INSTRUCTIONS:

(a) Using the equation $A - L = O$, show the effect of each of the transactions on assets, liabilities, and ownership.

(b) Prepare an income statement for January.

(c) Prepare a position statement as of January 31.

2-7

Indicate whether the following events would be a source of funds (S), use of funds (U), or have no effect on funds (NE):

(1) Bought merchandise on account
(2) Customer paid his account in cash
(3) Depreciation expense
(4) Gain on sale of land for cash
(5) Issuance of common stock for cash
(6) Issuance of common stock for patent
(7) Loss on sale of common stock investment
(8) Retirement of long-term bonds with cash
(9) Paid employee's wages in cash
(10) Bought merchandise for cash

2-8. Ajax Bottling Company (I)

The Ajax Bottling Company has been in business for a number of years. The company purchases various "raw materials," such as syrup, carbonated water, and empty bottles, and sells a bottled soft drink to retail stores. During the calendar year 19X5, Ajax was involved in the following events (listed in summary fashion):

(1) Purchased raw materials for $400,000 on account.
(2) Sold bottled soft drinks (costing $350,000) for $100,000 cash and $380,000 on account.
(3) Collected cash on account of $300,000.
(4) Paid interest (including that payable at the beginning of the year) of $6,000 in cash on notes payable.
(5) Paid cash on $115,000 for wages ($90,000) and utilities and other expenses ($25,000).
(6) Paid $350,000 cash on accounts payable.
(7) Sold marketable securities of $109,000 for cash.
(8) Collected interest on marketable securities of $3,000 in cash.
(9) Paid $58,000 cash for income taxes (including income taxes payable at the beginning of the year).
(10) Buildings and machinery have depreciated by $2,000 and $8,000, respectively.
(11) Purchased a new machine for $20,000, giving a note payable to the vendor for that amount.
(12) Sold new bonds (payable) for $30,000 cash.
(13) Paid $7,000 cash on notes payable.

INSTRUCTIONS:

(a) Following the format of Table 2-2 (p. 41), rewrite on separate paper and complete Table 2-7 by including the changes during 19X5 and the ending balances as of December 31, 19X5.

TABLE 2-7

Effect of Events of the Year 19X5 on Position Statement Items of Ajax Bottling Company

		Beginning Balance	*Change During Year*	*Ending Balance*
ASSETS				
Cash		$109,000		
Marketable Securities		209,000		
Accounts Receivable		52,000		
Inventories		105,000		
Land		20,000		
Buildings	$85,000			
Less: Allowance for Depreciation	25,000	60,000		
Machinery and Equipment	$58,000			
Less: Allowance for Depreciation	14,000	44,000		
TOTAL ASSETS		$599,000		
LIABILITIES				
Accounts Payable		$ 31,000		
Notes Payable		10,000		
Interest Accrued Payable		4,000		
Income Taxes Payable		55,000		
Bonds Payable		182,000		
TOTAL LIABILITIES		$282,000		
OWNERSHIP				
Common Stock		$180,000		
Retained Earnings:				
Beginning Balance		137,000		
Plus: Revenues				
Less: Expenses				
Equals: Ending Balance				
TOTAL OWNERSHIP		$317,000		

(b) Prepare an income statement for the year ended December 31, 19X5.

2-9. Ajax Bottling Company (II)

INSTRUCTIONS:

Refer to the data of Problem 2-8. Using the format of Table 2-5 (p. 48), prepare a reconciliation of income flows and cash flows for Ajax for the year ended December 31, 19X5.

2-10. Ajax Bottling Company (III)

INSTRUCTIONS:

Refer again to the data of Problem 2-8. Using the format of Table 2-6 (p. 49), prepare a reconciliation of income flows and funds flows for Ajax for the year ended December 31, 19X5.

CHAPTER 3

ASSETS, EQUITIES, AND INCOME FURTHER CONSIDERED

WHILE THE FUNDAMENTAL ACCOUNTING EQUATION ensures the internal consistency of double-entry accounting records, much of the explanatory value of accounting data stems from their aggregation into relatively homogeneous classes or subsets of assets, equities, and income which can then serve analytical and comparative purposes. Position and income statements and other reports prepared for internal use can be as detailed as management demands. Those prepared for external consumption are typically less detailed, but those published by publicly held corporations have improved substantially since the passage of the Securities Act in 1933 and the establishment of the Securities and Exchange Commission. Pressures for more detailed public disclosure have also come from stockholders and many in the accounting profession. Inadequacies and inequities in public reporting persist but accounting has come a long way since the 1920s when many firms reported little more than assets, liabilities, net worth, net income, and dividends.

The classes of assets and liabilities and the components of income normally portrayed in accounting statements represent the consensus of accountants and regulatory agencies on their value for analysis and evaluation of business firms. The discussion is, however, a continuing one, and the guidelines for preparing statements are subject to change. This chapter will outline presently accepted forms and the content of position and income statements and discuss the rationale underlying the choices that have been made.

THE POSITION STATEMENT

We have seen (in capsule form) a position statement for the firm
selling logs for fireplaces, a report on the status of its assets and equities
as of a particular moment in time. The statement is simply an expanded
form of the fundamental equation. In what is known as the *account
form* of statement, assets are listed on the left with the total equaling
that of the equities (liabilities and ownership) which are displayed on
the right. An example relating to a more complex, going concern is
shown in Table 3-1. In the *report form,* the position statement utilizes
the equation "assets minus liabilities equals ownership," listing the assets
first, subtracting the sum of the liabilities, and showing ownership as
a residual. This form is illustrated in Table 3-2. Variations in these
forms do, of course, exist, but they are primarily matters of taste which
need not concern us at this point. These two versions of the fundamental
equation were discussed in terms of a small corporation in Chapter
2. We now consider their significance for a more complex business
firm.

The account form focuses attention on the business as an entity.
It displays on one side the firm's assets—its resources for conducting
its business activities—and shows on the other side the various ways
in which those assets are now being financed—the array of external
claims against the firm. The emphasis is on the firm as an operating
entity, and creditors and owners are merely treated in terms of their
common feature—sources of finance to the firm.

The report form focuses attention on the status of owners and their
proprietary or residual interest in the business. It makes clear that
creditors have a prior and fixed claim against the firm by showing
the amount of liabilities as a subtraction that must be made from the
firm's total assets in order to determine the value of the owners' residual
claim against those assets. The mode of presentation makes apparent
the differences in status between creditors and owners. In particular
it draws attention to the greater risk borne by the owners. That risk
is of two kinds: (1) an *income risk* (shown more clearly on the income
statement), in that the return *on* owners' investment may fluctuate widely
because whatever the level of entity income (discussed later in this
chapter) interest *must* be paid to creditors, and (2) a *capital risk,* in
that the return *of* the amount invested in the event of liquidation is
subject to the prior claims of creditors.

With this overview, we can now look more closely at the components
of the position statement.

TABLE 3-1
WMR CORPORATION
POSITION STATEMENT
As of December 31, 19X1

ASSETS

Current:			
Cash		$ 250,000	
Marketable Securities		20,000	
Accounts Receivable	$ 450,000		
Less: Allowance for Bad Debts	45,000	405,000	
Merchandise Inventory		360,000	
Prepayments		80,000	$1,115,000
Investments:			
Stock of Affiliated Companies		$ 250,000	
Cash Surrender Value of Life Insurance		20,000	270,000
Plant:			
Land		$ 450,000	
Buildings	$2,200,000		
Less: Allowance for Depreciation	590,000	1,610,000	
Equipment:	$ 800,000		
Less: Allowance for Depreciation	150,000	650,000	2,710,000
Intangibles:			
Patents	$ 800,000		
Less: Allowance for Amortization	100,000	700,000	
Organization Costs		40,000	740,000
TOTAL ASSETS			$4,835,000

EQUITIES

Current Liabilities:			
Accounts Payable		$ 490,000	
Wages Payable		25,000	
Taxes Payable		60,000	
Dividends Payable		50,000	
Advances from Customers		20,000	$ 645,000
Long-Term Liabilities:			
Mortgage Payable		$ 300,000	
Bonds Payable		1,100,000	1,400,000
Total Liabilities			$2,045,000
Common Stockholders' Equity:			
Common Stock:			
$100 Par Value	$1,000,000		
Excess Over Par	800,000	$1,800,000	
Retained Earnings		990,000	
Total Common Stockholders' Equity			2,790,000
TOTAL EQUITIES			$4,835,000

TABLE 3-2

WMR CORPORATION
POSITION STATEMENT
As of December 31, 19X1

ASSETS
Current:
Cash		$ 250,000	
Marketable Securities		20,000	
Accounts Receivable	$ 450,000		
Less: Allowance for Bad Debts	45,000	405,000	
Merchandise Inventory		360,000	
Prepayments		80,000	$1,115,000

Investments:
Stock of Affiliated Companies		$ 250,000	
Cash Surrender Value of Life Insurance		20,000	270,000

Plant:
Land		$ 450,000	
Buildings	$2,200,000		
Less: Allowance for Depreciation	590,000	1,610,000	
Equipment	$ 800,000		
Less: Allowance for Depreciation	150,000	650,000	2,710,000

Intangibles:
Patents	$ 800,000		
Less: Allowance for Amortization	100,000	$ 700,000	
Organization Costs		40,000	740,000
TOTAL ASSETS			$4,835,000

LIABILITIES
Current:
Accounts Payable	$ 490,000		
Wages Payable	25,000		
Taxes Payable	60,000		
Dividends Payable	50,000		
Advances by Customers	20,000	$ 645,000	

Long-Term:
Mortgage Payable	$ 300,000		
Bonds Payable	1,100,000	1,400,000	
TOTAL LIABILITIES			$2,045,000

COMMON STOCKHOLDERS' EQUITY
Common Stock:
$100 Par Value	$1,000,000		
Excess Over Par	800,000	$1,800,000	
Retained Earnings		990,000	
TOTAL COMMON STOCKHOLDERS' EQUITY			$2,790,000

Assets

While all of a firm's assets are resources of the firm, all of the resources it may utilize in its activities are not listed among its assets. In other words,

$$\text{Firm } A\text{'s Assets} \leq \text{Firm } A\text{'s Resources}$$

For example, the air we breathe is certainly a technological "asset" to us (in the lay sense at least) for we could not continue to exist without it; but accountants do not regard it as an "asset," and, as it is free, economists do not regard it as among "economic resources," which by definition involve scarcity. Similarly, the systems of streets, highways, and freeways are clearly of benefit to business firms that must deliver goods to their customers, but these "resources" fail to qualify, in terms of accounting, as "assets" to those firms. The distinction by which some resources are defined as assets while others are not is one of ownership—only those resources owned by the entity are treated as its assets. Thus, even though the air we breathe is of considerable benefit to us, it is not an asset because we do not own it; similarly, the road systems are not assets of business firms because they are public property, not the private property of those firms.

The ownership distinction is subject to a serious shortcoming, however. Only legal entities, such as persons and corporations, are entitled to own property. But, as we have seen, accounting focuses upon economic rather than legal entities. Thus, when the economic entity being accounted for is not simultaneously a legal entity, the accountant willingly treats the economic entity as being assigned rights of ownership by its legal owners. Resources which have been committed to an economic entity, say, a proprietorship by its legal owner, are, therefore, regarded as the entity's own assets.

Having specified that assets are the resources "owned" by the entity, we need delve further into the nature of these resources. We may regard them as anything having a present value (a value today), that value stemming from benefits or services which are expected to be received at some date in the future. Indeed, assets themselves are often defined as "bundles" of expected future benefits or service potentials. Such definitions are *future-oriented*, however, and since we view accounting as being comprised of measurements of *present and past conditions*, at least so far as reporting and evaluation of decisions are concerned, we prefer to regard assets as those things having *current value*, even if such values are indirectly derived from the future. Indeed, the existence of market values at any point in time is an indication of the assessment by many people as to the likelihood of receiving future benefits or services. The notion that any given person entertains as to the course of future events is *subjective* in nature; when many persons act upon their individual subjective expectations, their collective actions produce present market prices which we regard as *objective* in nature. These objective prices form the basis for accounting measurements.

Assets, then, are those resources which have a market value and which are "owned" by the business entity. As such, they include: (1) cash, (2) claims to cash (such as marketable securities, accounts receivable, and notes receivable), (3) claims to goods and services (such as insurance coverage paid for in advance), (4) rights to the services inherent in the firm's physical properties, and (5) rights to the services derived from certain intangible assets (such as franchises and patents).

Normally, all of the assets of a firm are held in order to produce a profit. At any point in time, however, one asset can be exchanged for another at prices prevailing in the market place without changing the total market value of the firm's assets. At any moment, therefore, any composition of assets has the same market value as any other. It follows that market values at a moment in time cannot explain why a firm's management prefers one asset composition over another. Presumably, the asset composition preferred by management is the one which promises to grow in market value most rapidly through its profit-seeking activities. These activities must include one or more of the following:

(1) manufacturing—the combination and physical conversion of assets from one form to another;
(2) trading—the process of buying assets in one market or location and selling in another;
(3) servicing—the process of providing services to others, such as advice and assistance by accountants, lawyers, economists, and management consultants, and other services by banks (the use of money) and insurance companies;
(4) holding—the holding of an asset during a period of price changes.

In effect, the management attaches a higher (subjective) value to its array of assets than the market does and, indeed, if it is seeking to maximize profit, has chosen that array for which subjective value is the highest.

For reporting purposes, however, the firm must base values on objective data derived from the market place because subjective values are inherently not verifiable. Normally, the values reported are those dollar amounts actually paid at the time of purchase or the dollar values received at the time of sale.

Accountants have posited several different ways of categorizing assets on the position statement. Among the dichotomies are:

(1) tangible/intangible—the distinction being made between those assets having physical existence (such as buildings) and those not (such as notes receivable);

(2) monetary/nonmonetary—the distinction being made between those assets having exchange value (such as cash and accounts receivable) and those having use value (such as equipment);

(3) current/noncurrent—the distinction being made between them which reflects essentially a difference in time perspective, with one year being roughly the cut-off point (in effect, assets are divided into short-term and long-term groups).

Of these possible categorizations, the tangible/intangible distinction is perhaps the easiest operationally to make; however, it is a sterile concept in that such a distinction plays little or no role in either the making or evaluation of business decisions. The monetary/nonmonetary distinction, in contrast, has some basis in business decisions; moreover, as we shall see in later chapters, it is of importance in other accounting applications beyond position statement classifications of assets. Nevertheless, the categorization universally employed by American accounting practitioners is the current/noncurrent distinction. Although this distinction, resting heavily on how accountants have chosen to define "current," is perhaps the least obvious of the three to laymen, it has been adopted because of asset liquidity considerations and their role in business decisions.

Assets classified as current include: (1) cash or claims to cash, (2) those physical assets that in the normal course of business can or will be converted into cash in a relatively short time, and (3) rights to goods and services which have been paid for and are to be received in the relatively near future. In general, therefore, current assets are defined in terms of "nearness to cash," with nearness meaning generally one year. The nearness-to-cash criterion is obviously met by the first two categories, but the appropriateness of the third demands further amplification. The rationale for inclusion of this category rests upon cash *obviation;* in other words, by having already acquired these short-term claims to goods and services and paid for them, cash which would have been required to buy them is no longer needed. Thus, rather than leading to a short-term cash *inflow,* these assets—called prepayments—preclude the necessity of a short-term cash *outflow,* the net effect of which is regarded as the same as that of an inflow. Given these criteria for inclusion as current assets, therefore, all assets not meeting these requirements are excluded and classified as noncurrent.

Assets are reported in the position statement in accordance with the current/noncurrent designation, with current assets being listed first. Within the current asset group, assets are listed in descending order depending upon their nearness-to-cash. As illustrated in Tables 3-1 and 3-2, cash (both on hand and in banks) is shown first, followed by marketable securities (temporary investments of excess cash in the securities of other entities, usually debt instruments), and accounts and notes receivable (customer indebtedness). Together, these comprise the firm's *current monetary assets,* although they are not specifically identified as such. These assets (other than cash) are considered to be "near cash" in a substantive as well as a temporal sense. They are usually fixed in dollar amount, are readily marketable, and offer reasonable certainty of being converted into cash. The remaining current assets, inventories and prepayments (such as prepaid rent, prepaid insurance, and prepaid wages) conclude the descent from cash. These are, of course, nonmonetary assets that are expected either to be converted into cash or used up in the near future, i.e., usually within one year.

For most business firms, the noncurrent asset category contains the preponderance of its assets. Note in Tables 3-1 and 3-2, however, that nowhere in the position statement is the term "noncurrent assets" used. Because this group is so large and composed of so many disparate kinds of assets, it is usually divided into three groups: (1) investments, (2) plant assets, and (3) intangibles, or other assets.

The first heading which follows current assets in the position statement is *investments.* For the most part, these are the firm's holdings of the securities of affiliated companies—other firms over which the entity exercises control by virtue of share ownership—and long-term receivables. Certain funds are also included, such as pension funds and funds held for retirement of the firm's own outstanding liabilities. If life insurance policies are being carried by the firm on its key executives, the cash surrender values of those policies would be considered investments, too.

Except for inventories, which are usually regarded as current, all of the firm's other physical property generally falls under the heading of *plant assets.* In essence, plant assets constitute the firm's productive facilities which are used in the manufacture and marketing of its products. Among the assets included in this category are land, buildings, and equipment. Because buildings and equipment depreciate in value as they age and are used up in the process of production, accountants must estimate and record such declines in value. These amounts are termed *depreciation.* Land, in contrast, does not wear out or become obsolete; hence, it is not subject to depreciation; it remains 100 per cent physically intact. That is not to say that the value of land remains unchanged over time, only that any changes in its value are not the result of depreciation as that term is defined. Natural resources, sometimes known as *wasting assets,* are also included in the plant asset category. Oil and mineral reserves are examples of these natural resources and, because they are finite in quantity, they are subject to being used up as are buildings and equipment. The accounting process by which these decreases in value are estimated and recorded is termed *depletion.* Depletion is analogous (but not identical) to depreciation. Accounting for plant assets is the subject of a later chapter in this book.

The final broad noncurrent asset category is that of *intangibles,* the "advantages" which belong to the business. While not possessing physical form, these advantages have economic substance in that they are of value to the firm. Franchises, patents, copyrights, and trademarks are all examples of the exclusive rights inherent in advantages. Because such exclusive rights typically are of limited life in both legal and economic terms, the diminution in their value is recorded by a process of *amortization,* which is similar to depreciation and depletion. Intangibles are relegated to the bottom of the asset list because their values are subject to greater uncertainties of measurement than those of other assets, such as cash or inventories, both of which appear much higher on the list.

One intangible asset deserves special note. One frequently finds among the intangibles on a firm's position statement a figure for which the description is "goodwill." Every business firm likes to think, surely, that it generates "goodwill"—among its employees, its customers, and its stockholders. How is a value arrived at for this, and what does it really mean? When a firm receives an award for distinguished service to the community, can it enter X million dollars as an asset on its position statement under "goodwill" and an equal amount to "ownership equity" (say, retained earnings or a reserve for distinguished service contributions)? Not surprisingly, the answer is definitely "No, the firm cannot do this." Goodwill is entered on the position statement *only if it is purchased, i.e., paid for.* And that occurs usually only if a firm buys the assets of another firm and pays more for those assets (or assets minus liabilities) than the assets are *individually* worth. (Whether

individually worth in terms of market value or in terms of historical
costs as the assets are likely valued on the position statement of the
firm being bought out is a matter we shall consider in Chapter 10.)
A firm may pay more for a *group* of assets than the assets are worth
if purchased separately for any of a number of reasons—it may be
acquiring intangible assets (not valued on the position statement of
the firm being acquired) such as a trademark or the services of salesmen
with important contacts and loyalties among customers. The location
of the firm may have become strategic in terms of actual and/or expected
future population growth. It may be that certain management personnel
deemed especially valuable are agreeing to stay with the new combined
enterprise. We have said above that the market value of assets depends
on expected future net revenues which are thought will flow from
ownership of those assets. When the present value of these expected
future revenues minus costs exceeds the market value of the firm's
assets, we later term this excess of *subjective value* over and above *market
value* "subjective goodwill." The objective of the business is to turn
this "subjective goodwill" into "objective goodwill," i.e., into actual market
value. If a firm's assets minus liabilities contain an element of "subjective
goodwill" in the mind of a firm purchasing these assets, so that it
is willing to pay for it, the "subjective goodwill" becomes "objective
goodwill" at time of purchase and gets reported as "goodwill" on the
position statement of the purchasing firm.

Liabilities

Since liabilities and ownership are both of the same genre—equities—
any discussion of either of them individually must necessarily focus
upon their differences, which are many. One of the primary distinctions
is the *priority* that creditor claims have over owner claims. In liquidating
an entity, for instance, all creditor claims must be repaid before any
assets are tendered to the owners. Similarly, payments to creditors,
known as *interest,* must be made before any payments to owners, termed
dividends, can be made. Thus, the priority of creditor claims over owner
claims is a major distinguishing factor between liabilities and ownership.

Another differentiation is the relative *specificity* of liabilities. Credit
instruments, such as notes and bonds, usually denote both a due date
and a maturity amount in dollar terms. Moreover, a rate of return
(an interest rate) is quite often stated on the face of the instrument,
and the return is a legally enforceable claim against the entity. In
the event of the firm's failure to fulfill the requirements specified by
its creditor claims, certain legal remedies are often prescribed as part

of the contract. Further, some claims, like the mortgage for the retailer of fireplace logs treated in Chapter 2, may be specific to an asset of the firm, in that case, land. Such features are not common to ownership equities.

Liabilities or creditor claims, therefore, may be generally defined as *obligations of the entity either to convey assets or to provide services to parties outside the firm.* Asset conveyance obligations are frequently fulfilled in the form of cash payments, but they also may be satisfied by transferring goods, such as merchandise, to the claimants. For example, a customer might order merchandise from a business and attach payment for the goods to the order, thereby giving rise to a liability on the firm's part. Such liabilities are generally satisfied by the delivery of the merchandise ordered rather than by refunding cash. "Advances by Customers" in Table 3-2 is a liability of this type. Similarly, in cases where the business firm deals in services instead of goods, such prepaid orders are usually fulfilled by the rendering of the services ordered rather than by the tendering of cash. The converse situation is found where the firm's employees provide labor services prior to being paid for them (wages are rarely paid in advance) or when suppliers deliver merchandise to the firm on a credit basis. In these cases, goods and services are provided *to* the firm rather than *by* it, and the obligations so engendered must be discharged by the payment of cash.

Like assets, liabilities may be divided into current and noncurrent components. As with the delineation between current and noncurrent assets, the line of cleavage separating current from noncurrent (usually called "long-term") liabilities is normally one year. In treating liabilities, however, an additional criterion is added: As well as meeting the time requirement as specified, a liability, in order to be classified as current, must also be one which will be retired by the use of a current asset (such as cash or inventory). The purpose of this additional test is to eliminate from the current category those long-term debts coming due in the near future which will be retired by "refunding" them, i.e., replacing them with new long-term debt rather than paying them off. But in making such a determination the accountant is faced with the unpalatable choice of either accepting the firm's assertion as to how it intends to discharge the liability or else becoming a prognosticator in trying to predict an event which must necessarily occur subsequently to the position statement date. At best the accountant's task is difficult and at worst, impossible. Why is the burdensome task of differentiating between current and noncurrent liabilities imposed upon the accountant?

The answer lies with the apparent relevance to decision-makers of knowing the firm's ability to make good its obligations and thereby to avoid insolvency and bankruptcy. The ratio between a firm's current assets and its current liabilities, known as the *current ratio,* is generally regarded as one indicator of its financial health. Subject to certain limits, an excess of current assets over current liabilities suggests that the firm will be able to discharge its debts as they come due. An even more stringent indicator, the *acid-test* or *quick ratio* also is dependent upon a measure of current liabilities. This ratio, current monetary assets over current liabilities, is assumed to indicate financial health when it is approximately one-to-one, when current monetary assets equal current liabilities. Because these ratios are so widely used in the financial community and since both have current liabilities as their denominators, accountants are obligated to make the current/noncurrent distinction.

Once the current liabilities have been identified, they are simply listed together as a group, with no attempt being made to array them in order of maturity dates. Many liabilities, such as accounts payable to suppliers, have varying due dates; and some creditors offer multiple dates, with no single one being *the* due date. As a consequence, there is no priority implied in the list of current liabilities.

The same is true of noncurrent or long-term liabilities. All liabilities not meeting the tests to qualify as current are simply listed in another section following the current category. Whereas the current liabilities are usually comprised of wages payable, taxes payable, and accounts payable, long-term liabilities typically consist of bonds payable and mortgages payable. To be sure, the accounting for noncurrent liabilities is not bereft of its share of difficulties, although one might initially presume otherwise. Such presumptions are likely to be shattered when we consider the topic of income taxes in a subsequent chapter.

Ownership

The final or residual equity section is that of ownership, termed *proprietor's equity* (for proprietorships), *partners' equities* (for partnerships), and *stockholders' equity* (for corporations). As a general rule, when position statements are prepared for proprietorships and partnerships, only the names of the owners are displayed together with the dollar balances of their respective investments, and no distinction is made between capital originally invested and that reinvested from profits. In corporate position statements, however, direct capital investments are separated from indirect capital investments. Direct capital investments are those in which a transaction occurs between the firm and its owners, such as the exchange of stock certificates for cash (in the case of an incorporated business). With indirect capital investments, no transaction occurs; profits earned by the business remain there rather than being distributed to the owners. This "non-transaction" is known as *reinvested capital* or *retained earnings*. Obviously, in the case of corporations, owners exercise considerably greater control over the making of direct investments rather than indirect ones.

Direct capital investments by stockholders, known also as *invested* or *contributed capital*, have two components: (1) *legal* or *stated capital* and (2) *excess* over legal or stated capital. Many state laws (corporations are chartered by the states, not the federal government) require corporate stock to have a *par value*. This is the amount which must be permanently invested by stockholders as a "cushion" to absorb losses before they reach the creditors. Thus, the par value of shares represents the firm's legal capital. In some states, however, *no-par* stock may be issued, in which case the issue proceeds are then the legal capital. To further complicate matters, some states which permit the issuance of no-par stock require that each share have a *stated value*, which effectively is the same as par value. In any event, par value or stated value should not be taken to mean the *market value* of the share of stock but rather the amount the stockholders must leave permanently invested in the business so as to protect the interests of creditors. In practice most corporations tend to set the issue prices of their stocks higher than par or stated values, which reduces the value of the latter as a legal protection to creditors.

Commonalities

We must take care not to make too much of an issue of the creditor/owner distinction. From the viewpoint of the business entity, creditors and owners perform much the same role, that of "renting" their capital. In reality it is the degree of risk each is willing to assume which separates the two, creditors opting for less risk and a consequent lower rate of return on their investments than owners.

Moreover, business firms today often issue securities which can be described only as "hybrids," amalgamating various features of each class. Some of the messier problems confronting accountants today involve these hybrid securities which many times defy categorization as either liabilities or ownership. "Preferred stock," for example, is stock that typically bears a fixed dividend, usually slightly higher than the interest rate paid on bonds, to be paid before any dividends are paid on common stock. And, if the firm is liquidated, the preferred stockholders are entitled to be repaid their investment in full before common stockholders can recoup any part of their investment. Preferred stock, therefore, possesses features of both a liability and ownership. Accountants are frequently admonished to search for "substance over form" in evaluating economic events, but theirs is sometimes a herculean task given the innovations of many enterpreneurs in designing the contractual features of new security issues.

Finally, from the viewpoint of investors, the distinction between credit and ownership instruments often becomes blurred. Obviously the categorization of hybrid securities as either fish or fowl is no less difficult for investors than it is for accountants. But more importantly perhaps is the fact that ownership instruments issued by one company may very well be less risky than the credit instruments issued by another. A share of stock, for example, issued by a well-established public utility company may be a much safer investment both in terms of income risk and capital risk than a bond issued by a new mining company which has yet to locate any proven reserves of minerals. In comparison to the investor in securities, the accountant's task is the relatively easier one of categorizing the securities of only one business firm; the investor must assess those of many different companies.

THE INCOME STATEMENT

The income statement reports measurements of the changes in an entity's wealth or economic well-being as a consequence of its profit-seeking behavior during a finite period of time. Accordingly, the statement must be titled so that the particular entity being accounted for is identified to the exclusion of all other entities. Similarly, the finite time period covered by the statement must be explicitly identified, be it a week, month, quarter, or year, and the date at which the period ended must also be stated. Finally, the statement heading must, of course, identify the type of statement it is, i.e., an income statement rather than a position statement or some other kind. All of these requirements have been met in the heading of the statement illustrated in Table 3-3. Now let us consider the component parts of the statement in greater detail.

Revenues

Strictly speaking, revenues measure the increase in equity corresponding to the resource (asset) inflows to the entity received in return for the provision of goods or rendering of services to its customers during

TABLE 3-3

WMR CORPORATION
INCOME STATEMENT
For the Year Ended December 31, 19X2

REVENUES:		
Sales (net)	$5,824,000	
Interest	14,000	
Other	22,000	$5,860,000
EXPENSES:		
Cost of Goods Sold	$2,535,000	
Salaries and Wages	2,239,000	
Depreciation	325,000	
Other	185,000	5,284,000
OPERATING INCOME		$ 576,000
GAINS AND LOSSES ON ASSETS:		
Gain on Sale of Equipment	$ 54,000	
(Loss) on Sale of Land	(12,000)	42,000
ENTITY INCOME		$ 618,000
Interest Charges		168,000
OWNERSHIP INCOME		$ 450,000
Common Dividend Charges		240,000
INCREASE IN RETAINED EARNINGS		$ 210,000

a period. By definition, revenues comprise the positive component of the firm's operations; hence, the term "operating revenues," which is occasionally encountered, contains a redundancy.

For most business firms, sales constitute the bulk of revenues. As a consequence, the sales "event," the transaction between the firm and its customer, is crucial to the measurement of revenues. All transactions involve exchanges of one sort or another, so sales transactions must be a special subset. A sale is a transaction in which the entity gives up goods or services to a customer and receives, usually, current monetary assets. (Note that the reverse is true for a purchase: The firm gives up current monetary assets or incurs a current monetary liability and receives other assets.) Thus, a sale need not be made for cash; an account or note receivable would be sufficient in order to recognize a sale event because they fall into the monetary assets category. Because of the objectivity inherent in the transaction, the point of sale is generally considered as the moment at which revenues are usually measured with the transfer price (the selling price) corroborated by the value of the legal claim to cash against the customer.

Although sales revenues are by far the largest component of revenues for most firms, there are indeed other forms which revenues often take. As was pointed out in Chapter 1, accountants employ two tests in determining whether or not to record a revenue:

> 1. the provision of goods and/or services to customers must be substantially complete before revenue may be recognized;
> 2. in order to be recognized, revenue must be measurable with a reasonable degree of objectivity and certainty.

Obviously, an arm's-length transaction between buyer and seller in which the seller gives up goods or services in exchange for a claim to cash from the buyer usually meets both criteria, and that is why the point of sale is so commonly used as the signal for measuring revenue. Nevertheless, there are numerous economic events other than sales which satisfy both tests and, accordingly, qualify to be recorded as revenues.

Three common variants occur where revenues may be recorded either before or after the point of sale itself. An illustration of the former is where a firm is providing goods or services under a long-term contract, say, with the government, in which collectibility is assured. When such a contract spans several accounting periods and when work is being done continuously in fulfillment of the contractual terms, it is clear that some income must be applicable to each period, not just to the last one when the contract is completed. The work being done each period is typically monitored by the customer, who in turn usually makes periodic remittances of cash to the builder in the form of progress payments. Thus, the first criterion is generally regarded as having been fulfilled. Since ultimate collectibility of a specified amount of cash under the terms of the contract cannot reasonably be doubted, then the second test, measurability, is also met. Accordingly, the total revenue called for under the long-term contract is split up and applied to each period in which work is done in fulfillment of the contract. The amount of revenue recorded in each period is proportional to the ratio of the amount of work done in each period to the total amount required by the contract. The recording of a revenue necessitates an increase in the firm's asset values. If cash is received each period in proportion to the earning, naturally the increase in the asset, cash, satisfies this requirement. However, if cash is not to be collected until later, then a monetary asset, in the form of an "unbilled account receivable" from the customer, may be created in an amount equal to the amount earned in each period. When collection finally is made, the account receivable asset is simply exchanged for another monetary asset of equal value, cash.

Another illustration of when revenue may be recorded prior to the point of sale is when goods produced have a guaranteed as with certain agricultural commodities. Instead of the revenue being recorded *during* production, as with long-term contracts, it is recorded upon *completion* of production. So long as the producer is able to sell all that he produces at the current market price and so long as the costs of transporting the goods to market and selling them are incidental to the cost of producing them, both tests of revenue realization are thought to have been met. Thus, once production is complete, the goods produced are valued at an amount equal to their sales price less expected costs of transportation and sale; revenue is simultaneously recognized at a like amount.

The other common variant is where revenue is measured *after* the point of sale rather than before. In such instances, the business firm has usually fulfilled all of its obligations as called for under the terms of the sale (in other words, it already has provided goods or services to the customer), but there exists some reasonable doubt as to whether or not the buyer will fulfill the other side of the bargain. What usually happens is that the firm sells something to the customer and receives in exchange a long-term promissory note. When collectibility of the note is subject to question for whatever reason, it may be impossible to place a value on it and, accordingly, even though the first test has been met, the second one has not. In such cases, revenue is usually not recognized until the claim to cash is actually collected or until the doubts regarding collectibility of the note have been dispelled.

We have seen that revenues may be recorded before, after, and at the point of sale, depending upon whether or not the dual criteria have been satisfied. All three of these possibilities relate to situations involving a legal sale in which the firm transfers goods or services to a customer in exchange for cash or a claim to cash in the form of a receivable. There are, however, other types of revenues (besides those related to sales) with which firms are involved. For the most part, these concern the "renting" of certain of the firm's assets to outside parties. In return for permitting these parties to enjoy the use of its assets, the firm exacts a price from them in the form of what loosely may be termed "rent." Arrangements of this sort are customarily formalized by means of a contract which, among other things, specifies the term of use and the price to be paid for such use. An obvious example of this kind of arrangement is where the business firm leases to others its physical properties, such as land, buildings, and equipment. The revenues to be recorded in such circumstances might be termed "lease revenues" or "rental revenues." Less obvious perhaps are the situations in which the firm grants other firms or persons the right to use certain of the firm's so-called "advantages," such as its patents or trademarks, thereby giving rise to "royalty revenues." Finally, the firm may record "interest revenue" as a consequence of lending its cash to others (or by permitting them to postpone by means of an account or note receivable an amount due to the firm for goods and services rendered). Although the revenue titles differ, each of these situations is essentially analogous to each other in that all involve permitting someone or some firm to use certain of the firm's assets for a period of time in exchange for cash or a claim to cash. Once the assets have been conveyed to the user, the firm earns its revenues by: (1) the simple passage of time, (2) the receipt of certain benefits by the user, a portion of which must be passed on to the firm by operation of a pre-determined formula, or (3) some combination of (1) and (2). This process is known as the *accrual process* in that, once the firm has conveyed its assets to the user, for the most part it need take no further explicit actions in order to receive new assets in the form of cash or claims to cash. In other words, the firm need only be passive rather than active in fulfillment of its contractual obligations.

Having now explored the various types of revenues commonly generated by businesses, let us see how they fit into the income statement. The listing of revenues comprises the first section of the statement, as illustrated in Table 3-3, and they are usually arrayed in descending order of magnitude. Sales, representing the largest element of revenues for most firms, ordinarily comes first, followed by installments, rentals, royalties, interest, or whatever ranks second, and so on. If the firm has a wide range of different kinds of revenues, the total of which is quite small and incidental to the firm's primary revenues, these may be aggregated and listed as a single title, such as "other revenues" or "miscellaneous revenues." Traditionally, this listing would be the last one in the revenue section even though its total may be greater than some of those which precede it. Once all of the revenues have been listed, they are summed and the total is displayed in the column immediately to the right of the listing.

Expenses

Expenses are measures of the efforts expended by the firm in order to generate its revenues—its accomplishments. Because revenues can only be recorded when they have been realized, the efforts which produced them must necessarily have been made either in advance of the revenues or concurrently with them.

Expenses include the services of the firm's assets (say, machine services) and services directly acquired (say, labor) that have been used to produce the revenues with which these expenses are now matched. Therefore, although *efforts* must either precede or coincide with the revenues that they produce, they are classified and recorded as *expenses* only as revenues are recorded. As a general rule, we may say that *expenses are defined by the revenues* they generate (even though we shall later see that this rule is occasionally breached for the sake of convenience). The comparison of revenues with the expenses that gave rise to them is essentially the thrust of the matching concept.

Accountants usually categorize expenses either by the service that was performed (what was acquired) or by the purpose for which the expense was incurred (its function). The *service* approach (usually called the *natural* approach) classifies expenses by the characteristics of the asset or asset service that was used up in production and sale. Hence, expenses for such inputs as labor services, building space, and machine services are classified as wages, rent, and depreciation. In contrast, the *functional* approach classifies expenses in terms of the purposes served by the inputs used. Hence, it combines various service expenses into such categories as selling expenses and administrative expenses. Salesmen's wages, for example, might be combined with depreciation on their company cars and hotel bills to form the selling expense category. For internal analytical and evaluative purposes, the functional form is more frequently used because expenses then usually match the organizational and operational structure; the service classification is ordinarily employed in reports to outside users.

Given their knowledge of the firm's organizational structure, managers usually find that functional groupings permit greater disaggregation of data into components more relevant to their needs. These groupings are basic to the notion of *responsibility accounting,* expenses being aggregated into groups corresponding to the managers responsible for incurring them. On the other hand, external users often are not intimately aware of structural nuances of one firm as compared to another, nor are they interested in attaching responsibilities to individual managers. Moreover, since the evaluations and decisions they must make are couched in terms of the firm as a whole rather than its components, the service classification more readily permits them to make interfirm comparisons. Finally, because the firm's present and potential competitors are among the external users of its published accounting reports, the adoption of a service classification of expenses for external reporting serves to conceal important detailed interrelationships which could otherwise be used to the firm's own detriment.

How might expenses be reported in an income statement under each of these types of classifications? Let us consider first the functional expenses. If a firm is engaged in the manufacture and sale of goods, probably the largest single expense would be "cost of goods sold." This is an amalgamation of the purchase prices of component materials, the salaries and wages of factory workers, and overhead costs of the factory, such as depreciation, utilities, supplies, and property taxes. For a firm such as a department store which is not engaged in the manufacture of goods but rather only in merchandising them at retail, "cost of goods sold" probably still would be the largest expense item. In this case, the cost of any good sold would be comprised of its price when purchased from either the manufacturer or wholesaler, together with any freight or handling required to bring it to the store and make it ready for sale to consumers. Under the functional classification, the manufacturing firm and the department store alike would also report "selling expenses" and "administrative expenses," although selling expenses likely would be of relatively greater magnitude for the department store as opposed to the manufacturer. Each of these groupings, in terms of expense purpose and, hence, departmental organization or managerial responsibility, ordinarily includes an array of service expenses—salaries and wages, rent, depreciation, supplies, utilities, and so on—as applicable to each particular function. For internal purposes, selling expenses might very well be broken down into different product lines, just as administrative expenses might be subdivided into marketing, accounting, legal, and so on.

Under a service classification scheme, the purpose of the expense and the organizational structure of the business entity are totally disregarded and expenses are grouped simply by the kind of services entailed. The types of expenses which would be reported in an income statement might specify separately the following: materials, salaries and wages, depreciation, rent, utilities, professional services (usually accounting and legal obtained from outside the firm), and taxes. All of these expenses might appear, regardless of whether the firm being reported upon was a manufacturer or a merchandiser, but their relative magnitudes would probably differ. In any event, like revenues, expenses are traditionally listed in an income statement generally in descending order of magnitude (except, of course, if the final item is a composite of many small disparate kinds and titled "other expenses" or "miscellaneous expenses").

Operating Income

Once expenses have been deducted from revenues, the result is labeled "operating income" or "income from operations" and is highlighted on the face of the statement. This figure represents that component of profit which is the fruition of the firm's primary and related business activities. As such, it is an indicator of how well the firm has performed in the particular line(s) of endeavor that the firm itself has chosen and reveals, at least partially, whether or not the firm is a viable one in that industry. Moreover, the reporting of an operating income is generally thought to enhance comparability, both interfirm and interperiod, by excluding secondary activities which may be more volatile. Rightly or wrongly, many analysts use operating income figures to predict the future profitability of a particular entity, under the assumption that these primary activities are much more likely to recur in future periods than are the secondary, or nonoperating, items.

Gains and Losses

We have seen that operating items are divided into asset inflows (revenues) and asset outflows (expenses), with the difference between the two being reported as operating income. Such is not the case with nonoperating items, however. Although these secondary activities also involve asset inflows or outflows, only the net effect is reported, an excess of inflows over outflows being termed a *gain,* and the converse, a *loss.* For the most part, these gains and losses are related to the inflow and outflow of the firm's noncurrent assets, those which the firm acquired for their use value rather than their value in trade or exchange. Thus, if a firm decided to sell a machine instead of continuing to use it in production, the gain or loss on the sale would be classified as nonoperating. But occasionally a firm's current assets may be involved in nonoperating gains or losses. The firm's inventory of goods, for example, may have been acquired with the specific intent of resale, but if the goods are uninsured and subsequently destroyed in a fire, a loss would be recorded and reported in the income statement below operating income and along with other nonoperating items. Thus, any inflow or outflow of assets, be they current or noncurrent, may give rise to nonoperating gains or losses, even though most are related to noncurrent assets.

If nonoperating items cannot be distinguished from operating ones on the basis of the current/noncurrent asset dichotomy, upon what basis then is the distinction made? In theory, the line is drawn between the firm's primary and secondary activities, those which are normal and recurring versus those which are not. In practice, however, this delineation is often quite difficult to implement and has caused considerable controversy among accountants. While some items, such as the destruction of inventory in a fire, are easily classifiable, many others are not. Suffice it for now to say that nonoperating items are those affecting income which are not classifiable as either revenues or expenses and which do not involve direct investments or disinvestments by equity-holders, the firm's creditors and owners. Admittedly, we are leaving this matter in a rather unsatisfactory state for now, but we shall return to it once again in later chapters, treating it with greater precision at that time.

Entity Income

After expenses have been deducted from revenues and the net effect of gains and losses is either added to or subtracted from that figure, the balance arrived at is entity income. This figure is highlighted on the face of the income statement as was the case with operating income. Because entity income is measured *before* interest and dividend charges, it represents the profit of the firm as a unit independent of its creditors and owners. It is the total of the firm's profits from both primary and secondary activities, the sum of operating and nonoperating items before payment of interest and dividends.

The evaluative and analytical benefits which derive from reporting this figure are related to its focus upon the productive use of the firm's assets. Entity income is a reflection of how efficiently management has used the resources bequeathed to it regardless of the sources engaged in their financing. Such a measurement permits interfirm comparisons between companies which are otherwise identical except for the composition of their equities, one perhaps having a preponderance of long-term debt and the other not. Similarly, interperiod comparisons are facilitated if a significant shift between liabilities and ownership has occurred between two or more accounting periods. Probably the primary evaluative device using entity income is the rate of return on assets, the ratio of entity income to total assets.

Some accounting theorists have perceived entity income as being *the* income figure, and we feel their views possess considerable merit. However, we see substantial benefit in having a variety of different income figures, each of which may be useful for a different purpose. Accordingly, we have elected to draw the income statement in such a fashion that several different incomes are disclosed. For those who adhere to the tenet that there is only one "true income," they can select the one they prefer from among those provided and simply ignore the rest; others who agree with our stance will also find their needs generally satisfied. Hopefully in this manner, income statements will be servant to the needs of a variety of masters.

Creditor Charges

After entity income has been determined, the next task is to divide it into the components applicable to creditors and owners, respectively. This is accomplished by deducting from entity income the interest which has been earned by creditors during the period together with any gains or losses that have occurred with respect to the firm's liabilities. Such gains and losses are typically recorded when long-term debt is retired at prices other than those at which they are being carried. If there have been no gains or losses on debt during the period, then the only element of creditor charges to be reported on the income statement would be interest. We shall consider this subject in much greater detail in a succeeding chapter.

Ownership Income and Its Distribution

After creditor charges have been deducted from entity income, the residual balance is ownership income. In most conventional income statements, this is *the* income figure that is reported and it is generally titled, "net income" (or "net income after income taxes" if a figure for "net income before income taxes" has also been displayed).

The rationale for focusing so much attention upon this single number stems from the so-called proprietary theory of accounting. In conventional accounting practice all interest charges, as well as gains or losses on liabilities, are treated as *determinants* of income, interest being treated as an operating item and included among expenses and gains or losses on liabilities as nonoperating items.

As was the case with those who advocate the entity theory, proponents of the proprietary theory have offered meritorious arguments in their own behalf. To be sure, ownership income permits numerous analyses to be made which are relevant to certain users and which are different in purpose from those stemming from entity income. We prefer to recognize the merits of each concept and to report both incomes, entity and ownership alike.

Once ownership income has been determined, the income statement is essentially finished. However, when accountants stop at this point, they must then prepare an additional report for corporate entities called the "statement of changes in retained earnings" or "retained earnings statement." Usually, this report starts with the balance of retained earnings at the beginning of the period, adds to that amount any increases, subtracts any decreases which occurred during the period, and arrives at the ending balance of retained earnings. For the most part, increases consist of ownership income, and decreases are the dividends to common stockholders during the period. Thus, the change in retained earnings forms an important link between the income statement and position statement.

In cases where income and dividends represent the only changes in retained earnings during the period, however, the preparation of an additional statement can be avoided by incorporating retained earnings changes directly into the income statement. When this is done, the income statement technically should be retitled "statement of income and changes in retained earnings," but the absence of a retained earnings statement makes it readily apparent that such changes are included in the income statement itself. As a consequence, the income statement is often not retitled, nor do we recommend it to be.

Because changes in retained earnings consist mainly of ownership income and dividends and because other changes typically involving complex issues are beyond the scope of this book, we will simply include retained earnings changes in the income statement itself. By so doing, instead of ending with ownership income, our income statements will conclude with the retained earnings change during the period, labeled "increase (or decrease) in retained earnings." To arrive at that final figure, ownership income must be reduced by the amount of dividends to common stockholders during the period. It should be emphasized that the dividend charges and change in retained earnings are not *determinants* of ownership income but rather *distributions* of it. (Similarly, interest charges, dividend charges, and the change in retained earnings can be thought of as comprising the *distribution* of *entity income*.) This is a consequence of our having joined two distinct statements. The income statement itself ends with ownership income, and that is where the retained earnings statement begins.

THE COMPARATIVE POSITION STATEMENT

The income statement in Table 3-3 tells us that retained earnings of the WMR Corporation have increased by $210,000 during 19X2. Hence, at the end of the period, retained earnings must be $1,200,000 since they amounted to $990,000 at the beginning of the period (see Table 3-1, p. 65). This figure will appear opposite retained earnings in the position statement prepared for December 31, 19X2. Other values in the new position statement cannot be inferred directly from the income statement because (1) there may have been transactions during the year that did not affect the income statement (the purchase of marketable securities and the sale of more common stock are examples) and (2) the specific assets and liabilities affected by the changes depicted in the income statement are not disclosed in that statement.

The firm, however, has this information in its accounting records and can prepare a position statement for the end of the period under consideration. This is shown in the comparative position statement presented in account form in Table 3-4. This statement, which can also be presented in report form, enables the user to determine easily the changes in specific assets and equities which have taken place over the period.

In the table, we see, that retained earnings has increased by $210,000, an inference drawn from the income statement. As the firm's total assets have increased by $265,000, there must have been new direct investment by creditors and stockholders taken together of $55,000, the excess over indirect investment (the increase in retained earnings) by stockholders. The equity side of the position statement verifies this for us; total liabilities have increased by $55,000. As there was no new direct investment (or disinvestment) by stockholders, the fundamental check can be shown directly as follows:

Revenues	$5,860,000
− Expenses	5,284,000
= Operating Income	$ 576,000
+ Nonoperating Gains	42,000
= Entity Income	$ 618,000
− Interest	168,000
= Ownership Income	$ 450,000
− Dividends	240,000

$$\Delta A \quad - \quad \Delta L \quad = \quad \Delta O$$
$$\$265,000 - \$55,000 = \$210,000 \qquad = \qquad \$ \ 210,000$$

We shall return to the comparative position statement in Chapter 9; the changes it discloses are the basic data from which the sources and uses of funds statement is prepared. The immediate task before us, however, is to show how accountants accumulate their data as events transpire. That is the subject of the next chapter.

TABLE 3-4
WMR CORPORATION
COMPARATIVE POSITION STATEMENT
As of December 31, 19X1 and 19X2
(in thousands)

ASSETS

	Dec. 31, 19X2			Dec. 31, 19X1	
Current:					
Cash		$ 300			$ 250
Marketable Securities		150			20
Accounts Receivable	$ 500			$ 450	
Less: Allowance for Bad Debts	50	450		45	405
Merchandise Inventory		400			360
Prepayments		100	$1,400		80	$1,115
Investments:					
Stock of Affiliated Companies		$ 250			$ 250
Cash Surrender Value of Life Insurance		25	275		20	$ 270

EQUITIES

	Dec. 31, 19X2		Dec. 31, 19X1	
Current Liabilities:				
Accounts Payable	$ 520		$ 490	
Wages Payable	30		25	
Taxes Payable	80		60	
Dividends Payable	60		50	
Advances from Customers	10	$ 700	20	$ 645
Long-Term Liabilities:				
Mortgage Payable	$ 300		$ 300	
Bonds Payable	1,100	1,400	1,100	1,400
Total Liabilities		$2,100		$2,045

Plant:						
Land		$ 385			$ 450	
Buildings	$2,200			$2,200		
Less: Allowance for Depreciation	700	1,500		590	1,610	
Equipment	$1,125			$ 800		
Less: Allowance for Depreciation	225	900		150	650	
			2,785			2,710
Intangibles:						
Patents	$ 800			$ 800		
Less: Allowance for Amortization	200	$ 600		100	$ 700	
Organization Costs		40			40	
			640			740
TOTAL ASSETS			$5,100			$4,835

Common Stockholders' Equity:						
Common Stock:						
$100 Par Value	$1,000			$1,000		
Excess Over Par	800	$1,800		800	$1,800	
Retained Earnings		1,200			990	
Total Common Stockholders' Equity			3,000			2,790
TOTAL EQUITIES			$5,100			$4,835

Appendix A

All-Inclusive versus Current Operating Performance Approaches to Income

The approach to income reporting that accounting practitioners have opted for is essentially in accord with the *all-inclusive method* (sometimes called "concept") as opposed to the *current operating performance method* (also "concept"), which is more in keeping with our operating/nonoperating division but is not analogous to it. Under the "pure" all-inclusive method, all items having a positive effect upon income are grouped under one heading—usually titled "revenues"—and all negative items are grouped under a second heading—usually called "expenses" or "revenue deductions." The excess of positive over negative items, then, is income. The rationale for this approach is two-faceted: (1) any distinction between ordinary and extraordinary items is necessarily arbitrary and difficult to implement in practice, and (2) all items, both positive and negative, which affect income are given equal rank—there is no priority among the items and all must be considered before arriving at any figure which is to be labeled "income."

Over the years, the primary competitor to the all-inclusive method has been the current operating performance method, wherein only what we have called "operating items" are regarded as income. Nonoperating items are excluded from the income measurement process and treated as a direct adjustment to equities, in particular, owners' equities. The arguments traditionally given in behalf of this posture seem to be based on a belief that only normal items which recur from year-to-year constitute "true" income and that abnormal and irregular items are essentially aberrations which can be safely ignored. Because the primary purpose of income measurement is to assist in forecasting the firm's future incomes, the argument goes on, these aberrations tend to distort the series and mislead users as to the probable course of future events.

Although we feel there is merit to both methods of income reporting, we are not wholly satisfied with either. We view the current operating performance method as suffering from a fatal flaw in that it defines away certain elements—abnormal and nonrecurring items—which have as real an effect upon the firm's economic well-being as do the so-called ordinary items. The destruction of an asset as the result of a natural disaster (such as an earthquake) serves to reduce the firm's wealth just as much as if it had been used up by normal activities (such as wear and tear). In either event, assets (and equities) are diminished by equal amounts. Therefore, we view the exclusion of such "extraordinary" items from the income measure as a serious deficiency of the current operating performance method.

On the other hand, our quarrel with the all-inclusive method does not stem from its measurement of income as a whole, as is the case with the current operating performance method. Rather, we question its utility for purposes of analysis and evaluation. By aggregating all positive and negative elements into a single income figure, many important cause-and-effect relationships are either lost or obscured. For example, profits on speculative activities (actively or passively entered into) may conceal unprofitable manufacturing and trading activities. Proponents of the all-inclusive method are, of course, quite correct in pointing out that any distinctions made between classes such as ordinary/extraordinary items or operating/nonoperating items, while clear-cut in theory, are often ambiguous in practice. Nonetheless, it is our judgment that the analytical and evaluative benefits which accrue to users from attempting to make such distinctions are of sufficiently great importance as to justify the practical difficulties that inevitably will accompany them.

Our preference is an income reporting method which amalgamates the desirable features of both the all-inclusive and current operating performance methods and which, as a result, provides users with more relevant information than do either of the others taken individually. Moreover, it overcomes our objections to certain facets of the two alternatives and provides, we think, a useful vehicle for the discussion of certain major issues in subsequent chapters. Accordingly, we opt for a reporting method which incorporates into income all changes in asset values (except, of course, those stemming from payments to and receipts from equity-holders, the firm's creditors and owners). This method employs the operating/nonoperating dichotomy of income items and provides for several subdivisions of income, i.e., operating income, entity income, and ownership income, each of which has somewhat distinct analytical and evaluative uses. The application of such a method is illustrated in Table 3-3 (p. 77).

Appendix B

Product Costs versus Period Costs

Central to the matching concept is the association of efforts with accomplishments, of causes with effects, of costs with benefits. Implicit in this concept is a belief that a necessary relationship between the two exists and can be found by the accountant. Under the conventional approach to matching (i.e., revenue realization), it is assumed that once revenues have been identified, the costs that expired in giving rise to those revenues can be identified as well.

The difficulty that accountants encounter in attempting to apply the matching concept in practice stems from the fact that the association between costs and revenues is not always clear-cut and unambiguous. Some costs, of course, bear a clear and direct relationship with the revenues produced. The commission paid a salesman, the lumber used in building a house, the permit bought for holding a rock concert are all examples of a direct association between cost and revenue. But what is the relationship between, say, the property taxes paid on an automobile manufacturing plant and the sales of automobiles during the year? How is the cost of a major advertising campaign late in the year to introduce a new type of home video recorder related to sales of those recorders in that year and in subsequent years? And how can the costs of an employee-training program be related to the firm's revenues? Such indirect relationships are what cause difficulty for accountants.

On the presumption that all costs are incurred for the purpose of providing a product (or service) which in turn will generate a revenue, a cogent argument can be made that all costs conceptually are *product costs* which do not expire (becoming expenses) until the product is sold. But since only some costs are directly embodied in the product, hence, directly associated with revenue from sale of the product, the concept cannot be made operational for lack of a means of treating those costs not directly embodied.[1] To deal with this problem, accountants have developed the notion of *period costs*, those incurred during a particular accounting period but which bear no clear-cut relationship with the products (or services sold). Such costs are then simply treated as expenses of the period in which they were incurred, thereby eliminating the problem of associating these costs with any particular revenues. Thus, an arbitrary means has been adopted to rescue accountants from a problem from which there appears to be no practical solution. The problem itself is, however, a direct consequence of the revenue realization approach to matching, which accountants have adopted. As pointed out in Chapter 1, the revenue realization approach

1. Here we mean embodiment in the broad sense of the term. Consider the case of a new car dealer. Obviously, the price paid by the dealer to the manufacturer for a particular new car is a product cost. But what of the commission paid a salesperson for selling the car? Is that a product cost? A narrow interpretation would exclude it, but a broad one would not on the grounds that the commission was as essential to generating the sales revenue as the wages paid the workers who assembled the car.

requires that costs incurred during any period be split up between those expiring in the generation of revenues in that period and those that will expire in the generation of revenues in subsequent periods. Under the alternative approach to matching—the market value approach—all costs incurred during a given period are treated as expiring during that period, thereby obviating the need for allocating costs as between different periods.

DISCUSSION QUESTIONS

1. Discuss how each of the following affects a firm's assets, liabilities, or income if it affects one or more of these concepts at all:
   a. New contracts are signed committing customers to buy $1 million worth of output over the next three months.
   b. A patent, valued on the company's books as worth $100,000, is leased to a competitor for $100,000 a year for four years.
   c. The Los Angeles Dodgers are closing their books for the third quarter (on September 30), and advance sales of World Series tickets amount to $2 million.
   d. A new survey in September, costing ABC Television Network $500,000, shows that the network's new season's shows are being watched, on the average, by 20 per cent more Americans than the network's comparable shows last year.
   e. A new subsidiary is purchased by Company X for $30 million. The current market value of the subsidiary's assets minus its liabilities is $25 million. The value of the new subsidiary's stock on the American Stock Exchange, before purchase, had been $35 million.
   f. Company X expects to lose a lawsuit (for patent infringement) now in the courts; if it does, it will then have to pay Company Y $5 million.

2. A corporation executive was heard to say that the most valuable asset his company had was its reputation for craftsmanship and the quality of its products, and its most serious liability was its reputation for delivery delays because of outdated and inefficient equipment, purchased long ago, which frequently broke down. Presumably these two considerations will be reflected in future cash flows. Are they, however, reflected in valuing the present net worth of the business in accordance with the "generally accepted accounting principles" treated in Chapter 1? Should they be? Would either or both be *more* likely to be reflected in the value of the company's net worth if current value accounting were followed?

3. Is the WMR Company, whose income and position statements are illustrated in Chapter 3, in a sound "liquidity position"? What are the standard measures you would use to determine this?

4. How would you measure the WMR Company's rate of return on capital for 19X2? Would entity income or ownership income be in the numerator, assets or assets minus liabilities be in the denominator? What measure would a regulatory body establishing prices to be charged by the firm be likely to use? A securities analyst? A bondholder?

5. "A firm's 'entity income (loss)' is measured by the increase (decrease) in the value of its assets during the period." Is this statement true? Should it be qualified in some way? If so, how?

6. "All liabilities are assets to someone else but not all assets are liabilities for someone else. A *nation's* 'wealth,' then, must consist of the sum total of its assets which are *not* someone else's liabilities." Discuss. Which of the WMR Corporation assets shown in Table 3-1 (p. 65) would be included and which excluded in measuring the nation's wealth? How does this compare with the assets of a commercial bank which are mainly cash, securities, and loans to customers?

7. In somewhat analogous fashion, a nation's national income or product is determined for the most part by aggregating the *value added* by *all* economic entities in the nation (i.e., all costs *other than* purchased supplies and materials, plus profit) *or* by aggregating the value of all sales of *finished goods*. Why do these two measures come to the same thing?

8. a. You begin a business, say, a retail store specializing in imported consumer goods, by contributing $10,000 cash, using $2,000 of this for lawyer's fees and incorporation fees, $300 for the printing of articles of incorporation, and $700 for advertising announcements of your forthcoming venture. These outlays of $3,000 involved in getting started are treated as "organization costs" and are to be amortized over the first sixty months of operation at $50 a month. What are your assets and equities at this point in accordance with "generally accepted accounting principles"? (Is the "net worth" of the business, for example, $10,000? Or the remaining $7,000 cash that is all that could be realized if the venture never got off the ground? Or something else?)

   b. On June 1, you purchase imported consumer goods in exchange for $3,000 cash and $9,000 accounts payable, rent a store (prepaid rent $2,000 for two months), and hire a helper (wages of $600 a month to be paid in equal installments on the fifteenth and last day of every month). Your employee works from June 16 in helping you set up the store and is paid $300 on June 30, 19X8. You are set to open on July 1, 19X8. What are your assets, liabilities, and net worth at the end of the day on June 30, 19X8?

c. During the first fifteen days you sell nothing but pay your helper $300 on July 15. What would you report on your income and position statements at the close of business on July 15 in accordance with "generally accepted accounting principles"?

d. Between July 15 and July 31 you generate sales for cash of $3,000. At that point, you close the store, pay your helper $300, hold a "garage sale" for your inventory items and net $5,000 in cash, and go into bankruptcy, paying lawyers' fees of $2,000 cash. Prepare a final income and closing position statement for your venture for the month of July.

e. Compare and contrast the reports that you have drawn up under (b) and (d) with those that would be reported under a straight system of cash (rather than accrual) accounting. Discuss these two approaches in contrast with other approaches you might devise and consider for this problem—for example, suppose assets were to be valued at their liquidation value?

PROBLEMS

3-1

The items on a position statement are usually grouped according to these subdivisions: Current Assets, Investments, Plant Assets, Intangible Assets, Current Liabilities, Long-term Liabilities, and Stockholders' Equity. Indicate into which of these groups each of the following items would fit:

(1) Taxes Payable
(2) Merchandise Inventory
(3) Cash
(4) Common Stock
(5) Bonds Payable (if due in two years)
(6) Patents
(7) Building
(8) U.S. Government Bonds
(9) Retained Earnings
(10) Notes Payable (if due in two months)
(11) Advances from Customers
(12) Organization Costs
(13) Prepaid Rent (for the next three months)

(14) Accounts Payable
(15) Office Equipment
(16) Mortgage Payable
(17) Accounts Receivable
(18) Notes Payable (if due in one year and one day)
(19) Wages Payable
(20) Office Supplies

3-2. Busad Manufacturing Company

The accounts of the Busad Manufacturing Company fall into the following categories:

A. Current assets
B. Plant assets
C. Intangibles
D. Current liabilities
E. Long-term liabilities
F. Ownership equity
G. Revenues
H. Expenses
I. Entity income distributions

Below are listed some of the company's accounts. For each account, in which of the above-lettered sections of the income statement or the position statement would the account appear?

Example: If one of the items listed were Checking Account, First National Bank, the answer would appear thus:

<u>A</u> Checking Account, First National Bank

(1) Accounts Receivable
(2) Accrued Payrolls
(3) Advances from Customers
(4) Common Stock
(5) Common Dividends Payable
(6) Cost of Goods Sold
(7) Bonds Payable
(8) Dividends on Common Stock
(9) Equipment
(10) Interest Charges
(11) Machinery
(12) Materials Inventory
(13) Patents
(14) Petty Cash
(15) Prepaid Insurance
(16) Sales Revenue
(17) U.S. Government Bonds
(18) Work in Process Inventory
(19) Interest Accrued on Notes Receivable
(20) Interest Earned on Government Bonds

3-3

(a) If current liabilities are $10,000, noncurrent assets are $75,000, noncurrent liabilities are $25,000, and owner's equity is $65,000, what are current assets?

(b) If current assets are $15,000, total assets are $80,000, current liabilities are $8,000, and owner's equity is $50,000, what are noncurrent liabilities?

(c) If working capital is $20,000, total assets are $130,000, owner's equity is $60,000, and noncurrent liabilities are $40,000, what are current assets?

(d) If working capital is $15,000, owner's equity is $80,000, total equities are $200,000, and current liabilities are $75,000, what are noncurrent assets?

(e) If working capital is $20,000, noncurrent assets are $140,000, noncurrent liabilities are $85,000, and total liabilities are $110,000, what is owner's equity?

3-4. The Furst Company

Data regarding the Furst Company on December 31, 19X2 are as follows:

Cash in register, $300, and cash on deposit in checking account, $2,000.
Capital invested by stockholders, $40,000.
Building, originally cost $50,000 but now carried at $45,000 because of depreciation.
Furniture and fixtures, originally cost $10,000 but now carried at $8,000 because of depreciation.
Mortgage on building is $20,000 due on December 31, 19X7. Interest has been accruing for the past year at 6 per cent.
Merchandise inventory on hand is valued at $40,000, at cost.
Orders have been received from customers in the amount of $5,000. These orders have not yet been filled.
Customers owe Furst $8,000.
Furst owes wholesalers $6,000.
Furst plans to order $30,000 worth of goods from wholesalers during 19X3.
Taxes accrued during 19X2 are $3,000.
Furst owes its employees $800 in wages.
Land on which the building stands cost $7,000.
Furst has outstanding a loan from the bank in the amount of $15,000. The loan is due on March 15, 19X3 and interest accrued to date is $200.

INSTRUCTIONS:
Prepare, in good form, a position statement as of December 31, 19X2.

3-5. Ann Awder Corporation

The accounts of Ann Awder Corporation as of June 30, 19X1, are as follows:

Cash on Hand	800
Office Supplies	300
Notes Payable (due Sept. 30)	5,000
Advances from Customers	900
Accounts Payable	7,200
Cash in Bank	3,400
Improvements to Leased Buildings	12,000
Office Equipment	4,100
Accounts Receivable	15,200
Unexpired Insurance	2,600
Merchandise Inventory	31,300
Store Equipment	8,200
Store Equipment Note Payable (payable in four equal quarterly payments)	8,000
Common Stock—$10 Par Value	20,000
Dividends Payable	1,000
Taxes Payable	2,000
Interest Accrued on Notes	600
U.S. Government Bonds	1,000
Prepaid Rent	200
Retained Earnings	?
Delivery Equipment	4,400
Organization Costs	1,500
Wages Payable	900
Allowance for Depreciation	6,200

INSTRUCTIONS:

Prepare, in good form, a position statement as of June 30, 19X1.

3-6. Whitmire Company

Prepare a position statement for the Whitmire Company as of December 31, 19X7 with the following information:

Prepaid Insurance	$	800
Accounts Payable		4,600
Common Stock, $5 Par Value		150,000

Cash	22,300
Common Stock, ABC Co.	26,000
Retained Earnings	32,000
Bonds Payable	50,000
U.S. Treasury Bills	20,000
Wages Payable	4,200
Paid-in Capital in Excess of Par	30,000
Accounts Receivable	29,500
Building & Equipment	182,400
Inventory	24,000
Allowance for Depreciation	44,200
Land	10,000

ADDITIONAL INFORMATION:

(1) Fifteen per cent of the common stock of ABC Company is owned by the Whitmire Company to ensure a stable supply of materials.
(2) The bonds are repayable $10,000 per year beginning June 1, 19X8. Short-term securities will be sold if necessary to make the repayment.

3-7. Better Builders, Inc.

Better Builders, Inc., wants to apply for a short-term loan at a local bank and is advised to prepare a position statement as of the end of this month (March, 19X5). The following data are available:

(1) Cash on hand and in banks totals $300,000.
(2) Receivables from customers amount to $525,000 but past experience indicates that five per cent of these will be uncollectible.
(3) Life insurance policies, having a total face value of $1,000,000 and a cash surrender value of $50,000, have been purchased on key officers.
(4) Houses which have been completed and are on the market have a total sales price of $600,000 and total cost of $300,000.
(5) There is a mortgage of $750,000 on the headquarters building. The building originally cost $1,800,000 and now has a value of $1,200,000.
(6) There are five common stockholders in the company who originally invested $125/share for 10,000 shares of $100 par value stock. There have been no other stock transactions.
(7) Suppliers are owed $510,000 and employees are owed $31,000.
(8) The land the company's office is on cost $600,000 and the land the unsold houses are on cost $50,000.
(9) Interest of $75,000 on the mortgage is due.

(10) The company has invested its excess cash in commercial paper which cost $25,000.

INSTRUCTIONS:

Prepare the needed position statement as of March 31, 19X5.

3-8. Computex Corporation

In preparing the position statement as of December 31, 19X7 for Computex Corporation (a manufacturer of calculators and mini computers), the accountants encountered the following:

(1) $172,000 was classified as "repair parts inventory." This consists of parts used to repair defective calculators returned to the company for repairs, some of which are made under warranty. Because a number of the calculators returned are older models no longer being produced, the firm has decided to carry a large inventory of old parts to provide quick repair service to its customers rather than to make small batches periodically. As a result, the overall parts inventory is rather slow-moving; on the average, a part remains in inventory for a year-and-a-half before being installed in a defective unit.

(2) The company owes $100,000 to the First National Bank on a 90-day note due January 15, 19X8. The company's practice has been to "roll-over" this note every 90 days, replacing it with a new 90-day note. The original borrowing of the $100,000 occurred five years ago and the company does not foresee repaying the $100,000 for at least three more years. The First National Bank is apparently willing to continue with this arrangement indefinitely.

(3) The company has made an offer to buy a large tract of land as a future plant site. The offer price of $750,000 was accepted and Computex has already deposited $10,000 as "earnest money." Computex has applied to an insurance company for a loan amounting to 90 per cent of the purchase price. If the loan is disapproved, Computex will get its "earnest money" back. If the loan is approved, the $10,000 will be applied against the purchase price. If the loan is approved but Computex decides not to go through with the deal, the entire $10,000 will be forfeited. The closing date has been set for March 15, 19X8; and the loan application will be acted upon prior to that date.

(4) Computex has an old piece of equipment that was used in the manufacturing process until six months ago, when it was withdrawn from service and replaced by a newer, more efficient unit. The

equipment originally cost $28,000 and depreciation up to the point it was taken out of service amounted to $21,000 (no depreciation has been taken since that time). The company has no further use for the old equipment and hopes to sell it during 19X8 for $6,000 to $8,000.

(5) $37,000 of the accounts receivable represents the balance due from Titanic Company which is now in bankruptcy. The account is already over a year old. From the information presently available from Titanic's trustee in bankruptcy, Computex can reasonably expect to recover 50 cents on a dollar when the bankruptcy proceedings are completed. Titanic has been in bankruptcy for six months and it usually takes about two years to wind up such proceedings.

(6) Included among Computex's marketable securities are 300 shares of Computex's common stock which was purchased for $8,000 two months ago from a disgruntled stockholder. The price of the stock on December 31 is $8,500. Computex plans to sell these shares to new stockholders early in 19X8.

(7) Among Computex's liabilities are bonds payable in the amount of $500,000. These bonds have been outstanding for several years and begin maturing on June 30, 19X8 and each June 30 thereafter for the next four years at the rate of $100,000 per year.

(8) Among Computex's prepayments is $36,000 for a three-year fire insurance policy which was taken out on October 1, 19X7. Computex may cancel the policy at the end of any quarter (December 31, March 31, June 30, or September 30) and receive a refund of two-thirds of the remaining pro-rata portion of the original premium. For example, if Computex cancelled the policy on December 31, 19X7, it would receive a refund of $2/3 \left[\left(\dfrac{2.75 \text{ years}}{3.00 \text{ years}} \right) (\$36,000) \right]$ = $22,000. The company has no present plans to cancel the policy.

INSTRUCTIONS:

Determine how each of the above items (1) through (8) should be classified on Computex's December 31, 19X7 position statement. Explain briefly the reasons underlying your classification.

3-9

Indicate whether revenue would be recognized prior to (B), at (N), or after (A) the point of sale in the following situations:

(1) A farmer harvests a crop of grain for which there is a government support price.

(2) A ticket agency sells 1,500 tickets for a concert next month.
(3) A land developer sells lots at $10,000 to customers for a $100 down payment and a twenty-year note.
(4) An accountant prepares a regular client's tax return for the preceding year and bills him for the amount due for professional services.
(5) A dog breeder's prize cocker spaniel has a litter of five puppies for which the current selling rate is $200 per dog.

3-10. Super Sports, Inc.

Super Sports, Inc., has been in operation for one year. The president has asked you to help in the preparation of an income statement for the year ended December 31, 19X1 from his records. You find the following information:

(1) Ticket sales for sporting events amounted to $400,000, including $25,000 for a boxing match to be held on January 15, 19X2.
(2) The company had to borrow $250,000 on July 1, 19X1 at ten per cent interest per annum. The company repaid the loan on December 31, 19X1.
(3) The company paid $.25 per share as dividends on December 31, 19X1. There are 100,000 shares of common stock outstanding.
(4) Selling and administrative expenses amounted to $43,000.
(5) Super Sports paid commissions of 75 per cent of ticket revenues to the participants of events.
(6) A car bought for the president's use was totally destroyed one week after it was purchased for $6,500. The company had not insured the car.

INSTRUCTIONS:
Prepare the income statement needed for 19X1.

3-11. Bernie's Auto Shop

Bernie's Auto Shop wants to ascertain what its income was for the fiscal year ending June 30, 19X3. The following data are known about the year's operations:

(1) Receipts for services have amounted to $490,000. There are also ten cars in the shop which have been repaired for reliable customers who have not come in to get their cars and pay the charges, which amount to $10,000.

(2) The cost of supplies and parts used in the repairs amount to $140,000.

(3) The mechanics' and secretary's wages are $234,000 for the year.

(4) The property adjoining the shop is rented to a cafe for $10,000 per year.

(5) The mortgage on the land and building has a principal balance of $200,000.

(6) The company follows a policy of paying ten per cent of ownership income as dividends on the last day of the fiscal year.

(7) Two used gas pumps were sold to another competitor for $20,000. The pumps had a carrying value of $12,000.

(8) Depreciation expense for the year is $56,000.

(9) Interest on bank loans and mortgage totals $13,000.

INSTRUCTIONS:

Prepare an income statement in good form for Bernie's Auto Shop for fiscal 19X3.

3-12. The Montrose Corporation

During 19X8, The Montrose Corporation experienced the following changes with respect to its assets and equities:

(1) Total assets increased by $2,500,000.

(2) New contributions of capital consisted of:
   (a) an increase in current liabilities of $800,000;
   (b) an increase in bonds payable of $1,000,000;
   (c) the issuance of new common stock for $600,000, of which $50,000 was for a small stock dividend.

(3) New distributions of capital consisted of:
   (a) the payment of $350,000 in interest charges;
   (b) the payment of $250,000 in dividend charges, including the stock dividend.

INSTRUCTIONS:

Determine entity income and ownership income in two different ways:

(a) Using the change in assets, less new contributions from creditors and owners, plus new distributions to owners and/or owners and creditors;

(b) Determining the change in retained earnings and adding to that distributions to owners, then distributions to creditors.

CHAPTER 4

ACCOUNTING SYSTEMS AND ECONOMIC EVENTS

IN CHAPTERS 1–3 we delved into basic accounting concepts and principles, analyzing "aggregate events" over an accounting period in Chapters 2 and 3 in such a way that we could formulate and discuss finished income and position statements. Further, by virtue of the principles of double-entry theory and the fundamental equation, we determined that a basic check existed between the income statement and a comparative position statement: Entity income as shown on the income statement, has to equal the change in assets less the change in liabilities (before interest and dividend charges), as shown on the comparative position statement. Alternatively, entity income less interest charges (equals ownership income) less dividend charges on an expanded income statement has to equal the change in retained earnings (change in assets less change in liabilities after interest and dividend charges) on the comparative position statement.

In this chapter, we will investigate the basic procedures for keeping track of accounting data on economic events of the business enterprise and the problems that arise in so doing, so that body and substance are added to the skin and bones presentation in Chapters 2 and 3. We will see that the fundamental equation and double-entry principles stay very much with us; they are as important in everyday accounting problems as they seemed to be in our conceptualization of the basic accounting problem in Chapters 2–3.

Our approach in this chapter will be to discuss these basic accounting procedures, using as an example a simple trading model—a small corporation operating a retail store with a minimum set of complications.

We shall see how such an entity can maintain records for the myriad of similar transactions it faces each day and how it must adjust its accounts at the end of each period in order to incorporate information about other (nontransactional) events of the period. In subsequent chapters we will discuss principles and procedures involving more extensive short-term credit operations, manufacturing operations as opposed to trading operations, various types of organizations entailing different means of long-term financing, and the like.

ACCOUNTING SYSTEMS

Accounting systems are particular applications of the general accounting model. Each entity has its own accounting system. The design of an accounting system involves deciding (1) what information (data) is to be collected on the economic events experienced by the entity and (2) how that information is to be collected—what accounts are to be set up, how and when entries are to be made in these accounts, and so forth. The system is designed for a particular entity so that, given the activities of that entity, the data provided yield the best possible information that users (both internal and external) need to evaluate —at the lowest possible cost—decisions, overall performance, and current position of that entity. Because each entity is unique, there being no other exactly like it, each accounting system is likewise unique, there being no other system identical to it. A given accounting system may be similar to another system, but this is merely reflective of the fact that the respective entities to which each belongs are also similar to one another. Thus, two entities which are members of the same industry may be expected to have similar, although not quite identical, accounting systems.

Every accounting system is "custom-designed" to suit the particular entity involved. Such designs must take into consideration not only the informational needs of the users but also the resources (both human and material) which are available for the development and implementation of the system. In all probability, the demands for information by users will outstrip the capacity of the finite resources available to provide such information. When such is the case, a balance must be struck between the demands for information and the accounting system's capacity to provide it. There are trade-offs between quality of information and cost of information. Finally, the system that is designed must be flexible and must lend itself to later redesign whenever the nature of either information sources or information needs is altered.

Designing an accounting system is without doubt a difficult task and one of the most challenging ones faced by accountants. In order to design a particular accounting system, the accountant must first have an expert knowledge of the general accounting model applicable to all entities. Armed with this knowledge, the accountant must then dissect the organizational structure of the particular entity for which the accounting system is to be designed in order to determine both the sources and destinations of information. In consultation with the firm's management, the accountant must establish an order of priority of informational needs, both internal and external to the firm. Finally, given the finite human and material resources which have been made available, the accountant must design an accounting information system that fulfills as many needs as possible in descending order without exceeding the resource constraints. The task is clearly not one for a novice; given the constraints, considerable amounts of training, skill, and experience are required if the accountant is to devise a system that is an optimal one.

Our purpose in this book, however, is not to consider a particular accounting system designed for a particular firm. Rather, our concern is with the components that are indigenous to virtually all accounting systems, whether designed for large or small entities and regardless of the type of business the entities are engaged in—trading, manufacturing, or servicing.

Commonalities Among Accounting Systems: Journal and Ledgers

Accounting systems are designed and records kept according to the general double-entry theory that every economic event has two aspects which, when considered together, leave the fundamental equation in balance. In applying this theory to a business entity, two types of records are usually kept: (1) the *journal*, which is the book of original entry, in which economic events are recorded chronologically, and (2) the *ledger*, which is the book of secondary (or final) entry, in which the economic events originally recorded in the journal are posted to separate accounts, i.e., in which the aspects of various economic events are assembled into homogeneous bundles. Together, the journal and the ledger comprise the core of any accounting system.

The journal and the ledger designed along the lines of the double-entry theory were a development of the Renaissance. The use of "cross entries" is known to have been employed in Florence as early as 1211, but there is no record of complete double-entry accounts before 1340, when such a system was used in Genoa.[1] The famous treatise on bookkeeping, *Summa de Aritmetica, Geometria, Proportioni, et Proportionalita*, by Pacioli, was published in 1494. In this work, which forms a basis for most modern accounting systems, the journal and ledger were used substantially as they are today. Pacioli's instruction to merchants to "begin all their transactions in the name of God and put His Holy Name on every account," however, has not been retained.[2]

In developing these two types of records in accordance with the double-entry theory, accountants early devised a simple shorthand method of employing the fundamental equation—a process based on the familiar concepts, debit and credit.

Double-Entry Theory and "Debit" and "Credit"

In Chapters 2 and 3 we developed the fundamental equation

$$\text{Assets} = \text{Equities, or}$$
$$A = L + O, \text{ or}$$
$$A - L = O,$$

and we used arrows to denote the effect of transactions (and other nontransactional events) on this fundamental equation. In accord with double-entry theory, the equation must always remain in balance: What is owned or owed to the entity (assets) minus what it owes to others (liabilities) is the residual net worth, or ownership equity. Thus, (a) increases in assets must be equaled by (b) decreases in other assets and/or (c) increases in equities. And (d) decreases in equities must be equaled by (c) increases in other equities and/or (b) decreases in assets. Call (a) and (d) "debits," and call (b) and (c) "credits." Then we have:

DEBIT			CREDIT		
↑	increase		↑	increase	
Assets		=	Equities		
↓	decrease		↓	decrease	
CREDIT			DEBIT		

1. E. Peragallo, *Origin and Evolution of Double Entry Bookkeeping. A Study of Italian Practice from the Fourteenth Century* (New York: American Institute Publishing Company, 1938), p. 3.

2. Quoted in K. MacNeal, *Truth in Accounting* (Philadelphia: University of Pennsylvania Press, 1939), p. 62.

At any point in time, debit balances must always equal credit balances in the accounts of any enterprise. And any debit which records an increase in an asset or a decrease in an equity must be offset by an equal credit which records a decrease in an asset or an increase in an equity. The fundamental equation must always be in balance.

The terms "debit" and "credit" (abbreviated "dr." and "cr.") have a long history in accounting which need not concern us here.[3] What we must get used to—for we will use them freely throughout the rest of this book—are the basic rules of debit and credit. Dividing equities into liabilities and ownership, these rules are:

Increase in an asset	Debit
Decrease in a liability	Debit
Decrease in ownership	Debit
Increase in a liability	Credit
Increase in ownership	Credit
Decrease in an asset	Credit

These rules are not some mystical edict which one must simply accept; use of the terms "debit" and "credit" is simply accountants' shorthand for applying the basic principles of double-entry theory.

INITIAL JOURNAL ENTRIES, POSTING TO LEDGERS, AND THE POSITION STATEMENT

We have said above that there are two basic sets of records in accounting: the journal (or journals) and ledger accounts. One may well ask: "Why have *two* types of records, thus doubling the work involved, rather than simply one? Why 'post' data that are already recorded in one place (the journal) to another set of records (ledger accounts)? Why not keep only a journal or enter events directly into ledger accounts?" The answer is that each type of record serves a separate but unique and useful function. The *journal* is the only place where (1) *both aspects* of an economic event [involving debit(s) and equal

3. While debit and credit undoubtedly were associated originally with "debtor" and "creditor," respectively, with debit being used to record the amount owed by a debtor (as in the asset account "accounts receivable") and credit being used to record the amount owed to a creditor (as in the liability account "accounts payable"), such associations obviously do not apply to impersonal items such as buildings, land, and the like. The terms should be thought of purely as an arbitrary convention.

credit(s)] appear *together* and (2) events appear *chronologically*. In ledger accounts, on the other hand, *like events* are *grouped together*. Any good office procedure on correspondence will make *two* carbon copies of every letter sent out—one for a chronological file of outgoing correspondence and one for a file based on topics or particular people or groups being written to. "I know that we wrote them in early July, but I cannot imagine what it is filed under." (Search chronological file.) "Let me have all the correspondence with *x*, please." (Search main file.)

The General Journal

Let us then see how we enter events initially into a general journal. W. M. Jensen decides to start, with his own $20,000, a small corporation to operate a retail store specializing in durable consumer goods—radios and televisions, refrigerators, dishwashers, washing machines, and clothes dryers. The store opens for business on April 1, 19X7, and all "starting up" operations occur, we will say, on the day previous to this. "Starting up" operations include renting a temporary store for a year (involving payment of the first and last month's rent); purchase of land for future construction of a permanent store with cash (this land will be temporarily rented to a concessionaire who will use this land as a parking lot, the concessionaire sharing any profits on a 50–50 basis as payment for rent); purchase of merchandise inventory and supplies on credit, with accounts payable in thirty days; the taking out of an insurance policy for three years against loss of merchandise by fire or theft; and borrowing $12,000 cash from a local bank in exchange for a note payable, due in one year and carrying interest at 7.3 per cent per annum payable quarterly.

These starting-up events are entered in Jensen Corporation's general journal for March 31, 19X7, as shown in Table 4-1. In accord with double-entry theory and keeping our fundamental equation in balance, each event and each entry involve equal debits and credits. Each event can be pictured in terms of changes, as designated by arrows, in the components of our fundamental equation, as we did in Chapters 2 and 3, i.e., for our first entry:

$$\text{Cash} \uparrow \$20,000 \qquad \begin{array}{l}\text{Common} \uparrow \$20,000 \\ \text{Stock} \uparrow \end{array}$$

$$\Delta A \qquad\qquad\qquad = \Delta L + \Delta O$$

and for our second entry:

TABLE 4-1

General Journal Page 1
Jensen Corporation

Date		Ledger Acct. Number	Debit	Credit
19X7				
March 31	Cash	1	$20,000	
	Common Stock	9		$20,000
31	Prepaid Rent	4	4,000	
	Cash	1		4,000
31	Land	6	16,000	
	Cash	1		16,000
31	Merchandise Inventory	2	24,000	
	Accounts Payable	7		24,000
	Purchase Invoice Nos. 1–18, terms 30 days			
31	Prepaid Insurance	3	3,600	
	Cash	1		3,600
	Invoice No. 19—3 year policy			
31	Cash	1	12,000	
	Note Payable	8		12,000
	9-month note, County Bank, Interest 7.3% per annum			

Prepaid Rent ↑ $4,000

$\Delta A \qquad = \Delta L + \Delta O$

Cash ↓ $4,000

and so forth. As we move along, the student will do well to imagine each and every journal entry in this fashion in terms of how the event affects the components of our fundamental equation in such a way as to keep it in balance in accord with double-entry theory.

The accounts to be debited and credited are entered in the general journal as shown, with the debit(s) recorded first, followed by the credit(s), the account title(s) for the latter always indented at the left. The first letter of each major word in the account title is capitalized. Often the entry itself is sufficient explanation for the transaction, as in the initial receipt of capital and the prepayment of rent by cash. But in many transactions some information in addition to the entry itself is desirable. This should be written beneath the account titles involved, as in recording the purchase invoice numbers in the merchandise inventory entry. There is usually a single space skipped between entries, and entries are usually recorded in ink. Errors are not erased; a ruler is used to cross out the erroneous entry, and a new entry is made below or, if the space is not available, squeezed in above each line of the entry crossed out. The ledger account number column is considered below.

So much for standard form of the journal. The old style general journal has been largely replaced in modern accounting (except for nonroutine events) by special journals with special columns and other labor-saving substitutes, as are discussed in the first appendix to this chapter. Nevertheless, a familiarity with general journal entries is absolutely essential for our purposes; they are widely employed as a shorthand device for expository purposes in discussions of theoretical problems and will often be used in this book.

Although our simple initial journal entries would seem to be a rather routine process once double-entry theory is understood, in fact, setting up a journal and journalizing any non-routine economic event thereafter is a thinking process. When the accountant receives (in the form of a memorandum, a purchase invoice, a sales slip, or the like) the initial record of some economic event, he must decide first what accounts are involved. Is the rent paid for the store going to be debited initially as "rental expense" or as "prepaid rent"? In the former case, you are initially treating it as a reduction in ownership; in the latter, as an increase in an asset. In either case, as time elapses some "adjusting entry" at the end of a period (see below) will have to be made to incorporate in the records perhaps an "overstatement of expense" (if payment of two-months rental has been recorded all as "rental expense" but only one month has elapsed) or an "expiration of an asset" (if the entry was initially handled all as "prepaid rent"). Suppose the purchase of the land, currently used as a parking lot, involved a commitment to repair surrounding pavement? Should that fact be recorded now, perhaps as an "estimated liability," or only when the actual outlay is made? Certain "inventory" items are used as demonstration models and will not be sold—are they "supplies" or "merchandise inventory"? Some merchandise inventory was acquired at a discount.

Should the accountant journalize the entry at full price or at the discounted price? If at full price, what adjustment is to be made for the difference between price and cash paid out? These and many other kinds of decisions must be resolved in making journal entries.

Ledger Accounts

In contrast to the journalizing process, posting to ledger accounts is as routine a task as may be found anywhere. As indicated above, ledger accounts collect in one place information about like events—for example, the receipt and expenditure of cash—which may occur at different times and for different purposes. We have already established, with our journal entries, which separate ledger accounts to establish and use. In a ledger account, debits are (in accordance with American custom) entered to the left of a dividing line in the middle of the page, and credits are entered at the far right, as illustrated in Table 4-2. Journal entries involving this ledger account are posted to the ledger periodically, the number in the "ledger account number" column in the journal indicating both where the entry is posted to and the fact that it has been done. Thus, after postings on March 31, 19X7, Jensen's cash ledger account or "ledger folio" (LF) account might be as shown.

The columnar arrangement of the ledger account may differ among different entities. Table 4-2 might be considered standard form, but the student should take this and all other "standard forms" in this book with a grain of salt. For pedagogical purposes there must be some agreement on form, but in fact there may be only general limits

TABLE 4-2

Cash							LF1
Date	Explanation	Journal Page	Debit	Date	Explanation	Journal Page	Credit
19X7 March 31		1	$20,000	19X7 March 31		1	$ 4,000
31		1	12,000	31		1	16,000
				31		1	3,600
				31	To balance	√	8,400
			$32,000				$32,000
March 31	Balance	√	$ 8,400				

to that choice, either imposed externally or internally (by the profession). The first two columns on each side giving the month and day are followed by a wide column for explanations. Usually this will be blank because the nature of the account is specified in its title and any further explanation deemed necessary may be found in the journal, in which are recorded all entries prior to being posted to the ledger account. The page of the journal where the entry was originally recorded (and where, therefore, any explanation may be found) is listed in the third column just to the left of that giving the amounts of the changes in cash. Lines are never left blank in the ledger account. The same sequence is repeated on the right-hand side of the ledger account for the credit entries to cash.

Ledger accounts and the initial position statement

Our journal entries for establishing the Jensen Corporation have as yet involved no income items but rather only position statement items. In accord with double-entry theory, our ledger account balances, after posting, should comprise all the elements needed for our initial position statement and, as can be seen with abbreviated ledgers or "T-accounts" in Table 4-3, they indeed do just that. If Jensen Corporation closed its books at the end of the day on March 31, 19X7, in order to start business on April 1, it would balance and rule off its ledger accounts as shown in Table 4-2, adding the necessary balancing item above the line in whatever column (debit or credit) was "short," drawing a diagonal line, as shown, where there are blank lines so that nothing further can be written in, drawing a double line under the two now-equal "total" amounts, and entering the new balance in the appropriate column below the double lines to start the next period. Check marks are entered in the journal page column to indicate that the balancing entry (involving an equal credit and debit, one above the double line, one below the double line) is not journalized. Other ledger accounts—for prepaid rent, land, common stock, and others (which involve, in our initial simple case, only one entry)—are usually not balanced, the amounts contained therein simply carried forward into the next period.

JOURNAL AND LEDGER ACCOUNTS AND TRANSACTIONS DURING THE PERIOD

Let us now consider two days in the operation of Jenson Corporation, say, at mid-month: Imagine these events being repeated in diverse ways over other days of April and then consider adjusting procedures

TABLE 4-3
Illustration of Relationship Between Simple Position Statement and Ledger Accounts

JENSEN CORPORATION

POSITION STATEMENT

As of March 31, 19X7

ASSETS   EQUITIES

Current:
Cash	$ 8,400				
Merchandise Inventory	24,000		Current Liabilities:		
Prepaid Rent	4,000		Accounts Payable	$24,000	
Prepaid Insurance	3,600	$40,000	Note Payable	12,000	$36,000
Noncurrent:			Ownership:		
Land		16,000	Common Stock		20,000
		$56,000			$56,000

LEDGER ACCOUNTS

Assets = Equities

Cash			Accounts Payable	
Mar. 31 Balance $8,400			Mar. 31 Balance	$24,000

Merchandise Inventory			Note Payable	
Mar. 31 Balance $24,000			Mar. 31 Balance	$12,000

Prepaid Rent			Common Stock	
Mar. 31 Balance $4,000			Mar. 31 Balance	$20,000

Prepaid Insurance	
Mar. 31 Balance $3,600	

Land	
Mar. 31 Balance $16,000	

that must be undertaken at the end of the month if accounts are to be closed and an income and position statement drawn up for the month of April. Our general journal might be as shown in Table 4-4 for the dates of April 14 and 15.

The first transaction (involving a purchase of merchandise inventory) is straight-forward. Assets and liabilities increase. The second transaction

TABLE 4-4

General Journal	Ledger Acct. Number	Debit	Credit
Date			
19X7			
April 14 Merchandise Inventory	2	$1,864	
Accounts Payable—Simpson Appliances	7		$1,864
Purchase Invoice No. 26, terms 10 days			
14 Accounts Receivable—V. N. Hogue	5	798	
Sales Revenue	10		798
Cost of Goods Sold Expense	13	570	
Merchandise Inventory	2		570
Sales Invoice No. 37, terms 30 days			
14 Accounts Receivable—George Johnson	5	448	
Sales Revenue	10		448
Cost of Goods Sold Expense	13	320	
Merchandise Inventory	2		320
Sales Invoice No. 38, terms 30 days			
14 Sales—Returns	11	224	
Cash	1		224
Merchandise Inventory	2	160	
Cost of Goods Sold Expense	13		160
14 Wages Expense	12	4,100	
Cash	1		4,100
14 Cash	1	5,600	
Sales Revenue	12		5,600
Cost of Goods Sold Expense	13	4,000	
Merchandise Inventory	2		4,000
15 Accounts Receivable—Buckland County	5	3,600	
Sales Revenue	10		3,600
Cost of Goods Sold Expense	13	3,000	
Merchandise Inventory	2		3,000
Sales Invoice No. 39, terms 60 days			

Page 17

TABLE 4-4 CONTINUED

General Journal		Ledger Acct. Number	Page 18	
Date			Debit	Credit
15	Advertising Expense	15	240	
	Cash	1		240
15	Supplies Expense	14	98	
	Accounts Payable—Palace Stationery	7		98
	Purchase Invoice No. 77, terms 15 days			
15	Cash	1	340	
	Accounts Receivable—M. P. Smyth	5		340
15	Accounts Payable—Sunnyside Distributors	7	160	
	Merchandise Inventory	2		160
	Return of defective merchandise, Purchase Invoice No. 17			
15	Cash	1	7,980	
	Sales Revenue	10		7,980
	Cost of Goods Sold Expense	13	5,700	
	Merchandise Inventory	2		5,700
15	Accounts Payable—GEM Distributors	7	6,200	
	Cash	1		6,200
	Payment of Purchase Invoice No. 123			

concerns sales on credit acknowledging, under our perpetual inventory system, the cost of those goods sold. We have two entries to record this transaction:

$$\begin{array}{ccccccc}
\text{Accounts} & \uparrow & & \text{Sales} & \uparrow & & \\
\text{Receivable} & | & \$798 & \text{Revenue} & | & & \$798 \\
& \Delta A & = & \Delta L & + & \Delta O &
\end{array}$$

and

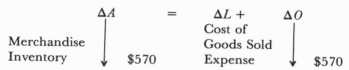

$$\Delta A \qquad = \qquad \Delta L + \qquad \Delta O$$

Merchandise		Cost of
Inventory $570		Goods Sold
		Expense $570

The third transaction (involving the sale to George Johnson) is, of course, similar to the second. The fourth transaction concerns the return of certain merchandise by a customer because it is defective. We will consider guarantees and other complications which might come into play at a later point (Chapter 7). In our case here we simply set up and debit an account, "sales-returns" (a contra-revenue account), and credit "cash," while at the same time debiting "merchandise inventory" (we have the goods back, defective as they may be) and crediting "cost of goods sold expense." In this way all aspects of a cash sale transaction recorded earlier have been effectively negated. Wages paid on April 14 to Jensen employees for the first two weeks of work are straight-forward, while the last entries for that day simply record the total of cash sales for the day as obtained by summing all the day's cash sales slips. The sales slips carefully record the item sold so that the accountant can record cost as well as sales value by referring to merchandise inventory records (see below).

The first three transactions for April 15 are straight-forward. The fourth merely records the collection of an outstanding account receivable (account of M. P. Smyth); one asset (cash) increases and is debited; one asset (accounts receivable) decreases and is credited. The fifth transaction for April 15 concerns the return to the distributor of the defective merchandise that the customer previously turned back on the 14th—in effect, "erasing" or negating Jensen's accounts payable with Sunnyside Distributors and the existence of that merchandise inventory. Finally, the last entry for the 15th records Jensen's paying off an outstanding account payable due two days hence.

All of these journal entries are duly posted to relevant ledger accounts—some of these being position statement accounts (all asset and liability accounts) and some being income statement accounts (sales revenue, sales returns, cost of goods sold expense, and all other expenses). Before considering how these are adjusted and closed at the end of the month, let us consider something that may have puzzled the student up to this point: How does the accountant keep track of (1) specific items making up merchandise inventory, (2) specific debtors in accounts receivable, (3) specific creditors in accounts payable, and specifics of other kinds?

Subsidiary Ledgers and Control Accounts

The large number and wide variety of economic events that must often be recorded suggests that subdivision and specialization may be as useful for efficient accounting as for efficiency in production. When detailed accounts of a particular kind, say, accounts payable, merchandise inventory, office expenses, or accounts receivable, become too numerous or cumbersome, they are often removed from the general ledger to a subsidiary ledger and replaced in the general ledger by a "control" account. In small firms these informational ledgers, which are not an integral part of the main accounting records, are usually limited to accounts receivable, accounts payable, and merchandise inventory accounts. In large concerns many subsidiary ledgers may be utilized, each containing numerous detail accounts and governed by a control account in the general ledger. Eliminating detail from main or control accounts and recording it in subsidiary ledger accounts serves three purposes: (1) reduces the size of the general ledger and, thus, makes the information contained therein more amenable to quick reference for the purposes of the higher executive staff and others; (2) facilitates the division of labor in the accounting department; and (3) aids in the detection of errors through comparison of the control account with the detailed subsidiary accounts which have been posted directly from a duplicate copy of the source document.

The main account in the general ledger—for example, accounts receivable or accounts payable—is said to be a *control* account because it serves as a check, or control, on individual postings to subsidiary ledgers; the posting to the control account and individual postings to subsidiary ledgers are made independently of each other. Modern special journals (see Appendix A to Chapter 4) usually have special columns for different purposes, and often the journal may be so set up that postings by special columnar totals may be made to commonly used general ledger accounts, such as accounts payable. Under these conditions there is a clear "control" relationship between a summary posting to the general ledger accounts payable-control account and a great many individual postings to the subsidiary accounts, such as those of GEM Distributors, Palace Stationery, and so on. An example of a typical control/subsidiary account relationship is that for Jensen Corporation, which appears in Table 4-5.

To derive maximum benefit from the use of subsidiary ledgers, posting to the detail accounts in the subsidiary should be made from a carbon copy of the same source document (such as a sales invoice or a purchase invoice) used in recording the economic event in the journal. In this

TABLE 4-5

Control/Subsidiary Account Relationships

Accounts Payable—Control

Total payments and returns during period {	√ $32,322 11,760 $44,082	√ $24,000 20,082 } Total purchases during period $44,082 √ $11,760	GENERAL LEDGER

Accounts Payable—GEM Distributors

Payments and returns during period {	4/6/X7 $8,900 4/9/X7 4,000 4/15/X7 6,200 √ 4,500 $23,600	√ $12,900 4/5/X7 6,200 4/21/X7 3,700 4/29/X7 800 } Purchases during period $23,600 √ $4,500

Accounts Payable—Palace Stationery

Payments and returns during period {	4/29/X7 $98 √ 160 $258	4/15/X7 $98 4/23/X7 160 } Purchases during period $258 √ $160	ACCOUNTS PAYABLE SUBSIDIARY LEDGER

Accounts Payable—Simpson Appliances

Payments and returns during period {	4/7/X7 $6,356 4/24/X7 1,864 √ 5,925 $14,145	√ $6,356 4/14/X7 1,864 4/29/X7 5,925 } Purchases during period $14,145 √ $5,925

Accounts Payable—Sunnyside Distributors

Payments and returns during period {	4/3/X7 $4,744 4/15/X7 160 √ 1,175 $6,079	√ $4,744 4/13/X7 1,335 } Purchases during period $6,079 √ $1,175

way an error made either in journalizing or posting will be disclosed by failure of the control account and subsidiary ledger to agree. If, as is sometimes done, subsidiary accounts are posted from entries in the journal, errors in journalizing will be perpetuated in the subsidiary ledger and may never be detected.

The Unadjusted Trial Balance

At any point in time, because of double-entry procedures, the total of debits should equal the total of credits, both in the journal and in the ledger accounts. This was true in our initial journal entries and ledgers; there were, of course, equal debits and credits, and these were reflected in a position statement that balanced. And since all economic events that we record continue to give rise to equal debits and credits, there is no reason for the basic equality in totals to change. Sometimes the practice is followed of "proving the journal" by summing the debit and credit columns of each page of the journal. A check on the equality of debits and credits after posting is obtained by a trial balance of balances in the ledger accounts, normally undertaken at the end of each accounting period after all the journal entries for the period have been posted. The preparation of a trial balance, it should be emphasized, is not critical to the accounting process; it serves merely as an indication that the arithmetic of the process was properly carried out.

An illustrative trial balance for Jensen Corporation for balances in ledger accounts on March 31, 19X7, plus entries made in the journal and posted to ledger accounts through April 30, 19X7, showing the net debit or credit balances in each ledger account, is given in Table 4-6. Accounts are listed in the order in which they appear in the ledger, with the ledger folio (account) number included at the left of the account title. Since the net debit or credit balance in each ledger account is listed, any account which is in balance (total debits equalling total credits—a balance of zero) would be omitted.

A trial balance is a check on the equality of debits and credits in the ledger accounts. It should not be construed as a complete check on the accuracy of the books. Items may have been listed in the wrong ledger accounts because either a mistake was made in the journal entry or an error was made in posting. For example, a box of cleaning supplies may have been inadvertently debited to merchandise inventory. Secondly, incorrect amounts may have been both debited and credited (equally) in the journal with consequent errors in the ledgers. As another example, the advertising entry for April 15 may have been erroneously entered as a debit to advertising expense and a credit to cash of $2,400. Thirdly, there may exist some events which occurred but which are unrecorded. None of these types of errors would be revealed by a trial balance.

The third type of error almost invariably is present in the initial trial balance because journal entries during the period have largely, if not entirely, been generated by source data on actual (arm's-length)

TABLE 4-6
JENSEN CORPORATION
UNADJUSTED TRIAL BALANCE
April 30, 19X7

LF	(Account Titles)	Dr.	Cr.
1	Cash	$ 15,211	
2	Merchandise Inventory	13,422	
3	Prepaid Insurance	3,600	
4	Prepaid Rent	4,000	
5	Accounts Receivable	15,440	
6	Land	16,000	
7	Accounts Payable		$ 11,760
8	Note Payable		12,000
9	Common Stock		20,000
10	Sales Revenues		178,610
11	Sales—Returns	3,025	
12	Wages Expense	8,420	
13	Cost of Goods Sold Expense	132,034	
14	Supplies Expense	6,208	
15	Advertising Expense	3,010	
16	Rental Expense	2,000	
		$222,370	$222,370

transactions during the period. But other types of events affecting the enterprise have occurred, even if they did not give rise to specific transactions: Some of the prepaid rent and insurance has been used up during April; interest on the note payable has accrued, even though no payment must be made for another two months (interest must be paid quarterly); the Jensen Corporation owes two days of wages although payment does not have to be made for another 12 days. When on an accrual system of accounting, such as is followed by most enterprises, "adjustments" must be made in the accounts at the time of closing the books to recognize events which affect the operation of the entity—its assets, equities, and income—but which have not yet entered the accounts. Normally, adjustments in the initial trial balance ledger accounts are set forth tentatively in a worksheet, which is then used to develop the final position and income statements. We will bypass the worksheet at this stage, however, leaving discussion of it for Chapter 9 when we will have treated more extensively some of the ingredients that go into a firm's system of accounts and into the firm's final statements. But end-of-period adjustments we must consider here.

ADJUSTING ENTRIES

Adjusting entries at the end of a period are needed to record events which have transpired but have not yet been entered in the firm's records. For one reason or another, revenue and expense accounts often either overstate or understate revenues earned and expenses incurred during the period. The counterpart to these is normally the overstatement or understatement of an asset or a liability. Let us consider six of the most usual types of adjustments that must be made in the accounts.

Expense Adjustments

Expenses recorded as assets. When a firm makes prepayments and time elapses, very likely some of those assets will normally have been used up during the period. What are actually expenses are still recorded as assets. The three-year prepaid fire and theft insurance policy is obviously a case in point. One month of the thirty-six has transpired. No claims have been made, but one month's insurance protection was paid for and received and that must be recorded as an expense for April. A journal entry accounting for this would be:

(a)   Insurance Expense $100
              Prepaid Insurance $100

This reduces the debit (asset) balance of $3,600 in prepaid insurance to $3,500 for the 35 months remaining in the policy and acknowledges that the one month's protection received was an expense of doing business.

The prepaid rent is another candidate for an adjusting entry but here ledger folio 16 shows that next month's rental was paid in April, presumably at the end of the month, i.e., the journal entry was:

Rental Expense $2,000
       Cash $2,000

Two month's rent is still prepaid (May, and the last month contracted for use of the store—March, 19X8), and so the rental accounts are in order as of April 30, 19X7.[4]

---

4. Recall that at the beginning of April, $4,000 was paid as rent for two months in advance (April, 19X7 and March, 19X8). By the end of April, therefore, half of that $4,000 prepayment has expired and the following adjusting entry could be made:

Rent Expense $2,000
       Prepaid Rent $2,000

Another candidate for adjustment of expenses recorded as assets involves depreciation on plant assets, but we are assuming that the Jensen Corporation owns no plant assets. We will consider this problem at length in Chapter 6.

Assets recorded as expenses. Ledger folio 14 records supplies purchased as expenses. We could have debited supplies as assets when they were purchased and then reduced that asset by the amount used up in the period—recording that amount as an expense—handling this account in the same way as prepaid insurance above. But the presumption here is that most supplies purchased will be used up during the period purchased, with perhaps only small inventories of supplies remaining at the end of the period. Nevertheless, clearly we will have overstated supplies expense by the amount of any inventory on hand—say, $900 worth. An entry correcting this expense overstatement and acknowledging the existence of the asset supplies inventory would be:

(b)	Supplies Inventory	$900
	Supplies Expense	$900

Unrecorded expenses. We have already hinted at two types of expenses which have been incurred during the month of April but are as yet unrecorded. Jensen has had the use of funds supplied by the bank against a one-year $12,000 note payable, 7.3 per cent per annum interest to be paid quarterly. The 7.3 per cent annual interest on $12,000 is $876 interest per year ($12,000 × .073 = $876). This figure divided by 365 days in the year yields a daily interest charge of $2.40 per day ($876 ÷ 365 = $2.40). Thirty days have elapsed; hence, $72 in interest charges have accrued for Jensen, as it has had use of those funds during all 30 days of the month. If the bank recalled the note on April 30, 19X7, Jensen would have to repay $12,000 principal *and* the $72 in accrued interest. Therefore, the $72 should now be recorded as a liability. We must make the following adjusting entry to Jensen's accounts:

This represents the rent for April. Recall also that late in April another rental payment of $2,000 was made, this time for the May rent—in effect, a prepayment. This payment could have been recorded in the following manner:

Prepaid Rent	$2,000	
Cash		$2,000

Once these two entries had been made, the rent expense account would have had a debit balance of $4,000. Although this two-entry procedure would correctly reflect the events as they occurred, the resulting account balances at the end of the period are exactly the same as when the "short-cut" procedure demonstrated in the text is used.

(c)   Interest Charges $72
         Interest Payable $72

A second as yet unrecorded expense (and liability) involves wages payable. Wages are paid by the Jensen Corporation at the end of every second week, and the last payday was April 28. Two days of the next pay period have elapsed; or 2/14 of a wage bill, say, of $4,200 (2/14 × $4,200 = $600), is an April expense and an April 30 liability. A journal entry must be made as follows:

(d)   Wages Expense $600
         Wages Payable $600

Total wage expenses for the month of April were not the $8,420 paid and recorded in the trial balance but rather $9,020 ($8,420 paid plus $600 owed at the end of April).

The supplies inventory account above and the wages payable account are "temporary asset and liability accounts," which should be erased in the normal course of events next period (at the end of which, however, new adjustments will have to be made). Frequently, adjusting entries involving "temporary asset and liability accounts" are "reversed" at the beginning of the subsequent period simply to make new entries in expense accounts easier during the period. This procedure is described, with its rationale, in Appendix B to this chapter.

Two of our expense adjustments, the first and third, involved correcting trial balance accounts for an *understatement* of expenses contained therein. The second adjustment involved correcting trial balance amounts for an *overstatement* of expenses. Obviously other types of understatement or overstatement might be involved—for example, taxes might have accrued. But we will ignore taxes at this point and move ahead to revenue adjustments.

Revenue Adjustments

End-of-period revenue adjustments are similar to end-of-period expense adjustments. They involve correcting trial balance amounts for: (1) an *overstatement* of revenue—revenue and assets have been recorded but, in fact, both are overstated (the latter because either an offsetting hidden "contra-asset" or liability account is involved); or (2) an *understatement* of revenue—revenue for the period and an asset are as yet unrecorded.

A contra-asset account recorded as revenue. Unless the Jensen Corporation has been extraordinarily fortunate in its choice of credit recipients, some of Jensen's credit sales will not be realized either in full or perhaps at all. To the extent that accounts receivable will not be collected, both revenues (sales) and assets (accounts receivable) are overstated. Accountants have developed two approaches for dealing with this "bad debt" problem: (1) the "direct write-off method" and (2) the "allowance method."

Of the two approaches, the direct write-off method is the simpler one. With this method, no entry is made for bad debts until a specific account, say, Accounts Receivable–John Dugan, is found to be uncollectible. Perhaps he has skipped town leaving no forwarding address; hence, it now appears highly unlikely that his account will be collected. At that point, the firm may well decide to write that particular account down to a zero balance, i.e., "write it off." Such an entry might be as follows:

Sales—Bad Debts[5]	XXX	
Accounts Receivable—John Dugan		XXX

The account debited is a contra-revenue; it reduces total revenues by the amount which, it is now recognized, cannot be collected, while the account credited recognizes the disappearance of what had been an asset. *If* the credit sale to John Dugan were made in the same period in which his account was written off as uncollectible, then net revenues for the period and total assets at end-of-period will be correctly stated. But suppose instead that the sale were made late in one accounting period and that the write-off was not made until the subsequent period. Clearly, both net revenues for the first period and assets at the end of the first period were *overstated* to the extent of John Dugan's account. By the end of the second period (the one in which his account was written off), assets will be correctly stated; but net revenues for that period would be *understated* by the amount of his account—and equal to the revenue *overstatement* in the preceding period. In other words, the contra-revenue account, sales-bad debts, was not correctly matched against the sales revenues account.

In an attempt to correct for these mismatchings that can stem from

---

5. In practice, rather than using a contra-revenue account, such as "sales-bad debts," accountants often use an expense account, such as "bad debts expense." Whichever account title is used, the impact on periodic income is the same, so the distinction is a minor one. We prefer the contra-revenue approach, as it emphasizes the fact that the revenue will never be collected (therefore, never existed) and that the account receivable was worthless from the outset. The expense approach seems to imply that the revenue did exist and that, at least at the point of sale, the account receivable had value; only because of some event subsequent to the sale did it become worthless.

the direct write-off method, accountants have developed an alternative procedure known as the allowance method. Under this method, it is recognized that some portion of credit sales and the related accounts receivable are not likely to be collected. This requires some write-down of revenues and assets in the same period in which the credit sales are made. At that point in time, however, it is still uncertain as to which *particular* accounts will prove to be uncollectible. Thus, even though perhaps two per cent of *all* credit sales may never be collected, it would be wrong to apply that percentage to *each* credit sale—most will be collected 100 per cent while a few will be collected either in part or not at all. Because of this uncertainty, the allowance method requires a two-entry process for implementation. The first of the two entries is known as the "provision entry" and is made at the end of the accounting period in the following manner:

Sales—Bad Debts	XXX	
Accounts Receivable—Allowance for Bad Debts		XXX

The amounts debited and credited above are usually (1) some pre-determined percentage of credit sales for the period or (2) some function of the outstanding accounts receivable at the end of the period as determined by means of an "aging schedule."[6] The first procedure is said to be an "income statement approach" since it emphasizes flows and the relationship between revenues and contra-revenues while the second is a "position statement approach," emphasizing stocks and the valuation of assets. In preparing financial statements, the first procedure is widely used and the amounts derived therefrom verified by means of the second procedure. The aging schedule percentages to be used in this exercise, say, at the end of a year, are in turn verified by experience during the year. An account that was deemed uncollectible after 180 days at some point in the second half of the year thus forms part of the (small) percentage of estimated uncollectible accounts for 0–30 days, a part of the (larger) percentage for 31–60 days, and so on.

---

6. An "aging schedule" is one in which a firm's accounts receivable are arrayed by their relative ages. The proportion of amounts that have been receivable for a shorter period of time and may be uncollectible is smaller than the proportion that may become uncollectible of those outstanding over a longer period. To illustrate, past experience may indicate that only one per cent of those accounts from 0–30 days old may become uncollectible, three per cent of those 31–60 days old, eight per cent of those 61–90 days old, twenty-five per cent of those 91–180 days old and fifty per cent of those 181 days to 365 days old; all accounts over one-year-old are considered uncollectible. Once the accounts have been arrayed by age and the total dollar amounts in each category multiplied by the appropriate percentage, the results are summed, with the total representing the dollar amount of expected bad debts.

When differences become apparent, consideration is then given to revising the percentage used in the first procedure.

We will assume that the Jensen Corporation adopts the "income statement approach." All credit sales are still reflected in accounts receivable outstanding at the end of its first month of operations—none have as yet been collected. Jensen predicts that five per cent of these outstanding accounts amounting to $15,440 will be uncollectible and, hence, makes the following adjusting entry in its books:

(e) Sales—Bad Debts $772
      Accounts Receivable—Allowance
      for Bad Debts $772

Note that with the allowance method approach above, the account credited is a contra-asset, thereby obviating the need for identifying which specific accounts are likely to become uncollectible. The primary impact of this entry is that it reduces both revenues for the period (by means of the contra-revenue, sales—bad debts) and assets at the end of the period (by means of the contra-asset, accounts receivable—allowance for bad debts).

Once it has been determined which specific receivables are uncollectible, the second entry—known as the "write-off entry"—is made to eliminate those accounts from the books. This entry is made as follows:

Accounts Receivable—Allowance
  for Bad Debts   XXX
      Accounts Receivable—John Dugan   XXX

This entry, taken alone, has no effect on revenues whatsoever and no effect on *total* assets. *Net* accounts receivable remains unchanged since the amount by which accounts receivable is reduced is exactly equal to the amount by which its contra-account (accounts receivable—allowance for bad debts) is decreased. All that has occurred, in effect, is a reclassification within the asset category.

A liability recorded as revenue. Another way revenue may be overstated in a period is by recording as revenue what is actually a liability. Let us say the Buckland County journal entry for April 15 involved a special order of closed-circuit TV for classroom use. The order was paid for when made (at a special discount price) with the understanding that the goods would be provided Buckland County when the new school building was ready—very likely before the end of the month. But April 30 comes, a strike has occurred at the school construction site, and it has not been possible to deliver the goods yet. In effect, cash has been received from the county but the sale has not been

consummated (and may never be—the Jensen Corporation may burn
down and all its merchandise go up in flames). Jensen owes the county
the goods or the cash paid for the goods. Jensen should therefore
write down sales revenues and record the liability as advances from
customers, viz.:

    (f)   Sales Revenues $3,600
           Advances from Customers $3,600

Simultaneously, of course, the expense which had been "matched" to
the revenue would have to be removed from the books as follows:

    (g)   Merchandise Inventory $3,000
           Cost of Goods Sold Expense $3,000

Alternatively, if uncertainty about timing (and perhaps ability to
deliver) existed at the time the order was received and collected for,
the liability advances from customers might have been created then,
rather than a credit entered for sales revenues, and the following entries
made if and when delivery was made:

    Advances from Customers $3,600
       Sales Revenues $3,600

    Cost of Goods Sold Expense $3,000
       Merchandise Inventory $3,000

If delivery has not been made by April 30, then no sale would be
recorded for April; but the cash receipt and liability, advances for
customers, would already be on the books, and no adjusting entry
would be necessary. As with other original entries and adjustments,
the choice between two perfectly valid procedures will often depend
on events the accountant considers most likely to occur. Hence, preference will be given to the original entry which is least likely to require
a subsequent adjusting entry. As a general rule, however, accountants
will try very hard, in accordance with the principle of conservatism,
never to record unearned revenue, as in effect we did with respect
to the entry for sales to Buckland County on April 15.

Unrecorded revenue. Inevitably there are often adjustments necessary
at the end of the period to record revenue which has accrued but
not yet been received, hence, perhaps not yet recorded. Interest accrued
but not yet received on marketable securities is an example, as, in
Jensen's case, the company's rental revenue (based on its share of the
profits) from its parking lot. This revenue has been earned but not
yet received. A telephone call to the concessionaire elicits that a check

for $1,640 is forthcoming from April parking lot revenues. The following entry records this:

(h)   Accounts Receivable—T. Casey $1,640
      Parking Lot Rental Revenue $1,640

The Adjusted Trial Balance and Financial Statements

It is clear that our (a) to (h) adjusting entries contribute equal debits and credits, some involving adjustments to existing ledger account

TABLE 4-7

JENSEN CORPORATION
Adjusted Trial Balance
April 30, 19X7

	LF	(Account Titles)	Dr.	Cr.
P	1	Cash	$ 15,211	
P	2	Merchandise Inventory	16,422	
P	3	Prepaid Insurance	3,500	
P	4	Prepaid Rent	4,000	
P	5	Accounts Receivable	17,080	
P	6	Land	16,000	
P	7	Accounts Payable		$ 11,760
P	8	Note Payable		12,000
P	9	Common Stock		20,000
I	10	Sales Revenue		175,010
I	11	Sales—Returns	3,025	
I	12	Wages Expense	9,020	
I	13	Cost of Goods Sold Expense	129,034	
I	14	Supplies Expense	5,308	
I	15	Advertising Expense	3,010	
I	16	Rental Expense	2,000	
I	17	Insurance Expense	100	
P	18	Supplies Inventory	900	
I	19	Interest Charges	72	
P	20	Interest Payable		72
P	21	Wages Payable		600
I	22	Sales—Bad Debts	772	
P	23	Accounts Receivable—Allowance for Bad Debts		772
P	24	Advances from Customers		3,600
I	25	Parking Lot Rental Revenue		1,640
			$225,454	$225,454

balances, some involving the setting up of new ledger accounts. We can now formulate an adjusted trial balance as in Table 4-7. All we have done to our unadjusted trial balance amounts is to include the adjusting entries. Thus, accounts receivable is $17,080 rather than $15,440 because adjusting entry (h) added a new debit of $1,640. Similarly a new debit entry appears for supplies inventory of $900 (LF 18) while the initial supplies expense debit amount of $6,208 is reduced to $5,308 because of adjusting entry (b). And so forth.

Given the adjusted trial balance in Table 4-7, the financial statements that appear in Tables 4-8 and 4-9 may be prepared. To facilitate statement preparation, each of the ledger accounts in the adjusted trial balance has been denoted with either an "I" (for income statement account) or a "P" (for position statement account). In designing systems of accounts, the ledgers are usually arranged in a fashion so that the accounts are numbered in accordance with their location in the financial statements. In other words, a numbering sequence may be established wherein, say, the 100 series is reserved for assets (cash being account number 101, accounts receivable being 102, and so forth), the 200 series for liabilities, the 300 series for ownership, the 400 series for revenues, and so on. In our simplified example of the Jensen Corpora-

TABLE 4-8

JENSEN CORPORATION
INCOME STATEMENT
For the Month Ended April 30, 19X7

REVENUES:				
Sales		$175,010		
Less: Returns	$3,025			
Bad Debts	772	3,797	$171,213	
Parking Lot Rental			1,640	$172,853
EXPENSES:				
Cost of Goods Sold			$129,034	
Wages			9,020	
Supplies			5,308	
Advertising			3,010	
Rental			2,000	
Insurance			100	148,472
ENTITY INCOME				$ 24,381
Interest Charges				72
OWNERSHIP INCOME				$ 24,309

TABLE 4-9

JENSEN CORPORATION
POSITION STATEMENT
As of April 30, 19X7

ASSETS

Current:

Cash		$15,211
Accounts Receivable	$17,080	
Less: Allowance for Bad Debts	772	16,308
Merchandise Inventory		16,422
Supplies Inventory		900
Prepaid Insurance		3,500
Prepaid Rent		4,000
		$56,341

Noncurrent:

Land	16,000
	$72,341

EQUITIES

Current Liabilities:

Accounts Payable	$11,760	
Note Payable	12,000	
Interest Payable	72	
Wages Payable	600	
Advances from Customers	3,600	$28,032

Ownership:

Common Stock	$20,000	
Retained Earnings	24,309	44,309
		$72,341

tion, we have not provided for such a planned ordering of accounts; rather we have merely added new accounts as the need arose. Nevertheless, it is important to be aware of the fact that most accounting systems are carefully designed in advance of their implementation and are not permitted to grow topsy-turvy as our simplified example may have implied.

The Process Summarized

Figure 4-1 summarizes the accounting process to this point as it is implemented by means of the journal and ledger accounts.

Closing Entries

Once the adjusting entries have been made and posted to the ledger accounts, the adjusted trial balance prepared to prove the equality of debits and credits, and the financial statements drawn up for dissemination to users, the books must then be closed. The closing process essentially involves bringing all income statement accounts (often referred to as "nominal" or "temporary" accounts) to zero balances, carrying the net change to the appropriate position statement accounts (known also as the "permanent" accounts). Once the closing process has been completed, the only accounts still having balances in them should be the permanent accounts. The rationale for this procedure relates to the notion of stocks and flows. At the end of the accounting period, all that exist are stocks, the position statement accounts. Thus, the flow accounts for the period just concluded must be emptied so as (1) to establish the final stock balances and (2) to prepare the flow accounts to receive the data of the ensuing accounting period so that the flows of different periods will not be intermingled with one another.

The vehicle for implementing the closing process is typically an account called "income summary" or "revenue and expense summary." This account *never* appears in either an income or position statement but instead serves as a temporary repository for the data that had been contained in the income statement (flow) accounts. In other words, income statement accounts are all simply emptied into the income summary account by means of "closing entries." The final closing entry then empties the income summary account by transferring its balance to the appropriate position statement account.

The question naturally arises as to how many closing entries are necessary. At one extreme, a separate closing entry could be made

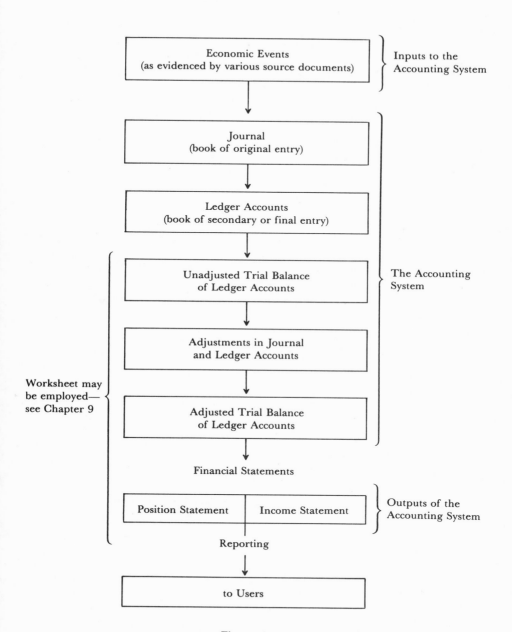

Figure 4-1

for each and every income statement account; at the other extreme, a single closing entry would be sufficient to do the job although, given the large number of accounts commonly involved, it would be a compound entry of the first magnitude. We shall take a middle-of-the-road approach here, utilizing several compound journal entries, one for each major section of the income statement. Thus, the first closing entry would involve the revenues section, closing out both revenue and contra-revenue accounts. In the case of the Jensen Corporation, this entry would be:

Sales Revenue	$175,010	
Parking Lot Rental Revenue	1,640	
Sales—Returns		$3,025
Sales—Bad Debts		772
Income Summary		172,853

Note that the credit to income summary is exactly equal to the net revenues appearing in the income statement in Table 4-8. Next, the various expense accounts would be closed by means of a single entry that has the effect of debiting income summary for the total expenses, as follows:

Income Summary	$148,472	
Cost of Goods Sold Expense		$129,034
Wages Expense		9,020
Supplies Expense		5,308
Advertising Expense		3,010
Rental Expense		2,000
Insurance Expense		100

(Had the firm had gains and losses during April, the next closing entry would empty those accounts.) At this point, were a balance to be struck in the income summary account, it would be equal to Jensen's "entity income" of $24,381. The next entry reduces the interest charges account to zero:

Income Summary	$72	
Interest Charges		$72

The effect of this entry is to reduce the balance in the income summary by the amount of entity income distributed to creditors so that the balance now equals ownership income. Since no ownership income was distributed in this case, the balance remaining in the income summary (a credit of $24,309) is closed out to ownership, in this case to the account, retained earnings. (This account is used in corporations to segregate capital directly invested by owners from that indirectly invested, i.e., income not paid out to owners.) The entry is as follows:

Income Summary	$24,309	
Retained Earnings		$24,309

Now the only accounts having non-zero balances are the stock accounts, those that appear in the position statement.

The nature of the income summary account should be clear by now—it serves merely as a bookkeeping convenience. The closing debits and credits could have been made just as easily to retained earnings directly, but having the income statement data (flows) temporarily condensed into a single account is often helpful. And again, we must reiterate that the income summary account itself *never* appears in either an income or position statement.

Once the closing entries have been made, all of the now-closed income statement accounts must be "ruled" so that the entries of the next period will not be confused with those of the period just ended. Since the totals of the debit and credit columns of each account should be equal (indicating a zero balance), "ruling" is accomplished simply by drawing a double line under each total (generally with a ruler, hence, the designation, "ruling"). This double line indicates to the accountant that the data contained above is from a now-closed period and is of no further concern. The position statement accounts—which contain non-zero balances—are also balanced and ruled at this time in the same manner as described earlier in this chapter.

SUMMARY

The logic of the accounting system used to develop the data from manifold source materials to an adjusted trial balance of ledger accounts, which then form the basis for the financial statements, is based on the same double-entry theory we first met in Chapter 2. All unadjusted and adjusted ledger balances must balance *in toto* (debits equal credits). Adjusted ledger balances of income statement accounts go into an income summary account, hence, to the ownership ledger. An excess of credits over debits in the income summary means an increase in ownership on the position statement, and it is that increase which, with the initial ownership balance, just provides for a balance of assets and equities in the ending position statement. Once all the closing entries have been made, assets at the end of the period must equal equities at the end of the period. Alternatively, the change in ownership which equals the change in assets less change in liabilitites on the *comparative* position statement will just equal the change in ownership on the income statement, the approach stressed in Chapter 2. For Jensen Corporation in April:

Revenues	$172,853
−Expenses	148,472
=Entity Income	$ 24,381
−Interest Charges	72
=Ownership Income (Change in Ownership before distributions to owners)	$ 24,309

From Comparative ⎱ ΔA $- \Delta L$ $= \Delta O$
Position Statement ⎰ $+ \$16,341 - (-\$7,968)$ $= \$24,309$
(Tables 4-3 and 4-9)

We must now turn to stretching our simple model of a trading firm in different directions, considering in the process some of the more difficult problems in basic financial accounting which up to now we have glossed over.

APPENDIX A

Special Journals in the Accounting System

In setting forth the nature of double-entry accounting, we have thus far used the simplest type of accounting techniques—based on individual entries in a general journal and postings to general ledger accounts. The days of the little bookkeeper with a green eye-shade, sitting on a high stool, bent over an old-fashioned desk, carefully recording entries and posting them individually to large leatherbound ledger folios, have, of course, passed long ago. In this appendix, we present a brief summary of more modern accounting techniques. This is not our primary interest, but it may be useful to visualize how accounting information is actually collected by American business firms. It should be remembered, however, that accounting principles are the same regardless of the actual procedures followed; even in a world of cybernetics, electronic brains will have to learn double-entry processes.

The general flow of records used to keep track of economic events is from *source documents* (sales slips, purchase invoices, time cards, bills of ladings, and so forth) to the *journal* and then to the *ledger accounts*, from which the financial statements are derived. Modern accounting systems permit greater speed and accuracy, offer more data for analysis, and frequently lower record-keeping costs as compared to the simple procedures pictured thus far by (1) replacing the general journal with *special journals* (typically having a number of columns, each for a different account) for the original entry of those economic events which are frequently repeated during the course of business and (2) summary posting of groups of entries to the ledger accounts. The basis of this improvement in accounting rests with the subdivision or elimination of clerical labor which it allows, with or without the introduction of machine processes, computer or otherwise.

As we have noted, the fundamental purpose of having special journals is to reduce the amount of accounting work to be done in recording and posting entries into the accounting system. Thus, the kinds of special journals to be designed and the fashion in which they are to be designed are a function of the types of economic events encountered most frequently by the firm. For most firms, these economic events are the transactions which involve (1) purchases, (2) sales, (3) cash receipts, and (4) cash payments. Accordingly, the four most commonly used special journals are (1) the purchases journal, (2) the sales journal, (3) the cash receipts journal, and (4) the cash disbursements journal. On occasion, one of these journals may be combined with another, such as (3) and (4) being combined to form a cash receipts and disbursements journal. Being custom-designed, the special journals used by any particular firm are dependent upon its own particular needs and the resources it has available. Accordingly, the journals we shall illustrate are by no means to be regarded as definitive, only fairly typical of the types found in practice.

Before we proceed, a word of caution is in order. *Special journals*—no matter how many a given firm has—*do not replace the general journal in entirety.* Indeed, all firms must maintain a general journal to record those relatively infrequent economic events that are not provided for in the special journals. All that a special journal does is to serve as the book of original entry for those events which occur most frequently, thereby eliminating the need to record each one individually in the general journal. Thus, special journals are substitutes *only in part* for the general journal.

Turning now to the most common types of special journals, let us begin our consideration with the *purchases journal.* Rather than being entered in the general journal, transactions involving the purchase of inventory items—merchandise, store supplies, office supplies, and the like—are initially entered into this journal. To be sure, other purchases (such as those of buildings, equipment, furniture, cars, and trucks, to mention a few) could also be entered in the purchases journal but generally are not because they occur relatively infrequently. This journal is usually used only for those routine and repetitive purchase transactions; thus, its use is commonly restricted to the purchase of various inventory items. Moreover, this type of purchase transaction is generally made on a credit basis, thereby giving rise to a short-term liability termed "accounts payable." A fairly standard form of the purchases journal appears in Table 4-A-1. Entries are made in the journal chronologically as the transactions occur. Then, depending upon the volume of such transactions entered into by the firm, the various columns are summed daily, weekly, or monthly, and the totals are posted to the appropriate ledger accounts. The fact that the column total has been posted is typically indicated by noting parenthetically the number of the account to which the total has been posted below the total itself.

TABLE 4-A-1

THE PURCHASES JOURNAL

Date	Merchandise Inventory Dr.	Store Supplies Inventory Dr.	Office Supplies Inventory Dr.	Accounts Payable Cr.	Vendor's Name
19X2 Jan. 2	$12,340			$12,340	Northland Co.
5		$260	$120	380	Jones Supply
9	6,190			6,190	Acme Corp.
12	4,740			4,740	Big State Co.
17			360	360	Stationer's Incorporated
20	14,920	430		15,350	Bark & Co.
23	2,870			2,870	Northland Co.
24	5,630			5,630	Kell Corp.
27	3,350			3,350	Greer Co.
30		105	75	180	Mid-Town
31	4,280			4,280	Central Wholesale Co.
	$54,320	$795	$555	$55,670	
	(151)	(153)	(155)	(204)	

Much of the benefit of special journals is derived from this "block posting" by saving the labor that would be required to post each transaction individually; the use of a special journal such as this permits a single posting to replace a multitude of individual postings. The other labor-saving advantage which stems from this special journal lies in the fact that account titles and related explanations need not be written out each time a transaction occurs; only the amounts and vendors need to be recorded in the columns provided.

The *sales journal* provides similar labor savings. In it, the routine, repetitive sales transactions are recorded in chronological order; and from it, "block postings" of the column totals are periodically made. Non-routine sales of the firm's other assets, such as buildings and equipment, are typically excluded from this journal. Thus, the "sales" referred to in its title should be taken to mean sales of merchandise. In contrast to purchases of merchandise and other inventories which are usually made on a credit basis, merchandise sales are typically made either on a cash or credit basis. Thus, if the sales journal is to record all sales of merchandise, whether for cash or credit, then both a column for cash and for accounts receivable must be provided; the alternative is to record only credit sales in the sales journal and cash sales in the cash receipts journal, but this would not provide a single record of total sales. The problem here lies with duplicate entries—if the sales journal is to record all sales, then cash sales must be provided for; and if the cash receipts journal is to record all cash inflows, then it, too, must provide for cash sales. As a result, cash sales are recorded twice, once in the sales journal and again in the cash receipts journal. The advantages of having a record of total sales in the sales journal and total cash receipts in the cash receipts journal must be weighed against the disadvantage of duplicate entries. If cash sales transactions are few in number and if it is deemed desirable to have all sales and all cash receipts recorded in their respective journals, then a column for cash should be provided in the sales journal and a column for sales provided in the cash receipts journal, and duplicate entries made. This is the assumption that underlies the sales journal illustrated in Table 4-A-2. When such is the case, however, the column total for cash is not posted; the total serves merely as a check when the debit and credit columns are "cross-footed" (the debit column totals being added together and compared with the sum of the credit column totals as a check against incomplete entries). When a total is intentionally not posted to an account, a check mark is parenthetically noted below the total instead of an account number.

As its title indicates, the *cash receipts journal* serves as the book of

TABLE 4-A-2

THE SALES JOURNAL

Date	Cash Dr.	Accounts Receivable Dr.	Customer's Name	Sales Cr.
19X2 Jan. 2	$ 1,840			$ 1,840
3		$ 2,165	J. R. Smyth	2,165
5		1,295	W. T. Bennett	1,295
6	3,610			3,610
9		1,245	W. J. Collins	1,245
11	5,590			5,590
11		1,310	H. S. Cohen	1,310
12		4,180	M. A. Holmes	4,180
13		5,070	S. M. Douglas	5,070
13	6,670			6,670
16		3,250	F. L. Hall	3,250
17		4,160	W. T. Bennett	4,160
17	3,520			3,520
18		1,200	P. J. Garrett	1,200
20		2,180	M. N. Cole	2,180
23		4,330	K. S. Bonner	4,330
23	3,640			3,640
24		1,620	T. R. Daily	1,620
25		1,910	J. R. Smyth	1,910
25	3,120			3,120
27		4,445	B. A. Butler	4,445
30		3,620	C. J. Rossetti	3,620
30		2,370	O. D. Schmidt	2,370
	$27,990	$44,350		$72,340
	(√)	(121)		(401)

original entry for all transactions involving the inflow of cash to the firm. For the most part, these transactions stem from collections on open, short-term accounts (accounts receivable) and from cash sales. However, other types of cash inflows, such as borrowings from creditors, cash investments by stockholders, and occasional disposals of firm assets like buildings and equipment, may occur, although infrequently. These relatively rare transactions are provided for by the provision of a money column entitled "Other Accounts," together with an attendant column, "Account Title," in which is written the name of the relevant account. Table 4-A-3 illustrates this format. The total of the "other accounts" money column is not posted because its sum represents heterogeneous

TABLE 4-A-3

THE CASH RECEIPTS JOURNAL

Date	Cash Dr.	Sales Cr.	Accounts Receivable Cr.	Customer's Name	Other Accounts Cr.	Account Title
19X2 Jan. 2	$ 1,840	$ 1,840				
	2,265		$ 2,265	F. O. Shields		
	1,880		1,880	C. R. Ferguson		
	3,115				$ 3,115	Notes Receivable
6	3,610	3,610				
	2,140		2,140	J. R. Smyth		
	1,605		1,605	T. N. Oldfield		
11	5,590	5,590				
	3,240		3,240	B. A. Butler		
	1,235		1,235	S. L. Tanner		
13	6,670	6,670				
14	10,000				10,000	Notes Payable
	4,815		4,815	D. A. Francois		
	2,620		2,620	E. F. Hunt		
17	3,520	3,520				
18	2,165		2,165	J. R. Smyth		
20	1,295		1,295	W. T. Bennett		
23	3,640	3,640				
24	1,245		1,245	W. J. Collins		
25	3,120	3,120				
26	1,310		1,310	H. S. Cohen		
27	4,180		4,180	M. A. Holmes		
27	5,070		5,070	S. N. Douglas		
	$76,170	$27,990	$35,065		$13,115	
	(101)	(√)	(121)		(√)	

items; rather its total serves only as a proof in cross-footing the journal. Instead, the column total is followed by a parenthetical check mark (as was the case for the cash column in the sales journal) and each individual amount is posted separately to the account listed alongside in the account title column. Also, the sales total is not posted so as to avoid double-counting, as cash sales have already been posted from the sales journal.

TABLE 4-A-4

THE CASH DISBURSEMENTS JOURNAL

Date	Vendor's Name	Payroll Payable Dr.	Utilities Payable Dr.	Accounts Payable Dr.	Other Accounts Dr.	Account Title	Cash Cr.
19X1 Jan.							
2	Merchants Wholesale			$ 5,925			$ 5,925
2					$ 7,200	Prepaid Insurance	7,200
3	Abco			2,805			2,805
5	Kell Corp.			6,265			6,265
6		$1,680					1,680
9					340	Advertising Expense	340
11	Control Wholesale			7,830			7,830
12	Northland Co.			12,340			12,340
13		1,680					1,680
13	Jones Supply			380			380
16					3,570	Store Equipment	3,570
19	Acme Corp.			6,190			6,190
20		1,680					1,680
20	Big State Co.			4,740			4,740
27	Stationer's Inc.			360			360
27		1,680					1,680
30	Bark & Co.			14,920			14,920
31			$125				125
31			340				340
31			55				55
		$6,720	$520	$61,755	$11,110		$80,105
		(212)	(217)	(204)	(✓)		(101)

The *cash disbursements journal* (sometimes termed the *check register* when all disbursements are made by check) is designed in a fashion similar to that of the cash receipts journal. An example of one having a standard format is provided in Table 4-A-4. In it, all outflows of cash are recorded, the most common being for inventories purchased on account (accounts payable), wages and salaries to employees (payroll payable), and the various utilities (utilities payable). Of course, these do not represent all of the payments that a business firm must make; accordingly, a money column must be provided for "Other Accounts," together with an attendant column entitled "Account Title," in which the relevant account names are listed. The column total of the money column for "other accounts" is handled in the same manner as in the cash receipts journal, and the individual amounts contained therein are posted directly to the relevant accounts listed alongside in the account title column.

Our brief digression into special journals is now complete although it has not been all-inclusive. The four special journals that have been illustrated are reasonably representative of those found in most business firms. Their form, however, may very well vary from firm to firm, depending upon individual needs; the forms we have illustrated should not be regarded as definitive but rather indicative. The actual formats used by firms in practice will usually include the features we have illustrated, but they will vary somewhat as do individual circumstances. In a similar vein, firms may employ more or fewer special journals than the four we have illustrated. As is the case with the accounting system itself, the number of special journals employed and the composition of each individual journal are custom-designed to fit the circumstances at hand. All that can be said for certain is that regardless of the number and type of special journals available, each firm must have a general journal to serve as a book of original entry in which to record those economic events not provided for in the various special journals.

APPENDIX B

Reversing Entries

The final—and optional—step of the end-of-period process involves the preparation of so-called "reversing entries." These entries are not critical to the accounting process and should be regarded as nothing more than a record-keeping convenience. Their purpose is to simplify the task of the accountant during the early part of the next period by eliminating the necessity of remembering to take into account the adjustments made at the end of the preceding period. In other words, the accountant can proceed to make journal entries when transactions or other economic events occur in the next period just as if no adjustments had been made.

An example may better clarify this process. Recall that one of the most common adjusting entries, and the one we made on April 30 for the Jensen Corporation, is as follows:

Wages Expense	$600	
Wages Payable		$600

When the next payday comes around, the accountant will have to make the following entry, remembering that one part of the total cash paid is for the liability, wages payable, and the rest is an expense of the current period:

Wages Payable	$ 600	
Wages Expense	3,600	
Cash		$4,200

Clearly, it would be easier if the accountant could simply follow the rule of debiting wages expense and crediting cash for the payroll total each payday. The process of reversing entries accomplishes this. If, at the beginning of the new period, the following reversing entry had been made,

Wages Payable	$600	
Wages Expense		$600

the liability account would have been eliminated and a temporary credit balance established in the expense account. This temporary credit balance does not square with reality but causes no real difficulties since financial statements would not be prepared during this relatively short interval anyway. When the regular payday arrived, the accountant could then make the following standard entry, just as would be done on any other payday:

Wages Expense	$4,200	
Cash		$4,200

Note that the net result of this entry, when coupled with the reversing entry, is the same as in the case where no reversing entry had been made; in either case, there is a debit balance of $3,600 in wages expense, a zero balance in wages payable, and a credit to cash for $4,200.

Reversing entries are made to reverse only adjusting entries—closing entries are *never* reversed. Moreover, not all adjusting entries are reversed, only those that either gave rise to an asset which will be used up in the subsequent period or a liability which will be liquidated during the ensuing accounting period (or what might be termed "temporary assets and liabilities"). Thus, an adjusting entry debiting depreciation expense and crediting allowance for depreciation would not be reversed, nor would an adjustment debiting sales-bad debts and crediting accounts receivable-allowance for bad debts. On the other hand, an adjusting entry debiting store supplies inventory (a "temporary asset") and crediting store supplies expense would be reversed as would an entry debiting wages expense and crediting wages payable (a "temporary liability").

In summary, then, reversing entries are nothing more than an optional accounting convenience and are made to reverse only those year-end adjusting entries which give rise to "temporary assets and liabilities."

DISCUSSION QUESTIONS

1. A baffled student says:

   I find the use of the terms "debit" and "credit" in accounting very confusing. Webster's New Collegiate Dictionary defines "credit" as "the balance in a person's favor in an account . . . an amount or sum placed at a person's disposal by a bank." I can understand that; you are made "better off" by a credit. The same source defines "debit" as "a record of indebtedness . . . a charge against a bank account." Again I can understand that; you are made "worse off" by a debit. Then I do not understand why *a business firm* "debits" an increase in an asset (which surely makes it better off) and "credits" an increase in a liability (which surely makes it worse off for it now owes someone some money). Surely the firm should "credit" the increase in the asset and "debit" the increase in indebtedness.

   Can you help this student out by untangling these apparent contradictions in accounting?

2. Another baffled student says:

   Accountants are the greatest "feather-bedders" (people who create unnecessary jobs to do unnecessary or no work) there are. There is simply no reason to do everything twice, once in a journal and then again in a ledger. You never use the journal again after posting to the ledger, it seems to me.

Why not enter everything directly in a ledger and *cross-reference* each ledger entry to its counterpart in another ledger (thereby being able to see both aspects of the single transaction together). Ledger entries are dated—you could easily put together a chronological history if you ever needed to.

Consider Appendix A to this chapter. If most large-scale businesses today do not, in fact, keep a full general journal, is there really any reason to learn "journal entries"? Why do you suppose the authors of this text (as well as every other text in accounting we know of) insist, in effect, that the student become familiar with simple general journal entries he or she may never see again in any practical accounting position?

3. Why do you suppose a "control" ledger account—for example, accounts receivable-control—is called a "control" account? Does it really exert any control over subsidiary accounts receivable ledger accounts—over Accounts Receivable-V. N. Hogue, Accounts Receivable-George Johnson, and so on? If there is a difference between the total balance in the subsidiary accounts and the total balance in the control accounts, is it not just as likely that the subsidiary accounts are correct and the control account is wrong, as vice versa?

4. Which of the following errors would be disclosed by a trial balance?
   a. A clerk recorded a cash sale erroneously as $22.50 on the sales slip instead of the correct amount received of $25.50.
   b. A clerk erroneously recorded a sale and the related account receivable as $22.50 instead of the correct amount of $25.50.
   c. The bookkeeper has not recorded interest due next month on a bank loan.
   d. A payment to a supplier was recorded by a credit to cash of $1,000 but a check was issued for the correct amount, $100.
   e. A purchase of office supplies was incorrectly recorded as utilities expense instead of supplies expense.
   f. The bookkeeper posted a collection on an account receivable to the customer's subsidiary ledger account but did not include it in the amount posted to the control accounts receivable ledger account.

5. What reasons, other than for income or loss, might cause the balance in the ownership equity account to change?

6. If you have two position statements for the XYZ Company, one dated 12-31-19X1 and one dated 12-31-19X2, can you deduce the income for year 19x2? Why or why not?

7. How could a liability account have a debit balance? An asset account a credit balance? Explain.

8. Would an investor in general be any more interested in a position statement than an income statement, or vice versa? Would one be more valuable for some purposes (for example, for evaluation of management performance) than another, or would it depend upon what aspects of management performance were being evaluated? Suppose growth in assets this year was greater than growth in assets last year but reported income this year was smaller than reported income last year: Which would be more meaningful in the evaluation of management performance—a two-year comparative position statement or a two-year income statement? Or can you say? Discuss.

PROBLEMS

4-1. *S. Owl's Bookstore*

S. Owl's Bookstore closes its books annually on December 31. Transactions for the last week in December and year-end adjustments are given below:

(1) Purchased textbooks on account for $710 from Hy Price, a wholesaler.
(2) Paid $260 on account to E. Z. Munee.
(3) Sold textbooks on account to Rick Trueblood, $120.
(4) Kathy Kohed returned textbooks for credit, $30.
(5) Collected $60 on account from A. Wehnie.
(6) Wrote off account of D. Dimwitte as worthless.
(7) Estimated bad debts for the year are ten per cent of credit sales (assume all sales were on a credit basis).
(8) Ending merchandise inventory is $8,400.

Certain relevant Bookstore ledger accounts have the following balances:

GENERAL LEDGER

	Debit	Credit
Cash	$ 980	
Accounts Receivable—Control	11,460	
Accounts Receivable—Allowance for Bad Debts		$ 180
Merchandise Inventory	27,900	
Accounts Payable—Control		6,900

Sales Revenue		32,300
Sales—Returns	6,100	
Sales—Bad Debts	-0-	
Cost of Goods Sold Expense	-0-	

ACCOUNTS RECEIVABLE SUBSIDIARY LEDGER

Kathy Kohed	$	90
Rick Trueblood		40
A. Wehnie		60
D. Dimwitte		50
Others		11,220

ACCOUNTS PAYABLE SUBSIDIARY LEDGER

Hy Price	$	220
E. Z. Munee		520
R. Mersiless		800
Others		5,360

INSTRUCTIONS:

(a) Journalize the transactions and year-end adjustments using only the above accounts.
(b) Post the journal entries to the ledger "T" accounts.

4-2. Sol's Store (I)

The transactions of Sol's Store for the month of January 19X3 and end-of-month adjustments are as follows:

(1) Purchased merchandise on account from Allied, $16,000.
(2) Sold merchandise on account to Adams for $2,000.
(3) Purchased supplies on account from Southland, $4,100.
(4) Paid freight on merchandise purchased in (1) above, $1,200.
(5) Sold merchandise on account to Carter, $8,000.
(6) Received payment on Brown's account, $15,000.
(7) Paid interest, $800.
(8) Carter returned merchandise for credit on his account, $1,400.
(9) Total cash sales for the month, $46,200.
(10) Paid wages to salesmen, $4,000, and office personnel, $1,500. Of this amount, $1,400 was due to salesmen and $600 to office personnel at the beginning of the month.
(11) Learned that Adams has skipped town. Wrote off balance in his account as worthless.
(12) Paid Federated $13,000 on account.

(13) Returned unsatisfactory merchandise to Allied for credit, $3,000.
(14) Accrued depreciation for the *month* of January on building and equipment. Both had been purchased on January 1, 19X0. The building had an expected useful life of 30 years and the equipment, 12 years. 80 per cent of the building depreciation and 60 per cent of the equipment depreciation is considered chargeable to the sales department. The remainder is chargeable to the administrative department.
(15) The insurance policy is a three-year policy which went into effect on January 1, 19X2. All expired insurance is considered chargeable to the administrative department.
(16) The portion of interest for the month which has not already been paid is accrued (you are to determine the amount).
(17) A physical count revealed selling supplies on hand to be $2,300.
(18) Wages due at month-end to salesmen, $300, and office personnel, $200.
(19) Bad debts for the month are expected to be two per cent of gross credit sales.
(20) A physical count revealed merchandise on hand of $15,700.

The general ledger contained these accounts and balances on January 1:

	Debit	Credit
Cash	$12,000	
Accounts Receivable—Control	26,000	
Accounts Receivable—Allowance for Bad Debts		$ 4,000
Merchandise	32,000	
Selling Supplies	5,400	
Prepaid Insurance	3,600	
Land	8,000	
Buildings	90,000	
Buildings—Allowance for Depreciation		9,000
Equipment	14,400	
Equipment—Allowance for Depreciation		3,600
Wages Payable		2,000
Accounts Payable—Control		42,000
10% Notes Payable		12,000
6% Mortgage Payable		60,000
Interest Accrued Payable		700
Common Stock		35,000

Retained Earnings		23,100
Sales Revenue		
Sales—Returns		
Sales—Bad Debts		
Cost of Goods Sold Expense		
Selling Expense		
Administrative Expense		
Interest Charges		
	$191,400	$191,400

The store maintained two subsidiary ledgers:

ACCOUNTS RECEIVABLE

	Debit	Credit
Adams	$ 1,000	
Brown	15,000	
Carter	10,000	

ACCOUNTS PAYABLE

	Debit	Credit
Allied		$18,000
Federated		13,000
Southland		11,000

INSTRUCTIONS:

(a) Journalize the transactions and end-of-month adjustments using only the above accounts.

(b) Post the journal entries to the ledger accounts.

4-3. Viebig and Ketchand, Incorporated

On September 1, 19X3, the general ledger and subsidiary ledgers of Viebig and Ketchand, Incorporated, contained the accounts and balances shown below:

GENERAL LEDGER

	Debit	Credit
Cash	$ 5,500	
Accounts Receivable—Control	20,000	
Accounts Receivable—Allowance for Bad Debts		$ 400
Merchandise Inventory	18,000	

Supplies Inventory	800	
Prepaid Insurance	2,800	
Land	9,000	
Building	75,000	
Building—Allowance for Depreciation		10,500
Equipment	16,000	
Equipment—Allowance for Depreciation		7,000
Wages Payable		1,200
Accounts Payable—Control		8,000
Interest Accrued Payable		1,400
Income Taxes Payable		4,200
Mortgage Payable		60,000
Common Stock		40,000
Retained Earnings		14,400
Sales Revenue		
Sales—Bad Debts		
Purchases		
Purchase Returns		
Freight-In		
Cost of Goods Sold Expense		
Wages Expense		
Depreciation Expense		
Supplies Expense		
Insurance Expense		
Utilities Expense		
Income Tax Expense		
Interest Charges		
	$147,100	$147,100

ACCOUNTS RECEIVABLE SUBSIDIARY LEDGER

	Debit	Credit
Beasley	$7,000	
Johnston	4,000	
Preston	9,000	

ACCOUNTS PAYABLE SUBSIDIARY LEDGER

	Debit	Credit
Aarons Co.		$2,000
Broarch Corp.		2,500
Callender, Inc.		3,500

The transactions that occurred during the month of September and the end-of-month adjustments were as follows:

(1) Purchased merchandise on account from Aarons, $8,100.

(2) Paid freight on merchandise purchased in (1) to Trailways Trucking, $300.

(3) Sold goods on account to Preston, $4,700.

(4) Paid interest on mortgage, $1,500.

(5) Paid principal on mortgage, $1,000.

(6) Received payment on account from Johnston, $4,000.

(7) Sold goods on account to Beasley, $3,100.

(8) Purchased equipment for cash, $2,000.

(9) Returned unsatisfactory merchandise to Aarons for credit on account, $100.

(10) Purchased supplies on account from Callender, $1,300, and debited them as expenses of this period.

(11) Sold additional common stock, $10,000.

(12) Received payment on account from Beasley, $10,000.

(13) Paid wages to employees, $6,200.

(14) Received notification Beasley is bankrupt. Wrote off balance in account as worthless.

(15) Purchased merchandise on account from Broach, $3,900.

(16) Paid income taxes, $4,800.

(17) Sold goods for cash, $22,300.

(18) Paid utilities, $700.

(19) Paid Aarons $6,700 on account.

(20) Paid freight on merchandise purchased in (15) to Fly-By-Nite Airways, $200.

(21) A physical count at month-end revealed unsold merchandise on hand to be worth $9,200.

(22) Depreciation for the month on the building and equipment is estimated at $300 and $200, respectively.

(23) Bad debts for the month are expected to be three per cent of credit sales.

(24) Interest on mortgage accrued at month-end is $400.

(25) Accrued payroll at month-end is $900.

(26) A physical count at month-end revealed supplies on hand worth $600.

(27) Prepaid insurance involves a three-year fire insurance policy which went into effect on January 1, 19X3.

(28) Income tax expense related to the month of September is estimated at $1,400.

INSTRUCTIONS:

Using *only* the accounts provided, journalize and post the foregoing transactions and all necessary end-of-month adjustments to the appropriate "T" accounts.

4-4. *Rea Sales Company (I)*

The general ledger of the Rea Sales Co., a furniture wholesaler, is as follows on January 1, 19X1:

	Dr.	Cr.
Cash	$ 5,000	
Accounts Receivable—Control	21,000	
Merchandise—Control	18,000	
Land	3,000	
Buildings and Equipment	24,000	
Allowance for Depreciation		$ 3,000
Accounts Payable—Control		12,000
Taxes Payable		2,000
Common Stock		50,000
Retained Earnings		4,000
Sales Revenue		-0-
Cost of Goods Sold Expense	-0-	
Selling Expenses	-0-	
Administrative Expenses	-0-	
Depreciation Expense	-0-	
Taxes Expense	-0-	
	$71,000	$71,000

The three subsidiary ledgers contain the following accounts:

Accounts Receivable:

Adams Furniture Co.	$ 3,000
Baker Home Supply	8,000
Cole Furnishings	4,000
Donaldson's	6,000
	$21,000

Merchandise:

Furniture	$12,500
Carpeting	3,500

Accessories	2,000
	$18,000

Accounts Payable:

Hemphill Mills	$ 1,500
American Company	3,500
Spring Valley	4,000
Essexville	3,000
	$12,000

During the month of January, the following transactions took place:

(1) Purchased $5,500 of furniture and $3,200 of accessories from American on account.
(2) Received $3,000 payment on account from Adams.
(3) Sold carpeting costing $1,000 and accessories costing $500 to Cole on account. The sales prices were $1,900 and $900 respectively.
(4) Sold furniture costing $6,600 to Adams for $8,900 on account.
(5) Paid $4,000 to Spring Valley.
(6) Purchased carpeting for $4,100 from Hemphill on account.
(7) Sold furniture costing $3,000 to Donaldson's for $4,500 on account.
(8) Received $6,000 from Baker as payment on account.
(9) Selling expenses amounting to $1,400 were paid.
(10) Taxes for January were estimated to be $800; this amount has not yet been paid.
(11) Administrative expenses amounting to $2,600 were paid.
(12) Purchased $10,700 of furniture and $3,200 of accessories from Essexville on account.
(13) Paid $4,200 on the Hemphill account.
(14) Sold furniture costing $1,800 to Donaldson's for $2,700 on account.
(15) Depreciation for the month was estimated to be $500.

INSTRUCTIONS:

(a) Journalize in a general journal and post the foregoing transactions to "T" accounts in both the general and subsidiary ledgers where relevant.
(b) Prepare an income statement and a comparative position statement for the month of January.

4-5. Kern's Book Store

On September 1, 19X3, the account balances in the general ledger of Kern's Book Co., a wholesaler, were as follows:

	Dr.	Cr.
Cash	$ 9,000	
Petty Cash	50	
Accounts Receivable—Control	7,040	
Merchandise Inventory—Control	6,250	
Building	20,000	
Building—Allowance for Depreciation		$ 2,000
Equipment	200	
Equipment—Allowance for Depreciation		20
Organization Costs	480	
Accounts Payable—Control		5,000
Salaries Payable		2,400
Common Stock		27,600
Retained Earnings		6,000
Sales Revenue		-0-
Cost of Goods Sold Expense	-0-	
Selling Expenses	-0-	
Salaries Expense	-0-	
Depreciation Expense	-0-	
	$43,020	$43,020

The balances in the subsidiary ledgers were as follows:

Accounts Receivable:

Johnson's Book Store	$2,150
Batt Stationeries	1,990
MacArthur Encyclopedias	2,900
	$7,040

Merchandise Inventory:

Paperbacks	$ 300
Hardbacks	2,950
Encyclopedias	3,000
	$6,250

Accounts Payable:

Reynolds & Co.	$1,300
Segal Paperbacks	200
American Publishers, Inc.	2,400
Caplan Press	1,100
	$5,000

During September, Kern's Book Store entered into the following transactions:

(1) Purchased $250 worth of paperbacks from Caplan Press for cash.
(2) Sold hardbacks which had cost Kern's Book Store $1,500 to Johnson's Book Store for $3,000 on account.
(3) Purchased encyclopedias from Reynolds & Co. for $500 on account.
(4) Paid Segal Paperbacks $200.
(5) Purchased $400 worth of paperbacks and $500 worth of hardbacks from American Publishers, Inc., on account.
(6) Purchased $200 worth of hardbacks from Caplan Press on account.
(7) Sold paperbacks costing $600 to Batt Stationeries for $1,000 on account.
(8) Received $2,000 from MacArthur Encyclopedias.
(9) Sold $1,600 worth of encyclopedias to MacArthur for $3,000 on account.
(10) Received $1,990 from Batt Stationeries.
(11) Selling supplies were purchased for $100 cash and are expensed as purchased. Other selling expenses amounting to $300 were paid in cash.
(12) Salaries of $400 which had accrued before September 1 were paid.
(13) Depreciation for the month was estimated at $250 for the building and $20 for the store equipment.
(14) This month's salaries of $1,000 were paid.

INSTRUCTIONS:

(a) Journalize and post the transactions to "T" accounts, beginning each account with the balance existing at September 1. Include both control and subsidiary ledgers.
(b) Prepare an income statement for September.
(c) Prepare a position statement as of September 30, 19X3.

4-6. Schaeffer, Inc.

INSTRUCTIONS:

Refer to Problem 2-6:
(a) Prepare journal entries to record the transactions.
(b) Post the entries to "T" accounts.

4-7. Smith and Jones, Inc. (I)

On June 1, 19X3, Smith and Jones were granted a corporate charter to operate a retail clothing store. During the month of June, the following transactions took place:

(1) Smith and Jones each invested $10,000 cash and received 100 shares of common stock.
(2) A store was leased for one year at a rental of $500 per month. The lease requires the payment of both the first and last month's rent immediately. Payment was made in cash.
(3) Showcases and counters were purchased for $4,000 cash.
(4) Merchandise was purchased for $20,000 from Gudthreds, a wholesaler, on account.
(5) Freight on the merchandise was paid, $250.
(6) A. Hammer, a carpenter, was paid $500 for installing the showcases and counters.
(7) Several schoolboys were paid $100 to unpack the merchandise and place it on shelves.
(8) A petty cash fund of $50 was established.
(9) Wrapping paper and other selling supplies were purchased for cash, $300.
(10) Two salesmen were hired and are to begin work on July 1. Their salaries will be $600 per month.
(11) A delivery truck was bought for $4,000 on June 30. A $1,000 down payment was made and the remainder was financed at Goldbag National Bank on a 10 per cent, 3-year note. Interest begins on July 1.
(12) A one-year insurance policy was acquired on June 30 by the payment of $1,200. The policy becomes effective July 1.

INSTRUCTIONS:
(a) Prepare all necessary journal entries for the month of June.
(b) Post all entries to "T" accounts.
(c) Prepare a position statement as of June 30, 19X3.

4-8. Smith and Jones, Inc. (II)

Refer to Problem 4-7. The store was opened for business on July 1 and transactions for July were as follows:

(13) Sales for the month totaled $25,000, of which $20,000 were credit sales.
(14) Merchandise was purchased from Van Hooten, a wholesaler, for $10,000, on account.
(15) Salesmen were paid $500 each during the month.
(16) Depreciation on the showcase and counters for the month was estimated at $100.
(17) Ending inventory of wrapping paper and other selling supplies was $100.

(18) Estimated depreciation for the month on the truck was $150.
(19) Collections on account totaled $9,000.
(20) Miscellaneous expenses for the month amounted to $1,500 and were paid in cash.
(21) Utilities bills totaling $250 were received.
(22) Merchandise on hand at the end of the month was valued at $12,000.
(23) Smith invested another $5,000 in cash for 50 shares.
(24) A loan from Goldbag National Bank was obtained on July 15 in the amount of $15,000. The note is due on July 15, 19X6 and bears interest at the rate of eight per cent.
(25) Jones sold his shares to Brown for $11,000.
(26) Accounts payable totalling $26,000 were paid.

INSTRUCTIONS:

(a) Prepare journal entries for the month of July and post them to "T" accounts. Use the "T" accounts in Problem 4-7. Assume that no other transactions than the above occurred in July. There must be adjusting entries for rent, interest, and insurance.
(b) Prepare an income statement for July.
(c) Prepare a position statement as of July 31, 19X3.

4-9. Sewhall Company

The position statement of Sewhall Company as of December 31, 19X7 was as follows:

ASSETS

Current:

Cash		$ 7,000	
Accounts Receivable	$97,000		
Less: Allowance for Bad Debts	3,000	94,000	
Merchandise Inventory		102,000	
Selling Supplies		6,000	
Prepaid Insurance		3,000	$212,000

Plant:

Land		$ 12,000	
Building	$80,000		
Less: Allowance for Depreciation	4,000	76,000	
Equipment	$20,000		

Less: Allowance for Depreciation	5,000	15,000	103,000
			$315,000

EQUITIES
Current Liabilities:

Accounts Payable	$ 82,000	
Wages Payable	8,000	
Advances on Customers' Orders	17,000	
Taxes Payable	13,000	$120,000

Stockholders' Equity:

Common Stock	$100,000	
Retained Earnings	95,000	195,000
		$315,000

The following transactions and adjustments occurred during 19X8:

(1) Merchandise purchases for the year were $310,000 on account.
(2) Sales recorded for the year were $320,000 on account and $130,000 for cash. In addition, all customers' orders outstanding at Dec. 31, 19X7 were filled.
(3) Customers returned goods for credit amounting to $8,000.
(4) Payments to suppliers totaled $290,000.
(5) Goods returned to suppliers for credit totaled $6,000.
(6) Payments to employees totaled $86,000.
(7) Collections on account amounted to $350,000.
(8) Payments for taxes totaled $29,000.
(9) Received orders accompanied by advance payments from customers amounting to $41,000. These were recorded as sales when received, but $9,000 of the orders were not filled during the year.
(10) Specific customers' accounts written off as worthless during the year amounted to $2,000.
(11) Various selling expenses paid during the year came to $25,000.
(12) Administrative expenses for the year totaled $35,000 of which $5,000 was unpaid at the year-end.
(13) A physical count of merchandise at year-end indicated $110,000 was on hand.
(14) The insurance policy was a three-year policy which has one year left to run at year-end.
(15) The building and equipment were purchased on January 1, 19X6. At that time the building and equipment had an expected useful live of 40 and 8 years, respectively.

(16) Bad debts for the year are expected to be two per cent of the credit sales.

(17) Wages due to employees at year-end amounted to $12,000.

INSTRUCTIONS:

(a) Prepare journal entries to record the foregoing.

(b) Prepare an income statement for 19X8 and a position statement as of December 31, 19X8.

(c) Does the "fundamental check" between income and comparative position statements prove out for the Sewhall Company for 19X8? Explain in a sentence or two.

4-10

INSTRUCTIONS:

Indicate, by writing across a row as shown in Table 4-10 for an example, the effect of each of the errors described below on the various elements of a company's financial statements. Use the following code:

$$O = \text{amount is overstated}$$
$$U = \text{amount is understated}$$
$$NE = \text{no effect}$$

TABLE 4-10

	Total Revenues	Total Expenses	Income	Total Assets	Total Liabilities	Total Owner's Equity
Example: Purchase of asset charged to expense	NE	O	U	U	NE	U

(1) Unexpired insurance, an asset account, was not adjusted at end of year to record portion expired.

(2) Interest on bank loan payable was not accrued at year-end.

(3) Failed to accrue interest earned to year-end on note receivable.

(4) Failed to record depreciation on building.

(5) Repair expense erroneously charged to Building account.

4-11. Gordon Company

Given below is the adjusted trial balance of the Gordon Company as of December 31, 19X1.

	Dr.	Cr.
Accounts Payable		$ 29,800
Accounts Receivable	$ 46,700	
Advances from Customers		3,700
Allowance for Bad Debts		2,400
Allowance for Depreciation		12,000
Bonds Payable		50,000
Buildings and Equipment	71,000	
Cash	16,000	
Common Dividends Payable		1,800
Common Dividend Charges	2,300	
Common Stock		20,000
Cost of Goods Sold Expense	82,100	
Depreciation Expense	4,000	
Income Tax Expense	2,900	
Income Taxes Payable		4,300
Interest Accrued Payable		2,300
Interest Charges	4,800	
Land	8,500	
Marketable Securities	12,200	
Merchandise Inventory	37,900	
Miscellaneous Revenues		7,100
Mortgage Payable		32,000
Organization Costs	1,700	
Other Expenses	6,200	
Patents	2,700	
Petty Cash	300	
Preferred Dividend Charges	1,800	
Preferred Stock		30,000
Prepayments	4,900	
Retained Earnings		5,800
Sales Revenue		162,300
Sales—Bad Debts	5,100	
Sales—Returns	11,400	
Supplies Expense	1,900	
Supplies Inventory	3,100	
Trademarks	1,400	
Wages Expense	36,200	
Wages Payable		1,600
	$365,100	$365,100

INSTRUCTIONS:

(a) Prepare all necessary closing entries.
(b) Prepare, in good form, a position statement as of December 31, 19X1.

PROBLEMS FOR APPENDIX A

4A-1. Rea Sales Company (II)

INSTRUCTIONS:
Refer to Problem 4-4. In that problem, the only journal used was the general journal and all transactions were recorded in it. In this problem, the general journal will be supplemented by four special journals which will contain the more frequent transactions; only relatively infrequent transactions will be recorded in the general journal. The special journals should have the headings given in Table 4-A-5. Record the transactions of Problem 4-4 in these journals on separate paper and make appropriate postings to the "T" accounts.

TABLE 4-A-5

				SALES JOURNAL		
Date	Accounts Receivable Dr.	Customer's Name		Sales Cr.		
				Furniture	Carpeting	Accessories

		PURCHASES JOURNAL				
Date		Merchandise Dr.		Accounts Payable Cr.	Creditor's Name	
	Furniture	Carpeting	Accessories			

TABLE 4-A-5 CONTINUED

		CASH DISBURSEMENTS JOURNAL			
Date	Accounts Payable Dr.	Creditor's Name	Other Accounts Dr.	Account Title	Cash Cr.

			CASH RECEIPTS JOURNAL		
Date	Cash Dr.	Accounts Receivable Cr.	Customer's Name	Other Accounts Cr.	Account Title

	GENERAL JOURNAL		
Date	Account Title	Dr.	Cr.

4A-2. *Young Corporation*

The two journals in Table 4-A-6 are the *only* ones used by Young Corporation to record its transactions. At the end of each week, data from these journals are posted to the general and subsidiary ledgers (the two subsidiary ledgers are for accounts receivable and accounts payable). Using the following schedule of possible posting instructions, indicate the proper posting of each column of Young's journals by listing the *letter* of the correct instruction beside the column number. Since debit and credit indications are omitted from the column headings, you will have to consider the kinds of entries which would use each of the columns marked by numbers (all of the possible columns where

TABLE 4-A-6

CASH RECEIPTS AND DISBURSEMENTS JOURNAL

Date	Cash		Accounts Receivable	Customer's Name	Accounts Payable	Creditor's Name	Sales	Other Accounts		Account Titles
	(1)	(2)	(3)		(4)		(5)	(6)	(7)	

SALES, PURCHASES, AND GENERAL JOURNAL

Date	Merchandise	Sales	Accounts Receivable		Customer's Name	Accounts Payable		Creditor's Name	Other Accounts		Account Titles
	(8)	(9)	(10)	(11)		(12)	(13)		(14)	(15)	

money amounts are entered) in forming your judgments as to the posting pattern.

The possible posting instructions for each column are as follows:

(a) Detailed items to subsidiary ledger as debits, total to general ledger as debit.
(b) Detailed items to subsidiary ledger as credits, total to general ledger as credit.
(c) Detailed items to general ledger as debits, total not posted.
(d) Detailed items to general ledger as credits, total not posted.
(e) Detailed items not posted, total to general ledger as debit.
(f) Detailed items not posted, total to general ledger as credit.
(g) Detailed items not posted, total not posted.
(h) None of the above describes the posting properly.

4A-3. Goodhew Company

The Goodhew Company uses certain special journals together with the general journal in recording transactions. The special journals are as seen in Table 4-A-7.

INSTRUCTIONS:

Using the following schedule of possible posting instructions, indicate the proper posting of each numbered column of the journals by putting the *letter* of the correct instruction beside the numbered column as listed on a separate piece of paper. Since debit and credit indications have been omitted from the column headings, you will have to consider the kinds of entries which would use the various columns in forming your judgments as to the posting pattern.

The possible posting instructions for each column are as follows:

(a) Total to general ledger as a debit, detailed items to subsidiary ledger as debits.
(b) Total to general ledger as a credit, detailed items to subsidiary ledger as credits.
(c) Total not posted, detailed items to general ledger as debits.
(d) Total not posted, detailed items to general ledger as credits.
(e) Total to general ledger as a debit, detailed items not posted.
(f) Total to general ledger as a credit, detailed items not posted.
(g) Total not posted, detailed items not posted.
(h) None of the above describes the posting properly.

TABLE 4-A-7

SALES JOURNAL				
Date	Cash	Accounts Receivable	Customer's Name	Sales
	(1)	(2)		(3)

PURCHASES JOURNAL			
Date	Merchandise	Accounts Payable	Creditor's Name
	(4)	(5)	

CASH RECEIPTS JOURNAL						
Date	Cash	Sales	Accounts Receivable	Customer's Name	Other Accounts	Account Title
	(6)	(7)	(8)		(9)	

CASH DISBURSEMENTS JOURNAL						
Date	Accounts Payable	Creditor's Name	Wages Expense	Other Accounts	Account Title	Cash
	(10)		(11)	(12)		(13)

PROBLEMS FOR APPENDIX B

4B-1. Sol's Store (II)

INSTRUCTIONS:

Refer to Problem 4-2. Assume that Sol's Store would like to embark on a policy of preparing reversing entries (a policy it has not followed to date). If the books were closed on January 31, 19X3, prepare all reversing entries that could *reasonably* be made on February 1.

4B-2. Gordon Company (II)

INSTRUCTIONS:

Refer to Problem 4-11. Assume that the Gordon Company would like to embark on a policy of preparing reversing entries (a policy it has not followed to date). If the books were closed on December 31, 19X1, prepare all reversing entries that could *reasonably* be made on January 1, 19X2.

CHAPTER 5

INVENTORY ASSETS

FOR A GREAT MANY BUSINESS FIRMS, inventories—primarily those for sale to customers—comprise their largest single asset item. This is certainly the case for merchandising establishments such as department stores and grocery stores. In firms such as manufacturers, where inventories are not the largest single asset item, they are typically second only to plant assets in magnitude. Only service enterprises have little in the way of inventories, but this is merely reflective of the fact that such firms have few assets at all—inventory, plant, or otherwise. Because the preponderance of business firms are engaged in either merchandising or manufacturing rather than service, it should be apparent that the manner in which their inventories are accounted for is of major import in any study of their accounting in general. Accordingly, it is appropriate at this juncture to devote an entire chapter to the topic of inventories.

THE VALUATION PROBLEM

As is the case with all assets, the primary problem encountered in accounting for inventories is one of *valuation*. What values should be recorded for inventories upon their initial acquisition? What values should be assigned to inventories undergoing physical transformation in the course of manufacturing? What values should be assigned to those units of inventory that are sold to customers during the accounting period? What values should be attributed to inventories still on hand at the end of the accounting period? These are basically the questions the accountant must answer with respect to inventories. Our role here initially will be to describe the manner in which accountants in day-to-day practice treat the questions of inventory valuation; later, we shall critically examine these procedures and suggest certain basic changes that we believe are both appropriate and necessary if accounting is to provide relevant information to users.

As applied to merchandise and manufacturing inventories, the usual accounting process is much like that just described in the preceding chapter. Inventories are initially recorded in the firm's accounting records at their *historical acquisition costs*—those costs incurred when the purchase transaction is concluded. Subsequent to the date of purchase, these historical costs are *allocated* either to expenses of the period or to the inventories remaining on hand at the end of the period. Since these inventories are carried on the books as assets prior to their disposal through sale to the firm's customers, when they are sold the asset account (inventories) must be reduced and the corresponding expense account (cost of goods sold expense) increased by similar amounts. Thus, merchandise inventories and manufacturing inventories are accounted for as are office supplies inventories and prepaid insurance—first as an asset and then as an expense. However, differences resulting from alternative methods of accounting for, say, office supplies inventories, may well be immaterial; but those same differences, when associated with merchandise or manufacturing inventories, assume considerably greater importance because of the magnitude of merchandise and manufacturing inventories in relation to the entity's total assets.

CLASSES OF INVENTORIES

Merchandise Inventories

The term *merchandise inventories* relates to the assets of merchandising firms which buy and sell finished products. No change in the physical nature of the product occurs while it is in the hands of the merchandiser—it is simply traded. Accordingly, merchandisers are often known as "trading companies" and their inventories are referred to as "stock-in-trade." Thus, groceries would constitute the stock-in-trade or merchandise inventory of a supermarket. Similarly, clothing, furniture, and household wares would bear the same relationship to a department store or discount house.

Manufacturing Inventories

Manufacturing firms, on the other hand, have three basic types of inventories: (1) raw materials, (2) work in process, and (3) finished goods. The terms themselves are fairly self-explanatory and together they describe the production process. The manufacturing firm buys raw materials (unfinished goods from the manufacturer's point-of-view), puts them into production (work in process) where they are physically transformed into a finished product (finished goods). It should be noted, however, that a product which constitutes one manufacturer's finished goods may be another manufacturer's raw materials. For example, iron ore would be a raw material for a steel mill while the mill's finished goods, steel, would be an automobile manufacturer's raw material. Thus, a product may well be the finished goods of many different manufacturers before it becomes finished goods in the eyes of the merchandiser who then trades it either to other merchandisers or to the ultimate consumer.

Supplies Inventories

Of course, merchandise inventories and manufacturing inventories are not the only inventory assets of merchandisers and manufacturers. Both will have on hand at all times certain inventories of supplies which are used in the course of their activities. Paper bags and string are examples of a merchandiser's supplies inventory as is machine oil for a manufacturer. However, since supplies inventories are generally immaterial in size and since adjustments of the accounts for supplies have been treated in the preceding chapter, we need no longer concern ourselves with them.

THE BASICS OF INVENTORY ACCOUNTING

Merchandise Inventories

The accounting procedures with respect to a merchandiser's principal inventories are quite simple. They may be expressed by means of a single equation which reads as follows:

$$BI + P = COGS + EI$$

It reads: Beginning inventory plus purchases minus ending inventory equals cost of goods sold. The sum of the first two components ($BI + P$) is referred to as "cost of goods available for sale." This "pool" of goods must be accounted for, then, either as having been sold ($COGS$) or remaining on hand at the end of the period (EI). Thus, the historical acquisition costs of merchandise inventories are allocated either to the expenses of the period (cost of goods sold expense) or to the assets remaining on hand at the end of the period (merchandise inventory).

Manufacturing Inventories

Accounting for inventories of manufacturers, however, is somewhat more complicated because of the fact that manufacturers have three different types of inventories. To be sure, the manufacturer would account for raw materials inventories in a manner similar to the merchandiser. The purchases of additional raw materials are added to beginning inventory and from that total the ending inventory is subtracted, leaving a residual, the raw materials transferred into production (used) during the period. The formula would read as follows:

> Beginning Inventory of Raw Materials
> + Raw Materials Purchased
> = Ending Inventory of Raw Materials
> + Raw Materials Used (transferred into production)

Likewise, the manufacturer's finished goods inventory would also be accounted for in a similar fashion except that where the merchandiser includes "purchases," the manufacturer would insert "cost of goods manufactured." In formula form, it would read:

> Beginning Inventory of Finished Goods
> + Cost of Goods Manufactured
> = Ending Inventory of Finished Goods
> + Cost of Goods Sold

The primary difference between accounting for manufacturing inventories and merchandise inventories lies not with raw materials or finished goods but with work in process. This is because the raw materials placed into production are physically transformed before being transferred out as finished goods. As a result, not only the cost of the raw materials but also the cost of transforming those raw materials into finished goods must be considered. These costs of transformation include the labor cost of those personnel actually working on the product (direct labor) and the costs of operating the factory in which the transformation occurs (factory overhead). Hence, there are three factor (and cost) inputs to work in process: (1) raw materials, (2) direct labor, and (3) factory overhead.

While the nature of raw materials and direct labor costs should be relatively clear, factory overhead may require additional explanation. Factory overhead includes all costs of manufacturing *other* than raw materials and direct labor. The following costs are typically included as factory overhead:

1. indirect labor costs, such as wage costs of supervisors, maintenance personnel, and janitors in the factory;

2. factory supplies, including machine oil, cleaning solvents, and so on;

3. property taxes on the factory;

4. insurance, such as fire, flood, windstorm, liability, and so forth, on the factory;

5. depreciation of factory buildings and equipment.

Since all factory overhead costs are not necessarily related directly to individual units of product or even overall levels of production, various methods for allocating these costs to inventory have been devised. These methods are generally subject matter of courses in managerial accounting. In the examples that follow in this chapter, it will be assumed that an appropriate method of allocating factory overhead costs to inventory is being applied.

If all the goods worked on during the period were *complete* at the end of the period, the formula for cost of goods manufactured would be as follows:

Raw Materials Used + Direct Labor + Factory Overhead
= Cost of Goods Manufactured

However, since there are almost always some goods in process that are only partially complete at the beginning and end of the period, the formula must be modified to read as follows:

Beginning Inventory of Work in Process
+ Raw Materials Used + Direct Labor + Factory Overhead
= Ending Inventory of Work in Process
+ Cost of Goods Manufactured

ACCOUNTING FOR INVENTORY ACQUISITIONS

The accounting procedures regarding the initial acquisition of inventory are essentially the same for both merchandisers and manufacturers. In the case of merchandisers, the inventory being purchased will simply be resold without being physically transformed in the interim. On the other hand, the inventory being purchased by the manufacturer (raw materials) will be physically transformed. Nevertheless, the accounting procedures are unaffected by these later events. The only event of relevance at this point is the acquisition.

At the date of acquisition, both merchandise and manufacturing inventories are valued in terms of the sacrifice made to acquire them. The value of the sacrifice made in terms of either cash assets surrendered or short-term monetary liabilities assumed is then imputed to the inventory assets acquired. This is, of course, the usual manner of recording purchase transactions, be they for inventories or any other assets. The amount so recorded is known as historical acquisition cost, or *historical cost* for short, and is *equal* to the *current market value* of the inventories at the date of acquisition (assuming that the purchase transaction entered into was made on an arm's-length basis).

Two alternative methods of accounting for the historical cost of inventories while in the entity's possession are available. One is known as the *periodic inventory method* and the other as the *perpetual inventory method*. In accounting for inventory acquisitions under the periodic method, all elements of the purchase transactions are maintained in separate "temporary" accounts until the end of the period. The sum of the balances in these temporary accounts represents the inventory "pool"—the historical cost of merchandise available for sale during the period in the case of the merchandiser and the historical cost of raw materials available for use in production during the period in the case of the manufacturer. At the end of the accounting period, a physical count is made of the goods remaining on hand and the appropriate historical cost of these goods is debited to an asset account, merchandise inventory (in the case of a merchandiser) or raw materials inventory (in the case of a manufacturer). The temporary accounts comprising the inventory pool are closed out and the residual debit balance becomes cost of goods sold expense for the merchandiser; for the manufacturer, the debit balance (which represents raw materials used) is transferred to work in process inventory.

When the perpetual inventory method is in use, no temporary pool accounts whatsoever are used. Rather, all historical costs associated with the inventory acquisition are debited directly to the asset account, merchandise inventory or raw materials inventory as the case may be.[1] Each time merchandise is sold or put into production, the inventory account is credited for the historical cost of the goods involved. Barring thievery, the balance in the inventory account should always be the historical cost of goods on hand. Thus, unlike the periodic inventory method, the perpetual inventory method requires no adjustment at the end of the accounting period except to eliminate discrepancies caused by theft or record-keeping error.[2]

The basic rule of asset valuation, "total cost in place, ready to use,"

1. Subsidiary accounts, however, would be used under a perpetual system, with the general ledger account, "merchandise inventory," serving as a control account.
2. Special problems arise in the valuation of manufactured goods. Because of their complex nature, a discussion of these is left to managerial accounting texts.

applies to inventories just as it does to other assets. In the case of inventories, this means that the value should be based on the initial purchase price (less any cash discounts available, whether or not they have been taken) plus all applicable freight and handling charges.

Purchases and Purchase Discounts

In its simplest form, accounting for a purchase transaction would involve nothing more than a debit and a credit. Assume that a firm purchased inventory from a vendor for $10,000 on account. If the purchaser employed the periodic method, the journal entry would be:

Purchases	$10,000	
Accounts Payable		$10,000

Under the perpetual method, the entry would read:

Merchandise (or Raw Materials) Inventory	$10,000	
Accounts Payable		$10,000

This simple case is not often found in practice, however. With the expanding use of credit in the purchase and sale of merchandise and raw materials, the success or failure of many businesses can be equated with the success or failure of their "credit policies." A successful credit policy is one that strikes a delicate balance between the large bad debt losses of a "too loose" credit policy and the restricted sales volume of a "too strict" credit policy. There is an obvious relationship between the speed with which a firm collects its accounts receivable and the size of its ultimate bad debt loss. Thus, an effective credit policy necessarily involves energetic collection efforts. A widely-used collection device is the offering of a *cash discount* to those customers who pay within a specified period of time, frequently ten days. The size of cash discounts naturally varies from one firm to the next, but the most widely used amount is two per cent. Firms offering cash discounts will print or type the fact in the "terms" section of their invoices. Thus, terms of "2/10, n/30" are known by all businessmen to mean that the purchaser is entitled to a two per cent discount if he pays within ten days, but that he may wait thirty days to pay the invoice, in which event he must pay the full amount.

The manner of handling cash discounts (hereafter called "purchase discounts") in the accounts of the purchasing firm depends upon the attitude of the firm with respect to the nature of the discount as well as on the inventory method (perpetual or periodic) in use. The following examples illustrate alternative ways of handling purchase discounts in the accounts of a firm using the periodic inventory method of accounting for inventories. The discount aspect of these examples would be essentially the same if the perpetual inventory method were used. Assume that a firm purchases goods at an invoice price of $1,000, terms 2/10, n/30 and pays for them within the discount period.

Purchases recorded at gross prices. Under this procedure, the gross purchase price is initially recorded in both the purchases and accounts payable accounts. If payment is made within the discount period, an account titled "purchase discounts" is credited with the amount of the discount. The journal entries would be made as follows:

Purchases	$1,000	
Accounts Payable		$1,000
Accounts Payable	$1,000	
Purchase Discounts		$ 20
Cash		980

If purchase discounts are regarded as a reduction in the cost of merchandise purchased, the balance of purchase discounts will be subtracted from the purchases account (along with purchase returns and allowances) in arriving at "net purchases." Those who feel that purchase discounts are a form of revenue would show them on the income statement as an addition to "operating income" in computing the entity's income. The latter method, however, is inconsistent with the revenue realization approach to matching (as discussed in Chapter 1) and would lead to the reporting of a profit even though no sales took place during the period.

Purchases recorded at net prices. Most accountants rightly feel that the "true" historical cost of merchandise or raw materials is the minimum amount for which they can be purchased and that, therefore, purchase transactions should be initially recorded net of the discount. Using this approach, the entries for the foregoing example would be:

Purchases	$980	
Accounts Payable		$980
Accounts Payable	$980	
Cash		$980

If the firm fails to pay within the discount period, $1,000 will be required to settle the account, in which event the second entry will be:

Accounts Payable	$980	
Loss from Lapsed Discounts	20	
Cash		$1,000

One of the strongest arguments in favor of recording purchases net of cash discounts is that data on discounts lost are more significant than are data on discounts taken. The typical two per cent discount means that $1,000 worth of goods can be bought for $20 less by paying twenty days early (in ten days instead of thirty). On an annual basis this saving is equivalent to interest at 36.5 per cent.[3] Since commercial bank interest rates seldom exceed 15 per cent and may be as low as seven per cent or eight per cent, the well-managed firm will take advantage of all the discounts offered to it within the limitations of its borrowing capacity. The taking of discounts is thus the expected or normal event and as such its measure is of no particular significance. The losing of discounts is a manifestation of carelessness or inefficiency, and its measure is thus of considerable significance in the evaluation of management performance.

The loss from lapsed discounts account may appear on the income statement as a cost addition in computing cost of goods sold, or it may be viewed as being in the nature of interest charges (and, indeed, may be so labeled). The latter treatment is to be preferred since it is consistent with the ideas involved in recording purchases net of the discount in the first place.

Firms using the perpetual inventory method may find it impractical to record purchases net of the discount because of the complexities resulting from the use of subsidiary inventory accounts which are a necessity for the perpetual method. Prices stated on an invoice must be reduced for the inventory records by the discount percentage. Obviously, for an invoice carrying ten different items, this requires ten computations. Further, the net prices may be awkward, involving fractional cents. Rounding would be feasible but would clearly complicate the control relationship between the parent and subsidiary inventory accounts. These complexities discourage many of those firms which use the perpetual system from recording purchases at net-of-discount prices.

---

3. If interest for 20 days is two per cent, the equivalent annual rate (interest for 365 days) may be determined as follows:

$$2\% = 20/365 \; X$$
$$36.5\% = X$$

Freight and Handling Costs

It is generally agreed that the historical acquisition cost of merchandise (or raw materials) to a firm is the cost delivered to the doorstep. Thus, freight charges are an element of cost and should be included in the inventory cost. In a perpetual inventory system, this would be accomplished by debiting the freight bill to the merchandise (or raw materials) inventory account. For example, assume that a company bought 100 units of product X at a price of $10 each and, in addition, paid $50 in freight charges to have the goods delivered. Entries to record these transactions in the control accounts would be as follows:

Merchandise (or Raw Materials) Inventory	$1,000	
Accounts Payable		$1,000
To record purchase of 100 units of product X.		
Merchandise (or Raw Materials) Inventory	$ 50	
Accounts Payable		$ 50
To record freight bill.		

Thus, the average unit cost of X would be $10.50 $\left(\dfrac{\$1,050}{100 \text{ units}}\right)$ for inventory valuation purposes. When a purchase involves several types of products and subsidiary inventory accounts are maintained as they are with a perpetual inventory method, the freight charges would have to be allocated among the several products in the subsidiary accounts. As a practical matter these allocations are difficult to make and, hence, freight charges are often written off as an expense of the period in which they were incurred rather than included in the inventory accounts when a perpetual method is in use. The resultant variations in income will be slight, especially if purchases are fairly constant from year to year.

Where the periodic inventory method is in use, freight charges are customarily segregated in an account called "Freight-In," which is combined with the beginning inventory and purchases accounts at the end of the period to arrive at the inventory pool of goods available for sale or use. Using the data in the foregoing example, entries for the periodic inventory method would be:

Purchases	$1,000	
Accounts Payable		$1,000
Freight-In	$ 50	
Accounts Payable		$ 50

Purchases Returns

Whether a firm is buying merchandise for resale or raw materials to be converted into a finished product, it will from time to time find it necessary or desirable to return some of the inventory items that it has purchased to the firm from which they were acquired. The decision to return goods may stem from the goods being defective, from the ordering of more goods than were needed, or from a decision to discontinue the handling of certain items. The willingness of the vendor to accept their return will depend upon the circumstances surrounding each case and the policies of the firm with regard to returns. Some have very liberal return policies; others are very strict. In any event, if items of inventory are returned for credit, the firm returning them must record the transaction in its accounts. If the perpetual inventory method is in use, this entry will be:

Accounts Payable	xxx	
Merchandise (or Raw		
Materials) Inventory		xxx

Where the periodic inventory method is being used, the entry will be:

Accounts Payable	xxx	
Purchases		xxx

or, preferably:

Accounts Payable	xxx	
Purchase Returns and		
Allowances		xxx

The latter entry is preferred because it segregates the cost of the goods which, for one reason or another, had to be returned to vendors during the year. Since such data may be indicative of careless purchasing practices, management usually desires that it be reflected in the accounts.

ACCOUNTING FOR INVENTORIES IN PRODUCTION

With the merchandiser, only two accounting problems regarding inventories are encountered: (1) accounting for their acquisition and

(2) accounting for their sale. A third problem, that of accounting for inventories while they are in the process of being physically transformed, is added when a manufacturer is considered. This transformation, of course, occurs between the acquisition date of raw materials and the date of sale of the finished products of which they become a part.

Essentially there are three elements of manufacturing costs which must be considered in valuing inventories: (1) raw materials, (2) direct labor, and (3) factory overhead. In the production process, raw materials (sometimes combining several different materials) are physically transformed into finished goods. Clearly, then, the cost of the raw materials alone cannot constitute the cost of the finished goods inventories that result. To these costs must be added the costs of transformation, direct labor (the wages of persons working directly on the materials being transformed), and factory overhead (the costs associated with operating and maintaining the factory itself so that production may occur).

The flow of costs in the production process may be more clearly seen in Figure 5-1. Assuming that a perpetual inventory method is

THE FLOW OF COSTS IN ACCOUNTING FOR INVENTORIES IN PRODUCTION

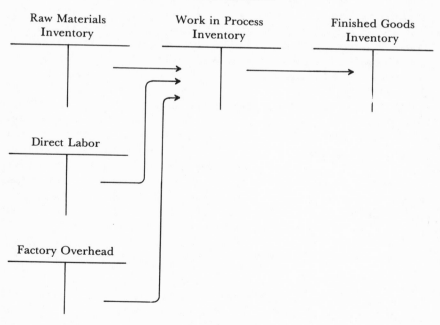

Figure 5-1

in use, as raw materials are purchased, their historical acquisition costs are debited to raw materials inventory and credited to either accounts payable or cash. When the materials are removed from the storeroom and placed into production, the associated costs of those materials are transferred by debiting work in process inventory and crediting raw materials inventory. The balance remaining in the raw materials inventory account is, of course, the historical acquisition cost of the ending inventory.

Unlike raw materials costs, neither direct labor nor factory overhead can be inventoried as such. Rather, since their asset values result only from their association with raw materials, they may be inventoried only as work in process. Most firms find it useful, however, to create temporary accounts in which the total direct labor and factory overhead costs of a period may be recorded. This simplifies the task of analysis somewhat because those costs are later "buried" in work in process inventory. Accordingly, all direct labor costs for a period are initially debited to direct labor and credited to payroll payable or cash. Similarly, all overhead costs of the period are first accumulated in factory overhead by debiting factory overhead and crediting various accounts such as allowance for depreciation, prepaid insurance, property taxes payable, accounts payable, cash, and even payroll payable (for the wages of supervisory, maintenance, and custodial personnel in the factory). The totals contained in direct labor and factory overhead are then transferred by crediting those accounts and debiting work in process. No balances should remain in either direct labor or factory overhead at the end of the period.

The debits to the work in process inventory account represent the sum of the beginning inventory, raw materials used in production, direct labor for the period, and factory overhead for the period. Assuming a perpetual inventory method is in use, an entry would be made debiting finished goods inventory and crediting work in process inventory each time completed goods were physically transferred from the factory to the warehouse where they would await sale. The balance then remaining in work in process inventory would be the allocated historical cost of the ending inventory of unfinished goods.

ACCOUNTING FOR INVENTORY SALES

When a sales transaction occurs, the inventory asset is exchanged for another asset, either cash or a receivable, generally of greater value. The inventory asset expires, becoming an expense to be matched against the revenue which it produces. Thus, the adjustment process as it relates to sales of inventory is similar to the adjustments of all other assets that are initially carried on the books as assets prior to their disposal.

Recording Revenues

Whichever inventory method (perpetual or periodic) is employed, the entry recording the sale is the same. Typically, the revenue entry will involve a debit to cash or accounts receivable and a credit to sales revenue for the selling price. Should a cash discount be permitted the customer, the sale can be recorded on either a gross or net basis. To illustrate the difference between the two, assume that a firm sells merchandise on account to a customer for $100, subject to terms of 2/10, n/30. If the gross method is employed, the revenue entry would be recorded as follows:

Accounts Receivable	$100	
Sales Revenue		$100

If the customer tenders payment within the discount period (ten days), the following entry would be made:

Cash	$98	
Sales—Discounts[4]	2	
Accounts Receivable		$100

Should the customer miss the discount, the collection entry would be:

Cash	$100	
Accounts Receivable		$100

If the net method is employed, the revenue entry would take the following form:

Accounts Receivable	$98	
Sales Revenue		$98

If the account is collected within the discount period, the collection entry would be:

Cash	$98	
Accounts Receivable		$98

---

4. "Sale-discounts" is a contra-revenue account which is deducted from sales revenue in the "revenues" section of the income statement to arrive at a net sales figure.

On the other hand, if the discount period lapses prior to collection, the following entry would be made:

Cash	$100	
Accounts Receivable		$98
Interest (or Lapsed		
Discount) Revenue		2

It should be apparent that, as was the case in recording purchases, the net method provides the best representation of the events that occurred. Had the customer chosen to pay cash for the merchandise rather than charging it, the selling price certainly would have been net rather than gross. Thus, the cash sales price of the goods is the net price; the gross price is actually a combination of the cash sales price ($98) and interest for not paying within the time allowed ($2).

In the case of purchases, the net method was preferred not only because it best reflected the events that occurred but also because of the control aspect it introduced. In accordance with the concept of "management by exception," it is expected that the discount should always be taken on purchases; when it is missed, that failure should be brought to management's attention for explanation and/or correction.

In accounting for sales, however, the control aspect is absent. Management cannot force its customers either to take or miss the discounts available to them; hence, the only advantage of accounting for sales on a net basis is that it better reflects the economic events. The net method is, however, more difficult to apply in practice as compared to the gross method. Since sales invoices are typically prepared in terms of gross prices, record-keeping is simplified if the accounting records are maintained on a similar basis. As both methods ultimately report the same profits for the period (assuming appropriate adjusting entries are made at the end of the period in each case), application of the gross method is not objectionable, even though theoretically less desirable.

Recording Cost of Goods Sold Expense

The frequency of entries recording cost of goods sold depends upon which inventory method, perpetual or periodic, is in use. Under the perpetual method, an entry is made each time a sale is consummated, whereas under the periodic method, an entry is made only at the end of the accounting period. Firms using the perpetual inventory method are able to determine gross profit over any period of time by simply subtracting the balance in cost of goods sold expense from the balance of the sales revenue account. Firms using the periodic inventory method must first count and price the goods on hand at the end of the period in question (i.e., take a physical inventory count) and compute the cost of goods sold; only then can they determine gross profit. Taking physical inventories is time-consuming, costly, and tends to disrupt normal production and sales activities.[5] It follows that firms using the periodic inventory method may find it inexpedient to compute entity and ownership income more often than once a year, while those using the perpetual inventory method can obtain quarterly, monthly, weekly, or even daily operating data with very little difficulty. The demands of both management and investors for interim accounting data has led to increasing use of the perpetual inventory method.

However, the perpetual inventory method has one serious disadvantage. Each sale requires two entries, as previously explained; and in order to make the entry debiting cost of goods sold expense and crediting merchandise (or finished goods) inventory, the firm must maintain detailed inventory records showing the historical cost of each article carried in stock. The cost of maintaining such records may be so great as to preclude use of the method by small concerns. This disadvantage has been overcome to some extent by the advent of electronic data processing equipment. And even the smallest firms may solve the record maintenance problem by marking the merchandise or finished goods inventories with the historical acquisition cost (in code, so that it will not be known to the customers) at the time it is placed in stock. When a sale is made, the historical acquisition cost (in code) is recorded on the sales ticket along with the selling price. Thus, data for the entry debiting cost of goods sold expense and crediting merchandise (or finished goods) inventory are obtained directly from the sales ticket without the necessity of referring to, or even maintaining, detailed perpetual inventory records.

With the perpetual inventory system in use by either merchandising or manufacturing firms, a single control account is the only general ledger account required. With a merchandiser, this control account is merchandise inventory; with a manufacturer, it is finished goods inventory. The entries made to merchandise inventory will record the

5. Firms using the perpetual inventory method take physical inventories from time to time in order to disclose inaccuracies in book inventories occasioned by theft or bookkeeping errors. However, these verification inventories need not be taken all at one time and, in practice, are usually taken on a cycle basis in such a way as to be relatively inexpensive and to cause a minimum of interference with normal operations.

data regarding the acquisition (purchase price, discounts, returns and allowances, and freight) and sale of the inventory. On the other hand, because all goods available for sale are produced within the firm, the manufacturer will debit finished goods only to record the allocated historical acquisition cost of goods received from the production department and credit it to record sales. Whichever account (merchandise inventory or finished goods inventory) is in use, the balance at all times represents the historical cost of goods available for sale (barring theft or bookkeeping errors).

When the periodic method of accounting for inventories is employed by a manufacturing concern, little changes in terms of the accounting procedures. Finished goods inventory continues to be debited to record the receipts of goods from the production department. At the end of the accounting period, a physical count is made of the finished goods remaining on hand. The difference between the debit total and the allocated historical cost of goods still on hand is then credited to finished goods inventory and debited to cost of goods sold expense. The residual balance, of course, represents the historical costs which have been allocated to the ending inventory.

Implementation of the periodic inventory method for a merchandiser, however, requires the use of a number of accounts which together comprise the inventory pool. This pool is composed of the following accounts: merchandise inventory (beginning inventory), purchases, purchase returns and allowances, freight-in, and handling costs. The sum of their balances is the historical cost of goods available for sale during the period. At the end of the accounting period, a physical count is made of the goods on hand and appropriate historical costs are attached, giving the historical cost of ending inventory. When this amount is deducted from the historical cost of goods available for sale for the period (the sum of the pool accounts), the result is cost of goods sold expense for the period. Accordingly, only one adjusting entry is necessary to record cost of goods sold under the periodic inventory method and that entry is made at the end of the accounting period.

To illustrate this procedure, let us suppose that at the end of the accounting period, the balances found in Figure 5-2 were contained in one firm's pool accounts. The $9,000 balance in merchandise inventory represents the beginning inventory. The balances in each of the other accounts represent the total of the activity for each category during the period (total purchases for the period equaled $78,000, and so on). Suppose that at the end of the period a physical count of the inventory quantity on hand was made and that, applying the appropriate cost flow assumption to the quantity, an ending inventory of $12,000

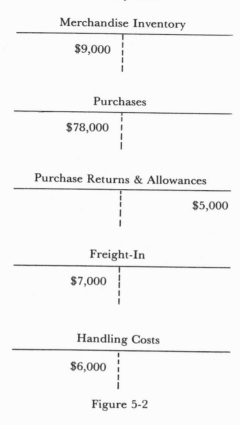

Figure 5-2

was determined. This includes, of course, the purchase price of the physical inventory on hand (however determined) plus the ending inventory share of other pool items—purchase returns and allowances, freight-in, and handling costs. The cost of goods sold during the period would then be computed as follows:

Beginning Inventory		$9,000
Add: Purchases	$78,000	
Less: Purchase returns and allowances	5,000	73,000
Freight-In		7,000
Handling Costs		6,000
Cost of goods available for sale ("pool")		$95,000
Less: Ending inventory		12,000
Cost of goods sold		$83,000

To close the pool accounts and to record the ending inventory and cost of goods sold, the following adjusting entry is made:

Merchandise Inventory	$12,000	
Cost of Goods Sold Expense	83,000	
Purchase Returns and Allowances	5,000	
Merchandise Inventory		$ 9,000
Purchases		78,000
Freight-In		7,000
Handling Costs		6,000

"pool" accounts (cost of goods available for sale)

Note that the asset account, merchandise inventory, is both debited and credited. The credit is to remove the beginning inventory balance ($9,000) from the account where it has been carried throughout the accounting period. The allocated historical cost of the ending inventory ($12,000) is then debited to the account. All of the other accounts in the entry are temporary rather than permanent accounts. Of these, only cost of goods sold expense appears in the financial statements; the rest are used only to facilitate record-keeping and managerial analysis and do not typically appear in published financial statements.

In practice, no separate inventory pool (cost of goods available for sale) account is established in the records, such an account being effectively bypassed by the compound journal entry illustrated above. However, by establishing such an account hypothetically, we may better illustrate (see Figure 5-3) the process of dividing the inventory pool into cost of goods sold expense and the ending balance of merchandise inventory.

INVENTORY COST FLOW ASSUMPTIONS

Up to this point, our attention has been primarily focused upon the mechanical operation of the accounting system for inventories. We have explained how inventory acquisitions are initially recorded and then how the accounting data are processed through the various accounts in arriving at cost of goods sold expense for the period and the related ending inventory balances. In so doing, however, we have rather cavalierly implied that there existed some *unique value* which could be attached to each inventory item as it moved through the accounting system from date of purchase to date of sale. Such, however, is not generally the case.

The primary exception arises in the case of merchandising firms that buy and sell products having high unit costs, such as automobiles, machinery, and jewelry. For the most part, these inventory items are

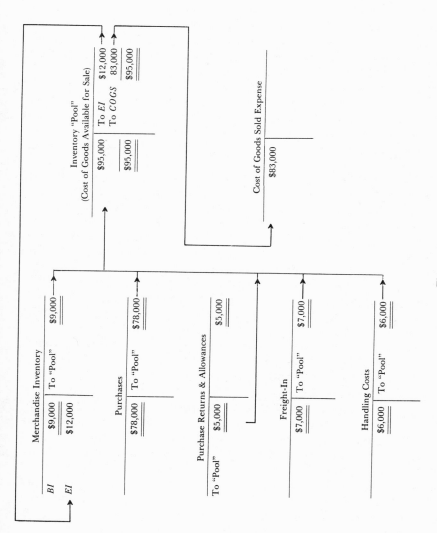

Figure 5-3

heterogeneous in nature, being perhaps custom-designed or custom-ordered; accordingly, each item is capable of being separately identified from the others which the firm has on hand. Moreover, the merchandising firm that deals in these goods does not transform them in any fashion—they remain physically the same from the day they are purchased from the manufacturer (or perhaps an intermediary merchandiser known as a wholesaler) until the day they are sold to customers. In other words, they are always finished goods. For these unique goods, as a consequence, it is usually possible to attach to each of them a unique value—their historical acquisition cost—from the day they enter the firm by purchase until the day they leave by sale. This method of inventory valuation is known as *specific identification*.

For merchandising firms that deal in homogeneous rather than heterogeneous items of inventory, it is, of course, possible to employ the specific identification method. Each item could perhaps be code-numbered on the day it is purchased and, when it is sold, its acquisition cost could be charged to cost of goods sold expense. However, when employed in conjunction with homogeneous items, this method is subject to a very serious shortcoming, that of "income manipulation" (sometimes more generously termed "income management"). By having the option of choosing from among the identical inventory items the ones that are to be sold, management may alter the amount to be reported as cost of goods sold expense and, hence, alter income as well. For example, management may elect to shore up a poor profit picture by selecting for sale those units having the lowest historical acquisition costs. Conversely, management may temper profits during a particularly robust period by selling off only those items having the highest historical acquisition costs. In effect, the players in the game are permitted to keep the score—clearly an undesirable state of affairs from almost any point of view (except, of course, management's). Thus, the specific identification method should be regarded as inappropriate in accounting for homogeneous inventory items.

When we turn to the case of a manufacturer producing homogeneous products, the specific identification method is similarly inappropriate. Many of the costs incurred in the manufacturing process are "joint costs"; that is to say, they are not attributable to a particular item of inventory but rather are incurred to facilitate the production process as a whole. As a consequence, any assignment of these costs, such as factory overhead, to a particular inventory item must necessarily be made on some arbitrary basis. And there exists a wide variety of arbitrary bases upon which such allocations of joint costs can be made, no one of which is clearly better than the others. It is simply not possible, therefore, to determine a unique value for an inventory item that is manufactured. Lacking such a unique value for each item, the specific identification method flounders.

In attempting to deal with the valuation problems engendered by homogeneous inventories and exacerbated in a dynamic economy characterized by changing prices, accountants have devised several alternative approaches to inventory valuations. These alternative approaches are founded upon differing assumptions as to the flow of historical acquisition costs through the business firm from date of purchase to date of sale. Of these, we shall discuss the three primary ones: (1) Last In First Out (LIFO), (2) First In First Out (FIFO), and (3) average cost. These three are the alternatives most widely used in practice, and all are generally acceptable for federal income tax purposes as well. The choice of which of the three approaches to use for financial reporting purposes, according to the accounting profession, is dependent upon which one "more appropriately measures income under the circumstances." To the best of our knowledge, no one has ever been able to specify the circumstances under which one method is more appropriate than the other; therefore, the choice should be regarded as essentially an arbitrary one.

LIFO versus FIFO

While LIFO and FIFO are usually referred to as inventory valuation methods, they are more properly methods for defining the expense known as cost of goods sold. The related inventory values are residuals, those appropriate for reaching the desired figure for cost of goods sold.

The LIFO approach proceeds on the assumption that the historical costs which should be assigned to the goods sold are those most recently incurred. The FIFO method, on the other hand, is based on the argument that the older costs should be assigned to goods sold. It follows, of course, that under LIFO, goods on hand at the end of a period must be assigned older costs (the more recent being allocated to goods sold), while under FIFO, the ending inventory must be assigned more recent costs (the older costs having been allocated to goods sold). Of the appropriately defined cost of goods available for sale, LIFO uses older costs for the ending inventory and the more recent costs for goods sold while FIFO reverses this allocation.

The two methods are frequently compared to an assumed physical flow of goods, though there is little reason to the argument that particular costs travel with particular goods, especially when the goods are homogeneous. The names of the methods have been developed in this way, however. Thus, LIFO assigns costs to goods sold as though the last in are first out (the more recent costs are assigned to goods sold) while FIFO allocates costs to goods sold as though the first in are first out (the older costs are allocated to goods sold). An example may clarify the effects of the LIFO and FIFO methods on the cost of goods sold expense and, consequently, on operating income.

Assume that two firms are identical in every respect except that one uses FIFO and the other LIFO. Both commence business at the same time with an initial stock of goods of 1,000 items purchased at $1.00 each. During the first period of operation both firms purchase 8,000 items at $1.10 each and sell 7,500 at $2.00 each. Both firms employ the periodic inventory method. Assuming no other expenses, we can make the following comparison:

	FIFO Company		LIFO Company	
Sales Revenue		$15,000		$15,000
Cost of Goods Sold Expense:				
Beginning Inventory	$1,000		$1,000	
Add: Purchases	8,800		8,800	
Cost of Goods Available for Sale	$9,800		$9,800	
Less: Ending Inventory	1,650	8,150	1,550	8,250
Operating Income		$ 6,850		$ 6,750

The FIFO company has assigned the older costs to goods sold (1,000 @ $1.00 plus 6,500 @ $1.10 = $8,150) and the more recent costs to inventory (1,500 @ $1.10 = $1,650). The LIFO company has allocated the more recent costs to goods sold (7,500 @ $1.10 = $8,250) and the older costs to inventory (1,000 @ $1.00 plus 500 @ $1.10 = $1,550). Thus, the cost of goods sold for the FIFO company is smaller (and, therefore, its reported income is larger) and its ending inventory value larger than the comparable figures for the LIFO company.

In the second period of operation, a further difference arises—the beginning inventory cost balances of the two firms are no longer identical, each firm starting the new period with its ending inventory from the preceding period. Assume each firm makes identical purchases of 10,000 units at $1.20 each and sales of 9,800 at $2.00 each. Still assuming no other expenses, we can compare results as follows:

	FIFO Company		LIFO Company	
Sales Revenue		$19,600		$19,600
Cost of Goods Sold Expense:				
Beginning Inventory	$ 1,650		$ 1,550	
Add: Purchases	12,000		12,000	
Cost of Goods Available for Sale	$13,650		$13,550	
Less: Ending Inventory	2,040	11,610	1,790	11,760
Operating Income		$ 7,990		$ 7,840

The ending inventories are valued as follows:

FIFO	LIFO
1,700 @ $1.20 = $2,040	1,000 @ $1.00 = $1,000
	500 @ 1.10 = 550
	200 @ 1.20 = 240
	$1,790

The cost of goods sold figures include for each method:

FIFO	LIFO
1,500 @ $1.10 = $ 1,650	9,800 @ $1.20 = $11,760
8,300 @ 1.20 = 9,960	
$11,610	

In general, both LIFO and FIFO are acceptable for federal income tax purposes, but a firm cannot arbitrarily abandon LIFO once that selection has been made; moreover, in order to use LIFO for tax purposes, the firm *must* adopt it for financial statement purposes as well. In periods of rising prices and increasing inventory size, perhaps the typical expectation for the successful firm in the United States, the use of LIFO leads to smaller reported taxable income and, hence, to lower current income tax payments. Its advantage in this respect has led more and more firms to adopt it, though many continue to employ FIFO. When prices have been falling over time, the advantage of LIFO over FIFO is reversed and FIFO leads to lower reported taxable income and income taxes.

But the advantages of LIFO to the growing firm do not rest solely on rising prices. If this were so, these advantages should disappear when rising and falling prices alternate so that the price trend is neither up nor down. Under these circumstances, however, the LIFO firm may still reap rewards that are not available to its FIFO counterpart. Periods of rising and falling prices can be expected to coincide roughly with prosperity and recession, with high and low profits (or losses). If this coincidence occurs, the LIFO firm will report lower profits when profits as a whole are high and larger profits (or smaller losses) when profits as a whole are low (or negative). The LIFO firm can, in effect, transfer profits from high-profit years (when income tax rates may be higher to stem inflationary pressure) to low-profit years (when rates may be lower to stimulate spending). This smoothing of cyclical income may also enable some smaller firms to avoid high marginal income tax rates on at least a part of their incomes. Despite these advantages, the apparent general tendency for prices to be flexible upward but not downward suggests that the greatest advantage of LIFO may be associated with expectations that the price trend will be upward.

For firms which are declining in size, the advantages of LIFO are much less certain, even though prices may be rising. The amount by which the inventory is reduced in each period is added to the cost of goods sold expense at the old prices assigned to that amount of inventory when the inventory quantity was last increased. These costs may be very old and also very low. The reduction in inventory may even make the cost of goods sold expense under LIFO lower than under FIFO, making reported taxable income and income taxes larger.

While LIFO tends to value goods sold at recent costs, it does so only by adopting ancient costs for inventory. When LIFO is used, inventory figures on the position statement usually bear little, if any, resemblance to the current market value of the goods. FIFO, on the other hand, usually leads to more current values on the position statement but achieves this effect by utilizing older costs for the goods sold on the income statement. A means for resolving this dilemma is suggested in the final chapters of this book.

Average Cost

The average cost method of valuing inventory assets and the cost of goods sold expense usually avoids the extremes of LIFO and FIFO and, under some circumstances, has computational advantages over both. It is a method which is acceptable for income tax purposes. Goods on hand at any moment are assigned an average cost, determined by dividing the total historical acquisition costs of all units on hand by the number of units on hand. When inventories are accounted for on a perpetual basis, each additional purchase is averaged in with existing goods to yield a new average cost, and goods sold are charged out at the average cost prevailing at time of sale. While a new average cost must be computed after each purchase, the records are not cluttered up with several prices related to those batches of goods still on hand or sold. Under the periodic method, a single average cost for the period is determined at the end of the period by dividing the cost of goods available for sale during the period by the number of units available for sale. The number of units sold during the period and those on hand at the end of the period are then multiplied by this average cost to yield the cost of goods sold and cost of ending inventory, respectively.

The data used to formulate examples of LIFO and FIFO would yield the following results under the average cost periodic method:

	Period 1		Period 2	
Sales Revenue		$15,000.00		$19,600.00
Cost of Goods Sold Expense:				
Beginning Inventory	$1,000.00		$ 1,633.33	
Add: Purchases	8,800.00		12,000.00	
Cost of Goods Available for Sale	$9,800.00		$13,633.33	
Less: Ending Inventory	1,633.33	8,166.67	2,015.36	11,617.97
Operating Income		$ 6,833.33		$ 7,982.03

In these simplified examples, the average cost of goods available for sale in the first period is $9,800 divided by 9,000 units, or $1.089/unit. This average cost, multiplied by the 1,500 items on hand at the end of the period, yields the figure for the ending inventory; multiplied by the 7,500 items sold, it yields the cost of goods sold expense. The appropriate average cost in Period 2 is similarly $\dfrac{\$13,633.33}{11,500 \text{ units}} =$ $1.1855/unit which, when multiplied by 1,700 items, yields the ending inventory figure and, when multiplied by 9,800, yields the cost of goods sold expense. Note that averaging leads to reported income figures which fall between the related FIFO and LIFO figures computed above. So long as prices are generally moving in one direction, either up or down, this condition will hold; however, such may not be the case when price movements are mixed.

NONCOMPARABILITY OF INCOMES UNDER ALTERNATIVE INVENTORY COST FLOW ASSUMPTIONS

As might be expected, when alternative assumptions are made regarding the flow of inventory costs, the resulting income and position statement data will differ. These differences are evidenced in the example appearing in Table 5-1.[6] Note that regardless of the cost flow assumption adopted, price and quantity data are identical for (1) beginning inventory in Period 1, (2) purchases in each period, and (3) sales in each period. Yet, even when working with the same raw data, the results differ significantly from method to method so long as purchase prices fluctuate over time. Only in the unlikely event that purchase prices remained constant over time would FIFO, LIFO, and average cost be expected to produce results comparable with one another.

Although comparable results between the various methods cannot be expected when prices vary from period to period, interperiod comparability for the *same* method might reasonably be expected. That is to say, given *identical* raw data in two different periods, consistent application of a particular cost flow assumption should produce identical results. Surprisingly enough, such is not necessarily the case. Consider the raw data for Period 1 and Period 4 in Table 5-1. Note that in each period the beginning and ending inventories amounted to ten and six units, respectively. Likewise during each period, twenty units were purchased at $17 apiece and twenty-four units were sold for $21 each. However, not one of the three methods—FIFO, LIFO, or average cost—produced an operating income in Period 4 that would be comparable to the Period 1 income determined by applying the same method. In this example, the most striking difference is with FIFO, from a $90 profit in Period 1 to a $115 profit in Period 4. It should be clear, therefore, that even consistent application of one method is no guarantee of comparability.

A Constraint: The Lower-of-Cost-or-Market

Accountants are inclined to be conservative in placing valuations on assets. They are willing to ride along with historical acquisition cost figures until prevailing market values fall below recorded costs. In these circumstances, conservatism may override historical costs and current market values may supplant historical costs in the valuation of inventories. To lend support to this practice, the accounting profession adheres closely to the rule of "cost or market, whichever is lower" in valuing inventories.

Those firms which measure cost according to the FIFO or average cost methods have this option for income tax purposes and must use

6. Adapted from E. O. Edwards and P. W. Bell, *The Theory and Measurement of Business Income* (Berkeley: University of California Press, 1961), Table 7, p. 156.

Table 5-1

THE EFFECTS OF ALTERNATIVE INVENTORY COST FLOW ASSUMPTIONS
ON REPORTED INCOME IN PERIODS OF CHANGING PRICES AND VOLUMES

	PERIOD			
	1	*2*	*3*	*4*
Sales	24 @$22 = $528	28 @$21 = $588	30 @$22.50 = $675	24 @$22 = $528
Beginning Inventory:				
FIFO	10 @$20 = $200	6 @$17 = $102	8 @$16 = $128	10 @$17.50 = $175
LIFO	10 @$20 = $200	6 @$20 = $120	6 @$20 / 2 @$16 } = $152	6 @$20 / 2 @$16 / 2 @$17.50 } = $187
Average Cost	10 @$20 = $200	6 @$18 = $108	8 @$16.33 1/3 = $130.67	10 @$17.26 2/3 = $172.67
Purchases	20 @$17 = $340	30 @$16 = $480	32 @$17.50 = $560	20 @$17 = $340
Ending Inventory:				
FIFO	6 @$17 = $102	8 @$16 = $128	10 @$17.50 = $175	6 @$17 = $102
LIFO	6 @$20 = $120	6 @$20 / 2 @$16 } = $152	6 @$20 / 2 @$16 / 2 @$17.50 } = $187	6 @$20 = $120
Average Cost	6 @$18 = $108	8 @$16.33 1/3 = $130.67	10 @$17.26 2/3 = $172.67	6 @$17.089 = $102.53
Operating Income (Loss):				
FIFO	$ 90	$134	$162	$115
LIFO	$108	$140	$150	$121
Average Cost	$ 96	$130.67	$157	$117.86

it for financial reporting purposes, but so far the pressure to permit it for firms employing LIFO has been unsuccessful. The rule is relatively unimportant so long as prices are generally rising, but it is possible that a fear of falling prices in the future may cause some firms to hesitate before adopting LIFO as a basis for inventory valuation.

For firms employing FIFO or average cost when prices are falling, the rule permits the substitution of a lower market valuation for a higher recorded cost figure. As a result, the cost of goods sold expense is raised, and reported income and income taxes are reduced.

As defined by the accounting profession, "current market value," for purposes of implementing the lower-of-cost-or-market rule, may be any one of a number of different current market values. Basically, "market value" is defined as the current cost of acquiring the item in question, i.e., its current replacement cost. However, the market value is subject to certain "ceiling" and "floor" constraints. On the one hand, the market value cannot be higher than "net realizable value," the price that could be obtained for the item by selling it to customers less costs of disposition (selling commissions, and so on). On the other hand, the market value cannot be lower than net realizable value less a "normal" profit margin. In other words, so long as current replacement cost falls between net realizable value and net realizable value less a normal profit margin, then current replacement cost is used as "market." However, if current replacement cost is higher than net realizable value (the "ceiling"), then net realizable value represents "market." Similarly, if current replacement cost is less than net realizable value less a normal profit margin (the "floor"), then the latter is used as "market."

Thus, current market value for purposes of the lower-of-cost-or-market rule may be any one of three different market values. Once the market value is selected from among the three possibilities, it is compared against historical cost and the lower of the two is used in assigning a value to the ending inventory. If market is the lower of the two, the difference between cost and market is usually charged to cost of goods sold expense for the period.

SUMMARY

This chapter has summarized the accounting techniques and valuation practices with respect to inventories that are currently in use by most firms in the United States. Considerable dissatisfaction with these methods has been expressed by many accountants and economists. Reported income is arbitrarily defined and position statement values are ambiguous, making comparisons among firms and over time extremely hazardous. These problems are discussed in more detail in the final chapters of this book, at which point another means of valuation is proposed with the objective of overcoming these problems.

DISCUSSION QUESTIONS

1. Mr. Clean is the owner of the Pick-up Company which manufactures and sells various models of compact vacuum cleaners. He is trying to decide if the inventory should be kept on a perpetual or a periodic inventory method. Discuss the advantages and disadvantages of each. Under what conditions would one method or the other be more advantageous for a company?

2. Where can the amounts represented by balances in the following accounts be found, either implicitly or explicitly, on the firm's financial statements:
   a. purchases
   b. work-in-process
   c. purchase discounts (under net and gross system)
   d. loss from lapsed discounts (under net and gross system)
   e. purchase returns
   f. allowance for sales discounts

3. The Coverup Company purchases wigs from its wholesale supplier who allows purchase terms of 2/15, n/30. The following transactions took place in October:
   a. A shipment of wigs was received on October 10. Gross price of the wigs is $5,200.
   b. Two wigs (gross price of $50 each) were defective and were returned on October 17.
   c. One-half of the invoiced amount was paid on October 20.
   d. The remaining portion of the invoiced amount was paid on October 27.

   Give the journal entries in the books of the Coverup Company under:
   (1) the gross price method
   (2) the net price method

4. If a company uses the LIFO cost flow assumption for tax purposes, it must also use the LIFO method in its financial statements.
   a. Do you think that it is appropriate for Congress to specify that in computing reported income the same procedures be followed

as in computing taxable income? If so, might it be well to extend this type of condition to other situations, i.e., FIFO or average cost? Why or why not?

b. What if the situation were reversed: If a company uses the LIFO cost flow assumption in valuing its inventory on its financial statements, it must use LIFO for tax purposes. Is this true or false? Explain.

5. Fill in the 2 × 4 matrix in Figure 5-4 with the cost flow assumption—LIFO, FIFO, or average cost—that would produce the result indicated at the top of the column.

6. The XYZ Company has been in operation for three years. At the close of its fiscal year, June 30, 19X3, the XYZ Company hired an independent auditor to verify its financial statements. Since this was a first audit, the prior statements were also examined. Assume the company uses a FIFO periodic inventory method. The following independent errors in the ending merchandise inventory were discovered:

a. Inventory amounting to $4,200 was temporarily placed in a back storeroom. This merchandise was accidentally overlooked during the inventory count on June 30, 19X1.

b. Inventory of $3,400 was ordered from the supplier. The goods arrived on June 28, 19X2, but the invoice was not received until July 4, 19X3.

c. XYZ Company recorded a sale of $7,300 on June 29, 19X3, but the merchandise was not shipped until July 2, 19X4.

	Highest *COGS*	Lowest *COGS*	Highest *EI*	Lowest *EI*
Inflation				
Deflation				

Figure 5-4

The reported income for each of these years was $4,020, $5,600, and $2,060, respectively.

(1) What is the correct net income for each of the three years?

(2) Make the appropriate correcting journal entries in 19X3, assuming the books are still open.

7. The ABC Company handles a single merchandise inventory item. For simplicity, assume that the company has no beginning inventory at January 1, 19X5. The following information is available:

Quarter Ending	Units Purchased	Cost	Units Sold	End of Quarter Market Price
March 31, 19X5	2000	$4.50	1000	$6.00
June 30, 19X5	1500	5.00	2000	6.00
Sept. 30, 19X5	3000	5.50	1500	5.50
Dec. 31, 19X5	2500	6.00	2500	5.50

What is the value of the ending inventory each quarter and at the end-of-year under the following flow assumptions:

a. LIFO

b. FIFO

c. FIFO (assuming lower-of-cost-or-market rule)

8. Some accountants feel it necessary to make artificial physical flow assumptions in accounting for inventories.

a. Is this because they believe that there must be some actual physical flow and accounting should reflect this? Or that they must find some means of allocating beginning inventory and purchases (goods available for sale) as between cost of goods sold and ending inventory? Discuss.

b. Is there normally any rationale having to do with measurement of book income (as opposed to taxable income) that would make a FIFO flow assumption better or worse than a LIFO flow assumption? Or either one better than the assumption that beginning inventory was held until mid-year, then sold, while ending inventory was purchased at mid-year? Discuss.

PROBLEMS

5-1. Marsh Company

Marsh Company began September 19X2 with no inventory on hand. The following transactions took place during the month:

Sept. 2 Purchased merchandise, $2,000 at invoice prices, terms 2/10, n/30.

 4 Received freight bill for $50 on Sept. 2 purchase.
 9 Purchased merchandise, $6,000 at invoice prices, terms 3/10, *n*/30.
10 Paid freight bill on Sept. 2 purchase.
11 Paid Sept. 2 invoice.
12 Sold merchandise costing $1,200 for $1,800 on account.
13 Received freight bill on Sept. 9 purchase, $150.
16 Returned merchandise from Sept. 9 purchase to creditor, $1,000 at invoice prices.
20 Purchased merchandise, $3,000 at invoice prices, terms *n*/30. (Supplier paid freight.)
24 Sold merchandise costing $600 for $900, on account.
27 Paid remainder of Sept. 9 invoice.

INSTRUCTIONS:

Prepare journal entries to record the foregoing, assuming Marsh records purchases on a net basis and prepares statements monthly (a) using the perpetual inventory method and (b) using the periodic inventory method.

5-2. Simonton Company

Simonton Company began business on the first of September and entered into the following transactions during the month:

Sept. 1 Purchased $9,000 worth of merchandise on account, terms 2/10, *n*/30.
    3 Sold goods costing $8,000 for $11,000 on account, terms 3/10 EOM. (EOM means the invoice price is due at the end of the month.)
    4 Purchased $10,000 (gross) worth of merchandise, terms 4/5, *n*/30. Payment was made immediately in cash.
    7 Received $60 freight bill for delivery of Sept. 4 purchase, terms *n*/30.
    9 Paid Sept. 1 invoice.
   10 Purchased $12,000 worth of merchandise on account, terms 3/10, *n*/30.
   11 Sold goods costing $10,000 for $14,000 on account, terms 3/10, *n*/30.
   12 Paid Sept. 7 freight bill.
   14 Received payment of Sept. 3 sale.
   19 Returned to suppliers $2,000 (gross) worth of merchandise from Sept. 10 purchase.

24 Customers returned $500 worth of merchandise (sold for $700) from Sept. 11 sale.

25 Received payment of remainder of Sept. 11 sale.

29 Paid remainder of Sept. 10 invoice.

INSTRUCTIONS:

Record the foregoing transactions and make the necessary end-of-month adjustments (if applicable), assuming that the Simonton Company:

(a) Uses the perpetual inventory method and records all purchases and sales on a gross basis;

(b) Uses the periodic inventory method, records all purchases on a net basis, and records all sales on a gross basis.

5-3. Bellaire Company

The Bellaire Company purchases all of its merchandise from several wholesalers, all of whom offer terms of 2/10, n/30. The wholesalers bill Bellaire in terms of gross prices, but Bellaire records all transactions in terms of net prices. All amounts given below are gross amounts. Bellaire uses the periodic inventory method.

INSTRUCTIONS:

Prepare journal entries to record the following:

(a) Purchases during the year from various wholesalers totaled $1,000,000.

(b) Freight costs on merchandise purchased amounted to $50,000 which was paid by Bellaire.

(c) Merchandise returned amounted to $100,000, half of which was returned after the discount period had lapsed. (Wholesalers pay freight costs of returning merchandise to them.)

(d) Bellaire's handling costs associated with the merchandise amounted to $60,000 for the year.

(e) Inventory on hand at the end of the year amounted to $200,000. (Prices based on wholesalers' invoices.)

5-4. Halletsville Company

The Halletsville Company began business at the first of the year. During the year the following transactions occurred. All amounts given below are gross amounts (unless otherwise indicated), but Halletsville records all transactions on a net basis.

INSTRUCTIONS:

Prepare journal entries to record the following:

(a) Sales on account during the year totaled $500,000. Terms were 2/10, n/30.
(b) Returns totaled $30,000. Of this amount, $10,000 of faulty goods was returned more than ten days following the sale.
(c) Collected accounts totaling $400,000, ten per cent of which were collected more than ten days following the sale.
(d) Bad debts were predicted at 1-1/2 per cent of recorded credit sales.
(e) Specific accounts deemed uncollectible during the year amounted to $4,000 (net of discounts).
(f) It is predicted at year-end that $5,000 worth of sales during the year will be returned early next year. All these returns will probably be made after the discount period has passed.
(g) At year end, it is estimated that discounts are still available on $15,000 worth of sales and that all of these discounts will be taken.

5-5. *Weir Company*

The Weir Company records all purchases on a net basis and all sales on a gross basis. Purchases are subject to terms of 2/10, n/30 while sales terms are 5/10, n/60. Relevant account balances on January 1 are as follows:

	Dr.	Cr.
Accounts Receivable	$162,000	
Accounts Receivable—Allowance for Bad Debts		$ 3,000
Accounts Receivable—Allowance for Sales Discounts		5,000
Accounts Receivable—Allowance for Sales Returns		4,000
Merchandise Inventory	73,000	
Merchandise to be Returned by Customers	2,400	
Accounts Payable		98,000

INSTRUCTIONS:

Assuming Weir Company accounts for its inventories on a FIFO periodic basis, prepare journal entries to record the following transactions for the month of January:

(a) Purchases for the month at invoice cost amounted to $150,000, all on account.

(b) Freight bills for merchandise purchased during the month amounted to $4,200 and were paid in cash.

(c) Merchandise returned to suppliers during the month amounted to $10,000 at invoice prices. All returns were made within ten days of purchase.

(d) Cash payments to suppliers on account amounted to $118,200. Discounts were taken on $90,000 gross amount of invoices.

(e) It was estimated at the end of January that discounts had been lost on $20,000 of payables at invoice prices.

(f) Sales during January amounted to $210,000, all on account.

(g) Merchandise returned by customers amounted to $10,000 at selling prices (gross). All returns were made within 20 days. Estimated cost of merchandise returned was $6,000.

(h) Collections on customers' accounts during January amounted to $172,000, cash. Customers took discounts on $160,000 gross amount of invoices.

(i) At the end of January, it was estimated that discounts were still outstanding on $30,000 gross amount of customers' accounts.

(j) At the end of January, it was predicted that customers would return merchandise amounting to $5,000 at gross selling prices. The estimated cost of such merchandise was $3,000.

(k) A physical count of the inventory on January 31 indicated $50,000 at gross invoice prices was still on hand.

5-6. *Gundy Company*

The Gundy Company records all purchases on a net basis and all credit sales on a gross basis. Normal trade terms for purchases are 3/10, *n*/30 and for sales, 2/10, *n*/30. Relevant account balances on January 1, 19X3 are as follows:

	Dr.	Cr.
Merchandise Inventory (including freight and handling)	$26,000	
Merchandise to be Returned	350	
Accounts Receivable	30,000	
Accounts Receivable—Allowance for Sales Discounts		$ 400
Accounts Receivable—Allowance for Sales Returns		500
Accounts Payable		1,940

Inventory records are maintained on the FIFO periodic inventory method. The transactions for the month of January are as follows:

(1) Purchases of merchandise totaled $50,000 at invoice prices are subject to terms of 3/10, n/30.
(2) Freight bills were received for merchandise purchased during the month, $2,000.
(3) Sales on account during the month totaled $82,000.
(4) Payments made to creditors on account were $43,800 (actual). Discounts were taken on $40,000 gross amount of invoices; discounts on the remainder were lost.
(5) Collections on account amounted to $98,200 (actual). Discounts were taken on $90,000 gross amount of invoices; discounts on the remainder were lost.
(6) Merchandise handling costs (other than freight) were $1,000 and were paid.
(7) Unsatisfactory merchandise returned to creditors amounted to $5,000 at invoice prices. Half of the merchandise had already been paid for, and of that half, discounts had lapsed on $600 of the invoices.
(8) Sales returns by customers amounted to $4,000 at invoice prices. The cost of merchandise returned was $2,800.
(9) Purchase allowances granted by creditors for damaged merchandise amounted to $300 at invoice prices.
(10) Predicted sales discounts to be taken by customers in February, $200 (on January sales).
(11) Predicted sales returns by customers in February (on January sales), $1,000 at invoice prices. Estimated cost of goods to be returned was $700 at net prices.
(12) As of the end of January, discounts had lapsed on $1,500 of payables at invoice prices.
(13) The physical inventory count on January 31 indicated goods on hand amounting to $15,000 at invoice prices.

INSTRUCTIONS:
Prepare journal entries to record the foregoing.

5-7. Manchester Machinery Company

The Manchester Machinery Company is a manufacturing firm. On January 1, 19X6 its inventory balances were as follows:

Raw Materials	$20,000
Work in Process	35,000
Finished Goods	30,000

Purchases of raw materials during the year totaled $270,000. Direct labor was $390,000 and overhead costs, $195,000. Sales during the year came to $950,000. Inventory balances on December 31, 19X6 were as follows:

Raw Materials	$10,000
Work in Process	25,000
Finished Goods	15,000

INSTRUCTIONS:

Compute the following:

(a) Cost of product added to process during 19X6.
(b) Cost of product finished during 19X6.
(c) Cost of product sold during 19X6.
(d) Income for 19X6.

5-8. *Adrian Corporation*

The Adrian Corporation is engaged in the manufacture of a single product. Each finished unit consists of the following:

Raw Materials:	3 lbs. @ $4/lb.	= $12
Direct Labor:	4 hrs. @ $5/hr.	= 20
Factory Overhead:	40% of Direct Labor	= 8
		$40

On January 1, 19X3, Adrian's inventory account balances were as follows:

Raw Materials (2,000 lbs.)	$ 8,000
Work in Process (1,000 units, 66 2/3% complete as to materials, 50% complete as to direct labor and factory overhead)	22,000
Finished Goods (500 units)	20,000

During the month of January, the following events took place:

(1) Purchased 7,000 lbs. of raw materials.
(2) Utilized 11,200 hours of direct labor.
(3) Incurred factory overhead costs of $22,400.

(4) Transferred 7,500 lbs. of raw materials into production.
(5) Sold 2,900 units.

On January 31, the finished goods inventory consisted of 600 units costing a total of $24,000. During the month, all costs remained constant (i.e., raw material was $4/lb., direct labor was $5/hr., and so on.).

INSTRUCTIONS:
Determine the following:

(a) Cost of goods completed and transferred to Finished Goods during January.
(b) Total costs added to Work in Process during January.
(c) Cost of raw materials included in Work in Process on January 31.
(d) Number of units of product started and finished during January.
(e) Cost of factory overhead included in Work in Process on January 31.

5-9. *Munising Corporation*

The Munising Corporation is engaged in the manufacture of a single product. Each unit of output contains two pounds of raw materials, five hours of direct labor, and overhead costs equal to three-fourths of the direct labor costs. Munising's inventory account balances on January 1, 19X3 are as follows:

Raw Materials (6,000 lbs.)	$18,000
Work in Process (2,000 units, 75% complete as to materials and 40% complete in terms of direct labor and overhead)	37,000
Finished Goods (1,500 units)	61,500

During 19X3, the following activities took place:

(1) Purchased in cash 40,000 lbs. of raw materials at $3/lb.
(2) Payroll payments to employees for services rendered during 19X3 totaled $557,000. Of this amount, $404,000 was for 101,000 hours of direct labor and the remainder for indirect labor.
(3) Other factory overhead costs paid in cash totaled $125,000 for 19X3.
(4) Depreciation on factory buildings and equipment for the year was estimated at $25,000.

(5) Raw materials requisitioned and transferred to production totaled 42,000 pounds.

(6) All direct labor costs were considered applicable to production.

(7) All factory overhead costs were considered applicable to production.

(8) The ending inventory of work in process consists of 5,000 units, half finished as to raw materials and 20 per cent complete as to direct labor and factory overhead.

(9) During the year, 17,000 units of product were sold for cash at $60 each.

(10) Selling expenses for the year totaled $185,000 while general and administrative expenses totaled $130,000. All were paid in cash.

INSTRUCTIONS:

(a) Prepare journal entries to record the foregoing.

(b) Prove the ending balances in raw materials, work in process, and finished goods.

5-10. Hoxie Company

The Hoxie Company, a retailing firm, began business on January 1, 19X3. On that date, Hoxie had a merchandise inventory (properly valued) of $10,000. Hoxie accounts for purchases on a net basis and sales on a gross basis. Normal trade terms are 3/5, n/30 for purchases and 2/10, n/30 for sales. Hoxie accounts for inventories using the FIFO periodic method. The following events (summarized) took place during 19X3.

(1) Sales, all on account, amounted to $300,000 (gross) for the year.

(2) Merchandise purchased on account during the year was $160,000 at invoice prices.

(3) Freight on merchandise was $14,000 and was paid in cash.

(4) Collections on account, $180,000 (at gross invoice prices). Discounts were taken on two-thirds of the accounts.

(5) Unsatisfactory merchandise returned to creditors for credit amounted to $20,000 at invoice prices.

(6) Customers returned merchandise amounting to $15,000 (gross). The cost of this merchandise was $8,000.

(7) Payments made on account to creditors totaled $130,000 at invoice prices. Discounts had lapsed on $20,000 gross amount of invoices.

(8) It is predicted at year-end that customers will return, in 19X4, $5,000 (gross) of goods they bought in 19X3. Hoxie estimated the cost of these goods to be $2,600.

(9) It is predicted at year-end that customers will take discounts on $70,000 (gross) of accounts receivable outstanding on December 31.

(10) A physical inventory count on December 31 reveals goods on hand amount to $20,000 at invoice prices.

INSTRUCTIONS:

Assuming Hoxie closes its books on December 31, prepare all necessary journal entries to record the foregoing. Closing entries are not required.

5-11. *Casart Company*

The Casart Company is a merchandising concern which prepares income statements monthly. On November 1, 19X2, Casart's merchandise inventory consisted of 100 units which had cost $12 each. During the month of November, the following transactions took place:

Nov. 3	Sold 70 units for $21 each
Nov. 12	Purchased 50 units for $13 each
Nov. 17	Sold 40 units for $22 each
Nov. 25	Purchased 30 units for $15 each
Nov. 28	Sold 20 units for $23 each

Casart has been using the FIFO periodic method of accounting for merchandise inventories but is considering switching to (1) FIFO perpetual, (2) LIFO periodic, (3) LIFO perpetual, (4) average cost periodic, (5) average cost perpetual.

INSTRUCTIONS:

Assuming all of Casart's other expenses totaled $500 in November, determine how much higher or lower income would be under methods (1) through (5) compared to the present method.

5-12. *Weimar Window Company*

The Weimar Window Company opened its doors for business on January 1. During the month of January, the following transactions took place:

Purchases:

January 1	5,000 units @ $7 per unit
January 15	7,000 units @ $8 per unit
January 30	3,000 units @ $9 per unit

Sales:

January 7	2,000 units
January 10	1,000 units
January 20	5,000 units
January 31	4,000 units

INSTRUCTIONS:

Determine the cost of the ending inventory on January 31 under each of the following methods:

(a) FIFO periodic inventory
(b) LIFO perpetual inventory
(c) Average cost periodic inventory

5-13. Hancock Company

Hancock Company's inventory of Widgets on January 1, 19X1 consisted of 200 units at a cost of $2.00 per unit. Purchases during January were as follows:

January 7	400 units @ $2.10
January 16	300 units @ $2.20
January 22	500 units @ $2.30

Sales during January were as follows:

January 3	100 units
January 10	300 units
January 18	200 units
January 25	500 units

INSTRUCTIONS:

Compute the cost of goods sold under each of the following inventory methods:

(a) FIFO periodic
(b) LIFO perpetual
(c) Average cost periodic
(d) FIFO perpetual

5-14. Willy Company

The Willy Company prepares its financial statements on a quarterly basis although its books are not formally closed until year-end. On

July 1, 19X3, the beginning of the third quarter, Willy's inventory consisted of 500 units, all of which had been acquired on June 25 at a unit cost of $2.00. During the third quarter (July 1–September 30), the following transactions occurred:

July	10	Sold 400 units @ $5.00
July	21	Purchased 300 units @ $2.10
Aug.	4	Purchased 200 units @ $2.20
Aug.	15	Sold 200 units @ $5.00
Aug.	30	Purchased 100 units @ $2.30
Sept.	8	Sold 300 units @ $5.50
Sept.	12	Purchased 200 units @ $2.40
Sept.	28	Sold 100 units @ $5.50

During the third quarter, Willy's total expenses other than cost of goods sold amounted to $3,100.

INSTRUCTIONS:

Determine Willy's income (or loss) for the third quarter under each of the following inventory methods:

(a) FIFO periodic
(b) LIFO periodic
(c) Average cost periodic
(d) FIFO perpetual
(e) LIFO perpetual

5-15. Hicks Co.

The Hicks Co.'s inventory of hamburger meat on June 1, 19X3 was 8,000 lbs. at a cost of $1.00 per lb. During the next three months the following sales and purchases were made:

Date		Purchases	Sales
June	4	4,000 lbs. @ $1.05	
	11		6,000 lbs.
	18	5,000 lbs. @ $1.10	
	25		3,000 lbs.
July	2	2,000 lbs. @ $1.05	
	9	6,000 lbs. @ $1.10	
	16		5,000 lbs.
	23	8,000 lbs. @ $1.15	
	30		10,000 lbs.

Aug. 6   5,000 lbs. @ $1.20
     13   4,000 lbs.
     20   4,000 lbs. @ $1.25
     27   2,000 lbs.

The inventory on August 31 was 12,000 lbs.

INSTRUCTIONS:

Compute the ending inventory and the cost of goods sold assuming that the firm uses:

(a) FIFO periodic
(b) LIFO periodic
(c) Average cost periodic
(d) FIFO perpetual
(e) LIFO perpetual
(f) Average cost perpetual

(Round average prices to four decimal places.)

5-16. Phuhl Company

The Phuhl Company's inventory of fuel oil on January 1, 19X2 consisted of 10,000 gallons costing $1.00 per gallon. Purchases and sales during 19X2 are as follows:

Jan.   6   Sold 4,000 gallons
Jan.   14   Purchased 5,000 gallons @ $1.05
Feb.   3   Sold 3,000 gallons
Feb.   27   Purchased 7,000 gallons @ $1.10
Mar.   15   Sold 8,000 gallons
Mar.   22   Purchased 4,000 gallons @ $1.15
June   16   Purchased 8,000 gallons @ $1.15
July   7   Sold 9,000 gallons
Aug.   24   Purchased 12,000 gallons @ $1.20
Sept. 26   Sold 15,000 gallons
Oct.   23   Purchased 3,000 gallons @ $1.25
Oct.   28   Purchased 11,000 gallons @ $1.30
Nov.   10   Sold 16,000 gallons
Nov.   30   Purchased 15,000 gallons @ $1.30
Dec.   2   Sold 4,000 gallons
Dec.   18   Purchased 9,000 gallons @ $1.35

The inventory on December 31 consists of 25,000 gallons.

INSTRUCTIONS:

Compute the cost of goods sold and cost of the ending inventory assuming:

(a) FIFO periodic
(b) LIFO periodic
(c) Average cost periodic
(d) FIFO perpetual
(e) LIFO perpetual
(f) Average cost perpetual

5-17. South Pearland Company

The South Pearland Company values its ending inventory on the lower-of-cost-or-market basis. At the end of the current year, it has five items on hand: A, B, C, D, and E. Their respective costs, expected selling prices, and expected selling expenses are as follows:

	A	B	C	D	E
Historical Cost	$26	$26	$42	$32	$55
Expected Selling Price	30	40	50	60	70
Expected Selling Expense	3	7	12	15	16
Cost to Replace	25	23	40	31	57

South Pearland Company's normal profit margin is 20 per cent of the selling price.

INSTRUCTIONS:

Determine the valuation of each of the foregoing items in accordance with the lower-of-cost-or-market rule.

5-18. Alvin Corporation

The Alvin Corporation sells four basic products, W, X, Y, and Z, and values its ending inventory in accordance with the lower-of-cost-or-market rule. On June 30, 19X9, the end of Alvin's fiscal year, the costs and expected selling prices of those four products are as follows:

	W	X	Y	Z
Historical Cost	$120	$170	$95	$220
Cost to Replace	140	130	85	150
Expected Selling Price	150	180	90	240

Alvin's selling expenses on each product are approximately 10 per cent of selling price and its normal profit margin is 20 per cent of selling price.

INSTRUCTIONS:

Determine the valuation of each of the foregoing items in accordance with the lower-of-cost-or-market rule.

CHAPTER 6

PLANT ASSETS

WHEREAS INVENTORY ASSETS usually represent the major asset category for merchandising firms, plant assets typically comprise the primary group for manufacturers. In the case of merchandisers, however, plant assets are also of great importance and usually are second only to inventories in terms of relative magnitude. Only service-type firms have little in the line of plant assets, just as they generally have few inventory assets or, for that matter, any other assets. Thus, the subject of plant assets is critical to the understanding of accounting for both manufacturing and merchandising firms and, accordingly, an entire chapter is devoted to this topic.

Plant assets are those tangible items of property essential to the conduct of a business that are held for the services they may render over a period of years, as contrasted with other tangible assets that are held for either direct sale to customers (merchandise inventories) or conversion into finished products to be sold to customers (raw materials and work in process inventories). Land, buildings, machinery, automobiles, and trucks are examples of plant assets. To be classed as a plant asset, the item must be used regularly in conducting business operations. Land purchased as an investment or as a possible future plant site, vacant buildings awaiting sale or demolition, and equipment no longer in service are not classed as plant assets but rather are shown in the position statement under an "Investments" or "Other Assets" caption, depending upon the perceived purpose for which they are held.

THE VALUATION PROBLEM

As is the case with inventory assets and, indeed, all assets, the primary problem in accounting for plant assets is one of valuation. What values should be recorded for plant assets upon their initial acquisition? What values of plant assets should be charged to expense during the accounting period? What values should be assigned to plant assets owned at the end of the period? These are perhaps the most complex issues that the accountant must face and, because of their complexity, they raise some of the most controversial and intriguing questions of accounting theory in general.

Most accounting theoreticians would probably concede that, in comparison to the problems of accounting for plant assets, the problems of accounting for inventory assets—especially merchandise inventories—are almost trivial. Merchandise inventory items, for example, are sold directly to the firm's customers: Thus, when a sale is consummated, the inventory item is *totally* consumed—100 per cent of its service potential disappears at the instant of the sale event. Moreover, most inventory items are consumed in the same period as when they were purchased.

In contrast to inventory assets, plant assets are not sold directly to the firm's customers but rather are sold *indirectly* to them in the sense that some portion (but not all) of their service potential is consumed in the garnering of revenues from customers. Furthermore, plant assets only rarely are fully consumed in the period of their acquisition; usually they are consumed over the course of several—and often a great many—accounting periods. A building, for example, is essentially the same in terms of square footage, height, shape, and number of rooms on the date of its retirement as on the day of acquisition. Its physical condition, of course, has deteriorated between those dates, the foundation, walls, windows, doors, and roof having decayed. Nevertheless, it is still *one* building on the day of retirement, just as it was *one* building on the day it was acquired. In terms of service potential and market value, however, it is a mere shadow of its former self.

Our initial interest with regard to plant assets is to describe the manner in which accountants in practice presently attempt to answer the questions of valuation. They do so by initially focusing upon the *historical acquisition cost* of a plant asset and then *allocating* that cost to the accounting periods that correspond to the asset's service life. This process of cost allocation is what accountants define as *depreciation*, although the meaning that they ascribe to the term is not necessarily the same as a layman's view. Suffice it to say at this point, *depreciation* in the practicing accountant's lexicon is not the antonym for *appreciation;* we shall explore this distinction in greater detail later.

Classes of Plant Assets

Land

Land owned by an entity is a unique asset in comparison to all others in the sense that its life is infinite. Long after inventories, buildings, equipment, and the like, have all departed, land will remain. Its service life may well transcend the lives of managers, owners, creditors, employers, and customers. It is perhaps one of the few perpetuities in a world of change; yet it, too, is subject to erosion—from the elements and abuses inflicted by man.

Not all land owned by a business entity is classed as a plant asset, only land that is routinely used in the firm's operations. The land upon which a store building, an office building, or a factory stands typically is treated as a plant asset, as is the land used for a parking lot, a test track, or a railroad right-of-way. Land purchased for speculative purposes, future uses, or that which is no longer used (having been taken "off-line" and awaiting ultimate disposition) is usually excluded from the plant asset category. Thus, the classification of land as a plant asset is dependent upon its present use in the firm's on-going operations. Although this distinction may at times be regarded as an arbitrary one, it is made on the grounds of assumed usefulness in the making of decisions by managers, investors, and other users of financial statements.

Buildings and Equipment

In contrast to land, buildings and equipment have finite lives. While it may be physically and technologically possible to extend the life of a building or a piece of equipment into perpetuity, it usually is not economically sensible to do so. Since accounting is concerned with economic events, economic life is necessarily a controlling factor.

Buildings and equipment which are classified as plant assets are those that are used in the firm's on-going operations, those which are productive of revenues. Accordingly, store buildings, office buildings, and factory buildings generally fall into this category unless, of course, they are "off-line" and awaiting ultimate disposition for some reason, such as retirement. In a similar fashion, equipment such as furniture, fixtures, factory machinery, trucks, and cars, when routinely used in the business firm's operations, is classed as plant assets.

ACCOUNTING FOR PLANT ASSET ACQUISITIONS AND DISPOSITIONS

Acquisitions

The acquisition cost of a piece of land, a building, a machine, or a piece of equipment is usually established in an open market transaction so that the costs recorded on the books are equal to current market values on that date. The acquisition cost should include, in addition to the invoice price of the asset itself, freight, installation, and any other costs incurred in installing the asset and readying it for use. In general, the acquisition cost is regarded as an objectively establishable amount.[1]

It is difficult, however, to decide whether or not some particular acquisitions are better recorded as expenses or assets at the time they are made; repair and maintenance expenses can often be confused with the plant assets to which they pertain. As a rough rule, the acquisition of an item which is expected to be wholly used up within the accounting period is originally recorded as an expense; the acquisition of an item which is expected to be used over a longer period is first recorded as an asset, the appropriate amount being transferred to expense at the close of each period. Repairs which occur regularly (such as oiling, cleaning, and adjusting) are clearly expenses; new machines are assets; but a new roof, a new motor, and a complete repainting of a building are less clear. Ideally, the item being replaced should have been completely charged off as an expense by the time of its replacement, in which case the new purchase should be treated as an asset.

The shorter the expected life of an acquisition, the more difficult it becomes to draw a line between expenses and assets. As a practical matter, minor acquisitions (say, under $100) are usually treated as expenses regardless of service life. Thus, the acquisition of a new typewriter may be classified as an asset while the purchase of a used one may be treated as an expense.

A special problem emerges when two or more assets are acquired in a single "basket" purchase, such as when both land and a building are bought for a single price. The accountant must then disaggregate the cost into components for each of the assets acquired because one may be depreciable and the other may not (as with buildings and land),

---

1. When plant assets are acquired in exchange for noncash items, such as shares of stock, cost may be more difficult to determine. If neither the asset nor the stock has an established current market value, say, when a new company exchanges its common stock for unique buildings or equipment, no independent value exists to serve as a basis for valuing the other as would be the case when, say, cash was either acquired or sacrificed.

and/or both may be depreciable but perhaps with different useful lives. The typical procedure for doing this is to ascertain the market value for each asset item in the "basket" purchase, sum those market values, and then allocate the "basket" purchase price to the assets on the basis of their relative market values. (When current market prices are not available because the assets are only irregularly traded, then recourse is usually made to appraisal values so long as they are obtained from qualified appraisers.) To illustrate this procedure, suppose Machine A and Machine B are bought for $45,000. An examination of current market prices reveals that Machine A, if purchased separately, would cost $30,000 and Machine B, $20,000. The "basket" purchase price of $45,000 is then allocated 60 per cent $\left(\dfrac{\$30,000}{\$30,000 + \$20,000}\right)$ to A

and 40 per cent $\left(\dfrac{\$20,000}{\$30,000 + \$20,000}\right)$ to B, giving Machine A a cost

for accounting purposes of $27,000 (60 per cent of $45,000) and B, $18,000 (40 per cent of $45,000).

Dispositions

The salvage (or disposal) value of a plant asset is the cash price that it can be sold for once it is deemed no longer suitable for use in the business and is retired. When accountants use the term "salvage value," they usually mean "net salvage value." Salvage value is the price at which the used plant asset can be sold; net salvage value, on the other hand, is the price at which the asset can be sold less any outlays required to sell it, such as outlays for the asset's removal, freight to transport it to the buyer, sales commissions, and so on. At any date prior to the date of sale, the net salvage value must be predicted because the future is unknowable; only when the date of sale has arrived may the net salvage value be known with certainty.

Although the concept of a net salvage value for a plant asset is generally unambiguous, complications arise when an asset is disposed of prior to the termination of its economic life. Such is the case for plant assets such as automobiles and certain kinds of factory and office equipment which are traded-in on new assets of the same kind long before their economic lives are entirely exhausted. The net salvage value of these assets is determined by the amount of reduction that is granted in the purchase price of the new asset being acquired. A trade-in, in effect, telescopes two transactions into one—the sale of the used asset to the dealer with the purchase of the new asset from the dealer. Thus, the amount by which the dealer is willing to reduce the cash price (to be differentiated from the list price or retail price) of the new asset represents the cash price—the net salvage value—of the used asset.

Upon disposal, any difference between the net salvage value of the retired asset and the value ascribed to it in the accounting records must be treated. Such differences may be the result of errors made in predicting the asset's useful life, its pattern of services rendered, or its net salvage value at the end of that life. Whatever the cause, the depreciation taken to date on the asset will be in error. As a result, income for the periods during which the asset was being used will also be in error. However, before discussing the accounting treatment of such errors, let us first see how plant assets in use are accounted for.

ACCOUNTING FOR PLANT ASSETS IN USE

The primary accounting problems with respect to the valuation of plant assets arise neither with their acquisition nor their retirement; instead, they are associated with their period of use by the business entity. Between the dates of acquisition and retirement, plant assets generally decline in value. This decline is caused by the concurrent action of many forces, among them wear and tear, obsolescence, and supply and demand in the marketplace. The process of accounting for the diminution value in plant assets between acquisition and disposal is generally referred to as *depreciation,* a nettlesome topic that arouses considerable controversy among accounting theorists.

The Nature of Depreciation

With the exception of land, all plant assets have a limited life. Sooner or later, they will wear out, be rendered obsolete, or become so inefficient that their continued use would impair the profitability of the business. Depreciation is the process whereby the difference between the plant asset's acquisition cost and its net salvage value is accounted for over the asset's limited life.

In lay language, depreciation is regarded as a *decline in value over time.* Thus, when referring to the first year's depreciation of an automobile, people usually mean the difference between its purchase price new and its current market value at the end of the year. Similarly, the second year's depreciation is usually taken to mean the difference between the car's current market values at the beginning and end of the second year. In effect, laymen regard depreciation as the antonym of appreciation, an *increase in value over time.*

Accountants, in contrast, do not regard depreciation as a decline in value over time but rather as a process of *cost allocation* to the accounting periods that comprise the asset's limited life. Thus, for accounting purposes, depreciation is the process by which the historical acquisition cost of a plant asset less its net salvage value (known as the "depreciable base") is systematically allocated among the accounting periods which make up its service or useful life. (Of course, if an asset has no salvage value, then its depreciable base is equal to its historical acquisition cost.) Only by coincidence would the accountant's depreciation for any given time period be equal to the layman's depreciation.

Accounting for the depreciation of plant assets is much like accounting for prepayments, a matter considered in Chapter 4. When a business pays the premium on a three-year insurance policy, it is purchasing a three-year supply of insurance protection services. At the end of each accounting period, that portion of the premium considered applicable to or expiring during that period is removed from the asset account, prepaid insurance, and debited to insurance expense. Similarly, when a business buys a plant asset, it buys a supply or bundle of future services. The depreciation expense of an accounting period is simply the historical cost of that portion of the bundle of services deemed to have been used up during the period. To determine the depreciation expense attributable to any particular period, the accountant must know the historical acquisition cost of the asset and must *predict* (1) its service life, (2) how its efficiency changes over time (the pattern in which its services will be rendered), and (3) its net salvage value.

Service Life

If a plant asset were to yield services forever at a constant rate, depreciation would be unnecessary. The services would, in effect, be costless (except for interest on the money invested) because after one period's services had been furnished, the asset would be equally as valuable as before. Land upon which a factory is built tends to meet these qualifications; buildings, machinery, and equipment do not.

There are physical limitations to the life of most plant assets. They tend to deteriorate simply with the passage of time. The wear and tear of actual operation is an even more important factor limiting physical life. For this reason, predictions of service life are sometimes stated in terms of units of output rather than in terms of time. *Technical limitations* such as these are often emphasized in discussions of depreciation, but they are effective limits only if no other factor enters to cut off an asset's life at some earlier point.

These other factors, *economic limitations,* are usually responsible for the termination of a plant asset's service life. Changes in tastes may reduce or destroy the demand for a product, and the plant asset used in producing the product may become useless; population shifts may make a factory obsolete because of its outdated location; the invention of a new machine may make another worthless. Taken together, elements such as these are termed "obsolescence." That obsolescence will occur in a dynamic society is certain; when and where are difficult to predict. Predictions of the service life of buildings, equipment, and machinery are, therefore, highly subjective and in that fact lies a source of major error in recording depreciation.

Efficiency Over Service Life

The technical efficiency path of a plant asset can be defined in terms of the pattern of services it renders in normal use over its lifetime. Efficiency may remain constant over service life; boilers, water pipes, and telephone lines are plausible examples. More often, efficiency declines with age as, for example, with precision instruments, automobiles, and typewriters. The efficiency of some assets may first increase and then decline, but few, if any, plant assets are characterized by increasing technical efficiency throughout service life.

The economic efficiency path of an asset describes the pattern of "earnings" it is expected to produce over its service life. As earnings in any period are usually determined by the "matching" of revenues produced and associated expenses incurred, economic efficiency paths depend not only on technical efficiency paths but also on expected patterns of asset use, the sale of related outputs, the prices at which outputs are sold, and the prices and quantities of related inputs.

The appropriate pattern of depreciation charges against revenues theoretically should depend upon the expected economic efficiency path of an asset and on the pattern of earnings this describes. If the pattern of earnings is to help in determining the pattern of depreciation charges, earnings (or "quasi-rents" in economic jargon) must be defined to *exclude* deductions for depreciation and interest on any money borrowed to purchase the asset, but net of all other expenses. After all, the questions to which answers are sought are "Will earnings cover depreciation charges?" and "If so, will the rate of return earned on the investment in the asset be sufficient to cover the cost of borrowing money to buy it?" It is, therefore, the pattern of earnings *before* deductions for depreciation and interest that determines whether economic efficiency is constant, rising, or falling. If a firm purchases an asset with its own funds, there is no interest charge in an accounting sense and we can speak simply of "earnings before depreciation," as in the following sections.

It should be noted before proceeding, however, that accountants in practice tend to ignore the efficiency paths of plant assets. In part, this is because of the difficulties that are encountered in attempting to discern such paths for certain assets. Unless there exists considerable evidence as to the efficiency path of an asset—evidence which has been garnered from past experience with similar or identical assets—any prediction as to the future efficiency path of an asset is an extremely tenuous one to make. Moreover, given the accountant's approach to depreciation as one of cost allocation rather than asset valuation and given that allocations by nature tend to be rather arbitrary anyway, perhaps there is little reason to aim for precision. Whichever the reason, practicing accountants tend to place little emphasis on efficiency paths of assets in choosing depreciation methods; instead, they subjectively select a "systematic and rational procedure" from among those deemed in accordance with "generally accepted accounting principles." We agree that most "accepted" depreciation methods are "systematic," but that they are "rational" is open to question.

Depreciation Methods

All depreciation methods have as their objective the splitting up of an asset's depreciable base over the asset's service life. Each method involves the determination of a percentage, fixed or variable, applicable to each portion of the asset's service life. Once these percentages have been established, then—depending upon the depreciation method adopted—they are multiplied by one of the following: (1) the asset's historical acquisition cost, (2) the asset's depreciable base, or (3) the net book value (historical acquisition cost less depreciation taken to date) of the asset at the beginning of the period. Thus, not only does the multiplier vary from method to method (and, in some methods, from period to period), but also the multiplicand.

Straight-line method. One of the most commonly used (and "generally accepted") depreciation methods in the United States is the straight-line method. The depreciable base (historical acquisition cost less net salvage value) is divided by the predicted number of periods of service life to obtain the depreciation expense applicable to each period. Thus, an asset costing $2,000 and having a predicted net salvage value of

$200 and a predicted useful life of five years would be depreciated at the rate of \$360 per year $\left(\dfrac{\$2,000 - \$200}{5 \text{ years}}\right)$. This periodic amount may be expressed as a percentage $\left(\dfrac{1}{n}\right)$ of the depreciable base (in this case, 20 per cent), or it is 18 per cent of the historical acquisition cost.

It is sometimes argued that straight-line depreciation is founded on the assumption of constant efficiency of assets apparently because the amounts of depreciation expense from year-to-year are constant. However, with constant efficiency, straight-line depreciation yields some queer results. Suppose that the use of a plant asset results, in each of five periods, in sales revenues of $12,344 and that associated expenses excluding depreciation amount to $9,000. Earnings before the deduction of depreciation are $3,344 each period, indicating constant efficiency. If the asset costs $10,000 and has no net salvage value at the end of its five-year life, depreciation expense computed according to the straight-line method would be $2,000 per period $\left(\dfrac{\$10,000}{5 \text{ years}}\right)$, leaving a reported income of $1,344 per period. These calculations are shown in Table 6-1. While the income reportedly derived from the use of

TABLE 6-1

	Period				
	1	*2*	*3*	*4*	*5*
(1) Revenue	$12,344	$12,344	$12,344	$12,344	$12,344
(2) Expenses other than depreciation	9,000	9,000	9,000	9,000	9,000
(3) Earnings before depreciation (index of efficiency)	$ 3,344	$ 3,344	$ 3,344	$ 3,344	$ 3,344
(4) Depreciation expense	2,000	2,000	2,000	2,000	2,000
(5) Income	$ 1,344	$ 1,344	$ 1,344	$ 1,344	$ 1,344
(6) Net book value of asset at beginning of period	$10,000	$ 8,000	$ 6,000	$ 4,000	$ 2,000
(7) Rate of return (5) ÷ (6)	13.4%	16.8%	22.4%	33.6%	67.2%

the asset is constant over time, the value of the plant asset on the books declines as each $2,000 portion of it is assigned to expense. The rate of return on asset value, i.e., income/book value, which indicates the percentage rate that the firm is earning on its remaining investment in the particular asset yielding the income, must therefore be rising over time. But if a firm can make a higher return by purchasing *old* assets than it can make by purchasing *new* ones, all firms would attempt to buy second-hand assets. A firm that could buy five assets (at $2,000 apiece), each having one year of life remaining, would earn $6,720 on a $10,000 investment as compared to $1,344 on a $10,000 investment in one new asset. Competitive bidding for old assets would raise their prices. Clearly, the book values specified by the straight-line method in this case are inconsistent; the rates of return should be equal in each period.[2]

An asset must be of some special *diminishing* efficiency type for the straight-line computation to yield consistent results. Efficiency (or earnings before depreciation charges) must diminish in such a way that income per period will decrease in proportion to the decrease in asset value. It is only then that the rate of return can be constant period after period. The hypothetical data in Table 6-2 represent such a situation.

The net book value of the asset at the beginning of a period is the *original acquisition cost* (C_0) minus accumulated depreciation, not the *depreciable base,* or amount to be depreciated. If there is a net salvage value contemplated at the end and everything goes according to plan, the book value at the beginning of the last period minus depreciation in the last period should yield an asset value at the end of the last period equal to planned net salvage value. And the total cumulative depreciation over the asset's life should just equal the depreciable base, or acquisition cost minus net salvage value. The reader may wish to verify this by positing that our asset's acquisition cost is $12,000 and a net salvage value of $2,000 at the end of the fifth period is contemplated. The earnings pattern consistent with straight-line depreciation (one-fifth of the depreciable base of $10,000, or $2,000 per period still) and a constant rate of return of 20 per cent per period would be $4,400 in period 1, with earnings declining by $400 a period

2. The book value of *plant* assets must be distinguished from the book value of the firm's *total* assets. If the firm retains funds equal to depreciation charges in the form of securities or other earning assets, the value of total assets ($2,000 in the above example) will exceed the value of the plant assets originally purchased. Revenues of the firm will also exceed the revenues attributable to the plant assets originally purchased by the amount earned on the reinvested funds.

TABLE 6-2

	Period				
	1	*2*	*3*	*4*	*5*
(1) Revenue	$13,000	$12,600	$12,200	$11,800	$11,400
(2) Expenses other than depreciation	9,000	9,000	9,000	9,000	9,000
(3) Earnings before depreciation (index of efficiency)	$ 4,000	$ 3,600	$ 3,200	$ 2,800	$ 2,400
(4) Depreciation Expense	2,000	2,000	2,000	2,000	2,000
(5) Income	$ 2,000	$ 1,600	$ 1,200	$ 800	$ 400
(6) Net book value of asset at beginning of period	$10,000	$ 8,000	$ 6,000	$ 4,000	$ 2,000
(7) Rate of return (5) ÷ (6)	20%	20%	20%	20%	20%

each period thereafter. Income would be $2,400 in period 1, $2,000 in period 2, and so on. Decreasing efficiency could have been demonstrated also by showing appropriate increases in expenses as the result, say, of rising repair and maintenance outlays.

Straight-line depreciation has in its favor several strong arguments: (1) most plant assets are probably of the diminishing efficiency type so that straight-line charges may approximate actual decreases in asset value; (2) the simple passage of time is an important element in the decline in value of many plant assets; and (3) the straight-line method is simple and easy to apply. Given the use of historical acquisition cost as a basis for depreciation and the large element of uncertainty in predictions of service life, efficiency paths, and net salvage value, it is doubtful that the use of more complicated methods is warranted under any but exceptional circumstances.

Our illustration, involving the appropriate depreciation rate for a particular pattern of declining efficiency assets (leading to straight-line depreciation) suggests a basic rule applicable to finding the appropriate depreciation method for *any* pattern of earnings. Basically, the problem is one of defining what portion of earnings (before depreciation) is to be termed depreciation in recognition of the expiration of asset value and what portion is to be called income. If the rate of return is to be constant, so that older assets are neither more nor less profitable to employ than newer assets, what one must do is find the internal rate of return (ρ), which applies to the investment where ρ is found by solving:

$$C_o = \frac{E_1}{1 + \rho} + \frac{E_2}{(1 + \rho)^2} + ... + \frac{E_n}{(1 + \rho)^n}$$

where C_o is the cost of the asset and E_1, E_2, ... are earnings in period 1, period 2, and so on. (E_n must include net salvage value, if any.) If we think of only one period and $C_o = \$100$ and $E_1 = \$120$, $(1 + \rho) = 1.2$, or $\rho = 20$ per cent. There would be a 20 per cent return in period 1 on an initial investment of \$100 in period 0. If the receipt were two periods away (rather than one), E_2 would have to be \$144, for \$100 at 20 per cent return per period would grow to \$144 in period 2.

We then apply this percentage (ρ) to the net book value of the asset at the beginning of each period to compute a *hypothetical* figure for income. This, of course, yields the necessary constant rate of return—the internal rate of return—period-by-period. Depreciation, then, is earnings minus income. This method of computing depreciation we call the *internal rate method* of depreciation.

Applying this basic formulation to our declining efficiency, straight-line case illustrated above shows that straight-line depreciation will apply to an asset only if earnings (before depreciation) are declining by ρD per period, where D is depreciation. We have in the illustration above:

Period	Earnings	$-$	Income	$=$	Depreciation
1	E_1	$-$	ρC_0	$=$	D
2	$E_2 = E_1 - \rho D$	$-$	$\rho(C_0 - D)$	$=$	$D - \rho D + \rho D = D$
3	$E_3 = E_2 - \rho D = E_1 - 2\rho D$	$-$	$\rho(C_0 - 2D)$	$=$	$D - 2\rho D + 2\rho D = D$
			etc.		

The compound interest method. Having seen that straight-line depreciation does *not* apply to constant efficiency assets but rather applies to a particular pattern of declining efficiency assets, it may be instructive to examine the depreciation method that *is* consistent with assets of constant efficiency. Consider the constant efficiency case depicted in Table 6-3. Our depreciation charges are *increasing* by a compound interest factor $(1 + \rho)$ per period. In the appendix to this chapter (p. 257), where we develop four basic interest table formulations involving compound interest and present values (useful here and in

TABLE 6-3

	Period				
	1	*2*	*3*	*4*	*5*
(1) Revenue	$12,344	$12,344	$12,344	$12,344	$12,344
(2) Expenses other than depreciation	9,000	9,000	9,000	9,000	9,000
(3) Earnings before depreciation (index of efficiency)	$ 3,344	$ 3,344	$ 3,344	$ 3,344	$ 3,344
(4) Depreciation expense	1,344	1,613	1,935	2,322	2,786
(5) Income	$ 2,000	$ 1,731	$ 1,409	$ 1,022	$ 558
(6) Net book value of asset at beginning of period	$10,000	$ 8,656	$ 7,043	$ 5,108	$ 2,786
(7) Rate of return (5) ÷ (6)	20%	20%	20%	20%	20%

Here it will be seen that:

Period	Earnings −	Income	=	Depreciation

Period 1: $E_1 - \rho C_0 = D_1$

Period 2: $E_2 - \rho(C_0 - D_1) = D_2 = \underline{D_1(1 + \rho)}$

Period 3: $E_3 - \rho(C_0 - D_1 - D_2) = D_3 = D_1 + \rho D_1 + \rho D_1(1 + \rho)$
$$= \underline{D_1(1 + \rho)^2}$$

etc.,
where $E_1 = E_2 = E_3$, etc.

later sections of the book), we show that the cumulative depreciation charges over *n* years exactly equal the cost of the investment, as indeed they do in Table 6-3.

Decreasing charge methods. If the efficiency of assets declines faster than the rate consistent with the straight-line method, some method which yields *declining* depreciation charges is appropriate. The method in most general use in England (and Canada), the diminishing balance method, is one example. A percentage is computed which, when applied in each period to the *net book value* of the asset at the beginning of the period, just exhausts the asset's depreciable base over its predicted service life.[3] The rate for a \$10,000 asset having a predicted life of five years with no salvage value is 84.2 per cent. Its application is illustrated in Table 6-4. The higher the net salvage value, the less rapidly the depreciation expenses decline (indeed, a salvage value of \$1,000 in Table 6-4 would make $r = 36.9$ per cent instead of 84.2 per cent); but the application of this method always assumes a *considerably* more rapid decline in asset efficiency than that which is consistent with the straight-line method. Indeed, it would be a rare asset that declines in efficiency as sharply as suggested by use of the diminishing balance method of depreciation (at least where there is zero salvage value).[4] If the method is employed but earnings do *not* fall as sharply as suggested in the table, the rate of return on book value will rise over the life of the asset, as it did when straight-line depreciation was employed for a constant efficiency asset.

A variant of the diminishing balance method which is used widely in the United States is the "double-declining-balance" method, which had its origins in the Internal Revenue Code. The annual straight-line precentage is computed (e.g., 20 per cent) and doubled (=40 per cent). This percentage is taken of each year's remaining net book value. The method does not yield precise recovery of the depreciable base and, for this reason, must be adjusted slightly toward the end of the asset's life. The method, assuming an earnings pattern which is appropriate for its use, is illustrated in Table 6-5.

Declining balance methods of depreciation which employ a *fixed percentage amount applied to a declining book value* frequently run into difficulties when there is a salvage value (S) expected because the amount

3. The formula used to compute the percentage rate, r, is $r = 1 - \sqrt[n]{\dfrac{S}{C}}$ where n = predicted periods of service life; S = net salvage value, which must be positive (if zero, it is stated as 1); and C is historical acquisition cost. The formula is derived as follows: The net book value, N, of the asset at the end of one period must be $N_1 = C(1 - r)$, at the end of two periods, $N_2 = C(1 - r)^2$, and at the end of n periods, $N_n = S = C(1 - r)^n$. The formula is obtained by solving this equation for $(1 - r)^n$.

4. If we trace the earnings-income-depreciation pattern symbolically for the diminishing balance method in similar fashion to what we did above for the straight-line and compound-interest methods, we see how the percentage rate r, where $r = 1 - \sqrt[n]{\dfrac{S}{C}}$ as per footnote 3, dominates the scene. We have:

Earnings	−	Income	=	Depreciation
E_1	−	ρC_o	=	$D_1 = rC_o$
$E_1(1 - r)$	−	$\rho C_o(1 - r)$	=	$D_2 = rC_o(1 - r)$
$E_1(1 - r)^2$	−	$\rho C_o(1 - r)^2$	=	$D_3 = rC_o(1 - r)^2$
		etc.		

TABLE 6-4

	Period				
	1	*2*	*3*	*4*	*5*
(1) Earnings before depreciation (index of efficiency)	$10,420	$1,646	$260	$42	$6
(2) Depreciation expense	8,420	1,330	210	34	5
(3) Income	$2,000	$ 316	$ 50	$ 8	$1
(4) Net book value of asset at beginning of period	$10,000	$1,580	$250	$40	$6
(5) Net salvage value					$1
(6) Rate of return (3) ÷ (4)	20%	20%	20%	20%	17%

TABLE 6-5

	Period				
	1	*2*	*3*	*4*	*5*
(1) Earnings before depreciation (index of efficiency)	$ 6,000	$3,600	$2,160	$1,296	$1,555
(2) Depreciation expense	4,000	2,400	1,440	864	1,296
(3) Income	$ 2,000	$1,200	$ 720	$ 432	$ 259
(4) Net book value of asset at beginning of period	$10,000	$6,000	$3,600	$2,160	$1,296
(5) Rate of return (3) ÷ (4)	20%	20%	20%	20%	20%

of salvage value is not reflected in the amount to be depreciated once the percentage amount is arrived at. (Indeed, the amount of the salvage value does not even enter the calculation of the percentage in the double-declining-balance method.) In the diminishing balance method, S must be positive (it is made to equal $1 if $S = 0$) and small changes in S greatly influence the percentage (and the depreciation expense each year)—the percentage to be applied dropping sharply with increases in S, hence, depreciation falling less rapidly over the life of the asset. When a multiple of the straight-line percentage $(1/n)$ is used and applied to net book value, as in the double-declining-balance method where the multiple is two (although the multiple may be less and not infrequently is 1.5), the existence of a salvage value may cause the asset to be fully depreciated (depreciation can never exceed the depreciable base) before the end of its service life. Applying the percentage amount to declining book value *less salvage value* would avoid this difficulty, but the method is not applied in this way.

One not uncommonly used decreasing charge method of depreciation, equally as arbitrary as the double-declining-balance method but one which avoids the salvage value problem and allows for the complete recovery of the depreciable base without requiring any corrections, is the sum-of-the-years'-digits method. The method itself is quite simple—the fraction of the depreciable base to be charged as depreciation in year t is given by the formula $\dfrac{1 + n - t}{1 + 2 + 3 + \ldots + n}$ where n is predicted service life and the denominator is the sum of the digits from 1 through n. For a five-year asset, for example, the denominator would be 15 $(1 + 2 + 3 + 4 + 5)$ and the numerator would be 5 in the first year, 4 in the second, and 1 in the fifth.[5] As the sum of the fractions so computed must always add to 1, the depreciable base will be fully allocated among the years of service life. An illustration of the appropriate earnings pattern which would equalize annual rates of return with this method applied to a five-year asset appears in Table 6-6.

Both the double-declining-balance method and the sum-of-the-years'-digits method of depreciation are allowed for tax purposes in the United States (as is the straight-line method). The *assumption* on earnings (necessary for a constant internal rate of return) under the double-declining-balance method is that they fall *each year* (until the final year, when the adjustment is made) by the percentage depreciation rate, i.e., by 40 per cent in Table 6-6,

$$\frac{\$6,000 - \$3,600}{\$6,000} = \frac{\$3,600 - \$2,160}{\$3,600} = 0.40$$

The assumption on earnings appropriate for the sum-of-the-years'-digits method is that earnings fall at *increasing* rates, i.e., in our previous example, earnings fall in year 2 by 25 per cent, in year 3 by 30 per cent, in year 4 by 38 per cent, and in year 5 by 54 per cent.

5. The denominator can also be determined through the use of the formula $\dfrac{n(n + 1)}{2}$.

TABLE 6-6

	Period				
	1	*2*	*3*	*4*	*5*
(1) Earnings before depreciation (index of efficiency)	$ 5,333	$4,000	$2,800	$1,733	$800
(2) Depreciation expense	3,333	2,667	2,000	1,333	667
(3) Income	$ 2,000	$1,333	$ 800	$ 400	$133
(4) Net book value of asset at beginning of period	$10,000	$6,667	$4,000	$2,000	$667
(5) Rate of return (3) ÷ (4)	20%	20%	20%	20%	20%

The units-of-production method. All of the depreciation methods discussed above assume that the service life of plant assets is related solely to time. Clearly some service life is related to use. The units-of-production method relates depreciation charges *solely* to asset use. The life prediction is specified in terms of the units of output predicted to be produced with the asset. The depreciation charge for any period is then determined by applying the fraction, (units-produced)/(total-units-predicted-to-be-produced), to the depreciable base. Thus, if it is expected that a machine will produce 10,000 units during its lifetime and 1,000 units are produced in the current period, ten per cent of the depreciable base is charged as an expense of this period.[6]

It is probably true generally that service life is a function of both time and use. It would seem logical, therefore, to divide depreciation charges into two parts and compute one on the basis of use and the other on the basis of time. The basis for making such a division, however, is difficult to determine.

Depreciation methods—an interpretative summary. While the preceding summary of some depreciation methods commonly employed in the United States and abroad is not in any way exhaustive, it does suggest

6. It should be pointed out that this measure may be subject to the same limitations as the straight-line method; if the amount produced is the same in every period, the two measures become identical. Depreciation, therefore, will be accurate in the sense of equality of rates of return for different periods only if repair and maintenance outlays are rising as the asset ages so that the asset is of the diminishing efficiency type.

the wide range of options available. For the most part, particular
depreciation methods employed for particular assets in particular firms
are likely to be chosen arbitrarily. A firm may simply have a policy
of using one particular method for all assets. Or it may employ for
its income and position statements the method adopted for tax purposes,
which is, of course, aimed at minimizing taxes. Or it may choose a
method or methods for its public statement reports which it thinks
will maximize reported income (or minimize it), given some projected
growth pattern for the firm (see below).

The suggestion here is that depreciation methods employed for
particular assets can be less arbitrary and more rational if they are
related to subjective predictions of earnings expected from use of the
assets so that the method chosen tends to equalize rates of return
year-by-year. The annual rates of return should conform to the internal
rate of return expected over the life of the asset.

In later chapters we shall argue that in the absence of changes in
the market prices of like assets of the same age, depreciation should
be computed as the decline in the asset's market value as it ages and
is used. This approach eliminates the need to make cost allocations
on the basis of either arbitrary methods or the internal rate of return
approach. For the present, however, let us stay within the realm of
present accounting practice and treat depreciation as the recovery of
historical cost.

The Recording of Depreciation

Once the amount of the depreciation expense for a period is determined, its recording is quite simple. The amount must be transferred
from the asset account to an expense account to indicate the portion
of the asset that has "expired." This is done by means of an end-of-period
adjusting journal entry such as:

Depreciation Expense $400
   Machinery—Allowance for
   Depreciation $400
   To record annual deprecia-
   tion for machinery.

The asset account, in this case, Machinery, is not credited directly because
the amount to be subtracted from it is clearly an estimate and subject,
therefore, to serious error. Instead, the credit is made to a contra-asset
account, Machinery—Allowance for Depreciation. The credit balance
which accumulates over time in this account is explicitly deducted from
the parent plant asset account balance on the position statement.

If the depreciation estimates prove to be correct over time, the amount accumulated in the allowance for depreciation account at the time the plant asset is retired from service will equal historical acquisition cost less net salvage value. Suppose an asset had an original cost of $2,200 and an expected net salvage value of $200. When that asset reached the end of its useful life, a total of $2,000 of depreciation would have been recorded on it. If, upon its retirement, the asset was sold as scrap for $200, the entry to record its disposal would be:

Cash	$ 200	
Machinery—Allowance for Depreciation	2,000	
Machinery		$2,200
To record sale of machinery		

Depreciation Corrections at Disposal Date

Because so many predictions—of useful life, pattern of services rendered over that life, and net salvage value of the end of life—must be made in order to apply conventional depreciation methods, errors frequently result. Such errors usually surface upon the plant asset's retirement and disposal, although some may appear earlier. In general, it is not possible to isolate the source or sources of error, but the net effect emerges as the difference between the asset's net book value and its net salvage value at date of disposition. To the extent that net book value exceeds net salvage value, the asset has been "under-depreciated"; in the opposite case, the asset is "over-depreciated." In either event, depreciation expense in prior periods was incorrect.

One manner in which such under- and over-depreciation might be treated would be by means of a special account, "Correction of Prior Years' Income—Depreciation," or "CPYI—Depreciation" for short. To illustrate the use of this account, suppose a machine that cost $5,000 has a net book value of $1,000 and is sold for $1,600 at the beginning of the accounting period. The amount by which its net salvage value exceeds its net book value represents over-depreciation in prior periods. The entry to record this asset's disposal, then, would be:

Cash	$1,600	
Machinery—Allowance for Depreciation	4,000	
Machinery		$5,000
CPYI—Depreciation		600
To record sale of machine and correction of over-deprecia- tion in prior years		

Had the selling price of the machine been, say, $700 rather than $1,600, then the entry would be:

Cash	$ 700	
Machinery—Allowance for Depreciation	4,000	
CPYI—Depreciation	300	
Machinery		$5,000

In either event, the balance in CPYI—Depreciation would be included in the current year's income statement as either an addition to income (when the account has a credit balance) or as a reduction of income (if a debit balance).

Since the corrections in the examples above clearly relate to prior years, the question may be raised as to why retained earnings is not charged directly instead of CPYI—Depreciation. Indeed, at one time accountants did make such charges directly to retained earnings. However, this practice tended to encourage firms to intentionally under-depreciate their assets in the knowledge that the ultimate correction would never reduce income in later years. Thus, the sum of reported incomes over a period of years would be greater than the sum of dividends plus changes in retained earnings. Recourse to the CPYI—Depreciation account approach, therefore, was thought to lessen, if not obviate, such temptations.

In practice, however, accountants do not generally use the CPYI—Depreciation account, preferring instead to record the difference between net salvage value and net book value on the disposal of plant assets through sale simply as either a gain or a loss. Using the example above, the appropriate entry to record the sale for $1,600 would be:

Cash	$1,600	
Machinery—Allowance for Depreciation	4,000	
Machinery		$5,000
Gain on Sale of Machinery		600

Similarly, to record the sale for $700, the entry would be:

Cash	$ 700	
Machinery—Allowance for Depreciation	4,000	
Loss on Sale of Machinery	300	
Machinery		$5,000

It should be noted that treatment of such differences between net salvage value and net book value as gains and losses rather than as corrections of prior years' income tends to cloak the tentative nature of depreciation in a garb of certainty that may not be justifiable.

When plant assets are disposed of by means of outright sale as in the examples above, realization is thought to be complete—a nonmonetary asset is exchanged for a monetary asset and a gain or a loss can be recognized. However, when plant assets are disposed of by exchanging them for other plant assets, as when they are traded in exchange for a new asset, realization may or may not be complete. Suppose that instead of selling the machine in the above examples, the firm traded it in on a new one having a cash price of $6,200. Suppose also that the firm is granted a trade-in allowance of $1,600 for its old machine so that it is able to acquire the new one by giving up its old machine plus $4,600 of cash. Because a nonmonetary asset (the new machine) is acquired in exchange for another nonmonetary asset (the old machine) plus a monetary asset (cash), realization has not occurred. As a result, no gain or loss is thought to emerge from the disposal of the old machine even though its apparent net salvage value (the trade-in allowance of $1,600) exceeds its net book value ($1,000). Thus, application of the realization convention in this instance leads to the following entry:

Machinery (new)	$5,600	
Machinery—Allowance for Depreciation (old)	4,000	
Machinery (old)		$5,000
Cash		4,600

To record disposal of old machine
by means of trade-in on new one

Instead of being treated as a gain, the $600 excess of apparent net salvage value over net book value serves as a reduction of the cost basis of the new machine (which is recorded at $5,600 rather than its cash price of $6,200). In effect, the "gain" will be deferred and realized over the life of the new machine by means of reduced depreciation (a $5,600 rather than a $6,200 machine being depreciated).

Suppose now that instead of a $1,600 trade-in allowance for its old machine, the firm was offered only a $700 allowance on the acquisition of the new one. In this case the net book value of the old machine ($1,000) exceeds its apparent net salvage value ($700). Realization has again not occurred since both a nonmonetary asset (the old machine) and a monetary asset (cash) were exchanged for another nonmonetary asset (the new machine). Accordingly, it would appear that the cost basis of the new machine should be $6,500, the sum of the net book value of the old machine plus the cash. However, in this case the accounting notion of conservatism sets an upper limit on the cost of the new machine at its cash price without trade, $6,200. Thus, accountants in practice would recognize a loss on the trade-in by means of the following entry:

Machinery (new)	$6,200	
Machinery—Allowance for Depreciation (old)	4,000	
Loss on Exchange of Machinery	300	
Machinery (old)		$5,000
Cash		5,500

To record disposal of old machine
by means of trade-in on new one.

We may generalize from the foregoing that for accounting purposes (1) whenever the net book value of a plant asset being disposed of exceeds its net salvage value, a loss is recognized, regardless of whether the asset is sold outright or traded-in; (2) whenever the net salvage value of a plant asset being disposed of by means of outright sale exceeds its net book value, a gain is recognized; (3) whenever the net salvage value of a plant asset being disposed of by means of trade-in on a similar asset exceeds its net book value *and* cash is being paid by the firm, no gain is recognized, but the cost basis of the plant asset so acquired is set equal to the sum of the cash paid plus the net book value of the plant asset being disposed of.

Depreciation Corrections During Service Life

Another type of correction would be required if the initial prediction of service life is revised prior to date of disposal of the plant asset. Suppose that a $2,000 asset (no salvage) originally predicted to last five years is predicted two years later to have a total life of only four years, i.e., two years of remaining life. Straight-line depreciation already taken, $800, would be $200 lower than that consistent with the revised prediction of service life; in other words, depreciation expense in each of the two previous years should have been $500 instead of $400. This correction would be effected by the following correcting journal entry:

CPYI—Depreciation	$200	
Machinery—Allowance for Depreciation		$200

To correct depreciation to date on Grinder #21
because of downward revision of predicted life
from five years to four years.

Subsequent period depreciation charges would be computed on the basis of the revised life prediction.

Although the foregoing procedure is preferable conceptually, in practice it is not widely employed. In its place, practicing accountants use what might be termed the "compensating-error method." In effect, depreciation errors made in previous periods are offset in subsequent periods by new depreciation errors that are opposite in sign (+ or −). Using our example, the depreciation should have been $200 higher in prior years than was actually recorded. Practicing accountants would make no correction on the date that the revised prediction of service life was made but would instead increase depreciation expenses in subsequent years by an amount totaling $200. At the date of the revision, the asset's remaining undepreciated base totaled $1,200. This amount would be spread over the remaining predicted life (two years) in accordance with the adopted method—in this case, straight-line at the rate of $600 per year. Although the correct depreciation expense was determined to be $500 per year [0.25($2,000)], the under-depreciation of prior years is "corrected" by over-depreciation in subsequent years. In effect, "two wrongs make a right."

Depreciation for the Firm as a Whole

The stationary firm and constant prices. Particular depreciation methods lose much of their apparent significance when their effects are aggregated for all plant assets acquired by a stationary firm at constant prices. A firm which is neither growing nor declining has probably reached this stationary state through the gradual acquisition of plant assets following which, by definition, the firm only replaces plant assets retired from use. Such a firm has an "even-age distribution" of plant assets. If the life of the firm's plant assets is ten years, for example, the firm's assets will include ten per cent which are nine years old, ten per cent which are eight years old, and so on; its total assets will be divided evenly among all possible ages. For such a firm, total depreciation expenses based on historical acquisition cost are independent of the depreciation method employed.

No matter what depreciation method is employed by the firm for each plant asset, total depreciation expenses on all assets having a life of n years will equal $1/n$ of the total depreciable base of its assets. If the straight-line method is used, each of the n groups of assets will be depreciated at the rate of $1/n$ per year. As each asset group has the same depreciable base (historical acquisition cost less net salvage value), total depreciation expense must be $1/n$ times the total depreciable base of all plant assets.

A different depreciation method also must yield the same total depreciation expense. An accelerated method applies a higher rate to newer assets which is compensated by applying a lower rate to older assets. Depreciation on assets in newer age groups will be larger than straight-line depreciation while depreciation on assets in older age groups will be smaller; but when these charges are summed, the effect for assets in all age groups must be identical.[7]

Growing and declining firms. The independence of total depreciation expense from the depreciation method used disappears when a firm is growing or declining. The growing firm is adding new assets faster than it is retiring old ones so its total plant assets must be weighted more heavily with assets in the newer age groups. If all groups of assets are depreciated at the same rate (the straight-line method), total depreciation charges will equal $1/n$ times the total depreciable base as before. But if an accelerated method is utilized, assets in the newer age groups, which are larger, are depreciated at higher rates while assets in the older age groups, which are smaller, are depreciated at lower rates. Total depreciation expenses will be weighted in favor of the higher rates, thus yielding a total expense in excess of that obtained when the straight-line method is utilized. The reverse effect would prevail if the depreciation method involved increasing charges as assets aged.

The effects described for growing firms would be reversed for declining firms whose total plant assets will generally be weighted more heavily with older assets. Accelerated methods which apply low rates

---

7. This can be demonstrated with simple mathematics as follows: Let $(C - S)$ equal the depreciable base of all the plant assets held by the firm. This amount is evenly divided among n age groups where n is predicted plant asset life. Let r_j stand for the depreciation rate applied to assets in the jth age group. As depreciation on each asset must be 100 per cent of depreciable cost, $\sum_{j=1}^{n} r_j = 1$. Total depreciation, D, on all of the firm's plant assets is

$$D = \frac{1}{n} r_1 (C - S) + \frac{1}{n} r_2 (C - S) + \frac{1}{n} r_3 (C - S) \dots + \frac{1}{n} r_n (C - S).$$

This reduces to

$$D = \frac{1}{n} (C - S)(r_1 + r_2 + r_3 \dots + r_n).$$

But as $(r_1 + r_2 + r_3 \dots + r_n)$ must equal one, we have $D = \frac{1}{n} (C - S)$, and total depreciation is independent of the particular depreciation method applied to the firm's plant assets.

to these older assets would yield total depreciation expenses for the firm which are below those obtained with the straight-line or increasing charge methods.

It follows, of course, that if prices are expected to be constant, a firm which wishes to minimize its current federal income tax bill should employ the accelerated methods now permitted by law on its tax returns only if it expects to grow in the future. A firm which expects to decline should prefer an increasing charge method for tax purposes.[8]

At first glance, it might appear that growing firms are permitted excessive depreciation even if they employ the straight-line method. As they are growing, the plant assets retired today are less than $1/n$ of their total plant assets because the acquisitions since these were acquired are all larger than the acquisition of assets now being retired. But their straight-line depreciation rate is applied to *all* plant assets, which in total are greater than n times those now retired. Their total depreciation (plus net salvage value) today must exceed the amount necessary to replace the assets retired.

This view involves a narrow definition of replacement. Depreciation charges are excessive in terms of the amount necessary to maintain a constant stock of *machines*, but they are not excessive in terms of the amount necessary to maintain a constant stock of *machine-years-of-service*. An example may help. Assume that a new firm commences business with one machine and increases its machine stock by one machine each year. Each machine has a life of five years, costs $100, and has no net salvage value. Table 6-7 shows the growth of the firm in both number of machines and number of machine-years-of-service. No machines are retired until the fifth year when the first machine acquired collapses. One machine is acquired in each period until year 6 when two machines are acquired, one to replace the one just retired and one to increase the machine stock. Depreciation during each of the first four years is "excessive" in the sense that no machines need be replaced in those periods. But depreciation is not excessive in terms of recovering the value of the machine-years-of-service which expired each year. Thus, depreciation in year 1 is $20 [0.2($100)], just equal to the value of the one machine-year-of-service used up in year 1 (see Table 6-8). Similarly, in year 4, when again no machines are

8. If the accelerated method can be applied only to assets acquired after the method is first permitted for income tax purposes, there is a transition period (no longer than the length of the asset life) during which the accelerated method is worth employing by *all* tax-minimizing firms whether growing or declining. In effect, each firm is starting new and its acquisitions, whether growing in size or declining, give it for tax purposes, at least at first, a dominance of newer assets.

TABLE 6-7

Year	Acquired	Number of Machines			Number of Machine-Years-of-Service	
		Beginning of Period	Retired	End of Period	Beginning of Period	End of Period
1	1	1	0	1	5	4
2	1	2	0	2	9	7
3	1	3	0	3	12	9
4	1	4	0	4	14	10
5	1	5	1	4	15	10
6	2	6	1	5	20	14
7	2	7	1	6	24	17

TABLE 6-8

Year	Depreciation	Cost to Replace Machines	Cost to Replace Machine-Years-of-Service Expired
1	$ 20	$ 0	$ 20
2	40	0	40
3	60	0	60
4	80	0	80
5	100	100	100
6	120	100	120
7	140	100	140

replaced, depreciation of $80 [0.2($400)] just recovers the value of the four machine-years-of-service used up in that period. And in year 7, when one machine must be replaced at a cost of $100, depreciation amounts to $140 [0.2($700)], the value of the seven machine-years-of-service which expire in that year.[9]

SUMMARY

In this chapter, we have considered the accounting issues that arise in connection with the acquisition, use, and disposition of plant assets. In so doing, we noted that many of the methods and procedures used

9. For a review of depreciation charges as a means of replacement, see E. Edwards, "Depreciation and the Maintenance of Real Capital," in J. L. Meij, *Depreciation and Replacement Policy* (Amsterdam: North Holland Publishing Company, 1961), pp. 46–140.

by practicing accountants are appropriate only if the assumption of a stationary state is made. Because such an assumption is not in accord with the "real world," many conventional accounting practices with respect to plant assets and their depreciation may be called into question—and have been by many accountants and economists. The "real world" is not described by the stationary state but rather is replete with changing prices and price-levels as well as with uncertainty regarding the course of future events, elements indigenous to the *dynamic state.* Accordingly, in the final chapters, we shall relax the assumption of the stationary state and, in so doing, shall re-examine the accounting processes with regard to plant assets in this light.

APPENDIX

Compound Interest and Present Value Concepts

The Nature of Interest

Even in the stationary state, where the future is known for certain, most people would exhibit what is called "positive time preference." If given the option of a sum of money today or the *same* sum of money next year, they would prefer the sum of money today. The existence of a predominance of "positive time preference" persons in the market gives rise to a "price" that people would be willing to pay and have money now and pay it back, say, next year; that "price" is *interest.* Because of "positive time preference" there would be more borrowers than lenders at a zero rate of interest, and the market is equilibrated by borrowers paying lenders interest. Interest is simply the rent which must be paid for the use of someone's capital over a period of time.[1]

In a stationary state there is no risk associated with any investment alternative since there is no change and no uncertainty; tastes, technology, and prices all remain constant. The real world, of course, does not conform to the stationary state assumptions since change and uncertainty are facts of life. Tastes are subject to the vagaries of human nature, technology is being constantly improved, prices fluctuate contin-

1. Perhaps the definitive work on time preference is Irving Fisher, *The Theory of Interest* (New York: Macmillan, 1907). For a very brief picture of how and why it gives rise to interest in the market, see Philip W. Bell and Michael P. Todaro, *Economic Theory* (Nairobi: Oxford University Press, 1969), pp. 165–170.

uously, and economies are plagued with inflation and deflation. Thus, interest as we know it consists not only of the "pure" interest associated with positive time preference and the stationary state but also of elements that adjust for the risks inherent in a dynamic world having an uncertain future. It is not mere coincidence that when the United States was enjoying relatively negligible annual inflation rates of two to three per cent, interest rates commonly ranged from three to five per cent. In more recent times, however, with inflation running six to eight per cent annually (or higher), interest rates are typically nine to twelve per cent. With inflation, lenders get back dollars worth less in terms of command over goods than the dollars they lent; not surprisingly, they charge more.

Compound Interest and Present Values

With the existence of positive interest rates in the market, there is a "time-value" of money. Interest serves as the medium through which two amounts of money, each due at different times, may be compared with one another. Consider first the familiar case of compound interest. If I have $100 today and my savings bank pays six per cent interest compounded annually, my $100, invested in the savings bank, will grow to $106 in a year's time. If reinvested or kept in the bank, my then $106 will grow to be worth $112.36 at the end of a second year. More generally, if p is the principal amount (in this case, $100), i is the interest rate per period (6% per year), n is the number of periods (years), and $a(n)$ is the amount to which the principal sum will accumulate to in the nth period, we have:

$$a(0) = p$$
$$a(1) = p(1 + i)$$
$$a(2) = p(1 + i)(1 + i) = p(1 + i)^2$$
$$a(3) = p(1 + i)^3$$
$$\vdots \qquad \vdots$$
$$a(n) = p(1 + i)^n. \qquad (6A.1a)$$

Consider now another savings bank which pays the same six per cent annual interest rate but compounds monthly during the year, or m times where $m = 12$. We would have:

$$a(0) \quad = p$$
$$a\left(\frac{1}{m}\right) = p\left(1 + \frac{i}{m}\right)$$

$$a\left(\frac{2}{m}\right) = p\left(1 + \frac{i}{m}\right)^2$$

$$a(1) = p\left(1 + \frac{i}{m}\right)^m$$

$$a(n) = p\left(1 + \frac{i}{m}\right)^{mn} = a(1)^n. \tag{6A.1b}$$

In our case, i/m is $.06/12 = .005$ and, using interest tables explained below, it can be seen that my \$100 invested in this savings bank for a year would be worth \$106.17, as compared with the \$106 above—*slightly more because it is compounded monthly rather than annually.*[2]

2. While it does not ordinarily concern accountants as much as economists, as we let m become larger and larger, i.e., compound more and more often during the year, we come closer and closer to regarding time as a continuous variable. If $i = 1$ and $p = 1$, then $a(1)$ takes on the following values as m grows larger:

$m = 1$	$a(1) = 2$
$m = 2$	$a(1) = 2.25$
$m = 3$	$a(1) = 2.37$
$m = 4$	$a(1) = 2.44$
. . .	
$m = 10$	$a(1) = 2.594$
$m = 100$	$a(1) = 2.704$
$m = 1,000$	$a(1) = 2.717$
$m = 10,000$	$a(1) = 2.71828$

The expression for $a(1)$ approaches a limit:

$$\lim_{m \to \infty} \left(1 + \frac{i}{m}\right)^m = e^i$$

And from (6A.1b), if

$$a(1) = e^i$$

and

$$a(2) = a(1)^n$$

then

$$a(n) = e^{in}$$

The number e, sometimes written "exp.," is the "exponential number" and happens to have the numerical value 2.71828. Tables of values of e^x are generally to be found along with tables of logarithms. "Compounding" an infinite number of times during the year—every second—in effect, having time serve as a continuous variable, is used a great deal in growth analysis in economics and sometimes in the world of accounting. If my savings bank had compounded continuously at six per cent per annum, my \$100 would have been worth at the end of a year

Suppose now we turn our question around and ask ourselves how much we would be willing to pay today for a sure promise to pay us $106 a year from now? Returning to a savings bank which compounded annually at six per cent as our option, it is clear that $106 a year from now is worth $100 to us today. (If we had it today and invested, we would have $106 in a year's time.) More generally, the *present value* p of an amount $a(n)$ n years away when the rate of interest is i is found by dividing both sides of (6A.1a) by $(1 + i)^n$, i.e.,

$$p = \frac{a(n)}{(1 + i)^n}. \qquad (6A.2a)$$

Compound interest and present value tables are available (such as Tables A1 and A2 on pp. 654–57 in the Appendix to the book) which simplify the computations considerably. These tables are based on the formulas:

$$a_{\overline{n}|i} = (1 + i)^n, \qquad (6A.1)$$

$$p_{\overline{n}|i} = \frac{1}{(1 + i)^n}, \qquad (6A.2)$$

which yield the *future* value in n periods of $1 invested today at i rate of interest compounded each period and the *present* value of $1 due n periods in the future when the interest rate is i per period, respectively. (The symbol $p_{\overline{n}|i}$ is read small p angle n at i.) Clearly the value of one is the *reciprocal* of the value of the other, i.e.,

$$a_{\overline{n}|i} = \frac{1}{p_{\overline{n}|i}}, \quad \text{or } p_{\overline{n}|i} = \frac{1}{a_{\overline{n}|i}}.$$

We actually need only one table if we are willing to make the added calculation.

Using Table A1 on pp. 654–55 let us ask how much our $100 will

---

$$e^{.06} = \$106.18$$

as can be seen from referring to an e^x table where $n = 1$ and $x = .06$. If population is growing (continuously) at three per cent per year and is today 10 million people, in how many years will it double?

$$10 \times e^{.03n} = 20$$

$$e^{.03n} = 2.$$

And again referring to an e^x table, this time finding what x equals when $e^x = 2$, we find $x = .69$, or $n = 23$ years.

grow to in five years compounded annually at six per cent per annum. We have:

$$\$100a_{\overline{5}|.06} = \$100 \times 1.33823 = \$133.82.$$

Or, using Table A2 on pp. 656–57 if we wish to find the present value of a single receipt of $1,000 ten years from today if the interest rate is six per cent per annum, we have:

$$\$1,000\, p_{\overline{10}|.06} = \$1,000 \times .55839 = \$558.39.$$

If we take the reciprocal of .55839, we get 1.79086. And that is the approximate value of $a_{\overline{10}|.06}$ in Table A1 on pp. 654–55.

Annuities—Future and Present Values

In much of accounting we are dealing with *annuities*—a single fixed payment once a period—over n periods when the interest rate in the market is i. Fixed interest payments on long-term bonds, payable annually or semi-annually, are annuities. Most life insurance transactions (payments and receipts) are annuities. Installment and mortgage payments—fixed in amount—are annuities. Our constant efficiency asset in Chapter 6, in effect, involves an annuity—a fixed amount of annual earnings over five years.

Suppose I put $100 a *month* into my savings bank which compounds monthly at six per cent per annum, or one-half per cent per month. How much money will I have at the end of two years? More generally, if $A(n)$ is the cumulative sum of payments of X dollars over n periods (starting *next* period, Period 1) into an investment yielding i interest, we have:

$$\begin{array}{ccccc} & & Period & & \\ \underline{1} & \underline{2} & \underline{3} & & \underline{n} \\ \end{array}$$
$$A(n) = X + X(1+i) + X(1+i)^2 + \ldots + X(1+i)^{n-1}$$

Let $(1+i) = b$. Then our series above can be expressed by our first equation below, while the second is the first multiplied by b.

$$A(n) = X(1 + b + b^2 + \ldots + b^{n-2} + b^{n-1})$$
$$b \times A(n) = X(b + b^2 + \ldots + b^{n-1} + b^n)$$

And subtracting the second from the first we get

$$(1-b)A(n) = X(1-b^n), \quad \text{or}$$
$$A(n) = X\left[\frac{(1-b^n)}{1-b}\right].$$

Substituting $(1 + i)$ for b,

$$A(n) = X\left[\frac{1 - (1 + i)^n}{1 - (1 + i)}\right] = X\left[\frac{(1 + i)^n - 1}{i}\right] \qquad (6A.3a)$$

Expression (6A.3a) is the cumulative value at the end of n periods of X dollars paid or received in each of n periods when the rate of interest is i. Interest Table A3 on pp. 658–59 gives the future value of an annuity of \$1 over n periods at i rate of interest, i.e.,

$$A_{\overline{n}|i} = \frac{(1 + i)^n - 1}{i}. \qquad (6A.3)$$

If we save \$100 a month at one-half per cent per month for 24 months,

$$\$100\ A_{\overline{24}|.05} = \$100 \times 25.4320 = \$2,543.20$$

If we want \$3,000 to buy a new car at the end of 24 months, we are going to have to save every month:

$$\frac{\$3,000}{25.4320} = \$117.96.$$

But what is the present value P of an annuity of X dollars over n periods if the interest rate is i? (Note that we use a capital A and capital P to denote values involving annuities and a small a and small p to denote values involving single payments.) We could arrive at P along much the same route as we took to arrive at $A(n)$ above, discounting each annuity payment to get *its* present value, then summing the series and doing above what we did with b except b would equal $1/(1 + i)^n$. But we do not need to. All we have to do is get the present value of what the annuity payments cumulate to at the end of n periods, i.e., the present value of $A(n)$. Obviously,

$$P_{\overline{n}|i} = A_{\overline{n}|i} \times p_{\overline{n}|i}, \text{ i.e.,}$$

$$P_{\overline{n}|i} = \left[\frac{(1 + i)^n - 1}{i}\right] \times \left[\frac{1}{(1 + i)^n}\right], \quad \text{or}$$

$$P_{\overline{n}|i} = \left(\frac{1 - (1 + i)^{-n}}{i}\right), \qquad (6A.4)$$

and if the annuity is X dollars per period, the total present value is

$$X \times P_{\overline{n}|i}, \quad \text{or}$$

$$P = X \times \left(\frac{1 - (1 + i)^{-n}}{i} \right). \tag{6A.4a}$$

$P_{\overline{n}|i}$ values are given in Interest Table A4 on pp. 660–61, although interest rates employed may sometimes exceed those given in the table. Thus, in our constant efficiency asset case in Chapter 6, where earnings (X) were \$3,344, the present value of those future earnings where i is now ρ or the internal rate of return, we have

$$P = \$3,344 \left(\frac{1 - (1.20)^{-5}}{0.20} \right) = \$10,000,$$

the original cost of the asset.

Note one last thing. If $n = \infty$ in our present value formulations (6A.4) or (6A.4a), clearly

$$P_{\overline{n}|i} = \frac{1}{i} \quad \text{and} \quad P = \frac{X}{i}$$

where i is any positive number or fraction, $(1 + i)^{\infty} = \infty$ and $1/(1 + i)^{\infty} = 0$. If $i = .10$, the present value of a permanent income stream of \$2,000 a year forever is \$20,000.

We thus have four fundamental interest formulations essential for work in accounting, embodied in Appendix Tables A1, A2, A3, and A4 on pages 654–661, giving values for different i's and n's for $a_{\overline{n}|i}$, $p_{\overline{n}|i}$, $A_{\overline{n}|i}$, and $P_{\overline{n}|i}$. We actually need only one small a or p table and one capital A or P table, for we can derive the other two values from the tables we then have. But it is much easier and better to have use of, and get used to using, all four tables. Let us now see how we can put our annuity formulations to work to prove rigorously that compound interest depreciation is appropriate for a constant efficiency asset and that the cumulative depreciation so recorded will always, at the end of the life of the asset, just equal its original cost less salvage value.

Compound Interest Depreciation

We illustrated in Chapter 6, without proving rigorously, that compound interest depreciation applies to constant efficiency assets. Using our two annuity formulations above, we can now prove this. We have [using our present value of an annuity formulation—equation (6A.4)]:

$$C_o = \frac{E}{1 + \rho} + \frac{E}{(1 + \rho)^2} + \ldots + \frac{E}{(1 + \rho)^n} = E\left(\frac{1 - (1 + \rho)^{-n}}{\rho}\right) \quad (6A.5)$$

Depreciation is earnings minus income, where income is ρ times the book value of the asset at the beginning of the period, i.e.,

$$D_1 = E - \rho C_0.$$
$$D_2 = E - \rho(C_0 - D_1) = D_1(1 + \rho).$$
$$D_3 = E - \rho(C_0 - D_1 - D_2) = D_1 + \rho D_1 + \rho D_1(1 + \rho)$$
$$= D_1(1 + \rho) + \rho D_1(1 + \rho) = D_1(1 + \rho)^2. \quad (6A.6)$$

We have shown in computing the cumulative value of an annuity over n periods [equation (6A.3)] that such a series cumulates in n periods to:

$$D_1 + D_1(1 + \rho) + D_1(1 + \rho)^2 + \ldots + D_1(1 + \rho)^{n-1} \quad (6A.7)$$
$$= D_1\left(\frac{(1 + \rho)^n - 1}{\rho}\right).$$

Substituting from (6A.6) for E in (6A.5), we have:

$$C_0 = D_1\left(\frac{1 - (1 + \rho)^{-n}}{\rho}\right) + \rho\, C_0\left(\frac{1 - (1 + \rho)^{-n}}{\rho}\right),$$

or

$$C_o\,[1 - (1 - (1 + \rho)^{-n}] = D_1\left(\frac{1 - (1 + \rho)^{-n}}{\rho}\right)$$

or

$$C_0 = D_1\left(\frac{1 - (1 + \rho)^{-n}}{\rho(1 + \rho)^{-n}}\right).$$

Dividing numerator and denominator by $(1 + \rho)^{-n}$,

$$C_0 = D_1\left(\frac{(1 + \rho)^n - 1}{\rho}\right). \quad (6A.8)$$

The cumulative sum of the depreciation charges over n periods just equals the initial value of the asset. If there were a salvage value, we would have to add S_n to the right-hand side of (6A.8), i.e., we would have:

$$C_0 = D_1 \left(\frac{(1 + \rho)^n - 1}{\rho} \right) + S_n, \qquad (6A.9')$$

or

$$C_0 = D_1 \times A_{\overline{n}|\rho} + S_n. \qquad (6A.9)$$

D_1 can then be readily determined if ρ, n, C_0, and S_n are known.

Our formulation follows from, and is consistent with, our basic internal rate of return formulation, wherein:

$$C_0 = E \times P_{\overline{n}|\rho} + S_n \times p_{\overline{n}|\rho}, \qquad (6A.10)$$

i.e., the discount factor which equates the present value of a stable stream of future earnings from use of an asset ($E_1 = E_2 = \ldots = E_n = E$), plus the present value of salvage (S_n) which is expected from sale of the asset at the end of period n, to original cost (C_0) is the "internal rate of return" (ρ). We know from our internal rate depreciation work that:

$$E - D_1 = \rho C_0, \quad \text{or} \quad E = D_1 + \rho C_0.$$

And we know from establishing fundamental relationships between our present value and future value formulations (see page 246) that:

$$P_{\overline{n}|i} = p_{\overline{n}|i} \times A_{\overline{n}|i},$$

or where ρ is the discount factor that

$$P_{\overline{n}|\rho} = p_{\overline{n}|\rho} \times A_{\overline{n}|\rho}.$$

Substituting the formulation above for E and this last formulation for $P_{\overline{n}|\rho}$ into (6A.10) we have:

$$C_0 = (D_1 + \rho C_0) \times p_{\overline{n}|\rho} \times A_{\overline{n}|\rho} + S_n \times p_{\overline{n}|\rho}$$

or

$$C_0 - \rho C_0 \times p_{\overline{n}|\rho} \times A_{\overline{n}|\rho} = D_1 \times p_{\overline{n}|\rho} \times A_{\overline{n}|\rho} + S_n \times p_{\overline{n}|\rho}.$$

Multiplying both sides by $\dfrac{1}{p_{\overline{n}|\rho}} = (1 + \rho)^n$, we obtain:

$$(1 + \rho)^n \left[C_0 - \rho C_0 \times \frac{1}{(1 + \rho)^n} \times \left(\frac{(1 + \rho)^n - 1}{\rho} \right) \right] = D_1 \times A_{\overline{n}|\rho} + S_n,$$

or

$$(1 + \rho)^n \times C_0 - (1 + \rho)^n \times C_0 + C_0 = D_1 \times A_{\overline{n}|\rho} + S_n,$$

or

$$C_0 = D_1 \times A_{\overline{n}|\rho} + S_n$$

which is our basic compound interest depreciation formulation (6A.9) above.[3]

Discussion Questions

1. In Chapter 6 it is suggested that the first problem to be handled in accounting for plant assets involves deciding on the *initial* value of the asset to be recorded on a company's books. This usually does not create any serious problems, since *acquisition cost* at that moment should equal *current market value*. But often there *are* issues over what to include in this acquisition cost. Consider the following:

> The De Right Company commissions a study to determine whether to locate its next sales branch in Pleasant Valley or Suburbia. In the interim, the company purchases an option to buy for $500,000 a piece of property with building in downtown Pleasant Valley and another option to buy for $400,000 a piece of property with building in Suburbia. Each option costs $15,000 and is effective for six months. As a result of the study alluded to above, the company, toward

---

3. A compound interest depreciation formula that is frequently found in the accounting literature is

$$D = \frac{C - S \times p_{\overline{n}|i}}{P_{\overline{n}|i}},$$

where C is the original cost, S is the expected salvage value, and D is, we think unfortunately, termed the basic depreciation charge. Under this formulation, D is, of course, simply equal to the net cash inflows generated each period by the asset or, in other words, what we have termed E (earnings); and the formula follows directly from equation (6A.10). From the basic depreciation charge so determined, interest on the beginning of the period book value of the asset is subtracted, yielding a net depreciation charge for the period. Because the "basic depreciation charge" is constant period to period and the interest on the asset is declining from period to period (a constant interest factor multiplied by a declining net book value yields an amount that declines from period to period), the net depreciation charge increases from period to period. Use of this method, then, produces a declining income pattern so that the asset's rate of return is constant over time.

Since the above formula for D $(= E)$ follows directly from (6A.10), i (the discount factor) must be equal to ρ (the internal rate of return on the asset). Although the accounting literature often seems to suggest that *any* interest rate or discount factor can be used to determine D, such is not the case. Since the formula for D is derived from (6A.10), i must be equal to ρ since (6A.10) is valid *only* for the internal rate of return, not some arbitrarily chosen interest rate or discount factor.

the end of the six-month option period, decides to purchase the property and building in Suburbia. The Pleasant Valley option expires. De Right's option agreement in Suburbia specified that if the option were taken up, the company would pay $400,000 for the property and building in Suburbia, i.e., the cost of the option could not be applied against the purchase price. Further, appraisals suggested the land on which the building sits is worth $20,000 unimproved and the building itself is worth $380,000. Finally, before the building could be used as a sales office, De Right had to devote $40,000 to modernize and repaint it.

What amount should be recorded as the acquisition cost of the building? Explain your position, indicating why you chose your answer over other possibilities.

2. The crux of the problem in accounting for plant assets, of course, lies not in determining acquisition amount to be capitalized or depreciated over the life of the asset but what should be treated as depreciation expense to measure the using up of that asset. As first hinted at in Question 7 at the end of Chapter 2 (when depreciation was first introduced) and again in the text of Chapter 6 (and the issue will be raised again, more substantively, in Chapters 11, 12, and 13), accountants are not of the same mind on this issue. Is the purpose of depreciation to:
   a. allocate, as an expense, over an asset's lifetime, the original acquisition cost of the asset, thus dividing the original historical cost into:
      (1) an expired cost, with the cumulative amount in that account being called allowance for depreciation, and
      (2) an unexpired cost representing amounts still on hand, to be used up in future periods; *or*
   b. measure the actual decline in an asset's market value period-by-period, depreciation expense then indicating the portion of the current market value of the asset which has been used up each period; *or*
   c. accumulate, within the firm (not pay these amounts out as dividends, for example), funds equivalent to that necessary to replace the asset at the end of its useful life; *or*
   d. two or more of the above?

Approach (a) emphasizes the past, approach (b) the present, approach (c) the future. Approaches (b) and, to some extent, (c) must await Chapters 11–13, when we finally introduce changing prices into our analysis. But consider (a) versus (c) *in the absence of price changes.* Does the accumulation, in a contra-asset account, of an allowance for depreciation, equal at the end of the life of the asset to its original acquisition cost less predicted salvage value, assure the firm that funds will be available to replace the asset? If not, what *does* the provision of accumulated depreciation on an asset assure the firm, if anything? What would you say to a stockholder who made the following comment:

> I always look to see that companies I invest in have made liberal depreciation allowances on their plant and equipment—preferably have depreciated their assets at a more rapid rate than would be provided for by straight-line depreciation. This way I am assured that (a) the firm can replace those assets, if they wear out early, for example; (b) the firm can take advantage of technological change and replace any old, outdated assets, even though not completely used up, by more up-to-date, modern equipment as needed; and (c) the firm will report higher earnings in the future so long as it retains its assets it now owns because it will have smaller depreciation expense amounts to charge against revenues.

(Hint: Consider this person's position, particularly with respect to (c), in terms of replacement chains discussed at the end of Chapter 6, as well as single assets.)

3. In fact, even in the simplest case our stockholder friend in Question 2 above might have some difficulty in finding out what he or she wishes to know from corporate reports, regardless of the merit or lack of merit of his or her argument. Suppose each company shown below has only one asset valued at historical cost:

	Besto Company	Greato Company
Equipment	$500,000	$500,000
Accumulated Allowance for Depreciation	(300,000)	(400,000)
Net Equipment	$200,000	$100,000

   a. Can you tell anything about which company has the newer asset?
   b. Can you tell anything about whether one company or the other has depreciated its assets more liberally to date?
   c. Even if we knew that both companies were using straight-line depreciation, can we tell anything about which company has the

newer asset? Or the asset nearer the end of its useful life? (Hint: Suppose the Greato Company's asset is predicted to have a ten-year life, the Besto Company's asset a five-year life?)

d. Suppose we knew that the lives of the two assets were both five years (indeed, they were identical assets) and that the assets were expected to have no salvage value at the end of that five-year period but that Besto was using straight-line depreciation while Greato was using sum-of-the-year-digits depreciation. Can we now say anything about which is the new asset and which is the asset nearer the end of its useful life? Explain.

e. Under the (d) assumptions above, can we necessarily conclude that the Greato Company will be in better shape to replace its asset early, if, for example, technological change makes this advisable? Or that either company is assured of having sufficient funds available so that it may replace its asset at the end of its useful life, assuming that the asset has not risen in price? Or that the Greato Company will show larger profits over the remaining life of its asset than the Besto Company (because of smaller depreciation charges)?

4. a. Let us see how the internal rate of return method works in practice. What depreciation in each of three years would be charged in accordance with this method on an asset costing $100,000, with a three-year life, no salvage value, and a pattern of expected earnings before depreciation as follows?

Year 1	Year 2	Year 3
$85,000	$42,000	$10,000

(Hint: The internal rate of return is 25 per cent—determine that this, in fact, is correct.)

b. The depreciation schedule you have worked out for your asset under (a) seems to conform to no standard depreciation method used in practice (such as straight-line, declining-balance, double-declining-balance, sum-of-the-years-digits). Let us devise a new depreciation method for our asset—a method we will call the "increasing-percentage-of-declining-value" method. For this method we will compute a "base percentage rate" equal to $75-5n$, where n is the number of years of life and $1 < n < 10$, and apply that percentage to the original book value of the asset to compute the first year's depreciation charge. We will then apply a percentage amount to each *subsequent* book value existing at the beginning of the year for which the depreciation expense is being computed equal to the previous year's percentage figure plus

$$\frac{100 - \text{previous year's percentage figure}}{\text{number of years of life remaining}}$$

It can be seen that our made-up "increasing-percentage-of-declining-value" method works nicely for our asset as follows:

	Beginning-of-year book value	Percentage applied	Depreciation
Year 1	$100,000	$75 - (5 \times 3) = 60\%$	$ 60,000
Year 2	40,000	$60 + \frac{40}{2} = 80\%$	32,000
Year 3	8,000	$80 + \frac{20}{1} = 100\%$	8,000
			$100,000

And our method will work well for any-age asset with $1 < n < 10$; try it on a five-year asset costing $100,000 with no salvage value. Is our "increasing-percentage-of-declining-value" depreciation method any better or worse than existing traditional depreciation methods—*in general? for our particular asset?* Compare the depreciation expense results achieved under the "increasing-percentage-of-declining-value" method with those that would be achieved under straight-line, declining-balance, double-declining-balance, and sum-of-the-years-digits methods; and discuss.

5. Krummee Coal Company has just purchased 1,000 acres of land on which are located extensive amounts of top quality coal. The acquisition price was $5,000,000. Krummee Coal plans to sell the land in five years when the company has completed the strip mining. The land will have an expected selling price of $500,000 at that time due to the destruction of the topsoil and plants. The controller of Krummee wants to depreciate the land over the five-year term of strip mining. Do you agree or disagree with this accounting treatment? Support your position, giving consideration to when, if ever, it is appropriate to depreciate land and when, if ever, it may be appropriate to appreciate land values on a company's books.

6. Jensen Enterprise manufactures plastic turkeys for which demand has been falling steadily. The president of Jensen has decided to shut down the Carloy plant unless or until demand picks up again and have the Garo plant produce all the plastic turkeys. While the

Carloy plant is inactive, the president wishes to stop taking depreciation on the productive assets there to reflect actual expenses more accurately and present a better profit picture for Jensen stockholders. Evaluate the president's position.

7. Mac's Machines employs 25 traveling salesmen who demonstrate drills, bits, and accessories to prospective customers. Each salesman must have a complete sample kit which costs $5,000. The samples last three to four years with virtually no repairs needed during this period and then must be replaced due to planned obsolescence: New patterns are being marketed every three years. The old sample kits can be sold for $500. Assume that the cost of the kits is material to the firm. How should the cost of the kits be accounted for?

8. Assume that a firm has an even-age distribution of 20 identical assets, each of which has a five-year life (the firm thus has four assets with five years of life remaining, four with four years of life remaining, and so on).

   a. Will the firm report higher, or lower, or the same income if it depreciates these assets on the basis of the sum-of-the-year-digits method as compared with the straight-line method? Explain, illustrating your answer.

   b. If our firm is not growing but rather has a stable capacity based on 20 machines, will its allowance for depreciation account be greater than, equal to, or less than the amount of outlay needed to replace worn-out machines at the end of each year under each depreciation method? Explain, illustrating your answer.

   c. If the firm is growing at the rate of five per cent per year, will its allowance for depreciation account be greater than, equal to, or less than the amount of outlay needed to replace worn-out machines at the end of each year under each depreciation method? Explain, illustrating your answer.

PROBLEMS

6-1. Dixon Company

Dixon Company purchased a completely operational factory from Patton, Inc. The purchase included the factory building, factory equipment, and the land the factory stands on. Patton's accounting records concerning the factory have the following balances:

Land	$ 50,000 Dr.
Building	300,000 Dr.

Building—Allowance for
            Depreciation   140,000 Cr.
Equipment   125,000 Dr.
Equipment—Allowance for
            Depreciation   45,000 Cr.

Dixon paid Patton $100,000 down and gave an installment note calling for payments of $10,000 per month for the next two years, plus interest at eight per cent. An appraiser called in by Dixon gave the following appraisals of the property:

Land $100,000
Building   180,000
Equipment   120,000

INSTRUCTIONS:

Prepare the necessary journal entries to record the purchase.

6-2. Cole Corporation

Cole Corporation was searching for a site for a new plant. It found three parcels of land in different locations, each of which might prove suitable. Accordingly, on February 10, Cole purchased options on the three sites for $1,000 each to hold the land until a final decision could be made. All options had to be exercised within 30 days.

On March 1, Cole decided to exercise the option on one of the parcels that had an old plant on it and let the other two options expire. The purchase price of the property acquired was $100,000 and was paid on March 1. In addition, Cole was required to assume the responsibility for back property taxes amounting to $4,000.

Cole immediately contracted with a wrecking company to tear down the old building for $5,000. Cole retained possession of any scrap building materials recovered. The wrecking job was completed on April 15 and the wrecking company was paid on that date. The scrap materials recovered were sold for $3,000 on April 20.

Cole then contracted with a construction company on May 1 to build a new plant on the site for $150,000. The contract called for an immediate payment of $25,000 and payments of $10,000 per month beginning June 1 and continuing until either the full contract price was paid or until the building was completed, whichever came first. If the building was completed first, the remaining balance was due when the building was approved by Cole. Cole made the May 1 payment and all other payments called for by the contract. Construction began immediately and the building was finished on November 15. Cole inspected the building, approved it, and paid the balance due on November 20.

INSTRUCTIONS:

Prepare journal entries to record the foregoing.

6-3. *Tomball Bearing Company*

The Tomball Bearing Company found itself in need of additional plant space. Tomball decided to acquire a piece of land adjacent to its factory and to construct a new factory wing on the land. Pursuant to the acquisition of the property and the construction, Tomball entered into the following transactions:

(1) The land was acquired at the price of $50,000 paid by check. Included in this price were title fees of $500 and a real estate commission of $3,000. In addition, Tomball agreed to assume property taxes in the amount of $4,000. The property acquired included an old house appraised at $4,000.

(2) The old house was razed and the land leveled at a total cost of $2,500 paid by check. By previous agreement, the wrecking company was to keep the scrap lumber, estimated to be worth $300.

(3) Tomball contracted with a construction company to build the new factory wing on the site for a total cost to Tomball of $100,000. Construction was to begin when the construction company completed a project it was already working on.

(4) Tomball received a bill from the city for $8,000. This amount represented property taxes of $5,500 and a sewerage assessment of $2,500.

INSTRUCTIONS:

Prepare journal entries to record the foregoing transactions.

6-4. *Brummett Corporation*

The Brummett Corporation was searching for a site for its Southwestern Regional offices. It located two potential sites, one an undeveloped piece of land upon which a suitable building could be erected and the other, a vacant manufacturing complex containing an office building and an old factory building. The office building on the second site would be adequate for Brummett's purposes, but the factory building would have to be demolished in order to provide parking space for customers and employees. The first site was being offered for $100,000 and the second for $250,000. Unable to decide which was the better choice, Brummett bought 60-day options on each, paying one per cent of the asking prices. In each case, if the option were exercised, the price of the option could be applied against the purchase price.

On June 30, the last day of the option period, Brummett elected to exercise the second option. Brummett paid $147,500 in cash and signed a note due in one year for $105,000. Legal fees relating to the purchase and title insurance totaling $1,300 were paid half by Brummett and half by the seller. The realtor's six per cent commission on the sale was paid by the seller. An appraiser was called in to establish the relative values for accounting purposes and submitted the following report:

Land	$ 90,000
Office Building	180,000
Factory Building	30,000
	$300,000

A wrecking company was hired for $10,000 to demolish the old factory building and was paid on July 10, the date of completion. A construction company paved the parking lot and submitted a bill for $15,000 upon completion, July 20. Various minor remodeling work on the office building was completed by July 30 and the contractors were paid $6,000 on that date.

Brummett moved into the building and began operations on August 1. Property taxes accrued for the last half of the year amounted to $9,000. It is expected that the building and parking lot would have useful lives of 30 years and 10 years, respectively, from the date they were put in service and they are both to be depreciated on a straight-line basis. Brummett closes its books on December 31.

INSTRUCTIONS:
Prepare all necessary journal entries through December 31. Be sure to date your entries.

6-5

(a) Define "depreciation" from an accountant's point of view.
(b) Identify the four most common methods of depreciation and state the *assumptions* underlying each of them (not how to calculate them).

6-6. *Chappell Company*

The Chappell Company has recently purchased a machine for $10,000. It has an expected life of four years and an expected net salvage value at the end of that time of $2,000.

INSTRUCTIONS:

(a) Compute depreciation expense for year 2 using the following methods:
   (1) straight-line
   (2) double-declining balance
   (3) sum-of-the-years' digits
(b) Compare methods (1), (2), and (3) with the internal rate of return method for year 2 if earnings are as follows over the four successive years: $5,500, $2,900, $1,800, and $1,220, and the internal rate of return is 15 per cent.
(c) What are the advantages and disadvantages in the internal rate method as compared with traditional methods such as those listed in (a)?

6-7. *Leavenworth Company*

The Leavenworth Company has just purchased a new machine for $5,200. It is anticipated that the machine will have a life of either ten years or will produce 45,000 units, whichever comes first. In either case, it is expected to have a net salvage value of $700 at the end of its useful life. Leavenworth has not yet decided which method of depreciation to use but is considering the following:

(1) straight-line
(2) double-declining balance
(3) sum-of-the-years' digits
(4) units-of-production (first year's production was 5,000 units).

INSTRUCTIONS:

Assuming Leavenworth's president prefers the straight-line method, demonstrate to him how much higher or lower income would be in the first year if (2), (3), and (4) were used instead.

6-8. *Hope Company*

The Hope Company has recently acquired a new piece of equipment for $16,000. The equipment is expected to have a useful life of five years, at the end of which its salvage value is anticipated to be $1,000. During each of the five years, it is expected that the equipment's output will be as follows:

Year	Units of Output
1	30,000
2	25,000
3	20,000
4	15,000
5	10,000

INSTRUCTIONS:

Determine each of the following:
(a) Depreciation for the third year under the sum-of-the-years' digits method.
(b) Depreciation for the second year under the double-declining balance method.
(c) Depreciation for the third year under the straight-line method.
(d) Depreciation for the fourth year under the units-of-production method.

6-9. Clarke Company

The Clarke Company purchased a machine for $8,500 on account, terms 2/10, *n*/30. Freight charges on the machine amounted to $200, paid in cash. The machine was installed and tested in four hours by three of Clarke's employees, each of whom earn $5 per hour. Materials used up in testing the machine cost $110. The expected life of the machine is four years and during that time it is expected to manufacture 10,000 units of product. At the end of the machine's useful life, it is expected that removal costs will amount to $300 and the machine can be sold for scrap for $1,000.

INSTRUCTIONS:

(a) Determine the amount to be capitalized for the machine.
(b) Prepare a table for depreciation over the life of the machine using the following methods:
    (1) straight-line
    (2) double-declining balance
    (3) sum-of-the-years' digits
    (4) units-of-production (assume 3,000 units are produced in year 1, 3,500 in year 2, 2,500 in year 3, and 1,000 in year 4).

6-10. Weisberg Co.

Weisberg Co. buys a new machine for $100,000 on account, terms 2/10, *n*/30, and pays for it within the discount period. It costs $300 to have the machine delivered to Weisberg's factory. Five men install the machine in three hours and are each paid $6.00 an hour for doing so. While installing and testing it, they use up $110 worth of materials. The machine has an expected life of five years and is expected to produce 50,000 units of product during that time. It is anticipated that at the end of the five-year period, it will cost $200 to have the machine removed and that it can then be sold for scrap for $1,000.

INSTRUCTIONS:

(a) Determine the original cost and the net salvage value of the machine.
(b) Compute the depreciation expense for each year of the machine's life and the total depreciation for the whole life, using the following methods:
   (1) straight-line
   (2) double-declining balance
   (3) sum-of-the-years' digits
   (4) units-of-production (assuming 11,000 units are produced the first year, 12,000 the second year, 10,000 the third, 9,000 the fourth, and 8,000 the fifth).
(c) Let us assume that expected earnings were $64,000, $46,000, $30,000, $18,000, and $7,000 in successive years and that, with expected net salvage value included as a receipt in the fifth year, the expected internal rate of return is approximately 30 per cent. Which of the above traditional and accepted depreciation methods most nearly fits depreciation by the internal rate method? Show your reasoning.

6-11. Greer Company

The Greer Company owned an office building which it had occupied since it was built 15 years ago. The building originally cost $100,000 and had an expected life of 40 years. Included in the cost of the building was the cost of the roof which was $5,000. The roof had an expected life of 20 years. Both the building and the roof were being depreciated on a straight-line basis. The account balances at the end of year 15 were as follows:

Building $100,000 Dr.

Building—Allowance for
Depreciation   39,375 Cr.

The old roof, having deteriorated badly, was removed at the end of year 15 and was replaced by a new roof costing $8,000, paid for in cash. The new roof had an anticipated life of 30 years. The original expectation of the building's life was not changed.

INSTRUCTIONS:

(a) Prepare journal entries to record the events of year 15 and depreciation for year 16 assuming the straight-line method is used for the new roof.

(b) Prepare journal entries to record the events of year 12 and depreciation for year 13 assuming the roof was retired at the end of year 12.

6-12. *Thomas Company*

The Thomas Company owns a high-rise apartment building which cost $1,200,000 when it was built. Included in the cost of the building was $200,000 for the air-conditioning/heating system. The building went into service on January 1, 19X9. At that time, it was expected that the building would have a useful life of 50 years and the air-conditioning/heating system, 20 years. Neither was expected to have any salvage value. Both the building and the system were being depreciated on the straight-line basis. The December 31, 19Y8 position statement included the following account balances:

Building	$1,200,000
Building—Allowance for Depreciation	300,000
	$ 900,000

On January 1, 19Y9, the company's depreciation policies were being reconsidered in light of changes in technology that had taken place in recent years.

INSTRUCTIONS:

Prepare journal entries that would be necessary to correct the accounts on January 1, 19Y9 (ten years after it went into service) and to record depreciation expense for the year 19Y9 under each of the following *independent* assumptions:

(a) It was anticipated that the air-conditioning/heating system would have a remaining useful life of two years from January 1, 19Y9 and that it would have a salvage value of $20,000. The original depreciation expectations regarding the building itself remained unchanged.

(b) It was expected that the air-conditioning/heating system would have a remaining useful life of 15 years from January 1, 19Y9 and the building would have a remaining useful life of 30 years from January 1. Neither was expected to have any salvage value.

6-13. Warren Co.

The owners and operators of Warren Co., a manufacturing firm, decided to close out their business and retire. During liquidation, they sold all of their machinery and equipment. These sales included:

(1) A piece of machinery which had been purchased seven years ago for $8,000. At that time, its service life had been expected to be eight years and its scrap value, $800. The straight-line method of depreciation had been used. It was sold for $1,700.

(2) Small pieces of furniture and equipment which had all been bought at once for $12,000 eight years ago when the firm had moved to a new location. It was then anticipated that they would last for ten years and have no scrap value. Again straight-line depreciation was employed. They were sold to another firm for $2,600.

(3) A machine which had cost $9,500 two years ago. At that time, its expected service life was three years and its predicted scrap value was $300. It had been expected to produce 15,000 units—5,000 each year—but had already produced 12,000 units in the first two years. The units-of-production method of depreciation had been used. The machine was sold for $1,800.

INSTRUCTIONS:
Make the necessary journal entries to record the above sales.

6-14. Purcell Company

The Purcell Company purchased equipment costing $6,000 on July 1, 19X7, at which time it was expected to have a ten-year life and a salvage value of $400. Installation costs amounting to $700 were charged to repairs expense. Entries were made on December 31, 19X7 and December 31, 19X8 recognizing straight-line depreciation. When the accountant was adjusting the books at the end of 19X9, he discovered the error relating to the installation costs. Also at that time, it was anticipated that the equipment would have a remaining useful life of ten years from December 31, 19X9 while salvage would remain unchanged at $400.

INSTRUCTIONS:

Prepare journal entries to correct Purcell's books, assuming that the accounts for 19X9 have not yet been closed.

6-15. Acme Taxi Company

The Acme Taxi Company was organized on January 1, 19X7. On that date it purchased four new cabs at a cost of $3,200 each. For depreciation purposes, it was decided to consider each cab as having two components—engine/transmission and body. Given the heavy usage each cab would receive, it was anticipated that the engine/transmission would have a service life of two years and the body, six years. It was estimated that the engine/transmission should be allocated $500 of the original cost of each vehicle and the remainder allocated to the body. Both were to be depreciated on a straight-line basis. The bodies were expected to have a salvage value of $300 each and the engine/transmissions, nothing. The cabs were put into service immediately.

On the evening of September 30, 19X8, one of the drivers inadvertently parked his cab in a most inopportune location at the railroad station while picking up a rider's luggage. The cab was totally destroyed. The impact of the incoming Limited scattered much of the cab over the surrounding countryside, hence, its value when sold to a junk dealer was only $100. Recovery on the cab's insurance policy amounted to $2,000. The cab was not replaced (but the driver was). On January 1, 19X9, the engine/transmission components of the remaining cabs were replaced for $600 apiece. A service life of two years is again anticipated.

INSTRUCTIONS:

Assuming Acme Taxi closes its books annually on December 31, prepare appropriate journal entries on:
(a) January 1, 19X7
(b) December 31, 19X7
(c) September 30, 19X8
(d) December 31, 19X8
(e) January 1, 19X9
(f) December 31, 19X9

6-16. Creaking Timbers Mining Company

The Creaking Timbers Mining Company recently acquired a new strip mine site for $1,000,000. It is expected that 300,000 tons of ore will be mined and that the residual land will be worth $100,000. The cost of removing the "overburden" (earth over the deposit) was $150,000. Structures costing $90,000 and equipment costing $120,000 were installed. During the first year of operations, 60,000 tons of ore were mined, of which 42,000 tons were sold. Labor costs for the first year totaled $75,000 and miscellaneous costs of production were $15,000.

INSTRUCTIONS:

Compute the following:
(a) Depletion rate per ton (units-of-production method).
(b) Rate of depreciation on structures and equipment per ton (units-of-production method).
(c) Total cost of ore production for the first year of operations.
(d) Total cost of ore inventory at year end.

6-17. Spiller's Offshore Oil Company

Spiller's Offshore Oil Company (SOOC) owns and operates a number of offshore oil wells in the North Sea. In late 19X3, SOOC acquired a site lease for $1,000,000 and began construction of another well and platform, No. 92, which was completed in mid-19X4. Production began on July 1, 19X4. Costs related to No. 92 were as follows:

Platform	$1,700,000
Well (drilling costs, piping, and so forth)	2,800,000
Pumping equipment	900,000

According to geologists' reports, the well is expected to produce 10,000,000 barrels of oil over four years from the date production commences. Once the well runs dry, the pumping equipment, which has an expected useful life of ten years, can be removed and transferred to another well at an estimated cost of $100,000. The platform and well cannot be removed, but the platform can be sold as a site for a "pirate" radio station for $200,000. SOOC closes its books annually on December 31. During 19X4, 1,300,000 barrels of oil were produced from No. 92.

INSTRUCTIONS:

Determine the cost of oil production from No. 92 during 19X4.

6-18. Myers Corporation

The Myers Corporation is in need of a new delivery truck to accommodate its rapidly expanding operations. After some shopping around, Myers found on January 1, 19X1 a truck that precisely met its needs at a new truck dealership. The dealer offered Myers these alternatives:

(1) Myers could buy the truck outright for $9,000 cash.
(2) Myers could buy the truck on time, paying $1,000 down and financing the balance over a three-year period with annual payments (including interest) of $3,331 commencing one year from date of purchase.
(3) Myers could lease the truck over a five-year period by making five annual payments of $2,335 with the first payment due on the date the lease commences. Under the lease, Myers must bear all outlays for repairs, maintenance, insurance, and so forth. At the end of the lease period, title to the truck will revert to the truck dealer.

The truck has an expected useful life of five years with an anticipated net salvage value of zero at the end of its life.

Myers Corporation is subject to a corporate income tax rate of 45 per cent and closes its books annually. For tax purposes, Myers elects to use the sum-of-the-years'-digits method of depreciation.

INSTRUCTIONS:

(a) Assuming that the time-value of money to Myers is 8 per cent per year, which alternative should the firm select?
(b) Assuming that the time-value of money to Myers is 20 per cent per year, which alternative should Myers select?
(c) Assuming that Myers opts for alternative (3), leasing the truck on January 1, 19X1, prepare all journal entries on Myers Corporation's books relative to the truck for 19X1 and 19X2.

Short Problems on Appendix

1. Consider each of the following cases, using Tables A1 through A4 on pages 654–661 to formulate your answers:
    a. John has just inherited $10,000. He plans to open a savings account, investing his inheritance to yield eight per cent per annum, and not withdraw any interest. In ten years, John's seven-year-old son, Jack, will be entering college and John hopes

to have a total of $20,000 available for Jack's education. Will John have enough money to finance Jack's education?

b. Refer to (a) above. Suppose now that John received no inheritance but that all other facts are the same. How much would he have to deposit in the savings account today in order to be able to finance Jack's education?

c. John's widowed mother Joanne has offered to sell John her lake cottage five years from now for $30,000. If John makes equal annual deposits of $5,000 beginning one year from today in another savings account yielding eight per cent per annum, would he have enough money to buy the cottage (assuming he withdraws no interest from the savings account during the five-year period)?

d. Refer to (c) above. Suppose that instead of selling the cottage to John five years from now, Joanne will sell it to him now, receiving as payment the same series of payments that John would have made to the savings account. Assuming that Joanne regards seven per cent per annum to be a fair rate of interest, at what price, in effect, today is she selling the cottage?

2. A friend needs a loan of $900 to pay his residential college fees. He intends to repay you in sixty days, with seven per cent interest based on a 360-day year. What is the amount of interest your friend will owe you at the end of the sixty-day period if you lend him the money? Show your calculations.

3. A piece of property you are considering investing in has appreciated at the rate of twenty per cent per year over the past ten years. The property is currently appraised to be worth $60,000. If this annual appreciation rate continues, how many years will it take for this property to double in value? Show your calculations.

4. What must be the average annual rate of growth of real per capita national output of a country if real per capita national output is to double in fifteen years?

5. Starting in exactly three years when you plan to begin a two-year MBA program in accounting, you are going to need $2,500 for tuition at the beginning of each six-month period over those two years. You have just inherited a substantial sum of money. You can deposit a lump sum today in a savings account that earns six per cent, compounded semi-annually. How much of your inheritance should you deposit today in the savings account to ensure payment of fees needed to pursue the MBA degree when you graduate, assuming your forecast of future fees is correct?

6. Your grandmother deposited $25 in a savings account for you when you were born and another $25 every birthday since, the account being turned over to you on your eighteenth birthday.
   a. If the account earned five per cent annual interest over eighteen years, how much would you have had when you reached your eighteenth birthday?
   b. If the account earned five per cent interest compounded daily over eighteen years, how much would you have had when you reached your eighteenth birthday?

7. If you figure you can pay $75 a month for your two remaining years in college and are willing to pay twelve per cent annual interest, how much can you afford to pay for a used car?

8. What is the semi-annual payment amount due twice a year on a 20-year, $48,000 mortgage at a 9.5 per cent annual interest rate?

9. Through an insurance fund, your father will accumulate by age 65 a total of $160,000 toward his retirement. How long can he withdraw $8,000 every six months (starting six months after retirement) if the fund earns six per cent per annum compounded semi-annually?

10. What is the internal rate of return on a two-year life asset expected to earn $75,000 in year 1 and $52,500 in year 2 if the original cost of the asset was $100,000 and it is expected to have a salvage value of $10,000 at the end of year 2?

11. Strapped for funds, you go to a loan shark who indicates that he is willing to make you an $1,800 loan at one per cent a month, or twelve per cent a year annual interest charge, involving repayment of principal at $75 a month plus the $18 a month interest charge, i.e., a monthly payment schedule of $93 a month. What effective annual interest charge will you *truly* be paying your loan shark friend? (Hint: Use formulation (6A.4) and experiment with different monthly i's and $n = 24$, starting with i equals the purported one per cent a month.)

12. Consider Problem 6-6 (p. 259). Let us assume expected earnings were a constant $3,888 a year over the four-year life of Chappell's machine. This would imply an expected internal rate of return of 25 per cent. (Check this out using your interest tables.)

Instructions:

Compute compound interest depreciation for each of the four years and show that it approximately accumulates to the depreciable base of the machine and leaves a book value at the end approximately equal to the anticipated net salvage value.

13. Consider Problem 6-9 (p. 260). Let us assume earnings were a constant $2,500 a year over the four-year life of Clarke's machine.

    Instructions:
    (a) Compute the internal rate of return on the asset.
    (b) Compute compound interest depreciation for each of the four years and show that it approximately accumulates to the depreciable base of the machine and leaves a book value at the end approximately equal to the anticipated net salvage value.

14. Consider Problem 6-10 (p. 261). Let us assume earnings were a constant $40,000 a year over the five-year life of Weisberg's machine.

    Instructions:
    (a) Compute the internal rate of return on the asset.
    (b) Compute compound interest depreciation for each of the five years and show that it approximately accumulates to the depreciable base of the machine and leaves a book value at the end approximately equal to the anticipated net salvage value.

CHAPTER 7

CREDITOR EQUITIES

WHEREAS *ASSETS*, the subject matter of the two preceding chapters, refer to the economic resources that a firm owns, *equities* may be interpreted as the claims of others (broadly known as "investors") against those resources. In total, equities must equal assets as stated in the fundamental accounting equation,

$$\text{Assets} = \text{Equities}$$

Thus, at any moment in time the firm must recognize obligations or claims against itself that equal in magnitude the book value of its resources.

CLASSES OF EQUITIES

Equities are composed of two broad groups: (1) creditor equities, or liabilities, and (2) owner equities. Creditor equities typically differ from owner equities in three important respects: (1) They generally require a date certain for repayment or fulfillment of the obligation (a maturity date); (2) they normally specify a rate of return that is fixed in amount and is stated as a percentage of the principal amount to be paid on the maturity date (an interest rate); and (3) they provide that, in the event of liquidation, creditors have priority over owners with respect to recovery of their claims.

Investors who attach a high value to the security of earnings and principal should invest in a firm's debt securities rather than its ownership securities. On the other hand, if an investor's primary goal is wealth maximization, he or she may prefer to invest in ownership securities (such as stock in the case of a corporation) because of the higher returns (prospective dividends and capital gains) typically associated with such securities. These higher returns reflect the relatively greater risks which owners must assume as compared to creditors. Ownership securities generally have no maturity date and usually do not specify a rate of return. Even where a return is specified, as with preferred stock, there is no guarantee that it will not be "passed over" (not paid) in any given year. The failure of the firm to pay the interest due on its liabilities will render the firm *insolvent* and, perhaps, ultimately bankrupt; such is not the case with returns on ownership equities. Finally, no assurances are made to owners that all or any of their capital will ever be returned to them and, if it is, they will be the last investors to be repaid since creditors have priority over them. Accordingly, the equity of owners is referred to as the *residual equity.*

The firm's periodic payments to its creditors are termed *interest charges.* The claims of creditors for interest must be satisfied before any payments can be made to owners. *Dividend charges* is the term used to describe payments to owners.

Classes of Creditor Equities

As is the case with assets, creditor equities may be categorized in either of two fashions, one being the monetary/nonmonetary distinction and the other, the current/noncurrent breakdown. *Monetary liabilities* are those which ultimately must be extinguished by the payment of cash to the claimant. Accounts payable, wages payable, and bonds payable are all examples of such liabilities. *Nonmonetary liabilities,* on the other hand, are those claims against the firm which ordinarily are not retired by the payment of cash to the claimant but rather by the rendering of a service or the delivery of a good. Warranties payable (which are extinguished by either the passage of time or the repairing or replacement of a faulty product) and subscriptions obligations (which are discharged by the delivery of a magazine or newspaper) are examples of nonmonetary liabilities. As we shall demonstrate in later chapters, the monetary/nonmonetary classification is an essential one in the preparation of certain types of funds statements. This distinction is also a critical one in financial reporting by multinational entities whose activities span many different countries and monetary systems.

Although the monetary/nonmonetary classification of liabilities is a useful one to make, in practice the most common distinction made is that between current and noncurrent (usually termed "long-term") liabilities. The general criterion for determining whether a liability is to be classified as current or long-term is whether the debt matures within less than or more than one year.[1] Thus, *current liabilities* are usually those due in less than a year while *long-term liabilities* include all those whose maturity dates extend beyond a year. In practice, however, not all debts coming due in less than a year are automatically classified as current; the overriding consideration depends on the anticipated means of extinguishment. If the debt coming due within a year is to be *refinanced* or "rolled-over" by exchanging it for new long-term debt, then it is classified as long-term. Thus, the primary criterion for classifying a liability may be stated as follows: If current assets will be used within a year to retire the liability (or if the liability is to be replaced by another liability that will be discharged within a year by the use of current assets), then it should be classified as a current liability; if not, it should be classified as a long-term liability.

In a position statement, liabilities are the first of the two equity classes listed, with current liabilities preceding long-term. Appearing below is the liabilities section of a position statement, which provides examples of the accounts usually found in each category:

Current Liabilities:		
Accounts Payable	$XX	
Wages Payable	XX	
Notes Payable (due within a year)	XX	
Income Taxes Payable (due within a year)	XX	
Bonds Payable (portion due within a year)	XX	
Interest Accrued Payable	XX	
Dividends Payable	XX	
Estimated Warranty Obligations	XX	
Subscription Obligations	XX	$XX
Long-Term Liabilities:		
Notes Payable	$XX	
Bonds Payable	XX	
Mortgage Payable	XX	
Income Taxes Payable	XX	XX
Total Liabilities		$XX

The order in which accounts are listed in either the current or long-term sections is of little importance. The usual procedure is simply to list them in order of decreasing magnitude, but even this tradition is

1. In those relatively rare instances where the entity's operating cycle is greater than one year, then the length of operating cycle is used instead. An operating cycle is the length of time required to go from cash-to-cash, i.e., cash is used to purchase inventory, which is later sold for cash (or for a receivable which is collected in cash).

frequently broached. Although it initially may be surprising that current liabilities are not arrayed according to relative liquidity as are current assets, upon reflection it should be obvious that "liquidity" among current liabilities would be difficult to deal with. Some accounts payable may fall due before, say, wages, but some bonds may fall due even before the trade accounts payable. In other words, the balance in each account does not represent a single sum due on a given date but rather is typcially composed of multiple amounts due at varying dates. Moreover, for some obligations such as warranties, the "due date" is uncertain. Finally, the informational benefits to be derived from arraying current liabilities in order of liquidity are minimal at best; of greater importance is their composition and total amount.

CURRENT LIABILITIES

As noted above, current liabilities are those which will be extinguished by the use of current assets within a year or by the incurrence of another current liability. Once distinguished from long-term liabilities, current liabilities may be categorized as either monetary or nonmonetary.

Current Monetary Liabilities

While current liabilities include all those liabilities that will be discharged within a year by the use of current assets, the addition of the monetary designation specifies the particular current asset to be used—cash. By definition, a monetary liability is one that is to be discharged by the rendering of cash. Short-term obligations, such as accounts payable, notes payable, payroll payable, and taxes payable, are typical of those falling into this category. In a similar vein, the portions of long-term liabilities coming due within a year and which are to be discharged by the payment of cash, such as mortgages payable and bonds payable, are also classified as current monetary liabilities.

For the most part, current monetary liabilities raise no particular accounting problems in terms of either theory or practice. The amounts borrowed (directly or indirectly for the purchase of goods and services) typically must be repaid dollar for dollar together with any charges for interest (or lapsed discounts). The procedures required in accounting for such "interest-bearing" notes and accounts have been treated in previous chapters; hence, no further attention is needed here.

Occasionally, however, problems arise when "noninterest-bearing" debt is incurred. In many cases, no interest whatever is charged because it is expected that the debt will be repaid in a very short time. Examples of such liabilities might be payroll payable and taxes payable, all of which create no special accounting problems. On the other hand, there sometimes exist certain debt instruments that bear no stated *explicit* interest rate but that contain an *implicit* interest factor. An obvious example is accounts payable which provide terms, such as 2/10, *n*/30, for cash discounts. If the account is not paid within ten days, a higher price will have to be paid because of implicit interest. Similarly, the firm may be liable for a so-called "noninterest-bearing note" which simply states the total dollar amount to be paid at the maturity date. The implicit interest arises in this case, however, from the fact that the amount borrowed (known as the *proceeds*) is less than the amount to be repaid. Assume, for example, a firm wishes to borrow $10,000 and repay it a year later. If the market rate of interest were six per cent, the firm might sign a noninterest-bearing note promising to repay $10,600 in one year. The note itself may contain no reference to the amount actually borrowed. On the dates of the borrowing and repayment, the firm would make the following entries:

Cash	$10,000	
Notes Payable—Discount	600	
Notes Payable—Maturity		
Amount		$10,600
To record borrowing		
Interest Charges	600	
Notes Payable—Discount		600
To record accrual of interest for		
one year		
Notes Payable—Maturity Amount	10,600	
Cash		10,600
To record repayment		

In some cases the implicit *interest* rate is replaced by an implicit *discount* factor, the result of which is the earning of a higher rate of return by the lender. To illustrate, assume a firm again wishes to borrow $10,000 with repayment set a year later. If a discount factor of six per cent is used in place of a six per cent rate of interest, the firm would be required to sign a note having a maturity amount of $10,638. This larger maturity amount results from the fact that the discount rate is multiplied times the maturity amount whereas the interest rate is multiplied by the proceeds or principal. Thus, if the maturity amount is X, then the total discount is .06X and the proceeds must be .94X. Since the firm wants to borrow $10,000 (the proceeds), then .94X equals

$10,000 and X equals $10,638. Clearly then, a six per cent discount rate is the equivalent of a 6.38 per cent interest rate because it is applied to a larger base. In this case, the borrowing and repayment would be recorded as follows:

Cash	$10,000	
Notes Payable—Discount	638	
Notes Payable		$10,638
To record borrowing		
Interest Charges	638	
Notes Payable—Discount		638
To record accrual of "interest" for one year		
Notes Payable	10,638	
Cash		10,638
To record repayment		

In the past, the substitution of a discount rate in place of an interest rate was commonly used to deceive unsuspecting borrowers. Today, however, the "truth-in-lending laws" require the lender to state the effective annual interest rate regardless of whether a discount or interest rate is being applied.

Current Nonmonetary Liabilities

In contrast to current monetary liabilities that are to be discharged by the payment of cash within a year, current nonmonetary liabilities are those that are to be extinguished by the delivery of goods or the provision of services. A generic name for these obligations is "advances from customers." For the most part, advances from customers are of two general types: (1) pre-revenue receipts from customers and (2) post-revenue obligations to customers.

The first of the two categories is perhaps the more common. This is when a customer pays cash to the firm for goods and services in advance of receiving them; thus, the receipt precedes the recognition of revenue by the firm. Examples of pre-revenue receipts from customers include magazine subscriptions, mail order sales, insurance premiums, rentals, tuition, and gift certificates. The receipt of cash by the firm is usually recorded by debiting cash and crediting an appropriately titled liability account such as subscription obligations or customer prepayments; titles like "unearned subscriptions revenue" are considered to be poor terminology as the term "revenues" should only appear in the income statement. Upon delivery of goods or provision of services to the customer, the liability account is debited and a corresponding revenue account is credited.

The second of the two types of customer advances arises when the sale calls for certain additional after-sale goods or services. In the typical case, these after-sale goods or services involve warranties on products sold by the firm. As a part of the sales contract for its products, the selling firm frequently includes a warranty to repair or replace faulty components of the product for some fixed period of time after the date of sale, such as 90 days or a year. An obvious example is a manufacturer's warranty on a new automobile. At the date the product is delivered, the seller is, in effect, selling two distinct things: (1) the product itself and (2) a warranty on the product. They could be sold separately, but usually they are not. Because they are not, on the date of sale the seller incurs a nonmonetary obligation to provide any necessary goods and services during the warranty period to repair the product sold. This obligation is recorded on the sale date in the following manner:

```
Warranty Expense                      XXX
    Estimated Warranty Obligations           XXX
```

As repairs are performed during the warranty period, the liability is discharged. These events are recorded as follows:

```
Estimated Warranty Obligations        XXX
    Parts Inventory                          XXX
    Wages Payable                            XXX
```

The credit to parts inventory records the decline in assets used in the repair work. The credit to wages payable is based on the assumption that a piece-work system prevails (common in automobile repair shops) and, thus, a new liability to the shop's workers is incurred as a result of the repair work.

The amount recorded in the estimated warranties payable account is the price to the seller of the amount of goods and services predicted to be rendered to customers over the warranty period. Usually not every unit sold will require the same amount of warranty work, and some may require none at all; accordingly, a probability estimate based on past experience is used as the basis of the amount initially recorded in the estimated warranty obligations account. No element of profit is usually assigned in practice to the warranty work, the entire profit on the sale of the product having been taken up at the point of sale. That is not to say that no profit could be attributed to the warranty.

Indeed, were the customer to have the option of purchasing either the product alone or the product together with the warranty, the differential between the price of the former and that of the latter would be the price of the warranty itself and that amount could be recorded as warranty revenue over the warranty period. In journal form, the following entry would be made at the date the customer purchased both the product and the warranty:

Cash	XXX	
Sales Revenue		XXX
Warranty Advances from Customers		XXX

Again during the warranty period, the rendering of goods and services to customers in fulfillment of warranty obligations would be recorded as follows:

Warranty Expense	XXX	
Parts Inventory		XXX
Wages Payable		XXX

By the end of the warranty period, the advances account (a liability) would be closed to a revenue account in the following manner:

Warranty Advances from Customers	XXX	
Warranty Revenue		XXX [2]

Thus, in cases where customers have the option of purchasing a warranty, an element of profit (the excess of warranty revenues over warranty expenses) may be attributed to the warranty activities. When such is the case, the accounting process is identical to that for pre-revenue receipts from customers as discussed above with reference to subscriptions, rentals, and so forth.

LONG-TERM LIABILITIES

Except in rare instances, all long-term liabilities are monetary in nature. Moreover, since virtually all long-term debt instruments have a stated interest rate on their face, a few problems of accounting for noninterest-bearing notes arise. In general, long-term liabilities may be categorized into two groups: (1) those where repayment of principal occurs throughout the life of the obligation, thereby leaving only the final payment

2. Should the warranty period extend beyond the close of an accounting period, a portion of the total warranty revenue would, of course, be recognized at the close of the accounting period by means of a similar entry.

due at maturity, and (2) those where repayment of principal occurs only at maturity. Mortgages and installment notes payable are examples of liabilities falling into the first group while bonds are typical of the second group.

Periodic Principal Repayment

Since in the first group, each periodic payment includes both principal and interest, the accounting problem involves the determination of the amount of each. Some obligations call for a schedule of payments which decline in amount over the life of the debt. In this case, the periodic principal repaid remains constant while the interest payment declines, reflecting the declining principal balance of the debt. Other obligations call for a schedule of payments which remain constant in amount throughout the life of the obligation. When this situation exists, the relative proportions of the payment applying to principal repayment and to interest vary. The interest portion, of course, declines over the life of the debt while the principal portion increases. Let us now consider examples of each of these types of repayment plans.

Assume that on December 31, 19X1, the Evans Company borrows $60,000 from a bank on a three-year, six per cent note, repayable in three installments of $20,000 principal plus interest to date due each December 31. Evans would account for the borrowing and repayment as follows:

19X1
December 31   Cash $60,000
                   6% Notes Payable $60,000
               To record borrowing on a
               three-year 6% note from bank

19X2
December 31   Interest Charges $ 3,600
               6% Notes Payable   20,000
                   Cash $23,600
               To record repayment of $20,000
               plus 6% interest on $60,000

19X3
December 31   Interest Charges $ 2,400
               6% Notes Payable   20,000
                   Cash $22,400
               To record repayment of $20,000
               plus 6% interest on $40,000

19X4
December 31

Interest Charges	$ 1,200	
6% Notes Payable	20,000	
Cash		$21,200

To record repayment of final
$20,000 principal plus 6%
interest on $20,000

To illustrate the case of equal annual payments, let us slightly modify the terms of Evans Company's borrowing. Assume that instead of making three equal annual principal payments of $20,000 per year plus interest, Evans agrees to pay equal total dollar amounts, including both principal and interest each year. To determine the amount of the equal annual payments, we will find it necessary to refer to our interest tables (pp. 654–61) since these three payments constitute an ordinary annuity.[3] The $60,000 borrowed represents the present value of a three-year ordinary annuity (of R per period), hence,

$$\$60,000 = R\,P_{\overline{n}|i}$$
$$\$60,000 = R\,P_{\overline{3}|.06}$$
$$\$60,000 = 2.67301R$$
$$R = \frac{\$60,000}{2.67301}$$
$$R = \$22,446.61$$

Given the amount of the total annual payment including principal and interest, the accounting for the note is as follows:

19X1
December 31

Cash	$60,000.00	
6% Notes Payable		$60,000.00

19X2
December 31

Interest Charges	$ 3,600.00	
6% Notes Payable	18,846.61	
Cash		$22,446.61

To record first annual
payment of $22,446.61

---

3. For a discussion of the nature of an annuity, see the appendix to Chapter 6, "Compound Interest and Present Value Concepts."

19X3

December 31	Interest Charges	$ 2,469.20	
	6% Notes Payable	19,977.41	
	Cash		$22,446.61
	To record second annual payment of $22,446.61		

19X4

December 31	Interest Charges	$ 1,270.63	
	6% Notes Payable	21,175.98	
	Cash		$22,446.61
	To record final annual payment of $22,446.61		

The amount recorded for interest charges in each year equals six per cent of the outstanding principal balance for the year. Thus, interest for 19X2 is six per cent times $60,000, or $3,600, while for 19X3 it is $2,469.20 [6% ($60,000.00 − $18,846.61)]. Interest for 19X4 computed exactly would be $1,270.56 [6% ($60,000 − $18,846.61 − $19,977.41)]. However, since the equal annual payment contracted for was $22,446.61 and since the principal balance due was $21,175.98, we simply assumed the difference to be interest. The $0.07 error in interest ($1,270.63 − $1,270.56) resulted from our interest tables not extending to a sufficient number of decimal places.

The student will quickly see that it is this kind of fixed periodic payments on borrowings that is used in installment loans for automobiles and household durable goods (where n, then, is usually months) and for most mortgages on property (where n may be years, half-years, and so on). In installment loans and mortgages, it is a necessary and convenient way to establish the repayment pattern, for coming up with one single repayment of principal at the end may very well be impractical.

Principal Repayment at Maturity

Having considered the cases where principal repayment occurs throughout the life of the debt instrument, we shall now turn to the case where repayment occurs at the maturity of the obligation. Corporate bonds are perhaps the most common form of this type of debt.

Corporations frequently issue bonds as a means of financing assets, particularly when the company's earning stream is relatively stable, as is the case with many public utilities. Without such an earning stream, a firm could be in serious difficulty because of the legal requirements of the bond contract that calls for the periodic payment of interest and the repayment of the debt at maturity.[4] Failure to comply with either of these requirements could result in the corporation's bankruptcy. Thus, a firm having fluctuating earnings may be well-advised to issue preferred or common stock rather than bonds since dividends need not be paid every year on stock.

In cases where a company may safely issue bonds, however, a number of advantages accrue to the issuer. First, interest rates on bonds are generally lower than the rate of return earned on its total assets, thereby allowing the company to "trade on its equity." In this manner, the firm can provide its common stockholders with a higher rate of return on their equity (in the form of either dividends or increments to their equity via retained earnings) than would otherwise be possible. Second, interest is deductible on the company's income tax return while preferred and common dividends are not. Given a corporate income tax rate approximating 50 per cent, the *effective* rate of interest to the corporation is only half of the rate actually paid to bondholders. Thus, bonds often are an extremely attractive method of securing additional capital.

Virtually all bond contracts contain two promises made by the issuer: (1) a promise to make a regular series of cash payments over the life of the bond (interest) and (2) a promise to make a lump-sum payment at the termination of the bond's life (face value). In a simple case, a corporation might issue, say, $1 million of six per cent, ten-year bonds, receiving $1 million in cash from the bondholders in return for ten annual cash payments of $60,000 and one payment of $1 million at the end of ten years.

This simple case is not often found in practice, however, for a number of reasons. In the first place, the market rate of interest may fluctuate between the date the plan is made for the bond issue and the date the bonds actually are issued. Alternatively, the bond interest rate (known as the "stated rate" or "face rate") may intentionally be set substantially lower than the market rate so as to defer payment of some of the interest until the bonds mature, thereby conserving some of the corporation's cash resources. If the stated rate is less than the market rate, the bond will sell at a *discount;* if it is higher, the bond will sell at a *premium.*

Bonds Issued at "Par"

To illustrate, let us assume that the Graymen Company plans to issue $1 million of six per cent, ten-year bonds. If the market rate

4. Income bonds, which require payment of interest only when income is sufficient to bear the charge, are an exception.

of interest is also six per cent, Graymen's two promises to the bondholders can be evaluated as follows:

		(rounded to nearest ten)
(1) Present value of the annuity ("interest" stream): $60,000 $P_{\overline{10}|.06}$ = $60,000 × 7.36009 =		$441,610
(2) Present value of the single-sum (maturity amount or face value): $1,000,000 $p_{\overline{10}|.06}$ = $1,000,000 × .55839 =		558,390
	Proceeds	$1,000,000

Thus, it can be seen that if the investor could purchase either of the two promises separately, the price would be $441,610 for the stream of payments alone and/or $558,390 for the lump sum due ten years hence. By buying both promises, the investor will pay $1,000,000. Upon receipt of the cash from the investor (the "proceeds"), Graymen would make the following entry:

Cash	$1,000,000	
Bonds Payable		$1,000,000

At the end of each of ten years of the bond's life, Graymen would record interest as follows:

Interest Charges	$60,000	
Cash		$60,000

Finally, on the maturity date, Graymen would repay the debt and make the following entry:

Bonds Payable	$1,000,000	
Cash		$1,000,000

Bonds Issued at a Discount

Now, let us take the case where bonds are issued at a *discount*, i.e., the stated rate is less than the market rate of interest. Assume the Graymen Company plans to issue the same bonds as before, but now the market rate is eight per cent while the stated rate remains at six per cent. The proceeds of the bond issue would be determined as follows:

(1) Present value of the annuity:
$60,000P_{\overline{10}|.08} = \$60,000 \times 6.71008 = \qquad \$402,605$

(2) Present value of the single-sum:
$\$1,000,000p_{\overline{10}|.08} = \$1,000,000 \times .46319 = \qquad \underline{463,190}$

$$\text{Proceeds} \quad \underline{\underline{\$865,795}}$$

Clearly, investors will pay less than the maturity amount of the bonds so as to earn the higher market rate of interest. The difference between the maturity amount and the proceeds ($1,000,000 − $865,795 = $134,205) is the discount. Because Graymen ultimately will repay $1,000,000 for the use of only $865,805, the discount will constitute a portion of the total interest earned by the bondholders. Graymen would record the issuance of the bonds as follows:

Cash	$865,795	
Bonds Payable—Discount	134,205	
Bonds Payable—Maturity Amount		$1,000,000

Note that Bonds Payable—Discount is a contra to Bonds Payable—Maturity Amount; the *net* liability would be reported on the position statement. Over the ten-year life of these bonds, the liability will grow until it reaches $1,000,000, which is done by amortizing the bond discount each year. Thus, at the end of the first year, Graymen would pay cash of $60,000 to the bondholders and make the following entry:

Interest Charges	$69,264	
Bonds Payable—Discount		$9,264
Cash		$60,000

The amount debited to interest charges is the market rate of interest times the net liability outstanding that year. At the end of the first year, it would be eight per cent times $865,795, or $69,264. Since only $60,000 was paid in cash, the remainder was an increase in the net liability, recognized by the amortization of the discount. And, if we computed the present value of the bond paying six per cent, when the market rate of interest is eight per cent, for the nine *remaining* years of its life as above, we would find that it has indeed crept approximately $9,264 closer to its face or maturity value, i.e.,

(1) Present value of the annuity:
$\$60,000 \ P_{\overline{9}|.08} = \$60,000 \times 6.24689 = \qquad \$374,813$

(2) Present value of the single-sum:

$1,000,000 $p_{\overline{9}|.08}$ = $1,000,000 × .50025 =   500,250
                                                                    $875,063

which approximately equals $865,795 + $9,264 (the difference of $4 due to the rounding to five decimal points in our tables). At the end of the second year, the debit to interest charges would be $70,005 [8% ($865,795 + $9,264)]. Thus, both the net liability and interest charges will increase from year to year until maturity, reflecting the *effective* interest rate on the *effective* debt. At maturity, the balance in the discount account will be zero, leaving the $1,000,000 in the parent account as the full liability to be repaid on that date.

Bonds Issued at a Premium

The case of a bond *premium* is handled similarly to that of the discount. Once again assume Graymen plans to issue the same bonds but that the market rate of interest is now five per cent. The proceeds of the issue would be as follows:

(1) Present value of the annuity:

$60,000$P_{\overline{10}|.05}$ = $60,000 × 7.72173 = $463,304

(2) Present value of the single-sum:

$1,000,000$p_{\overline{10}|.05}$ = $1,000,000 × .61391 = $613,910

                                       Proceeds $1,077,214

Here, because the periodic payments are larger than investors are demanding, the investors are willing to lend more than will be returned to them at maturity. Actually, each $60,000 periodic payment will include a return of principal as well as interest, so that by the maturity date, $77,214 (the premium) of their capital will have already been returned to them. Graymen would record the issuance of the bonds and the first interest payment a year later as follows:

Cash	$1,077,214	
Bonds Payable—Maturity Amount		$1,000,000
Bonds Payable—Premium		77,214
Interest Charges	53,861	
Bonds Payable—Premium	6,139	
Cash		60,000

The account, Bonds Payable—Premium, is an adjunct account and is amortized in the same manner as the discount account was (the difference between the cash actually paid out each period and the product of the market rate of interest times the net liability). As the premium is amortized each year, the net liability decreases as does the interest charge so that at all times the effective rate of interest to Graymen is five per cent.[5]

Recording Bond Retirement at Maturity

When the maturity date of a bond issue rolls around, the liability balance should be exactly equal to the maturity amount. If the bonds were initially issued at par, the liability balance from date of issue through the bonds' life to date of maturity would remain constant at the maturity amount. On the other hand, if the bonds were initially issued at either a premium or a discount, the related adjunct account (Bonds Payable—Premium) or contra-account (Bonds Payable—Discount) would be amortized over the life of the bond so that by maturity date, the net liability balance would be the same, regardless of whether the bonds were initially issued at par or at a premium or a discount. That entry would consist simply of a debit to Bonds Payable—Maturity amount and a credit to cash for the amount repaid. No gain or loss would result from the retirement.

Recording Bond Retirement Prior to Maturity

All bonds are not retired at their maturity dates; indeed, they are frequently retired considerably in advance of that date. The reasons that give rise to such events are manifold as, for example: The firm may not have need for the borrowed monies as long as originally anticipated; the firm may have an unexpected surplus of cash and near-cash assets with no attractive investment alternatives available; a decline in market interest rates may make it attractive for the firm to issue new bonds at lower rates in place of the old bonds which pay interest at higher rates; an increase in market interest rates may

5. Occasionally, accountants use the straight-line method of amortization where the total premium or discount is divided by the number of periods, with the result being amortized each period. Accordingly, interest charges remain constant in dollar amount each period, but this causes the *effective* rate to change since the net liability is either increasing (in the case of a discount) or decreasing (in the case of a premium). The straight-line method should not be used except in instances where the differences between the two methods are so small as to be immaterial.

make it attractive for the firm to retire the old bonds by paying their now-reduced market price, the cash for retirement being obtained by issuing new bonds at a higher interest *rate* but a lower principal amount (thus, without much change in total interest *payments*), thereby enabling the recognition of a gain on bond retirement.

Bonds that are retired prior to their maturity dates may be discharged by one of two means: repayment or refunding. *Repayment* is where bonds are discharged by the payment of available cash to the bondholders either by means of exercising a "call" provision in the bond contract or by purchasing the bonds on the open market.[6] *Refunding* is where new bonds are issued either in exchange for old bonds or where the proceeds of a new issue are used to retire the older one. Regardless of the means, early retirement of bonds usually results in the recognition of a gain or loss on the retirement. The gain or loss is equal to the difference between the value of the sacrifice (cash or new bonds payable) made to retire the old bonds and the book value of the old bonds.

The gain or loss on early retirement of bonds arises as a consequence of a change in the market rate of interest between date of issue and date of retirement or in the market's evaluation of the riskiness of the bonds outstanding. The liability balance initially recorded for bonds at date of issue is equal to the market value of the bonds at that date, that market value being in turn a function of the market rate of interest at that time. However, at any subsequent point in the life of the bonds, their book value would be equal to their current market value *only* if the current market rate of interest is equal to the market rate on the issue date or if the market rate change is offset by a change in risk evaluation. This is unlikely to be the case, however, as market interest rates fluctuate frequently and widely and market reassessments of risk are regularly made. As a consequence, if bonds are retired by buying them in the open market, it is likely that the price paid will differ from their book value at that point in time, thereby giving rise to a gain or loss on retirement. Similarly, if the bonds are retired

6. Quite often, bond contracts include a provision whereby the issuing entity may redeem all or part of a bond issue from bondholders prior to maturity date. This is known as "calling" the bonds. A predetermined "call price" is stated in the contract and, although the price may vary as the bonds approach maturity, it is usually set somewhat in excess of maturity amount, the difference being known as the "call premium." The call price effectively sets a ceiling on the amount the issuer has to pay in order to redeem the bonds prior to maturity. Should market interest rates decline sufficiently as compared to the stated interest rate on the bonds, the market price of the bonds may climb substantially above their maturity amount. Because the call price sets an upper limit on the operation of these market forces, bondholders generally would prefer not to have such a provision inserted in the bond contract, all else being equal, whereas bond issuers would want such protection.

by "calling" them from the bondholders, the established call price is likely to differ from the book value at that time, also giving rise to a gain or a loss on retirement.

A special case arises if the firm issuing the bonds defaults on the bond contract or goes into bankruptcy. Under such circumstances, the par or face amount of the bonds becomes payable and the difference between the book value and face value would be treated as a gain or loss. In dire situations of this sort, however, creditors may not be able to collect the full amounts due them and may be forced to settle for less, in which event the bonds should be written down to their net realizable value.

Before leaving the subject of gains and losses on bonds, a final word is in order. Instead of being included in the gains and losses section of the income statement, gains and losses on bonds should be deducted from entity income in arriving at ownership income. Such a procedure correlates with the treatment of interest charges on bonds. Entity income, the result of the revenues, expenses, gains, and losses associated with the firm's assets, accrues to the firm's equity-holders as a group and is computed without regard to the firm's equity structure. By contrast, ownership income is concerned only with that aspect of entity income available to preferred and common stockholders. When bonds held by creditors are retired at a gain, the ownership group benefits vis-a-vis the creditor group; when retired at a loss, the reverse is the case. In other words, the gain or loss on bonds accrues to the owners rather than to the firm as a whole.

A SPECIAL CASE: INCOME TAXES PAYABLE

Although it may initially seem odd to regard the government as a creditor of the business firm, upon further reflection this relationship may become more apparent. The payment of taxes (income, property, franchise, and so on) is a condition of doing business. In the case of income taxes, taxes are assessed as a function of income earned by the firm. Thus, income taxes accrue as income is earned, but remittances are made to the government only periodically. Since there is a time lag between the accrual of income taxes and their payment, an obligation to the government arises which is recorded as a liability.

Accounting for income tax obligations is not as simple and straight-forward as it may seem at first blush. Although it has been assumed or implied thus far that taxable income and accounting income are identical, this is rarely the case. Taxable income is defined by the tax laws, and while the laws incorporate a considerable amount of conventional accounting practices in that definition, the basic objectives of the income tax laws differ from the objectives of accounting. *Accounting should be concerned with the optimal allocation of scarce resources* within the economy while the tax laws are concerned with the generation of revenues for the government as well as the implementation of certain public policy goals of Congress (only one of which may be optimal resource allocation). In addition, the tax laws are conditioned by rulings made for administrative convenience in applying the law. Given the differences in objectives, differences between accounting (book) income and taxable income in any particular period of time are likely to occur. These differences between accounting and taxable income may be classified either as *permanent* or *temporary*.

Permanent Differences

Differences between accounting and taxable income that may never be reconciled with one another are known as permanent differences. The causes of permanent differences are as follows:

1. Certain revenues and gains are included in the determination of accounting income but not taxable income. An example of a revenue is interest earned on municipal bonds which clearly qualifies as a revenue for accounting purposes but which is non-taxable to the recipient. Capital gains which qualify as "long-term" under the tax code are another example as such gains are taxable to corporations at a flat 28 per cent rather than at the usually higher ordinary income rate.

2. Certain deductions are included in the determination of accounting income, but these deductions are excluded, limited, or afforded special treatment under the tax laws. An example of a deduction for accounting purposes which is not allowable for tax purposes is the amortization of goodwill. Under certain conditions, for example, deductions for charitable contributions and capital losses on investment properties may be limited for tax purposes while the entire amounts would be deductible for accounting purposes. An example of a special treatment is "percentage depletion," which is deductible on the tax return, while "cost-based depletion" is all that can be deducted for accounting purposes.[7]

Although there are relatively few permanent differences, when such differences do exist the taxable incomes and accounting incomes that

---

7. In essence, where "percentage depletion" is permitted for tax purposes, the deduction is a fixed percentage of *revenues* without reference to the cost of the properties being depleted. For accounting purposes, on the other hand, the most that can be depleted over the life of the property is its *cost*, hence, the term "cost-based depletion."

result may thus *never* coincide with one another either for a particular period or over the lifetime of the taxable entity. If all else is equal, however, no special accounting problems are created since income tax expense would be equal to the taxes assessed during the year.

Temporary Differences

Much more important are the temporary differences, for these do create special problems for the accountant. The temporary differences result from differences in *timing* of the recognition of revenues or in the deduction of expenses. Thus, over the life of an entity, taxable income ultimately may be identical with accounting income but not necessarily within every individual period. In any given period, one of two situations may occur:

1. Accounting income (before income taxes) will be greater than taxable income because (a) certain revenues are recognized on the books before they are reported on the tax return (such as an installment sale which is recorded as revenue on the books on the date it occurs but which is reported on the installment basis for tax purposes) or (b) certain expenses are deducted on the tax return before they are deducted on the books (such as using accelerated depreciation for tax purposes and straight-line for the books).

2. Taxable income is greater than accounting income (before income taxes) because (a) a revenue is reported on the tax return before it is recognized on the books (such as payments received from customers in advance of delivery of goods or services) or (b) an expense is deducted on the books before it is deducted on the tax return (such as warranty expenses which are estimated on the books in advance of their payment but which cannot be deducted on the tax return until payment is made).

These timing differences wreak havoc with the matching concept which requires that revenues be matched with the expenses that produced them. Since income taxes are generally regarded by accountants as expenses rather than as distributions of income, the income tax expense for a particular period, according to the matching concept, should be related to the income of the period for which the payment of taxes is required.

To illustrate the problem, assume that the Jones Company owns plant assets having an historical acquisition cost of $100,000 and an expected service life of four years with no salvage. These assets are being depreciated on a straight-line basis for book purposes and on a sum-of-years'-digits basis for tax purposes. For each of the four years, Jones' revenues are $80,000 and its expenses, other than depreciation and income taxes, are $20,000. Assuming Jones Company is subject to an income tax rate of forty per cent, income taxes for each of the four years will be computed on its tax return as seen in Table 7-1. If the income taxes payable for the year as determined above are simply deducted as an expense of the year for financial reporting purposes, Jones Company's income statements would appear as seen in Table 7-2. The unsuspecting reader of Jones Company's statements would be surprised to find that the income tax expense is *rising* in each of the four years while revenues and all other expenses remain constant.

To remedy this, a procedure known as *interperiod income tax allocation* has been devised. The income tax expense used in determining book income for the period is based on all items of revenue and expense constituting book income which, in the past, present, or future, either

TABLE 7-1

	Years			
	1	2	3	4
Revenues	$80,000	$80,000	$80,000	$80,000
Depreciation Expense	$40,000	$30,000	$20,000	$10,000
Other Expenses (excluding income taxes)	20,000	20,000	20,000	20,000
Total Deductible Expenses	$60,000	$50,000	$40,000	$30,000
Taxable Income	$20,000	$30,000	$40,000	$50,000
Income Tax Rate	×40%	×40%	×40%	×40%
Income Taxes	$ 8,000	$12,000	$16,000	$20,000

TABLE 7-2

	Years			
	1	2	3	4
Revenues	$80,000	$80,000	$80,000	$80,000
Depreciation Expense	$25,000	$25,000	$25,000	$25,000
Income Tax Expense	8,000	12,000	16,000	20,000
Other Expenses	20,000	20,000	20,000	20,000
Total Expenses	$53,000	$57,000	$61,000	$65,000
Entity and Ownership Income	$27,000	$23,000	$19,000	$15,000

have given or will give rise to an income tax liability. If the income tax expense so determined is larger than the taxes currently due, the difference is credited to either a long-term liability (if the taxes will be paid in the future) or an asset (if the taxes have already been paid in the past). Conversely, if the income tax expense is smaller than the taxes currently due, the difference is debited to either a long-term liability (to reflect payment of an obligation recorded in a previous period) or an asset (to reflect prepayment of an expense to be recorded in a future period).[8]

Income Tax Deferrals

To illustrate, let us continue with the Jones Company example. In each of the four years, the income tax expense would be $14,000 (the forty per cent tax rate multiplied times the remainder of $80,000 of revenues less straight-line depreciation of $25,000 and other expenses of $20,000). Since the income taxes that will actually have to be paid in year 1 are $8,000, as previously determined, the following journal entry is made:

Income Tax Expense	$14,000	
Income Taxes Payable—Current		$8,000
Income Taxes Payable—Long-Term		6,000

Likewise, in year 2 the income tax expense will be $14,000 while the taxes currently due amount to $12,000, requiring the following entry:

Income Tax Expense	$14,000	
Income Taxes Payable—Current		$12,000
Income Taxes Payable—Long-Term		2,000

In years 3 and 4, the taxes currently due will be greater than the expenses for each year, thereby reducing and finally eliminating the long-term liability.

Income Tax Expense	$14,000	
Income Taxes Payable—Long-Term	2,000	
Income Taxes Payable—Current		$16,000

8. As a curious consequence of the matching concept, practicing accountants often treat the debit and credit balances that arise from interperiod income tax allocation as deferred charges and deferred credits, respectively, on the position statement. This choice of titles apparently has been made as a compromise between the advocates and opponents of tax allocation. We believe that the use of such nondescript titles in place of "prepaid income taxes" (an asset) and "income taxes payable—long-term" (a liability) is indefensible in terms of sound accounting concepts.

Income Tax Expense	$14,000	
Income Taxes Payable—Long-Term	6,000	
Income Taxes Payable—Current		$20,000

Jones Company's income statements for the four years after implementing income tax allocation would appear as seen in Table 7-3. Note that Jones Company's income over the four years is $84,000, the same as it was without income tax allocation. It will be seen that the $14,000 per year charged in our amended statement over the four years adds up to the $56,000 that the company must pay in cash for taxes over the four years, i.e., $8,000 + $12,000 + $16,000 + $20,000.

TABLE 7-3

	Year			
	1	2	3	4
Revenues	$80,000	$80,000	$80,000	$80,000
Depreciation Expense	$25,000	$25,000	$25,000	$25,000
Income Tax Expense	14,000	14,000	14,000	14,000
Other Expenses	20,000	20,000	20,000	20,000
Total Expenses	$59,000	$59,000	$59,000	$59,000
Entity and Ownership Income	$21,000	$21,000	$21,000	$21,000

Income Tax Prepayments

Let us now turn to the case where taxes are paid in advance of their being written off on the books as an expense. Assume the Smith Company has leased some property to another firm for $10,000 per year and has received $30,000 for three years' rent in advance. For book purposes, the rental revenue will be recorded at the rate of $10,000 per year for each of the three years; but for income tax purposes, the full $30,000 is taxable when it is received. Assume no expenses other than income taxes are involved and that the tax rate is forty per cent. The tax returns for the three years would be as follows:

	Years		
	1	2	3
Taxable Income	$30,000	-0-	-0-
Income Tax Rate	×40%	×40%	×40%
Income Taxes	$12,000	-0-	-0-

Without income tax allocation, Smith's income statements would appear as follows:

	Years		
	1	*2*	*3*
Revenues	$10,000	$10,000	$10,000
Income Tax Expense	12,000	-0-	-0-
Entity and Ownership Income (Loss)	($ 2,000)	$10,000	$10,000

Without income tax allocation, the statements appear rather queer since Smith's activities for each of the three years have remained unchanged, yet a loss is indicated in the first year while all revenues in the second and third years go directly into income.

To incorporate tax allocation into its records, Smith Company would have to make the following entries:

Year 1	Income Tax Expense	$4,000	
	Prepaid Income Taxes	8,000	
	Income Taxes Payable—Current		$12,000
Year 2	Income Tax Expense	$4,000	
	Prepaid Income Taxes		$4,000
Year 3	Income Tax Expense	$4,000	
	Prepaid Income Taxes		$4,000

With income tax allocation, Smith Company's income statements would appear as follows:

	Years		
	1	*2*	*3*
Revenues	$10,000	$10,000	$10,000
Income Tax Expense	4,000	4,000	4,000
Entity and Ownership Income	$ 6,000	$ 6,000	$ 6,000

Income Tax Carry-Back and Carry-Forward

One additional knotty problem confronts the accountant in attempting to arrive at the appropriate income tax expense figure to be reported on the income statement, that of the "carry-back, carry-forward" provision of the tax law. This provision was devised to allow for equitable treatment of companies whose earnings are erratic to the degree that they have income in some years and losses in others. Without this provision, such companies would end up paying more income taxes than other companies whose total earnings over a period of years were equal to the net earnings (annual incomes and losses combined) of the companies having erratic earnings.

Basically, this provision works as follows. A company that has suffered a loss for the year is permitted, for tax purposes, to apply that loss against the income that was earned and taxed in the three preceding years. This would reduce the taxable income in the preceding years and permit the company to apply for a refund of the taxes previously paid. If, however, there is insufficient income in the preceding years to offset the loss, any excess loss may be applied to earnings for the next seven years, thereby reducing tax payments in the later years.

To demonstrate this, assume the Brown Company is subject to a forty per cent tax rate and had earnings and taxes in years 1 through 3 as follows:

Year	Taxable Income	Income Taxes Paid
1	$10,000	$4,000
2	12,000	4,800
3	9,000	3,600

If, in year 4, Brown incurred a loss for tax purposes of $25,000, it would "carry-back" this loss—first to year 1 in the amount of $10,000, to year 2 for $12,000, and to year 3 for $3,000. Totally, Brown Corporation could claim tax refunds of $10,000 [40% ($10,000 + $12,000 + $3,000)]. Brown's income statement for year 4 would include a "negative tax" of $10,000, thereby reducing the loss from $25,000 to $15,000. The journal entry to record this would be:

Income Tax Refund Receivable $10,000
    Reduction of Loss Due to Income
    Tax Carry-back $10,000

The account debited would be classified as a current asset while the account credited would be closed to the income summary as a "negative expense."

To illustrate the "carry-forward" case, assume that instead of $25,000, Brown Company's loss for tax purposes in year 4 was $50,000. Brown could "carry-back" only $31,000 of the loss to the three prior years (equal to the taxable income in those years), leaving $19,000 to "carry-forward" to apply against future earnings. The entry to record this might be as follows:

Income Tax Refund Receivable	$12,400	
Prepaid Income Taxes	7,600	
Reduction of Loss Due to Income		
Tax Carry-back and Carry-forward		$20,000

Accordingly, Brown Company's loss on its income statement would be reduced from $50,000 to $30,000.

While this method of handling the carry-forward is consistent with the treatment of the carry-back, a great deal of uncertainty surrounds the prepaid income taxes account. This asset has value only if there are sufficient earnings in the seven succeeding years against which the loss can be applied. Since Brown has incurred a substantial loss in year 4, its future earnings prospects may be bleak; hence, the carry-for-ward tax benefit may never be realized. When such doubt exists, accountants conservatively do not record the asset but rather disclose its contingent nature in a footnote to the financial statements. The entry made would merely reflect the refund of taxes from prior years, an amount which is certain.

Income Tax Refund Receivable	$12,400	
Reduction of Loss Due to Income		
Tax Carry-back		$12,400

Thus, the loss on Brown Company's income statement for year 4 would be $37,600 ($50,000 − $12,400). Should taxable income materialize in the succeeding seven years, income tax expense should be recorded just as it would have been had there been no carry-forward, and the tax reduction that results should be recorded as a gain in that year. To illustrate, suppose that Brown Company had accounting and taxable income in year 5 of $7,000. Brown would make the following journal entries to record income taxes for that year:

Income Tax Expense	$2,800	
Income Taxes Payable—Current		$2,800
Income Taxes Payable—Current	$2,800	
Gain Due to Income Tax Carry-		
Forward		$2,800

The Income Tax Expense of $2,800 would be reported among expenses in Brown Company's income statement for year 5, while the Gain Due to Income Tax Carry-Forward would be reported among gains and losses. The net effect on Brown's income for year 5 would, of course, be zero. Similarly, the debit and credit to Income Taxes Payable—Current would cancel each other out.

DISCUSSION QUESTIONS

1. In a discussion of the handling of preferred stock and present
   accounting practice, two accounting students argue as follows:

   Leonard:

   > I believe that preferred stock should be listed as a long-term
   > liability. Preferred stockholders have preference over com-
   > mon stockholders in the payment of dividends and have
   > a prior claim on the company's net assets in case of liquidation.
   > Also preferred stock is usually callable, like a bond issue.

   Martha:

   > Preferred stock dividends are not accrued in a liability account
   > if unpaid (although admittedly in the case of cumulative
   > preferred stock, past as well as present unpaid dividends
   > must be paid to preferred shareholders before any dividends
   > can be paid to common shareholders), and no specific maturity
   > date is set as it is normally in the case of long-term debt.
   > Therefore, preferred stock is rightfully part of stockholders'
   > (ownership) equity.

   Which view accords with present accounting practice? Do you think
   that present accounting practice is correct on this issue? Explain.

2. Would you prefer to borrow on the basis of a note paying 8.5 per
   cent interest or a note sold at an 8 per cent discount? Explain,
   and justify your answer.

3. The Mulcahey Office Supply Company sells typewriters under a
   one-year warranty contract that obligates the company to repair,
   free of charge, any typewriters sold, if it can be shown that difficulties
   in the first year of use are due to defective parts. In its first year
   of operations, Mulcahey sells 1,000 typewriters at an average price,
   including warranty, of $165. Mulcahey estimates that these typewrit-
   ers, without the warranty agreement, could have been sold for an
   average price of $150, i.e., that buyers believe the warranty is worth
   ten per cent of purchase price. Mulcahey estimates that warranty
   expenses in the year following sale, on the 1,000 typewriters sold
   in year 0, will amount to only $7,000; hence, it expects to make
   a profit of $8,000 on its warranty arrangements. In fact, Mulcahey
   has no warranty expenses in year 0 but, largely because of a faulty
   mechanism on a popular new model, has warranty expenses in year
   1, on year 0 sales, of $18,000. Assuming Mulcahey adjusts its estimated

warranty expenses on year 1 sales to reflect experience and that it again sells 1,000 typewriters in year 1 at an average price of $165 and further that expenses other than those involving the warranty contract were $120,000 in both years 0 and 1,

a. show aggregate journal and ledger entries connected with sales and warranty obligations for years 0 and 1 under each of the methods which are suggested in the text as a means of handling warranty obligations in a firm's accounts;

b. compute the income for both years 0 and 1 under the two methods and discuss whether you think the income is (1) overstated or (2) understated in each year under each method and, if so, by how much.

How might your answer to (b) be affected if the warranty agreement were for three years? Can you suggest a better method for handling warranties which extend for more than one year than either of those suggested in the text (and generally followed in the profession)? Explain your position.

4. The Slowdrip Faucet Company needs cash for improvements and negotiates with a bank for the amount required. Four thousand five hundred dollars ($4,500) is borrowed on December 31, 19X3 on a two-year, seven per cent note.

a. If the principal is to be repaid in two equal payments, one on December 31, 19X4 and one on December 31, 19X5, and interest due at that time also paid then, what are the journal entries for December 31, 19X3, 19X4, and 19X5?

b. If the total dollar amount to be paid at the end of 19X4 and 19X5 (principal and interest) are to be the same in each year, what are the journal entries for these dates?

5. Suppose in Question 4, Slowdrip had been offered the option of repaying the principal of the loan in two equal installments over two years, plus annual interest on the amount outstanding, or alternatively repaying equal dollar amounts (principal and interest) at the end of every six months over two-and-a-half years. Under which method would it pay less total interest to the bank (show your calculations)? Would it, then, necessarily prefer that method assuming that it had no liquidity problems? (Hint: Consider the *present value* of scheduled cash outpayments under each method on the basis of an interest factor of seven per cent.)

6. What considerations do you think might influence a company's treasurer in considering whether to issue bonds at par, at a discount, or at a premium? Why may one company call a bond selling at

a discount and pay for it by issuing a new bond at par, while another company may at the same time call a bond selling at a premium and pay for it by issuing a new bond at par?

7. Classify the following as a timing difference (T) or as a permanent difference (P) that may exist as between accounting (book) income and taxable income. Note in each case whether an amount needs to be added to or subtracted from accounting income to arrive at taxable income for the year under consideration.
   a. Amortization of goodwill
   b. Long-term contracts where percentage-of-completion basis is used for the measurement of accounting income and completed-contract basis is used in the measurement of taxable income
   c. Warranty costs
   d. Life insurance premiums on company officers
   e. Accelerated depreciation used for tax purposes but straight-line depreciation used in measuring accounting income
   f. Prepaid rental revenue
   g. Interest earned on municipal bonds
   h. Fines and penalties paid because of violation of antitrust laws or other statutes

8. The following is a before-tax income statement for a small local conglomerate company for 19X5, specializing itself in the taxi business but having other interests as well:

Revenue from Sales	$168,000	
Dividends from Investments (in related firms)	25,000	
Interest on Municipal Bonds	30,000	$223,000
Wage Expenses	$ 60,000	
Depreciation on Taxis	25,000	
Amortization of Goodwill	6,000	
Rental Expenses	12,000	$103,000
OPERATING INCOME BEFORE INCOME TAXES		120,000
Gain on Sale of Equipment		$ 14,000
ENTITY INCOME BEFORE INCOME TAXES		$134,000
Interest Charges		$ 9,000
OWNERSHIP INCOME BEFORE INCOME TAXES		$125,000

The company uses straight-line depreciation on their taxis for book purposes and they are assumed to all have been bought for the same price and all to have a four-year life expectancy, half of them being two years old at the end of 19X5, half of them being four years old at that time. The company uses sum-of-the-years'-digits depreciation for tax purposes.

a. Compute the company's current tax liability for 19X5 assuming that: (1) 85 per cent of dividends received from related firms are excluded from taxation; (2) interest on municipal bonds are nontaxable; (3) goodwill amortization is not deductible for tax purposes; (4) capital gains are taxed at 25 per cent; (5) all other income is taxed at 45 per cent.

b. Assuming identical events in 19X6, except that the half of the taxis which are four years old are replaced by new ones (at constant prices) while the other half are now three years old rather than two years old, show the journal entries for 19X5 and 19X6 which would be used to handle income tax expense were the company to employ interperiod income tax allocation procedures.

c. What is the basic purpose of interperiod income tax allocations?

9. Assume that the Burkman Company had the following taxable income between 19X1 and 19X5:

Year		Taxable Income	Tax Rate
19X1		$ 2,000	20%
19X2		6,000	40
19X3		4,000	30
19X4	assumption 1:	(7,000)	30
	assumption 2:	(15,000)	30
19X5		5,000	40

a. Record the aggregate journal entry for income tax expense for 19X4 under each of assumptions 1 and 2.

b. Record the aggregate journal entry for income tax expense for 19X5 under each of assumptions 1 and 2.

PROBLEMS

7-1. *Wausaukee Winch Company*

On January 10, 19X9, Wiley Fingers arrived at the offices of Wausaukee Winch Company to begin the annual audit of Wausaukee's financial statements for the year ended December 31, 19X8. The controller has been having some difficulties in preparing the year-end statements. In particular, he is concerned with how to treat the following liabilities:

(1) The Accounts Payable—Control account has a net credit balance of $172,000. A detailed review of the accounts payable ledger accounts indicated 237 individual accounts with credit balances totaling to $178,000 and four accounts having debit balances of $6,000. Also, all payables are recorded at gross prices. An analysis reveals that purchase discounts still available to Wausaukee on December 31 amount to $2,800.

(2) On July 1, 19X8, Wausaukee borrowed $6,209 cash from one of its customers, issuing to the customer a noninterest-bearing five-year note with a face amount of $10,000.

(3) A 90-day note payable due on January 8, 19X9 in the amount of $7,500 was retired on that date by transferring title to a piece of unused land that Wausaukee owned.

(4) Several years ago, Wausaukee borrowed $25,000 from a life insurance company, using as collateral for the note the cash surrender value of life insurance policies that the company holds on certain of its key officers. As of December 31, 19X8, the cash surrender value of those policies aggregated to $37,000. The note bears interest at nine per cent per year payable on March 1 and September 1 each year. The due date on the note is September 1, 19X9.

(5) A two-year bank note in the amount of $50,000 falls due on March 15, 19X9. The note bears interest at eight per cent, payable annually on March 15. Wausaukee and the bank have just entered into an agreement whereby the note will be refinanced by the issuance of another two-year eight per cent note on March 15.

(6) $150,000 maturity amount of seven per cent convertible bonds issued by Wausaukee several years ago will be due on June 30, 19X9. Interest is payable semi-annually on December 31 and June 30 (the December payment has been made). Each of the $1,000 bonds is convertible on the demand of the bondholder into fifteen shares of Wausaukee's common stock. The market price of the stock has been climbing at a rate of twenty per cent per year for the past several years and on December 31, 19X8 stands at $62 per share.

INSTRUCTIONS:
As Wiley Fingers, prepare a schedule of the current and long-term liabilities of Wausaukee as of December 31, 19X8.

7-2. Downtown Department Store

The Downtown Department Store began selling gift certificates for the first time just before the Christmas season in 19X8. Certificates are offered in $5 multiples, up to a maximum of $50, and expire three months from date of issuance. During that period, $750,000 of gift certificates were sold; 60 per cent were redeemed prior to December 31.

Downtown's controller, never having confronted this issue before, has asked for your advice on this matter. In particular, the controller is concerned about the dollar amount to report as a current liability on the store's December 31, 19X8 position statement. In talking with officials from other department stores, the controller learned that their experience has been that 85 per cent of such certificates are redeemed and the rest simply expire unused. Also, in reviewing a sample of the redemptions to date, the controller found that cost of goods sold was equal to 65 per cent of the face amount of the certificates, which is the same ratio that the store has experienced on its regular cash and credit sales.

INSTRUCTIONS:

(a) Present the controller with all the alternative amounts that could be recorded as a current liability with respect to certificates outstanding on December 31, 19X8. For each alternative, indicate its impact upon income in 19X8 and 19X9.
(b) Indicate which of the alternatives presented in (a) above you prefer. Give reasons for your preference and an explanation of why you rejected the other possibilities. Your discussion should be supported by reference to particular accounting principles.

7-3. American Car Company

The American Car Company (ACCo) manufactures automobiles which it sells to its franchised dealers, who in turn sell them directly to the public. Each car is sold with a one-year warranty which commences on the date the car is delivered by the dealer to the customer. When warranty work is required, the customer returns the car to the dealer who provides the necessary repairs. The dealer then notifies ACCo of the warranty work, requesting repayment in cash for labor services rendered and for replenishment of parts used.

On the basis of its past experience with its warranties, ACCo expects that, on the average, each car sold will require warranty work equal to one per cent of ACCo's selling price of the car to its dealers. Data from prior years indicates that 76 per cent of the dollar amount of warranty work will be performed evenly over the first four months that the warranty is in effect and the remainder evenly over the last eight months. Of the cost of warranty work, 60 per cent is typically for labor and 40 per cent for parts. The average time between sale of a car to a dealer until the dealer delivers the car to the customer is one month.

ACCo's sales records for the years 19X1 and 19X2 are as follows:

| | (in millions) | |
	19X1	*19X2*
January	$195	$210
February	180	190
March	185	195
April	195	200
May	205	210
June	200	205
July	195	195
August	305	325
September	295	315
October	275	290
November	250	275
December	230	270

(For simplicity, assume that all sales are made on the first day of each month.)

On December 31, 19X1, the balance in ACCo's estimated warranty obligations account was $9,674,500. During 19X2, dealers submitted claims to ACCo for $33.6 million for labor and $22.4 million for parts. Upon receipt of these claims, ACCo immediately issued checks and shipped parts. ACCo makes no entries during the year to reflect warranty obligations but rather makes a single adjusting entry at year-end.

INSTRUCTIONS:

Prepare all necessary journal entries on ACCo's books to reflect its activities during 19X2 with respect to warranties. You may assume that sales for the year have been properly recorded. (Hint: A schedule of warranty claims still outstanding by month would be helpful.)

7-4. *Westside Place and South University Place*

The City of Westside Place and the City of South University Place both issued $1,000,000 face value bonds due in twenty years. Interest of two-and-a-half per cent was payable annually on January 1. Westside Place issued its bonds on an annual yield basis of three per cent while

South University Place issued its bonds at an effective annual rate of two per cent.

INSTRUCTIONS:

Calculate the cash proceeds that each city will receive.

7-5. *Wichita Falls Widget Company*

On January 1, 19X0, the Wichita Falls Widget Company issued $1,000,000 maturity amount five per cent, ten-year bonds at a price to yield six per cent. Interest is payable semi-annually on July 1 and January 1. The cash received for the bonds was $925,618.

INSTRUCTIONS:

Assuming Wichita Falls Widget closes its books annually on December 31, prepare the necessary journal entries on:

(a) January 1, 19X0
(b) July 1, 19X0
(c) December 31, 19X0
(d) January 1, 19X1

7-6. *Gelband Company*

The Gelband Company issued $1,000,000 of five per cent debenture bonds on January 1, 1968 at a price so as to yield an effective interest rate of six per cent compounded annually. Interest is payable annually on January 1 and the bonds will mature on January 1, 1983. Gelband closes its books annually on December 31.

INSTRUCTIONS:

Prepare journal entries on Gelband's books for December 31, 1977 and January 1, 1978.

7-7. *Prescott Company*

The Prescott Company issued $1,000,000 maturity amount of five per cent bonds on January 1, 19X2. Interest is payable semi-annually on July 1 and January 1. The bonds mature on January 1, 19X7. The market rate of interest on January 1, 19X2 was six per cent, compounded semi-annually.

INSTRUCTIONS:

Assuming Prescott closes its books annually on December 31, prepare relevant journal entries on Prescott's books for the following dates:

(a) January 1, 19X2
(b) July 1, 19X2
(c) December 31, 19X2
(d) January 1, 19X3

7-8. Bonner Company

On January 1, 19X4, Bonner Company issued $10,000 maturity amount of eight per cent, three-year bonds. The market rate of interest on that date was six per cent. Interest is payable on January 1 of each year, and the bonds mature on January 1, 19X7.

INSTRUCTIONS:

Make the necessary journal entries to record the issuance of the bonds, the yearly payments, and the repayment at maturity.

7-9. Harold Company

On January 1, 19X3 the Harold Company issued $10 million of eight per cent debenture bonds which mature on January 1, 19X8. Interest is payable semi-annually on July 1 and January 1. The market rate of interest for bonds of comparable quality on January 1, 19X3 was six per cent, compounded semi-annually. Harold closes its books annually on December 31.

INSTRUCTIONS:

Prepare relevant journal entries on Harold's books for

(a) January 1, 19X3   (e) July 1, 19X7
(b) July 1, 19X3   (f) December 31, 19X7
(c) December 31, 19X3   (g) January 1, 19X8
(d) January 1, 19X4

7-10. Albion Corporation

On January 1, 19X3, the Albion Corporation issued $1,000,000 of eight per cent debenture bonds due January 1, 19X8. Interest on the bonds is payable semi-annually on January 1 and July 1. The bonds are callable at 103 plus accrued interest to date on any date of interest payment subsequent to January 1, 19X5. On the date of issue, the market rate of interest for bonds of comparable quality was ten per cent, compounded semi-annually. Albion closes its books annually on December 31.

INSTRUCTIONS:

Determine the following:

(a) The proceeds of the bond issue on January 1, 19X3.
(b) The amount to be recorded for interest charges on July 1, 19X6.
(c) The total cash payment required if all the bonds were called and redeemed on January 1, 19X7.

7-11. Smith Company

The Smith Company issued $1,000,000 of six per cent, ten-year mortgage bonds on April 1, 19X8. The bonds are callable at 102 and interest is payable quarterly on the first of July, October, January, and April. On the issue date, the market rate of interest for similar bonds was eight per cent, compounded quarterly. Smith closes its books annually on June 30.

INSTRUCTIONS:

Prepare journal entries to record:

(a) Issuance of the bonds on April 1.
(b) Accrual and payment of interest on June 30 and July 1, 19X8, respectively.
(c) Redemption of the bonds assuming they are called on October 1, 19X9.

7-12. Nottingham & Sons, Inc.

Nottingham & Sons, Inc., needs to borrow $20,000 to finance a research project. Mr. Nottingham and his three sons each found a loan company from which they could borrow the money. They discovered that the firm could borrow the $20,000 on any of the following terms:

(1) On a note with a five per cent discount factor, with repayment set at one year later,
(2) On a note with a six per cent rate of interest, with repayment set at one year later,

(3) On a two-year note with a six per cent interest rate, with payments of interest plus $10,000 on the principal to be made at the end of each year, or

(4) On a three-year, five per cent note, with equal annual payments at the end of each year which would include both interest and principal.

INSTRUCTIONS:

(a) Calculate the *present value* (using an interest factor of six per cent) for interest and repayment of principal on each of the four notes, and indicate which alternative, other things being equal, you would recommend for Nottingham and Sons to use in solving its present financial problem.

(b) Prepare the necessary journal entries to account for each note, its interest, and the repayments, and determine the total interest charges required by each.

7-13. Malvern Company

The Malvern Company owns a single asset, a piece of machinery which was acquired on January 1, 19X1 for $65,000. The machine has an expected depreciable life of three years at the end of which its value as scrap is anticipated to be $5,000. During each year of its expected life, the machine will produce revenues of $70,000 while it incurs expenses (other than depreciation and income taxes) of $40,000. Malvern Company is depreciating the machine on its books using the straight-line basis but is using sum-of-the-years'-digits for tax purposes. Malvern is subject to an income tax rate of 40 per cent and closes its books annually on December 31.

INSTRUCTIONS:

Assuming all expectations are correct, prepare journal entries to record income tax expense (reflecting interperiod income tax allocation) for each of the three years.

7-14. Taggart Corporation

The Taggart Corporation is in the process of adjusting and closing its books at year-end, December 31, 19X3. Income tax expense for 19X3 has not yet been determined nor has the income tax liability at year-end. During 19X3, Taggart's total revenues were $500,000, and its expenses were $400,000. All items of revenue and expense are identical for book and tax purposes except for depreciation. Taggart acquired equipment for $90,000 on January 1, 19X3 which is being depreciated on its books on a straight-line basis with an expected life of five years and no salvage value. On its tax return, Taggart plans to depreciate the building on the same basis, except using the sum-of-the-years'-digits method.

INSTRUCTIONS:

Prepare the appropriate journal entry to record taxes for 19X3 on Taggart's books, using interperiod income tax allocation procedures. Assume Taggart is subject to a tax rate of 40 per cent.

7-15. *Bluegate Company*

The Bluegate Company is primarily in the business of leasing equipment. Bluegate closes its books on December 31, 19X2, and prior to closing on that date, the balances in the nominal accounts are as follows:

	Dr.	Cr.
Administrative Expenses	$17,000	
Depreciation Expenses	51,000	
Maintenance Expenses	25,000	
Other Revenues		6,000
Rental Revenues		110,000

Income tax expense for the year has not yet been determined. All items that will appear on Bluegate's published income statement and on its tax return are identical with two exceptions:

(1) On July 1, 19X2, Bluegate received an advance payment on future rentals amounting to $15,000. This payment covers a rental period from July 1, 19X2 through December 31, 19X3 and is taxable in full when received.
(2) On January 1, 19X1, Bluegate purchased a piece of equipment for $32,000. The equipment has an expected life of four years at the end of which its salvage value is anticipated to be $2,000. Bluegate is depreciating the equipment on a sum-of-the-years'-digits basis for tax purposes and straight-line for book purposes.

INSTRUCTIONS:

(a) Determine Bluegate's taxable income for 19X2, assuming Bluegate is subject to a tax rate of 40 per cent.

(b) Prepare the journal entry or entries necessary to reflect interperiod tax allocation.

7-16. *Hart Company*

The Hart Company commenced operations on July 1, 19X3. The company is engaged in the manufacture of heavy machinery which generally requires from between four to eighteen months to complete. Accordingly, Hart requires advance deposits for 25 per cent of selling price from customers who order such machinery. Although Hart does not consider these deposits to be revenue until the completed machinery is delivered to the customer, they are taxable to Hart when received. During 19X3, Hart received deposits totaling $150,000. Of this amount, $20,000 applied to 19X3 deliveries, $80,000 to 19X4 deliveries, and $50,000 to 19X5 deliveries. In 19X4, Hart received deposits amounting to $200,000, of which $70,000 applies to 19X4 deliveries, $90,000 to 19X5 deliveries, and $40,000 to 19X6 deliveries. On July 1, 19X3, Hart purchased manufacturing machinery for use in its factory. The machinery cost $300,000 and has an expected useful life of three years with no salvage value at the end of that time. Hart is depreciating its machinery on a straight-line basis for book purposes and double-declining-balance for tax purposes. Hart reported revenues of $560,000 and expenses (other than income taxes) of $290,000 for 19X3 on its own financial statements. For 19X4, Hart reported revenues of $980,000 and expenses (other than income taxes) of $620,000. Hart closes its books each year on December 31 and is subject to an income tax rate of 40 per cent.

INSTRUCTIONS:

Prepare the appropriate journal entries to reflect interperiod tax allocation on December 31, 19X3 and December 31, 19X4, assuming all items of revenue and expense other than those referred to above are identical for book and for tax purposes.

7-17. *Houston Poultry Co.*

In fiscal year 19X7, the Houston Poultry Co. suffered a loss for tax purposes of $60,000. The firm had started operating in 19X1, and its income in previous years had been the following:

Fiscal year	Taxable income
19X1	($19,000)
19X2	12,000
19X3	6,000
19X4	(1,000)
19X5	10,000
19X6	15,000

The firm is subject to an income tax rate of 40 per cent and has paid its taxes correctly each year, taking advantage of the "carry-back, carry-forward" provision when possible.

INSTRUCTIONS:

Make the journal entry which would be made at the end of 19X7 to account for income taxes.

CHAPTER 8

OWNER EQUITIES

HAVING CONSIDERED CREDITOR EQUITIES, we turn now to the other major equity category, owner equities. The term "owner equities" does not appear in position statements in practice but rather is replaced by one that identifies the type of business organization that the firm has adopted. The most commonly used forms in the United States today are the sole proprietorship, the partnership, and the corporation. When the first two forms are employed, the ownership section of the position statement is titled simply "proprietor's equity" or "partners' equity." However, when the corporate form is adopted, more than one title may be required if several different classes of corporate stock have been issued and are outstanding. Thus, ownership in a corporate position statement may be represented by both "preferred stockholders' equity" and "common stockholders' equity," each representing a different class of ownership.

There are approximately 10.2 million sole proprietorships, 1 million partnerships, and 1.8 million corporations in the United States.[1] Yet corporations alone accounted for over 74 per cent of the income originating in business in 1976 and the data in Table 8-1 indicate that the corporate share has been increasing.[2] That so few corporations produce so much suggests that the corporation is a form of organization well-adapted to large-scale business activities while the proprietorship and partnership forms are more typical of the small-scale operations associated largely with farming, fishing, and servicing. The different

---

1. Other forms of business organization, such as the trust, are relatively unimportant both in numbers and in output.

2. The data also suggest that the share of income generated by corporations varies directly with the general level of business activity; the corporation appears to be less stable as a generator of incomes than are other forms of business organization.

forms do exist side-by-side, however, and some proprietorships and partnerships are larger than the smaller corporations.

The differing legal characteristics that define types of business organization are matched, unfortunately, by differences in the legal and accounting definitions of their incomes. It is not surprising, therefore, that the adaptation of accounting procedures to the needs of the several types of organizations has resulted in data on total income and its distribution that are difficult to interpret and to compare. These are the problems that occupy us in this chapter.

TABLE 8-1

*INCOME ORIGINATING IN BUSINESS**

(IN BILLIONS OF DOLLARS)

Year	All Business	Corporate Business	Corporate Business as Percentage of All Business
1929	78.2	45.2	57.8
1933	32.9	17.3	52.6
1935	48.3	27.0	55.9
1940	70.1	42.4	60.5
1944	145.8	90.1	61.8
1945	141.0	82.4	58.4
1946	154.5	86.3	55.9
1947	174.6	104.7	60.0
1948	198.2	120.4	60.7
1949	189.9	115.5	60.8
1950	211.5	132.3	62.6
1951	241.6	153.3	63.5
1952	250.1	158.5	63.4
1953	261.6	169.0	64.6
1954	256.5	163.3	63.7
1955	281.8	184.2	65.4
1956	298.3	195.2	65.4
1957	310.5	202.9	65.3
1958	307.4	195.8	63.7
1959	336.6	220.8	65.6
1960	345.5	226.2	65.5
1961	352.8	228.6	64.9
1962	384.8	256.4	66.5
1963	404.4	270.4	66.8
1964	433.8	292.2	67.3
1965	473.9	320.5	67.7
1966	519.7	353.7	68.1

TABLE 8-1 CONTINUED

*INCOME ORIGINATING IN BUSINESS**

(IN BILLIONS OF DOLLARS)

Year	All Business	Corporate Business	Corporate Business as Percentage of All Business
1967	541.2	366.7	67.8
1968	586.0	400.1	68.3
1969	629.8	428.4	68.2
1970	650.3	438.7	67.5
1971	693.3	468.1	67.5
1972	770.3	564.3	73.3
1973	866.0	630.6	72.8
1974	916.7	671.4	73.2
1975	977.8	717.6	73.4
1976	1,102.0	821.8	74.6

*Income originating in a business unit is roughly the amount paid factors of production. It includes wages and salaries, rent, interest, and profits. It excludes payments and accruals for indirect business taxes, gifts, and depreciation charges.

Income originating in business includes income generated by government enterprises (approximately 1% of the total).

Source: 1929-55: U.S. Department of Commerce, *Survey of Current Business, U.S. Income and Output* (1958), Table 1-12, pp. 134-5; 1956-58. *Survey of Current Business* (July, 1960), Table 9, p. 13.
  1959-61: *Survey of Current Business* (July, 1964), Table 8, p. 13.
  1962-63: *Survey of Current Business* (July, 1966), Table 1.13, p. 15.
  1964-65: *Survey of Current Business* (July, 1968), Table 1.13, p. 23.
  1966-67: *Survey of Current Business* (July, 1970), Table 1.13, p. 21.
  1968-69: *Survey of Current Business* (July, 1972), Table 1.13, p. 20.
  1970-71: *Survey of Current Business* (July, 1974), Table 1.13, p. 20.
  1972: *Survey of Current Business* (July, 1976), Table 1.14, p. 29.
  1973-76: *Survey of Current Business* (July, 1977), Table 1.14, p. 24.

THE SOLE PROPRIETORSHIP

The sole proprietorship is a business firm that is owned, and usually managed, by one person. It is regarded as an economic entity for accounting purposes although it may represent only a part of the assets (and income) of the individual owner (the proprietor). The law, however, does not recognize the sole proprietorship as being separate and distinct from the other assets and economic activities of the individual. It is, for example, the *individual*'s total income, whatever its source, that is subject to income tax—the income of the business entity is not taxed separately. The proprietor is also held by law to be liable without limit for the debts of the business; creditors of the proprietorship can exercise claims against the total assets of the individual and are not limited to those assets employed in the business firm. Thus, the law does not recognize the sole proprietorship as a separate legal entity even though accountants treat it as if it were by regarding it as an economic entity. Because the accounting problems indigenous to the proprietorship are much the same as with the partnership, we shall turn directly to a consideration of that form of business organization. In so doing, we will deal with those problems affecting proprietorships and partnerships conjointly as well as those unique to the partnership.

THE PARTNERSHIP

We may define a partnership as "an association of two or more persons to carry on as co-owners a business for profit." As it stands, this definition is equally applicable to the corporation, yet it does emphasize the partnership's principal economic advantages over the sole proprietorship form of business organization. These derive from the fact that more than one person has an ownership interest in the firm. First, the capital available to the firm is likely to be greater because the sources of owner equity are larger in number and, as a consequence, the firm's borrowing opportunities may also be greater. Second, the risks of management and ownership are spread over a larger number of people. Finally, specialization at the management level becomes possible without the delegation of authority to persons lacking the interest of ownership in the enterprise.

In addition to its advantages over the sole proprietorship, the partnership enjoys several advantages over the corporate form of business organization as well. Far and away the primary advantage has to do with taxation. Partnerships, *per se,* are not subject to taxation of their incomes although the partners themselves must pay income taxes on their individual shares of partnership income. In contrast, corporate income is taxed twice—first, to the corporation itself as an entity, and second, to the stockholders to the extent they receive dividends from the corporation. A secondary advantage of partnerships over corporations is that greater control can be exercised over the firm and its co-owners. This aspect is particularly important in the case of professional firms—law firms, CPA firms, medical practices, and the like—wherein personal responsibility of the professional practitioner assumes paramount importance. Indeed, many states prohibit professional practice in corporate form to protect this responsibility of the professional to his or her client or patient. In some states, however, statutes have been passed providing for a special form of corporation—the "professional corporation"—which preserves certain desirable aspects of the partnership while permitting certain advantages of the corporate form of organization.

Investment in the Partnership

A partnership may be formed by any two or more persons without the legal formalities that are required in forming certain other types of business organizations, such as the corporation. Nevertheless, it is generally desirable to have a written partnership agreement that specifically delineates such things as the rights and duties of each partner, the amounts and types of capital to be contributed by each, the manner in which partnership profits and losses are to be distributed among the partners, and the procedures for disinvestment. Many friends have entered into partnerships with one another only to witness their friendships disintegrate as a direct result of disagreements that could have been averted through an explicit, written partnership agreement.

In forming a partnership, the partners each usually contribute assets to the entity. The assets so contributed do not become the property of the partnership itself because, not being a legal entity, the partnership cannot own property; instead, the property is jointly owned by all the partners, the partner investing the property relinquishing personal rights to it. For accounting purposes, however, property contributed to a partnership by the various partners is treated as if it were owned by the partnership since the partnership is regarded as an economic entity by accountants.

The process of recording initial investments by partners is quite simple. An asset account is opened for each type of property received and an owner equity account is opened for each partner. Thus, the entry to record the contribution by, say, Allen of $10,000 cash would be recorded in the following fashion:

Cash $10,000
    Allen, Capital $10,000
    To record initial investment
    by Allen

Great care must be taken by the accountant in recording contributions of noncash assets, however. The current market values of such assets must be ascertained and recorded to assure equitable treatment of all the partners because: (1) the valuation may be used as a basis for distributing partnership profits and losses in accordance with the partnership agreement, (2) any gains or losses on the subsequent sale of the contributed assets accrue to the partnership rather than the individual partner who contributed the asset, and (3) distributions of partnership assets in liquidation are based on the balances in the partners' capital accounts. It should be readily evident that if a partner contributed, say, land having a current market value of $25,000 but which was recorded on the partnership's books at that partner's original acquisition cost several years ago of $18,000, an inequitable treatment of that partner would result. Similarly, if that same property had a current market value of only $14,000 at date of contribution, it should be equally apparent that the other partners would be treated unfairly.

In a partnership position statement, the ownership section is usually called "partners' equity." The only accounts that appear in this section are the capital accounts—one for each partner—the balances in those accounts representing the sum of the capital originally contributed plus or minus each partner's share of partnership's profits or losses plus any additional investments and minus any withdrawals. The primary accounting problems with regard to partners' equities subsequent to the date of initial investment, however, relate to the determination and distribution of partnership profits and losses.

Income Determination in the Partnership

There are two particular aspects of the determination of income in partnerships (and sole proprietorships as well) that are worthy of special consideration: (1) adoption of the "proprietary theory" and (2) treatment of factor returns to partners (or proprietors).

Adoption of the proprietary theory. The partnership, like the sole proprietorship, is an economic entity accounted for separately from the identities of the individuals who comprise its ownership. Even though accountants regard it as an accountable entity, they do not account for it under the so-called "entity theory" but rather in accordance with the "proprietary theory."

The proprietary theory is thought to be particularly germane to proprietorships and partnerships as opposed to corporations, in part, at least, because of the status of its assets and liabilities. In corporations, assets are the legal property of the corporation itself, but with proprietorships and partnerships, assets are the property of the owners. In a similar fashion, while corporate liabilities represent claims against the corporation itself, liabilities of proprietorships and partnerships are claims against the owners rather than the entity. Furthermore, there is generally a personal relationship between management and ownership of proprietorships and partnerships, the managers and owners usually being the same persons, where such is often not the case with corporations. Under the proprietary theory, assuming no additional investments or disinvestments (including withdrawals) by the owner(s), income for the period is defined as the change in the value of net assets, or

$$\Delta \text{Assets} - \Delta \text{Liabilities} = \text{Ownership Income}$$

The entity view of income is most readily understood in terms of the corporation. Being a recognized legal entity in its own right, it can be conceived as viewing creditors and stockholders as simply alternative sources of funds for financing the assets which the firm uses to generate income. Conceptually, the corporation's income derives from its assets. Some of that entity income (EI) is used to pay interest to creditors (IC), and some may be used to pay dividends to stockholders (DC). The residual represents an increase in retained earnings (ΔRE). Hence, these different concepts of income are related as follows:

$$
\begin{array}{rl}
 & EI \\
 & -IC \\
\hline
= & OI \\
- & DC \\
\hline
= & \Delta RE
\end{array}
$$

We shall discuss entity income for the corporation later in this chapter.

The difference between these two approaches to income centers upon the treatment of creditors. Under the entity theory, interest to creditors as well as dividends to stockholders is a *distribution* of income—entity income is income before interest is deducted. Under the proprietary theory, interest is a *determinant* of income, interest being deducted from net revenues minus other expenses to arrive at income. This leaves only dividends as a distribution of income.

Partnership (and proprietorship) income is determined in accord with the proprietary theory. Since otherwise identical partnerships may have different capitalization structures (combinations of liabilities and owner-ship), comparisons of their proprietary incomes may be misleading because of differences in interest charges. The problem is easily remedied, however, given the fact that partnership income is not taxable to the partnership. By simply adding back the amount of interest charges for the period to the partnership income, one may arrive at entity income. Thus, if one wishes to see how the partnership *as an entity* performed income-wise during a period, the conversion can be made with little difficulty.

Treatment of factor returns to partners. Not so easily resolved is the question of accounting for factor returns to partners. To compute the income of the partnership, only those activities of its owners that are functionally related to the operation of the business may be considered—unrelated activities are excluded from the books of the business entity. On the other hand, the income of the partnership can only be determined after all expenses of operating the business have been deducted. These must include the expenses of all functions performed for the partnership by the owners themselves; from the point of view of the business, expense is related to the function performed, not to the identity of its supplier. The owners will ultimately receive the earnings of the partnership but as individuals they may serve the partnership in several capacities and, therefore, receive "factor incomes" as well. A partner may contribute the use of a building to the business and/or labor services as a manager or a salesman. The cost of these services should be deducted from revenue as rent and salaries and wages in determining the partnership's income just as it would be deducted if these services were performed by non-owners.

The problem of such expenses arises in determining their amounts. When the business purchases services from outsiders, the payment is generally determined in an open market or by arm's-length bargaining. The value assigned to services contributed by partners, on the other hand, is usually established by agreement among the partners themselves and as such may not reflect open market prices. Nevertheless, the expense to the partnership of such services is the amount that would have to be paid to outsiders for comparable services. An approximation to this expense can be obtained by determining the largest amount the partner could have obtained for the same services had they been performed for someone else (economists term this the "opportunity cost"). Thus, the rent of a building accountable as an expense to the business is the largest amount that the partner could have obtained by renting it to someone else. Ascertaining amounts of this kind with any degree of precision is clearly difficult. Once the amounts are established, however, the accounting entries to record them should follow the pattern established for other expenses. The income that results after the deduction of all expenses can then be distributed among the partners, as owners, in whatever ratio they have agreed upon. The individual who owns a share in the business may, therefore, receive payments from the partnership (1) for services rendered, i.e., as a supplier of factors of production, and (2) as a distribution of income, i.e., as part owner of the business.

In a great many cases the members of a partnership contribute approximately equal amounts of capital and render services to the partnership of approximately equal value (or at least the partnership agreement stipulates that they are of equal value). Under such circumstances there is little reason for the partners to concern themselves with what their compensation or interest on invested capital ought to be since it makes no difference in the division of partnership income. For this reason it is quite common for partners' salaries and interest on capital to be ignored and for the partnership to report an income figure that ignores the expenses associated with partners' services and capital contributions.

This tendency for partnerships to give little or no consideration in practice to the imputed expenses associated with the provision of managerial services and capital by partners in arriving at their income is encouraged by the income tax status of partnerships. For most income tax purposes, partnerships are treated as an aggregation of individual taxpayers rather than as a separate taxable entity. Partnerships as such pay no income taxes. Instead, they file an information return in which they disclose their revenues, expenses, income, and the amount of income allocable to each member of the firm. The tax on partnership income is then paid by the individual members of the firm who must include on their individual income tax returns their respective shares of the partnership income (*whether or not that income is actually distributed to them*). Interest paid to a partner for use of capital is not recognized as a deduction in computing the income of the partnership but rather is treated as a partial allocation of partnership income to that partner. Although partners' salaries are deducted on the partnership information return in arriving at partnership income, the partners do not report such amounts as salaries on their individual income tax returns but instead show the sum of their salaries and shares of partnership income as a single figure under the heading "Income from Partnerships."

Income Distribution in the Partnership

In the absence of any agreement, partners share profits or losses equally. An agreement, whether oral or written, is usual, however, so that the possible patterns for the distribution of profit are unlimited. The agreement should be carefully drawn to include provisions for salaries, interest, rent, and other elements of profit distributions, together with arrangements for withdrawing or contributing capital, adding new partners, selling a partnership interest, and providing for partnership dissolution. If an agreement is inclusive and unambiguous, it can be easily interpreted and applied in the accounts. Many of the problems of accounting for partnerships stem from loosely-phrased, incomplete, or nonexistent agreements. A good agreement minimizes a second difficulty also—the confusion of personal activities of the partners with those of the partnership. This problem arises whenever an owner in his or her capacity as an individual has dealings with or through the partnership of which he or she is also an owner.[3]

Because of the endless variety of possible distribution patterns, the distribution of income among partners can only be illustrated. Let us assume that Ashcraft and Bunch decide to form a partnership for the purpose of conducting a hardware business. Ashcraft is to contribute land and a building to be used as a store; Bunch is to contribute $20,000 in cash. It is agreed that Bunch, as manager, will be paid a salary of $12,000 annually while Ashcraft, who will work only part-time, will be paid $6,000. The partnership will pay Bunch an annual rental of $2,400 for use of a warehouse he personally owns. Partnership income, after deducting all expenses, will be divided in proportion to the balance in their capital accounts at the beginning of the period.

Let us assume that the land and building contributed by Ashcraft are correctly recorded at their current market values of $5,000 and $25,000, respectively. The journal entry to open the partnership books would be as follows:

Cash	$20,000	
Land	5,000	
Building	25,000	
Ashcraft, Capital		$30,000
Bunch, Capital		20,000

The accounting problems peculiar to partnership operation are related to the determination and distribution of partnership income as affected by (1) the dual nature of the partners (as both owners and suppliers of factors of production) and (2) the necessity of keeping a record for each partner of his or her total earnings from the business (whether partnership income or factor return) so that the balance in this account

3. We have seen that an owner may also be a supplier of factors of production. That owner may also be a customer. If he or she secures discounts that are not available to other customers, a record of the sale at the lower price transfers profit to the owner without its ever appearing on the records of the entity. If one partner does this extensively, that partner may secure a disproportionate share of the partnership's profits. Proper accounting procedures, if they are utilized, can prevent this.

can be included with any outside income in making up his or her personal income tax return. We need a record of partnership income for the business and a record for each partner of the taxable income derived from the enterprise.

The latter objective is accomplished by setting up a "drawing" or "personal" account for each partner. Credits to this account are made for factor returns (salaries, rent, and so on) as they accrue to the partner as well as for the partner's share of partnership income. Debits are made for actual withdrawals from the business (be they in the form of cash or noncash assets) and for the partner's share in partnership losses. Each drawing account includes, therefore, a record of the partner's total earnings from the business (factor returns plus share of partnership income—or minus share of partnership loss) which can be used for personal income tax purposes. At the end of the accounting period, the balance in the account represents the increase or decrease over the period in the partner's capital; the drawing accounts are, therefore, closed to the respective capital accounts at that time. Some illustrative entries for one 12-month accounting period follow which show that a meaningful statement of partnership income can also be derived.[4]

1. Salaries are recorded at the end of each month.

Salary Expense	$1,500	
Ashcraft, Drawings		$500
Bunch, Drawings		1,000

The credits record salaries as elements of individual earnings. The debit records them as expenses from the point of view of the business.

2. Ashcraft withdraws her total salary each month; Bunch withdraws $750 of his $1,000 salary each month. (Entries for withdrawals are made when the withdrawals occur, which may be *before* salary accrual, in anticipation of profit or as a withdrawal of capital itself depending upon the partnership agreement.)

Ashcraft, Drawings	$500	
Cash		$500
Bunch, Drawings	$750	
Cash		$750

3. Rent payable to Bunch is recorded monthly.

Rent Expense	$200	
Bunch, Drawings		$200

4. The revenue and expense data developed over the period and

---

4. The uniformity of the monthly entries below is not realistic. It is adopted only to conserve space.

grouped in the income summary account reveal a net loss of $3,000. This is distributed between the partners on the 60–40 relationship between their capital accounts at the beginning of the period.

Ashcraft, Drawings	$1,800	
Bunch, Drawings	1,200	
Income Summary		$3,000

5. The balances in the drawings accounts would now be closed to the respective capital accounts.

Ashcraft, Capital	$1,800	
Bunch, Drawings	4,200	
Ashcraft, Drawings		$1,800
Bunch, Capital		4,200

The drawings accounts of the two partners after these entries are shown in summary in Table 8-2. While Ashcraft's earnings generated by the business were only $4,200 (salary minus share of partnership loss), her cash withdrawals amounted to $6,000. The difference, $1,800, represents a withdrawal of part of her capital. Bunch's earnings generated by the business, $13,200, exceeded his cash withdrawals of $9,000 so that his equity in the partnership was increased by $4,200. The end-of-year capital balances would be: Ashcraft, $28,200 ($30,000 − $1,800); Bunch, $24,200 ($20,000 + $4,200). Thus, assuming no additional investments or disinvestments by either partner, next year's

TABLE 8-2

Ashcraft, Drawings

Withdrawals	$6,000	Salary	$6,000
Share of partnership		To Ashcraft, Capital	
loss	1,800	account	1,800
	$7,800		$7,800

Bunch, Drawings

Withdrawals	$9,000	Salary	$12,000
Share of partnership		Rent	2,400
loss	1,200		
To Bunch, Capital			
account	4,200		
	$14,400		$14,400

profit-sharing ratio would be about 54–46. The principal differences
between partnership income as we have construed it (treating factor
returns to partners as *determinants* of income) and partnership income
as commonly reported in practice (treating factor returns to partners
as *distributions* of income) are clarified in the tabulation that appears
in Table 8-3.

In both cases, the partners had total taxable earnings of $17,400.
Of this amount, Ashcraft's share was $4,200 (her $6,000 salary minus
her $1,800 share of the loss), while Bunch's share was $13,200 (his
$12,000 salary plus rent on his warehouse of $2,400 minus his $1,200
share of the loss).

These data reveal that in this instance the business was operated
at a loss; the revenues did not cover total expenses including factor
returns to partners. The partners as individuals secured earnings from
the partnership, but their earnings were less than they could have
earned by furnishing their services to someone else. Conversely, if they
had not provided the services themselves, they would have had to pay
salaries and rent to others for the equivalent services. They have been
forced to pay a price ($3,000 plus whatever interest they could have
earned on their capital accounts) for the privilege of operating their
own firm.

TABLE 8-3

	Partnership Income Statement with Factor Returns to Partners Treated as Determinants of Income		Partnership Income Statement with Factor Returns to Partners Treated as Distributions of Income	
REVENUES:				
Sales		$200,000		$200,000
EXPENSES:				
Cost of Goods Sold	$160,000		$160,000	
Salaries	18,000		-0-	
Rent	2,400		-0-	
Other	22,600	203,000	22,600	182,600
OWNERS' INCOME (LOSS)		($ 3,000)		$ 17,400
ALLOCATED TO:				
Ashcraft		($1,800)		$ 4,200
Bunch		(1,200)		13,200
		($3,000)		$17,400

It will be noted that no provision for income taxes has been made on the books of the partnership. Recall that the partnership itself pays no income taxes and the income taxes paid by each partner are an individual problem. Each must report for income tax purposes his or her total earnings from whatever the source; the earnings each has received from the partnership (Ashcraft, $4,200; Bunch, $13,200) may be only one element of his or her total earnings. The amount received from the partnership must be computed without regard to reinvestment in the enterprise; income is taxed whether or not the partner permits its retention in the business (Bunch must pay a tax on $13,200 although his cash withdrawals were only $9,000).

Limitations of the Partnership Form of Organization

Ideal for the small, easily liquidated business, the partnership form of business organization suffers from several defects which have become increasingly apparent in the modern era of big business where mass production, research, advertising, trademarks, and patents necessitate large accumulations of capital, more or less perpetual existence of the firm, and the organization of a management team composed of a relatively large number of highly skilled specialists. These defects are inherent in certain of the legal characteristics of the partnership: (1) mutual agency, (2) unlimited liability, (3) restrictions on transfer of ownership, and (4) limited life.

Mutual agency. Each partner is an agent of the partnership and as such may sign contracts and enter into agreements, without the knowledge or consent of co-partners, which are legally binding on the partnership. An individual partner's ability to bind the partnership in this way is, as a general rule, limited to agreements within the apparent scope of the business. For example, a partner in a retail lumber business can enter into agreements in the name of the partnership to purchase or sell lumber, borrow money, or hire new employees. But the partner, acting alone, could not bind the others to a contract to buy a carload of potatoes or to lend money to firms or individuals other than those with whom the partnership regularly did business.

Partners may agree among themselves to limit the rights of partners to negotiate certain kinds of contracts and specifically delegate such authority to one or more of the partner group. For example, one partner may be authorized to enter into purchase agreements, another given exclusive jurisdiction over sales contracts, and a third made solely responsible for managing the firm's finances. While such internal arrangements are binding upon the partners and upon outsiders who know of the agreement, they are not binding upon outsiders who are not aware of the agreement's existence. Outsiders dealing with the partnership have the right to believe that each partner has the normal agency rights of a partner unless they have been advised to the contrary.[5]

Mutual agency is a distinct disadvantage of the partnership form of business organization. It requires the exercise of extreme care in the selection of partners and thereby seriously limits accumulation of the large amounts of capital and specialized managerial talents essential to the conduct of large-scale business enterprises.

Unlimited liability. If a partnership suffers losses and the assets of the firm are insufficient to pay its liabilities, the creditors of the partnership may satisfy their claims out of the *personal* assets of the individual partners. In so doing the partnership creditors are not required to look to each of the partners for their pro-rata portion of the partnership debts but rather may press their entire claim against whichever of the partners seems most likely to be able to pay.[6] Although this rule may appear harsh, it is essential to the protection of partnership creditors because of the unlimited right of the partners to withdraw partnership assets (however, the partnership agreement may limit withdrawal powers of the partners vis-a-vis one another). Indeed, if it were not for this rule, it would be impossible for a partnership to obtain credit without the personal guaranty of one or more of the partners.

The unlimited liability of each general partner is an important defect of the partnership form of organization. To obtain the capital necessary to the conduct of large enterprises (such as General Motors or Exxon),

---

5. For example, *A*, *B*, and *C* form a partnership to engage in the wholesale jewelry business. Their agreement specifies that only *B* may enter into contracts for the purchase of goods for resale. *C*, without the knowledge of *A* or *B*, signs a contract with *X* Company to purchase $100,000 worth of diamonds. *X* Company has no knowledge of the special agreement among the partners. The partnership is bound by *C*'s contract with *X* Company. However, *C* is guilty of breaching the contract with *A* and *B* and may be liable to them if the partnership sustains a loss in disposing of the diamonds.

6. For example, suppose that *X*, *Y*, and *Z* form a partnership in which each invests $10,000 in cash with the understanding that profits and losses are to be shared equally. Operations are immediately unsuccessful and at the end of one year the firm has suffered losses of $50,000 with the result that the partners' capital contributions have been wiped out and the firm's liabilities exceed its assets by $20,000. *X* is a person of substantial means with extensive holdings of stocks, bonds, and real estate. *Y* and *Z* have invested their life savings in the partnership and have no other assets aside from the usual personal effects. The creditors of the partnership could, and undoubtedly would, require *X* to make good the entire $20,000 partnership deficit. *Y* and *Z* would then be liable to *X* for their respective one-thirds of the $20,000 but, since they are without assets, such claims would be of little value to *X*.

it is necessary to bring in thousands of "owners," most of whom have no effective voice in the conduct of the business. It would be virtually impossible to obtain investment funds from such absentee owners if their ownership of an interest in the business carried with it unlimited liability for the business firm's debts. As a matter of fact, many relatively small businesses, otherwise suitable for operation in partnership form, are deterred from organizing as partnerships because one or more of the owners is unwilling to be subjected to the risk of unlimited liability.

Restrictions on transfer of ownership. The mutual trust and confidence that necessarily characterize relations between partners (because of the rules of mutual agency and unlimited liability) make necessary another rule of partnership law—that no new partner may be admitted to the firm without the consent of *all* existing partners. This not only means that the concurrence of all the partners is necessary to the creation of a new partnership interest but that an existing partnership interest cannot change hands unless all of the partners consent to the admission of the transferee. Although a deceased partner's interest may be bequeathed to anyone that partner chooses and a living partner's interest can likewise be sold to the purchaser of that partner's choice, in either case the transferee does not acquire the right to participate in the firm as a partner but only to an accounting from the firm for the value of that interest. If the remaining partners are all agreed, the transferee may be admitted to the firm and effectively succeed into all of the rights of the transferor. If, however, one or more of the remaining partners is unwilling to admit the transferee into the firm, the transferee may require that his or her interest be liquidated. Many partnership agreements further restrict the transfer of interests by giving the remaining partners the right to buy the interest of a partner who retires from the partnership for any reason.

These restrictions on the transfer of partnership interests render investment in a partnership highly illiquid and limit expansion through the admission of a large number of partners. Unlimited liability for business debts plus the highly illiquid character of a partnership interest is enough to discourage the most intrepid investor.

Limited life. A partnership is based upon a contract, express or implied, whereby two or more individuals join together for the conduct of some kind of business. The partnership agreement may fix a definite future date for termination of the enterprise or, as is more often the case, provide for indefinite duration. In either event, however, the life of a partnership is limited. It may be terminated voluntarily by agreement of the partners or it may terminate automatically by operation of law in the event of death, withdrawal, bankruptcy, or proved incapacitation of *any* partner, or in the event a new partner is admitted to the firm. The fact that a partnership is automatically dissolved whenever any one of these events occurs does *not* mean that the business must be terminated and the partnership's assets (after payment of liabilities) divided among the partners. Those partners other than the one who died, withdrew, became bankrupt, or was judged incompetent, may, if they wish, form a new partnership and continue to carry on the business. However, the necessity of liquidating the interest of their former partner may require the disposition of assets essential to the conduct of the enterprise and make continuation a virtual impossibility. Clearly, the continuity of a partnership cannot be depended upon by suppliers, customers, creditors, or even the partners themselves; and the life of a partnership is likely to vary inversely with the number of partners involved, thereby seriously restricting growth of the firm both from the standpoint of capital requirements and the attraction of skilled management.

THE CORPORATION

As it is presently constituted, the corporation effectively remedies all of the defects inherent in the partnership. Ownership of corporate shares carries with it no right whatsoever to enter into binding agreements on behalf of the corporation. Instead, management of a corporation is vested in a board of directors, and the participation of shareholders in company affairs is limited to their right to elect the directors.

The liability of each owner is limited to the capital he or she has invested in the corporation; there are no restrictions on the transferability of ownership shares and, in most states, a corporation has a perpetual existence subject to the right of its shareholders to elect to terminate its existence. These advantages are gained by bequeathing to the corporation an existence separate and apart from that of its owners as a "legal entity" just as if it were a person. The separate states confer this privilege of corporate existence by the granting of charters to those who desire to operate a business in corporate form. The continuity of a corporation, together with the transferability of its ownership shares and the limited liability of its owners, facilitates long-range planning and long-term borrowing and makes possible the accumulation of huge amounts of capital by selling shares to the public without regard to the ability or integrity of the purchasers.

The advantages of the corporation are not obtained without certain disadvantages, however, It often happens with widespread stock ownership that the intimate relationship between the ownership and management of the firm vanishes. Management may become more interested in maximizing their salaries than in maximizing corporate income and dividends. In addition, the corporation must pay an organization fee to the state in which it is incorporated and an annual franchise tax, usually based upon the amount of its stockholders' equity, to all of the states having such taxes.

Undoubtedly, the greatest disadvantage in the corporate form of doing business is the taxation of corporate income. The incomes of a sole proprietorship or partnership, whether distributed to owners or not, are subjected to income tax only through their inclusion in the individual income tax returns of their owners. Corporate income, on the other hand, is subjected to a corporate income tax and, in addition, owners must include as taxable income on their personal tax returns that part of after-tax corporate income which is distributed to them in the form of dividends. This treatment has led to claims of "double taxation."[7] Congress has acknowledged these claims in token fashion with a provision exempting from taxation the first $100 of dividends received by each individual taxpayer.

In 1958, Congress took a new and interesting approach to the double-tax problem of the corporation by the addition to the Internal

7. As an offset, however, that part of corporate income that is retained in the firm is not taxed as a part of owners' incomes. When owners' incomes are in the upper tax bracket and considerable corporate income is retained in the firm, total taxes may be less under the corporate form than under the partnership. To the extent that income retained in the firm leads to an increase in the market price of the firm's stock, stockholders may benefit if they sell the stock at a gain and the gain is taxed at the lower long-term capital gains rate. This is because only 40 per cent of a gain qualifying for long-term capital gains treatment is subject to taxation to individuals.

To illustrate, suppose a firm has $100 in income and its owner is in a 70 per cent income tax bracket. If the firm is a proprietorship or a partnership, the $100 would be subject to taxation at the 70 per cent rate, or total income taxes of $70 would be paid by the owner (regardless of whether or not the $100 income was distributed or retained in the firm), leaving only $30. Now, suppose the firm is a corporation subject to a corporate income tax rate of, say, 40 per cent. The corporation would, in any event, have to pay income taxes of $40. If the remaining $60 is distributed to the owner, it would again be taxed at the owner's 70 per cent rate, thereby leaving $18. In such an event, clearly the proprietorship or partnership form would be preferable from the owner's point of view since the owner would have more left ($30) after taxes. However, suppose that instead of paying out $60 in dividends, the corporation retains the whole $60, thereby leading to a $60 increase in the market price of its stock. If the owner sells the stock at the higher price and the $60 gain is subject to long-term capital gains treatment, the owner will have to pay only $16.80 in taxes [.7 × .4 ($60)], thereby leaving $43.20 out of the original $100 of firm income. In this event, the owner should prefer the corporate form over either the proprietorship or the partnership.

Revenue Code of Subchapter S which permits certain corporations to elect to be taxed in a manner similar (but not identical) to that of partnerships. Corporations making the election under Subchapter S are no longer required to pay the corporate income tax. Instead, they file an information return setting out their revenues, expenses, and income and indicating the name and address of each shareholder and the amount of corporate income allocable to the stockholder by virtue of stock ownership. The shareholders then report their respective shares of the corporate income on their individual income tax returns in much the same way as partners do.

Certain restrictive features of Subchapter S limit its application to a relatively few corporations. In the first place, only corporations with ten or fewer shareholders are eligible to make the election. In addition, the law provides that no shares may be owned in trust, that all shareholders must consent to the election, and that new shareholders must file a formal consent to the election within a certain number of days after they acquire their stock. In the event that shares are transferred in trust or a shareholder fails to consent to the election, the corporation ceases to be a Subchapter S corporation retroactive to the first of the year. The law further provides that the income which had been taxed to the shareholders while the election was in effect but which had not been withdrawn prior to the automatic termination of Subchapter S status will be taxed again to the shareholders if and when withdrawn.

Investment in The Corporation

A corporation is organized and chartered in a particular state by one or more persons who become the firm's original stockholders. Among its primary provisions, the corporate charter specifies the classes of stock to be issued, the number of shares authorized in each class, and, if appropriate, the "par value" or "stated value" of those shares.

A corporation may issue one or more classes of stock. When only one class is issued, it is known as *common stock;* however, other classes, such as *preferred stock,* may be issued in addition to the common. When two or more classes of stock are outstanding, they are differentiated from one another in terms of the rights and privileges conferred upon stockholders. In brief, common stockholders have the right (1) to elect the board of directors of the corporation; (2) to participate in corporate profits as paid out in dividends by vote of the board of directors; (3) to participate in any asset distribution when the corporation is liquidated but only after all senior claims (liabilities, preferred stock) are first fully satisfied; and (4) in the absence of statute, charter, or bylaw to the contrary, to maintain their proportionate ownership interest in the corporation whenever new common stock is issued by means of their "preemptive rights." In essence, therefore, the common stockholders constitute the "residual equity" of the corporation and, as such, are the owners of the corporation much as are proprietors of proprietorships and partners of partnerships.

In contrast, preferred stockholders are a sort of hybrid between owners and creditors, their rights being in some respects akin to those of owners but in others being more like creditors. Preferred stockholders generally have preference over common stockholders in receipt of dividends and in return of their capital upon liquidation of the corporation, but both of these rights are subservient to those of creditors. Creditors must be paid all interest that has accrued to them before any dividends may be paid on preferred stock; likewise, in liquidation, creditors must be repaid fully all obligations due them before any assets may be distributed to preferred stockholders. Generally, preferred stock contracts provide for a stated rate of return (the preferred dividend rate) as well as a specified amount to be returned in event of liquidation (the liquidation value). Preferred stockholders typically have no voting rights in the corporation except in special circumstances, such as when their dividends are *in arrears* (when any or all of their regular dividends are omitted in a given year). Most preferred stocks are *cumulative* (all dividends in arrears from preceding years plus the current preferred dividend must be paid before any dividends can be paid on common stock) and *callable* (the corporation may redeem the preferred stock outstanding by the payment of a pre-determined price—the call price—which is usually set slightly higher than the issuance price). In addition, preferred stocks are frequently *convertible* (exchangeable at the option of the stockholder into common stock at some pre-determined ratio) and are occasionally *participating* (entitled to receive an extra dividend once common stock has been paid a dividend equal to the regular dividend on preferred). Clearly, preferred stockholders benefit from the cumulative, convertible, and participating features when offered, but not from a callable provision.

In many states, both common and preferred stock are required to have a *par value*. This requirement is intended for the benefit of the corporation's creditors by providing a "cushion" to absorb losses before impinging on creditor equities since corporate creditors have no recourse to the personal assets of the firm's owners, as do proprietorship and partnership creditors. When the par value per share is multiplied by the number of shares outstanding, the result is the corporation's *legal capital,* an amount from which dividends cannot be paid. Because par values in practice are usually set at quite minimal amounts, most shares are initially issued at prices considerably in excess of those amounts; however, when shares are issued at prices below par value, the stockholders generally may be assessed for the amount of the deficiency. As a consequence, disclosure of par value amounts in financial statements has meaning primarily when shares are issued at a discount, thereby indicating to shareholders the amount of their contingent obligations to the firm. Nevertheless, accountants as a rule routinely disclose par value amounts whether or not the shares were issued at a discount.

Not all states have par value requirements but instead permit corporations to issue *no-par* stock. But even in those states where such stock may be issued, often the stock must have a *stated value.* This amount, when multiplied by the number of shares issued and outstanding, produces what is known as the firm's *stated capital,* which is not subject to withdrawal by stockholders. For accounting purposes, there is little difference between the treatment of par value stock and no-par stock having a stated value.

Little difficulty is encountered in recording the issuance of stock for cash. Suppose, for example, that a corporation issues 100 shares of $10 par value common stock in exchange for $1,400. This investment transaction would be entered on the corporation's books in the following manner:

Cash	$1,400	
Common Stock—$10 Par Value		$1,000
Common Stock—Excess Over Par Value		400

Had the stock in the foregoing example had a $10 per share stated value rather than par value, the entries would have been the same except that the words "stated value" would have been inserted in place of "par value." In either event, it is important to note that *only by chance* would the market value of the stock be equal to its par or stated value.

When stock is issued in exchange for non-cash assets, the problem of accounting for such an investment becomes more complex. Suppose that a corporation received a tract of land in exchange for 1,000 shares of its $5 par value common stock. How would such an entry be recorded? Should the current market value of the land be imputed to the stock, or vice-versa? As a general rule, accountants in practice use the value of the item (land or common stock) which is more clearly evident and impute that value to the other. Thus, if the stock were not actively traded (therefore, its current market price were not readily determinable) but the current market value of the land acquired were found to be $8,000, the following entry would be made to record the investment transaction:

Land	$8,000	
Common Stock—$5 Par Value		$5,000
Common Stock—Excess Over Par Value		3,000

On the other hand, supposing that no current market value were available for the land but that the stock were being actively traded for $7 per share, then the imputed value of the land would be $7,000 (1,000 shares @ $7/share) and the following entry would be made:

Land	$7,000	
Common Stock—$5 Par Value		$5,000
Common Stock—Excess Over Par Value		2,000

As can be seen, a certain amount of subjective judgment on the part of the accountant enters into the picture when one value must be selected for imputation. The accountant's task becomes a particularly onerous one when neither item has a readily apparent market value.

In a corporation's position statement, the ownership section is usually titled "stockholders' equity." Even when several different classes of stock are outstanding, all issues are usually grouped under this heading; however, if both preferred and common are outstanding, it may well be desirable (because of the significant differences in the rights of the two classes) to separate them into separate sections, one titled "preferred stockholders' equity" and the other, "common stockholders' equity." As mentioned previously, preferred stock is essentially a hybrid, an amalgamation of certain aspects of both creditors' and owners' equities. Common stock, on the other hand, may be regarded as being strictly ownership in nature. Combining the two into a single section, therefore, is akin to mixing apples and oranges. When the two are separated, the equity side of a position statement would appear as in Table 8-4. Note that the retained earnings account is not apportioned between the preferred and common but rather is placed intact in the common section. This is because, in the absence of special circumstances, all income accrues to the residual equity holders—the common stockholders.

Income Determination in the Corporation

The income reported for a firm should not be altered by the form of organization adopted by the firm. Two firms that perform the same

TABLE 8-4

ILLUSTRATION OF THE EQUITY SIDE
OF A MODEL POSITION STATEMENT

EQUITIES
  Current Liabilities:
    Accounts Payable $XX
    Payroll Payable   XX
    Income Taxes Payable   XX
    Other   XX $XX

  Long-Term Liabilities:
    Bonds Payable $XX
    Less: Discount   XX $XX
    Income Taxes Payable   XX   XX $XX

  Preferred Stockholders' Equity:
    Preferred Stock:
      $100 Par Value $XX
      Excess Over Par Value   XX   XX

  Common Stockholders' Equity:
    Common Stock:
      $10 Par Value $XX
      Excess Over Par Value   XX $XX
    Retained Earnings   XX   XX
                                                          $XX

economic function and use identical asset structures with equal efficiency
should produce identical income figures. Present-day accounting practices often will not produce such results, however, for two reasons.

First, as applied to proprietorships and partnerships, conventional
accounting practices frequently result in a non-economic definition of
income because certain expenses—factor payments to owners—are not
usually deducted in the determination of income. We corrected for
such deficiencies by defining such factor payments as expenses so that
all factors of production (such as salaries and rent) were treated similarly,
regardless of whether they were provided to the firm by owners or
outsiders. For the most part, no similar problem exists in accounting
for corporations. If rent or salary payments are made to a stockholder
for factor services rendered, the amounts paid are simply treated as
expenses at the outset. Unless abused, the relationship to the corporation
of the recipient of such factor payments is irrelevant for either financial
reporting or income tax purposes.

The second reason stems from the treatment of interest to equity-providers (the creditors and owners). In present-day accounting practice, the proprietary theory is employed virtually universally to all forms of business organization—sole proprietorships, partnerships, and corporations alike—to the exclusion of the entity theory. As a consequence, payments made to creditors for the use of their capital are treated as expenses and deducted in the determination of income while similar payments to owners are treated as distributions of income. The same is true of taxable income as defined by the income tax laws. But the adoption of such a definition of income yields figures which are not comparable for different companies. Two firms which are identical in every respect except for their equity structures would report vastly different income figures if one existed largely on borrowed capital (creditor equities) while the other relied mainly on owner contributions (owner equities); what would be interest expense to one firm would be part of the reported income of the other. This difficulty is overcome if the firm's income is defined so that interest is treated as a distribution of income (rather than as a determinant of income), regardless of whether it is paid to creditors or owners. Entity income, therefore, has been defined throughout this text to include (1) interest paid to creditors, (2) dividends paid to stockholders, and (3) increases—or decreases—in retained earnings. In so doing, we have sacrificed economic theory for the sake of comparability. From an economic point of view, interest on capital provided is regarded as an expense of doing business, whether paid to creditors or owners, and *all* expenses must be deducted before arriving at economic profit. As a consequence, entity income as we have defined it is not equal to the economic concept of profit. However, because dividends include not only an interest element but also a profit element and because it is extremely difficult to differentiate between the two, we are forced to treat all interest as though it were an element in the distribution of income in order to achieve comparability among financial statements. (For further consideration of this matter, see the discussion of "Excess Current Income" in Chapter 11.)

Income Distribution in the Corporation

Equity structure. If the equity structure of the firm (i.e., the proportions and amounts of a firm's equities that derive from creditors and owners) is given, a part of the pattern of income distribution is also given. Interest payments to creditors are a fixed charge (they must be met if the firm is to remain solvent) so, in the short run, management can alter income to the firm's owners only by altering the entity income level itself. In the long run, however, management can determine these amounts by altering the equity structure of the firm. The effect of differing equity structures on the owners' rate of return is illustrated below:

	Corporation	
	Stock-Heavy	Debt-Heavy
Equities Contributed by:		
Creditors	$ 10,000	$ 90,000
Owners	90,000	10,000
	$100,000	$100,000
Entity Income before Income Taxes (15% on assets of $100,000)	$ 15,000	$ 15,000
Distributed to Creditors (at 8% interest)	800	7,200
Taxable Income	$ 14,200	$ 7,800
Income Taxes (40% of Taxable Income)	5,680	3,120
Ownership Income	$ 8,520	$ 4,680
Rate of Return on Owner's Equity	9.5%	46.8%

By "trading on the equity" (that is, operating with a large proportion of borrowed capital), the stockholders stand to increase the rate of return they earn on their investment because the rate of return earned by the firm ($15,000/$100,000 = 15%) exceeds the rate payable to creditors.[8] This advantage may accrue to the firm as an entity if management pays cash dividends at a given rate to stockholders; the

8. Note particularly that heavy indebtedness operates to the detriment of stockholders if the firm earns less than eight per cent on its total equities. For example:

	Corporation	
	Stock-Heavy	Debt-Heavy
Entity Income before Income Taxes (7.5% on assets of $100,000)	$7,500	$7,500
Distributed to Creditors (at 8% interest)	800	7,200
Taxable Income	$6,700	$ 300
Income Taxes (40% of taxable income)	2,680	120
Ownership Income	$4,020	$ 180
Rate of Return on Owners' Equity	4.5%	1.8%

larger the proportion of borrowed capital, the more income the firm can retain, so long as the firm earns at a rate in excess of the interest rate.

The determination of dividend payments. The amount and nature of dividends to be paid are also matters of financial policy. In the short run, both entity income and interest are given; but management controls cash dividend payments and, thus, the amount of ownership income to be retained in the business. This decision is sometimes reduced to a tradition, however, and a firm continues to pay a constant cash dividend per share or an established percentage of ownership income year after year. Genuine decisions regarding cash dividends are complex; they are inextricably bound up in the financing of expansion because the amounts paid out cannot at the same time be retained, and yet the issuance of new blocks of stock may be influenced by the amounts and regularity of past cash dividend payments.

The amount of a cash dividend also depends on the cash position of the firm. If sales have resulted largely in an increase in accounts receivable or if cash from sales has been used through the year to retire bonds or other liabilities or to purchase new plant, equipment, inventories, or other assets, the income of the firm will not be reflected by an increase in cash. On the other hand, if replacement of worn-out equipment is not undertaken during the year or if liabilities are run up and receivables are cut, an increase in cash may accompany a loss. Thus, the directors of a corporation cannot look solely at income in determining the amount of a cash dividend payment.

There are three significant dates with respect to cash dividends: the date of declaration, the date of record, and the date of payment. When the corporation's board of directors declares a cash dividend, at that instant the dividend becomes a current liability of the firm to its stockholders. This action is recorded by means of the following entry:

Common (or Preferred) Dividend Charges	XXX	
Common (or Preferred) Dividends Payable		XXX

The date of record occurs between the dates of declaration and payment. No entry is made on this date, but a listing of the owners of the corporation's stock is obtained at the close of trading on that date so as to identify who will receive the dividends. Only those persons owning shares on the date of record are entitled to receive the dividends when paid (on the date of payment). After the date of record the shares will trade "ex dividend," and their market price should fall by an amount equal to the dividend (assuming no other factors affect share prices). Finally, on the date of payment, the following entry is made:

> Common (or Preferred) Dividends Payable   XXX
> Cash   XXX

At the close of the accounting period, the dividend charges account is closed to the income summary account or, perhaps, directly to retained earnings.

If income is high but the cash position of the firm is low, the corporation may pay a *stock dividend*—the firm may give its stockholders additional shares of stock. The immediate effect of a stock dividend is nil. Total assets and equities of the firm are unaffected. Each owner holds the same relative share in the firm as before; the stockholder simply has more pieces of paper as evidence of that share. Each piece of paper reflects an ownership interest in a smaller asset value than it did just before the stock dividend was issued; therefore, the value of each piece of paper should be expected to fall. The issuance of such stock dividends may arouse the expectation, however, that future cash dividends per owner will rise; i.e., the same cash dividend per share of stock multiplied by a larger number of shares will yield a larger total.[9] Therefore, the value of a stockholder's shares in terms of the firm's assets is unchanged by the stock dividend, but the value of his or her holdings on the stock market may rise. Should the stockholder choose to convert a part of those holdings into cash, he or she does so only by reducing his or her percentage of ownership in the firm.

The accounting procedures for recording stock dividends are analogous to those for cash dividends with two major exceptions. First, the amount to be recorded for the dividend on the declaration date is dependent upon the magnitude of the dividend. For so-called "small stock dividends" (under 20 to 25 per cent), the amount to be recorded is equal to the current market value of the shares to be distributed, whereas for "large stock dividends" it is equal to the par or stated value of the shares.[10] Second, the dividend payable account is replaced

---

9. This line of reasoning is valid if the stock dividend is issued in lieu of a *cash* dividend, for the expansion made possible by the retained cash should increase the firm's profitability. If the stock dividend is paid in lieu of *no* dividend, the preceding argument holds. Taken by itself, however, a stock dividend simply adds to the slips of paper signifying ownership.

10. The rationale for this treatment is as follows. With a "small stock dividend," it is assumed that the same cash dividend rate per share will be maintained for the new shares as for the old; thus, the *per share* market price should remain unchanged and the *total* market value of the stockholders' holdings will increase, thereby resulting in benefit to the stockholder. A "large stock dividend," on the other hand, is assumed

by a "stock dividend to be distributed" account. Because the stock dividend will be "paid" by the distribution of new stock rather than cash, no liability results. Instead, the stock dividend to be distributed account remains in the stockholders' equity section and the total amount of stockholders' equity remains unchanged both before declaration and after payment.

The retention of earnings. The retention of earnings year after year is usually reflected by increases in the retained earnings account. To the uninformed this amount may appear to be available for cash dividend payments, and at many stockholder meetings the amount recorded in this account is used as an argument for larger cash dividends. The account, however, merely represents a form of ownership interest in the total assets of the firm; it does not indicate that the form of these assets is such that they could readily be used for cash dividend payments. It is more likely that the assets are necessary to the continued operation of the firm in much the same way that the original investments of the stockholders are necessary. Retained earnings indicates additional capital; it indicates nothing about the uses to which the capital has been put nor about its present availability for cash dividend payments.

In order to emphasize to stockholders that a large balance in the retained earnings account does not necessarily mean an equivalent ability to pay cash dividends, some corporations have taken the perhaps questionable step of establishing "reserves" out of retained earnings; i.e., they have earmarked portions of retained earnings to indicate the uses to which the corresponding assets have been or are expected to be put. Take the following entry as an example:

Retained Earnings	XXX	
Retained Earnings—Reserve for		
Bond Retirement		XXX

As the result of such an entry, unappropriated retained earnings on the position statement would be reduced and a reserve for bond retirement would be created. The latter should be shown in the common stockholders' equity section of the position statement as an appropriation or division of retained earnings in the following manner:

---

to be the equivalent of a *stock split* and the *per share* market price is expected to fall by an amount proportionate to the size of the dividend; thus, the *total* market value of the stockholders' shares is expected to remain unchanged, thereby resulting in no benefit to the stockholder.

Chapter 8

Retained Earnings:
  Reserve for Bond Retirement   XXX
  Unappropriated   XXX   XXX

The reserve account indicates only that a part of retained earnings
has been kept within the business for the purpose of retiring bonds
payable as they come due. Once the purpose for which the reserve
was established is completed (in this case, the bonds having been paid
off), the reserve is usually eliminated by an entry which reverses the
original entry that established the reserve, i.e.,

  Reserve for Bond Retirement   XXX
    Retained Earnings   XXX

Other types of retained earnings reserves that are encountered in
financial statements may include reserve for plant expansion, reserve
for redemption of preferred stock, and reserve for general contingencies,
to name but a few.

Appropriations of retained earnings by means of reserve accounts
are of dubious merit. No transaction has occurred; the board of directors
has simply ordered that a particular journal entry be made which
rearranges the components of ownership equity. The making of that
entry has in no sense earmarked any of the firm's assets but rather
is intended merely to communicate information concerning contingencies, debt covenants, expansion plans, and the like, any of which
may tend to limit future dividend payments. Such communications can
be accomplished much less ambiguously by means of notes or footnotes
to the financial statements. Notes to the statements provide the opportunity for complete explanation without the implication that something
has been "set aside" when, in fact, nothing but an accounting entry
has been made.

Reserves versus funds. All retained earnings reserves have one thing
in common—they do *not* indicate an accumulation of *funds* but rather
only the reason why the owners have been asked to invest additional
funds (by accepting cash dividends that are smaller than ownership
income) in the firm. Total assets less total liabilities have been increased
by a corresponding amount; but reserve accounts, no more than retained
earnings itself, do not necessarily indicate the specific form this increase
has taken. Thus, a reserve for bond retirement indicates a reason for
retaining earnings but does not indicate that cash is being accumulated.

If a firm wishes to accumulate monetary assets for bond retirement
or any other purpose, this can be done with or without a reserve account;
the accumulation of funds is a distinct and entirely different decision

and activity. Management can simply accumulate cash and other monetary assets in excess of immediate operating needs, keeping in mind the reason for doing so. Excess monetary assets may lead to demands for higher cash dividends or higher wage payments, however, so management will often make clear on the position statement the reason for accumulating such excess liquidity by listing certain assets as being held for a particular purpose. This segregation of assets is usually accomplished by adopting a new account title, say, fund for new plant construction. The actual assets making up a fund should be shown in a footnote to the position statement. In the case of bond retirement, the firm may make the following entry periodically:

Fund for Bond Retirement	XXX	
Cash		XXX

This may simply be an accounting entry, the cash remaining in a bank account together with the cash held for routine operations. Nevertheless, the purpose of indicating to stockholders and other interested parties that the cash being accumulated is not excessive is accomplished. On the other hand, the firm may actually appoint a trustee and transfer cash to the trustee's control to hold in whatever relatively liquid asset form that the trustee prudently chooses. However, unless the funds are actually deposited with a trustee and are out of the firm's control, there is little reason to set up a fund. As is the case with retained earnings reserves, communication can be better accomplished by means of notes to the financial statements.

Although of dubious merit in many cases, the establishment of a fund and the appropriation of retained earnings to a reserve account are intended to serve two different purposes, the first to accumulate liquidity for a specific purpose, the second to acquaint stockholders and others with the reason for retaining earnings regardless of the form of the corresponding assets. A special fund may be established without a special reserve; a reserve may be set up without a corresponding fund; on occasion both are introduced.

The term "reserve" should be restricted to appropriations of retained earnings. Frequently in the past and occasionally today, however, "reserve" has been used otherwise—to indicate contra-asset accounts and as a title for liability accounts. Thus, the allowance for depreciation account, which merely indicates the estimated amount of plant asset costs that have expired, is occasionally labeled "Reserve for Depreciation." In the past, some firms have made position statement interpretation more difficult by carrying this account on the credit side rather than as a deduction from plant assets, thus inflating both sides of the statement. A reserve for income taxes account is an example of a liability account incorrectly labeled; a reserve for accrued interest is another. Such accounts should be titled "Income Taxes Payable" and "Interest Accrued Payable." These inconsistent uses of the word "reserve" should be kept in mind in examining any position statement.

DISCUSSION QUESTIONS

1. a. Most firms in the professions—law, accounting, architecture, for example—have traditionally tended to prefer to operate as partnerships rather than as corporations. What factors *other than tax considerations,* both pro and con, influence them in this decision? Do you think that the non-tax advantages of a partnership form of organization are real or largely illusory? How about the disadvantages?

   b. Of course, tax considerations often *do* play a key role in deciding on the form of business organization to be adopted. If the corporate income tax rate is 50 per cent, if capital gains are taxed at half the personal income tax rate (i.e., only half of any long-term capital gain is taxed at the full personal income tax rate), and if the whole after-tax income is retained in a corporate structure and is reflected in proportionately higher stock prices, partners in what tax brackets would find it advantageous, from a *tax point of view,* to incorporate? Suppose the corporate income tax rate, t', were 40 per cent? [Hint: The tax on every dollar of a partner's earnings in a partnership would be t—based on the partner's tax bracket—while if incorporated, it would be t' (the corporate tax rate) $+ .5(1 - t')t.$]

   c. Considering (a) and (b) together, would taking advantage of the possibility of lower taxes (in the case of very high partnership incomes) through incorporation depend on giving up certain non-tax advantages of a partnership form of organization? Explain. (Hint: To take full advantage of the benefits of the capital gains tax, the securities must be "saleable," i.e., presumably traded on an open market somewhere.)

2. Three students—A (the artist), C (the capitalist), and S (the salesman)—decide to form a partnership, duly notarized, to sell paintings of campus scenes to the faculty and student body. A paints the scenes, working a total of 30 hours; C contributes the $600 needed to reproduce 1,000 copies; and S spends 100 hours of time selling them door-to-door. The students had expected to be able to sell

the reproductions for $2 apiece but quickly recognized that no one would buy them at this price and they ended up selling all 1,000 at $1 apiece. No agreement had been drawn up specifying wage rates, any specific return on capital for C, nor on the distribution of any income. A claims she can earn $10 an hour as a commercial artist and should receive at least $300. S claims he earned $4 an hour as a door-to-door salesman over the summer and he should receive at least $400. C says he put up the $600 knowing it was a risky venture and, given the riskiness of the venture, he should receive at least a 25 per cent return, or $150 over and above the $600 contributed.

a. How would you suggest resolving their difficulties?
b. How do you think a court of law might resolve their difficulties?
c. Draw up a partnership agreement that you think might have provided for a "fair" distribution of income (or division of loss) as between A, C, and S at the start of this venture.

3. If capital contributions accurately reflect current values in the market place and factor payments accurately reflect current values in the market place of factor contributions, surely the only fair way to distribute any income over and above factor payments (or divide losses) among partners is in proportion to their existing capital contributions (say, at the beginning of the period).

a. Would you agree or disagree with this statement. Why?
b. How could you apply the principles suggested by the statement to a case where Smith and Jones start a law practice with equal capital contributions of $10,000 each and they consider themselves, and are, equally capable as lawyers. Over the first three years income and drawings of the partners are as follows (with the excess of the former over the latter going largely toward office equipment):

	Year		
	1	2	3
Partnership Income	$60,000	$100,000	$120,000
Smith, Drawings	30,000	45,000	50,000
Jones, Drawings	15,000	20,000	20,000

Work is shared equally, but both partners agree, that Smith is far better at public relations and, in fact, is largely responsible for at least 75 per cent of the firm's total billings over the first three years.

4. If you were a doctor considering going into a small group practice with six other doctors, would you elect to form a partnership, a general corporation, or a corporation under Subchapter S of the Internal Revenue Code? Explain your preference.

5. A student named Shirley Harrison does not have a dime to her name, but she has developed—and has obtained a patent on—a remarkable new copier which is extremely cheap to construct and reproduces colors as well as black and white. If she can get $50,000 initial capital, she has every reason to expect that while it may take five years to gain market acceptance of her product, during which period she may suffer losses and may well be subjected to lengthy and costly suits by one or more firms currently in the copying field, eventually—say, after five years—she should be able to reap enormous profits from her invention. How would you suggest she go about raising the initial capital required? (Consider, among other things, the relative advantages and disadvantages of bonds, preferred stock, and common stock under these circumstances.)

6. Both R Company and S Company are in the toy manufacturing business and both have been in business for five years. Can you tell from the following information on long-term equities in their latest position statements which company has been more profitable during its first five years of existence? If not, what other information would you need? (Assume the comparison is to be made in terms of cumulative entity income.)

	R Company	S Company
Bonds Payable	$40,000,000	$20,000,000
Common Stock—$5 Par Value	10,000,000	15,000,000
Paid-in Capital in Excess of		
Par Value	15,000,000	20,000,000
Retained Earnings	2,000,000	7,000,000

7. As illustrated in the text (p. 334), "trading on the equity" has such obvious advantages for shareholders and/or company that it may appear surprising that the practice is not engaged in more extensively than it is. Can you suggest some reasons for caution? (Try out some alternative entity income figures in the example on p. 334, such as $10,000, $7,500, and $5,000.)

8. a. Which of the following companies do you think would be more likely to pay a cash dividend this year to shareholders, all other considerations being equal?

	X Company	Y Company
Ownership Income	$10,000,000	$15,000,000
Depreciation on Plant and Equipment	20,000,000	10,000,000
Increase in Accounts Receivable	6,000,000	15,000,000
Increase in Property, Plant and Equipment	35,000,000	30,000,000
Increase in Bonds Payable	20,000,000	15,000,000

b. If either the X Company or the Y Company foregoes a cash dividend this year but issues a stock dividend of $5 million while the other company issues a cash dividend of $5 million—and total shareholder equity amounts are the same in the case of the two companies—which company would you rather own stock in, or can you say?

9. Given the financial woes of the social security system in the late 1970s in the United States, it is obvious that any corporate official operating a company pension program should establish both a reserve account and an equal fund asset account which would be sure to accumulate to, with interest, actuarial estimates of expected pension payment obligations of the company's present labor force when these workers retire. To do anything less than this is irresponsible.

Do you agree? Are there perhaps reasons to think that present shareholders and present wage earners might disagree on this issue? Might a shareholder argue, for example, for establishment of a fund but not a reserve, or for neither perhaps, whereas a wage earner might prefer a reserve and not a fund or perhaps neither? Discuss.

PROBLEMS

8-1. McCosh Clothing Company

At the end of 19X0, the account balances of A. McCosh Clothing Company, a sole proprietorship, were:

ASSETS

Cash	$ 5,000
Accounts Receivable	17,000
Merchandise	30,000

Prepayments		9,000
Store Equipment	$14,000	
Less: Allowance for Depreciation	3,000	11,000
		$72,000

EQUITIES

Accounts Payable	$18,000
Accrued Liabilities	10,000
A. McCosh, Capital	44,000
	$72,000

Finding himself in need of larger quarters than those he was renting, McCosh approached McTavish, the owner of a large, vacant store building downtown. McCosh proposed that they form a partnership with McTavish investing his land and store building for a 40 per cent interest. An appraisal indicated the land was worth $10,000 and the building, $60,000. The property was subject to an 8 per cent mortgage of $45,000 which the partnership would assume. McTavish insisted that an allowance for bad debts be set up in the amount of $2,000 to cover doubtful accounts but agreed otherwise to accept all of McCosh's other book values as approximating fair market value. The partnership agreement was drawn up, McCosh and McTavish both invested their properties (McTavish also had to invest additional cash for his 40 per cent interest), and McCosh and McTavish Clothiers commenced business January 1, 19X1. McCosh closed the books for his proprietorship and a new set of books was opened for the partnership.

INSTRUCTIONS:

(a) Prepare journal entries to close McCosh's books.
(b) Prepare journal entries for the partnership's books to record the foregoing and prepare a position statement for the partnership as of January 1, 19X1.

8-2. McCosh and McTavish, Clothiers

Refer to problem 8-1. The year of 19X1 was a prosperous year for the new partnership. The following were the transactions for the year.

(1) Credit sales, $80,000; cash sales, $33,000.
(2) Collections on account, $77,000.
(3) Specific receivables written off as bad debts, $1,000.

(4) Purchases of merchandise on account, $60,000.
(5) Payments on account, $55,000.
(6) Selling expenses, paid in cash, $14,000.
(7) Administrative expenses (including annual mortgage interest), paid in cash, $9,000.
(8) At year-end, the balance in prepayments was $6,000 and in accrued liabilities, $12,000 (both charged to administrative expenses).
(9) Depreciation for the year: building, $4,000; equipment, $1,000.
(10) Estimated bad debts for the year amounted to two-and-a-half per cent of credit sales.
(11) A physical count of merchandise at year-end indicated a balance of $32,000.

In addition, the partnership agreement called for the payment of salaries to both McCosh and McTavish. McCosh, who worked full-time at the store, was to have a salary of $1,000 per month and McTavish, who worked half-time, $500 per month. Any remaining profits or losses were to be divided in the 60 per cent–40 per cent ratio. McCosh withdrew $800 per month and McTavish, $500.

INSTRUCTIONS:

(a) Prepare journal entries to record the foregoing and to close the books.
(b) Prepare a position statement as of December 31, 19X1.
(c) Prepare an income statement for 19X1 (1) treating factor returns as expenses and, thus, determinants of income and (2) treating factor returns as distributions of income.
(d) What is McCosh's taxable income for 19X1? McTavish's taxable income for 19X1?

8-3. *Finerty, Lefkowitz, and Oshima*

Finerty, Lefkowitz, and Oshima are partners in a retailing firm. The profit-and-loss sharing agreement calls for the following:

(1) Salaries of $8,000 and $12,000 annually are to be paid to Lefkowitz and Oshima, respectively, for their services. Finerty receives no salary.
(2) Rent of $18,000 annually is to be paid to Finerty for the use of his store building. Lefkowitz is to receive $2,000 per year for the use of a warehouse he owns.
(3) Each partner is to be paid ten per cent "interest" per year on the balance in his capital account at the beginning of the year.

(4) After the foregoing allocations have been made, any remaining profits or losses are to be divided among Finerty, Lefkowitz, and Oshima on a 40-30-30 basis.

At the end of the current year, the partnership's pre-closing trial balance (in condensed form), *before* any factor payments or distribution of income (normally these are entered in the accounting records only at the end of the year), appears as follows:

	Dr.	Cr.
Assets	$320,000	
Liabilities		$ 90,000
Finerty, Capital		110,000
Finerty, Drawings	15,000	
Lefkowitz, Capital		40,000
Lefkowitz, Drawings	25,000	
Oshima, Capital		70,000
Oshima, Drawings	20,000	
Revenues		410,000
Expenses (other than factor payments made to partners)	340,000	
	$720,000	$720,000

INSTRUCTIONS:

(a) Compute (1) entity income and (2) ownership income for the partnership for the year.
(b) Compute each partner's taxable income for the year.
(c) Determine the post-closing balances in each of the partner's capital accounts and prepare an end-of-year position statement.

8-4. Jones, Levy, and Brandt

Jones, Levy, and Brandt were partners in an accounting firm restructured on January 1, 19X1 at the time of Brandt's retirement. During 19X1 fee revenues were $200,000 and office expenses, $120,000. None of the revenues and expenses were the result of any transactions the partnership had with any of the individual partners.

The profit-and-loss-sharing agreement provides for the following:

(1) Jones, who works full-time for the partnership, is to receive an annual salary of $30,000. Levy, who works half-time, is to receive

$15,000. Brandt is retired and no longer works for the partnership but retains his capital interest in the firm.

(2) Brandt is to receive an annual rent payment for the use of his building in the amount of $18,000.

(3) Any remaining profits or losses are to be divided on the following basis:

Jones	40 per cent
Levy	40 per cent
Brandt	20 per cent

The credit balances in the partners' capital accounts on January 1 were as follows:

Jones	$50,000
Levy	50,000
Brandt	25,000

During the year, the partners each withdrew the following amounts in cash in anticipation of their share of the profits for the year:

Jones	$ 8,000
Levy	5,000
Brandt	16,000

No additional investments were made by any of the partners during the year.

INSTRUCTIONS:

Calculate the post-closing December 31 balances for each of the partners' capital accounts.

8-5. Cohen, O'Banion, and Schmidt

The partnership of Cohen, O'Banion, and Schmidt had the following profit-sharing agreement: (1) Cohen and O'Banion were each to receive monthly salaries of $1,000 while Schmidt received $500 monthly, (2) Schmidt was to receive rent on facilities he owned in the amount of $750 per month, and (3) any remaining profits or losses were to be divided among the partners in proportion to their capital account balances at the beginning of the year.

On December 31, 19X2, the partnership's account balances were as follows:

	Dr.	Cr.
Cash	$ 5,000	
Accounts Receivable	25,000	
Merchandise	15,000	
Buildings and Equipment	60,000	
Allowance for Depreciation		$ 20,000
Accounts Payable		15,000
Mortgage Payable		30,000
Cohen, Capital		10,000
Cohen, Drawings	8,000	
O'Banion, Capital		20,000
O'Banion, Drawings	17,000	
Schmidt, Capital		15,000
Schmidt, Drawings	10,000	
Sales Revenue		250,000
Cost of Goods Sold Expense	150,000	
Salaries Expense	15,000	
Depreciation Expense	10,000	
Rent Expense	-0-	
Other Expenses	45,000	
	$360,000	$360,000

No entries have yet been made to record partners' salaries, rent, and shares of remaining profits or losses. Withdrawals of cash during the year by partners have been recorded by debits to the drawing accounts.

INSTRUCTIONS:

Prepare journal entries allocating profits or losses pursuant to the partnership agreement and prepare closing entries.

8-6. *Loper and Lopez*

When the partnership of Loper and Lopez was formed, the following profit-sharing agreements were made:

(1) Monthly salaries were to be $1,000 for Loper and $500 for Lopez.
(2) Lopez was to receive $700 per month rent for use of the building he owned.
(3) The first $10,000 of any remaining profits or losses were to be

divided equally among the two partners, and the rest was to be divided in proportion to their capital account balances at the beginning of the year.

(4) Salaries and rent would not be accounted for or paid until the end of the year, but the partners could withdraw cash during the year. These withdrawals would be recorded as debits to the drawing accounts.

On December 30, 19X3, the partnership's account balances were as follows:

Cash	$ 10,000	
Account Receivable	25,000	
Merchandise	15,500	
Building and Equipment	50,000	
Allowance for Depreciation		$ 5,000
Accounts Payable		12,000
Notes Payable (long-term)		23,000
Loper, Capital		10,000
Loper, Drawings	6,000	
Lopez, Capital		20,000
Lopez, Drawings	7,200	
Sales Revenue		200,000
Cost of Goods Sold Expense	100,000	
Wages Expense	15,000	
Salaries Expense	-0-	
Depreciation Expense	2,500	
Rent Expense	-0-	
Other Expenses	38,800	
	$270,000	$270,000

No transactions with outsiders were made on December 31.

INSTRUCTIONS:

(a) Prepare the necessary December 31 journal entries to account for salaries, rents, and allocation of profits or losses to the partners according to the agreement, and prepare closing entries.

(b) Prepare a position statement as of December 31, 19X3.

(c) Prepare a statement showing (1) entity income and (2) ownership income for 19X3.

8-7. McCosh and McTavish, Inc.

Refer to Problem 8-2. On January 1, 19X2, the partners decide to incorporate their business. A corporation charter is secured from the state which authorizes the issuance of 25,000 shares of $10 par value stock. Each partner is issued the appropriate par value amount of stock in accordance with his respective capital account, and all assets and liabilities of the partnership are transferred to the corporation. On January 1, 3,000 shares of stock are sold to outsiders for $30,000.

INSTRUCTIONS:

(a) Prepare journal entries to close the partnership's books.
(b) Prepare journal entries to open the corporation's books, and prepare the stockholders' equity section of the corporation's position statement as of January 1, 19X2.

8-8. McKinnon and Tanaka

Two entrepeneurs, McKinnon and Tanaka, decide to embark upon an automobile dealership together (selling new Yahama cars), with McKinnon putting up all of the estimated capital requirement of $100,000 and Tanaka agreeing to run the dealership in return for a $10,000 salary and 20 per cent of the profits, with the remaining 80 per cent going to McKinnon. They are in the process of deciding whether to form (a) a partnership, (b) a regular corporation, or (c) a Subchapter S corporation and are looking into tax considerations and other matters involved in this decision. Their best estimate of before-tax income for the dealership in the first five years is that it will average $250,000 a year. The two men agree that if they form a corporation and either wants out for any reason, he must sell his shares of stock (divided 80 per cent and 20 per cent between the two) at the then prevailing book value; they agree further that $50,000 of the firm's income is to be left in the firm each year for the first five years, the retained earnings thus increasing the book value of the stock of a corporation. The increase in book value if sold would then be subject to the capital gains tax of one-half the capital gain taxed at each man's personal income tax rate. Assume that income from the dealership is all the income each man earns, that any firm income over and above the $50,000 to be retained, after all firm taxes are paid, is to be distributed to the two men divided 80 per cent and 20 per cent, and that personal income tax rates are:

Income	Tax Rate
$20,000–$34,999	30%
$35,000–$49,999	40%
$50,000–$64,999	50%
$65,000–$79,999	60%
>$80,000	70%

The corporate income tax rate is 20 per cent on the first $50,000 of income and 45 per cent of all income above that figure.

INSTRUCTIONS:

(a) If each man wishes to maximize his after-tax income over the five-year period, can they agree on a form of organization? What will be the annual after-tax income of each under each of the three possible forms of organization suggested above?

(b) What are the principal factors other than tax considerations that might influence the preference of each man with respect to form of organization?

8-9. *Speedtreck and Electroscopic (I)*

Two firms in a "hot" new electronics field have grown rapidly in the last few years. Speedtreck Corporation, a closely held firm, financed its growth by issuing bonds; Electroscopic Corporation financed its growth with retained earnings, issues of new stock, and the payment of stock rather than cash dividends. The financial positions of the two firms today are as follows:

Speedtreck Corporation

Assets	$1,000,000	Current Liabilities	-0-
		8% Bonds Payable	$ 800,000
		Common Stock—$100 Par Value (2,000 shares issued & outstanding)	$ 200,000
		Retained Earnings	-0-
	$1,000,000		$1,000,000

Electroscopic Corporation

Assets	$1,000,000	Current Liabilities	$ 200,000
		6% Preferred Stock—$100	

	Par Value (cumulative and convertible*; 4,000 shares issued & outstanding)	$ 400,000
	Common Stock—$100 Par Value (3,000 shares issued & outstanding)	$ 300,000
	Retained Earnings	100,000
$1,000,000		$1,000,000

*Electroscopic's preferred stock is convertible into common stock on a share-for-share basis at the option of the preferred stockholder.

Both firms are subject to a corporate income tax rate of 40 per cent.

INSTRUCTIONS:

Compare the rates of return to the holders of (1) Speedtreck's bonds, (2) Speedtreck's common stock, (3) Electroscopic's preferred stock, and (4) Electroscopic's common stock under each of the following assumptions:

(a) Each firm has entity income of $250,000.
(b) Each firm has entity income of $5,000.

8-10. *Speedtreck and Electroscopic (II)*

Refer to Problem 8-9. Assume that Speedtreck and Electroscopic each earned entity incomes of $150,000, $30,000, $10,000, $75,000, and $125,000 over the next five years and distributed all after-tax income available to common shareholders after making due provisions for bondholders and preferred shareholders, with the bondholders of Speedtreck paid the interest due them sach year and the preferred shareholders of Electroscopic paid dividends on their cumulative preferred stock whenever this was earned.

INSTRUCTIONS:

Prepare a schedule showing entity income, ownership income, and the rate of return per share of common stock for each firm over the five-year period. The schedule should show the companies' distribution policies.

8-11. *Madisonville Manufacturing*

The Madisonville Manufacturing Company has among its position statement accounts the following "reserves" (each has a credit balance):

Reserve for Income Taxes
Reserve for Depreciation
Reserve for Warranties Outstanding
Reserve for Future Plant Expansion
Reserve for Bad Debts
Reserve for General Contingencies
Reserve for Bond Retirement
Reserve for Sales Returns and Allowances
Reserve for Risks Not Covered by Insurance
Reserve for Restoration of Leased Properties
Reserve for Sales Discounts Outstanding
Reserve for Reduction of Inventories from Cost to Market
Reserve for Vacation Pay
Reserve for Expropriation of Foreign Assets
Reserve for Future Inventory Price Declines

INSTRUCTIONS:

(a) For each account, identify the nature of the account and its likely location on Madisonville's position statement.

(b) For each account that is inappropriately titled, provide a title that better reflects the nature of the account.

CHAPTER 9

PRODUCING THE BASIC FINANCIAL STATEMENTS

THE LAST SEVERAL CHAPTERS have been concerned wtth *inputs* to the accounting system. In this chapter, we return to a consideration of *outputs,* the financial statements. In Chapters 2 and 3, we analyzed the fundamental principles of double-entry theory and demonstrated with the two traditional statements (the income statement and the position statement) the fundamental relationship that exists between income and change in position over a period. Each describes events over the period in a different way but in a manner that depicts, because of double-entry theory, a fundamental consistency between ownership income, on the one hand, and changes in assets minus liabilities, on the other. At the same time we discussed in those chapters the formulation of a third statement, the funds statement, which would provide additional but different information on events of the period. The earning of income, which is the fundamental objective of the business enterprise, is not necessarily synonymous with augmentations of cash, or liquid funds, as we saw in the simple example in Chapter 2.

Since the introductory chapters, which dealt with finished statements and double-entry theory, we have explored the workings of the accounting system itself and considered in greater depth several of the major components of financial statements—inventory and plant assets as well as creditor and owner equities. It seems appropriate at this juncture, therefore, to tie together these diverse topics and, in so doing, to introduce a widely-used accountants' tool, the worksheet. Before getting into these matters, however, let us try to put a little perspective on the end-products that will be generated.

It has become common in business terminology to think and talk in terms of the extent to which such-and-such an activity will generate a "cash flow," loosely meaning—usually—an increase in liquid funds. From here it is but a short step to thinking that changes in the liquidity position of the enterprise, as shown in the funds statement, are more important than the earning of income, as shown in the income statement. The funds statement, however, while an important *adjunct* to the income and comparative position statements, is just that—indeed, as we shall see, it proves to be simply an embellishment and reorganization of the two traditional statements. By viewing operations from a somewhat different perspective, the funds statement adds in important ways to our total knowledge of the functioning and performance of the enterprise. In fact, most income that is earned generates additional funds; indeed, the funds supplied by operating activities normally exceed income because one key expense, depreciation, does not use up funds. But what becomes of those funds, how they are supplemented by other sources of funds (through sale of assets, new borrowing, and so on), and how the total funds thus generated are used or applied (to pay interest and dividends, to replace existing assets or purchase new ones, or to call long-term liabilities, for example) is important supplementary information needed for a full appraisal of business performance. Changes in liquidity have attracted special attention in recent years in part because of the difficulties some firms have had in replacing assets which have gone up in price. Does income generate sufficient funds to "maintain capital"? This is a matter which we shall get into in some detail in Chapters 11–13. Suffice it for now to say, the earning of income is still the *primary* aim of business enterprises; the generation of funds is largely, directly and indirectly, dependent upon it (one cannot normally borrow or obtain new ownership capital unless projected income justifies it); and, thus, the income statement is still the key measure of performance (the funds statement a supplementary measure of use in evaluating liquidity considerations connected with performance).

Let us then start with the income and position statements, and the worksheet used to generate them, and then turn to a modified worksheet and see how it is used to fashion a statement of sources and applications of funds.

The Worksheet for Income and Position Statements

In order to prepare financial statements as soon as possible after the end of an accounting period and to avoid errors in the formal adjusting and closing process, the accountant usually performs all of the necessary work in an informal fashion first. This is done by use of a worksheet, a columnar tool of the accountant which is used to bring together in a systematic manner the data needed to adjust the accounts and prepare the financial statements. The worksheet, then, serves as the basis for drawing up the financial statements and making the formal adjusting, closing, and reversing entries. Use of the worksheet *does not* obviate the making of any of these entries in the books.

The worksheet appears in many different forms, shapes, and sizes. Perhaps the most common form, a ten-column affair, is shown in Table 9-1. The first two columns contain the December 31, 19X1 "Unadjusted Trial Balance" of the Jameson Company. In the second pair of columns, "Adjusting Entries" (involving accruals, prepayments, and depreciation) are entered in the debit and credit columns and are identified with letters (a), (b), and so on, to indicate the two aspects of each adjustment. Later, these adjusting entries will be recorded in the journals and posted to the ledgers the same as other entries. The explanations of the adjustments on the Jameson Company worksheet are as follows:

(a) To record the $1,600 estimated bad debts that are expected to occur as a result of sales made during 19X1.
(b) To record $1,400 of wages that have accrued but are unpaid as of December 31, 19X1.
(c) To record $800 of supplies on hand at year-end.
(d) To record estimated depreciation of $3,000 on buildings and equipment for the year.
(e) To record estimated patent amortization of $1,000 for the year.
(f) To record $200 of interest that has accrued and remains unpaid at year-end.
(g) To record estimated income taxes for 19X1 of $8,100.

Once these adjusting entries are made, we have (by summing horizontally the rows across our worksheet), in effect, *adjusted* trial balances for almost all the ledger accounts. If we think back to the work with the fundamental accounting equation in Chapters 2 and 3, and the process of accumulating data in ledger accounts in Chapter 4, we will recognize that the ledger balances after adjusting entries contain amounts that either go to the firm's position statement (all account balances for assets and equities) or to the firm's income statement (all account balances involving revenues and matching expenses as well as the gain on sale of equipment and interest and dividend charges).

But one further set of adjusting and closing entries must still be made before we can continue with this process. In the third pair of columns, headed "Cost of Goods Sold Expense," are entered the adjusted account balances that pertain to the computation of cost of goods sold.[1] The merchandise inventory of $18,100 at January 1, 19X1 (to which no adjustments have been made) is transferred laterally to the cost of goods sold expense debit column. Purchases and freight-in, which when combined with the beginning inventory represent the cost of goods available for sale, are likewise transferred laterally to the cost of goods sold expense debit column. The only other data required for the computation of cost of goods sold is the December 31, 19X1 ending inventory. This is determined by actual count (a physical inventory) and pricing of the goods on hand at the end of the year. The amount, $19,500, is entered in the cost of goods sold expense credit column and also in the position statement debit column. By entering the same amount in the position statement debit column, the heretofore unrecorded asset, merchandise inventory at December 31, 19X1, is introduced into the space reserved for position statement data. The cost of goods sold expense columns now reflect the cost of goods sold as the difference between the total of the debit column (goods available for sale during the year) and the total of the credit column (goods not yet sold at year end).[2]

Now debit and credit balances in asset and equity accounts other than merchandise inventory can be moved rightward to columns 9 and 10, thus comprising, with the ending inventory already there, the fundamental ingredients for the position statement. The columns for cost of goods sold expense show a debit balance of $64,100 and consist of beginning inventory plus purchases and freight-in minus ending inventory. A credit entry in the cost of goods sold expense columns at the bottom (column 6) balances these columns, and a debit entry for cost of goods sold expense in column 7 (depicting expenses related to the income statement) effectively enters this figure in the income statement columns as an expense. Other revenue and expense items, as well as interest and dividend charges and the gain on sale of equipment, are transferred laterally across the worksheet to columns 7 and 8, which then contain all the items needed for our income statement. The credit balance of $9,900 in this pair of columns is, then, the change in retained earnings. The fundamental check tells us that this should be reflected also by a debit balance of $9,900 in our position statement columns;

1. It should be recognized that this pair of columns is necessary only when a periodic inventory system is in use.
2. If the Jameson Company had accounts for purchase returns and allowances, they, too, would be entered in the cost of goods sold credit column.

TABLE 9-1
JAMESON COMPANY
WORKSHEET FOR INCOME AND POSITION STATEMENTS
For the Year Ended December 31, 19X1

Account Titles	Unadjusted Trial Balance Dr.	Cr.	Adjusting Entries Dr.	Cr.	Cost of Goods Sold Expense Dr.	Cr.	Income Statement Dr.	Cr.	Position Statement Dr.	Cr.
Cash	$ 12,700								$ 12,700	
Marketable Securities	20,900								20,900	
Accounts Receivable	36,400								36,400	
Accts. Rec.—Allowance for Bad Debts		$ 800		(a) $1,600						$ 2,400
Merchandise Inventory	18,100				$18,100	$19,500			19,500	
Supplies Inventory			(c)$ 800						800	
Prepayments	7,300								7,300	
Investment in Brompton Company	16,400								16,400	
Land	13,600								13,600	
Buildings & Equipment	73,100								73,100	
Bldgs. & Equip.—Allow. for Depr.		15,000		(d) 3,000						18,000
Patents	9,000								9,000	
Patents—Allow. for Amortization		3,000		(e) 1,000						4,000
Accounts Payable		30,900								30,900
Wages Payable				(b) 1,400						1,400
Interest Accrued Payable				(f) 200						200
Income Taxes Payable				(g) 8,100						8,100
Bonds Payable		70,000								70,000
Preferred Stock—$100 Par Value		15,000								15,000
Preferred Stock—Excess over Par Value		5,000								5,000
Common Stock—$10 Par Value		10,000								10,000
Common Stock—Excess Over Par Value		20,000								20,000
Retained Earnings		14,800								14,800
Sales Revenue		138,000						$138,000		
Interest Revenue		1,200						1,200		
Gain on Sale of Equipment		3,600						3,600		
Purchases	63,700				63,700					
Freight-In	1,800				1,800					
Wages Expense	42,000		(b) 1,400				43,400			

TABLE 9-1 CONTINUED
JAMESON COMPANY
WORKSHEET FOR INCOME AND POSITION STATEMENTS
For the Year Ended December 31, 19X1

Account Titles	Unadjusted Trial Balance Dr.	Unadjusted Trial Balance Cr.	Adjusting Entries Dr.	Adjusting Entries Cr.	Cost of Goods Sold Expense Dr.	Cost of Goods Sold Expense Cr.	Income Statement Dr.	Income Statement Cr.	Position Statement Dr.	Position Statement Cr.
Supplies Expense	3,100			(c) 800			2,300			
Miscellaneous Expense	3,800						3,800			
Interest Charges	1,800		(f) 200				2,000			
Preferred Dividend Charges	600						600			
Common Dividend Charges	3,000						3,000			
Sales—Bad Debts			(a) 1,600				1,600			
Depreciation Expense			(d) 3,000				3,000			
Patent Amortization Expense			(e) 1,000				1,000			
Income Tax Expense			(g) 8,100				8,100			
	$327,300	$327,300	$16,100	$16,100		$19,500				
Cost of Goods Sold Expense to Income Statement						64,100	64,100			
					$83,600	$83,600	$132,900	$142,800		
Increase in Retained Earnings to Position Statement							9,900			9,900
							$142,800	$142,800	$209,700	$209,700

assets at the end of the period should exceed equities at the end of
the period by the amount of any *increase* in retained earnings. And
indeed this proves to be the case. A *debit* for increase in retained earnings
at the bottom of column 7 and a *credit* for increase in retained earnings
at the bottom of column 10 effectively balance out the income statement
and position statement columns, and we have, from the worksheet,
all the needed ingredients for the two finished statements. Needless
to say, a net *debit* balance before this final entry in the income statement
columns and a net *credit* balance in the position statement columns
would have indicated a decrease in retained earnings over the year
and would have to be represented by a balancing credit entry at the
bottom of column 8 and a debit entry at the bottom of column 9.
In terms of journal and ledger, the total increase (decrease) in retained
earnings entries on the worksheet would be reflected by transferring
the balance in the income summary account, which includes interest
and dividend charges and the gain on sale of equipment, to the retained
earnings account and balancing this out.

THE FINISHED PRODUCTS: PREPARATION OF THE INCOME AND POSITION STATEMENTS

The construction of financial statements from worksheet data is a
relatively simple task. All that needs to be done is to consider how
best to present the data collected in the worksheet: (1) what sort of
rearrangement to make in the ordering of data; (2) what accounts
should be combined (in practice, the worksheet is detailed and complicated; but in our simple case, which has relatively few accounts, each
may be displayed individually); (3) what changes, if any, should be
made in descriptive titles; and (4) what new balances, sub-totals, and
the like, should be included in the firm's statements which are not
formulated on the worksheet. When drawing up statements prescribed
by regulatory authorities, such as the Securities Exchange Commission,
the Interstate Commerce Commission, or the Federal Power Commission, the accountant, of course, has no latitude. When not restricted
by external regulations, however, the accountant must and should use
good judgment in statement preparation.

The financial statements which can be prepared are shown in Tables
9-2 and 9-3. These particular statements might be considered model
statements although the form they take may vary considerably, some
presentations being considered better than others. In earlier chapters,
we discussed what we believe to be good presentation format; thus,

further discussion at this point is unwarranted. However, we have introduced two elements in the statements in Tables 9-2 and 9-3 that have not appeared in previous chapters and which we should briefly consider before turning our attention to the topic of the funds statement.

Intrastatement Income Tax Allocation

In the Jameson Company's income statement, income taxes appear not in one place (as in all our previous illustrations) but in three different locations: (1) as an expense, (2) as a reduction of the gain on sale of equipment, and (3) as a reduction of the interest charges. The Jameson Company actually accrued tax liabilities during the year amounting

TABLE 9-2

JAMESON COMPANY
INCOME STATEMENT
For the Year Ended December 31, 19X1

REVENUES:			
Sales	$138,000		
Less: Sales—Bad Debts	1,600	$136,400	
Interest		1,200	$137,600
EXPENSES:			
Cost of Goods Sold		$ 64,100	
Wages		43,400	
Depreciation		3,000	
Supplies		2,300	
Patent Amortization		1,000	
Miscellaneous		3,800	
Income Taxes		8,000	125,600
OPERATING INCOME			$ 12,000
GAINS AND LOSSES ON ASSETS:			
Gain on Sale of Equipment		$ 3,600	
Less: Applicable Income Taxes		900	2,700
ENTITY INCOME			$ 14,700
Interest Charges		$ 2,000	
Less: Applicable Income Tax Savings		800	1,200
OWNERSHIP INCOME			$ 13,500
Preferred Dividend Charges			600
Income to Common Stockholders			$ 12,900
Common Dividend Charges			3,000
INCREASE IN RETAINED EARNINGS			$ 9,900

TABLE 9-3
JAMESON COMPANY
POSITION STATEMENT
As of December 31, 19X1

ASSETS

Current:			
Cash		$12,700	
Marketable Securities		20,900	
Accounts Receivable	$36,400		
Less: Allowance for Bad Debts	2,400	34,000	
Merchandise Inventory		19,500	
Supplies Inventory		800	
Prepayments		7,300	$ 95,200
Investments:			
Investment in Brompton Company			16,400
Plant:			
Land		$13,600	
Buildings & Equipment	$73,100		
Less: Allowance for Depreciation	18,000	55,100	68,700
Intangibles:			
Patents		$ 9,000	
Less: Allowance for Amortization		4,000	5,000
			$185,300

EQUITIES

Current Liabilities:			
Accounts Payable	$30,900		
Income Taxes Payable	8,100		
Wages Payable	1,400		
Interest Accrued Payables	200	$40,600	
Long-Term Liabilities:			
Bonds Payable		70,000	$110,600
Preferred Stockholders' Equity:			
Preferred Stock:			
$100 Par Value		$15,000	
Excess Over Par Value		5,000	20,000
Common Stockholders' Equity:			
Common Stock:			
$10 Par Value		$10,000	
Excess Over Par Value		20,000	$30,000
Retained Earnings		24,700	54,700
			$185,300

to $8,100, as shown on the worksheet; these consisted of ordinary income taxes of $7,200 and a capital gains tax of $900. But because we treat interest charges as a distribution of income rather than as an expense in arriving at income, we must compute the tax attributable to operating income *before* interest charge deductions and then treat the smaller tax that must actually be paid because interest charges are deductible in computing corporate income taxes as a *saving* or a reduction in interest charges. Thus, total taxes of $8,100 are broken down in accordance with the above divisions as $8,100 = (1) $8,000 + (2) $900 − (3) $800. These computations can be further explained as follows.

In Jameson's case, we have assumed that the applicable corporate tax rate on ordinary income is 40 per cent and on capital gains, 25 per cent. Furthermore, we have assumed that all items appearing on its 19X1 income statement are subject to tax in the same year, thereby removing the need for interperiod income tax allocation. It can be seen that, without taxes, Jameson's operating income would have been $20,000 (net revenues of $137,600 less expenses other than income taxes of $117,600). Thus, given the tax rate on ordinary income of 40 per cent, the applicable income tax on Jameson's operating income would be $8,000. Likewise, without considering income taxes, the gain on the sale of equipment would have added $3,600 to income, but this gain has been assumed to be subject to the capital gains rate of 25 per cent; hence, an additional $900 of taxes stems directly from the gain, leaving a net-of-tax gain of $2,700. Finally, since Jameson's interest charges are deductible on its tax return as an expense (subject to the ordinary income tax rate of 40 per cent), $800 of income tax has been saved as a direct consequence of the $2,000 interest deduction [40% ($2,000) = $800]. Looking at it another way, without the interest deduction, Jameson would have had to pay $8,900 in income taxes. Similarly, if Jameson had not had both the interest and the gain, its income taxes (on operating income alone) for 19X1 would have been $8,000. Thus, application of the intrastatement income tax allocation procedure has resulted in the apportionment of Jameson's $8,900 of taxes for 19X1 to the components that gave rise to that amount, while, since interest is a deductible expense for federal income tax purposes, the saving thereby engendered of $800 on interest charges yields the net result that a total of $8,100 in taxes was paid during the year.

The purpose of the intrastatement allocation procedure ostensibly is to assist statement users in making predictions of an entity's future results. Given expectations as to whether or not the gain will recur in future years or if Jameson's future interest burden will be increased or decreased, users can better determine what Jameson's after-tax income will be in subsequent periods. Because of the perceived benefit that accrues to statement users as a consequence of intrastatement income tax allocation, this procedure is routinely employed by accountants.

Intangible Assets and Amortization Expense

Another new element, having to do with patents and their related amortization, appears in Jameson's financial statements. Patents are classified on the position statement under the heading of "Intangibles," which generally appears as the last category among the assets. This category is reserved for those noncurrent, nonmonetary assets that have an economic, but not a physical, existence. Their values lie in the advantages or rights that they bestow upon their owner. Examples of items typically falling into this category include trademarks, copyrights, franchises, and patents.

The process by which intangibles are written off as expenses is known as *amortization,* which is analogous to depreciation for plant assets. An intangible, such as a patent, has both a legal and an economic life. The legal life of a patent is the 17–year period that the federal government grants the owner of the patent the exclusive right to manufacture and sell a particular product or use a specific process. Its economic life is usually shorter than its legal life, however, because the demand for the product may dissipate long before 17 years have passed, frequently because newer patents have rendered the older patent obsolete. Thus, the effective useful life of a patent is the shorter of its legal life or its economic life. The straight-line method is generally used for amortizing a patent's cost over its effective useful life. In the Jameson Company example, we have assumed that the patent cost $9,000 and is being written off using the straight-line method over a nine-year life.

THE NATURE AND IMPORTANCE OF THE FUNDS STATEMENT

We touched upon the nature of the funds statement at the end of Chapter 2 and again at the beginning of this chapter. The relationship (or apparent lack thereof) between reported income of the period and changes in cash, net current monetary assets, and net working capital (total current assets less current liabilities) over the same period, which was noted in Chapter 2, is frequently misunderstood. The accountant who presents to statement users an income statement showing substantial income is frequently asked the question, "Where is it? What happened to it? The firm's liquid assets have deteriorated yet your statement says that it made money. What is wrong?" The accountant should point out that not all income is necessarily produced in liquid form and, to the extent that it is, these monies may have been used to purchase new equipment, to retire long-term debt, or to pay dividends to stockholders. In order to provide statement users with a complete explanation of what happened to the liquid resources available to the firm during the year, however, it is customary to add to the income statement and position statement a third basic statement on the firm's sources and applications of funds. As already indicated, such a statement should in no way be thought of as a substitute for the other two statements nor, we believe, should it be thought of as any more important than the other two statements. It simply provides in a useful format additional information on the firm's behavior and performance.

The precise definition of "funds" and the format for a "sources and applications of funds" statement are not matters on which all accountants can agree.

The Cash Approach

In its narrowest interpretation, funds may be regarded simply as cash (on hand and in demand accounts at banks); in this context, a funds statement would be nothing more than a statement of cash receipts and disbursements. This interpretation has been generally rejected by accountants because its use is limited primarily to short-run planning (cash forecasting, in particular), a matter of lesser importance to top management and parties external to the firm than longer run considerations with respect to net current monetary assets or net working capital. Moreover, a statement of cash receipts and disbursements, being encumbered with details, is often an unwieldy document from which to glean general perspectives regarding the firm as a whole. Finally, cash is frequently subject to short-term fluctuations stemming from uneven collections of receivables or payment of payables. As a result, an interpretation of funds as cash is of little utility except to those persons charged with the responsibility for the firm's cash management.

The Net Current Monetary Asset Approach

Another possible interpretation is to define funds somewhat more broadly as the firm's net monetary items. However, because monetary items may often include noncurrent accounts, such as bonds payable, that may be of little import in the firm's short-, intermediate-, or even long-run plans, this definition is generally narrowed to net *current* monetary items, i.e., to net current monetary assets (current monetary assets less current monetary liabilities). This approach has much to commend it and is the one we prefer. It avoids the narrowness objection to the cash approach by including those "near-cash" items, such as accounts receivable and payable, yet focuses directly upon the firm's liquidity, an essential element to any interpretation of funds. Moreover, net current monetary assets are generally subject to less fluctuation than is cash; therefore, relatively unimportant aberrations stemming from whether a sale was made for cash or on account are avoided. Finally, this interpretation of funds avoids several of the shortcomings of the other, broader interpretations that we shall discuss below. However, this approach does suffer from a serious deficiency in that the concept of net current monetary assets is not one widely understood by statement users. Of course, any concept that is not widely understood is not widely used.

The Net Working Capital Approach

For many years, the most widely accepted interpretation of funds among practicing accountants was that of net working capital, current assets less current liabilities. A primary advantage of this approach is that the concept of net working capital is widely understood by statement users. In fact, many firms array their position statements in such a fashion as to focus upon net working capital. Usually, such a statement is set up in the following manner:

> Current Assets
> − Current Liabilities
> = Net Working Capital
> + Noncurrent Assets
> − Long-Term Liabilities
> = Ownership

This approach also squares nicely with the accountant's accrual procedures and, as such, ties in nicely with the other financial statements. The net working capital approach suffers, however, from a serious deficiency that stems from its broadness. By including nonmonetary current assets and liabilities in the definition of funds, an inventory build-up will create the impression of enhancing the firm's liquidity which, of course, may not be accurate, particularly if the inventory is slow-moving. Indeed, many firms that have let their inventories build up to excessive levels have found themselves in difficult financial straits because the money that otherwise could have been used to pay their bills as they came due was tied up in inventories. We believe that any definition of funds should reflect a firm's liquidity, and for this reason we would reject the net working capital approach even though for many years it was widely accepted among practicing accountants.

The "All Financial Resources" Approach

Despite its apparent shortcomings, the net working capital interpretation of funds has been rejected by the accounting profession in favor of an even broader view, that of "all financial resources." The reason for rejecting the net working capital approach appears to stem from its failure to take account of transactions such as the acquisition of noncurrent assets for such equity securities as common stock. Because this kind of transaction would technically neither increase nor decrease net working capital, it would not be disclosed on a net working capital funds statement in a strict interpretation of such a statement. Similarly, a transaction in which bonds payable were converted into common stock would not appear in such a funds statement. The accounting profession apparently was of the view that in substance such transactions were merely "telescoped transactions," essentially no different from those in which, say, common stock was sold for cash and the cash was used to purchase noncurrent assets or to redeem outstanding bonds payable. In our view, the term "all financial resources" has never been adequately defined; it appears to be a combination of the net working capital approach plus "telescoped transactions."

Putting aside a strict cash approach for reasons suggested above, we can illustrate our other two options with respect to the definition of "funds"—net current monetary assets versus net working capital (generally net current monetary assets plus inventories and prepayments)—and our option on format (a narrow approach limited to sources which actually gave rise to funds and applications which actually used funds versus the all-inclusive approach) by one central example for the Jameson Company. We will use our preferred definition of "funds" as being net current monetary assets but will show how this could readily be extended to the more widely used net working capital concept, i.e., net current assets. And we will utilize the now generally accepted "all-inclusive approach" but will show, by footnoting "telescoped transactions," how this could be readily altered to the narrower approach.

THE WORKSHEET AND THE FUNDS STATEMENT

A funds statement can be derived from a worksheet in a manner similar to that of income and position statements. In fact, our starting point is a comparative position statement yielding assets and equities at the beginning and end of the period and, thus, changes in assets and equities over the period. We know that (ignoring additional direct investments or disinvestments by owners)

$$\Delta A - \Delta L = \Delta RE,$$

where RE is retained earnings. If we now divide assets and liabilities into current monetary assets and liabilities, labeling the difference as "funds" $(\Delta A_F - \Delta L_F)$, on the one hand, and other (non-fund, or NF) assets and liabilities, on the other, we have

$$\Delta A_F + \Delta A_{NF} - \Delta L_F - \Delta L_{NF} = \Delta RE, \text{ or}$$
$$\Delta A_F - \Delta L_F = \Delta RE + \Delta L_{NF} - \Delta A_{NF}. \tag{9.1}$$

On the left, positive elements (an increase in fund assets or a decrease in fund liabilities—both of which would be *debits*) indicate increases in funds, and negative elements (a decrease in fund assets or an increase in fund liabilities—both of which would be *credits*) indicate decreases in funds. For example, an increase in accounts receivable, by itself, represents an increase in funds; an increase in wages payable, by itself, represents a diminution of funds.

The right-hand side of equation (9.1) is thought of as sources and applications of funds. Positive elements (an increase in retained earnings and/or non-fund liabilities and/or a decrease in non-fund assets—all of which are *credits*) are *sources* of funds. Funds have, as a first approximation, been increased by income from operations retained in the business and/or new issues of, say, bonds, and/or the sale of, say, land. Negative elements (a decrease in retained earnings and/or non-fund liabilities and/or an increase in non-fund assets—all of which are *debits*) are *applications* of funds. Funds have been decreased by losses on operations (expenses requiring use of funds exceeding revenues contributing funds) and/or repurchasing outstanding bonds and/or the purchase of, say, equipment.

If the comparative position statement is organized along these lines, as we have done in the first two columns of the worksheet shown in Table 9-4, the changes then derived in columns 3 and 4 comprise a first approximation of a funds statement. The total of debits minus credits above the dotted line indicates the increase (+) or decrease (−) in Jameson's funds over the year. The total of credits below that line indicates the firm's sources of funds, while the total of debits below the line indicates uses or applications of funds. Sources (credits) less applications (debits) below the line must equal any increase in funds (debits minus credits) above the line; if applications (debits) exceed sources (credits) below the line, there must be a net decrease in funds (credits exceed debits) shown above the line. This follows from the fact that overall debits must equal credits—position statements must balance. If we added up the totals in the "changes" for the Jameson Company, we would find:

	Sources of funds (credits below the dotted line)	$40,600
less	Applications of funds (debits below the dotted line)	39,300
equals	Increase in funds (debits minus credits above the dotted line)	$ 1,300

While such a statement could, mechanically, be shown to provide some sort of explanation for the $1,300 increase in funds (as compared with the $9,900 increase in retained earnings), we can formulate a much more intelligible and informative funds statement by making certain adjustments, such as are given in the third pair of columns in the middle of the worksheet.

The necessary adjustments in this simple illustration are three in number. First, we *expand* the change in retained earnings by crediting and debiting the various components that were shown on the income statement to yield the change in retained earnings (see Figure 9-1). The excess of credits over debits inside the box [the entries labeled (a)] of Figure 9-1 just equals the $9,900 increase in retained earnings. Hence, the adjustment labeled (a) in the adjustments column of the worksheet merely substitutes the *components* of the change in the retained earnings for the single aggregate figure.

		Dr.	Cr.	
	Sales and Other Revenues		$137,600 (a)	
less	Expenses	$125,600 (a)		
equals	Income from Operations			$12,000
plus	Gain on Sale of Equipment		2,700 (a)	
equals	Entity Income			14,700
less	Interest and Dividend Charges	4,800 (a)		
equals	Change in Retained Earnings			9,900

Figure 9-1

TABLE 9-4

JAMESON COMPANY

WORKSHEET FOR FUNDS STATEMENT

For the Year Ended December 31, 19X1

| | Dec. 31 19X0 Dr. (Cr.) | Dec. 31 19X1 Dr. (Cr.) | Changes | | Adjustments | | Funds Statement | | | |
| | | | | | | | Net Changes in Funds | | Applications | Sources |
			Dr.	Cr.	Dr.	Cr.	Dr.	Cr.	Dr.	Cr.
Cash	$ 9,700	$12,700	3,000				$3,000			
Marketable Securities	22,100	20,900		$ 1,200				$1,200		
Accounts Receivable	32,800	36,400	3,600				3,600			
Accounts Receivable—Allowance for Bad Debts	(2,000)	(2,400)		400				400		
Accounts Payable	(29,300)	(30,900)		1,600				1,600		
Wages Payable	(1,100)	(1,400)		300				300		
Interest Accrued Payable	(600)	(200)	400				400			
Income Taxes Payable	(5,900)	(8,100)		2,200				2,200		
Merchandise Inventory	18,100	19,500	1,400						$ 1,400	
Supplies Inventory	900	800		100						$ 100
Prepayments	6,800	7,300	500						500	
Investment in Brompton Co.	13,400	16,400	3,000		(c) $5,700				3,000	
Land	11,600	13,600	2,000						2,000	
Buildings and Equipment	60,700	73,100	12,400						18,100	
Bldgs. & Equip.—Allowance for Depreciation	(16,400)	(18,000)		1,600	(b) 3,000					
Patents	9,000	9,000				(c) $1,400				
Patents—Allowance for Amortization	(3,000)	(4,000)		1,000	(b) 1,000					

TABLE 9-4 CONTINUED

JAMESON COMPANY

WORKSHEET FOR FUNDS STATEMENT

For the Year Ended December 31, 19X1

	Dec. 31 19X0 Dr. (Cr.)	Dec. 31 19X1 Dr. (Cr.)	Changes Dr.	Changes Cr.	Adjustments Dr.	Adjustments Cr.	Net Changes in Funds Dr.	Net Changes in Funds Cr.	Applications Dr.	Sources Cr.
Bonds Payable	(90,000)	(70,000)	20,000						20,000	
Preferred Stock—$100 Par Value	-0-	(15,000)		15,000						15,000
Preferred Stock—Excess Over Par Value	-0-	(5,000)		5,000						5,000
Common Stock—$10 Par Value	(8,000)	(10,000)		2,000						2,000
Common Stock—Excess Over Par Value	(14,000)	(20,000)		6,000						6,000
Retained Earnings	(14,800)	(24,700)		9,900	(a) 9,900					
	-0-	-0-	$46,300	$46,300						
Sales and Other Revenues						(a) 137,600				137,600
Expenses					(a) 125,600				125,600	
Gain on Sale of Equipment					(c) 2,700	(a) 2,700				
Dividend and Interest Charges					(a) 4,800				4,800	
Expenses Not Requiring Funds						(b) 4,000				4,000
Funds Received from Sale of Equipment (net of taxes)						(c) 7,000				7,000
					$152,700	$152,700		$5,700	$175,400	$176,700
Increase in Funds								1,300	1,300	
							$7,000	$7,000	$176,700	$176,700

The second and third adjustments amend the expanded sources and applications of funds arrived at following the first adjustment to eliminate all credits not involving the receipt of funds and all debits not involving the application of funds. Inspection of the "revenues" section reveals that all revenues either brought in cash or gave rise to receivables, i.e., they all increased funds—no sales revenues were earned, for example, by exchanging goods for stock in another company, or for some other nonmonetary asset, such as inventories. Inspection of the expenses section indicates that all expenses *except two* involved an application of funds, i.e., were paid for by cash or gave rise to current payables. The two expenses which did not decrease funds are depreciation expense on buildings and equipment ($3,000) and the amortization of patents ($1,000). Our first "mechanical" approximation of a sources and applications of funds statement included as credits allowances for depreciation and amortization which were, therefore, treated as sources of funds [although the allowance for depreciation on buildings and equipment was a netted figure, involving a reduction in the allowance on equipment which was sold, as well as amounts still in the ledger on buildings and equipment held at the end of the period (see below)]. And, in a way, these allowances *were* a source of funds—they appear under the allowance for depreciation and amortization categories because these expenses were deducted from revenues in arriving at entity income and the change in retained earnings whereas they did not really involve a *use* of funds. The items making up the increase in retained earnings are understated as a source of funds, and that understatement is in the allowance for depreciation and amortization items. Better, then, to credit these amounts ($3,000 depreciation expense plus $1,000 amortization expense equals $4,000) in our grouping of operating items in the lower part of the worksheet (below the dotted line) and debit the allowance for depreciation and allowance for amortization lines to cancel, in effect, the credits there. This is accomplished through adjusting entry (b). Funds provided by operations were not the $137,600 sales minus $125,600 expenses equals $12,000 but rather the $137,600 sales minus $121,600 of funds used equals $16,000.

Our third and last adjustment (c) involves reinterpreting the funds obtained from sale of equipment. A check of our records shows that the journal entry describing this sale was as follows:

Cash	$7,900	
Buildings and Equipment—		
Allowance for Depreciation	1,400	
Buildings and Equipment		$5,700
Gain on Sale of Equipment		3,600

On this gain we paid a capital gains tax of $900, which was deducted from the gross gain to arrive at the gain (net of taxes) of $2,700 used in computing entity income and change in retained earnings. The funds (net of taxes) received actually amounted to $7,000, but this fact is essentially hidden in our original data by incorporating it in the three items—buildings and equipment—allowance for depreciation (as a debit of $1,400 there), buildings and equipment (as a credit of $5,700 there), and the gain on sale of equipment (net of taxes) (as a credit of $2,700 there). Better, then, to reverse these entries in our adjustments columns and enter the net amount of funds received in one place below. This adjustment is accomplished by the four items marked (c) in the fifth and sixth columns.

None of our adjustments altered the residual of sources and applications of funds which explained the $1,300 increase in funds found in our first mechanical approximation in columns 3 and 4. The adjustments merely expanded and reinterpreted sources and applications to provide more meaningful information. We are now in a position to sum laterally columns 3, 4, 5, and 6 in order to obtain data for a schedule of changes in funds (using the figures above the dotted line in our worksheet) and a schedule of sources and applications of funds (using the data below the dotted line), the two together comprising the funds statement shown in Table 9-5.

Our worksheet is flexible and can be adapted to any kind of conceptualization of the funds statement desired. If, for example, we use our broader definition of funds and interpret changes in funds as changes in net working capital (as indicated, the generally accepted interpretation but not one we would choose for a funds statement), we simply draw the single line in our worksheet below inventories and prepayments, thus including this net increase as an increase in funds rather than as an application of (the narrower definition of) funds. The net increase in funds generated by sources less applications would then be $3,100 rather than $1,300. We prefer an approach more geared to changes in the firm's liquidity, and increases in inventories and prepayments may well not be liquid.

Similarly, we could easily adapt our worksheet to yield a narrower or stricter funds statement rather than the all-inclusive format shown. We would simply enter adjustments [say (d) and (e)] in our middle pair of columns, which effectively deletes the stock issues, the purchase of bonds payable, and the additions to investment in the Brompton Company—all of which did not strictly involve sources and uses of funds because they involved direct exchanges of noncurrent assets and liabilities (see footnotes to Table 9-5). Thus, we would debit in column 5 Preferred Stock—$100 Par Value for $15,000(d), debit

TABLE 9-5
JAMESON COMPANY
FUNDS STATEMENT
For the Year Ended December 31, 19X1

SOURCES:

From:	Operations	$16,000	
	Sale of Equipment (net of taxes)	7,000	
	Issuance of Preferred Stock	20,000[1]	
	Issuance of Common Stock	8,000[2]	$51,000

APPLICATIONS:

To:	Net Increase in Inventories	$ 1,800	
	Repurchase of Bonds Payable	20,000[1]	
	Purchase of Brompton Investment	3,000[2]	
	Purchase of Land	2,000	
	Purchase of Buildings and Equipment	18,100	
	Payment of Interest (net of taxes)	1,200	
	Payment of Preferred Dividends	600	
	Payment of Common Dividends	3,000	49,700

INCREASE IN FUNDS (See Supporting Schedule) $ 1,300

JAMESON COMPANY
SCHEDULE OF CHANGES IN FUNDS
For the Year Ended December 31, 1971

	Dec. 31 19X0	Dec. 31 19X1	Increase (Decrease)
CURRENT ASSETS:			
Cash	$ 9,700	$12,700	$3,000
Marketable Securities	22,100	20,900	(1,200)
Accounts Receivable (net)	30,800	34,000	3,200
	$62,600	$67,600	$5,000
CURRENT LIABILITIES:			
Accounts Payable	$29,300	$30,900	$1,600
Wages Payable	1,100	1,400	300
Interest Accrued Payable	600	200	(400)
	$36,900	$40,600	$3,700
Income Taxes Payable	5,900	8,100	2,200
FUNDS	$25,700	$27,000	$1,300

1. The newly issued $20,000 in preferred stock was exchanged directly for bonds payable and, thus, did not strictly give rise to funds nor was the repurchase of the bonds strictly an application of funds. The two offsetting items are included here as if they involved funds for purposes of completeness.

2. Of the $8,000 in new common stock issued, only $5,000 actually directly involved receipt of new funds; $3,000 in new common stock (involving $750 par value and $2,250 excess over par value) was exchanged directly for the purchase of new investment in the Brompton Company. As above, the two offsetting items are included here as if they involved funds for purposes of completeness.

Preferred Stock—Excess over Par Value for $5,000(d), and credit Bonds Payable in column 6 for $20,000(d). And we would debit in column 5 Common Stock—$10 Par Value for $750(e) and Common Stock—Excess over Par Value for $2,250(e), while crediting in column 6 Investment in Brompton Company for $3,000(e). Our funds statement, then, would not include these items as sources and uses of funds.

It goes without saying, but perhaps better with saying, that our worksheet in reality may be considerably more complicated than shown here. But more extensive adjustments and/or a more complicated initial change in position statement will not alter the principles to be followed. The adjustments simply involve asking oneself whether or not the changes shown on the comparative position statement adequately portray sources and applications; if not, adjustments must be entered in such a way that sources and applications are portrayed in a more meaningful fashion.

Conclusions

The three basic statements are mutually compatible and complementary, and there are interrelationships in their formulation and in their interpretation. The Jameson Company did earn operating income of $12,000, which generated additions to funds of $16,000. Yet only $1,300 in (our concept of) funds were generated *in toto* over the year. In fact, Jameson generated considerably more than the $16,000 funds reported from operations—through sale of equipment and, if the all-inclusive approach is used, through substantial amounts of newly issued stock. But Jameson did not sit idly by simply accumulating liquid funds. Its initial liquidity position was deemed satisfactory. (Its initial current ratio was 2.3 to 1 and its initial "quick" ratio 1.7 to 1.) It, therefore, used much of its accumulation of funds for new activities which it thought would generate more income than interest on marketable securities. Nonmonetary assets costing $23,900 were acquired and the long-term debt of $20,000 was retired over the year. It paid its interest charges, and it paid dividends on common stock of $3,000, amounting to ten percent of the book value of the stock at the end of the year. Its current ratio at the end of the year was the same as at the beginning, 2.3 to 1, and its "quick" ratio was down only slightly, to 1.6 to 1. Whether or not Jameson's use of its accumulated funds was in accord with stockholder wishes or, indeed, even wise, is not known. But clearly the fact that the increase in funds was substantially less than income is no cause for alarm from a financial point of view. However, this is not always the case.

Discussion Questions

1. The owner of a taxi company argues:

   The "bottom line" on the basis of which I judge the performance of my managers is cash flows or funds generated, not
   income. It is increases in cash flows which determine how
   many taxicabs I can have in the field at any given time and,
   thus, how many more funds can be generated and, thus,
   in the end, how many dollars I can take out in dividends.

   His accountant argues:

   But, sir, if our taxis are driven harder in order to generate
   more funds, they will wear out more quickly. If the increase
   in depreciation exceeds the increase in funds generated
   (hence, in effect, income is lower), we are worse off. Our
   funds position is important, but the "bottom line" has got
   to be income.

   Discuss the relative merits of the two positions.

2. The text suggests that a worksheet involves simply the carrying
   through to final statement form the essential logic of double-entry
   accounting theory, which we first met in Chapter 2 and put into
   bookkeeping practice in Chapter 4. Review in your mind the essential
   aspects of double-entry theory as applied in the accounts and explain
   clearly why this approach leads, with unfailing logic, to the finished
   income and position statements, as exemplified in the worksheet
   tabulation (Table 9-1).

3. a. How would the worksheet for income and position statements
      of the Jameson Company (Table 9-1) be affected if an internal
      audit performed at the time the worksheet was drawn up showed
      the following errors in Jameson's records:
      (1) Accounts receivable amounting to $900, which had been
          written off as bad debts in 19X1, were eventually collected
          but were never recorded as collected;
      (2) Accounts payable amounting to $7,000, which were listed in
          the books as having been paid, had, in fact, not been paid;
      (3) While the final inventory count "proved" the ending inventory
          figure of $19,500, purchases recorded as received and paid
          for amounting to $8,000 had evidently never been received
          or paid for.
   b. Since the audit showed that Jameson's cash position was as recorded
      and all other ledgers were correct, what can you surmise has

happened? What recommendations might you as the internal auditor make with respect to internal controls in the Jameson Company?

4. Suppose the president of the Jameson Company, for whatever reasons, wanted to show either a higher or a lower ownership income figure for 19X1. What might be the principal options available to him to accomplish his wish, given present "generally accepted accounting principles"? Would an external audit necessarily force the company to disclose what it had done to alter reported income? Explain.

5. The principal rationale for reporting a separate figure for entity income on a company's income statement is to have an income figure which is independent of the way in which a company finances its assets, thereby making earnings comparisons among companies easier when one wishes to compare earnings from operations (as a ratio to total assets, for example). How does the intrastatement income tax allocation procedure practiced by the Jameson Company further this entity income report objective? Explain.

6. Which of the following events, had they occurred in 19X1, would have affected the reported increase in funds shown on the Jameson statement (Table 9-5), by how much, and why?
   a. purchase of an option to buy a new land site for possible future expansion, in exchange for $2,000 cash;
   b. purchase of the land in exchange for $3,000 cash and a $27,000, 20-year mortgage;
   c. the granting of stock option rights to the president of the Jameson Company to reward his service to the company—the option involving the right to purchase 500 shares of Jameson stock from the company at $20 a share (current market value $40);
   d. the exercise of these stock option rights by Jameson's president;
   e. a decision to use double-declining-balance depreciation on new buildings and equipment purchased in 19X1 over their ten-year life rather than the straight-line depreciation originally contemplated and used in Table 9-5;
   f. a decision to switch from FIFO to LIFO which reduces to zero the net increase in inventories figure in Table 9-5.

7. How would your answers to Question 6 be altered, if at all, if Jameson employed (a) an "all-inclusive net working capital" funds statement approach or, alternatively, (b) the narrower approach to a net current monetary asset funds statement as opposed to the all-inclusive approach?

8. Suppose the president of the Jameson Company, for whatever reasons, wanted—in a manner analogous to his desires with respect to reported income treated in Question 4—to make his liquidity position look better or worse than that shown in Table 9-5. Could he do it? If so, how, and if not, why not?

PROBLEMS

9-1. Lembke Company

The unadjusted trial balance of the Lembke Company as of December 31, 19X1 is as follows:

	Dr.	Cr.
Cash	$ 36,000	
Marketable Securities	27,000	
Accounts Receivable	82,000	
Accounts Receivable—		
Allowance for Bad Debts		$ 4,000
Merchandise Inventory	126,000	
Supplies	23,000	
Prepayments	42,000	
Land	58,000	
Buildings	172,000	
Buildings—		
Allowance for Depreciation		38,000
Equipment	97,000	
Equipment—		
Allowance for Depreciation		22,000
Trademarks	18,000	
Accounts Payable		103,000
Mortgage Payable		136,000
Common Stock		150,000
Retained Earnings		153,000
Sales Revenue		562,000
Sales—Discounts	13,000	
Sales—Returns	28,000	
Interest Revenue		14,000
Purchases	312,000	
Purchases—Returns		29,000
Freight-In	17,000	
Selling Expense	73,000	

Administrative Expense	52,000	
Income Tax Expense	14,000	
Interest Charges	21,000	
	$1,211,000	$1,211,000

Additional Information:

(1) Depreciation expense for the year is estimated as follows: buildings, $8,000; equipment, $6,000.

(2) Bad debts, based on the year's sales, are estimated at $11,000.

(3) Interest accrued receivable at year-end is $3,000.

(4) Income tax liability at year-end is $9,000.

(5) Interest accrued payable at year-end is $5,000.

(6) Salaries payable at year-end are: selling, $4,000; administrative, $1,000.

(7) Physical inventory count of supplies at year-end is $13,000.

(8) Physical inventory count of merchandise inventory at year-end is $133,000.

INSTRUCTIONS:

(a) Prepare a worksheet with pairs of columns for unadjusted trial balance, adjusting entries, cost of goods sold, income statement, and position statement. Enter the data above.

(b) Prepare an income statement and position statement in good form.

(c) Prepare, in journal entry form, adjusting and closing entries.

9-2. Worthington Company

The fiscal year for Worthington Company ends on August 31. As of August 31, 19X3, the firm's unadjusted trial balance is as follows:

	Dr.	Cr.
Cash	$ 33,000	
Accounts Receivable	32,000	
Merchandise Inventory	19,000	
Office Supplies	-0-	
Prepayments	8,000	
Investment in Harrison Co.	15,000	
Fund for Plant Expansion	20,000	
Land	13,500	
Buildings and Equipment	60,000	

Buildings and Equipment—		
Allowance for Depreciation		$ 9,000
Patent	4,000	
Patent—Allowance for Amortization		940
Accounts Payable		12,000
Salaries Payable		-0-
Other Accrued Payables		8,000
Bonds Payable		40,000
Preferred Stock		10,000
Common Stock		20,000
Retained Earnings:		
Unappropriated		42,060
Reserve for Plant Expansion		40,000
Reserve for Contingencies		10,000
Sales Revenue		152,000
Purchases	80,000	
Freight-In	1,000	
Salaries Expense	50,000	
Supplies Expense	4,000	
Miscellaneous Expense	1,200	
Interest Charges	1,000	
Preferred Dividend Charges	300	
Common Dividend Charges	2,000	
	$344,000	$344,000

Adjustments need to be made for the following:

(1) Salaries of $4,600 have accrued but have not yet been paid.
(2) Depreciation on buildings and equipment of $3,000 for the year has not been recorded.
(3) Patent amortization of $235 for the year has not yet been recorded.
(4) Interest charges of $200 have accrued during the year.
(5) Income taxes for the year are estimated at $3,306.
(6) $1,000 of prepaid insurance has been used up during the year.
(7) A physical inventory shows that $500 of office supplies are on hand on August 31.
(8) A physical inventory shows that $21,000 of merchandise is on hand.

It was decided that no cash would be transferred to the fund for plant expansion at this time but that if the company made money this year, the first $1,000 would go into the reserve for plant expansion, the second $1,000 would go into the reserve for contingencies, and the rest would remain unappropriated.

INSTRUCTIONS:

Prepare (a) a worksheet for the year; (b) journal entries to formally record your worksheet adjustments in the general journal and to close the books; (c) an income statement with instrastatement tax allocation (where the tax rate is 40 per cent on ordinary income); and (d) a position statement as of August 31, 19X3.

9-3. Northwestern Corporation

The pre-closing balances in Northwestern Corporation's nominal accounts at year-end on December 31, 19X3 are as follows:

	Dr.	Cr.
Administrative Expenses	$15,000	
Common Dividend Charges	13,000	
Cost of Goods Sold Expense	54,000	
Gain on Sale of Securities		$ 12,000
Interest Charges	10,000	
Interest Revenue		7,000
Loss from Flood Damage	4,000	
Sales Revenue		126,000
Selling Expenses	22,000	

Northwestern has not yet determined the amount of income taxes due on 19X3 income. Northwestern is subject to a 40 per cent tax rate on all items of ordinary income and 25 per cent on capital gains.

Additional Information:

(1) Interest revenue includes $2,000 of interest on municipal bonds which is nontaxable.
(2) The gain on sale of securities qualifies for capital gains treatment.
(3) The loss from flood damage is fully deductible in the determination of ordinary taxable income.

INSTRUCTIONS:

Prepare, in good form, an income statement reflecting intrastatement tax allocation.

9-4. Weir Company

The Weir Company closes its books annually on March 31. On that date in 19X3, the pre-closing balances in Weir's nominal accounts are as follows:

	Dr.	Cr.
Cost of Goods Sold Expense	$60,000	
Depreciation Expense	6,000	
Gain on Sale of Land		$ 8,000
Insurance Expense	1,000	
Interest Charges	3,500	
Interest Revenue		5,000
Loss from Wind Storm	7,500	
Sales Revenue		100,000
Supplies Expense	2,000	
Utilities Expense	3,000	
Wages Expense	18,000	

Weir is subject to an income tax rate of 40 per cent on all items of ordinary income and 25 per cent on all items that qualify as capital gains.

Additional Information:
(1) Included in interest revenue is $3,000 of interest on municipal bonds which is nontaxable.
(2) The loss from wind storm is fully deductible in the determination of ordinary taxable income.
(3) The gain on sale of land qualifies for capital gains treatment.

INSTRUCTIONS:
(a) Determine the amount of Weir's income taxes for the fiscal year ended March 31, 19X3.
(b) Prepare an income statement for the year ended March 31, 19X3 in good form and fully reflecting intrastatement tax allocation.

9-5. Chase Company

The nominal accounts of the Chase Company at December 31, 19X2 are as follows:

	Dr.	Cr.
Administrative Expenses	$ 35,000	
Common Dividend Charges	9,000	
Cost of Goods Sold Expense	190,000	
Fire Loss	20,000	
Gain on Sale of Land		$ 12,000
Interest Charges	10,000	

Interest and Dividend Revenue		30,000
Sales Revenue		320,000
Selling Expenses	55,000	

The amount of income taxes for 19X2 has not yet been determined. Chase is subject to a corporate income tax rate of 40 per cent on ordinary income and 25 per cent on capital gains. During the year, Chase received interest on municipal bonds (included in interest and dividend revenue) of $5,000. The gain on sale of land is the only item which qualifies for capital gains treatment.

INSTRUCTIONS:

Prepare, in good form, Chase's 19X2 income statement.

9-6. *Sterling Corporation*

The following nominal (temporary) accounts appear in the Sterling Corporation's general ledger prior to closing on December 31, 19X3.

	Dr.	Cr.
Common Dividend Charges	$ 25,000	
Cost of Goods Sold Expense	290,000	
Gain on Sale of Building		$ 40,000
General and Administrative Expenses	70,000	
Income Tax Expense	24,000	
Interest Charges	30,000	
Interest Revenue		20,000
Loss on Fire Damage	10,000	
Preferred Dividend Charges	5,000	
Sales Revenue		480,000
Selling Expenses	60,000	

Included in interest revenue is $5,000 of interest on municipal bonds which is nontaxable. The fire loss is deductible in the determination of ordinary income. The amount recorded in the account, income tax expense, correctly reflects the total amount of taxes applicable for the year 19X3. Sterling Coproration is subject to a 40 per cent tax rate on ordinary income and 25 per cent on capital gains.

INSTRUCTIONS:

Prepare, in good form, an income statement for the year ended December 31, 19X3 reflecting intrastatement income tax allocation.

9–7 Gilbert Company

INSTRUCTIONS:

Given below is a list of economic events with respect to the Gilbert Company for the current year. For each item, indicate its effect on Gilbert's funds statement for the year as one of the following:

S = source of funds A = application of funds N = no effect on funds assuming "funds" are defined as (a) cash, (b) net current monetary assets, (c) net working capital.

    (1) Cash sales
    (2) Purchase of a building for cash
    (3) Borrowing on a 90-day note
    (4) Purchase of merchandise on account
    (5) Declaration of cash dividend
    (6) Annual amortization of patents
    (7) Sale of common stock
    (8) Sales on account
    (9) Uninsured inventories destroyed by fire
   (10) Payment of accounts payable
   (11) Payment of a cash dividend
   (12) Retirement of bonds with cash
   (13) Write-off of specific receivables to allowance
   (14) Payment of stock dividend
   (15) Sale of long-term bonds

9-8. Mesa Manufacturing Company

INSTRUCTIONS:

Given below is a list of economic events with respect to Mesa Manufacturing Company for the current year. For each item, indicate its effect on Mesa's funds statement for the year as one of the following:

S = source of funds A = application of funds N = no effect on funds assuming "funds" are defined as (a) cash, (b) net current monetary assets, (c) net working capital.

    (1) Declaration of a cash dividend
    (2) Declaration of a stock dividend
    (3) Acquisition of land with payment in cash
    (4) Acquisition of land with assumption of a mortgage
    (5) Purchase of office equipment on account

(6) Annual accrual of bond interest
(7) Transfer of cash from general account to payroll account
(8) Annual accrual of estimated bad debts
(9) Annual accrual of depreciation, chargeable to expenses
(10) Annual accrual of depreciation, chargeable to work-in-process inventories
(11) Recognition of loss of building (uninsured) destroyed by fire
(12) Annual amortization of patents
(13) Annual accrual of oil depletion
(14) Annual amortization of bond discount
(15) Annual amortization of bond premium
(16) Conversion of bonds to common stock
(17) Recognition of land appreciation
(18) Recognition of loss of uninsured inventories destroyed by fire

9-9. Henkel Company

Given below are Henkel Company's financial statements for 19X1:

Henkel Company
Comparative Position Statements

	As of December 31, 19X1			As of December 31,19X1		
ASSETS:						
Current:						
Cash		$ 38,000			$ 30,000	
Accounts Receivable (net)		80,000			90,000	
Merchandise Inventory		125,000	$243,000		70,000	$190,000
Plant:						
Land		$ 32,000			$ 25,000	
Buildings and Equipment	$105,000			$110,000		
Less: Allowance for						
Depreciation	30,000	75,000	107,000	18,000	92,000	117,000
Intangibles:						
Trademarks (net of amortization)			50,000			60,000
			$400,000			$367,000
EQUITIES:						
Current Liabilities:						
Accounts Payable		$ 30,000			$ 75,000	
Payroll Payable		3,000	$ 33,000		5,000	$ 80,000
Common Stockholders' Equity:						
Common Stock		$250,000			$200,000	
Retained Earnings		117,000	367,000		87,000	287,000
			$400,000			$367,000

Henkel Company
Income Statement
For the Year Ended December 31, 19X1

REVENUES:

Sales		$300,000

EXPENSES:

Cost of Goods Sold	$180,000	
Depreciation	20,000	
Trademark Amortization	10,000	
Other	40,000	250,000

OPERATING INCOME	$ 50,000

GAINS AND LOSSES ON ASSETS:

Gain on Sale of Land	$ 3,000	
(Loss) on Sale of Building	(8,000)	(5,000)

ENTITY AND OWNERSHIP INCOME	$ 45,000
Common Dividend Charges	15,000

INCREASE IN RETAINED EARNINGS	$ 30,000

Additional Information:

(1) The original cost of the land that was sold was $5,000.
(2) The original cost of the buildings and equipment that were sold was $25,000.

INSTRUCTIONS:

Prepare a sources and uses of funds statement for the year ended December 31, 19X1, supported by a schedule of changes in net current monetary assets.

9-10. Emmert Corporation

Given below are Emmert Corporation's income statement and condensed beginning and ending position statements for the calendar year 19X3.

Emmert Corporation
Comparative Position Statement
As of January 1 and December 31, 19X3

	Dec. 31, 19X3		Jan. 1, 19X3	
ASSETS:				
Current Assets		$130,000		$100,000
Plant Assets—Cost	$350,000		$360,000	
Allowance for Depreciation	60,000	290,000	50,000	310,000
		$420,000		$410,000

EQUITIES:

Current Liabilities		$ 95,000		$100,000
10% Bonds Payable:				
Maturity Amount	$ 90,000		$180,000	
Premium	15,000	105,000	20,000	200,000
		$200,000		$300,000
Common Stockholders' Equity:				
Common Stock	$180,000		$100,000	
Retained Earnings	40,000	220,000	10,000	110,000
		$420,000		$410,000

Emmert Corporation
Income Statement
For the Year Ended December 31, 19X3

REVENUES:		
Sales		$385,000
EXPENSES:		
Cost of Goods Sold	$220,000	
Depreciation	40,000	
Other	90,000	350,000
OPERATING INCOME		$ 35,000
GAINS AND LOSSES ON ASSETS:		
Gain of Sale of Building		32,000
ENTITY INCOME		$ 67,000
Interest Charges	$ 23,000	
Loss on Redemption of Bonds	6,000	$ 29,000
OWNERSHIP INCOME		$ 38,000
Common Dividend Charges		8,000
INCREASE IN RETAINED EARNINGS		$ 30,000

Additional Information:

(1) During 19X3 Emmert Company sold a building which originally cost $90,000. No other plant assets were sold or retired during 19X3.

(2) Half of the total bonds outstanding were retired on December 31. No new bonds were issued during 19X3.

(3) Common stock of $80,000 was issued during the year in exchange for equipment of equal value.

INSTRUCTIONS:

Prepare an all-inclusive statement of sources and uses of funds for 19X3 adequately supported by footnotes and by a schedule of changes in net current monetary assets.

9-11. *Cantrell Company*

Given below are the income statement and beginning and ending position statements for the Cantrell Company for the calendar year 19X2:

Cantrell Company
Comparative Position Statements
As of January 1 and December 31, 19X2

		As of December 31, 19X2			As of January 1, 19X2	
ASSETS:						
Current:						
Cash		$13,000			$11,000	
Accounts Receivable (net)		32,000			26,000	
Merchandise Inventory		24,000	$ 69,000		23,000	$ 60,000
Plant:						
Land		$14,000			$17,000	
Buildings and Equipment	$109,000			$80,000		
Less: Allowance for Depreciation	19,000	$90,000	104,000	16,000	64,000	81,000
			$173,000			$141,000
EQUITIES:						
Current Liabilities:						
Accounts Payable		$ 18,000			$ 15,000	
Long-Term Liabilities:						
Notes Payable		46,000	$64,000		31,000	$46,000
Common Stockholders' Equity:						
Common Stock		$75,000			$70,000	
Retained Earnings		34,000	109,000		25,000	95,000
			$173,000			$141,000

Cantrell Company
Income Statement
For the Year Ended December 31, 19X1

REVENUES:		
Sales		$340,000
EXPENSES:		
Cost of Goods Sold	$210,000	
Depreciation	5,000	
Other	103,000	318,000
OPERATING INCOME		$ 22,000
GAINS AND LOSSES ON ASSETS:		
Gain on Sale of Land	$ 1,000	
(Loss) on Retirement of Equipment	(3,000)	(2,000)
ENTITY INCOME		$ 20,000
Interest Charges		3,000

OWNERSHIP INCOME	$ 17,000
Common Dividend Charges	8,000
INCREASE IN RETAINED EARNINGS	$ 9,000

Additional Information:

(1) $5,000 of common stock was issued in exchange for new equipment.
(2) Equipment retired during the year had originally cost $5,000. No other equipment or buildings were sold or retired during the year.
(3) No land was acquired during the year.

INSTRUCTIONS:

Prepare an all-inclusive statement of sources and uses of funds for the year ended December 31, 19X2 adequately supported by footnotes and by a schedule of changes in net current monetary assets.

9-12. Garland Company

Given below are the income statement and beginning and ending position statements for the Garland Company for the calendar year 19X2:

Garland Company
Comparative Position Statements
As of January 1 and December 31, 19X2

	As of December 31, 19X2			As of January 1, 19X2		
ASSETS:						
Current:						
Cash		$24,000			$11,000	
Accounts Receivable (net)		32,000			26,000	
Merchandise Inventory		24,000	$ 80,000		23,000	$ 60,000
Plant:						
Land		$13,000			$17,000	
Buildings and Equipment	$99,000			$80,000		
Less: Allowance for Depreciation	19,000	80,000	93,000	16,000	64,000	81,000
			$173,000			$141,000
EQUITIES:						
Current Liabilities:						
Accounts Payable		$21,000			$15,000	
Long-Term Liabilities:						
Notes Payable		37,000	$58,000		31,000	$46,000
Common Stockholders' Equity:						
Common Stock		$81,000			$70,000	
Retained Earnings		34,000	115,000		25,000	95,000
			$173,000			$141,000

Garland Company
Income Statement
For the Year Ended December 31, 19X2

REVENUES:		
Sales		$340,000
EXPENSES:		
Cost of Goods Sold	$210,000	
Depreciation	10,000	
Other	96,000	316,000
OPERATING INCOME		$ 24,000
GAINS AND LOSSES ON ASSETS:		
Gain on Sale of Land	$ 2,000	
(Loss) on Retirement of Equipment	(4,000)	(2,000)
ENTITY INCOME		$ 22,000
Interest Charges		3,000
OWNERSHIP INCOME		$ 19,000
Common Dividend Charges		10,000
INCREASE IN RETAINED EARNINGS		$ 9,000

Additional Information:

(1) $5,000 of common stock was issued in exchange for new equipment.

(2) Equipment retired during the year had originally cost $11,000. No other equipment or buildings were sold or retired during the year.

(3) No land was acquired during the year.

INSTRUCTIONS:

Prepare an all-inclusive statement of sources and uses of funds for the year ended December 31, 19X2 adequately footnoted and supported by a schedule of changes in net current monetary assets.

9-13. Worthington Company

Refer to Problem 9-2. The post-closing account balances for Worthington Company as of August 31, 19X2, were as follows:

	Dr.	Cr.
Cash	$ 18,800	
Accounts Receivable	34,000	
Merchandise Inventory	20,000	
Office Supplies	200	
Prepayments	4,000	

Investment in Harrison Co.	12,000	
Fund for Plant Expansion	19,000	
Land	10,000	
Buildings and Equipment	60,000	
Buildings and Equipment—		
Allowance for Depreciation		$ 9,000
Patent	4,000	
Patent—Allowance for Amortization		940
Accounts Payable		13,000
Salaries Payable		-0-
Other Accrued Payables		11,500
Bonds Payable		30,000
Preferred Stock		6,500
Common Stock		19,000
Retained Earnings:		
Unappropriated		42,060
Reserve for Plant Expansion		40,000
Reserve for Contingencies		10,000
	$182,000	$182,000

Additional Information:

(1) The $3,000 increase in investment in Harrison Co. was the result of the following journal entry:

Investment in Harrison Co.	$ 3,000	
Cash		$ 2,000
Common Stock		1,000

(2) The $3,500 increase in land was the result of the following entry:

Land	$ 3,500	
Preferred Stock		$ 3,500

(3) The $10,000 increase in bonds payable was the result of the following entry:

Cash	$10,000	
Bonds Payable		$10,000

INSTRUCTIONS:

Prepare (a) an all-inclusive sources and uses of funds worksheet for Worthington Company for the year ended August 31, 19X3; (b) a sources and uses of funds statement; and (c) a schedule of changes in net current monetary assets.

Chapter 9

9-14. Lampe Company

Lampe Company
Comparative Position Statements

	December 31, 19X1			December 31, 19X0		
ASSETS:						
Current:						
Cash		$ 12,000			$ 10,000	
Marketable Securities		9,000			15,000	
Accounts Receivable	$ 76,000			$ 65,000		
Less: Allowance for Bad Debts	7,000	69,000		5,000	60,000	
Merchandise Inventory		61,000			40,000	
Prepayments		23,000	$174,000		20,000	$145,000
Investments			82,000			50,000
Plant:						
Land		$ 20,000			$ 25,000	
Buildings	$110,000			$150,000		
Less: Allowance for Depreciation	25,000	85,000		30,000	120,000	
Equipment	$ 95,000			$ 75,000		
Less: Allowance for Depreciation	30,000	65,000	170,000	25,000	50,000	195,000
Intangibles:						
Patents (net of amortization)			24,000			30,000
			$450,000			$420,000
EQUITIES:						
Current Liabilities:						
Accounts Payable		$ 62,000			$ 50,000	
Accrued Payables		48,000	$110,000		45,000	$ 95,000
Long-Term Liabilities:						
Bonds Payable			130,000			150,000
Common Stockholders' Equity:						
Common Stock		$125,000			$100,000	
Retained Earnings		85,000	210,000		75,000	175,000
			$450,000			$420,000

Lampe Company
Income Statement
Year Ended December 31, 19X1

REVENUES:		
Sales		$382,000
Less: Discounts	$ 6,000	
Bad Debts	8,000	14,000
		$368,000
EXPENSES:		
Cost of Goods Sold	$222,000	
Salaries	63,000	
Depreciation	21,000	
Patent Amortization	6,000	
Other	9,000	321,000
OPERATING INCOME		$ 47,000

GAINS AND LOSSES ON ASSETS		
(Loss) on Sale of Canyon City Plant	($ 12,000)	
(Loss) on Sale of Investment in		
Phlybinite Company	($ 7,000)	(19,000)
ENTITY INCOME		$ 28,000
Gain on Redemption of Bonds		2,000
OWNERSHIP INCOME		$ 30,000
Common Dividends		20,000
INCREASE IN RETAINED EARNINGS		$ 10,000

Additional Information:

(1) The Canyon City Plant consisted of a factory building and the land it stood on. No equipment was included in the sale. The original cost of the land was $14,000 and the building, $80,000. No other land or buildings were sold during the year.

(2) The Phlybinite Company stock had been acquired for $18,000 and was included with "Investments."

INSTRUCTIONS:

(a) Prepare a source and uses of funds statement in good form, supported by a schedule of changes in net current monetary assets.

(b) Prepare a statement of sources and uses of working capital, supported by a schedule of changes in working capital.

CHAPTER 10

PREPARING CONSOLIDATED STATEMENTS

THE ACCOUNTING PRINCIPLES discussed so far have related to the records and statements of specific economic entities such as a trading corporation or a manufacturing firm. But such an economic entity may itself be a collection of economic entities—such as the several stores which may be operated by a trading corporation or the various plants in which a firm might conduct its manufacturing activities—and accounts would normally be kept for each of these component entities. In addition, the trading corporation or the manufacturing firm may in turn be a part of a larger business organization for which records may be kept and statements must be prepared. Hence, any set of accounts and statements may be both a disaggregated component of a more comprehensive set and an aggregation of a number of component sets.

In theory, problems of aggregation and disaggregation of financial accounts are mirror images of one another. One can go in either direction—disaggregate into component parts what is already a whole, or aggregate what are initially component parts into a whole. In practice, it is often simpler to account for disaggregated units and then consolidate the results in order to fashion statements for the larger entity. General Motors divisions—Chevrolet, Pontiac, Electro-Motive, Delco-Remy, and others—are not legal entities, but GM treats them as separate economic entities with each having its own accounting records. Their statements are then consolidated into reports for GM as a whole, these being all that shareholders and other outsiders see.

The process of consolidation and the preparation of consolidated statements are the subjects addressed in this chapter. In order to discuss them, two preliminary issues must be resolved, namely, whether or not such statements should be fashioned from component parts for some larger entity, and what determines the nature and definition of the consolidated entity for which reports are to be formulated.

In many cases, these two preliminary issues are easily settled. The only relevant entity for consolidation may be determined by legal considerations. If an economic entity is also a *legal* entity, reports on that entity must be fashioned. Consolidating divisional statements of a single company is a case in point. (Whether or not *also* to publish reports for the principal divisions, however, is a touchy issue. They might well be relevant and useful to shareholders, analysts, and other interested outsiders. Companies usually prefer not to publish these for they do not wish to give away, unnecessarily, information that may be valuable to competitors or perhaps embarrassing to the company.)

In many other cases, however, the issues of whether or not to consolidate and, if so, for what entity, are more nebulous. Take the case of Corporation A (the parent company) which owns 40 per cent of the shares of Corporation B (a partially owned subsidiary). Should Corporation A report simply investments equivalent to its shareholdings in Corporation B (however that value is determined) as an asset and the dividends received from Corporation B as income, thus reporting on the basis of its strict legal relationships? Should Corporation A report its purchased share of B's net worth as investments but *all* of its share of B's income (whether distributed or not) as income, adding its share of B's increase in retained earnings to its investments? Or, perhaps because Corporation A exercises *de facto* control over Corporation B's operations as a result of its substantial shareholdings in B, should there be a full A-B consolidated position, income, and funds statement?

The key word in the above questions is "control." Whenever actual or potential control can be exercised, through whatever means, there is presumably a case for financial statements appropriate to that control function, i.e., reports which circumscribe the same boundaries as those over which decisions and control can be exercised. We have emphasized throughout this book that in order to make sound new decisions one must evaluate old decisions; for this, one needs relevant data. If, in fact, decisions are being made on a consolidated entity basis, one needs consolidated data.

The range of business activities over which a single individual, a group of individuals, or a firm may exercise decisions and, thus, influence or control is often not easy to define. Majority ownership should guarantee control, but so may substantial minority ownership. Control may also be exercised through interlocking directorates, by a single shareholder holding substantial shares of stock in two or more companies (the companies having no ownership interest among themselves), and in other ways. Whether or not consolidated statements should be formulated and, if so, for what entity are not easy questions to answer, and accountants have had to fall back largely on rules of thumb based on degree of ownership of one or more firms by another. As suggested above, however, there may be other reasons connected with business objectives for the formulation of consolidated statements, and such statements may thus be drawn up for private use, although not distributed publicly.

When we move beyond the realm of the desirability of consolidated statements to serve private business objectives, we come to a whole new rationale and need. A comparative study of the activities of two industries may necessitate the fashioning of consolidated statements for each industry, even though no ownership or indirect control is involved. The formulation of national income accounts involves further consolidation to obtain accounts for the business sector as a whole (vis-a-vis the household, government, and foreign sectors). Clearly principles of consolidation have applications extending beyond the business community itself.

Let us first distinguish between the *combination* of data and the *consolidation* of data. Combination requires only the adding together of data of like kinds. Suppose, for example, that Firm A has sales of $300,000 and Firm B has sales of $200,000. Combination discloses that, taken together, the two firms had sales of $500,000. Consolidation requires more information because the process seeks to disclose the consolidated entity's transactions *with outsiders only*. If, for example, Firm B had sold $50,000 of its output (say, leather) to Firm A and Firm A had incorporated that purchase into its own output and sales (say, shoes), then the sales to outsiders of the two firms taken together are only $450,000. Similarly, if Firm A has accounts payable of $40,000 and Firm B of $25,000 but $12,000 of Firm's A debt is owed to Firm B, the amount owed to outsiders by the consolidated entity is not $65,000 but only $53,000. As another example, suppose that Firm A has income of $24,000, which includes dividends of $2,000 received from Firm B, whose income is $8,000. The two firms taken together have income of $30,000, not $32,000.

The process of consolidation is intended to eliminate double-counting, i.e., transactions between the two entities for whom statements are being consolidated, in order to reveal the consolidated entity's standing (position, income, or flow of funds) with the rest of the economy.[1]

1. For some purposes intra-family, intra-firm, or intra-industry transactions are significant. If data on the dollar value of steel used in making automobiles is wanted, it could not be gotten from statements that eliminate intra-firm transactions if one firm

The simple combination of data will yield consolidated results only if the entities for which consolidation is being undertaken have no transactions with each other.

Much of the rationale for consolidation in the business world arises as a result of relationships between a parent corporation and its subsidiaries. We shall begin with the problems involved in accounting for intercompany investments on the books of the parent. This discussion lays important groundwork for the discussion of consolidated income statements and consolidated position statements, which forms the major share of this chapter. The principles of consolidation are the same, regardless of rationale.

ACCOUNTING FOR INTER-ENTITY OWNERSHIP

When one business firm acquires an ownership interest in another, the only accounting recognition of the transaction is made in the records of the investor firm; the investee firm simply notes a change in the names of its owners. Usually such a transaction is consummated between corporations, wherein the investor corporation acquires shares of the investee corporation's common stock from the investee's stockholders, giving them in exchange cash, equity securities (debt, preferred stock, or common stock of the investor corporation), or some combination of the two. Regardless of what is given up in exchange, a new asset is recorded on the investor corporation's books, Investment in X Corporation.

Classification of the Investment Account

The first problem that we encounter in accounting for inter-entity ownership involves the classification of the new asset account. If the acquisition of investee corporation common stock were made as a temporary investment so as to earn some rate of return on temporarily excess cash assets, then the asset account is classified among marketable securities in the current asset section of the investor corporation's position statement. If, however, investments are made in the common stock of other corporations with some longer-term objective in mind—for example, to influence the activities of another entity (say, to assure supplies of raw materials or markets for one's products) or to obtain outright control of another firm—they are classified as noncurrent

owns both a steel plant and an automobile plant. Input-output analysis is designed to reveal interrelationships of this kind and, hence, is based on principles of combination rather than consolidation, although whole industries in the end may be consolidated.

assets in the "investments" section of the investor corporation's position statement. It is with this kind of investment that we are primarily concerned.

Initial Valuation of the Investment Account

The second problem that we encounter in accounting for inter-entity ownership involves the dollar amount to be recorded in the investment account; the valuation question arises once again. The answer is, of course, *cost*, but the specific cost to be used is dependent in part upon the nature of the consideration that was exchanged for the investee corporation's common stock. We will consider in this chapter only the common types of consideration, namely, cash and common stock. If cash is paid, the stock acquired is valued accordingly just as in the case of the purchase of any asset for cash. If, on the other hand, the investor's common stock is used in the exchange, accounting rules specify the circumstances under which either of two valuation methods must be used. These two methods are (1) purchase and (2) pooling of interests.

If the purchase method is required, the value of the common stock acquired is imputed from the value of the common stock given in exchange for it. In a sense the transaction is "telescoped," it being treated as though the investor's stock had been sold for cash, the cash then being used to acquire the investee's common stock. If the pooling-of-interests method is required, it is the value of the stock given in exchange that is imputed from the value of the stock acquired. Moreover, the value of the stock acquired must be valued at its book value in the records of the investee corporation. These valuation methods are discussed further toward the end of this chapter. In the meanwhile, the essentials of consolidation, as distinct from issues of initial valuation, are discussed on the assumption that stock is acquired for cash and that the price paid is equal to the book value of the stock so that no *goodwill* arises in the exchange.

Subsequent Valuation of the Investment Account

Once the investment account has been classified as current or noncurrent and the acquisition has been defined as either a purchase or a pooling of interests, a third accounting problem arises—that of how to account for the investee corporation's income and dividends subsequent to the date of acquisition. Accountants have devised two methods for dealing with them: the cost method and the equity method. Similar to the purchase-pooling dichotomy, the two are not generally inter-changeable, and specific rules have been promulgated that designate the circumstances under which each is to be adopted.

Cost method. Under the cost method, the balance in the investment account remains basically unchanged subsequent to the acquisition date of the investee's shares, provided, of course, that the investor corporation neither acquires additional shares nor disposes of any already owned. Any undistributed income reported by the investee as earned after the acquisition date is ignored on the books of the investor corporation. Only dividends paid by the investee to the investor are accounted for by the investor. The usual entry to record the dividends would be:

Dividends Receivable	XXX	
Intercompany Dividend Revenue		XXX

If the dividends are paid out of earnings retained prior to the acquisition, however, receipt of those dividends is regarded as a reduction in the cost of the investment—in effect, a return of capital. Any dividends paid out of income earned subsequent to the acquisition date are treated by the investor corporation as revenue and reported as such on investor corporation's income statement.

Since the investor corporation's reported income is in part a function of the dividend policy of the investee, it would be possible for the investor to alter its income in any period by influencing or exercising control over the investee's dividend policy. Because of the income manipulation that could result from the adoption of the cost method, the accounting profession has limited its use to those situations wherein it is unlikely that the investor corporation could exercise such control. Specifically, the cost method is deemed appropriate in cases where the investor corporation owns less than 20 per cent of the investee's outstanding common stock; only if it can be convincingly demonstrated that the investor is not in a position to exercise control may this method be used when the investor owns 20 per cent or more of the stock. Thus, 20 per cent—although an arbitrary figure—has been selected as the point delineating control from lack thereof.

The cost basis, therefore, is primarily used in accounting for short-term investments classified as marketable securities (where control is not the intent) or when an investor is embarking on an acquisition program with perhaps the ultimate intent of exercising influence or control but has not yet acquired many shares. In either instance, the purchase rather than the pooling method would be appropriate in recording the initial acquisition.

Equity method. In those cases not falling within the purview of the cost method, the equity method is to be employed. This method is deemed appropriate whenever the investor owns 20 per cent or more of the investee's outstanding common stock unless it can be convincingly shown that, despite such ownership, significant influence or control does not exist.

In contrast to the cost method, under the equity method, both the investee's income and dividends subsequent to the date of acquisition are accounted for on the books of the investor. With regard to income, the investor debits its investment account and credits a revenue account for its pro-rata share of investee's reported income before any dividend charges, such as in the following:

Investment in X Company   XXX
    Intercompany Investment Revenue   XXX

(Following our simplified assumption that the cash price paid by the investor company for the investee's common stock was equal to its book value, no adjustment of the investee's income is required. When such is *not* the case, certain adjustments might be necessary to reflect the difference between the book value and the price paid, but we will leave these discussions for more advanced texts.) Dividends are recorded on the declaration date by a debit to an asset account and a credit to the investment account, i.e., simply the exchange of one asset for another since income (which included any dividends) has already been reported, as follows:

Dividends Receivable   XXX
    Investment in X Company   XXX

As with the cost method, any dividends from earnings retained prior to acquisition are treated as a reduction in the investment account. At any point in time subsequent to the acquisition date, therefore, the balance in the investor's investment account will be essentially equal to the sum of the original acquisition cost plus the investor's pro-rata share of the investee's earnings retained subsequent to acquisition. (It should be recalled that the amount recorded as the original acquisition cost will depend upon whether the purchase method or the pooling method is employed.)

As previously pointed out, the equity method is predicated on a presumption of influence or control over the activities of the investee corporation. Whenever the ownership of the investee's other stock is widely dispersed, no other stockholder owning many shares, the investor corporation can exercise *de facto* control even though its ownership is less than 50 per cent. However, when the investor's holdings are more than 50 per cent, the investor's control becomes *de jure* as well. At that point, accountants usually prepare consolidated financial statements for investor and investee, just as if the two separate entities were one and the same. In other words, the combination of investor and investee is regarded as an economic entity, even if it has no legal standing, i.e., is not, say, a conglomerate corporation. Although separate sets of financial statements will continue to be prepared for each of the two entities, the investor's annual report will usually contain only the consolidated statements since they are prepared primarily for the benefit of the investor corporation's managers, investors, and the like. (It should be noted that if *only* consolidated statements are prepared, it makes no difference whether the investment is accounted for under the cost or equity basis because the investment account will be eliminated in the consolidation process; the cost/equity rule is thus applicable only for unconsolidated financial statements on the part of the investor company.) We shall now turn our attention to the problems involved in the preparation of consolidated statements.

THE CONSOLIDATED INCOME STATEMENT

Because consolidated statements are designed on the basis that only a single entity is being reported upon, care must be taken to ensure that no intra-family transactions are included among the income statement items. That is to say, only those revenues, expenses, gains, and losses that stem from the family's relations with the outside world should be included.

In order to prepare a consolidated income statement, the separate entity income statements of both the parent company and the subsidiary company must be obtained. As a basis for our subsequent discussion, we shall use the highly simplified statements of P Company (the parent) and S Company (the subsidiary) that are presented in Table 10-1. A consolidating worksheet, such as that illustrated in Table 10-2, is then prepared using the data from the two statements. The first pair of columns in the worksheet contain the data from P's income statement; S's data are entered into the second pair of columns. Revenues are entered into the credit columns just as they would appear on the books of P and S, while expenses appear in the debit columns. In order for the columns to be self-balancing, P's and S's incomes (in this simplified case, entity and ownership income are one and the same) are also entered into the debit columns. The third pair of columns are provided

TABLE 10-1
P COMPANY
INCOME STATEMENT
For the Year Ended December 31, 19X1

REVENUES:
Sales	$500,000	
Intercompany Investment	10,000	$510,000

EXPENSES:
Cost of Goods Sold	$350,000	
Other	50,000	400,000

ENTITY AND OWNERSHIP INCOME $110,000

S COMPANY
INCOME STATEMENT
For the Year Ended December 31, 19X1

REVENUES:
Sales		$100,000

EXPENSES:
Cost of Goods Sold	$ 60,000	
Other	30,000	90,000

ENTITY AND OWNERSHIP INCOME $ 10,000

for the necessary eliminating entries. It should be emphasized that these entries are made *only* on the working papers and are never formally entered into the accounting records of either P Company or S Company because their books represent the separate entities, not the two taken together. The data from the first two pairs of columns, as modified by the eliminations in the third pair, are then extended into the last pair of columns, which then contains the data for the preparation of the consolidated income statement, i.e., the income statement for the consolidated entity. Using this basic worksheet, let us now consider a variety of possible relationships between P Company and S Company.

One Hundred Per Cent Ownership, No Intercompany Purchases/Sales

Let us begin with the simplest case where the parent company is the solitary owner of the subsidiary and the price it paid when it acquired the subsidiary in some year prior to 19X1 was equal to the book value of the subsidiary's ownership equity at that time (so the question of

TABLE 10-2

P COMPANY AND SUBSIDIARY S COMPANY

WORKSHEET FOR CONSOLIDATED INCOME STATEMENT

For the Year Ended December 31, 19X1

Account Titles	P Company Dr.	P Company Cr.	S Company Dr.	S Company Cr.	Eliminations Dr.	Eliminations Cr.	Consolidated Income Statement Dr.	Consolidated Income Statement Cr.
Sales Revenue		$500,000		$100,000				
Intercompany Investment Revenue		10,000						
Cost of Goods Sold Expense	$350,000		$60,000					
Other Expenses	50,000		30,000					
Entity and Ownership Income	110,000		10,000					
	$510,000	$510,000	$100,000	$100,000				

whether the acquisition was accounted for as a purchase or a pooling is avoided for now). Furthermore, let us assume that the two have not entered into any transactions with one another, including the payment of dividends by the subsidiary to the parent. Given such a simple, straight-forward situation, it might be expected that all that need be done in preparing a consolidated income statement for P and S would be to add the like items of revenue, expense, and income. To do so, however, would be to overlook one important element that would result in double-counting.

Recall that once a company owns 20 per cent or more of another, it must adopt the equity method of accounting for its investment in that firm. Since P owns 100 per cent of S, then P must be using the equity method. Accordingly, at the end of the period, P must have made the following entry to record its share (100 per cent) of S's income for 19X1:

| Investment in S Company | $10,000 | |
| Intercompany Investment Revenue | | $10,000 |

Since S paid no dividends during the period, P would have made no other entries during the period with respect to its investment in S. The credit item, of course, appears as a revenue in P's income statement, thereby increasing P's income by $10,000. As a consequence, if we were simply to add P's and S's income statements, we would have a consolidated income figure of $120,000. We would be double-counting S's $10,000 income, once from S's income statement and again from P's income statement.

In order to correct for this double-counting, a single elimination is required. Note that the double-counting appears only on P's income statement since the revenue (and resultant income) reported there is purely intercompany in nature; in contrast, all of S's revenues, expenses, and income stemmed from its relations with outsiders. Thus, our elimination must be solely concerned with the items on P's statement. We eliminate these items by making the following entry, labeled (a), in the consolidating worksheet that appears in Table 10-3:

| Intercompany Investment Revenue (P Co.) | $10,000 | |
| Entity and Ownership Income (P Co.) | | $10,000 |

Then, once the appropriate extensions are made to the final pair of columns on the worksheet, the consolidated income statement that appears in Table 10-4 can be prepared.

TABLE 10-3
P COMPANY AND SUBSIDIARY S COMPANY
WORKSHEET FOR CONSOLIDATED INCOME STATEMENT
For the Year Ended December 31, 19X1

Account Titles	P Company		S Company		Eliminations		Consolidated Income Statement	
	Dr.	Cr.	Dr.	Cr.	Dr.	Cr.	Dr.	Cr.
Sales Revenue		$500,000		$100,000				$600,000
Intercompany Investment Revenue		10,000			(a)$10,000			
Cost of Goods Sold Expense	$350,000		$ 60,000				$410,000	
Other Expenses	50,000		30,000				80,000	
Entity and Ownership Income	110,000		10,000			(a)$10,000	110,000	
	$510,000	$510,000	$100,000	$100,000	$10,000	$10,000	$600,000	$600,000

TABLE 10-4

P COMPANY AND SUBSIDIARY S COMPANY
CONSOLIDATED INCOME STATEMENT
For the Year Ended December 31, 19X1

REVENUES:		
Sales		$600,000
EXPENSES:		
Cost of Goods Sold	$410,000	
Other	80,000	490,000
CONSOLIDATED ENTITY AND OWNERSHIP		
INCOME		$110,000

One Hundred Per Cent Ownership, Intercompany Purchases / Sales with Complete Resale

Having considered a simple case, let us now add a slight complication, that of transactions between the two companies. Keeping all other facts as in the preceding example, let us assume that P Company and S Company had intercompany purchases and sales, S making all of its sales to P during the period and P in turn selling to outsiders all of the goods it purchased from S during the year. Since all the goods ultimately ended up in the hands of outsiders, S's $10,000 income may be regarded as fully realized, as may P's $100,000 profit on its sales. However, as in the preceding example, P's investment revenue is double-counting S's income so it will have to be eliminated just as before. This elimination appears as entry (a) in Table 10-5. Moreover, S's sales of $100,000 were not made to outsiders but rather to P so they, too, will have to be eliminated. Along the same lines, $100,000 of P's $350,000 of cost of goods sold were the result of purchases from S; only $250,000 resulted from purchases from outsiders. Thus, these two "mirror-image" items would be eliminated by means of the following entry:

Sales Revenue (S Co.)	$100,000	
Cost of Goods Sold Expense (P Co.)		$100,000

Once this entry, labeled (b), is entered into the eliminations columns of Table 10-5 and the data extended to the last pair of columns, the consolidated income statement in Table 10-6 can then be prepared. With regard to that statement, the following should be noted: (1) the sales of $500,000 are composed entirely of P's sales to outsiders; (2) the cost of goods sold of $310,000 is composed of $250,000 that P

TABLE 10-5

P COMPANY AND SUBSIDIARY S COMPANY

WORKSHEET FOR CONSOLIDATED INCOME STATEMENT

For the Year Ended December 31, 19X1

Account Titles	P Company		S Company		Eliminations		Consolidated Income Statement	
	Dr.	Cr.	Dr.	Cr.	Dr.	Cr.	Dr.	Cr.
Sales Revenue		$500,000		$100,000	(b)$100,000			$500,000
Intercompany Investment Revenue		10,000			(a) 10,000			
Cost of Goods Sold Expense	$350,000		$ 60,000			(b)$100,000	$310,000	
Other Expenses	50,000		30,000				80,000	
Entity and Ownership Income	110,000		10,000			(a) 10,000	110,000	
	$510,000	$510,000	$100,000	$100,000	$110,000	$110,000	$500,000	$500,000

TABLE 10-6

P COMPANY AND SUBSIDIARY S COMPANY
CONSOLIDATED INCOME STATEMENT
For the Year Ended December 31, 19X1

REVENUES:		
Sales		$500,000
EXPENSES:		
Cost of Goods Sold	$310,000	
Other	80,000	390,000
CONSOLIDATED ENTITY AND OWNERSHIP		
INCOME		$110,000

purchased from outsiders and $60,000 that S purchased from outsiders; (3) the other expenses of $80,000 are composed of P's $50,000 and S's $30,000, both paid to outsiders; and (4) the $110,000 of consolidated income is made up of $100,000 earned by P and $10,000 earned by S.

As a slight twist on the preceding case, let us assume that some of S's sales are made directly to outsiders rather than all being made to P. The introduction of differential sales requires that we add for expository purposes a simplifying assumption (one that we shall retain throughout the remaining examples concerning consolidated income statements), namely, that S sells a single homogeneous product at a uniform price regardless of whether the sales are made to outsiders or to P Company. Having made that assumption, suppose that S makes 35 per cent of its sales directly to outsiders and 65 per cent to P Company, all of which P resells prior to the end of the period. In this instance, consolidated income will remain at $110,000 as before, but the revenue and expense components leading to this figure will be different. In particular, only $65,000 of S's sales revenue will be eliminated, together with an equal amount of P's cost of goods sold expense, because only these items are being double-counted. All of S Company's separately reported $10,000 entity and ownership income may be considered realized because all of the goods sold by S during the period ultimately made their way into the hands of outsiders, either through direct sale by S or indirect sale by P. A worksheet prepared under these circumstances would be identical to that appearing in Table 10-5 except that the eliminating entry (b) would be for $65,000 rather than $100,000, thereby making consolidated sales $535,000 and consolidated cost of goods sold $345,000. Because other expenses on a consolidated basis would remain unchanged at $80,000, consolidated entity and ownership income would, therefore, be $110,000.

One Hundred Per Cent Ownership, Intercompany Purchases / Sales with Incomplete Resales

The preceding examples involved only the element of double-counting intercompany purchases and sales since all goods were resold to outsiders by the end of the period; let us now consider a case having the additional element of unrealized profits from the consolidated entity's viewpoint. Let us continue to assume that P owns 100 per cent of S and, for simplicity's sake, return to our earlier assumption that all of S's sales are made to P. In addition, let us relax our assumption that all goods purchased by P and S are resold to outsiders and substitute the assumption that only 85 per cent of those goods are resold during the period. In other words, 15 per cent of the goods sold by S to P during the period remain in P's ending inventory. There are now three aspects to this consolidation: (1) the double-counting by P of S's income by means of the intercompany investment revenue account, (2) the double-counting of purchases and sales involving those goods resold by P, and (3) the unrealized profit stemming from those goods not resold by P.

Since the first aspect is exactly the same as in the preceding examples, it is eliminated in precisely the same manner and is labeled entry (a) in Tables 10-7 and 10-9. The second aspect may also be treated in a manner similar to the preceding examples. Instead of eliminating all of S's sales to P as before, however, we now eliminate only 85 per cent, together with a corresponding amount of P's cost of goods sold. The appropriate entry is:

Sales Revenue (S Co.)	$85,000	
Cost of Goods Sold Expense (P Co.)		$85,000

This entry, labeled (b), appears in the consolidating worksheets in Tables 10-7 and 10-9.

The third aspect, that involving the profit on the goods not yet resold to outsiders by P, is somewhat more complicated. From the consolidated viewpoint, clearly some portion of S's separately reported profit must be regarded as unrealized. The question, however, is how much of that profit should be eliminated in the preparation of the consolidated income statement.

The gross margin approach. There are several possible approaches to this question. The one most widely used in practice is to eliminate a proportionate amount of S Company's *gross margin* (sales less cost of goods sold), which in this case would be .15 ($100,000 − $60,000), or $6,000. This approach is predicated upon a particular assumption

Table 10-7

P COMPANY AND SUBSIDIARY S COMPANY

WORKSHEET FOR CONSOLIDATED INCOME STATEMENT

For the Year Ended December 31, 19X1

Account Titles	P Company		S Company		Eliminations		Consolidated Income Statement	
	Dr.	Cr.	Dr.	Cr.	Dr.	Cr.	Dr.	Cr.
Sales Revenue		$500,000		$100,000	(b)$ 85,000 (c) 15,000 (a) 10,000			$500,000
Intercompany Investment Revenue		10,000						
Cost of Goods Sold Expense	$350,000		$ 60,000			(b)$ 85,000 (c) 9,000	$316,000	
Other Expenses	50,000		30,000				80,000	
Entity and Ownership Income	110,000		10,000			(a) 10,000 (c) 6,000	104,000	
	$510,000	$510,000	$100,000	$100,000	$110,000	$110,000	$500,000	$500,000

with respect to S's expense other than cost of goods sold. It should be recalled that costs (see Appendix 3B) can be divided into two categories: product and periodic. From S's viewpoint, cost of goods sold expense is a product cost while other expenses are periodic. Whether or not this dichotomy can be extended to the consolidated entity, however, depends upon the nature of S's other expenses. If they are *nonvariable,* that is, if they do not change from period to period in concert with changes in sales, then they may be regarded as periodic expenses from the combined entity point of view as well. It is this assumption that underlies the gross margin approach. If these expenses (other than cost of goods sold) would have been incurred regardless of the quantity of goods S sold to P during the period, then the cost to the combined entity of those goods must be equal to S's inventoriable (or product) costs. Following the gross margin elimination approach, the appropriate eliminating entry would be:

Sales Revenue (S Co.)	$15,000	
Cost of Goods Sold Expense (S Co.)		$9,000
Entity and Ownership Income (S Co.)		6,000

This entry, labeled (c), appears in Table 10-7. The consolidated income statement that results from that worksheet is presented in Table 10-8.

TABLE 10-8

P COMPANY AND SUBSIDIARY S COMPANY
CONSOLIDATED INCOME STATEMENT
For the Year Ended December 31, 19X1

REVENUES:		
Sales		$500,000
EXPENSES:		
Cost of Goods Sold	$316,000	
Other	80,000	396,000
CONSOLIDATED ENTITY AND OWNERSHIP		
INCOME		$104,000

The income approach. On the other hand, suppose that S's other expenses varied directly in proportion to the quantity of goods sold to P. These expenses would then be termed *variable* expenses, and even though S treats them as periodic, they might very well be regarded as product costs from the combined entity point of view. For example, selling expenses might vary directly with sales revenues, especially when sales people are paid only commissions which are a fixed percentage

TABLE 10-9

P COMPANY AND SUBSIDIARY S COMPANY
WORKSHEET FOR CONSOLIDATED INCOME STATEMENT
For the Year Ended December 31, 19X1

Account Titles	P Company Dr.	P Company Cr.	S Company Dr.	S Company Cr.	Eliminations Dr.	Eliminations Cr.	Consolidated Income Statement Dr.	Consolidated Income Statement Cr.
Sales Revenue		$500,000		$100,000	(b)$ 85,000			$500,000
Intercompany Investment Revenue		10,000			(c) 15,000			
Cost of Goods Sold Expense	$350,000		$ 60,000		(a) 10,000	(b)$ 85,000	$316,000	
						(c) 9,000		
Other Expenses	50,000		30,000			(c) 4,500	75,500	
Entity and Ownership Income	110,000		10,000			(a) 10,000	108,500	
						(c) 1,500		
	$510,000	$510,000	$100,000	$100,000	$110,000	$110,000	$500,000	$500,000

of selling prices. In a number of instances, delivery expenses might also bear a direct relationship to sales revenues. Assuming that S's other expenses are all variable in such a fashion, had P not acquired goods from S for its ending inventory, S would not have incurred 15 per cent of its other expenses, or $4,500 [.15 ($30,000)]. Accordingly, it would seem appropriate that such costs be capitalized as a part of P's ending inventory. This is accomplished, in effect, by eliminating only that portion of S's *income* that relates to those goods in P's year-end inventory, $1,500 [.15 ($10,000)]. Note that this amount is exactly the difference between the amount eliminated under the gross margin approach ($6,000) and that portion of S's other expenses to be capitalized as part of the consolidated entity's ending inventory ($4,500). Following the income elimination approach, the necessary eliminating entry would be:

Sales Revenue (S Co.)	$15,000	
Cost of Goods Sold Expense (S Co.)		$9,000
Other Expenses (S Co.)		4,500
Entity and Ownership Income (S Co.)		1,500

This entry, labeled (c), appears in the worksheet in Table 10-9. The consolidated income statement prepared from that worksheet appears in Table 10-10.

TABLE 10-10

P COMPANY AND SUBSIDIARY S COMPANY
CONSOLIDATED INCOME STATEMENT
For the Year Ended December 31, 19X1

REVENUES:		
Sales		$500,000
EXPENSES:		
Cost of Goods Sold	$316,000	
Other	75,500	391,500
CONSOLIDATED ENTITY AND OWNERSHIP		
INCOME		$108,500

Combined approach. In the majority of instances, it is likely that S's other expenses would be neither exclusively variable nor nonvariable. When such is the case, a combination of the gross margin and the income approaches would be appropriate. To illustrate, assume the same facts as in the preceding case, except that P Company has selling expense of $37,000 and administrative expense of $13,000 rather than

other expenses of $50,000. Similarly, instead of other expenses of
$30,000, assume S Company has selling expense and administrative
expense of $21,000 and $9,000, respectively. For both companies, selling
expenses are completely variable while administrative expenses are
completely nonvariable. These data are contained in the worksheet
displayed in Table 10-11.

Given these assumptions, three eliminating entries will be required
in order to prepare a consolidated income statement. The first entry,
(a), as in preceding examples, merely eliminates the double-counting
of S's income. The second entry, labeled (b), eliminates the double-
counting of sales and cost of goods sold for those goods sold by S
to P and then resold by P to outsiders. The third entry, (c), eliminates
S company's unrealized profit on the goods sold to P during the period
but which remain in P's inventory at the end of the year. This entry
is as follows:

(c) Sales Revenue (S Co.)	$15,000	
Cost of Goods Sold Expense (S Co.)		$9,000
Selling Expense (S Co.)		3,150
Entity and Ownership Income (S Co.)		2,850

Note that, as before, 15 per cent of S's sales and cost of goods sold
are eliminated; this is the same regardless of whether the gross margin
or the income approach is used. The difference appears with respect
to the selling and the administrative expenses, the former being treated
in accordance with the income approach (hence, 15 per cent of S's
selling expenses are eliminated) and the latter in accordance with the
gross margin approach (none eliminated). The amount of S's income
eliminated, $2,850, is then a simple "plug" figure. The effect of the
foregoing is to establish the capitalized cost of P's ending inventory
purchased from S at $12,150 (S's variable cost of goods sold, $9,000,
plus S's variable selling expenses, $3,150). The consolidated income
statement that results appears in Table 10-12.

Upstream versus downstream intercompany purchases/sales. In all of the
examples we have examined thus far, the sales have been from the
subsidiary company to its parent. Such intercompany transactions are
known as "upstream sales." As might be expected, the converse—sales
from the parent to the subsidiary—are known as "downstream sales."
Regardless of the direction of the sales, the basic elimination procedures
remain unchanged, the only difference being whose accounts are
eliminated. To illustrate, when S Company made all of its sales to
P Company and P subsequently resold all of those goods prior to the

TABLE 10-11

P COMPANY AND SUBSIDIARY S COMPANY
WORKSHEET FOR CONSOLIDATED INCOME STATEMENT
For the Year Ended December 31, 19X1

Account Titles	P Company		S Company		Eliminations		Consolidated Income Statement	
	Dr.	Cr.	Dr.	Cr.	Dr.	Cr.	Dr.	Cr.
Sales Revenue		$500,000		$100,000	(b)$ 85,000 (c) 15,000 (a) 10,000			$500,000
Intercompany Investment Revenue		10,000						
Cost of Goods Sold Expense	$350,000		$ 60,000			(b) $85,000	$316,000	
						(c) 9,000		
Selling Expense	37,000		21,000			(c) 3,150	54,850	
Administrative Expense	13,000		9,000				22,000	
Entity and Ownership Income	110,000		10,000			(a) 10,000 (c) 2,850	107,150	
	$510,000	$510,000	$100,000	$100,000	$110,000	$110,000	$500,000	$500,000

TABLE 10-12
P COMPANY AND SUBSIDIARY S COMPANY
CONSOLIDATED INCOME STATEMENT
For the Year Ended December 31, 19X1

REVENUES:		
Sales		$500,000
EXPENSES:		
Cost of Goods Sold	$316,000	
Selling	54,850	
Administrative	22,000	392,850
CONSOLIDATED ENTITY AND OWNERSHIP		
INCOME		$107,150

end of the period, we made the following eliminations:

Sales Revenue (S Co.)   XXX
    Cost of Goods Sold Expense (P Co.)   XXX

Had the facts been the same but the sales "downstream" instead, we would make the following elimination:

Sales Revenue (P Co.)   XXX
    Cost of Goods Sold Expense (S Co.)   XXX

The entry is the same; only the company identifications are affected. This difference is of no particular significance so long as the parent company owns 100 per cent of the subsidiary; however, when the parent owns less than 100 per cent, it is of great importance because consolidated income must then be divided between majority and minority ownership interests.

Minority Interest

Before leaving consolidated income statements, we must consider one additional situation—that where the parent does not have complete ownership of the subsidiary. Rather than assuming that P owns 100 per cent of S, let us assume instead that P owns 90 per cent of S. This leads to the existence of a so-called "minority interest," that represented by the 10 per cent not held by P. Actually, this does not complicate matters as much as might be expected. While from the minority's point of view all sales made by S to P are realized whether or not the goods have ultimately been resold by P to outsiders, the basic purpose of the consolidation must be kept in mind. The consolidated statements are prepared for the use of those parties (parent company's managers and equity-holders, external analysts, prospective investors, and economists) who are concerned with the activities of the family of companies as a whole, regardless of the legal distinctions between the two companies. The consolidated statements reflect the activities of the consolidated entity, not the activities of the two separate legal entities, as those are reflected in the individual financial statements of the two companies. Thus, while all of the profits from S's sales to P are legally realized from the point of view of the minority owners, they are not realized in terms of the "family." As a result, the minority owners should look to S's separate income statement for the information they need, not to the consolidated statement.

Keeping in mind the purpose of the consolidated statement, it should be clear, then, that all of the eliminations made in the preceding examples where 100 per cent ownership was assumed are equally applicable to situations where ownership is less than 100 per cent. There would be no change in the worksheet whatsoever; the only difference between this case and those preceding would appear in the consolidated income statement itself. Here it will be necessary to break down the consolidated income into two components, income to minority interest and income to majority interest. Returning to our example in which consolidated entity income and ownership income are the same, it is actually the consolidated ownership income that is being divided between the minority and majority interests. Since the ownership income to majority interest is of prime importance on the consolidated statement, we will merely subtract the minority's share from consolidated ownership income to arrive at the majority interest.

The next question that arises is how much of the income is attributable to the minority. The answer is fairly straight-forward. In the immediately preceding example, of the $107,150 consolidated entity and ownership income, $100,000 was contributed by P and $7,150 by S. Clearly, the minority owners are entitled to no share of P's contribution, only S's. Their share of S's contribution, then, is proportional to their holdings, i.e., ten per cent of the $7,150 or $715. The statement that results is presented in Table 10-13. Note that the only difference between this statement and that in Table 10-12 is the division of consolidated income between majority and minority interests. Thus, it is possible to make comparisons between two "families" that are identical in all respects except percentage of ownership by the parent.

This breakdown of income into two parts, that derived from the parent company ($100,000) and that earned by the subsidiary ($7,150), may be viewed with a degree of skepticism. The prices at which goods

TABLE 10-13

P COMPANY AND SUBSIDIARY S COMPANY
CONSOLIDATED INCOME STATEMENT
For the Year Ended December 31, 19X1

REVENUES:		
Sales		$500,000
EXPENSES:		
Cost of Goods Sold	$316,000	
Selling	54,850	
Administrative	22,000	392,850
CONSOLIDATED ENTITY AND OWNERSHIP INCOME		$107,150
Minority Interest in Ownership Income (10% of $7,150)		715
OWNERSHIP INCOME TO MAJORITY INTEREST		$106,435

are transferred from one company to another within the family are accounting transfer prices which may not necessarily be the same as market prices. If goods are transferred to the parent at higher prices, the subsidiary reports a larger income while the parent reports a smaller one. Conversely, if transfer prices are lower than market prices, the parent will report a larger income and the subsidiary a smaller one. If a subsidiary sells its product to outsiders as well as to the parent, there is a market price which may or may not be applied to intra-family transfers. If it is, the income division is relatively reliable. (Recall that in our examples we assumed that S was selling a single product for which it charged the same price to both P Company and outsiders.) If a subsidiary sells only to the parent, however, the determination of a price is often arbitrary and the division of income between parent and subsidiary is equally arbitrary. A consolidated income, therefore, does not necessarily mean that each of the firms consolidated was profitable.

The accounting techniques for handling parent-subsidiary relationships open the door for many activities that are highly unethical or even illegal when minority interest is involved. The owners of a parent company may milk the minority owners of a subsidiary by transferring goods from the subsidiary to the parent at such low prices (or from the parent to the subsidiary at such high prices) that the subsidiary reports zero or negative income. Profit distributions that would have gone to minority owners may actually end up in the hands of the owners of the parent company. On the other hand, an influential officer in a parent company who is personally a heavy minority owner in a subsidiary may reverse this procedure to his or her personal gain. By setting accounting transfer prices appropriately, the earnings of the family may all be reported as earnings of the subsidiary. A portion of its profit distributions would then accrue to the minority owner-officer. The possibility of these and similar manipulations are enhanced when the number of interrelated companies is large and the relationships are complex. The need for constant surveillance of and a well-defined legal framework for such complicated organizations is well recognized, although the precise nature and extent of these controls is the subject of some dispute.

With the advent of multinational corporations having overseas subsidiaries, the accounting transfer price problem assumes added importance. Differing income tax rates between nations may encourage firms to alter accounting transfer prices so as to minimize the overall tax burden on the family of companies. This is particularly true when the subsidiaries are wholly-owned so that all ownership profits will ultimately accrue to the parent company's stockholders. If income tax rates are higher in country A as compared with country B, goods sold by a family firm in country A to another in country B will be priced below the market price so as to deflate the selling firm's profits and inflate the buying firm's earnings. If the goods are moving in the opposite direction, transfer prices will be set at a level above the market price so as again to minimize the amount of income exposed to higher tax rates. Ultimately, such international transactions hold implications for balance of payments matters and international money flows which must be recognized by the respective governments of countries A and B.

THE CONSOLIDATED POSITION STATEMENT

The preparation of the consolidated position statement is similar in many respects to that of the consolidated income statement. The consolidation takes place on a worksheet which combines data from the statements of the parent and subsidiary companies in the first two pairs of columns. Another pair is provided for eliminations and a final pair for the consolidated statement data.

A sample worksheet for A Company and its subsidiary, Z Company, is illustrated in Table 10-14. Data from the individual position statements have already been entered on the worksheet. Note that the data from

TABLE 10-14

A COMPANY AND SUBSIDIARY Z COMPANY

WORKSHEET FOR CONSOLIDATED POSITION STATEMENT

December 31, 19X1

Account Titles	A Company Dr.	A Company Cr.	Z Company Dr.	Z Company Cr.	Eliminations Dr.	Eliminations Cr.	Consolidated Position Statement Dr.	Consolidated Position Statement Cr.
Cash	$ 20,000		$ 15,000				$ 35,000	
Accounts Receivable	55,000		40,000				95,000	
Merchandise Inventory	35,000		30,000				65,000	
Investment in Z Company	125,000					(a) 25,000 (b) $100,000		
Land	60,000		20,000				80,000	
Buildings and Equipment	115,000		65,000				180,000	
Allowance for Depreciation		$ 25,000		$ 10,000				$ 35,000
Accounts Payable		45,000		15,000				60,000
Other Payables		50,000		20,000				70,000
Z Company:								
Common Stock—$10 Par Value				50,000	(b) $ 50,000			
Common Stock—Excess Over Par Value				30,000	(b) 30,000			
Retained Earnings				45,000	(b) 20,000 (c) 25,000			
A Company:								
Common Stock—$5 Par Value		60,000						60,000
Common Stock—Excess Over Par Value		90,000						90,000
Retained Earnings		140,000			(a) 25,000 (c) 115,000			
Consolidated Retained Earnings						(c) 140,000		140,000
	$410,000	$410,000	$170,000	$170,000	$265,000	$265,000	$455,000	$455,000

the common stockholders' equity sections of the two companies have been placed on separate lines, a convenience that will become apparent later.

One Hundred Per Cent Ownership, No Intercompany Receivables / Payables, No Unrealized Intercompany Profits

To keep matters simple (initially at least), let us assume that there are no intercompany payables or receivables and no unrealized intercompany profits on any of the assets. Furthermore, assume that A Company acquired 100 per cent of Z Company's outstanding common stock several years ago for $100,000 cash, a price exactly equal to the book value of Z's shares at that time. Because Z's former shareholders were paid in cash and have no continuing ownership interests, this acquisition is being accounted for as a purchase rather than as a pooling of interests. At the date of acquisition, the book value of Z Company's common stockholders' equity was composed of the following:

Common Stock:		
$10 Par Value	$50,000	
Excess Over Par Value	30,000	$ 80,000
Retained Earnings		20,000
		$100,000

The difference between the $100,000 purchase price and the $125,000 balance in A Company's investment in Z Company account reflects A's share (100 per cent) of the income that Z has retained since the date of acquisition. (Because A owns more than 20 per cent of Z, A will account for its investment using the equity method.)

In this simple case, the only eliminations required are those involving A Company's account, "Investment in Z Company." The $125,000 balance in that account may be eliminated by a single entry, but for expository purposes it will be clearer if we use several entries instead. First, we shall eliminate the double-counting of the income that has been retained by Z Company since it was acquired by A. This income has been accounted for once on Z's records, where it resides in Z's assets and retained earnings, and again on A's books, where it appears as a part of the investment account and as a component of A's retained earnings. Since the income originated with Z Company, we shall eliminate A's double-counting of it by means of the following entry:

Retained Earnings (A Co.)	$25,000	
Investment in Z Co. (A Co.)		$25,000

This entry, labeled (a), appears in the worksheet in Table 10-14.

The uneliminated balance in A's investment account, $100,000, represents the cost of the investment. We may eliminate this balance by crediting the investment account and debiting Z Company's corresponding stockholders' equity accounts. Since A acquired 100 per cent of Z's stock, we must debit these accounts for their entire balances as of that date (had A acquired a lesser percentage, we would eliminate only that percentage of the account balances as of date of acquisition). The appropriate eliminating entry, therefore, is as follows:

Common Stock—$10 Par Value (Z Co.)	$50,000	
Common Stock—Excess Over Par Value (Z Co.)	30,000	
Retained Earnings (Z Co.)	20,000	
Investment in Z Co. (A Co.)		$100,000

This entry is labeled (b) in Table 10-14.

After entry (b) has been made, the only balance remaining in any of Z Company's stockholders' equity accounts is the $25,000 appearing in retained earnings. This amount represents the income that Z has earned and retained subsequent to the date of acquisition by A. The balance in A's retained earnings account, once entry (a) has been made, represents only those earnings generated and retained by A itself; none of Z's earnings have been intermingled. It would seem curious, however, to display two retained earnings accounts, one for Z and one for A, in the consolidated position statement. Z's retained earnings, of course, could simply be added to A's, but then it would appear as if all earnings had been generated by A alone which is not the case. The solution is to merge the two retained earnings balances into a single balance titled "Consolidated Retained Earnings." This is accomplished by means of the following entry:

Retained Earnings (Z Co.)	$ 25,000	
Retained Earnings (A Co.)	115,000	
Consolidated Retained Earnings		$140,000

This entry appears in Table 10-14 as entry (c). Note that the account, consolidated retained earnings, is merely an artifact of the consolidation and does not appear on the books of either A or Z.

With entry (c), the eliminations required for our simple case are now complete. The data from the first two pairs of columns of Table 10-14 may now be extended through the eliminations columns and into the final pair of columns from whence can be prepared the consolidated position statement. That statement appears in Table 10-15.

TABLE 10-15
A COMPANY AND SUBSIDIARY Z COMPANY
CONSOLIDATED POSITION STATEMENT
December 31, 19X1

ASSETS:
  Current:
    Cash — $ 35,000
    Accounts Receivable — 95,000
    Merchandise Inventory — 65,000 — $195,000
  Plant:
    Land — $ 80,000
    Buildings and Equipment — $180,000
    Less: Allowance for Depreciation — 35,000 — 145,000 — 225,000
    $420,000

EQUITIES:
  Current Liabilities:
    Accounts Payable — $ 60,000
    Other Payables — 70,000 — $130,000
  Common Stockholders' Equity:
    Common Stock:
      $5 Par Value — $ 60,000
      Excess Over Par Value — 90,000 — $150,000
    Consolidated Retained Earnings — 140,000 — 290,000
    $420,000

One Hundred Per Cent Ownership, Intercompany Receivables/Payables, Unrealized Intercompany Profits

Assuming the same basic facts as in the preceding case, let us now relax the assumptions that there are no intercompany payables or receivables and no unrealized intercompany profits on any of the assets. Specifically, let us assume that A Company purchased goods for $50,000 from Z Company during 19X1 and resold $40,000 of these to outsiders. Z has recorded a profit of $2,000 on the goods remaining in A's inventory (assume that the profit has been correctly determined in accordance with one of the methods—gross margin, income, or combined—discussed earlier in the chapter). Furthermore, A still owes Z $8,000 on account for these purchases.

The elimination procedure for this more complex case begins in the same manner as before. First, entry (a) in Table 10-16 eliminates the double-counting by A Company of Z's earnings that have been retained since acquisition. Second, entry (b) eliminates the cost of the investment by A, together with the corresponding stockholders' equity accounts of Z as of the date of acquisition. These two entries are identical to those appearing in Table 10-14 and need no further elaboration.

One aspect that does require elaboration, however, concerns the intercompany receivable/payable. Of Z Company's receivables, $8,000 is due from A Company, which has recorded a like amount as a payable on its books. Since neither Z's asset nor A's liability stem from transactions with outsiders, both must be eliminated. The entry that does so is as follows:

Accounts Payable (A Co.)	$8,000	
Accounts Receivable (Z Co.)		$8,000

Once this entry, labeled (c) in Table 10-16, is made, the remaining balance in Z's receivables and A's payables represents only claims against and obligations to outsiders.

Another aspect in need of consideration has to do with the $2,000 unrealized intercompany profit residing in A's inventory. As a consequence, A's inventory balance must be reduced by $2,000 in order to represent its cost to the consolidated entity. Similarly, Z Company's retained earnings must be reduced by a like amount so as to leave only those earnings that have been realized by transactions with outsiders. The elimination is accomplished in the following manner:

Retained Earnings (Z Co.)	$2,000	
Merchandise Inventory (A Co.)		$2,000

This appears in Table 10-16 as entry (d).

The final entry to be made in the worksheet is analogous to the last entry we made in Table 10-14, where both A's and Z's remaining retained earnings balances were transferred to a new account, consolidated retained earnings. In this case, the final entry differs from that in the preceding case only in amount (because $2,000 of Z's retained earnings are unrealized in this example) and is as follows:

Retained Earnings (Z Co.)	$ 23,000	
Retained Earnings (A Co.)	115,000	
Consolidated Retained Earnings		$138,000

This entry, labeled (e) in Table 10-16, concludes the eliminations required in this case. Once the worksheet has been completed, the consolidated position statement that appears in Table 10-17 can be prepared.

TABLE 10-16

A COMPANY AND SUBSIDIARY Z COMPANY

WORKSHEET FOR CONSOLIDATED POSITION STATEMENT

December 31, 19X1

Account Title	A Company Dr.	A Company Cr.	Z Company Dr.	Z Company Cr.	Eliminations Dr.	Eliminations Cr.	Consolidated Position Statement Dr.	Consolidated Position Statement Cr.
Cash	$ 20,000		$ 15,000				$ 35,000	
Accounts Receivable	55,000		40,000			(c) $ 8,000	87,000	
Merchandise Inventory	35,000		30,000			(d) 2,000	63,000	
Investment in Z Company	125,000					(a) 25,000		
						(b) 100,000		
Land	60,000		20,000				80,000	
Buildings and Equipment	115,000		65,000				180,000	
Allowance for Depreciation		$ 25,000		$ 10,000				$ 35,000
Accounts Payable		45,000		15,000	(c) $ 8,000			52,000
Other Payables		50,000		20,000				70,000
Z Company:								
Common Stock—$10 Par Value				50,000	(b) 50,000			
Common Stock—Excess Over Par				30,000	(b) 30,000			
Retained Earnings				45,000	(b) 20,000			
					(d) 2,000			
					(e) 23,000			
A Company:								
Common Stock—$5 Par Value		60,000						60,000
Common Stock—Excess Over Par		90,000						90,000
Retained Earnings		140,000			(a) 25,000			
					(e) 115,000			
Consolidated Retained Earnings						(e) 138,000		138,000
	$410,000	$410,000	$170,000	$170,000	$273,000	$273,000	$445,000	$445,000

TABLE 10-17
A COMPANY AND SUBSIDIARY Z COMPANY
CONSOLIDATED POSITION STATEMENT
December 13, 19X1

ASSETS:
  Current:
    Cash $ 35,000
    Accounts Receivable   87,000
    Merchandise Inventory   63,000 $185,000

  Plant:
    Land $80,000
    Buildings and Equipment $180,000
    Less: Allowance for Depreciation   35,000   145,000   225,000
                                                                            $410,000

EQUITIES:
  Current Liabilities:
    Accounts Payable $ 52,000
    Other Payables   70,000 $122,000

  Common Stockholders' Equity:
    Common Stock:
      $5 Par Value $ 60,000
      Excess Over Par Value   90,000 $150,000

    Consolidated Retained Earnings   138,000   288,000
                                                                            $410,000

Minority Interests, Intercompany Receivables / Payables, Unrealized
Intercompany Profits

Up to this point in our discussion of consolidated position statements, we have assumed 100 per cent ownership of the subsidiary by the parent; now let us turn to a situation involving something less than complete ownership. Keeping facts essentially as they were in the immediately preceding example, let us assume that A Company acquired only 80 per cent of Z's outstanding common stock, paying $80,000 in cash to Z's stockholders. This price is exactly equal to 80 per cent of the book value of Z's stockholders' equity on that date [.80 ($50,000 par value + $30,000 excess over par + $20,000 retained earnings)]; in other words, the shares were purchased at their book value. Since the date of acquisition, Z has earned and retained $25,000 as before, but now A would record only 80 per cent of that amount, $20,000, in its investment account. Accordingly, at December 31, 19X1, the balance in A's investment account is only $100,000 rather than $125,000 as in our preceding examples. To make A's position statement balance, we have reduced A's retained earnings from $140,000, as in the earlier examples, to $115,000. Thus, in all respects other than A's investment and retained earnings accounts, the amounts appearing in the first two pairs of columns in the worksheet in Table 10-18 are the same as in Table 10-16. Let us see now how the existence of a minority interest affects the eliminations.

As before, the first eliminating entry, labeled (a) in Table 10-18, does away with A Company's double-counting of its share of the earnings that Z has retained since acquisition. Because Z has retained $25,000, we therefore must eliminate A's 80 per cent share as follows:

Retained Earnings (A Co.)	$20,000	
Investment in Z Co. (A Co.)		$20,000

The entry differs only in amount from entry (a) in Table 10-16, the difference reflecting the interest of the minority stockholders in Z's earnings retained since A's acquisition.

In a similar vein, entry (b) in Table 10-18 differs from its counterpart in Table 10-16 only in amount. This entry eliminates the cost of A's investment together with 80 per cent—A's ownership percentage—of Z's stockholders' equity accounts at date of acquisition:

Common Stock—$10 Par Value (Z Co.)	$40,000	
Common Stock—Excess Over Par Value (Z Co.)	24,000	
Retained Earnings (Z Co.)	16,000	
Investment in Z Co. (A Co.)		$80,000

Entries (c) and (d) in Table 10-18, to eliminate intercompany receivables/payables and unrealized intercompany profit in inventory, are exactly the same as they were in Table 10-16. The existence of a minority interest changes that not one iota; hence, no further discussion of these two eliminations is required.

The last entry in Table 10-18, labeled (e), is similar to its counterpart in Table 10-16 but, as with (a) and (b), differs in amount. The entry appears below:

Retained Earnings (Z Co.)	$18,400	
Retained Earnings (A Co.)	95,000	
Consolidated Retained Earnings		$113,400

As before, the entire balance that remains in A's retained earnings

TABLE 10-18

A COMPANY AND SUBSIDIARY Z COMPANY

WORKSHEET FOR CONSOLIDATED POSITION STATEMENT

December 31, 19X1

	A Company		Z Company		Eliminations		Consolidated Position Statement	
	Dr.	Cr.	Dr.	Cr.	Dr.	Cr.	Dr.	Cr.
Cash	$ 20,000		$ 15,000				$ 35,000	
Accounts Receivable	55,000		40,000			(c) $ 8,000	87,000	
Merchandise Inventory	35,000		30,000			(d) 2,000	63,000	
Investment in Z Company	100,000					(a) 20,000		
						(b) 80,000		
Land	60,000		20,000				80,000	
Buildings and Equipment	115,000		65,000				180,000	
Allowance for Depreciation		$ 25,000		$ 10,000				$ 35,000
Accounts Payable		45,000		15,000	(c) $ 8,000			52,000
Other Payables		50,000		20,000				70,000
Z Company:								
Common Stock—$10 Par Value				50,000	(b) 40,000			10,000
Common Stock—Excess Over Par				30,000	(b) 24,000			6,000
Retained Earnings				45,000	(b) 16,000			8,600
					(d) 2,000			
					(e) 18,400			
A Company:								
Common Stock—$5 Par Value		60,000						60,000
Common Stock—Excess Over Par		90,000						90,000
Retained Earnings		115,000			(a) 20,000			
					(e) 95,000			
Consolidated Retained Earnings						(e) 113,400		113,400
	$385,000	$385,000	$170,000	$170,000	$223,400	$223,400	$445,000	$445,000

Minority Interest (bracket over Consolidated Position Statement Cr. amounts 10,000; 6,000; 8,600) is transferred to consolidated retained earnings (recall that we had to change the initial balance earlier in the example from $140,000 to $115,000 to accord with the change in A's initial investment account balance). However, because of the existence of a minority interest in Z, we cannot transfer the entire remaining balance in Z's retained earnings account to consolidated retained earnings. All that we can transfer is an amount equal to A's proportionate share of Z's *realized* earnings that have been retained since acquisition, or 80 per cent of $25,000 *less* the unrealized intercompany profit of $2,000. After this entry is made, the residual balance in Z's retained earnings represents the minority's share, $8,600. This amount is comprised of the minority's 20 per cent share of earnings retained *at* the date of acquisition plus 20 per cent of the $23,000 of realized earnings retained *since* the date of acquisition.

Once the foregoing entries have been made in the worksheet in Table 10-18, the appropriate extensions are made into the last pair of columns. Note that there are balances now remaining in Z's stockholders' equity accounts, something that did not occur in the preceding examples. These amounts represent the 20 per cent minority interest in Z Company. Accordingly, when a consolidated position statement is prepared from the worksheet, a new section must be provided for minority interest. That section follows all liabilities but precedes common stockholders' equity in the statement in Table 10-19. Placement in that location, although virtually universal in practice, reflects an ambiguity in accounting thought. Some accountants regard minority interest essentially as a liability while others regard it more as an element of ownership. Those who adopt the former viewpoint seem to be subscribing to a proprietary theory approach, while those who opt for the latter appear to embrace an entity theory approach. Strictly speaking, if minority interest is regarded as a liability, it should be included among the liabilities; conversely, if it is an element of ownership, it should be included in that section. The decision by the profession to place it between liabilities and ownership (a sort of "purgatory" for nondescript accounts) appears to have been made as a compromise, one not wholly consistent with either the proprietary or entity approaches.

A FINAL CONSIDERATION:
PROBLEMS CONCERNING VALUATION OF THE INVESTMENT ACCOUNT

In our discussions throughout this chapter, we treated all acquisitions of the stock of a subsidiary by a parent as purchases because those acquisitions were made by the payment of cash to previous shareholders.

TABLE 10-19
A COMPANY AND SUBSIDIARY Z COMPANY
CONSOLIDATED POSITION STATEMENT
December 31, 19X1

ASSETS:
  Current:
    Cash $ 35,000
    Accounts Receivable   87,000
    Merchandise Inventory   63,000 $185,000

  Plant:
    Land $ 80,000
    Buildings and Equipment $180,000
    Less: Allowance for Depreciation   35,000   145,000   225,000
                                                                                            $410,000

EQUITIES:
  Current Liabilities:
    Accounts Payable $ 52,000
    Other Payables   70,000 $122,000

  Minority Interest in Z Co.:
    Common Stock:
      $10 Par Value $ 10,000
      Excess Over Par   6,000 $ 16,000

    Retained Earnings   8,600   24,600

  Common Stockholders' Equity:
    Common Stock:
      $5 Par Value $ 60,000
      Excess Over Par Value   90,000 $150,000

    Consolidated Retained Earnings   113,400   263,400
                                                                                           $410,000

To simplify matters further, we assumed that the price paid was equal to the subsidiary's book value of the shares acquired. This permitted us to focus our attention on the consolidation procedures alone to the exclusion of questions of initial valuation. However, our assumption regarding the price paid was quite unrealistic because only in extremely rare situations would it be equal to the subsidiary's book value. In an era of generally rising prices, book values tend to lag behind current market values; therefore, the cash price paid for subsidiary stock usually exceeds book value.

Moreover, by limiting our examples of acquisitions to those effected by cash purchases, we ignored situations involving "stock-for-stock swaps," that is, where the parent company issues its own shares in exchange for those of the subsidiary. When stock is acquired by the payment of cash, the valuation problem is a trivial one as the value of the sacrifice (cash) is simply imputed to the investment account. However, when subsidiary stock is acquired by the issuance of parent company stock, the problem of valuation often becomes quite formidable. Because one value must be imputed from the other, which stock should be imputed from the other, and which stock should be valued independently—the parent's or the subsidiary's? It is to these questions that we must attend before closing our discussion of consolidated statements.

Acquisitions for Cash at Prices Other Than Book Value

Even if stock is acquired for cash, a problem in consolidation does arise if the price that was paid for the stock differed from its book value. Consider the eliminating entry that is made to offset the parent's investment account against the subsidiary's stockholders' equity accounts [which appeared as entry (b) in Tables 10-14, 10-16, and 10-18]. When the amount recorded in the investment account is not equal to the book value of the shares acquired, the entry will not balance. Because the price paid for the shares typically exceeds their book value, the difference needed to balance the entry will usually be a debit. This difference could be the result of any one or a combination of the following:

1. The subsidiary's books may contain certain errors that understate both its assets and equities.
2. The subsidiary's books may be errorless, but the current market values of certain of its assets—usually its nonmonetary ones—may be higher than their unexpired historical acquisition costs.
3. The subsidiary may have certain unrecorded assets, particularly "goodwill," which have caused the value of the company as a going concern to be greater than the sum of the values of its physical assets.
4. The parent company may expect certain economic advantages to result from the union of the two firms, leading in turn to greater profits for one or both firms than would have been earned otherwise. As a consequence, the parent may have paid more than current market value to acquire

the subsidiary, this difference being termed "goodwill from consolidation."

Clearly, if the debit difference resulted from errors in the subsidiary's records as in (1) above, the subsidiary should simply correct its assets and equities by writing them up; once that has been done, the debit difference disappears and the consolidating eliminations can proceed as in our preceding examples. However, when the difference stems from items (2), (3), or (4), another tack must be taken.

With regard to item (2), it is not at all unlikely that the price paid for the subsidiary's stock will reflect the current market values of its assets rather than their unexpired historical acquisition costs. The solution here is to dispose of the debit difference by assigning higher values to the particular assets involved. To illustrate, suppose the price paid for 100 per cent of the stock exceeded its book value by $20,000 (the debit difference). Suppose also that the subsidiary's only asset whose current market value differs from its unexpired historical acquisition cost is land and that difference is $20,000. The subsidiary's land would be written up as a part of the eliminating entry as follows:

Common Stock—$XX Par Value (Subsidiary)	XXX	
Common Stock—Excess Over Par Value (Subsidiary)	XXX	
Retained Earnings (Subsidiary)	XXX	
Land (Subsidiary)	20,000	
Investment in Subsidiary (Parent)		XXX

The eliminating entry would then balance, and the amount reported for land on the consolidated position statement would exceed by $20,000 the sum of the amounts reported for land on the parent's and subsidiary's separate financial statements.

So long as the subsidiary's assets that are being written up have nothing to do with the income statement, then the only effects will be on the consolidated position statement. However, most assets ultimately expire—merchandise inventories disappearing into cost of goods sold expense, building and equipment disappearing into depreciation expense, and so on—and if these assets are written up, income statement items must also be altered. The problems associated with such write-ups are numerous and complex; hence, we shall defer their consideration to a more advanced text. Note only that if, say, a depreciable asset is written up, depreciation expense must likewise be written up. The result is that consolidated income will be less than the sum of the reported incomes on the separate financial statements of the parent and the subsidiary. Needless to say, management frequently regards this consequence as unattractive.

With regard to items (3) and (4) involving goodwill, the solution is similar to the one just proffered. The debit difference is assigned to a new asset, goodwill, which then appears on the consolidated position statement under the "intangibles" heading (along with patents, trademarks, and others). According to the profession's present rules, this asset must then be amortized over a period not to exceed 40 years, thereby creating a new expense item, amortization expense, in the consolidated income statement. This, too, reduces the income of the consolidated entity below the sum of those reported by its component firms. Since the amortization of goodwill cannot be expensed for tax purposes (see p. 288), it is fair to say that management generally would prefer not to have goodwill recorded and amortized.

Acquisitions for Stock

In contrast to acquisitions made for cash, acquisitions effected by stock swaps present difficult problems in the initial valuation of the parent's investment account. As noted earlier in this chapter, two different approaches have been employed in practice by accountants. One is to determine the current market value of the stock issued by the parent and to impute that value to the investment account. The other is to determine the subsidiary's book value of the stock being acquired and to impute that amount to the parent's investment account. As may be apparent, these two approaches frequently produce dramatically different results.

The first approach works much like an acquisition of a subsidiary's stock for cash. In effect, the transaction is viewed as if two separate transactions were being telescoped into one, the first being the issuance of parent company stock for cash and the second being the use of that cash to buy subsidiary company stock. In reality, of course, no cash changes hands, and the subsidiary's previous stockholders simply become owners of parent company stock. However, viewed in this manner, the resulting consolidated financial statements turn out about the same as if the acquisition had been made for cash. Any debit differences that emerge in the consolidating eliminations are treated as asset write-ups (including the recognition of goodwill), and any related expenses (cost of goods sold, depreciation, goodwill amortization) are also appropriately increased. Thus, this approach as well as acquisitions actually made for cash are collectively known as the *purchase method* of accounting for intercompany investments.

Contrasted to the purchase method is the *pooling-of-interests* method. Instead of viewing one firm as a parent purchasing an interest in a smaller, subsidiary firm, the two consolidating companies are viewed as essentially equal partners simply joining their interests together. Since there is a "joining together" rather than a purchase of one by another, no basis is thought to exist for restating the book values of either of the two partners. All that happens in consolidations treated as poolings is that the book values of the two firms are simply added together. As a consequence, the totals reported for assets, equities, and income in the consolidated financial statements are exactly equal to the sum of those amounts on the parent's and subsidiary's separate financial statements. No assets (or expenses) are written up to reflect current market values. The attractiveness to management of this approach as compared to the purchase method should be obvious—more reported income is usually preferable to less income.

For many years, the purchase and pooling methods were regarded as substitutes for each other when acquisitions were effected by stock swaps, the pooling method being the more popular of the two. Indeed, the availability of the pooling method is thought by many to have spawned the great merger movement of the sixties. As a reaction to many abuses of the method, however, the accounting profession imposed many restrictions upon its use. The most important of these is that 90 per cent or more of the subsidiary's stock must be swapped for parent company stock, thus implying that the corporations must previously have been independent of each other. When any of the required conditions is not met, the acquisition must be accounted for as a purchase.[2]

A Critique

The profession's compromise solution permitting both methods to be used (although not interchangeably) is, in our view, inadequate. The fundamental problem evidenced by the purchase-pooling controversy is not one of *consolidation* but rather one of *valuation*. As time passes, book values diverge from current market values, but accountants in practice generally recognize value changes only when a transaction occurs, the transaction serving as the basis for a change in accountability. In effect, the pooling method disavows the existence of a transaction, thus no change in accountability is permitted. The purchase method,

---

2. For a complete discussion of the conditions underlying pooling-of-interests accounting, see "Business Combinations," *Accounting Principles Board Opinion No. 16* (American Institute of Certified Public Accountants: New York, 1970).

in contrast, recognizes the acquisition as a transaction, but the only accounts that are affected are essentially those of the subsidiary, the parent's remaining basically at book value. Even under the purchase method, therefore, the balances reported in consolidated financial statements are a potpourri of book values and current market values. We believe this to be a major flaw in present-day consolidated statements (and, indeed, in separate entity financial statements as well). The values reported should be homogeneous, and it is to this fundamental issue that we address ourselves in the remaining chapters.

DISCUSSION QUESTIONS

1. The Praeger family, consisting of Mom, Pop, son Jim, and daughter Margaret, all work during July and August, and Father George worries about confusion in the family accounts. He is an amateur "accounting buff" and insists that the family keep its records just as if it were a business enterprise. Toward the end of June, after school gets out, Father George establishes Jim, who wants to do neighborhood lawn and gardening work over the summer, in business by buying $200 worth of "stock" in "Jim Praeger Enterprises," providing that amount of cash which just enables Jim to purchase a good, used power mower and other equipment needed to get started. Not wishing to saddle Jim with debt, Father George enters an agreement whereby the stock in Jim Praeger Enterprises is set up as cumulative preferred stock paying six per cent dividends (when earned), repurchasable by Jim Praeger Enterprises at any time at par value ($200). Margaret's lemonade stand business is simpler to set up; she purchases supplies from her mother on account and repays her "accounts payable" as revenue is received. During the month of July, the following aggregate transactions occur with respect to the family conglomerate:

    a. Father George brings home $800 take-home pay from his job as a mechanic, and Mother Grace brings home $400 take-home pay from her part-time job teaching English as a second language to foreign students in the area. These revenues are pooled and $900 is spent out of this account on household expenses, including $6 to Margaret for lemonade and $20 to Jim for yard work. George and Grace agree to share the residual equally for personal expenses, and George spends $130 in this way, Grace $70.

    b. Jim earns $200 cash in gross revenues, of which $20 is from his mother and father, and has no operating expenses.

   c. Margaret earns $30 cash in gross revenues, of which $6 is from her parents, and has $10 in expenses paid to her mother (her mother's purchases of these supplies is included in the $900 family household expenses above).

What would each member of the family report as revenues, expenses, and income for the month of July; and what would be reported as revenues, expenses, and income for the family as a whole, as a single economic unit? Set up a table as follows:

	Reported Separately			*Reported as a Family Unit*		
	Revenues	*Expenses*	*Income*	*Revenues*	*Expenses*	*Income*
George						
Grace						
Jim						
Margaret						
Total						

2. *Irrespective* of any legal obligations any of the constituent parts in a conglomerate might have with respect to financial reporting, how do you feel about the *economic* and *social* reasoning involved in each of the following positions with respect to reporting for a conglomerate entity which has a number of subsidiaries (either wholly or partially owned)?

   a. Conglomerate A is run in a tightly centralized fashion, the central office making all investment decisions as well as all operating decisions—on where inputs should be purchased (from other conglomerate subsidiaries or outside suppliers) and where outputs should be sold (to other conglomerate subsidiaries or outside demanders), and, in both cases, at what price. All decisions are made for the common good (of the conglomerate as a whole). The manager of Conglomerate A feels that one consolidated set of reports, for managers and outsiders alike, is *all* that is needed.

   b. Conglomerate B is run as a completely *de*centralized entity, each of the subsidiaries making its own operating and investment decisions independently. The manager of Conglomerate B feels that financial reports for each subsidiary's operations are all that is needed for both internal and external reporting purposes. No consolidated report is necessary, and, indeed, such a report would be misleading.

   c. Conglomerate C is run in "in-between" fashion, as between (a) and (b) above; what are, for the most part, decentralized *operating* decisions by subsidiaries are subject from time to time to being overruled in the central office for the common good, and the central office makes all investment decisions in the interests of the conglomerate as a whole. The manager of Conglomerate C feels that financial reports for each subsidiary's operations *and* the conglomerate as a whole are needed for *internal use* but that only the latter should be made public and available to *external* users.

d. Economist X feels that for the good of both the enterprise and society, financial reports for individual subsidiary operations separately and consolidated statements for the conglomerate as a whole should be formulated *and published* for all three conglomerates, A, B, and C.

e. Accountant Y feels that both individual and consolidated reports for the conglomerates should be formulated and published and that these reports should not only detail economic events as they affected the reporting unit but also detail, so far as possible, the gains and losses (e.g., smoke damage to residences) accruing to outsiders as a result of the firm's actions. Accountant Y feels that an economic entity should report the full *social* benefits and costs which result from its operations so far as it can do this, not just the *private* benefits and costs which result from its operations.

3. It has been argued that the reason acquisitions and mergers by conglomerates are so popular today is that one can do almost anything one wants to with one's books in the process and stay within generally accepted accounting principles (GAAP)—raise profits, lower profits (and taxes), expand assets substantially or by only a little, obtain loss-carryforwards to offset future profits, hence, taxes, and so on. Accountants have "guidelines" for the application of purchase versus pooling-of-interests methods in the valuation of assets acquired and for the application of cost versus equity methods for subsequent valuation of those investments. But all one has to do is to see that the category one will be placed in conforms to one's objective.

a. Defend the accounting profession with respect to the application of purchase versus pooling-of-interests and cost versus equity in handling the initial valuation and subsequent accounting for stock acquired of one firm by another.

b. Given the possibility of your firm acquiring all or part of the assets of another firm, how might you best proceed if you wished to:
(1) enlarge the ratio of income to assets by the largest amount;
(2) minimize taxes;

(3) report the largest growth in assets possible.

c. What suggestions, if any, would you make to the Financial Accounting Standards Board (FASB) on reform in accounting for mergers and acquisitions? Justify your position.

4. Accountants do not treat a parent's share of the undistributed profits of a subsidiary as part of the parent's income unless the parent owns 20 per cent or more of the subsidiary's outstanding common stock. On the other hand, with entities embarking on a "pooling of interests," ownership in excess of 10 per cent of the outstanding common stock of one of the entities is regarded as evidence of a lack of independence between them.

a. Why do the percentages differ?

b. Why make a distinction in either case?

5. The matter of distribution—whether income is paid out as dividends to the parent or retained and perhaps reinvested by the subsidiary—has certain tax implications. In the case of a domestic subsidiary, the corporate profits tax applies to all of the income earned by the subsidiary whether distributed or not, and, if distributed, the parent must pay taxes on the 15 per cent not excluded under the "85 per cent dividends exclusion" provision of the income tax law. In the case of foreign subsidiaries, however, whether or not income is distributed to the parent *does* have tax implications—in many cases, very significant implications. In the case of a foreign subsidiary, the parent pays U.S. corporate profits taxes only if the subsidiary's income is repatriated to the United States, the parent then paying any differential in tax which may be created by the United States which has a higher corporate tax rate than that prevailing in the country where the subsidiary is domiciled (the foreign tax rate being zero in the case of a pure "tax haven," such as the Bahamas, which has no corporate income tax).

a. Can you, as an *accountant,* add anything to the *economic* arguments that have raged during the Kennedy years and again during the Carter years in favor of, and opposed to, treating foreign and domestic subsidiaries alike in the matter of U.S. taxation of corporate profits? Does an "entity approach," as suggested by some accountants, imply that profits belong to the corporation (subsidiary) rather than the owners (the parent) unless or until such profits that are distributed have a bearing on this matter? (See Chapter 13 and discussion of the replacement cost income approach for more on this issue.) If one adheres to such a version of the "entity theory" in accounting (and should one?), would the matter of percentage of ownership, hence, perhaps degree of control, be a relevant issue, as accountants today feel it is, in deciding whether or not a parent's share of undistributed profits of a domestic subsidiary should be reported as income to the parent company?

b. If the undistributed profits of foreign subsidiaries are to be subject to the U.S. corporate profits tax, can you, as a tax accountant, suggest any way legally to avoid at least part of this tax while still retaining control of the foreign subsidiary's operations for the American parent? [Hint: Could the American parent distribute, say, up to 49 per cent of its shares in the foreign subsidiary to its (the parent's) shareholders in exchange for owner's shareholdings in the parent and thus bypass U.S. corporate taxation of at least part of the foreign subsidiary's profits?]

6. Is there any *substantive* difference in reporting an increase in a parent's "investments" in a subsidiary on the parent's position statement and the parent's share of all income of the subsidiary (distributed or not) on its income statement, on the one hand (when the parent's ownership share is at least 20 per cent but not more than 50 per cent); and reporting assets, liabilities, and retained earnings in consolidated fashion (when ownership is 50 per cent or more), with due account taken of income accruing to majority and minority shareholders on the consolidated income statement, and in the retained earnings figure on the consolidated position statement, on the other hand? Explain.

7. American CPA firms face *many* complicated issues in auditing the financial reports of foreign subsidiaries of American multinational corporations prior to auditing consolidated statements for the multinational as a whole. Discuss each of the following from the point of view of an auditor of the financial reports of Subsidiary X, say, in Germany, and Parent P ("Global Enterprises") in the United States, which owns 60 per cent of the shares of common stock outstanding of Subsidiary X, the rest being owned by German nationals:

a. In order to take advantage of a "tax holiday" granted another wholly-owned subsidiary (Subsidiary Y) in Malaysia, Subsidiary X pays Subsidiary Y exhorbitant prices for X's purchases from Y, or so it seems to you the auditor, thus channeling virtually all of the profits on Subsidiary X's subsequent sales of the good to Subsidiary Y in Malaysia where the profits are subject neither to local tax nor to U.S. tax (unless repatriated to the United States).

b. The German mark has fluctuated substantially vis-a-vis the United States dollar during the year for which the audit is being made, and at the end of the year the mark is 20 per cent higher in value vis-a-vis the dollar than it was at the beginning of the year. Values in marks for Subsidiary X must be translated into values in dollars if consolidated statements are to be formulated for the parent and its subsidiaries.

c. In Germany it is becoming "generally accepted accounting practice" to exclude from reported shareholder or ownership income that which can be shown to have been generated by assets which have been financed by long-term debt, on the grounds that such income is in no way connected with shareholder contributions of capital. Subsidiary X adheres to this practice and appropriates all income which it attributes to long-run creditor contributions of capital, over and above interest charges, to a special reserve rather than including it as ownership income.

d. Although American "generally accepted accounting principles" do not yet allow "replacement costs" [current market (entry) values] to be used as a base for depreciation estimates, German practice (and, to some extent, practice elsewhere in Europe as well) does allow this. Subsidiary X uses "replacement costs" in computing its depreciation estimates.

e. German practice is considerably more liberal than American practice in allowing payments of commissions to third-country nationals for help in facilitating sales, and Subsidiary X has used this greater freedom extensively in its sales promotion efforts.

(Note: Remember, in considering each of the above, that Subsidiary X is 60 per cent owned by Global Enterprises, the U.S. parent, and 40 per cent owned by German nationals. This may be relevant or irrelevant in your decisions as an auditor, but it is a fact that you must consider.)

PROBLEMS

10-1. Carroll Corporation and Doty Company

At the beginning of January, 19X4, Carroll Corporation acquired a block of Doty Company's outstanding common stock by purchase in the open market. The acquisition of the stock was made at a price equal to its value on Doty's books.

During the next several years, the two firms entered into no transactions with one another other than the payment of dividends by Doty to Carroll. Doty reported income and paid dividends during those years as follows:

For the Year Ended December 31

	19X4	19X5	19X6
Entity Income (Loss)	$90,000	$125,000	($25,000)
Less: Interest Charges	10,000	10,000	15,000
Ownership Income (Loss)	$80,000	$115,000	($40,000)
Less: Common Dividend Charges	30,000	60,000	60,000
Increase (Decrease) in Retained Earnings	$50,000	$55,000	($100,000)

INSTRUCTIONS:

(a) Assuming that Carroll acquired 15 per cent of Doty's outstanding common stock in January 19X4, prepare all relevant journal entries on Carroll's books relating to its holdings of Doty's stock through 19X6. Carroll closes its books annually on December 31.

(b) Same as (a) except assume that Carroll acquired 30 per cent of Doty's common stock.

10-2. Allied Corporation and General Corporation

On the first of January 19X1, Allied Corporation acquired a block of General Corporation's outstanding common stock from one individual at a price equal to its book value on General's books.

The two corporations had no dealings with each other except for the payment of dividends by General to Allied. General reported income and paid dividends over the next few years as follows:

For the Year Ended December 31

	19X1	19X2	19X3
Entity Income (Loss)	$15,000	$70,000	$95,000
Less: Interest Charges	40,000	40,000	40,000
Ownership Income (Loss)	($25,000)	$30,000	$55,000
Less: Common Dividend Charges	20,000	20,000	30,000
Increase (Decrease) in Retained Earnings	($45,000)	$10,000	$25,000

INSTRUCTIONS:

(a) Under the assumption that Allied had acquired 40 per cent of General's common stock in January 19X1, prepare all relevant journal entries on Allied's books relating to its holdings of General's stock through 19X3. Allied closes its books annually on December 31.

(b) Same as (a) except assume that Allied acquired only 10 per cent of General's stock.

10-3. Large Company and Small Company

Large Company acquired 80 per cent of Small Company's common stock when the latter was organized late in 19X8 (the price of the stock acquired being exactly equal to its book value). Small sells a single, homogenous product, charging the same price whether to parent company or outsiders. During 19X9, 75 per cent of Small's sales were made to Large. Both Small and Large are on a calendar year basis and their income statements for 19X9 are as follows:

	Large		Small	
REVENUES:				
Sales	$500,000		$150,000	
Intercompany Investment	20,000	$520,000	-0-	$150,000
EXPENSES:				
Cost of Goods Sold	$300,000		$100,000	
Other	100,000	400,000	25,000	125,000
ENTITY AND OWNER-SHIP INCOME		$120,000		$ 25,000

Small Company's Other Expenses are nonvariable.

INSTRUCTIONS:

(a) Under the assumption all goods sold to Large by Small were re-sold to outsiders by Large, prepare in good form the 19X9 consolidated income statement for Large and Small.

(b) Same as (a) except assume that 20 per cent of the goods sold to Large remained in Large's inventory on December 31, 19X9.

10-4. Smith Company and Davis Company

Smith Company acquired 90 per cent of Davis Company's common stock on January 1, 19X0 at a price equal to the stock's book value.

Both firms are on a calendar year basis and their income statements
for the year ended December 31, 19X0 appear below:

	Smith		Davis	
REVENUES:				
Sales	$500,000		$100,000	
Intercompany				
Investment	13,500	$513,500	-0-	$100,000
EXPENSES:				
Cost of Goods Sold	$350,000		$60,000	
Selling	65,000		14,000	
Administrative	35,000	450,000	11,000	85,000
ENTITY INCOME		$ 63,500		$ 15,000
Interest Charges		12,000		-0-
OWNERSHIP INCOME		$ 51,500		$ 15,000
Common Dividend Charges		6,500		18,000
INCREASE (DECREASE)				
IN RETAINED EARNINGS		$ 45,000		($3,000)

Smith manufactures and sells a single product. During 19X0, Smith
made ten per cent of its sales to Davis, all at the same prices charged
to outsiders. Davis resold four-fifths of the goods so acquired to outsiders
during the year.

Davis is a retailing firm that buys merchandise from a variety of
vendors other than Smith. Although Davis sells a wide variety of goods,
its gross margin percentage is the same on all goods. Later in 19X0,
Davis sold some of these goods to Smith (to be used in Smith's factory)
for $15,000. At year-end, none of these goods had been put into service.

Smith's selling expenses are variable and its administrative expenses
and Davis' selling and administrative expenses are nonvariable.

INSTRUCTIONS:

Prepare a worksheet for a consolidated income statement for the year
ended December 31, 19X0 and the resulting income statement.

10-5. *American Foods and Houston Grocery*

The income statements for American Foods Corporation and its
subsidiary, Houston Grocery Company, for the year ended December
31, 19X3, are as follows:

	American Foods		Houston Grocery	
REVENUES:				
Sales	$2,000,000		$200,000	
Intercompany				
Investment	15,000	$2,015,000	-0-	$200,000
EXPENSES:				
Cost of Goods Sold	$1,100,000		$100,000	
Selling	400,000		50,000	
Administrative	300,000	1,800,000	30,000	180,000
ENTITY AND OWNERSHIP INCOME		$ 215,000		$ 20,000

American Foods owns 75 per cent of Houston Grocery's common stock which it acquired early in 19X1 at a per-share price equal to book value per share.

During 19X3, 60 per cent of Houston's sales were made to American; by year-end American had re-sold to outsiders 80 per cent of the goods it bought from Houston. Houston maintains the same gross margin percentage on all its sales and all sales to American were made at the same prices Houston charges outsiders.

INSTRUCTIONS:

(a) Assuming that Houston's selling expenses are variable and its administrative expenses are nonvariable, prepare a worksheet for a consolidated income statement for the year ended December 31, 19X3 and the resulting consolidated income statement.

(b) Assuming that both Houston's selling expenses and its administrative expenses are nonvariable, prepare a consolidated income statement for the year ended December 31, 19X3.

10-6. *Mono Corporation and Polly Company*

Given below are the income statements of Mono Corporation and its subsidiary, the Polly Company, for the year ended December 31, 19X5.

	Mono	Polly
REVENUES:		
Sales	$500,000	$200,000

Intercompany Investment	17,000		-0-	
Other	10,000	$527,000	-0-	$200,000

EXPENSES:

Cost of Goods Sold	$250,000		$120,000	
Selling	100,000		35,000	
Administrative	90,000	440,000	25,000	180,000

OPERATING INCOME	$ 87,000	$ 20,000
GAINS AND LOSSES:		
Gain on Sale of Land	5,000	-0-

ENTITY AND OWN- ERSHIP INCOME	$ 92,000	$ 20,000

Mono owns 85 per cent of Polly's outstanding common stock which it acquired in mid-19X4 in the open market at a per-share price equal to the book value per share.

Polly manufactures and sells a single, homogeneous product. During 19X5, Polly's sales to Mono totaled $160,000, all of which were made at the same price that Polly charges outsiders. Of the goods it purchased from Polly during the year, Mono re-sold 60 per cent to outsiders. Also during 19X5, Mono sold Polly a piece of land which had cost $12,000 for $17,000 and collected a $10,000 "management fee" from Polly (classified as other revenue by Mono and as administrative expense by Polly). Mono incurred no expenses with regard to either the sale of the land or the "management fee."

Polly's selling expenses are variable and its administrative expenses exclusive of the "management fee" are half variable and half nonvariable.

INSTRUCTIONS:

Prepare a consolidated income worksheet for the year ended December 31, 19X5 and the resulting statement.

10-7. *Wilkes Corporation and Barre Company*

Income statements for the year ended December 31, 19X6 for Wilkes Corporation and its subsidiary, Barre Company, are given below:

	Wilkes	Barre
REVENUES:		
Sales	$650,000	$150,000

Intercompany				
Investment	20,000		-0-	
Other	35,000	$705,000	10,000	$160,000

EXPENSES:				
Cost of Goods Sold	$390,000		$ 85,000	
Selling	140,000		20,000	
Administrative	70,000	600,000	15,000	120,000
OPERATING INCOME		$105,000		$ 40,000
GAINS AND LOSSES:				
(Loss) on Sale				
of Equipment		(20,000)		-0-
ENTITY INCOME		$ 85,000		$ 40,000
Interest Charges		55,000		15,000
OWNERSHIP INCOME		$ 30,000		$ 25,000
Common Dividend				
Charges		50,000		20,000
INCREASE (DECREASE)				
IN RETAINED EARNINGS		($ 20,000)		$ 5,000

Wilkes owns 80 per cent of Barre's outstanding common stock. The stock had been acquired late in 19X2 at a per-share price equal to its book value per share.

Both Wilkes and Barre manufacture and sell single homogeneous products. The product manufactured by Wilkes serves as a raw material for Barre in its manufacturing. All sales between the two firms are made at regular market prices.

During 19X6, Wilkes made sales of $65,000 to Barre. Of the raw materials Barre purchased from Wilkes, 20 per cent remain in Barre's raw materials inventory. Of the other 80 per cent that were used, three-quarters ended up in finished products and one-quarter are still in process. Of those finished during the year, two-thirds were sold to Barre's customers, the remainder being in finished goods inventory at year-end.

Late in 19X6, Wilkes sold a piece of used equipment to Barre for $37,000. The equipment had originally cost Wilkes $78,000 and had a net book value of $57,000 on the date of sale.

On July 1, 19X3, Barre borrowed $150,000 from Wilkes on a five-year, ten per cent note. Interest on the note is payable semi-annually on June 30 and December 31. Wilkes classifies interest as other revenue.

Wilkes incurred no specific costs during 19X6 with respect to either the sale of equipment or the loan to Barre.

Wilkes' and Barre's selling expenses are variable and their administrative expenses are nonvariable.

INSTRUCTIONS:

Prepare a worksheet for a consolidated income statement for the year ended December 31, 19X6 and the resulting statement.

10-8. *Williams Company and Miller Company*

Given below are the December 31, 19X2 position statements for the Williams Company and its subsidiary, the Miller Company:

	Williams Co.		Miller Co.	
ASSETS:				
Current:				
Cash	$ 13,500		$ 5,000	
Accounts Receivable	50,000		25,000	
Merchandise Inventory	45,000	$108,500	20,000	$50,000
Investments:				
Investment in				
Miller Co. Stock		45,000		
Plant:				
Land	$ 25,000		$10,000	
Buildings & Equipment	90,000		35,000	
Less: Allowance for				
Depreciation	(15,000)	100,000	(5,000)	40,000
		$253,500		$90,000
EQUITIES:				
Current Liabilities:				
Accounts Payable	$ 30,000		$20,000	
Other Payables	48,500	$ 78,500	5,000	$25,000
Common Stockholders'				
Equity:				
Common Stock	$150,000		$50,000	
Retained Earnings	25,000	175,000	15,000	65,000
		$253,500		$90,000

Williams had acquired 70 per cent of Miller's outstanding stock on January 1, 19X2 at which time Miller's common stock and retained earnings balances stood at $50,000 and $5,000, respectively.

During 19X2, Miller sold merchandise costing $12,000 to Williams on account for $20,000. At year-end, $5,000 of this merchandise was still in Williams's inventory and Williams still owed Miller $4,000 on account. During the year, Miller also sold Williams land costing $4,000 for $7,000.

INSTRUCTIONS:

Prepare a worksheet for a consolidated position statement as of December 31, 19X2 and the resulting statement.

10-9. *Alpha Company and Beta Company*

Given below are the unclassified position statements of Alpha Company and its subsidiary, Beta Company, on December 31, 19X0:

	Alpha Co.	Beta Co.
Cash	$ 21,000	$ 15,000
Accounts Receivable	63,000	72,000
Merchandise Inventory	49,000	41,000
Investment in Beta Co. Stock	119,000	-0-
Land	22,000	13,000
Buildings & Equipment	113,000	87,000
Allowance for Depreciation	(21,000)	(19,000)
	$366,000	$209,000
Accounts Payable	$ 71,000	$ 37,000
Accrued Liabilities	33,000	2,000
Common Stock	200,000	100,000
Retained Earnings	62,000 .	70,000
	$366,000	$209,000

Alpha purchased 70 per cent of Beta's stock on January 1, 19X0. At that time, Beta had $100,000 in common stock and $60,000 in retained earnings.

Included in Alpha's year-end inventory is $13,000 of merchandise purchased from Beta. The merchandise had cost Beta $9,000. Alpha owed Beta $21,000 at year-end for merchandise purchased during the year. During 19X0 Alpha sold Beta land for $7,000 which had cost Alpha $4,000.

INSTRUCTIONS:

Prepare a worksheet for a consolidated position statement as of December 31, 19X0 and the resulting statement.

10-10. *Acme Corporation and Zeta Company*

The Acme Corporation acquired 70 per cent of Zeta Company's outstanding stock on January 1, 19X3 for $84,000. On that date, Zeta's common stockholders' equity consisted of $100,000 of common stock and $20,000 of retained earnings. On December 31, 19X3 the position statements of the two companies were as follows:

	Acme Corp.		Zeta Co.	
ASSETS:				
Current:				
Cash	$ 35,000		$ 20,000	
Accounts Receivable	80,000		30,000	
Merchandise Inventory	60,000	$175,000	45,000	$ 95,000
Investments:				
Investment in Zeta Co.		105,000		
Plant:				
Land	$ 35,000		$ 15,000	
Buildings and Equipment				
(net of depreciation)	120,000	155,000	85,000	100,000
		$435,000		$195,000
EQUITIES:				
Current Liabilities:				
Accounts Payable	$ 80,000		$ 35,000	
Other Payables	25,000	$105,000	10,000	$ 45,000
Common Stockholders'				
Equity:				
Common Stock	$200,000		$100,000	
Retained Earnings	130,000	330,000	50,000	150,000
		$435,000		$195,000

During the year, Acme purchased merchandise from Zeta for $50,000, of which 40 per cent remained unsold at year-end. Zeta's profit on these goods was 10 per cent of selling price. At year-end, Acme owed

Zeta $25,000 on account. During 19X3 Acme sold to Zeta, for $8,000, land which had originally cost Acme $5,000.

INSTRUCTIONS:

Prepare a worksheet for a consolidated position statement as of December 31, 19X3 and the resulting statement.

10-11. *Large Company and Small Company*

Given below are the position statements of Large Company and its subsidiary, Small Company, as of December 31, 19X9:

	Large Company			Small Company		
ASSETS:						
Cash		$ 30,000			$ 20,000	
Accounts Receivable (net)		72,000			35,000	
Merchandise Inventory		170,000	$272,000		60,000	$115,000
Investments:						
Investment in Small						
Company Plant			128,000			
Land		$ 15,000			$ 20,000	
Buildings and Equipment	$130,000			$105,000		
Less: Allowance for						
Depreciation	45,000	85,000	100,000	40,000	65,000	85,000
			$500,000			$200,000
EQUITIES:						
Current Liabilities:						
Accounts Payable		$ 90,000			$ 30,000	
Accrued Payables		50,000	$140,000		10,000	$ 40,000
Common Stockholders' Equity:						
Common Stock		$250,000			$100,000	
Retained Earnings		110,000	360,000		60,000	160,000
			$500,000			$200,000

Large Company acquired 80 per cent of Small Company's outstanding common stock on January 1, 19X6, at which time Small's common stock and retained earnings were $100,000 and $50,000, respectively.

During 19X9, Small sold merchandise which cost $18,000 to Large for $30,000. Of this merchandise, one-third remained in Large's inventory at year-end. Also at year-end, Large still owed Small $8,000 for merchandise purchased during the year.

During 19X7, Large had sold Small a piece of land for $5,000. The cost of this land to Large was $3,000.

INSTRUCTIONS:

Prepare a worksheet for a consolidated position statement as of December 31, 19X9 and the resulting statement.

10-12. Allied Corporation and Zapata Company

Given below are the position statements of the Allied Corporation and its subsidiary, Zapata Company, as of December 31, 19X3:

	Allied Corporation		Zapata Company	
ASSETS:				
Current:				
Cash	$ 38,000		$ 25,000	
Accounts Receivable	105,000		75,000	
Merchandise Inventory	160,000	$303,000	80,000	$180,000
Investments:				
Investment in				
Zapata Company		152,000		
Plant:				
Land	$ 85,000		$ 20,000	
Buildings & Equipment				
(net of depreciation)	260,000	345,000	50,000	70,000
		$800,000		$250,000
EQUITIES:				
Current Liabilities:				
Accounts Payable	$110,000		$ 40,000	
Other Payables	40,000	$150,000	20,000	$ 60,000
Common Stockholders'				
Equity:				
Common Stock	$400,000		$100,000	
Retained Earnings	250,000	650,000	90,000	190,000
		$800,000		$250,000

Allied currently owns 80 per cent of Zapata's outstanding common stock. Sixty per cent was acquired on December 31, 19X0, at which time Zapata's retained earnings balance stood at $50,000. The other 20 per cent was acquired on December 31, 19X2 when Zapata's retained earnings totaled $75,000. Zapata's balance in common stock has been $100,000 since the company was organized 15 years ago.

During 19X3 Allied sold Zapata merchandise on account for $30,000, merchandise which had cost Allied $24,000. By year-end, Zapata had re-sold two-thirds of this merchandise to its customers. Zapata still owed Allied $7,000 on these purchases.

In 19X1, Allied had sold Zapata some land costing $9,000 for $12,000.

INSTRUCTIONS:
Prepare a worksheet for a consolidated position statement as of December 31, 19X3 and the resulting statement.

10-13. *Southwest Sugar Corporation and Southern Refining Company*

On January 1, 19X2, Southwest Sugar Corp. bought 75 per cent of the common stock of Southern Refining Co. for $120,000. At that time, the balances in the equity accounts of Southern Refining Co. were common stock, $80,000, and retained earnings, $20,000. The current market values of all of Southern's assets and liabilities were equal to their book values, except for land which had a current market value of $55,000 and a book value of $30,000.

As of December 31, 19X5, the position statements of each were as follows:

	Southwest Sugar Corporation		Southern Refining Company	
ASSETS:				
Current:				
Cash	$ 50,000		$ 25,000	
Accounts Receivable	90,000		50,000	
Merchandise Inventory	71,000	$211,000	25,000	$100,000
Investments:				
Investment in Southern Refining Company		144,000		
Plant:				
Land	$ 75,000		$ 50,000	
Buildings and Equipment	$100,000		$250,000	
Less: Allowance for Depreciation	10,000	90,000 165,000	40,000	210,000 260,000
		$520,000		$360,000
EQUITIES:				
Current Liabilities:				
Accounts Payable	$ 90,000		$ 95,000	
Other Accrued Liabilities	55,000	$145,000	125,000	$220,000
Common Stockholders' Equity:				
Common Stock	$300,000		$ 80,000	
Retained Earnings	75,000	375,000	60,000	140,000
		$520,000		$360,000

During the year, Southwest Sugar Corp. bought $40,000 worth of goods on account from its subsidiary, Southern Refining Co. By year-end, it had repaid half of this amount and had re-sold 80 per cent of these goods to outsiders. Southern Refining Co. had recorded a 10 per cent profit on the sales to its parent company.

During 19X4, Southwest Sugar Corp. sold some land which had cost $18,000 to Southern Refining Co. for $20,000.

INSTRUCTIONS:

Prepare a worksheet for a consolidated position statement as of December 31, 19X5 and the resulting consolidated position statement.

10-14. *Duluth Distributing Corporation and Superior Sales Company*

Given below are the position statements as of December 31, 19X6 for the Duluth Distributing Corporation and its subsidiary, the Superior Sales Company:

	Duluth Distributing Corporation			Superior Sales Company		
ASSETS:						
Current:						
Cash		$ 65,000			$ 20,000	
Accounts Receivable		220,000			105,000	
Merchandise Inventory		195,000	$ 480,000		85,000	$210,000
Investments:						
Investment in Superior						
Sales Company			288,500			
Plant:						
Land		$ 75,000			$ 35,000	
Buildings & Equipment	$380,000			$260,000		
Less: Allowance for						
Depreciation	110,000	270,000	345,000	150,000	110,000	145,000
TOTAL ASSETS			$1,113,500			$355,000
EQUITIES:						
Current Liabilities:						
Accounts Payable		$240,000			$ 90,000	
Other Payables		135,000	$ 375,000		55,000	$145,000
Common Stockholders' Equity:						
Common Stock		$400,000			$100,000	
Retained Earnings		338,500	738,500		110,000	210,000
TOTAL EQUITIES			$1,113,500			$355,000

Duluth acquired 95 per cent of Superior's outstanding common stock on January 1, 19X4 by issuing new shares of Duluth's common which then had a current market value of $266,000. The balances in Superior's common stock and retained earnings accounts on January 1, 19X4 were $100,000 and $80,000, respectively. On that date, the current market values of Superior's assets and liabilities approximated their book values with one exception: Superior's land had a current market value of $45,000 and a book value of $25,000. This combination did not qualify for treatment as a "pooling-of-interests" and was appropriately accounted for as a "purchase."

During 19X4, Duluth sold Superior a tract of land for $10,000. This land had cost Duluth $3,000 when it was acquired in 19X0.

At the beginning of 19X6, Duluth owed Superior $45,000 on account for purchases of merchandise in 19X5 (all of which had been sold by December 31, 19X5). During 19X6, Duluth purchased merchandise from Superior for $120,000 on account. Superior's profit on these goods amounted to $12,000. By year-end, Duluth had resold two-thirds of this merchandise to its own customers. Duluth's total payments on account to Superior during 19X6 amounted to $115,000.

INSTRUCTIONS:

Prepare a worksheet for a consolidated position statement as of December 31, 19X6 and the resulting position statement.

CHAPTER 11

CURRENT VALUE THEORY

THE CENTRAL PURPOSE of accounting, as outlined in Chapter 1, is to measure for a business entity its accomplishments (revenues), its efforts (expenses), its success or failure (income or loss) over a given period of time, and its position (what it owns and owes) at any moment of time. In preceding chapters we have described the system of accounting principles and techniques generally recognized by industry, government, and the accounting profession as the proper way to record financial transactions and to prepare financial statements for a business enterprise.

So far little has been said about the effects that changes in the general price level and in specific prices of a firm's assets and liabilities and of its outputs and inputs might have on the meaningfulness of the statements being compiled. Traditionally, the accounting profession has ignored effects of price changes until gains or losses have been realized through the direct sale of an asset (or retirement of a liability), has recorded asset and liability values in terms of historical costs, and has treated expenses in the income statement as allocations of historical purchase prices. It is the purpose of this chapter to examine critically the implications of relying on historical costs and to investigate certain approaches—in particular, current value theory—presently being put forward as an alternative to strict reliance on historical costs. The traditional and the newer approaches will be evaluated according to the usefulness and relevance of the data obtained to the needs of those who use the data, both inside and outside the firm.[1]

---

1. Much of the analysis of this chapter is worked out in detail in E. O. Edwards and P. W. Bell, *The Theory and Measurement of Business Income* (Berkeley: University of California Press, 1961). The analysis there was amended in substantive fashion in E. O. Edwards, "The Primacy of Accounting Income in Decisions On Expansion: An Exercise in Arithmetic," in Cees van Dam (Ed.), *Trends in Managerial and Financial*

Users of accounting data need information primarily to evaluate the decisions and performance of the firm. The needs of managers can best be seen in the perspective of the planning process of the individual firm. Most firms draw up detailed plans—over some "planning horizon"—of expected future revenues and expenses, involving use of an initial posited set of assets (which may, then, change over the planning period through increments, decrements, or changes in composition). The "planning horizon," which may be of any length and which will differ for different firms (five or, perhaps, ten years might be normal, but it may well be shorter or longer), is as far ahead as the firm can see itself in terms of its objectives. Plans are constantly updated—as one period elapses, another is added at the other end. The objective of the firm is to "outguess the market," i.e., generate income over and above the income that could be earned simply by investing, at interest, in risk-free securities. *Subjective estimates* of profit must be turned into *objective market value. Evaluation* involves ascertaining whether or not this is being done, i.e., *actual events* are measured and compared with *expected events.* If there are deviations from plan, managers must be able to learn from the data being provided how and why deviations are occurring in order (1) to take any appropriate action in terms of the existing plan (pat the purchasing manager on the back or fire him or her); (2) to modify or, perhaps, alter drastically the updated plan for the next planning period (expand a product line or get out of it and go into another, buy some new labor-saving machinery to correct for what is turning out to be much higher labor costs than expected, and so on); and (3) to improve the decision-making process itself. Managers may well wish to compare performance this period with past performances and/or with performances of other competing firms.

Interested *outsiders* (investors, creditors, labor unions, government regulatory bodies) may or may not be privy to the firm's plan.[2] But they clearly have the same interest as the managers in ascertaining objective events—in measuring actual performance, often in comparison

Accounting (Leiden: Martinus Nijhoff, 1978). And we have benefited by discussions of others in the literature since 1961, as represented, at least partially, by footnote references in this chapter.

2. Whether or not outsiders should be privy to the management's *plans*—based on their forecasts of the future—so that they, too, can ascertain deviations from plan is an open question. The Securities and Exchange Commission, the regulatory body primarily protecting investors, which at one point encouraged firms to make financial forecasts available to the public, has since retreated on this issue. But certainly reliable data on actual performance are a legitimate concern of investors, creditors, and others.

with past periods and/or other firms but also in terms of their own expectations and standards of performance.

If accounting data are to serve properly these needs of insiders and interested outsiders, such data must, we suggest, meet four criteria—requirements that will become clear as our analysis proceeds.

1. The accounting model should be designed to classify change in such a way as to make clear why the change occurred.
2. The accounting model should measure events as they occur; that is, the actual events of a period should be recorded to the exclusion of events which occurred in earlier periods or which may occur in future periods—*all* the events of a period and *only* the events of that period.
3. The operating results and financial position of one year should be comparable with those of prior and subsequent years.
4. The financial statements of one company within an industry should be comparable with those of another company in the same industry as well as with those of firms in other industries. (this criterion will be met only if the other three are met as we shall see.)

INCOME CONCEPTS AND THE EVALUATION OF DECISIONS AND PERFORMANCE: A SIMPLE CASE

Consider, then, a simplified version of a firm's plan. We will compress what might be 20 years into two representative periods, and we will assume that the firm purchases only one (plant) asset—for $10,000, with funds committed by owners. That asset is expected to depreciate at the rate of 50 per cent per period; but, unlike our previous methods of measuring depreciation internally, that percentage is now derived from the values of new and one-period-old plant assets in the market place. There, a one-period-old asset can be acquired for one-half the price of a new asset and a two-period-old asset is worthless. In our firm the asset is expected to yield 20 per cent over its lifetime on "earnings" of $7,000 in period 1 and $6,000 in period 2. Here and in what follows, we use the term "earnings" *not* as traditionally employed by accountants to denote "income" (as in "earnings per share") but rather to denote "income plus depreciation," i.e., the *increase in net current monetary assets from operations,* or what is often loosely called "cash flows" from an investment. Hence:

	Period	
	1	2
(1) Expected earnings before depreciation	$ 7,000	$6,000
(2) Depreciation	5,000	5,000
(3) Income	$ 2,000	$1,000
(4) Book Value of asset at beginning of period	$10,000	$5,000
(5) Rate of return: (3) ÷ (4)	20%	20%

Depreciation as determined in the market is consistent with that determined by the internal rate of return method as outlined in Chapter 6, but that compatibility will disappear at a later stage of our analysis and then the market will be our overriding guide. The interest rate on risk-free securities is ten per cent. And we will assume throughout the early portions of this chapter that there are no expected changes in the general price level and that none occur.

At the outset, the firm's subjective estimate of the asset's value, based on anticipated future earnings discounted at the market rate of interest, exceeds the asset's market value or cost, i.e.,

$$\text{Subjective Value} = V_0 = \frac{\$7,000}{1.1} + \frac{\$6,000}{(1.1)^2}$$
$$= \$6,364 + \$4,958 \quad = \$11,322$$
$$\text{Market Value} = C_0 \qquad\qquad = \ 10,000$$

$$\text{Subjective Goodwill} \quad = \quad V_0 - C_0 \quad = \$ \ 1,322$$

The expected increase in the market value of the firm in period 1 is $2,000. At the end of period 1, it expects to have $7,000 in cash (from earnings) and an asset then worth $5,000, as compared with an asset worth $10,000 at the beginning of the period. Call this increase in market value of the firm *current income*. If the firm pays the $7,000 earnings out in dividends at the end of period 1, its market value is expected to increase from $5,000 to $6,000 in period 2; and its expected current income in period 2 would be $1,000.

Part of this increase in market value, or current income, each period represents *implicit interest* on the investment, that which could have been earned simply by investing what is tied up in the business in risk-free securities. Only part of it represents "outguessing the market," i.e., earning over and above what could be earned at interest. Call this latter *excess current income*. Over the life of the plan the firm intends to turn its subjective goodwill, which is a measure of the present value (at the outset of the plan) of the extent to which the firm *thinks* it can "outguess the market," into market value in the form of excess current income. We have:

	Period	
	1	2
Expected Current Income from investment	$2,000	$1,000
less Interest on previous period's asset value tied up in investment	1,000	500
equals Excess Current Income	$1,000	$ 500

The present value in period 0 of the excess current income stream is:

$$\frac{\$1,000}{1.1} + \frac{\$500}{(1.1)^2} = \$909 + \$413 = \$1,322.$$

This is *subjective goodwill*. If events go according to plan, the firm will just turn its subjective goodwill into market value in the form of excess current income. Its expectations will have been realized.[3]

Alternatively, we can determine ownership income as follows:

Receipts of investor	Period		
	1	2	
From chosen investment	$7,000 (earnings)	+ $ 700 (interest)	All received by end of period 2
		+ $ 6,000 (earnings)	= $13,700
From alternative investment at interest	1,000 (interest)	+ $ 1,100 (interest)	
		+ $10,000 (principal)	= 12,100
Net advantage of chosen investment			$ 1,600

3. Robert Anthony has urged that imputed interest on owners' investment in the firm be explicitly deducted, along with any actual interest paid to creditors, from entity income in arriving at ownership income. See Robert N. Anthony, "Let's Account for Interest," Collected Papers of the *American Accounting Association's Annual Meeting,* Tucson, Arizona, August 18–20, 1975 (Sarasota, Florida: American Accounting Association, 1975), pp. 268–271.

It is assumed that the $7,000 income (from the chosen investment which the investor receives in period 1) is reinvested at the ten per cent interest rate prevailing in the market in period 2. The present value in period 0 of $1,600 in period 2 is:

$$\frac{\$1,600}{(1.1)^2} = \$1,322$$

which again is subjective goodwill.

Thus, if the investor's own capital is employed, the investor must have more value at the end than simply investing at interest if the investment is to generate excess profits. The subjective estimate of this ability to outguess the market is subjective goodwill. If the investor borrows the capital to finance the investment (at the same market rate of interest), more must be generated than is required to pay interest on the debt and repay the principal at the end in order to do better than the market. In that case we would have:

	Period					
	1		2			
Earnings of investor	$7,000	+	[$600 (interest) + $6,000 =	$6,600]	=	$13,600
less Interest on debt	1,000	+			1,000 =	2,000
Dividends	$6,000	+			$5,600 =	$11,600

The investor could repay the principal on the debt of $10,000 and have $1,600 left, the present value of which is the subjective goodwill of $1,322, as shown above.

Such is the firm's plan with respect to its initial asset. We could build into its initial plan tentative plans for reinvestment at the end of period 1 (for example, in such a way as to maintain the market value of the firm); but we will say that this is left open, any such decision being dependent upon the actual events of period 1.

Events unfold in period 1, and the firm does, in fact, earn the expected $7,000 from using the asset in period 1. The asset the firm purchased for $10,000 in period 0, however, jumps in value in the market on the first day of period 1 to $12,000. In considering price changes throughout this chapter, unless otherwise specified, we will assume these arbitrary beginning-of-the-period jumps or declines to save on calculations and simplify the problem. (In Chapter 12, when we show in more detail how such changes can be incorporated into accounting records, we will be more realistic and assume the changes occur gradually over the period.) The 20 per cent jump in the value of the asset new is reflected in a 20 per cent higher value than that expected at the end of period 1 for a one-period-old asset, i.e., the asset is then worth $6,000 in the market. In this chapter we will assume that the purchase price of the (either new or one-period-old) asset (*entry price*) is the same as the selling price of the asset (*exit price*), leaving consideration of possible divergence between these two prices to Chapter 13.

The central question now is what accounting information, particularly with respect to income generated from use of the asset, is relevant for evaluating the plan at the end of period 1 in preparation for drawing up a new plan to extend to periods 2 and now 3. And what concept is relevant for the basic decision we have to make at the end of period 1 of how much of our income should be paid out in dividends and how much should be reinvested in the entity? Income clearly plays a key role in these exercises. The nub is in defining "income."

Economic Income and Its Components

The accepted *economic* concept of income is that given by Hicks (1946), following Fisher (1906) and Lindahl (1939): "The maximum amount which an individual can spend [consume] this week and still be able to expect to spend [consume] the same amount in real terms in each ensuing week."[4] Some accountants seem to accept this concept of income as the ideal for accounting and argue that the accounting concept will differ from the economic concept only because practical difficulties of measurement prevent accountants from directly measuring the ideal itself.

Applied to the firm, the usual concept of economic income, $\overline{EI}$, is that it is the increase over the period in the subjective value attached to the net assets of the enterprise or that it is interest (used in the discount factor) on subjective value prevailing at the beginning of the period. In accordance with our basic plan above, *expected* economic income in period 1 is thus defined as follows:

$$\overline{EI}_1 = V_1 - V_0 = iV_0,$$

where all values are those which are expected at the beginning of period 1 (or the end of period 0).[5] We have already found V_0 to

---

4. J. R. Hicks, *Value and Capital*, 2nd ed. (Oxford: Clarendon Press, 1946), p. 174. See also I. Fisher, *The Nature of Capital and Income* (New York: Macmillan, 1906) and E. Lindahl, *Studies in the Theory of Money and Capital* (London: Allen and Unwin, 1939).

5. We have:

$$V_0 = \frac{E_1}{(1 + i)} + \frac{E_2}{(1 + i)^2},$$

be equal to \$11,322 above. V_1 can be obtained by adding to receipts expected to be generated in period 1 before dividends, \$7,000, the then present value of expected receipts in period 2, $\dfrac{\$6,000}{1.1}$,

$$V_1 = \$7,000 + \frac{\$6,000}{1.1} = \$12,454,$$

and from the above,

$$\overline{EI}_1 = \$12,454 - \$11,322 = .10(\$11,322) = \$1,132.$$

If the firm received \$7,000 in period 1 as expected and paid out economic income of \$1,132 in dividends, it could buy \$5,868 of securities with the remainder and earn \$587 interest in period 2. In period 2 it would then receive \$6,000 + \$587 = \$6,587. It could again pay out economic income of \$1,132 as dividends and purchase \$5,455 in securities, which, with the securities carried over from period 1, would give it \$11,322 in securities (equal to its original subjective value); and it could, assuming no change in the rate of interest, then pay out economic income of \$1,132 forever. Our *expected economic income*, which we could pay out in periods 1, 2, and forever, was based on expected receipts during the plan period—which is as far as we could see in thinking of outguessing the market. After that, we had to count on just matching the market, i.e., getting interest on risk-free securities.

It is useful to view expected economic income in one further sense. If we add and subtract market value in period 0 (M_0) and expected market value in period 1 (M_1) to our first equation above and rearrange terms, we obtain the following:

$$\begin{aligned}
\overline{EI}_1 &= V_1 - V_0 + [M_1 - M_1 + M_0 - M_0], \\
&= [M_1 - M_0] - [(V_0 - M_0) - (V_1 - M_1)],
\end{aligned}$$

or, in our case,

$$\begin{aligned}
\overline{EI}_1 = &[\$12,000 - \$10,000] - [(\$11,322 - \$10,000) \\
&- (\$12,454 - \$12,000)]
\end{aligned}$$

$$V_1 = E_1 + \frac{E_2}{(1 + i)},$$

and

$$V_1 - V_0 = \frac{E_1 + iE_1 - E_1}{(1 + i)} + \frac{E_2 + iE_2 - E_2}{(1 + i)^2} = iV_0.$$

$$= [\$2{,}000] - [(\$1{,}322) - (\$454)]$$
$$= [\$2{,}000] - [\$868]$$
$$= \$1{,}132$$

At the outset there is a certain subjective goodwill, $V_0 - M_0$, which it is expected will be turned into market value by the end of the plan. Expected economic income in period 1 consists of the increase in market value which will have been generated in period 1 (if expectations are realized) $[M_1 - M_0]$ less the decline in this subjective goodwill $[(V_0 - M_0) - (V_1 - M_1)]$—this decline occurring because some of the initial subjective goodwill has already been turned into market value and less remains to be converted into market value in the future.

It is probable that, when the period has passed, expectations will not prove to have been entirely correct. The *evaluation process* consists of analyzing the deviations of actual events from expected events. Suppose that, after the first period has passed but before any dividend has been paid, the subjective value then assigned to the firm's plan of operation (now extended to cover period 3) is V_1', and this value differs from the expected value (V_1) by the amount c. Then actual economic income $(\overline{EI}_1')$ will differ from the economic income originally anticipated for this period $(\overline{EI}_1)$ by c, i.e.,

$$\overline{EI}_1' = V_1' - V_0 = (V_1 + c) - V_0.$$

Suppose, in our example, that $V_1' = \$13{,}222$.[6] Then actual economic income is

$$\overline{EI}_1' = V_1' - V_0 = \$13{,}222 - \$11{,}322 = \$1{,}900.$$

---

6. This is based, say, on the assumption that the original asset, wisely or unwisely, is kept, and is still expected to earn \$6,000 in period 2 and that any income not paid out as dividends in period 1 can be reinvested in an asset which would yield 20 per cent on book value in each of periods 2 and 3 (with straight-line depreciation appropriate). Then V_1'', *after dividends in period 1,* is as follows:

$$V_1'' = \frac{\$6{,}000}{1.1} + \frac{.2(\$7{,}000 - .1V_1'') + \dfrac{\$7{,}000 - .1V_1''}{2}}{1.1}$$

$$+ \frac{.2\left(\dfrac{\$7{,}000 - .1V_1''}{2}\right) + \dfrac{\$7{,}000 - .1V_1''}{2}}{(1.1)^2}$$

$$= \$5{,}455 + \$4{,}454 - .0636\,V_1'' + \$3{,}471 - .0496\,V_1''$$

Unexpected economic income, c, is then

$$\overline{EI\,'_1} - \overline{EI}_1 = \$1,900 - \$1,132 = \$768.$$

The deviation c tells us very little by itself. V'_1 at the end of period 1 may differ from its originally expected value (a) because the market value of the firm's assets at the end of period 1 just before dividend payments (its earnings in period 1 plus the value of its plant asset at the end of the period) differs from expectations and/or (b) because expectations of changes in market value in subsequent periods (as reflected in differences in actual from expected subjective goodwill at the end of period 1) are now different from those entertained at the beginning of the period. Hence, the amount that the firm could now pay as dividends and still feel as well off as it did at the beginning of the period may differ from expected economic income not only because events of period 1 deviated from expectations but also because expectations about still future events have changed. We have, thus,

$$c = a + b.$$

The *deviation* components a and b are analogous to the components of economic income ascertained above, i.e., we have:

$$\overline{EI\,'_1} = [M'_1 - M_0] - [(V_0 - M_0) - (V'_1 - M'_1)],$$

$$\overline{EI}_1 = [M_1 - M_0] - [(V_0 - M_0) - (V_1 - M_1)],$$

or, subtracting,

$$[\overline{EI\,'_1} - \overline{EI}_1] = \quad [M'_1 - M_1] \quad + [(V'_1 - M'_1) - (V_1 - M_1)]$$
$$\quad c \qquad = \qquad a \qquad + \qquad\qquad b$$

Consider first the market value of the firm's assets before dividend payments. Those were originally expected to be worth \$12,000 ($=M_1$), composed of \$7,000 in cash (earnings) and \$5,000 as the value of

---

$$1.1132 V''_1 = \$13,380$$
$$V''_1 = \$12,020.$$

The first term is earnings on the original asset in period 2, the second is earnings on the period 1 reinvestment in period 2 [where earnings are income plus depreciation and (\$7,000 − .1V''_1) is the amount reinvested], and the third is earnings on the period 1 reinvestment in period 3. An amount iV''_1 can be paid out in dividends in period 1 (and forever if expectations are realized), and so V''_1 before dividends in period 1 is \$12,020 + \$1,202 = \$13,222. The reader can verify that if expectations in periods 2 and 3 are realized, sufficient securities can be bought at the end of each of those periods (\$8,857 in period 2 and \$3,163 in period 3 = \$12,020) after payment of dividends of \$1,202 each period so that the dividends could be continued forever.

the plant asset now one-period-old. In fact, the firm's assets are now worth \$13,000 ($=M_1'$), composed of \$7,000 in cash and a one-period-old asset worth \$6,000. Instead of the expected increase in market value of \$12,000 $-$ \$10,000 $=$ \$2,000, the increase has turned out to be \$3,000. Hence, component a of unexpected economic income is \$1,000. Component b is

$$[(\$13,222 - \$13,000) - (\$12,454 - \$12,000)] = -\$232.$$

Thus,

$$
\begin{array}{ccc}
c & = & a & + & b \\
\$768 = & \$1,000 & - \$232.
\end{array}
$$

While we will make no further substantive use of component b (and, therefore, none of unexpected economic income c), its nature must be explained in order to justify its rejection for accounting purposes. Subjective goodwill, the excess of subjective value over market value at the end of period 1 before dividends, was originally expected to be \$12,454 $-$ \$12,000 $=$ \$454. It has turned out to be \$13,222 $-$ \$13,000 $=$ \$222. It is, in fact, \$232 less than originally expected. This is the amount by which the unexpected increase in market value in period 1 exceeds the unexpected increase in subjective value deriving from changes in expectations about events in periods 2 and 3. Hence, less subjective goodwill is now expected to be converted into market value in subsequent periods than was originally expected to remain for future conversion at this time. If expectations about still future events improved sufficiently, the unexpected change in goodwill at the end of period 0, component b, could be positive. Clearly, component b and unexpected economic income itself, component c, contain changes in expectations about still future events, and these cannot be tested against objective market events of this period. It follows that economic income in either its expected or actual forms is useless as a means of evaluating expectations about present and past events in order to improve expectations about future events, to make dividend and reinvestment decisions, and to formulate a new plan for the future. It is, then, the measurement and analysis of component a, the deviation of actual events from expected events *of the same period*, on which the evaluation of expectations must be based.

How much of the subjective goodwill prevailing at the start of period 1 was expected to be turned into market value and how much *was actually* turned into market value in period 1—and why the difference? This question relates to measurable events of period 1. How much subjective goodwill exists and remains to be turned into market value in the future and how expectations may have changed between period 0 and period 1 with respect to this are matters to be tested against future events. It is only component a of unexpected economic income that is relevant for accounting and the evaluation of decisions and performance because only component a depends solely on actual and expected events of period 1; component b depends solely upon changes in subjective expectations about still future events. The fundamental question we must address is what are the actual events and the original expectations about them which together determine component a and how can these events be classified and measured in order to improve decisions and the decision-making process and properly evaluate performance.

Current Income and Its Components

We have defined current income for a period as the increase in market value of the firm from the beginning to the end of the period. The deviation of actual current income from expected current income is, therefore, our component a of unexpected economic income derived above. Further, we can and, we believe, should separate current income into two components: (1) *current operating income* (COI), the excess over a period of the current value of output sold over the current cost of related inputs—when both are expressed in terms of prices prevailing during the period; and (2) *realizable cost savings or holding gains* (RHG), which consist of any increases during the period in the values of assets and any decreases in the values of liabilities while these assets and liabilities are held by the firm. These two types of gains arise from totally different types of events—one involving the transformation of inputs into goods which are sold at a higher value, and the other involving increases in the values of assets (or decreases in the values of liabilities) simply because of changes in market conditions outside the firm. Even if some or, indeed, all of the holding gains are related to operations in the sense that the assets and liabilities involved are required to generate operating income, it is useful to distinguish between the two types of gains and measure actual events against expected events with respect to each.

If we apply these concepts to evaluating component a and our plan in period 1, we have the following:

	Expected	Actual	Variance
Earnings	$7,000	$7,000	0
Depreciation	5,000	6,000	+$1,000

Current Operating Income	$2,000	$1,000	−$1,000
Realizable Holding Gains	0	2,000	+ 2,000
Current Income	$2,000	$3,000	+$1,000

The *current cost* of using the asset over the period is its decline in market value over the period from $12,000 to $6,000. That decline is no longer consistent with internal rate of return depreciation. Our expected earnings pattern applied to a $12,000 asset yields a 5.65 per cent internal rate of return and depreciation of $6,322 in period 1 and $5,678 in period 2. Nevertheless, in working with market values as we must now do, it is the decline in the market value of the asset during the period (because of aging and use) which is the appropriate figure to use for current cost depreciation, not our estimate of what the market value should be if others shared our experience and expectations.[7]

The *realizable cost savings or holding gains* on our asset in period 1 are, of course, based on the fact that the asset rose in price from $10,000 to $12,000—while we held it—at the very beginning of the period. We paid only $10,000 for an asset worth $12,000 the next day. As we use the asset, we use up or *realize* this $2,000 realizable holding gain or *cost saving*. In period 1 we realize half the gain (the excess of current cost depreciation of $6,000 over historic cost depreciation of $5,000); and if prices do not change further and our earnings expectations for period 2 materialize, we will realize the remainder of the gain in period 2.

Now what does our current income tabulation tell us? First, it tells us clearly that our investment is not *currently* profitable. On an asset whose market value was $12,000 at the beginning of the period, we earned only $1,000 income on operations (not the $2,000 income from operations reported in traditional accounting income—that figure includes as operating income the portion of the *cost saving* or holding gain that was realized in period 1) for an 8.33 per cent return, less than risk-free interest. If expected earnings in period 2 remain $6,000, we will earn a zero rate of return in period 2—$6,000 earnings from an asset worth $6,000. Not only should we not reinvest in this activity, we should sell our one-period-old asset—we can do better by investing

7. If there is no used-asset market, we may have to apply some use pattern and assume used assets change in value in accordance with this use pattern being applied to new asset prices. That most assuredly will yield a *better* approximation of market value than depreciation based on historical cost. But if used-asset prices exist, we should certainly use these.

the proceeds in risk-free securities. But, of course, the original investor
is not badly off, as the reporting of our realizable holding gain shows.
Indeed, the investor is better off than anticipated, given expected current
income in period 1 of $2,000 and actual current income of $3,000.

With our data on current income and its components in hand, we
are surely now in a better position to make dividend-reinvestment
decisions at the end of period 1 and to formulate a plan for periods
2 and 3. The first thing we must do is assess carefully the $6,000
expected earnings figure from our one-period-old plant asset in period
2. If this figure remains as our expected earnings from using the asset
in period 2, we should, unless we are constrained by contract commitments or the like, either consider alternative uses for the asset or sell
the asset immediately for $6,000.

What *alternative* investment options do we have? Perhaps we could
use our asset differently (for example, more intensively) or produce
different products with it. Suppose none of these possibilities yields
an expected rate of return in excess of the market rate of interest.
Then we should sell the asset and pay the owner $13,000 and go
out of business. The owner will have gotten income equal to the current
income figure of $3,000 on a $10,000 investment, generated a 30 per
cent rate of return, and surely be happy. Even if the owner now invests
the $13,000 only at interest, he or she will be better off at the end
of the plan period, with $14,300 in cash, than expected—he or she
expected $13,700, as shown in the outline of the plan.

But few firms go out of business when they have done well by their
owners. Suppose our firm casts about and finds a new activity that
is expected to yield a 20 per cent return over periods 2 and 3. How
much should the firm pay out in dividends and how much should
be reinvested? There is no simple answer to this question; it turns
not only on expectations of future events but also on the amount and
composition of a firm's assets and liabilities. But the current income
measure for period 1 yields a better view of the firm's accomplishments
and, hence, provides a better basis for judging its future options than
other measures.

Suppose we set as an arbitrary goal for the firm the continuous
maintenance of market value, i.e., the firm pays out in dividends any
excess over and above the amount necessary to maintain market value.
Then clearly it can pay out current income, which by definition is
the increase in market value of the firm over the period. If the firm
sells the one-period-old asset at the end of period 1 for $6,000, it
has $13,000 in cash, can pay out the $3,000 current income in dividends,
and start over, buying a new asset for $10,000 which is to yield a
20 per cent return in periods 2 and 3.

Suppose, however, it is constrained by advance commitments from selling the asset at the end of period 1. It can still pay out $3,000 and maintain market value. But dividends will then be reduced even more than anticipated in period 2. In accordance with the original plan, current income was expected to fall from $2,000 in period 1 to $1,000 in period 2; now it will fall from $3,000 to $800—20 per cent on the $4,000 invested ($7,000 earnings less $3,000 dividends) in the new asset and a zero rate of return on the old asset.

Under these circumstances a firm might well decide to even out its dividends, period-by-period. In the example, management can do this by paying out in dividends only current operating income plus that portion of a period's realizable cost savings or holding gains which is realized (through use or sale) in that period. Since we are assuming new assets can be purchased to yield a 20 per cent return on invested capital, like the old asset, it can be seen that dividends can then be $2,000 in each period and the firm can continue to maintain its market value at the end of the (new) plan, assuming management's new expectations on earnings are exactly realized and there are no price changes on the firm's assets (see Table 11-1). The new asset purchased at the end of period 1 for $5,000 has an expected life of two periods and is expected to yield 20 per cent each period on book value (increasing

TABLE 11-1

	Actual	Planned						
		Period						
	1	2				3		
	Original Asset	Old Asset	New Asset	Total		Old Asset	New Asset	Total
1. Earnings	$ 7,000	$6,000	$2,750	$ 8,750		$3,900	$8,100	$12,000
2. Depreciation	6,000	6,000	1,750	7,750		3,250	6,750	10,000
3. Current Operating Income	$ 1,000			$ 1,000				$ 2,000
4. Realizable Holding Gains	2,000			0				0
5. Current Income	$ 3,000			$ 1,000				$ 2,000
6. Dividends	2,000			2,000				2,000
7. Reinvestment (1) − (6)	5,000			6,750				10,000
8. Book Value, beginning of period	10,000			11,000				10,000
9. Rate of return (5) ÷ (8)	30%			9%				20%

depreciation charges are required, given its expected earnings pattern). The asset to be purchased at the end of period 2 is a one-period-life asset yielding 20 per cent, a yield we continue to use for purposes of simplicity. By the end of period 3, if things go as planned, the firm will be back on track, just maintaining its market value, and will have maintained a steady dividend stream.

But this is only one of many new plans that could be evolved. The point is that managers can fashion a *better* plan if they have current value data than if they do not. And interested outsiders have the same interest in and need for current value information. Current income as a concept is not a poor substitute to be used in accounting in place of the ideal of economic income. Current income is the *component* of economic income—and the only portion of it—that is relevant for accounting, which must measure present and past events, and as such is a concept having validity in its own right. For evaluative purposes it *is* the ideal, not a poor substitute for it. By contrasting the usefulness of current value information with that which is formulated today in accordance with present accounting practices, let us see why this is so.

CURRENT INCOME AND TRADITIONAL ACCOUNTING INCOME CONTRASTED AND COMPARED

It can be seen from the simple example above that under our present assumptions (allowing individual asset prices to change but not, as yet, the general price level), current income meets our first two tests set forth in the introduction. It properly classifies change into operating income and holding gains so as to make clear why the change occurred. Second, current income reports *all* the events of the period and *only* the events of the period. Traditional accounting income, in terms of present practice, meets neither of these tests.

Traditional accounting income, which is based on historical costs and ignores price changes which occur while an asset is held, would consist of expected and actual income for our example as follows:

Traditional Accounting Income

	Expected	Actual	Variance
Earnings	$7,000	$7,000	0
Depreciation	5,000	5,000	0
Operating Income	$2,000	$2,000	0

We may alter our projections of expected events in period 2 and amend our thoughts on the worth of our initial investment, but the accounting data provided do not suggest any reason to do this. Traditional accounting income does not include holding gains that have occurred but are as yet unrealized (such as the $1,000 gain in value in period 1 on our one-period-old asset which we have not used up yet). And it not only reports some holding gains that were *generated* in past periods but *realized* in this period as gains of this period (thus violating the other part of our "*all . . . only*" requirement), it also reports those (realized) holding gains as part of operating income. Thus, if events went in accordance with the new plan for period 2 (p. 469), traditional accounting income would consist of $2,000 income from operations for that period because it would combine current operating income of $1,000 with a holding gain of $1,000 which *accrued* in period 1 but was *realized* in period 2, i.e., traditional accounting income would simply deduct historical cost depreciation of $5,000 on the old asset and $1,750 on the new from earnings of $8,750 and report the difference as income from operations.

The two income concepts can be contrasted as follows. If

A represents *current operating income*—the excess over a period of the current value of output sold over the current cost of related inputs;

B represents *realizable cost savings* or *holding gains*—the increase in the current cost of assets while held by the firm during the period;

C represents *realized holding gains through sale*—the excess of proceeds over (depreciated) historical costs on the irregular sale or disposal of assets (not illustrated in the example); and

D represents *realized holding gains through use*—the excess of the current cost over the historical cost of inputs used in producing output sold;

	Income elements included as operating income	as holding gains
Traditional Accounting Income	$A + D$	C
Current Income	A	B

Note that *B* is *not* simply the sum of $C + D +$ unrealized gains that have accrued this period because *D* may, and normally will, include gains that have accrued in past periods but are realized in this period.

B is $C + D +$ unrealized gains accruing in this period *minus gains that have accrued in past periods* (and are, thus, part of past period B's) but are realized in this period, or it is the total of all (realized and unrealized) holding gains that have accrued in this period.

Because current income meets our first two tests—properly classifying change and reporting all the events of a period and only the events of that period—and traditional accounting income does not, current income is a vastly superior measure in the essential evaluation process which both insiders and interested outsiders must continuously perform. We have seen how current income and its components, which properly showed that there were significant variances from plan in period 1 (whereas traditional accounting income indicated no variances), opened up new options for the managers of the business and influenced their decision-making with respect to the next planning period. Specifically, current value data make clear to managers the advisability of selling the existing asset (if there is no change in earnings expectations—and, since actual earnings in period 1 did equal expected earnings, there is perhaps little reason to change expectations for period 2). To do so increases the subjective goodwill available from the original investment.[8] Second, the information directs management to look for new, profitable alternative investments for any reinvestment of earnings. Only if such alternatives can be found is reinvestment justified, i.e., reinvestment in the existing line of activity is *not* justified under our assumptions.

The argument is often made that many businesses, for reasons such as the above, do indeed develop current value data for their own use

8. A change in asset value, earnings expectations remaining unchanged, does not alter subjective goodwill; but it does change the *timing* of the turning of subjective goodwill into market value, and this may well affect decisions. Thus, the new current income and excess current income stream on our original asset (as seen from period 0) is:

	Period	
	1	2
	Actual	Expected
Current Income from investment	$3,000	0
less Interest on previous period's asset value tied up in investment	1,000	$600
equals Excess Current Income	$2,000	−$600

The present value in period 0 of this new excess current income stream is still $1,322, equal to the original subjective goodwill. But if the asset is sold at the end of period 1 and the proceeds invested at interest in period 2, the negative excess current income in period 2 is avoided and subjective goodwill as seen from period 0 would be $1,818.

but do not feel that it is justifiable to supplement the required traditional accounting income data with current value data in their public reports. Such data are relevant for managers but not outsiders. But interested outsiders—for example, actual or prospective stockholders, security analysts, creditors, and government regulators—*also* have a legitimate interest in and need for current value information. They, too, need to know that our firm is not in a currently profitable line of activity (as shown by the current operating income figure, in particular with reference to current values of assets on the position statement) but that *existing* shareholders have not yet been hurt and, indeed, may be quite well off (because of the realizable holding gains that accrued in period 1).

The advantages of current income and current values on the comparative position statement over traditional accounting income and historical costs on the comparative position statement are also evident when we apply our other two tests—performance comparisons between firms and over time. Suppose a second firm, identical in size to the firm in our example, buys a *different* $10,000 two-period-life machine in period 0, for which straight-line depreciation is appropriate. That machine produces the same $7,000 in earnings in period 1 but does *not* rise in price. Both firms would report traditional accounting income in period 1 of $2,000. But as we have made clear, current income data show that our firm is in serious trouble in terms of operating income in its chosen line of activity. The reporting of realizable holding gains on the income statement and current values on the position statement shows that our shareholders are not suffering—yet—and, indeed, may be better off than firm 2's shareholders if the firm can change direction, sell its assets, and reinvest so as to earn, say, a 20 per cent return, or use its assets differently. It is surely wrong to report the performance of these two firms in period 1 as being identical.

On comparison of performance over time, if our firm carries through on its period 2–3 plan, traditional accounting income would be $2,000 in period 1 and $2,000 in period 2, all reported as income on operations from assets worth $10,000 each period on the position statement— identical performance in the two periods. Current income would report $1,000 for current operating income in each period (identical, but lower performance on operations) but a realizable cost saving or holding gain of $2,000 in period 1. The current income components highlight the fact that the firm made a good purchasing and timing decision, reflected in its period 1 holding gains and rise in value of the assets on the position statement, but not necessarily a good long-run operating decision. The holding gain should all be recognized in the period when it occurred, not part of it in period 1 and part of it in period 2, as the holding gain or cost saving was *realized* through use of an asset which had gone up in price. Only then can performance be properly attributed to the time—and managers responsible at that time—that the event occurred. If holding gains are reported only when realized (and they may be realized over a long time span, say, in the case of a 20-year asset), later managers of the firm get credit (reported income is higher) for decisions made by earlier managers. And if these realized holding gains are reported as income from operations, as traditional accounting income does, later managers get credit for *current operating performance*, whereas the gain is actually attributable to an *earlier purchasing decision.*

CURRENT VALUES FOR OTHER ASSETS AND LIABILITIES

The reporting of current values in the position statement and of current income in the income statement, as applied to plant assets and revenues and expenses associated with those assets, should clearly apply to other assets and liabilities of the firm. We will consider three such items, two assets and one liability.

Marketable Securities

Perhaps the easiest and most obvious asset to put into current value terms is marketable securities held by the firm. Assuming that they are regularly traded in stock and bond markets, their current market values are readily available. Indeed, most firms are constantly trading in these securities themselves. If securities go up in value while held by the firm and are sold, a gain is recognized in present accounting records. If they go up in value but are not sold this period, a realizable holding gain should be recorded and would be, following the current value method.

The reasoning is essentially the same as that employed in analyzing the effects of a price change on our plant asset. But here it is more obvious because treasurers of firms and investment analysts readily *think* in terms of *current yields* on marketable securities. Their decision-making process is based on analysis in these terms and on thinking in terms of holding gains as well as earnings from the security. If one purchases in year 0 for $100 a five-year $100 bond yielding eight per cent interest, one is inevitably thinking in terms of what interest rates are going to do in the future. If interest rates go up to ten per cent in the first year of the bond, the value of the bond should drop to $93.66 and there is a realizable holding loss.[9] That loss should be recognized in year 1 when it occurred, whether or not the bond is sold in year 1. The treasurer of the firm which bought the bond in year 0 has generated only $1.64 current income on the security in year 1, having earned interest of $8, and suffered a realizable holding loss of $6.34. It is the investment merits of this treasurer that management and outsiders must assess. Suppose a new treasurer comes in year 1 and decides to hold the bond in the belief that interest rates are going to go down in year 2 to eight per cent—and they do. Then the new treasurer should get credit for the realizable holding gain of $6.34 in year 2. It is no good to say that the first treasurer *expected* that after rising to ten per cent in year 1 interest rates would fall back to eight per cent in year 2 and the realizable loss occurring in year 1 would be recouped in year 2. If the treasurer had expected that, he or she should have bought a one-year-to-maturity bond in year 0 yielding eight per cent, earning $8 in current income (the bond matures and so there is no realizable loss) in year 1. The first treasurer (or the new one) could then have invested in a new ten per cent bond in year 1 and gotten the realizable holding gain consequent upon the fall in interest rates in year 2.

Again, it is *current income* generated by an asset, the change in its market value which occurred in the period in question, that is important in the making and evaluation of decisions. The reporting of an income of $8 in year 1 and year 2, as would be done using historical costs, overstates income in year 1 and understates income in year 2. It cannot be used to evaluate effectively the decision to buy in year 0 or the decision to hold and not to sell in year 1 or to point to what should have been done, i.e., buy a one-year-to-maturity bond in year 0 and a ten per cent bond in year 1. And again it is current income and current values on the position statement that are essential in comparing performance among firms. Suppose Firm A invested in the eight per cent bond in year 0 and retained it in year 1 as above, while Firm B invested in the one-year-to-maturity eight per cent bond at the end of year 0 and bought a ten per cent four-year bond at the end of year 1 with the proceeds from the repayment of principal. Interest rates were eight per cent in year zero, ten per cent in year 1, and

---

9. Using the present value formulas developed in the appendix to the chapter on plant assets and employed in the chapter on creditor equities, we have:

$$V_1 = \$8P_{\overline{4}|.10} + \$100p_{\overline{4}|.10} = \$93.66.$$

eight per cent thereafter. Reported income under our two methods
would be:

	Year			
	1		2	
	Firm A	Firm B	Firm A	Firm B
Traditional Accounting Income	$8	$8	$8	$10
Current Income	1.66	8	14.34	15.15

Traditional accounting income only marginally shows the better performance of Firm B, and then only in year 2, whereas its markedly
better performance was in year 1. Firm A (with its new treasurer)
did as well as could be expected in year 2, given its poor performance
in year 1 and the consequent decline in the market value of what
it had to invest in year 2.

Our illustration clearly shows the weakness of the "cost or market,
whichever is lower" convention that is sometimes used in traditional
accounting for both inventories and marketable securities (see Chapter
5 on "Inventory Assets"). Presumably one would recognize the realizable
holding loss of Firm A in year 1 and report holdings of $93.66 on
one's position statement. Current income would be reported for both
firms in year 1. Presumably one would have to recognize Firm A's
realizable cost saving or holding gain in year 2 as market value went
back up to historical cost, if this is recognized on the position statement,
so that marketable securities were reported as $100 there; it would
have to be recognized on the income statement for consistency. But
Firm B's realizable holding gain in year 2 would *not* be reported. This
makes no sense whatever and simply confuses both internal decision-
making and external comparisons among firms.

Inventories

The other principal asset for which prices often change sharply over
time is inventories. The effects of price changes in creating a divergence
between current costs and historical costs are not so prolonged as with
plant assets where the effect of using historical cost accounting may
be felt many years after the event, but the effects in any given period
may be sharper.[10]

10. See Edwards and Bell, *op. cit.*, Table 6, p. 138, for estimates of the percentage
overstatement and understatement of total corporate profits in the United States because
of failure to value inventories at current costs for 1929-1959. Perusal of recent U.S.

TABLE 11-2

Current Value Accounting for Inventories as Compared with LIFO and FIFO Historical Cost

	Period 1	Period 2	Period 3	Period 4
(1) Sales	24@$22 = $528	28@$21 = $588	30@$22.50 = $675	24@$22 = $528
(2) Purchases	20@$17 = $340	30@$16 = $480	32@$17.50 = $560	20@$17 = $340
(3) Beginning Inventory-FIFO	10@$20 = $200	6@$17 = $102	8@$16 = $128	10@$17.50 = $175
(4) Ending Inventory-FIFO	6@$17 = $102	8@$16 = $128	10@$17.50 = $175	6@$17 = $102
(5) Cost of Goods Sold-FIFO	$438	$454	$513	$413
(6) Income (Loss)-FIFO	$90	$134	$162	$115
(7) Beginning Inventory-LIFO	10@$20 = $200	6@$20 = $120	8 = $152	10 = $187
(8) Ending Inventory-LIFO	6@$20 = $120	6@$20+2@$16 = $152	6@$20+2@$16+2@$17.50 = $187	6@$20 = $120
(9) Cost of Goods Sold-LIFO	$420	$448	$525	$407
(10) Income-LIFO	$108	$140	$150	$121
(11) Beginning Inventory-Current Cost	10@$20 = $200	6@$15 = $90	8@$17 = $136	10@$20 = $200
(12) Ending Inventory-Current Cost	6@$15 = $90	8@$17 = $136	10@$20 = $200	6@$15 = $90
(13) Cost of Goods Sold-Current Cost	24@$17 = $408	28@$16 = $448	30@$17.50 = $525	24@$17 = $408
(14) Current Operating Income (COI)-Current Cost [=(1)−(13)]	$120	$140	$150	$120
(15) Realizable Holding Gains (RHG)-Current Cost[1]	$(42)	$14	$29	$(42)
(16) Current Income (CI)-Current Cost [=(14)+(15)]	$78	$154	$179	$78

1. There are alternative ways to compute realizable holding gains. Perhaps the easiest is to assume that the beginning inventory is sold (at purchase prices) during the period and the ending inventory is bought (at purchase prices) during the period. Thus, the realizable holding gain (loss) in period 1 would be $10 \times (-3) + 6(-2) = -42$ and in period 2 $6 \times (1) + 8(1) = 14$, and so on. We could get the same thing by assuming that 4 inventory in period 1 worth $20 at the beginning of the period were held and sold for $17 in period 2 [$RHG = 4 \times (-3) = -12$] and 6 inventory were held throughout the period [$RHG = 6 \times (-5) = -30$], for a total RHG of -42. No special "flow" assumption is necessary. This matter is considered further in Chapter 12 through use of an "input-output" approach.

We have shown in the chapter on inventory assets that *none* of the methods currently being used to value inventories and cost of goods sold (*including LIFO*) will normally yield the same figure for income in two different periods when the events of those two periods are identical. But current income can and does do this. The LIFO method is not a substitute for the use of current value accounting for inventories.

We can investigate the current income concept as it would apply to inventories and the cost of goods sold by reference to Table 11-2, which is an extension of the example used to illustrate FIFO, LIFO, and average cost concepts in the chapter on inventories.[11] For purposes of simplicity we assume that purchase prices for inventories change in each period in two discrete jumps, from the beginning of the period to the middle of the period when all purchases are made (which, in effect, can be considered an average of purchase prices during the period) and from the middle of the period to the end of the period. The beginning and ending inventories at current costs in lines 11 and 12 of Table 11-2 are simply the number of units held times the prices prevailing at the beginning and end of the period, respectively. The cost of goods sold (at current costs) in line 13 is simply the number of units sold (in line 1) times the average purchase price prevailing in the period. Current operating income is then line 1 minus line 13. Realizable holding gains in line 14 is, of course, the gain or loss experienced because inventories were held while their price changed (see footnote 1 to Table). Current income, then, is the sum of current operating income plus realizable holding gains. It is the change in the market value of the firm from the end of the previous period (after dividends) to the end of the current period (before dividends), i.e., in period 1 one starts off with no cash and inventories worth $200 and ends up, before dividends, with $188 in cash (revenues minus purchases) and $90 worth of inventories—market value has increased by $78, which is what the current income figure reports.

It is clear from a study of the table that neither FIFO- nor LIFO-reported income in any way approximates the current income figure or even current operating income (LIFO equals this figure when inventory volume increases—or stays the same—but misses, erratically, when inventory volume falls). The failure of traditional inventory methods to report a meaningful income figure—and the success of

---

Department of Commerce data show that generally overstatement is much more marked for inflationary years since 1968.

11. See Table 5-1, the illustration being adapted from Edwards and Bell, *op. cit.,* Table 7, p. 156.

current income in doing this—is brought out dramatically by comparing periods 1 and 4 in Table 11-2. Events in these two periods were identical. Yet FIFO reports a 28 per cent larger profit in the fourth period; LIFO, a 12 per cent larger profit in period four. The current income figure, on the other hand, is the same for the two periods and correctly reports a $78 increase in the market value of the firm in each period.

Nor do differences in reported incomes under the different methods "wash out" over the four-period cycle. If we sum the reported incomes by each of the four methods for the four periods, we get:

FIFO	$501
LIFO	519
Current Income	489

If we sum cash receipts and subtract the sum of cash expenditures (assuming that the excess of the former over the latter is left idle—otherwise we would have to add interest in computing incomes), add our period 4 ending inventory at market value, and subtract our initial investment, we get:

Cash receipts	$2,319
less Cash expenditures	1,720
	$ 599
plus Ending Inventory	90
	$ 689
less Initial Investment	200
equals Gain in Market Value	$ 489

The cumulative current income figure correctly reflects the four-period profit to the firm; the other three methods overstate it in varying degrees.

Not only does current income, and only current income, show the gain in market value over the four periods and in each of the four periods (and so serve in a valuable way in decision-making and evaluation—such as whether to stay in or get out of the business), but the components of current income pinpoint the problem.

The problem lies not in operations, wherein the firm is earning at better than a 100 per cent rate of return on invested capital, but in the purchasing manager's office. Suppose the purchasing manager were limited to a minimum inventory of six (for purposes of operations) and a maximum inventory of ten (because of storage limitations). Clearly he should have held six (not ten) inventory at the beginning of period 1 and ten (not six and eight) inventory at the beginning of periods 2 and 3, stocking up from six to ten at the end of periods 1 and 2. And he should have run his inventory down to six again (not ten) at the end of period 3. He would then have had a cumulative realizable holding loss over the four periods of −$10 rather than −$41. Realizable holding gains in the four periods under the new assumptions would be:

1	2	3	4
$6 \times (-3) = -18$	$10 \times (1) = 10$	$10 \times (.50) = 5$	$6 \times (-3) = -18$
$6 \times (-2) = -12$	$10 \times (1) = 10$	$10 \times (2.50) = 25$	$6 \times (-2) = -12$
−30	20	30	−30

Finally, our illustration shows again the value of the current income concept in making comparisons among firms. One has great difficulty in comparing performance between, say, two identical firms if they report different incomes because of using a different inventory system (LIFO, FIFO, or average cost). Our FIFO firm would report a smaller profit in period 1 than our LIFO firm. If both use current income, they report the same income in period 1 and in every other period. (Of course, if they both use LIFO, they report the same income, too, but it is not the income that portrays the events of that period; the evaluator is misled with respect to *both* firms.)

Long-Term Liabilities

If decision-making and evaluation and performance comparison are improved by current value accounting for assets, the same should apply to liabilities. Consider again the basic model developed at the beginning of this chapter of an asset initially valued at $10,000 to generate $7,000 in period 1 and $6,000 in period 2 and to be worth nothing at the end of period 2 (see page 469). Suppose, further, that the initial investment of $10,000 was financed half by owner capital and half by issuance of two-year ten per cent bonds paying $500 a year interest and having an initial value and a final maturity value of $5,000.

Suppose now that there are no price changes and expected earnings of $7,000 materialize, but interest rates rise in the market at the beginning of period 1 to 15 per cent. As we have seen in the chapter on creditor equities, this should cause a fall in the market value of the firm's long-term liability to $4,594 at the beginning of period 1, and at the end of period 1 its market value would be $4,783.[12] Dividends paid, we assume, are now current (entity) income minus interest payments of $500, or $1,500; cash receipts ($7,000) less interest ($500) less dividends ($1,500) equals cash reinvested ($5,000). Let us say that the $5,000 reinvested, perhaps in a one-period-old machine like our original (for that is turning out to be profitable), earns 20 per cent in period 2. In accordance with current value income concepts, we should then report:

		Period	
		1	2
	Earnings	$7,000	$12,000
less	Current Cost Depreciation	5,000	10,000
	Current Entity Income	$2,000	$ 2,000
less	Current Interest Charges	689	717
		$1,311	$ 1,283
plus	Realizable Holding Gain of Owners	406	—
	Current Ownership Income	$1,717	$ 1,283
less	Dividends	1,500	1,500
	Contribution to Current Capital	$ 217	$ (217)

Current entity income is unaffected by matters which simply rearrange equities, for it is defined as the change in the market value of assets from one period to the next other than those changes due to new contributions by creditors (any increase in the market value of liabilities) and/or owners and before any distribution of assets to creditors (in the form of interest) and/or to owners (in the form of dividends or other income paid to owners). But from current entity income we now subtract *current interest charges,* i.e., the current value of long-term liabilities at the beginning of the period times the current rate of interest

12. The present value of the annuity ("interest" stream) after the change in interest rate at the beginning of period 1 is:

$$500 \, P_{\overline{2}|.15} = \$500 \times 1.62571 = \$812.85.$$

The present value of the single-sum payable at maturity is:

$$\$5,000 \, p_{\overline{2}|.15} = \$5,000 \times .75614 = \$3,780.70.$$

The total present value is $812.85 + 3,780.70 = $4,593.55. For the end of period 1,

$$\$500 \, P_{\overline{1}|.15} = \quad \$500 \times .86957 = \quad \$434.78$$
$$\$5,000 \, p_{\overline{1}|.15} = \quad \$5,000 \times .86957 = \$4,347.85$$

Total $4,782.63

which we would have to pay were we borrowing money this period ($4,594 × .15 = $689 in period 1, and $4,783 × .15 = $717 in period 2).

The realizable holding gain of owners stems from the decline in the value of the long-term liability which occurred at the beginning of period 1 because of the rise in interest rates, i.e., $406 = $5,000.00 − $4,594). This gain is realized through use of the borrowed money, $189 in period 1 (the excess of the current interest charge over nominal, or historical cost charge) and $217 in period 2 ($189 + $217 = $406).

It will be seen that after dividends in period 1 there will be a contribution to current capital of owners of $217 which is just equal to the decline in the market value of long-term liabilities, as should be shown on the position statement in period 1 and compared with period 0; i.e., we have:

Comparative Position Statement
end of periods 0 and 1

(Current Values)

	Period			Period	
	0	1		0	1
Assets	$10,000	$10,000	Bonds payable	$ 5,000	$ 4,783
			Ownership	5,000	5,217
	$10,000	$10,000		$10,000	$10,000

In period 2 the bonds payable go back up to $5,000 at the end of the period, and ownership goes back down to $5,000 with a negative contribution to current capital of $217, as shown above.

Again we can show the significance for decision-making and evaluation of performance of current value accounting. Let us suppose that the prices of the original $10,000 machine and of a one-period-old machine went up only six per cent, to $10,600 and $5,300, respectively. It was in part the consequent decline in current operating income and the forecast, say, of significantly lower current (entity) income in period 2 by some security analysts that threw a scare into bondholders and caused the price of this firm's bonds to fall to $4,783 in the market by the end of period 1 and, thus, the effective *borrowing* rate of interest for this company to become fifteen per cent. The interest on risk-free securities is still ten per cent; hence, that continues to be the rate to be used in calculating the present value of future earnings of the firm in decision-making on *investments*. And the earnings projected by the firm's manager-owners are unchanged—it is only outside lenders who have adjusted this projection downward.

The firm can then show owners that further investment in its activity will earn excess current income, that it has positive subjective goodwill. At the end of period 1, it has a convincing case to put to owners that if only $1,200 of cash earnings of $7,000 less interest of $500 is paid in dividends and the remaining $5,300 invested in a one-period-old machine, owners will be better off by the end of period 2 (when we will again say the firm liquidates) than if the $5,300 were invested in risk-free securities (by owners or by the firm). The present values of the two options at the end of period 1 (assuming the firm invests in the risk-free securities at ten per cent) show:

	Dividends in period		Present Value (end of period 1)
	1	*2*	
I. Firm invests in machine	$1,200	$6,500	$1,200 + \dfrac{\$6,500}{1.1} = \$7,109$
II. Firm invests in securities	$1,200	$6,330	$1,200 + \dfrac{\$6,330}{1.1} = \$6,955$

But now current value accounting has thrown up a third option for the firm and its owners. It could pay off its bonds payable at a price of $4,783 (buying the bonds in the market); and it, or the owners, will earn interest of ten per cent on the residual cash.

	Dividends in period		Present Value (end of period 1)
	1	*2*	
III. Firm pays off bonds	$1,200	$6,569	$1,200 + \dfrac{\$6,569}{1.1} = \$7,172$

Clearly, Option III is the preferred option. It comes to light only if current values are reported for liabilities as well as for assets.[13] Further, it is the treasurer of periods 0 and 1 who should be applauded by

---

13. Dividends in period 2 in this exercise are cash receipts less payments, i.e.,

I $12,000 (from two machines) − $5,500 (interest and principal on bond) = $6,500

II $6,000 (from one machine) + $5,830 (interest and principal on securities) − $5,500 (interest and principal on bond) = $6,330

III $6,000 (from one machine) + $569 [interest and principal on securities, i.e., $517 ($5,300 − $4,783) was reinvested at 10% interest and $517 × 1.1 = $569] = $6,569

owners (and perhaps chastised by creditors) for having opened up the possibility of Option III. The gains that the treasurer produced for owners (at the expense of creditors) should be recorded when he or she was in charge.

CHANGES IN THE GENERAL PRICE LEVEL AND COMPARISONS OVER TIME

We have tried to show that changing individual prices of assets and liabilities of a firm can have significant effects on decision-making and evaluation of performance, by insiders and interested outsiders, and that therefore to measure and assess this performance we must have data which incorporates these changes into the firm's reports—as current value accounting does. Under the assumption that there are no changes in the general price level, current income meets all four of the tests set out at the beginning of the chapter, whereas traditional accounting income meets none of the four. What happens if we introduce changes in the general price level (inflation and deflation) in the economy?

There was a period when some students of the problem thought of corrections for individual price changes and corrections for changes in the general price level as an either/or proposition—either you corrected for individual price changes or the general price level but not for both. But if one holds some Xerox stock and wants to see how he or she fared this week, one does not look at *just* the price of a share of Xerox stock *nor certainly* just at the Dow-Jones or Standard and Poor's index. One looks at both and compares. If the price of Xerox rises by ten per cent, and so, too, the prices of all other stocks on the stock exchange, the Xerox owner experiences an increase in command over dollars but not in command over shares of stocks. On the other hand, if Xerox rises by ten per cent and other share prices are unchanged, he or she has greater command over both dollars and stocks.

It is the same way with business firms and changes in individual prices of their assets and liabilities and changes in the general price level. The existence of positive current income in a period recognizes increased *command over dollars* on the part of owners. But the value of a dollar changes over time in terms of its *command over goods*. If the market value (in dollars) of a firm rises by ten per cent but *all* prices in the economy also rise by ten per cent, the shareholder experiences a ten per cent increase in the dollars owned; but these cannot be turned into more commodities or services to consume. In other words, the *real* position of the stockholder is unchanged.

The value of money is thus measured by the quantity of goods a dollar can buy. If bread is the only good in question and its price rises from $0.50 in period 1 to $1.00 in period 2, then the value of a dollar has been halved—from two loaves to one loaf. Where many goods are involved, we must relate the purchasing power of a dollar to a "basket" of goods, with their prices weighted by proportionate volumes that are normally consumed. If the basket normally consumed is one loaf of bread and two pounds of fish and the price of bread doubles while the price of a pound of fish rises from $1.25 to $1.50, the basket of one loaf of bread and two pounds of fish which cost $3.00 in period 1 will cost $4.00 in period 2. The price index rises 33 per cent, i.e., goes from 100 in period 1 to 133 in period 2. To make period 1 dollars comparable to period 2 dollars, we must *multiply* period 1 dollars by 133/100 or 1.33 to show that one "period 1 dollar" is worth 4/3 of one "period 2 dollar," or $1.33. To make period 2 dollars comparable to period 1 dollars, we must *divide* them by 1.33 to show that one "period 2 dollar" is worth $1 ÷ 1.33 = three-quarters of one "period 1 dollar," or $.75.

It follows that if a firm had assets worth $10,000 in 1960 dollars and assets worth $15,000 in 1980 dollars and the general price level had doubled over this period, it cannot, or should not, be said that the firm has grown 50 per cent in size or that owners are 50 per cent richer. Nor can it or should it be said that if current income were $2,000 in 1960 and $3,000 in 1980, income was 50 per cent higher. To make any comparisons over time when the general price level is changing, i.e., the value of a dollar is changing, the dollars of one period must first be converted to equivalent dollars of the other period. The firm clearly declined in size and earnings *in real terms* over the period—by 25 per cent—i.e., its 1960 assets stated in 1980 dollars (in order to make them comparable to 1980 assets stated in 1980 dollars) would disclose that real assets had declined from $20,000 to $15,000; in terms of 1960 dollars the decline was from $10,000 to $7,500, again 25 per cent. And real income, too, declined by 25 per cent. When the dollar changes in value over time, a new monetary unit is automatically created. It can be 1960 dollars or it can be 1980 dollars (or 1970 dollars). But data for the two periods can be meaningfully compared only in dollars of the same value and vintage.

Traditionally, the accounting profession has adhered to what is known as the *money convention*, using money as a unit of account and refusing to take cognizance of the fact that the unit of measurement itself might change in value over time—not because the profession denied the

existence of what is known to be true (that the value of money is
subject to change) but rather because it held that it is not a proper
function of accounting to account for changes in the value of the
monetary unit itself. This position is defended on the ground that
financial statements prepared in compliance with the money convention
are based on verifiable objective evidence and contain a minimum of
subjective speculation, whereas statements adjusted for changes in the
value of the dollar would presumably be subject to manipulation at
the will of owners or management. The availability of reliable price
indexes, such as the U.S. Bureau of Labor Statistics' *Consumer Price
Index* and the U.S. Department of Commerce's *Wholesale Commodity
Price Index*, and GNP price deflators casts considerable doubt on the
validity of this position.

Which of the several generally accepted price indexes should be used
to make dollars of one period comparable with dollars of another period
is the subject of some dispute. We believe, with Robert R. Sterling,
that it should be a *consumer* price index, related to the final goods
a consumer buys.[14] It is the real income and real value of net worth
of *people*, of *owners*, that we are measuring, and their interest is
presumably in command over consumer goods, not producer goods
(whose prices are, however, reflected in the prices of consumer goods).
This leads us to prefer the *Consumer Price Index* of the U.S. Bureau
of Labor Statistics or the GNP deflator for consumption goods of the
U.S. Department of Commerce. The former is more familiar and, thus,
perhaps more acceptable, but the latter covers a wider range of consumer
goods and might perhaps be more applicable to measure real gains
or losses of owners of American business firms.

Our method for adjusting current value income and position statements for changes in the general price level to express changes that
have taken place in real terms and make them comparable one with
another can be expressed by the following five equations. Let

M = Net current monetary assets,
N = Nonmonetary assets expressed in current values,
L = Long-term liabilities expressed in current values,
R = Residual or owners' equity expressed in current values.

Subscripts 1 and 2 attached to these variables denote value at end
of periods 1 and 2, in current dollar values applicable to that time,

14. See his perceptive comments on this issue in Robert R. Sterling, *Theory of the
Measurement of Enterprise Income, op. cit.*, pp. 340–341, especially footnote 6 where he
cites economists from Smith to Keynes in support of his position.

i.e., N_1 is the current value of nonmonetary assets at the end of period 1 in "period 1 dollars," and so forth. Further, let

$$CRI = \text{Current Real Income,}$$
$$S = \text{Sales receipts,}$$
$$C = \text{Current costs other than depreciation,}$$
$$D = \text{Current cost depreciation,}$$

all relating to events of period 2 as expressed in "period 2 dollars."

Assume, then, that prices change abruptly on the first day of period 2. (We will modify this in Chapter 12 to allow, more realistically, for gradual price changes over the period.) There are three relevant price changes:

$p = $ the percentage increase in the general price level,
$q = $ the percentage increase in the dollar price of nonmonetary assets,
$r = $ the percentage increase in the dollar value of long-term liabilities,

all occurring abruptly on the first day of period 2. Then for our comparative position statement expressed in end-of-period-2 dollars, we have:

$$M_2 - M_1(1 + p) + N_2 - N_1(1 + p) - [L_2 - L_1(1 + p)]$$
$$= R_2 - R_1(1 + p) = CRI_2. \qquad (11.1)$$

Further, any change in net current monetary assets in dollar terms must be due to revenue from sales less outlays (1) for current costs other than depreciation and (2) for gross investment expenditures on new nonmonetary assets (GI_2) plus any increase in new long-term borrowing (B_2) where these are assumed to occur at the end of the period, i.e.,

$$M_2 - M_1 = S_2 - C_2 - GI_2 + B_2. \qquad (11.2)$$

We can express period 2 nonmonetary assets and long-term liabilities in terms of period 1 values, both in dollars of their own period, as:

$$N_2 = N_1(1 + q) - D_2 + GI_2 \qquad (11.3)$$
$$L_2 = L_1(1 + r) + B_2. \qquad (11.4)$$

Substituting (11.2), (11.3), and (11.4) into the left-hand side of (11.1), we get:

$$CRI_2 = S_2 - C_2 - GI_2 + B_2 - M_1 p + N_1(1 + q) - D_2 + GI_2 -$$
$$N_1(1 + p) - [L_1(1 + r) + B_2 - L_1(1 + p)], \text{ or}$$
$$CRI_2 = [S_2 - C_2 - D_2] + N_1(q - p) + L_1(p - r) - M_1 p. \quad (11.5)$$

The first term on the right (in brackets) is current operating income already expressed in period 2 dollars. The second term is the realizable *real* cost savings (or realizable real holding gains) on nonmonetary assets. The third term is the realizable *real* cost savings (or holding gains) on long-term liabilities; there is a gain if the general price level rises, for you then owe less in real terms, and there is a loss if their dollar value rises. The fourth term is the realizable real holding gain on net current monetary assets, which will be a loss so long as M_1 is positive and the general price level rises (because money is then worth less).

Let us, then, apply this framework to the following adaptation of our basic plant asset example in this chapter. We will assume that our firm starts off in period 0 with a $10,000, two-period-life-no-salvage-value asset, and $5,000 cash. In the absence of price changes, the asset is again expected to yield earnings before depreciation of $7,000 in period 1 and $6,000 in period 2. The value of the asset (new) jumps ten per cent at the beginning of each period but so do revenues and operating costs; hence, actual earnings become $7,700 in period 1 and $7,260 (= $6,000 × 1.21) in period 2. Straight-line depreciation is then appropriate throughout. Since the asset continues to yield a 20 per cent current rate of return, current cost depreciation is reinvested in a one-period-old used asset of the same type at the end of period 1 and perhaps in a new asset at the end of period 2 (although this does not concern us). Our two-period picture in the absence of any general price level changes may be seen in Table 11-3.

Now suppose the general price level rose by five per cent, in a sudden jump, at the beginning of period 1. Our comparative current real position statement and current real income statement, both expressed in period 1 dollars before dividends, would be as seen in Table 11-4. Period 0 assets and equities have been expressed in period 1 dollars by multiplying their period 0 dollar amounts by 1.05, in accordance with equation (11.1). The increase in cash in dollars is given by equation (11.2), i.e.,

$$M_2 - M_1 = [S_2 - C_2] - GI_2 + B_2$$
$$\$7,200 - \$5,000 = [\$7,700] - \$5,500 + 0$$

The realizable real holding gain on nonmonetary assets and realizable real holding loss on monetary assets are in accordance with equation (11.5), i.e.,

$$N_1 (q - p) - M_1 p$$
$$\$10,000 (.10 - .05) - \$5,000 (.05)$$

TABLE 11-3

	0	1 Before dividends and reinvestment	1 After dividends and reinvestment	2 Before dividends and reinvestment	2 After dividends and reinvestment
		Period			
Cash	$ 5,000	$12,700	$ 5,000	$19,520	$ 5,000
Machine(s)	10,000	$11,000		$12,100	
Less: Current cost depreciation	0	5,500		12,100	
Net value	$10,000	5,500	5,500	0	
Reinvestment	0		5,500		12,100
Total assets (= ownership equity)	$15,000	$18,200	$16,000	$19,520	$17,100

	Period 1	Period 2
Earnings before depreciation	$7,700	$14,520
Current Cost Depreciation	5,500	12,100
Current Operating Income	$2,200	$ 2,420
Realizable Holding Gains	1,000	1,100
Current Income	$3,200	$ 3,520
Dividends (= Current Operating Income)	2,200	2,420
Change in Retained Earnings	$1,000	$ 1,100

Current real income of $2,450 equals the change in ownership equity as shown on the current real position statement.

If we think of comparing actual income with expected income in period 1 (the latter being $2,000) in accordance with the model set forth at the beginning of this chapter (see p. 458), we see that in spite of a five per cent rise in the general price level, actual current real income is higher than expected current real income because the increases in specific prices related to earnings and plant assets produced real gains (unexpected real income) which exceeded the (unexpected) real loss on net current monetary assets. Corrected for individual asset price changes but uncorrected for changes in the general price level, our current income was $3,200 (the current operating income of $2,200 plus the *nominal* realizable holding gain on plant assets of $1,000). The *nominal* holding gain consists of two elements: a *real* total holding gain of $250 and a *fictional* total holding gain of $750, which is

TABLE 11-4

COMPARATIVE CURRENT REAL POSITION STATEMENT
End of Period, Periods 0 and 1
(in Period 1 Dollars)
(*before* dividends but *after* Period 1 reinvestment)

Assets	Period		Equities	Period	
	0	1		0	1
Cash	$ 5,250	$ 7,200	Ownership Equity	$15,750	$18,200
Plant	10,500	11,000			
Total	$15,750	$18,200		$15,750	$18,200

CURRENT REAL INCOME STATEMENT
Period 1
(in Period 1 Dollars)

	Sales less Expenses other than Depreciation	$7,700
Less:	Current Cost Depreciation	5,500
	Current Operating Income	$2,200
Plus:	Real Realizable Holding Gain (Loss) on Nonmonetary Assets	500
Plus:	Real Realizable Holding Gain (Loss) on Monetary Assets	(250)
	Current Real Income	$2,450

represented by the write-up of period 0 ownership equity from $15,000 to $15,750 to reflect the rise in the general price level or reflect the changing value of the dollar, i.e., put period 0 dollar amounts into period 1 dollar values.

We leave it to the student to puzzle out how to put periods 0, 1, and 2 position statements and periods 1 and 2 income statements in period *2* dollars so that we can compare in meaningful fashion our performance in period 2 with previous years. If the rise in the general price level in period 2 is 15 per cent, i.e., the general price index moves from 100 to 105 to 120.75 over the three periods (so that period 0 dollars must be multiplied by $1.2075 = \dfrac{120.75}{100}$ and period 1 dollars by $1.15 = \dfrac{120.75}{105}$ to put dollar amounts of those periods into period

TABLE 11-5
COMPARATIVE CURRENT REAL POSITION STATEMENT
End of Period, Periods 0, 1 and 2
(In Period 2 Dollars)

Assets				*Equities*			
	Period				*Period*		
	0	*1*	*2*		*0*	*1*	*2*
Cash	$ 6,038	$ 5,750	$ 5,000	Ownership Equity	$18,113	$18,400	$17,100
Plant	12,075	12,650	12,100				
	$18,113	$18,400	$17,100		$18,113	$18,400	$17,100

COMPARATIVE CURRENT REAL INCOME STATEMENT
for Periods 1 and 2
(In Period 2 Dollars)

		1	*2*
	Sales less expenses other than Depreciation	$8,855	$14,520
Less:	Current Cost Depreciation	6,325	12,100
	Current Operating Income	$2,530	$ 2,420
Plus:	Real Realizable Holding Gain (Loss) on Nonmonetary Assets	575	(550)
Plus:	Real Realizable Holding Gain (Loss) on Net Monetary Assets	(288)	(750)
	Current Real Income	$2,817	$ 1,120
	Dividends	2,530	2,420
	Change in Retained Earnings	287	(1,300)

2 dollars), the answer, *after*, let us say, current operating income ($2,200) is paid out in dividends in period 1 and current cost depreciation is reinvested and the same is done in period 2, would be as seen in Table 11-5.

Needless to say, this exercise illustrates in striking fashion how necessary it is *both* to adjust historical cost values for changing *individual* prices of assets and liabilities (i.e., put statements in current value terms) *and* to adjust those current values for the changing value of the dollar (i.e., put statements in *real* current value terms). Consider again initial expectations for a no-price-change economy where we reinvest current cost (= historical cost) depreciation of $5,000 at the end of period 1 to maintain market value. Expected current income (= traditional accounting income) is $2,000 each period. With rising prices we decide to reinvest current cost depreciation of $5,500 at the end of period 1 and produce the results as above (p. 489). To make the first correction without the second yields current income of $3,200 in period 1 and $3,520 in period 2, whereas current real income in period 1 is only $2,450 in period 1 dollars and in period 2 is only $1,120 in period 2 dollars. As we shall illustrate in Appendix A to Chapter 12, an income statement making the second correction but not the first, i.e., adjusting *historical costs* for changes in the general price level, as many accountants advocate, would yield wrong figures as well.

We believe strongly that real current value accounting, or price level adjusted current costs, is what we need. We proceed, therefore, in Chapter 12 to show how current value concepts can be translated into practice in realistic accounting terms. Then, in Chapter 13, we shall consider the wide variety of alternative, essentially partial, concepts espoused by different accountants and accounting groups in various parts of the world and compare these with what we have set up as an ideal.

Discussion Questions

1. While many words, phrases, and concepts have been employed by accountants and official accounting bodies in trying to develop "generally accepted accounting standards" [GAAS—a term we substitute for "generally accepted accounting principles" (GAAP)], the text in Chapter 1 and here in Chapter 11 seems to center on three key words which the authors feel are critical in this effort: *objectivity, usefulness,* and *comparability.* Many of the other ideas accountants have employed in talking about "standards" or "principles" could, it would seem, be subsumed under one or another of these three vital concepts. The condition that accounting data be "measurable," "quantifiable," "verifiable," and/or "unbiased"— terms that have been used at one time or another in the attempt to establish standards—would all seem to be bound with the notion of "objectivity." "*Objectivity*" implies that two competent, unbiased (or at least differently biased) accountants, provided with the same raw data, would each arrive at approximately the same information to be communicated to users. Information arrived at *subjectively,* related to forecasts of future events, for example, would normally not meet this condition. Such information might be expressed in "quantifiable" terms but would not really be "measurable" in a

scientific sense, for it would not be "verifiable" until at least events have transpired which can be measured "objectively" against the "subjective" forecasts. Similarly, the terms "relevant," "intelligible," "material," "reliable," or "timely" would seem to imply concepts that are a *sine qua non* for "usefulness." It might seem that our third basic concept, "comparability," would be subsumed under the necessity of "usefulness" as well. But some information may be useful but not provide for comparability—highly specialized information related to a specific process or plant, for example. On the other hand, information which provides data that are irrelevant, immaterial, unreliable, inconsistent, or excessively outdated will not normally be useful, nor will data which cannot be used to draw comparisons with similar activities—within a firm or among firms, in the present or over time. "Consistency" (but not "foolish consistency") is a *sine qua non* for "comparability" and "usefulness," but putting data together by means of "consistent" methods (e.g., FIFO or LIFO, a particular depreciation method) does not *ensure* "comparability" or "usefulness."

a. Chapter 11 suggests that two critical conditions (Criteria 1 and 2 on p. 457) must be met if accounting information is to lead to "comparability" and be truly "useful" to those needing such information, whether they be insiders (managers) or interested outsiders (potential and actual shareholders and others), if no changes in the *general price level* occur over the time period being considered, and one further condition (Criterion 3) if such changes do occur. Discuss these conditions and explain why the authors deem them so important. Do you agree with them or disagree with them? Explain your position.

b. Do you feel that there are other conditions, embodying perhaps other concepts which either cannot or should not be subsumed under the above three ideas of objectivity, usefulness, and comparability, that are as important or perhaps more important in establishing standards for the provision of accounting information than the conditions stressed by the authors? Explain your thinking.

c. It can be argued that if errors are consistent (say, income is always overstated by 30 per cent by all firms), rates and direction of change over time and the relative profitability of different firms and industries can be adequately judged. Is this argument, in your opinion, sufficient to rescue historic-cost-based accounting from the arguments advanced by the authors in this chapter? Why, or why not?

2. Assume that a firm buys a $10,000 asset expected to earn $8,000 in the first year of use and $6,000 in the second year of use, at the end of which time it will not be economical for the firm to continue to use the asset; but it expects it can net $500 in salvage value from sale of the used asset as scrap metal. The price of the asset new rises 15 per cent at the very beginning of the first period and stays at this value to the end of period 1, while a one-period-old asset, identical to that used by the firm, is worth $5,750 at the end of the first period. [Purchase (entry) price equals sale (exit) price.] Further, a one-year-old asset identical to that used by the firm is being bought and sold on used-asset markets at the end of period 2 for only $3,000, the decline in value occurring abruptly at the beginning of period 2 because of an announcement of a new breakthrough in technology which will make new assets of a like nature to our firm's asset produce nearly twice as much revenue and yet cost the same as the old asset. What is current income and current operating income of our firm in periods 1 and 2, and how do these amounts compare with traditional accounting (historical cost) income, assuming the firm uses the "internal rate" method of depreciation? Assume that expectations regarding earnings and salvage value are, in fact, realized.

3. Most managements of companies in the United States have not taken enthusiastically to SEC requirements that they provide information in their annual reports, perhaps only in footnotes, beginning in December 1976, on replacement cost values for inventories and plant assets. The *Annual Report* for 1976 of MAPCO included the following statement by MAPCO's Chief Executive Officer:

> . . . I strongly urge . . . stockholders to join with me in ignoring the one-sided story on replacement-cost accounting made mandatory by current accounting rules of the SEC. It is truly expensive hogwash . . . [15]

In the 1976 United States Steel *Annual Report* we find:

> By Accounting Series Release 190 (ASR 190) issued March 23, 1976, the Securities and Exchange Commission established a new rule. Its stated purposes are: (1) to provide information to investors which will assist them in obtaining an understanding of the current costs of operating the business; and (2)

15. Arthur Young and Company, *Disclosure of Replacement Cost Data—Illustrations and Analysis* (1977), p. 16.

to provide information which will enable investors to determine the current cost of inventories and productive capacity as a measure of the current economic investment in these assets. In the opinion of U.S. Steel management, the required replacement cost disclosure does not satisfy either of the stated objectives.[16]

While the authors, like some managements, have qualms about the specific methods advocated by the SEC to determine "replacement cost" (see Chapter 13, Footnote 6), many, if not most, managers seem to see little value in current cost information of any variety, and security prices seem not to have responded very much, nor in any noticeable pattern, to the provision of such information in annual reports.

a. Suppose you were a manager considering alternative investment in support activities for Basic Activity A versus Basic Activity B (say, foreign versus domestic activities, or two quite different domestic products). Activity A is yielding a 15 per cent return on the *book* value (based on historical costs) of assets invested in the activity, whereas Activity B is yielding a 25 per cent return on the *book* value of assets invested in the activity. Assume that both activities have the same degree of risk. When income is measured in current value terms, *current operating income* is 12 per cent of the current value of assets invested in Activity A, 8 per cent of the current value of assets invested in Activity B. *Current income* is 20 per cent of the current value of assets invested in Activity A, 17 per cent of the current value of assets invested in Activity B. Would *you* be interested in the information provided by current value accounting; and if so, how might it affect your decision to invest in support activities for Basic Activity A versus Basic Activity B?

b. If you were a *potential* shareholder and Activity A were being pursued by Company A, Activity B by Company B, and those were the only activities being pursued by each company, would *you* be interested in the information provided by current value accounting? How might it affect your decision to invest in the shares of Company A versus Company B?

4. *The Wall Street Journal*, September 7, 1977, p. 39, reported on a research finding by the T. Rowe Price organization, which manages

16. *Ibid.*

$4 billion of pension and other private accounts and $2 billion of
mutual funds, to the effect that the 30 stocks comprising the Dow
Jones industrial average were selling at 10.3 times reported earnings
but if those reported earnings were "adjusted for the effects of
replacement-cost accounting," the average price-earnings multiple
would be 33.7. A similar comparison for a sample of growth stocks
suggested a multiple of 16.5 in terms of present stock prices and
reported earnings, 20.2 in terms of present prices and reported
earnings "adjusted for the effects of replacement-cost accounting."

   a. What kind of adjustment do you think the Price organization
      probably made to reported earnings to reflect "the effects of
      replacement-cost accounting"? Specifically, do you think their
      adjusted income figure probably reflects current operating income
      or total current income as those terms are used in the text? Why?
   b. Might a *potential* new investor and an *existing investor* have different
      ideas on which of the two current income concepts should be
      used in any price/income multiple calculation (the reciprocal of
      which is the ratio of current earnings to current value of assets
      or current rate of return), if only one multiple were to be quoted?
      What would each prefer in the denominator? Why? Discuss how
      both concepts might be useful to *both* types of investors, explaining
      why, as well as what the two different multiples tend to depict.
   c. Why do you think the Price organization's adjustment of reported
      earnings had a much more marked effect on the price/earnings
      multiple for the 30 Dow Jones stocks as compared with the sample
      of growth stocks? Do the differential effects perhaps tend to reflect
      older versus newer companies, hence, older versus newer assets?
      Explain why this might be the answer.
5. Make a table in the format shown below, by entering a 1 for the
   reported income figure you would expect to be highest, by entering
   a 3 for the reported income figure you would expect to be lowest,
   and by entering a 2 for the reported income figure you would
   expect to be in between the other two.

Assumption A: Plant asset prices have risen by 15 per cent since
              purchase at the beginning of the year and there have
              been no other price changes.
Assumption B: Plant asset prices have fallen steadily during the first
              two years of ownership due to technological change,
              but they leveled out toward the end of last year and
              there has been no further change this year nor have
              there been any other price changes over the three year
              period.

Assumption C: Inventory prices for materials the firm uses have risen
sharply since the beginning of the year because of the
operations of an international cartel, there have been
no other price changes, and the firm:
(1) has maintained inventory stocks constant and used
FIFO;
(2) has maintained inventory stocks constant and used
LIFO;
(3) has decreased inventory stocks and used LIFO;
(4) has increased inventory stocks and used FIFO.

	A	B	C(1)	C(2)	C(3)	C(4)
			Assumption			
1. Traditional Accounting (Historical Cost) Income						
2. Current Operating Income						
3. (Total) Current Income						

6. What can you say about where the value of *current real income* would
fit into your hierarchy of reported income values in Question 5
under specific price assumptions of Assumption A, on the one hand,
and Assumption B, on the other, if there were a rise in the general
price level of eight per cent during the relevant period? Explain.

7. The implementation of current values presents a new
dimension and will force reconsideration of many aspects
of financial reporting. We believe, however, that it is now
more urgent to implement current-value accounting than
to debate these other aspects of financial reporting.

> Touche Ross, *Current Value
> Accounting: Economic Realty in
> Financial Reporting* (1975), p. 16.

One can only conjecture about the total range of asset
valuation practices that would be proposed as acceptable
if current value amounts were injected into financial
statements. Certainly the discipline now incorporated in
conventional accounting, the hard-earned results of de-
cades of work by many individuals and organizations, is
likely to be sacrificed if a new basis of accounting is adopted
and the long, tedious, and painful process of developing
authoritative standards will have to commence anew.

> Ernst & Ernst, *Accounting Under
> Inflationary Conditions* (1976), p. 26.

Discuss these two statements on current value accounting by "Big Eight" firms, commenting especially on the Ernst and Ernst suggestions (a) that introduction of current values into accounting would broaden enormously the range of options which business firms would propose as acceptable, presumably with sound arguments, as compared with options open to them under present "generally accepted accounting principles"; and (b) that if "sunk costs" are sufficiently large, one keeps and uses one's asset even if "present value of future benefits" (PV) lies below "replacement cost" (RC)—perhaps involving technological change and more modern methods—at least so long as PV lies above NRV ("net realizable liquidation value").

PROBLEMS

11-1. Tronix Corporation (I)

Assume that there is a new machine which can be used to produce an electronic product. The machine will be worth nothing at the end of two years because rapid technological change in the field is likely to produce a new machine making a radically different and better product by that time. But during those two years the Tronix Corporation estimates that if it purchases the machine for $120,000 it can earn revenues less expenses other than depreciation of $128,000 in the first year of operations and $56,000 in the next. The company's view of the *pattern* of earnings which can be expected from use of the machine is shared in the market place, although the market does not anticipate such a high rate of return from its use of the asset; specifically, the market expects earnings to be $104,000 and $48,000 in years 1 and 2, respectively, and a rate of return of only 20 per cent as compared with Tronix's expected rate of return of 40 per cent.

INSTRUCTIONS:

(a) Set up a two-year plan for the Tronix Corporation given the above projections, showing expected earnings, a depreciation plan appropriate for that projected earnings pattern (indicating whether or not this fits any standard depreciation method), expected income, and the rate of return on end-of-previous-year's book value that is expected by Tronix from use of the machine, assuming it keeps and uses it for the two years.

(b) Even though the market expects lower earnings from the machine than does Tronix, should the Tronix plan accurately forecast the *market value* of the asset over its life if there is full information about market expectations (but not about Tronix's expectations), if the market's expected 20 per cent rate of return just compensates for risk, and if the expectations of both Tronix and the market are exactly realized? How do you explain this? (You may wish to refer back to the material in Chapter 6.)

(c) Show that the expected subjective goodwill to be turned into market value over the life of the plan is equal to (1) the present value of expected earnings (cash inflows) less the original cost of the machine and (2) the present value of the excess current income stream. Assume a discount rate of ten per cent.

11-2. *Oil Well Rescue Operations, Inc. (I)*

An individual has a patent on a tertiary recovery technique which allows an oil well to produce oil profitably for an extra two years. He has formed a company, Oil Well Rescue Operations, Inc. (OWRO), which purchases sites of old wells, operates the wells for two years, and then sells the land. The firm is considering two projects. Project A, geologists suggest, is likely to produce 2,200 bbls. of oil in each of two years. The price of crude is $12/bbl. The land and well can be purchased for $50,000 and could, it is predicted, be sold for $9,365 at the end of the two-year period. Company geologists estimate that Project B could produce 2,000 bbls. of oil a year for two years. The land and well can be purchased for $35,000 and it is expected that the land could be sold for $3,950 at the end of the two-year period. Given the risks involved, OWRO executives feel they have to generate a better than 20 per cent rate of return on invested capital to undertake either project.

INSTRUCTIONS:

(a) Set up a two-year plan for Projects A and B showing expected earnings, an appropriate depreciation schedule given those expected earnings, the current income that can be expected from each project, the change in book value of the property, and the expected rate of return on book value each year. You should include in the second year earnings a "final dividend" based on the resale of the property, assuming expectations can be realized. (Note: Refer to the last section of Appendix 6-A. It is best to think in terms of a pattern of earnings *from production* on each project and a "salvage value." The salvage value must be added to second-year earnings to arrive at the internal rate of return, but in setting up the plan the original cost less salvage value is depreciated and the salvage value appears as the book value at the end of the second year and constitutes a "final dividend." The depreciation method chosen is therefore the method appropriate for a constant efficiency asset.)

(b) Given OWRO rate of return objectives, will it undertake one, both, or neither of the projects? Compute subjective goodwill in each case, using the "target" rate of return as the discount factor, and indicate why *in this case* this approach yields the same conclusion as that involving comparison of internal rates of return with the "target" rate of return.

Optional:

(c) Investment decisions based on comparing internal rates of return to a "target" rate of interest do not always yield the same results as a decision based on comparing subjective goodwills. Suppose Project A had expected earnings of $5,000 in Year 1 and $66,105 in Year 2, which, with consideration of salvage value, yields an internal rate of return of 27 per cent. Suppose Project B had expected earnings of $55,000 in Year 1 and $3,635 in Year 2, which, with consideration of salvage value, yields an internal rate of return of 30 per cent. Which investment would you choose if the risk-adjusted "target" rate of return were 20 per cent in both cases? Why?

11-3. Executive Travel, Inc. (I)

Two pilots decided to establish an air travel service for executives in the Metro City area. They found that they could buy a good used jet for $360,000. After testing the market carefully and accumulating a core list of client contracts, they predicted that over a three-year plan period they could generate revenues less expenses other than depreciation (the expenses including a good salary for each of the pilots) of $154,000, $138,000, and $122,000 in each of three successive years. The decline in earnings over the period reflects increasing revenues but greater increasing costs, especially repair and maintenance charges for the plane. The projected pattern of prices, allowing for anticipated price increases, for the eight-year-old plane they were purchasing was as follows:

	Year			
	0	1	2	3
Eight-year-old plane	$360,000	$402,000		
Nine-year-old plane		296,000	$329,000	
Ten-year-old plane			232,000	$260,000
Eleven-year-old plane				168,000

The expected value of the aircraft in three years, *if there were no price changes,* was $120,000. No new investments are made over the three years; all revenues less costs other than depreciation are paid out as dividends to the owners.

INSTRUCTIONS:

(a) Assuming that the plane's price jumps to its new amount on the first day of each year, set up a three-year plan for the firm showing expected earnings (cash flows), current cost depreciation, current operating income, realizable holding gains (cost savings), current income, and rate of return (current income/end-of-previous-period book value) for each of the three years.

(b) Compute subjective goodwill by summing the present value of earnings (cash flows) over the three-year period and adding the present value of the expected worth of the plane at the end of the three-year plan period, using a discount factor of ten per cent each year. Show that this figure is identical to the present value of the *excess* current income stream over the plan period.

(c) Compare your results in (a) and (b) with those that would be obtained by planning in terms of traditional historical costs, i.e., ignoring any expected future price changes for the plane. For these purposes use a standard depreciation method that is most consistent with internal rate depreciation.

11-4. Tronix Corporation (II)

Refer to Problem 11-1. A machine introduced by competitors on the first day of year 1 is similar to the one just purchased by Tronix. The new machine produces twice as much as Tronix's machine but has the same initial cost, $120,000. The new machine, like the old, has a two-year expected life with no salvage value. The lure of higher profits draws more firms into the industry and as a result the selling price of the new product went down. Earnings, not including depreciation, for the users of the new machine were $188,000 during the first year and should be $76,000 during the second. Tronix's income before depreciation was $94,000 in year 1 and should be $38,000 in year 2.

INSTRUCTIONS:

(a) Calculate the market value of Tronix's machine immediately after the introduction of the new machine. Assume that the market and Tronix have identical views as to earnings on both machines and that perfect information exists in the market place.

(b) Calculate earnings, internal rate current cost depreciation, current operating income, realizable holding gains (losses), current income, and rate of return on *current market value* over two years on the new machine and the old machine Tronix purchased on the last day of year 0. If the net realizable (sale) value of Tronix's machine is less than its current replacement cost, should Tronix continue to use its old machine in year 2, or sell it and purchase one of the new machines? [Note: For such decision-making with respect to alternative *future* courses of action, Tronix will wish to compare current operating income relative to the current value of the asset before use during the period at prices prevailing or expected to prevail during the period under consideration. Thus, the denominator in our expected rate of return calculation on the old asset for year 2 should be the book value (which is equal to market value given the assumptions under (a).] Any forecast of future earnings should, of course, take past experience into consideration.

(c) Prepare traditional historical cost income statements using sum-of-the-years'-digits depreciation. Compare and contrast these statements with the current income statements you prepared in part (b) above. Given a risk-free interest rate (discount factor) of ten per cent, what do historical cost records suggest to management, shareholders, and others about the virtues (or lack thereof) of Tronix staying in this business and continuing to use its original machine another year? Explain.

11-5. *Oil Well Rescue Operations, Inc. (II)*

Refer to Problem 11-2 (a) and (b). Having chosen whichever Project, A or B, seemed wise, OWRO re-thinks its options at the end of year 1.

The expected decline in land values over the two-year period is based on recovering the remaining oil reserves. The company is bound to restore the land to the state existing before drilling operations; hence, we can say that the land, without oil, of Project A was initially worth $9,365 and that of Project B $3,950. The sites are located in California and soon after OWRO has made its decision and purchased one of the project sites Proposition 13 was passed. Land values fall by almost two-thirds in the Project B county, and OWRO finds that at the end of the two-year period it will be able to realize only $1,325, rather than the original expected $3,950, from sale of the land after drilling on it. On the other hand, land values rise close to 50 per cent in the Project A county because county supervisors there adopt, partly in consequence of Proposition 13, a drastic "no-growth" ordinance and sharply restrict new construction. OWRO can expect to realize $13,920 rather than $9,365 on the sale of the Project A property after drilling on it.

INSTRUCTIONS:

(a) Assume all of the above occurs on the very first day of year 1 when the supervisors in each county announce their respective answers to the new legislation cutting property taxes drastically. Earnings and depreciation as a result of drilling are as originally expected in year 1 and the expectations for drilling operations in year 2 are unchanged. Set up an income statement which would include earnings, depreciation (based on the drilling operations), current operating income, realizable holding gains, current income, the book value of the land and equipment initially and at the end of periods 1 and 2 (in current value terms—remember, realizable holding gains (losses) are involved), and rates of return of both current operating income and current income, actual in year 1, expected in year 2.

(b) Evaluate concisely, giving your reasons, (1) what OWRO management should do now at the end of year 1, given the earnings assumptions in Problem 11-2 and the appropriate decision made at that time on the basis of value assumptions prevailing at time of the initial investment, and (2) what OWRO management *should have done* initially if the advent of Proposition 13 and its effects in the two counties had been foreseen.

11-6. *Executive Travel, Inc. (II)*

Refer to Problem 11-3. There our pilots planned in terms of expected price increases on their fixed asset as well as current earnings. Their estimate of the price increase in the market for this type of plane (new and used) turned out to be exactly on the mark in year 1. In year 2 the prices for this type of plane (new and used) jumped approximately 20 per cent at the beginning of the period, rather than the expected 12 per cent. This rate of increase was expected to drop at the beginning of year 3 to 15 per cent. It was felt that the plane would have to be sold at least by the end of year 3 and a newer, more modern plane purchased if they were going to continue in business. Earnings were as expected in years 1 and 2, and expectations for year 3 were unchanged. The new actual and expected values for the plane are as shown below.

			20% rise	15 % rise
	0	1	2	3
Eight-year-old	$360,000	$402,000		
Nine-year-old		296,000	$355,000	
Ten-year-old			248,000	$285,000
Eleven-year-old				183,000

INSTRUCTIONS:

(a) Recalculate year 2 earnings, current cost depreciation, current operating income, realizable holding gains, current income, market value at the end of the period, and rate of return (current operating income / market value and current income / market value separately) which were actually achieved. Recalculate these data for expected values in year 3.

(b) If the market for used planes were a perfect market so that the buying price equals the selling price and, given the riskiness of the business, the minimum rate of return the pilots will accept given their best estimates of current income is 25 per cent, what will our two pilots do at the end of year 2? (Hint: Discount earnings in year 3 plus market value of the asset at the end of year 3 by a discount factor of 25 per cent and compare this with the value of the asset at the end of year 2.) Given the uncertainty of price changes in this world, what would the expected current operating income rate of return on market value suggest the pilots do if the risk-free rate of return in the market is 10 per cent?

11-7. Eliza Harmon Trust

You are a shareholder in a small family investment trust, with assets of only $30,000 on December 31, 19X5. The financial report of the trust on that date was as follows:

Report of the Eliza Harmon Trust
December 31, 19X5

Assets Held	No. of Shares Held	Cost	Market Value	Indicated Yield
Cash			-0-	
Security A	120	$ 3,850	$12,000	4.0%
Security B	360	10,800	18,000	6.0%
Total		$14,650	$30,000	

Early in April you receive another report on the trust as follows:

Report of the Eliza Harmon Trust
March 31, 19X6

Assets Held	No. of Shares Held	Cost	Market Value	Indicated Yield
Cash			$ 440	
Security A	150	$ 7,000	16,500	3.6%
Security B	280	8,400	19,600	4.3%
Total		$15,400	$36,540	

Accompanying the first quarter 19X6 report is a letter from the managers of the trust stating that, while the Standard and Poors (500 major stock) index rose by only 14.1 per cent during the first quarter of 19X6, the stocks held by the Eliza Harmon Trust rose in value by 20.3 per cent ($36,100/$30,000), that you are in good hands, and that the managers feel that they can declare a dividend of $3.90 per share on the trust's 100 shares outstanding—a dividend equal in total to the dividends collected by the trust from their investments.

You feel "unsettled" by the Eliza Harmon Trust financial reports. They give you, in effect, a comparative position statement but no income statement. How do you evaluate performance? The trust did better than the Standard and Poors average, evidently, but perhaps Securities A and B were a good bet to begin with—securities chosen long ago by your Great-Aunt Eliza Harmon or by her financial adviser. Besides, shares were clearly bought and sold during the period. What sense does it make to compare a simple aggregative total of shares held at the end of 19X5 and at the end of the first quarter of 19X6? (The Eliza Harmon Trust financial reports are typical of those in the investment management field in the United States—even of large investment trusts, managing millions of dollars of pension money.)

Having recently read an accounting text devoted, in part, to current value theory, you recognize that in order to get a "handle" on this matter, you must sort even income earned from marketable securities into two parts: current operating income and realizable holding gains. The sum of the two over a period must equal the increase in market value of assets held by the Trust. That is surely what the Trust should be trying to maximize. But more important, you must ascertain this information security-by-security in order to evaluate the investment decisions of the managers of the Trust.

In order to evaluate performance, you must learn what happend to the market value of a *fixed number of shares* of each security held by the Trust over the period under consideration. Obviously if securities are bought and sold over the period (as was the case for Securities A and B in the Eliza Harmon Trust), little can be ascertained from a *general* comparative position statement, as suggested above.

Pressing the managers of the Trust, you ascertain the following for the first quarter of 19X6:

	December 31, 19X5	Purchase	Sale	March 31, 19X6
		Price of Security At Time of		
Security A	$100	$105		$110
Security B	50		$40	70

Given that and the above position statements, you set about to fashion an income statement for the first quarter of 19X6 that will enable you to evaluate the management's performance.

INSTRUCTIONS:

(a) Develop a comprehensive statement, with three rows for each security held during the period: shares held throughout the period [showing dividends paid (current operating income) and realizable (but as yet unrealized) holding gains], shares bought and/or sold during the period showing dividends (if any) and realizable holding gains accruing during the period on these (before sale or after purchase), and totals. Columns might consist of number of shares held; original cost; market value—December 31, 19X5; bought; sold; market value—March 31, 19X6; change in market value; current operating income (dividends received); *realizable* holding gains; *realized* holding gains; current income; and realized income (current operating income plus realized holding gains, some of which may have accrued in former periods). Assuming that only two security transactions were made during the period, all the information you need is above. Your revised financial report should contain a row for cash, which should be the sum of the value of securities sold plus dividends received less securities bought. [Since the Trust has told you that $390 in dividends were received, a little detective work with "indicated yields" (over a year period) suggests that Securities A paid a quarterly dividend of $1 per share for the quarter and that the new Security A shares were purchased *after* the date of record on the quarterly dividend. Security B paid a quarterly dividend of $.75 per share for the quarter and Security B shares sold during the quarter were sold *after* the date of record on the quarterly dividend.]

(b) In not more than a single page, write a statement evaluating the performance of the managers of the Eliza Harmon Trust for the first quarter of 19X6 (granting that the managers have to have some longer view in prospect but should also be evaluated quarter-by-quarter).

11-8. Kurst Publishers (I)

The Kurst newspaper chain is considering investing in one of two major paper mills to ensure its raw materials supply. Both mills produce the same product using machinery of the same type and vintage. Mill B is about 50 per cent larger than Mill A. Mill B can be bought for $60 million, Mill A for $40 million. Income statements for the two mills for last year (these relative revenues and expenses seem to reflect reasonably well the activities of previous years) are as follows (in millions of dollars):

	Mill A			Mill B		
REVENUES			$200			$300
EXPENSES:						
Cost of Goods Sold						
Pulp	$150			$195		
Wages	30			50		
Other	15	$195		30	$275	
Selling and Administration		5	200		10	285
ENTITY INCOME			$ 0			$ 15

On the face of it, Mill B would seem to be the more efficient operation; it is earning a 25 per cent profit on the value of its ownership equity while Mill A's rate of return is zero per cent. The primary reason for Mill B's better performance would appear to be its more efficient use of pulp. Mill A reports cost of goods sold on a FIFO periodic inventory basis while Mill B uses a LIFO periodic inventory method. Kurst's analysts decide to put both income statements on a current cost basis so far as cost of goods sold are concerned, using the following facts provided by the two mills (units, hence, values, in millions):

	Mill A	Mill B
Sales, paper	10 units @ $20.00 = $200.00	15 units @ $20.00 = $300.00
Purchases, pulp	15 units @ $10.00 = $150.00	21 units @ $10.00 = $210.00
Beginning Inventory	1 unit @ $15.00 = $ 15.00	1 unit @ $ 7.50 = $ 7.50
Ending Inventory	2 units @ $ 7.50 = $ 15.00	1 unit @ $ 7.50 = $ 7.50
		+1 unit @ $15.00 = $ 22.50

INSTRUCTIONS:

(a) Assuming the (average) purchase price of $10 is the current cost of pulp for the year, put Mill A's and Mill B's income statements into current value terms so far as the cost of goods sold is concerned.

(b) Which mill do you think is the better investment for Kurst Publishers, all other things being equal? Why?

11-9. Swift Family Mopeds

Ten years ago Philip Swift, an aerospace engineer, decided that the high-pressure, always-on-the-road life of a top business executive was not for him. He "retired" to a town in California, on the Pacific Ocean, which he had always wanted to live in and set up a bicycle center with his family. The business thrived, and three years ago the Swifts decided to extend their operations. They opened up a new branch store managed by Philip Swift, Jr., to sell the new craze, mopeds. The new branch did well the first two years. On an initial investment of $116,000 ($16,000 inventory and $100,000 for a store), the new activity netted its owners only $23,200 in cash dividends (all increases in cash were to be paid to the parent enterprise), but it earned a rate of return considerably in excess of the 20 per cent return earned in the bicycle store. The low cash returns were the result of expanding inventory in response to sharply increasing sales volume. Things took a tumble last year (the third year of operations), however, as sales fell sharply and the rate of return dropped to 8 per cent. Father Swift was worried and considered abandoning the moped operation, but his son's accountant convinced him that the trouble was in the accounting system, not the moped operation. The store was on a FIFO (periodic) system of accounting for inventories and the cost of goods sold. If the store had been on an LIFO system, which, the accountant argued, would eliminate artificial "inventory profits and losses," it could be shown that over the three-year period, profits averaged better than 20 per cent *and* the rate of return was actually highest in the last (third) year. Another accountant that Swift Senior consulted warned him that LIFO, too, had its defects, but that on a *current value accounting* basis it was probably worth staying in the moped business. Current value accounting data, however, suggested that Swift Senior should talk to his son about inventory purchasing policy, the accountant added. Swift Senior decided to carry on another year, and he was glad that he did because profits were generally better than ever in the branch's fourth year of operation.

INSTRUCTIONS:

(a) Set up a table, similar to Table 11-2 in the text, showing beginning and ending inventory, cost of goods sold, and all relevant income figures and rates of return for the three different inventory methods being discussed (i.e., FIFO, LIFO, and current value accounting methods) over the four-year period. The table should be based on the following information you cull from Swift Jr.'s records plus a few telephone calls.

(1) Depreciation of the building is on a straight-line basis over a 20-year-life, with the assumption that there will be no salvage value;

(2) Selling costs other than those related to purchase of the mopeds for resale were $40,000 in year 1 and increased $4,000 a year in each of the next three years;

(3) Quantities and average prices of mopeds sold and purchased initially and for each of the four years were as follows:

	0	1	2	3	4
			Year		
Units Sold		300	400	280	300
Average Price		$500	$520	$565	$540
Units Purchased	80	360	440	180	360
Average Price	$200	$250	$320	$250	$250

(4) Ending inventory price figures as would be used for valuation under each of the three approaches were as follows:

	1	2	3	4
		Year		
FIFO	$285	$350	$250	$260
LIFO	210	220	200	230
Current Value	300	360	200	300

(b) Answer briefly, in a short paragraph, the following questions about the information accumulated under (a):

(1) Does the standard "flow" formula, $BI + Purchases - EI = COGS$, work for the computation of $COGS$ under the current value approach? Why, or why not?

(2) Does the fact that realizable holding losses in the third year exceeded realizable holding gains of years 1 and 2 justify the second accountant's oblique criticism of Swift Jrs.'s purchasing operations? If prices changed smoothly over the course of each

year, what can you say of Swift Jr.'s purchasing performance?

(3) Using comparisons with the current value accounting results, indicate in what way FIFO yields a misleading impression of profitability, and why.

(4) Using comparisons with the current value accounting results, indicate in what way LIFO yields a misleading impression of profitability, and why.

(5) How much do cash-flow-from-operations figures differ from (a) current operating income, (b) current income, and why the difference in each case? Would cash flows differ from current operating income if inventory volume was unchanged, albeit prices changed?

(6) In years 1 and 4 identical events occurred and current value accounting recorded identical results, but FIFO and LIFO did not. How do you explain this?

11-10. Kurst Publishers (II)

Refer to Problem 11-8. Elements of the position statement must be considered along with income, efficiency, and rate of return when making investment decisions. When Kurst was considering the acquisition of a paper mill, Mills A and B presented the following position statements (in millions of dollars):

	A	B		A	B
Current Monetary Assets	$15	$ 40	Current Liabilities	$22	$ 43
Inventories	35	35	Bonds Payable	28	42
Noncurrent Assets	40	60	Stockholder's Equity	40	50
	$90	$135		$90	$135

Both firms are in a somewhat weak liquidity situation, especially Mill A, but that is because they have both been trying to build up their stocks of pulp in the expectation that the recent sharp rise in pulp prices will continue. Basically there would seem to be little basis for choice on the basis of position statement items—in general, Mill B is one-and-a-half times Mill A in every way.

On investigating the bonds payable of the two mills, however, the Kurst analysts find that Mill B issued its bonds considerably earlier than Mill A and at lower interest rates. The current market rate for these types of bonds is ten per cent. The situation is as follows:

	Maturity Value	Interest Rate	Years Remaining
Mill A, Set I	$20	8%	20
Set II	8	10	25
Mill B, Set I	30	6	10
Set II	12	7	15

INSTRUCTIONS:

(a) Determine the nominal worth of this situation to Kurst Publishers in each case.
(b) If each mill is willing to sell to Kurst at the book value of its stockholders' equity, which mill should Kurst buy, considering only the position statements? Why?

11-11. Tronix Corporation (III)

Refer to Problem 11-1. Let us assume that after carefully working out its plan *without* considering the possibility of price changes, with respect to the economy as a whole and its own assets in particular, Tronix management gets a new directive from its major shareholders, viz., there must be at least *a 25 per cent real return on invested capital* in "the first year" (i.e., over the first half of the plan period) or the management team had better start looking for new jobs.

This causes management to rethink its projected investment. An economic consulting firm suggests that Tronix's expected subjective goodwill to be derived from the investment is well-known in the industry, and one should expect new entrants, which will drive down earnings and drive up the price of the machinery to be purchased and used. The consulting firm suggests that planning be based on the following assumptions:

(1) Tronix's projected machine will rise in price by 20 per cent in year 1—let us say all price changes occur abruptly on the first day of the year for ease of computation;
(2) Nominal money earnings in the absence of changes in the general price level might be expected to be $110,000 rather than $128,000 (suggesting a 25 per cent return on invested capital), and these will rise in proportion to any increase in the general price level;
(3) The general price level is expected to advance by ten per cent in (on the first day of) year 1;
(4) $30,000 of net current monetary assets will be needed to be retained

throughout year 1 and this money can be borrowed at a ten per cent rate of interest.

INSTRUCTIONS:

(a) Compute projected *current real income* and its components for year 1 in year 1 dollars.
(b) Adjust these year-1-dollar amounts to year 0 dollars and compare the resultant figure for year 1 current real income with the initial year 0 investment.
(c) If management undertakes the investment and all expectations are exactly realized, will the management team have a job with Tronix at the end of year 1? Explain briefly.

11-12. Oil Well Rescue Operations, Inc. (III)

Refer to Problems 11-2 and 11-5. Actual events are as given in 11-5, except that the general price level in the economy increases by five per cent a year in years 1 and 2, jumping upwards on the first day of each year, we will assume, to make computations easier.

INSTRUCTIONS:

(a) Compute a statement detailing *current real income* and its components for years 1 and 2, in year 1 and year 2 dollars, respectively.
(b) If the managers of OWRO require a *real rate of return on invested capital of 15 per cent* in order to undertake an investment, should they have undertaken Project A, Project B, both, or neither? Show the calculations used to arrive at your answer. [Hint: Compare the present value of the current real income flow *measured in year 0 dollars* with the initial outlays of $50,000 on Project A and $35,000 on Project B and ascertain whether the rate of return is greater or less than the required 15 per cent.]

11-13. Executive Travel, Inc. (III)

Refer to Problem 11-3.

INSTRUCTIONS:

(a) In formulating their plan in accordance with the assumptions given in Problem 11-3, our pilots also adjusted their thinking to take account of a general rate of inflation of eight per cent per year in each of the three years. Compute a statement for planned *current real income* and its components for each of the three years, measured in year 1, year 2, and year 3 dollars, assuming that all other expected events (earnings and specific price changes) are as assumed in Problem 11-3.

(b) What is the *expected real rate of return on invested capital* of Executive Travel, Inc. over the plan period if the pilots invest in the airplane? [Hint: Vintage dollars of years 1, 2, and 3 must be deflated so as to be expressed in year 0 dollars in comparing the expected current real income stream with the initial outlay.]

11-14. Executive Travel, Inc. (IV)

Refer to Problem 11-6. Suppose that our pilot friends were entering the air taxi business primarily to pay themselves a substantial salary, and their requirement so far as return on capital was concerned was that they simply "break even" in real terms, i.e., current real income per dollars invested must be greater than zero. In effect, they are willing to give up interest on invested capital in exchange for the salaries they pay themselves, which exceed their opportunity cost salaries by approximately the interest they could earn on their investment.

INSTRUCTIONS:

(a) If the general inflation rate in the economy proves to be six per cent per year in years 1 and 2, will our pilots have met their investment-rate-of-return condition if they acquire the plane and keep it for years 1 and 2? Show your computations.

(b) If earnings and specific asset price expectations for year 3 are still as given in Problem 11-6 but the inflation rate is expected to rise to ten per cent in year 3, would the pilots expect to meet their investment-rate-of-return condition in year 3, or should they sell the airplane if they still have it, assuming sale price equals purchase price in the market (as given in the table in Problem 11-6)? Show your computations.

CHAPTER 12

CURRENT VALUE ACCOUNTING

ALL OF THE SUGGESTED MODIFICATIONS of traditional historical cost data treated in Chapter 11 would involve amending or supplementing historical cost records in one form or fashion. Clearly, the basic records of transactions must be kept in terms of historical costs. The accounts cannot be altered daily for every slight price change that occurs. But periodically those accounts must be amended so as to provide the information we have argued is so urgently needed. How frequently this is done depends on the benefits a firm's managers attach to having such current value data. At any rate, it must be done at the end of the accounting period when the financial statements are prepared, and that is what we will concentrate on here.

Our objective in this chapter is to develop income and position statements in terms of current costs. To differentiate these from the traditional historical cost statements, we shall title them the *current income statement* (which will be divided into two components, one for operating activities and the other for holding gains involving price changes) and the *current position statement*. Later, when we adjust our current cost data for changes in the general price level, we shall term them the *current real income statement* and the *current real position statement*. We have argued that these statements are the most informative and useful insofar as the evaluation of decisions and performance is concerned. In addition, however, the data required for most of the alternative concepts that we shall treat in Chapter 13 "fall out" of our current cost data, and thus we shall be able to compare our current cost-based income and position statements with those statements that would result from other approaches to current value accounting.

We shall amend our records in two distinct steps. First, we will record the changes in *specific prices* during the period for the affected asset,

514

liability, and expense accounts so as to state each in terms of its current cost without regard for changes in the purchasing power of the dollar. Second, we shall adjust for changes in the *general price level*, converting the current cost data reported in terms of nominal dollars into *real* dollars (i.e., dollars of constant purchasing power). Although both amendments could be made simultaneously, we think it far better pedagogically to show the necessary adjustments in these two steps.

Adjustments in the Accounts to Reflect Changes in Specific Prices

For purposes of illustration, let us consider the accounts of the Leavenworth Corporation, which commenced its activities on January 1, 19X8. Leavenworth employs traditional historical cost accounting methods, and its post-closing ledger accounts as of December 31, 19X8 appear in Table 12-1. Leavenworth's comparative position statement as of January 1 and December 31, 19X8 and its income statement for the year ended December 31, 19X8 (all in terms of historical costs) are shown in Tables 12-2 and 12-3.

TABLE 12-1

Cash		Accounts Receivable	
$72,000		$120,000	

Merchandise Inventory				Land	
(Beginning Inventory)	$50,000	(Cost of Goods Sold)	$700,000	$40,000	
(Purchases)	780,000	(Ending Inventory) √	130,000		
	$830,000		$830,000		
√	$130,000				

Building		Building—Allowance for Depreciation	
$200,000			$10,000

TABLE 12-1 CONTINUED

Equipment		Equipment—Allowance for Depreciation	
$110,000			$22,000

Accounts Payable		Bonds Payable	
	$100,000		$100,000

Other Payables	
	$40,000

Common Stock		Retained Earnings	
	$350,000		(c-5) $50,000

Sales Revenue	
(c-1) $1,000,000	$1,000,000

Cost of Goods Sold Expense		Depreciation Expense	
$700,000	(c-2) $700,000	$32,000	(c-2) $32,000

Other Expenses		Interest Charges	
$200,000	(c-2) $200,000	$8,000	(c-3) $8,000

Common Dividend Charges		Income Summary	
$10,000	(c-4) $10,000	(c-2) $932,000	(c-1) $1,000,000
		(c-3) 8,000	
		(c-4) 10,000	
		(c-5) 50,000	
		$1,000,000	$1,000,000

TABLE 12-2
LEAVENWORTH CORPORATION
COMPARATIVE POSITION STATEMENT
As of January 1 and December 31, 19X8

	December 31, 19X8			January 1, 19X8		
ASSETS:						
Current:						
Cash		$ 72,000			$ 85,000	
Accounts Receivable		120,000			-0-	
Merchandise Inventory		130,000	$322,000		50,000	$135,000
Plant:						
Land		$ 40,000			$ 40,000	
Building	$200,000			$200,000		
Less: Allowance for Depreciation	10,000	190,000		-0-	200,000	
Equipment	$110,000			$110,000		
Less: Allowance for Depreciation	22,000	88,000	318,000	-0-	110,000	350,000
			$640,000			$485,000
EQUITIES:						
Current Liabilities:						
Accounts Payable	$100,000			$ 35,000		
Other Payables	40,000	$140,000		-0-	$ 35,000	
Long-Term Liabilities:						
Bonds Payable		100,000	$240,000		100,000	$135,000
Common Stockholders' Equity:						
Common Stock		$350,000			$350,000	
Retained Earnings		50,000	400,000		-0-	350,000
			$640,000			$485,000

TABLE 12-3

LEAVENWORTH CORPORATION
INCOME STATEMENT
For the Year Ended December 31, 19X8

REVENUES:		
Sales		$1,000,000
EXPENSES:		
Cost of Goods Sold	$700,000	
Depreciation	32,000	
Other	200,000	932,000
OPERATING INCOME AND ENTITY INCOME		$ 68,000
Interest Charges		8,000
OWNERSHIP INCOME		$ 60,000
Common Dividend Charges		10,000
INCREASE IN RETAINED EARNINGS		$ 50,000

A few of the figures contained in the accounts require further explanation. The decrease in cash from $85,000 at the beginning of the year to $72,000 at year-end was the result of:

Sales revenue	+	$1,000,000
less: Increases in accounts receivable	−	120,000
less: Merchandise purchases	−	780,000
less: Other expenses	−	200,000
plus: Increases in current liabilities	+	105,000
less: Interest charges	−	8,000
less: Common dividend charges	−	10,000
	−$	13,000

Leavenworth is a retailing firm that buys at wholesale and sells at retail a single product. The firm has adopted the FIFO cost flow method, and its cost of goods sold for the year was determined as follows:

Beginning inventory		
5,000 units @ $10/unit	=	$ 50,000
Add: Purchases		
65,000 units @ $12/unit (average price)	=	780,000
Cost of goods available for sale		$830,000
Less: Ending inventory		
10,000 units @ $13/unit	=	130,000
Cost of goods sold (60,000 units)		$700,000

Purchases of merchandise were evenly distributed throughout the year so that $12/unit represents the average price at which Leavenworth purchased merchandise during the year.

The building and equipment are both being depreciated on a straight-line basis. Their expected useful lives are 20 years and 5 years, respectively, at the end of which neither is expected to have a net salvage value. Thus, annual depreciation on the building is $10,000 $\left(\dfrac{\$200,000}{20 \text{ years}}\right)$ and on the equipment, $22,000 $\left(\dfrac{\$110,000}{5 \text{ years}}\right)$.

At the beginning of the year, Leavenworth issued $100,000 maturity amount of eight per cent bonds at par. The bonds are noncallable and nonconvertible, mature in five years, and pay interest of $4,000 every six months. Accordingly, the amount reported for interest charges for the year ($8,000) represents the cash paid to bondholders during the year.

At year-end, the following current cost information is available to Leavenworth Corporation:

a. Price lists provided by suppliers indicate that the current cost of the merchandise that Leavenworth deals in is $13.50/unit at year-end.

b. An examination of real estate records of recent transactions in similar nearby property indicates that, were Leavenworth to have purchased its land at year-end, the cost would have been approximately $52,000.

c. Because buildings of the type owned by Leavenworth are not regularly bought and sold, no current market prices as such are available. However, recourse to government-prepared construction cost indexes indicates that, were Leavenworth to have built its building at year-end, the cost would have been approximately $230,000. The price indexes have risen steadily throughout the year.

d. The type of equipment owned by Leavenworth is quite common and has a wide variety of applications. As such, an active market exists for used equipment of this type. At year-end, the following prices are available from equipment dealers:

| | Current Purchase Price at December 31 | |
	19X7	19X8
New	$110,000	$126,500
One-year-old	77,000	88,550
Two-years-old	49,500	56,925

The rise in prices of new and used equipment has been steady throughout the year.

e. Interest rates for bonds similar to those issued by Leavenworth have gradually declined from eight per cent to six per cent over the year. As such, the market price for such bonds at year-end is as follows:

$$\$100,000\, p_{\overline{8}|.03} = \$100,000 \times .78941 = \$78,941$$
$$\$\ \ \ 4,000\, P_{\overline{8}|.03} = \$\ \ \ 4,000 \times 7.01969 = \underline{\ \ 28,079}$$

$$\underline{\underline{\$107,020}}$$

Despite the fact that certain individual prices have changed during the year, we will assume that there was no change in the general price level during the year (i.e., no change in the purchasing power of the dollar). We will relax this assumption once the general principles of adjustment for individual price changes have been presented.

General Principles of Adjustment

Since we have assumed that there has been no change in the general price level, Leavenworth has clearly benefited by having acquired its merchandise, land, building, and equipment at a time when their purchase prices were lower. Conversely, Leavenworth's stockholders have been hurt by the decline in interest rates that drove up the price of the bond liabilities. Had Leavenworth waited until year-end to issue its bonds, it could have borrowed the $100,000 at a cheaper rate; alternatively, to retire the bonds today would cost more (by $7,020) than if the interest rate had remained unchanged. The overall effect of these price changes is as yet unclear; to ascertain their effect, we must adjust Leavenworth's historical cost based accounts to reflect current costs.

We shall make these adjustments in such a fashion as not to disturb or obscure the firm's conventional accounting records, using a series of adjunct accounts and preparing only year-end entries to make the adjustments to current costs. The adjunct accounts will be established for each asset, liability, and related expense account subject to changes in price. (In this particular example, no revenue adjunct accounts are necessary, but in other cases they might be required.) These accounts will contain only the increments or decrements from historical costs to current costs and, as such, will be titled "current cost increment (or decrement)." In general, the only accounts requiring adjuncts of this sort will be those whose balances are stated in terms of historical costs; accounts with balances stated in current monetary terms (such as cash and accounts payable) will not require modification as they already represent current values.

It should be noted at this juncture, however, that this adjunct account procedure is necessary only if historical cost data must be preserved. Otherwise, no adjunct accounts would be needed since all entries would be made into the primary accounts. Transactions during the year would be recorded in the conventional manner, but the regular year-end adjusting entries to record *historical* cost depreciation expense, *historical* cost of goods sold expense, and so forth, would *not* be made. In their place would be year-end adjusting entries to record *current* cost depreciation expense, *current* cost of goods sold expense, and so on. Indeed, we believe there is little to be gained by preserving historical cost data. Pedagogically, however, there is an important advantage in using the adjunct account procedure in that it facilitates comparison of current cost data with historical cost data; as a result, our exposition will be couched in terms of adjunct accounts.

Mechanically, the procedure for making the adjustments to current cost at year-end involves two steps: (1) a journal entry to record the change during the year in the current cost of the asset or liability and to recognize the related gain or loss and (2) a journal entry to adjust the related expense to a current cost basis. For example, in the case of a depreciable asset whose current cost has risen during the year, the first entry would involve a debit to an "asset—current cost increment" account and a credit to a holding gain account to reflect the effects of the price increase that occurred during the year. The second entry would then consist of a debit to "depreciation expense—current cost increment" and a credit to "asset—allowance for depreciation—current cost increment" for the difference between current cost and historical cost depreciation for the year.

The determination of the amounts involved in making year-end current cost adjustments is somewhat more complex. For this purpose, it is helpful to think in terms of *inputs to* and *outputs from* the accounting period. In terms of quantities (rather than prices), this is fairly easy to do. Suppose a firm had 150 units of inventory on hand at the beginning of the accounting period and purchased 600 more during the period. These are the quantity *inputs* to the accounting period. Suppose also that the firm sold 625 units during the year and had 125 left on hand at the end. These are the quantity *outputs* from the period. In terms of quantities, then, quantity inputs will be *equal* to quantity outputs from the period. On the other hand, prices of inputs and prices of outputs will differ from one another by the *price changes* that occur during the period.

When we multiply quantity by price, the result, of course, is *cost*. Under conventional accounting, we multiply a present quantity by a historical price to arrive at the historical cost of the item in question. Once established, the historical price is assumed not to change over time. In other words, historical price inputs to the period will be equal to historical price outputs from the period. Therefore, under conventional accounting, the historical cost of inputs to the accounting period will be equal to the historical cost of outputs from the period. Gains and losses stemming from price changes are generally not recognized.

When we turn our focus to *current prices* rather than historical prices, the situation changes. The current price of an item is the price that would be required to purchase it on a given day. Thus, the current price to purchase an item on day 2 may differ from its current price on day 1. As a consequence, the current prices of inputs to an accounting period may very well differ from the current prices of outputs from the period, the differences being due to price changes during the period.

Under current cost accounting (as opposed to historical cost accounting), current prices rather than historical prices are used. We multiply the present quantity of an item by its current (or present) price to yield the item's current cost. Because current prices can and often do change over time, the current cost of an item at one point in time may differ from its current cost at another point in time by the amount of the change in its current price multiplied by the quantity held over that time.

This difference we call a *realizable* holding gain (or loss). We do so to distinguish it from the gains and losses that arise under historical cost accounting, those being *realized* gains (or losses) because they typically are recognized only when the item in question is sold (i.e., realization occurs).

For an asset, the realizable holding gain (or loss) for the accounting period is determined by means of the following formula:

$$
\begin{bmatrix} \text{Increase (decrease) in market} \\ \text{value of assets while held by} \\ \text{the firm} \end{bmatrix} = \begin{bmatrix} \text{Realizable holding gain} \\ \text{(loss) for the period} \end{bmatrix}
$$

$$
= \begin{bmatrix} \text{Current cost of outputs from} \\ \text{the period at date of output} \end{bmatrix} - \begin{bmatrix} \text{Current cost of inputs to} \\ \text{the period at date of input} \end{bmatrix}
$$

$$
= \begin{bmatrix} \begin{pmatrix} \text{Current cost} \\ \text{at end of} \\ \text{period of} \\ \text{asset on} \\ \text{hand at end} \\ \text{of period} \end{pmatrix} + \begin{pmatrix} \text{Current cost} \\ \text{at date of} \\ \text{consumption or} \\ \text{disposition of} \\ \text{asset consumed} \\ \text{or disposed} \\ \text{of during} \\ \text{the period} \end{pmatrix} \end{bmatrix} - \begin{bmatrix} \begin{pmatrix} \text{Current cost} \\ \text{at beginning} \\ \text{of period of} \\ \text{asset on hand} \\ \text{at beginning} \\ \text{of period} \end{pmatrix} + \begin{pmatrix} \text{Cost at} \\ \text{date of} \\ \text{acquisition} \\ \text{of asset} \\ \text{acquired} \\ \text{during} \\ \text{the period} \end{pmatrix} \end{bmatrix}
$$

Whenever the current cost of asset outputs from the period exceed the current cost of asset inputs to the period, a realizable holding gain has occurred; when the opposite is the case, the difference is a realizable holding loss on the asset.

Liabilities are, of course, the opposite side of the coin from assets. Accordingly, the realizable holding gain (or loss) for the period on a liability is determined as follows:

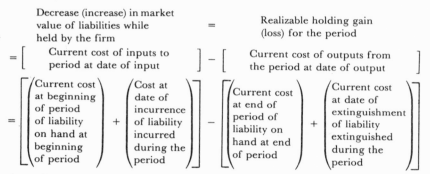

A realizable holding gain has occurred whenever the current cost of liability inputs to the period exceed the current cost of liability outputs from the period; an entity is "better off" if the current cost of what it owes declines in value. In the opposite case, a realizable holding loss in the amount of the difference has occurred. Let us now apply these formulations to the Leavenworth Corporation example.

Land

Because it is the simplest to understand, let us consider first the current cost adjustment required for Leavenworth's land. Adapting our general formula for determining holding gains to the specific instance of land, we have:

$$\begin{array}{c}\text{Change in market value} \\ \text{of land during the year} \\ \text{while held by the firm.}\end{array} \doteq \begin{array}{c}\text{Realizable holding} \\ \text{gain on land}\end{array} =$$

$$= \left[\begin{array}{c}\text{Current cost of land} \\ \text{outputs from the period} \\ \text{at date of output}\end{array}\right] - \left[\begin{array}{c}\text{Current cost of land} \\ \text{inputs to the period} \\ \text{at date of input}\end{array}\right]$$

$$= \left[\left(\begin{array}{c}\text{Current cost} \\ \text{at year-end} \\ \text{of land} \\ \text{owned at} \\ \text{year-end}\end{array}\right) + \left(\begin{array}{c}\text{Current cost} \\ \text{at date of} \\ \text{sale of land} \\ \text{sold during} \\ \text{the year}\end{array}\right)\right] - \left[\left(\begin{array}{c}\text{Current cost at} \\ \text{beginning of} \\ \text{year of land} \\ \text{owned at} \\ \text{beginning} \\ \text{of year}\end{array}\right) + \left(\begin{array}{c}\text{Current cost} \\ (= \text{historical} \\ \text{cost) of land} \\ \text{purchased} \\ \text{during the} \\ \text{year}\end{array}\right)\right]$$

Because Leavenworth neither bought any additional land nor sold any
land during the year, we then have:

Realizable
holding gain $= [(\$52,000) + (\text{-0-})] - [(\$40,000) + (\text{-0-})]$
on land
$= \underline{\underline{\$12,000}}$

It should be stressed that only because the land was purchased at the
first of the year will its current cost at that date be the same as its
historical cost. In subsequent years, such will not be the case (except
by accident); for example, the current cost of land at the beginning
of the next year, 19X9, will be $52,000. Current cost increments to
asset accounts are *cumulative* in nature, the total in the account being
balanced out every year.

Since no expense adjustments are required, a single year-end adjusting
journal entry is sufficient in the case of land:

(1)   Land—Current Cost Increment $12,000
           Realizable Holding Gain on Land $12,000

The account debited is an asset adjunct account, the balance in which
($12,000), when added to the historical cost of land ($40,000), yields
the current cost of land at year-end ($52,000). This is the amount
to be reported in Leavenworth's year-end current cost position statement.
The account credited is an income statement account, the balance in
which will be reported in Leavenworth's current cost income statement
for 19X8.

Merchandise Inventory

Next, let us determine the amount of realizable holding gain (or
loss) that occurred during 19X8 with respect to Leavenworth's inventory.
Adapting our formula for realizable holding gains (or losses) on assets
to the inventory situation, we have:

Realizable holding gain (or loss) =
on merchandise inventory

$= \begin{bmatrix} \text{Current cost of inventory} \\ \text{outputs from the period} \\ \text{at date of output} \end{bmatrix} - \begin{bmatrix} \text{Current cost of inventory} \\ \text{inputs to the period} \\ \text{at date of input} \end{bmatrix}$

$$
\begin{aligned}
= & \left[\begin{pmatrix}\text{Current} \\ \text{cost at} \\ \text{end of} \\ \text{year of} \\ \text{inventory} \\ \text{on hand} \\ \text{at} \\ \text{year-end}\end{pmatrix} + \begin{pmatrix}\text{Current} \\ \text{cost at} \\ \text{date of} \\ \text{sale of} \\ \text{goods} \\ \text{sold} \\ \text{during} \\ \text{the year}\end{pmatrix}\right] - \left[\begin{pmatrix}\text{Current} \\ \text{cost at} \\ \text{beginning} \\ \text{of year of} \\ \text{inventory} \\ \text{on hand at} \\ \text{beginning} \\ \text{of year}\end{pmatrix} + \begin{pmatrix}\text{Current} \\ \text{cost (=} \\ \text{historical} \\ \text{cost) of} \\ \text{inventory} \\ \text{purchases} \\ \text{made} \\ \text{during} \\ \text{the year}\end{pmatrix}\right]
\end{aligned}
$$

$$
\begin{aligned}
= & \left[\begin{pmatrix}\text{Units on} \\ \text{hand at} \\ \text{year-end} \\ \times \\ \text{Current} \\ \text{cost per} \\ \text{unit at} \\ \text{year end}\end{pmatrix} + \begin{pmatrix}\text{Units} \\ \text{sold} \\ \text{during} \\ \text{the year} \\ \times \\ \text{Average} \\ \text{current} \\ \text{cost of} \\ \text{units} \\ \text{during} \\ \text{the year}\end{pmatrix}\right] - \left[\begin{pmatrix}\text{Units on} \\ \text{hand at} \\ \text{beginning} \\ \text{of year} \\ \times \\ \text{Current} \\ \text{cost per} \\ \text{unit at} \\ \text{beginning} \\ \text{of year}\end{pmatrix} + \begin{pmatrix}\text{Units} \\ \text{purchased} \\ \text{during} \\ \text{the year} \\ \times \\ \text{Cost} \\ \text{per unit} \\ \text{during} \\ \text{the year}\end{pmatrix}\right]
\end{aligned}
$$

$$
= \left[\begin{pmatrix}10{,}000 \\ \text{units @} \\ \$13.50/ \\ \text{unit}\end{pmatrix} + \begin{pmatrix}60{,}000 \\ \text{units @} \\ \$12/\text{unit}\end{pmatrix}\right] - \left[\begin{pmatrix}5{,}000 \\ \text{units @} \\ \$10/\text{unit}\end{pmatrix} + \begin{pmatrix}65{,}000 \\ \text{units @} \\ \$12/\text{unit}\end{pmatrix}\right]
$$

$$
\begin{aligned}
&= [\quad \$135{,}000 \quad + \quad \$720{,}000 \quad] \quad - \quad [\ \$\ 50{,}000 \quad + \quad \$780{,}000 \quad] \\
&= \quad \$855{,}000 \qquad\qquad\qquad\qquad - \quad \$830{,}000 \\
&= \quad \$\ 25{,}000
\end{aligned}
$$

Unlike the case of land, Leavenworth's realizable holding gain on merchandise inventory involves quantity as well as price changes during the period (because the quantity of goods purchased exceeds the quantity of goods sold, hence, ending inventory exceeds beginning inventory). We have a second (right-hand) term in each of our brackets and these two terms do not cancel out.[1]

A few further words of explanation are in order:

1. The ending inventory is priced as of December 31, 19X8 to yield the current cost of the ending inventory, $135,000.

2. The current cost of goods sold, $720,000, is determined by using the *average* current purchase price during the year. Since Leavenworth's

---

1. If there were no *changes* in inventory stocks, i.e., the quantity of goods purchased exactly equaled the quantity of goods sold, the second and fourth entries across the page would cancel each other out under our assumption of evenly distributed purchases and sales, and we would then have the same (no net *quantity change*) situation as in land, where these two entries were both zero.

merchandise purchases were evenly distributed over the year, the average price Leavenworth paid for goods during the year, $12/unit, is the average current price. In essence, then, current cost of goods sold is computed on a "hand-to-mouth" basis, just as if Leavenworth had bought the goods on the same day it sold them.

3. The beginning inventory's current cost of $50,000 is exactly equal to its historical cost. This occurred only because, having begun business on the first of the year, Leavenworth actually purchased the inventory on that date. Usually, such would not be the case, the beginning inventory having been purchased in some preceding accounting period.

4. Purchases for the year, $780,000 in this case, will *always* be stated at current cost. This is because on the date of purchase and—except by accident—only on that date will historical cost and current cost be identical.

There are, of course, other ways in which Leavenworth's realizable holding gain on merchandise for 19X8 could have been determined. For expository purposes, let us consider some of these other alternatives, using various arbitrary flow assumptions. As we shall discover, the final result will be the same under *any* flow assumption.

First, we could assume that all sales and purchases were made at mid-year and that the beginning inventory was sold at that time. The beginning inventory of 5,000 units is assumed to have been held during the first half of the year while its current purchase price rose from $10/unit to $12/unit (the average or mid-year price). The realizable holding gain, then, on the beginning inventory would have been $10,000 (5,000 units @ $2/unit increase in price). Of the 65,000 units purchased at mid-year, 55,000 are assumed to have been sold immediately; there would be no realizable holding gain on these units. The remaining 10,000 units that were purchased at mid-year were held for the second half of the year, becoming the ending inventory. During this period, their current purchase price rose from $12/unit to $13.50/unit, yielding a realizable holding gain on the ending inventory of $15,000 (10,000 units @ $1.50/unit increase in price). In total, then, Leavenworth's realizable holding gain would be $25,000 ($10,000 on beginning inventory and $15,000 on ending inventory), the same amount as was determined earlier.

As a slight variant on the foregoing, we could again assume that all purchases and sales were made at mid-year but that instead of being sold the beginning inventory was held throughout the year (becoming part of the ending inventory). Thus, that inventory would have been held throughout a period during which the current purchase price rose from $10/unit to $13.50/unit, yielding a realizable holding gain of $17,500. Of the 65,000 units purchased at midyear, 60,000 would have been sold immediately (no realizable holding gain on them), leaving 5,000 units to be held throughout the second half of the year, becoming part of the ending inventory. Because the current price rose from $12/unit to $13.50/unit during this period, the realizable holding gain on these units would be $7,500 (5,000 units @ $1.50/unit price increase). In total, the realizable holding gain for the year would again be $25,000 ($17,500 + $7,500 in this case).

As a third alternative, we can gear our assumptions to correspond with the FIFO cost flow method being employed by Leavenworth and still get the same answer. Consider first the ending inventory. These 10,000 units were purchased at a time when their purchase price was $13/unit and held until the end of the period at which time their current price was $13.50/unit. The realizable holding gain on these units was $5,000 (10,000 units @ $.50/unit price increase), all of which would be regarded as *unrealized* in conventional accounting terms. On the other inventory units Leavenworth had during the year—all of which were sold—the realizable holding gain results from the rise in value from beginning of year to time of sale, or it is the difference between the $720,000 current cost of goods sold and the $700,000 historical cost of goods sold, or $20,000. Under conventional accounting, this gain would be regarded as *realized* since the goods were sold. Again, the total realizable holding gain for 19X8 would be $25,000 ($5,000 + $20,000 in this case). Moreover, the total realizable holding gain would still be $25,000, regardless of the cost flow method adopted by Leavenworth—LIFO, average cost, whatever. (The student may wish to prove this by running through the computations.) In accounting on a current cost basis, *no cost flow assumption is required* (or, alternatively, *any* cost flow assumption may be employed without changing the result), and this in itself is a major advantage over the arbitrariness necessitated by historical cost accounting.

However determined, the change in current cost of the inventory, the recognition of the realizable holding gain for the period, and the adjustment of cost of goods sold expense to a current cost basis are accomplished by two year-end adjusting journal entries. The first entry recognizes the realizable holding gain for the period, to wit:

(2)	Merchandise Inventory—Current Cost Increment	$25,000	
	Realizable Holding Gain on Merchandise Inventory		$25,000

The account debited is an asset adjunct account, created for the express purpose of adjusting inventory historical costs to a current cost basis without altering the original historical cost record. The account credited is an income statement account which will appear on Leavenworth's current cost income statement but not its historical cost statement.

The second entry adjusts cost of goods sold to a current cost basis and simultaneously further adjusts the balance in the asset adjunct account:

(3)   Cost of Goods Sold Expense—
      Current Cost Increment $20,000
         Merchandise Inventory—
         Current Cost Increment $20,000

When the account debited is added to the historical cost of goods sold account, the sum is current cost of goods sold, an amount which will be reported on Leavenworth's current cost income statement. The amount credited in entry (3) represents a reduction in the balance of the inventory adjunct account created in entry (2) because goods were sold. The balance *left* in this account after entry (3), i.e., $5,000, is the amount which, when added to the historical cost of ending inventory ($130,000), yields the current cost of ending inventory ($135,000). This is the amount that will be reported on Leavenworth's year-end current cost position statement.

Building

In contrast to land and inventories, the year-end adjustments to current cost for Leavenworth's building are more complex. Not only are two year-end entries required (because the building is gradually being consumed while its current price is changing), but also the computations are more involved. The concept, however, remains the same; we compute the realizable holding gain as the excess of *current cost outputs from* the accounting period over the *current cost inputs to* the period.

We shall demonstrate first how this is done and then explain the rationale afterward:

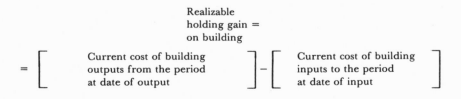

$$
= \left[\left(\begin{array}{c} \text{Estimated} \\ \text{current} \\ \text{cost at} \\ \text{year-end} \\ \text{of portion} \\ \text{of new} \\ \text{building} \\ \text{on hand at} \\ \text{year-end} \end{array} \right) + \left(\begin{array}{c} \text{Estimated current} \\ \text{cost at date} \\ \text{of consumption} \\ \text{(or disposition)} \\ \text{of portion of} \\ \text{new building} \\ \text{consumed (or} \\ \text{disposed of)} \\ \text{during} \\ \text{the year} \end{array} \right) \right] - \left[\left(\begin{array}{c} \text{Estimated} \\ \text{current} \\ \text{cost at} \\ \text{beginning} \\ \text{of year of} \\ \text{portion} \\ \text{of new} \\ \text{building} \\ \text{on hand at} \\ \text{beginning} \\ \text{of year} \end{array} \right) + \left(\begin{array}{c} \text{Current} \\ \text{cost (=} \\ \text{historical} \\ \text{cost) of} \\ \text{additions} \\ \text{at date} \\ \text{made to} \\ \text{building} \\ \text{during} \\ \text{the year} \end{array} \right) \right]
$$

$$
= \left[\left(\begin{array}{c} \text{Portion} \\ \text{of new} \\ \text{building on} \\ \text{hand at} \\ \text{year-end} \\ \times \\ \text{Current} \\ \text{cost at} \\ \text{year-end} \\ \text{of new} \\ \text{building} \end{array} \right) + \left(\begin{array}{c} \text{Portion} \\ \text{of new} \\ \text{building} \\ \text{consumed} \\ \text{during} \\ \text{the year} \\ \times \\ \text{Average} \\ \text{current} \\ \text{cost during} \\ \text{the year} \\ \text{of new} \\ \text{building} \end{array} \right) \right] - \left[\left(\begin{array}{c} \text{Portion} \\ \text{of new} \\ \text{building} \\ \text{on hand at} \\ \text{beginning} \\ \text{of year} \\ \times \\ \text{Current} \\ \text{cost at} \\ \text{beginning} \\ \text{of year} \\ \text{of new} \\ \text{building} \end{array} \right) + \left(\begin{array}{c} \text{NONE} \\ \text{(in this} \\ \text{example)} \end{array} \right) \right]
$$

$$
= \left[\left(\begin{array}{c} 95\% \\ \times \\ \$230,000 \end{array} \right) + \left(\begin{array}{c} 5\% \\ \times \\ \dfrac{\$200,000 + \$230,000}{2} \end{array} \right) \right] - \left[\left(\begin{array}{c} 100\% \\ \times \\ \$200,000 \end{array} \right) + \left(\text{-0-} \right) \right]
$$

$$
= [\quad \$218,500 \quad + \quad \$10,750 \quad] - [\quad \$200,000 \quad] + (\quad \text{-0-} \quad)]
$$

$$
= \quad \$229,250 \quad\quad - \quad\quad \$200,000
$$

$$
= \quad \$\;29,250
$$

Now, a few words of explanation:

1. The first item in the equation represents the current cost of Leavenworth's now-used building at year-end. This is analogous to the current cost of ending inventory in the merchandise case. Since Leavenworth's straight-line depreciation method on a useful life of 20 years with no expected salvage was thought to approximate the *quantity* of building services consumed, then 5 per cent of the building was consumed during the year, leaving 95 per cent on hand at year-end. Multiplying 95 per cent by the current cost of a *new* building at year-end yields the approximate current cost of Leavenworth's *used* building at the end of 19X8.

2. The second item in the equation is current cost depreciation expense
for 19X8 and is analogous to cost of goods sold expense. It should
be remembered that all expenses on a current cost basis are computed
as if the asset were acquired on the same date that it was consumed
or disposed of (a "hand-to-mouth" basis). Technically, this should be
done on a day-by-day basis, finding the current price of new building
services on that day and multiplying that by the quantity of building
services consumed on that same day. Because such a task is impractical,
we simply compute the approximate quantity of building services
consumed during the year (5 per cent) and multiply it by the average
current cost of a new building for the year $\left(\dfrac{\$200{,}000 + \$230{,}000}{2} \right)^2$.

3. The third item in the equation is analogous to the current cost
of beginning inventory. Since the building was acquired new at the
first of the year, its services were 100 per cent intact. We simply multiply
this amount by the current price of a new building on that date ($200,000)
to yield current cost, which is the same as historical cost. However,
at the beginning of *next year* (19X9), the current cost of the building
will *not* be its historical cost but rather the current cost of the (by
then) used building, $218,500. Current cost, not historical cost, is what
we are interested in, and the two will coincide only at date of purchase
(except by accident).

4. The last item in the equation is analogous to merchandise purchases
during the year. Had Leavenworth's building been added on to during
the year (such as a new wing), been remodeled, or had some other
improvement made, the cost of such would be added here as another
input. Of course, the current cost and historical cost of any input during
the period will always be the same. Since Leavenworth added nothing
to the building during the year, this factor is zero. We included it
in the equation simply for expository purposes to indicate what might
occur in other circumstances.[3]

2. Using the average building price over the year is equivalent to assuming that the
price jumped at mid-year (rather than on the first day of the year, as in our Chapter
11 examples), when the 20-year-life building is two-and-a-half per cent depreciated.
We could compute the current cost depreciation adjustment, to be added to the historical
cost depreciation of $10,000, to get total current cost depreciation, as 0.025 × $30,000
= $750, and assume that this added amount all resulted from a price rise occurring
at mid-year. Under-depreciation on a current cost basis in the first half of the year
is then just compensated for by over-depreciation on a current cost basis in the second
half of the year. The resultant figure for current cost depreciation is the same as that
calculated by using our averaging concept.

3. If buildings were sold during the year—a further complication we have avoided
in the Leavenworth example—a third term would be added to our bracketed output

As noted earlier, two journal entries are necessary to make the required current cost adjustments for Leavenworth's building. As with merchandise inventory, the first entry recognizes the increase in current cost of the asset as well as the realizable holding gain that occurred during the year. Because it is generally regarded as useful to know the relationship between the cost of an entity's used depreciable assets vis-a-vis the cost of new ones, both the building account and its related allowance for depreciation must be adjusted. The building account is adjusted by the amount necessary to bring its balance up to year-end current cost. Since the amount of the realizable holding gain is already known, the adjustment to allowance for depreciation is simply a "plug" figure, although it can be computed directly.[4]

Thus, the first entry is as follows:

(4)	Building—Current Cost Increment	$30,000	
	Building—Allowance for Depreciation—Current Cost Increment		$750
	Realizable Holding Gain on Building		$29,250

The second entry simply adjusts historical cost depreciation for 19X8 to a current cost basis, i.e., it is the excess of current cost depreciation over historical cost depreciation:

(5)	Depreciation Expense—Current Cost Increment	$750	
	Building—Allowance for Depreciation—Current Cost Increment		$750

Once these two entries have been made, the asset and contra-asset accounts together with their respective adjunct accounts represent the

---

amounts, and we would have to calculate the realizable holding gain *accruing this period* on those buildings before sale. The portion of any total *realized* holding gain which accrued in *former periods* is *not* part of this year's current income.

4. If the building's services had remained intact for the entire year of 19X8, Leavenworth's realizable holding gain would have been $30,000, the difference between the current cost of a new building at year-end ($230,000) and at the beginning of the year ($200,000). However, Leavenworth had, on the average, only 97.5 per cent of a new building on hand during the year (100 per cent at the beginning of the year and 95 per cent at the end). Accordingly, Leavenworth's gain was equal to 97.5 per cent of the potential holding gain of $30,000. The portion of the potential gain that Leavenworth did *not* get (2.5 per cent of $30,000), because it was using up the building's services during the year, is the adjustment to the allowance for depreciation.

current cost of Leavenworth's used building at year-end. The building is 5 per cent "used up," or 95 per cent remains, and 0.95 × $230,000 = $218,500, which is the value that will be reported on the current cost position statement.

Equipment

Because current market prices are available for *both* new and used equipment, the process of determining current cost increments, realizable holding gain, and current cost depreciation expense for Leavenworth's equipment is somewhat different from that for the building. Although our basic formulation remains the same as before—comparing current cost outputs from the period against current cost inputs to the period—some of the components will differ because, in this instance, more precise data are available. In particular, it is no longer necessary to use some conventional depreciation method applied to the current cost of a new asset to approximate current cost of a used asset and current cost depreciation. To illustrate how this difference works, let us compute the realizable holding gain for 19X8 on Leavenworth's equipment:

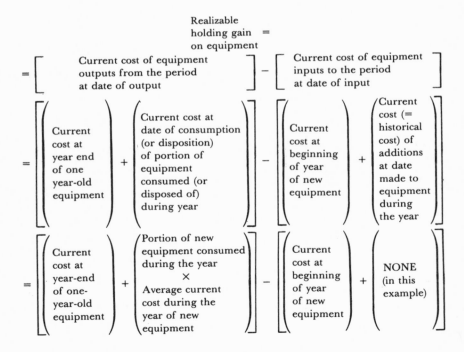

$$= \left[\left(\$88,550 \right) + \left(\frac{\$126,500 - \$88,550}{\$126,500} \times \frac{\$110,000 + \$126,500}{2} \right) \right] - \left[\$110,000 + (\text{-0-}) \right]$$

$$= [(\ \$ \ 88,550 \ ) + (\ 30\% \ \times \ \$118,250 \ )] - [\ \$110,000 \ + (\ \text{-0-} \ )]$$

$$= [\qquad \$ \ 88,550 \qquad + \qquad \$35,475 \qquad] - [\ \$110,000 \ + (\ \text{-0-} \ )]$$

$$= \qquad \$124,025 \qquad\qquad\qquad - \qquad \$110,000$$

$$= \qquad \$ \ 14,025$$

Of the components of this equation, all should be self-evident (from the market price data given on p. 519) except for the second, which is the computation of current cost depreciation for 19X8. As was the case with Leavenworth's building, current cost depreciation is the portion of a new equipment's services consumed during the year multiplied by the average current cost of new equipment during the year. The average current cost is computed the same as with the building; the portion of a new asset's services consumed is not. Instead, it is determined by relating new and used equipment prices to one another to establish the market's assessment as to the portion of the asset's services consumed during the year. This is done by subtracting the current cost at year-end of one-year-old equipment from the current cost at year-end of new equipment and dividing the result by the current cost at year-end of new equipment. In other words, it is the decrease in current cost that resulted from use of the equipment that is related to the current cost of unused equipment. In the case of Leavenworth's equipment, a one-year-old unit is worth only 70 per cent of a new unit at year-end, hence, the depreciation rate for the year was 30 per cent, and this percentage is then applied to its average current price during the period.[5]

The two journal entries that result from our computations are:

(6) Equipment—Current Cost Increment $16,500
      Equipment—Allowance for
      Depreciation—Current
      Cost Increment $ 2,475
      Realizable Holding Gain
      on Equipment   14,025

5. This seemingly elaborate computation is necessitated by the assumption of gradual price changes over the year. In Chapter 11, where we assumed that prices jumped on the first day of the year, we could simply subtract the market value of a one-year-old

(7)   Depreciation Expense—Current
      Cost Increment $13,475
          Equipment—Allowance for
          Depreciation—Current
          Cost Increment $13,475

These two entries will affect Leavenworth's current cost financial statements in the same manner as entries (4) and (5) with respect to the building. The primary difference is that the net current cost (after depreciation) on the equipment represents an exact market value, whereas with the building the figure is only an approximation.

Bonds Payable

The final current cost adjustments for the Leavenworth Corporation have to do with its bonds outstanding. The concept is basically the same as with assets except that—since bonds are a liability and the opposite of an asset—outputs from the period are subtracted from inputs to the period rather than the other way around. As we shall see, Leavenworth had a realizable holding loss on its bonds during 19X8 because the drop in interest rates drove the price of its bonds up. Our computations are as follows:

$$
\begin{aligned}
&\text{Realizable holding gain (loss) on bonds payable} \\[4pt]
&= \left[\begin{array}{c}\text{Current cost of bonds}\\ \text{inputs to the period}\\ \text{at date of input}\end{array}\right] - \left[\begin{array}{c}\text{Current cost of bonds outputs}\\ \text{from the period at}\\ \text{date of output}\end{array}\right] \\[6pt]
&= \left[\left(\begin{array}{c}\text{Current}\\ \text{cost of}\\ \text{bonds at}\\ \text{beginning}\\ \text{of year}\end{array}\right) + \left(\begin{array}{c}\text{Interest}\\ \text{charges}\\ \text{at}\\ \text{current}\\ \text{cost}\\ \text{during}\\ \text{the year}\end{array}\right)\right] - \left[\left(\begin{array}{c}\text{Current}\\ \text{cost of}\\ \text{bonds at}\\ \text{year-end}\end{array}\right) + \left(\begin{array}{c}\text{Cash}\\ \text{paid for}\\ \text{interest}\\ \text{during}\\ \text{the year}\end{array}\right) + \left(\begin{array}{c}\text{Cash paid}\\ \text{for bond}\\ \text{retirements}\\ \text{during}\\ \text{the year}\end{array}\right)\right] \\[6pt]
&= \left[\left(\$100{,}000\right) + \left(\$7{,}234\right)\right] - \left[\left(\$107{,}020\right) + \left(\$8{,}000\right) + \left(\begin{array}{c}\text{NONE (in}\\ \text{this case)}\end{array}\right)\right] \\[6pt]
&= \quad \$107{,}234 \qquad\qquad - \qquad \$115{,}020 \\[4pt]
&= \quad (\$\ \ 7{,}786)
\end{aligned}
$$

---

asset from the current market value of the asset new and the resultant figure would be current cost depreciation.

Of the five items in the equation, the second and third deserve explanation.

The second item, what we have termed "interest charges at current cost during the year," will appear in Leavenworth's current cost income statements as "current interest charges." They represent the amount Leavenworth would have had to pay during the year had its borrowings been on a "hand-to-mouth" basis, i.e., borrowing for one day at a time. As such, they are analogous to the current cost depreciation on Leavenworth's building and equipment. Because the decline in interest rates on Leavenworth's bonds occurred gradually over the course of the year, we approximate the current cost interest changes by: (a) assuming that the entire interest rate change occurred at mid-year (after the mid-year interest payment), (b) multiplying the assumed market interest rate for the first half of the year by the current cost of the bonds at the beginning of the year, (c) multiplying the assumed market interest rate for the second half of the year by the current cost of the bonds at mid-year after the assumed interest rate change, and (d) summing the amounts determined in (c) and (d). Assuming that the market rate of interest declined from eight per cent to six per cent at mid-year, the current cost of Leavenworth's bonds after the rate change (and after the mid-year interest payment) would have been:

Present value of maturity amount:
$\$100,000\, p_{\overline{9}|.03} = \$100,000 \times .76642 = $ \hfill $\$ 76,642$
Present value of future interest payments:
$\$4,000\, P_{\overline{9}|.03} = \$4,000 \times 7.78611 = $ \hfill $\underline{31,144}$

\hfill $\underline{\underline{\$107,786}}$

Given the assumed current cost of the bonds at mid-year, the current cost interest for 19X8 is computed as follows:

$$
\begin{aligned}
\text{Current cost interest charges} = {} & \left(\begin{array}{c} \text{Current} \\ \text{cost of} \\ \text{bonds at} \\ \text{beginning} \\ \text{of year} \end{array} \times \begin{array}{c} \text{Assumed} \\ \text{market} \\ \text{rate of} \\ \text{interest} \\ \text{for} \\ \text{first} \\ \text{half of} \\ \text{year} \end{array} \right) \\
+ {} & \left(\begin{array}{c} \text{Assumed} \\ \text{current} \\ \text{cost of} \\ \text{bonds at} \\ \text{mid-year} \\ \text{(after} \\ \text{mid-year} \\ \text{interest} \\ \text{payment)} \end{array} \times \begin{array}{c} \text{Assumed} \\ \text{market} \\ \text{rate of} \\ \text{interest} \\ \text{for} \\ \text{second} \\ \text{half} \\ \text{of year} \end{array} \right)
\end{aligned}
$$

$$= [\quad \$100,000 \quad \times \quad .04 \quad] + [\$107,786 \quad \times \quad .03 \quad]$$
$$= \quad \$ \quad 4,000 \qquad\qquad + \quad \$ \quad 3,234$$
$$= \quad \underline{\$ \quad 7,234}$$

At year-end, the market rate of interest was six per cent. Hence, the current cost of Leavenworth's bonds at that date—the third item in our equation—was computed as follows:

Present value of maturity amount:
$$\$100,000 p_{\overline{5}|.03} = \$100,000 \times .78941 \quad = \quad \$ \ 78,941$$
Present value of future interest payments:
$$\$ \quad 4,000 P_{\overline{5}|.03} = \$ \quad 4,000 \times 7.01969 \quad = \quad \underline{\quad 28,079}$$
$$\underline{\$107,020}$$

With our foregoing computations completed, we can prepare the required adjusting journal entries at year-end in a manner similar to those we have prepared earlier with respect to Leavenworth's assets. They are as follows:

(8) Realizable Holding Loss on
     Bonds Payable $7,786
         Bonds Payable—Current Cost
         Increment $7,786
(9) Bonds Payable—Current Cost Increment $ 766
         Interest Charges—Current
         Cost Decrement $ 766

Once the foregoing entries have been made, the balance in the current cost increment account ($7,020), when added to the balance in the historical cost bonds account ($100,000), represents the current cost of Leavenworth's bonds at year-end ($107,020). The current cost decrement for interest ($766) is simply the current cost interest charges for 19X8 ($7,234) less the historical cost interest charges ($8,000), the former amount, then, being reported as interest charges on Leavenworth's current cost income statement.

SUMMARY OF ADJUSTMENTS AND CURRENT COST FINANCIAL STATEMENTS

In the course of making our nine year-end adjusting journal entries, we created a number of new adjunct accounts for current cost increments and realizable holding gains. These accounts are displayed in Table

TABLE 12-4

Merchandise Inventory- Current Cost Increment

(2) $25,000	(3) $20,000
$25,000	✓ 5,000
✓ $ 5,000	$25,000

Land- Current Cost Increment

(1) $12,000	

Building- Current Cost Increment

(4) $30,000	

Building-Allowance for Depreciation-Current Cost Increment

	(4) $ 750
$1,500	(5) $ 750
$1,500	$1,500
	✓ 1,500

Equipment- Current Cost Increment

(6) $16,500	

Equipment-Allowance for Depreciation-Current Cost Increment

	(6) $ 2,475
✓ $15,950	(7) 13,475
$15,950	$15,950
	✓ 15,950

Bonds Payable- Current Cost Increment

(9) $ 766	(8) $7,786
✓ 7,020	
$7,786	$7,786
	✓ $7,020

Retained Earnings- Current Cost Increment

(c-1) $20,000	(c-3) $ 766
(c-2) 14,225	(c-4) 25,000
(c-8) 7,786	(c-5) 12,000
	(c-6) 29,250
✓ 39,030	(c-7) 14,025
$81,041	$81,041
	✓ $39,030

TABLE 12-4 CONTINUED

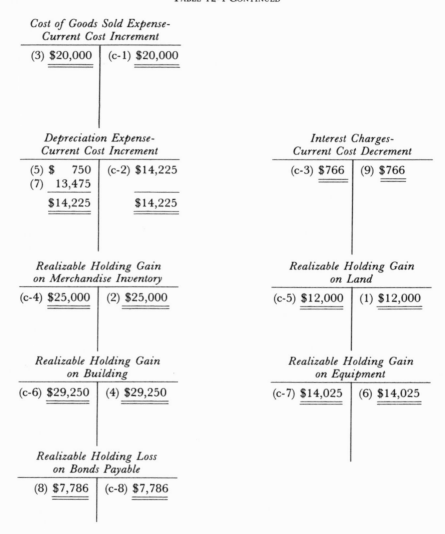

Cost of Goods Sold Expense-
Current Cost Increment

(3) $20,000	(c-1) $20,000

Depreciation Expense-
Current Cost Increment

(5) $ 750	(c-2) $14,225
(7) 13,475	
$14,225	$14,225

Interest Charges-
Current Cost Decrement

(c-3) $766	(9) $766

Realizable Holding Gain
on Merchandise Inventory

(c-4) $25,000	(2) $25,000

Realizable Holding Gain
on Land

(c-5) $12,000	(1) $12,000

Realizable Holding Gain
on Building

(c-6) $29,250	(4) $29,250

Realizable Holding Gain
on Equipment

(c-7) $14,025	(6) $14,025

Realizable Holding Loss
on Bonds Payable

(8) $7,786	(c-8) $7,786

12-4, complete with appropriate postings and closings.

When these additional accounts are coupled to Leavenworth's historical cost accounts, it becomes possible to prepare financial statements on a current cost basis. These statements, Leavenworth's comparative current position statement and its current income statement, appear as Tables 12-5 and 12-6, respectively.

TABLE 12-5

LEAVENWORTH CORPORATION
COMPARATIVE CURRENT POSITION STATEMENT
As of January 1 and December 31, 19X8

	December 31, 19X8			January 1, 19X8		
ASSETS:						
Current:						
Cash		$ 72,000			$ 85,000	
Accounts Receivable		120,000			-0-	
Merchandise Inventory		135,000	$327,000		50,000	$135,000
Plant:						
Land		$ 52,000			$ 40,000	
Building	$230,000			$200,000		
Less: Allowance for Depreciation	11,500	218,500		-0-	200,000	
Equipment	$126,500			$110,000		
Less: Allowance for Depreciation	37,950	88,550	359,050	-0-	110,000	350,000
			$686,050			$485,000
EQUITIES:						
Current Liabilities:						
Accounts Payable	$100,000			$ 35,000		
Other Payables	40,000	$140,000		-0-	$ 35,000	
Long-Term Liabilities:						
Bonds Payable		107,020	$247,020		100,000	$135,000
Common Stockholders' Equity:						
Common Stock		$350,000			$350,000	
Retained Earnings		89,030	439,030		-0-	350,000
			$686,050			$485,000

TABLE 12-6

LEAVENWORTH CORPORATION
CURRENT INCOME STATEMENT
For the Year Ended December 31, 19X8

REVENUES:
Sales		$1,000,000

EXPENSES:

Cost of Goods Sold	$720,000	
Depreciation	46,225	
Other	200,000	966,225

CURRENT OPERATING INCOME		$ 33,775

REALIZABLE HOLDING GAINS
(LOSSES) ON ASSETS:

On Merchandise Inventory	$ 25,000	
On Land	12,000	
On Building	29,250	
On Equipment	14,025	80,275

CURRENT ENTITY INCOME		$ 114,050
Interest Charges		7,234
Realizable Holding Gain		
(Loss) on Bonds Payable		(7,786)
CURRENT OWNERSHIP INCOME		$ 99,030
Common Dividend Charges		10,000
INCREASE IN RETAINED EARNINGS		$ 89,030

ADJUSTMENTS IN THE ACCOUNTS TO REFLECT CHANGES IN THE GENERAL PRICE LEVEL

Having the accounts and financial statements of the Leavenworth Corporation in current cost rather than historical cost terms is a major step toward having more realistic and usable data for the evaluation of managerial decisions and performance. Indeed, so long as the purchasing power of the dollar remains constant over time, it is the only step required. Even though the prices of specific goods and services move upward or downward, the general level of prices (i.e., the purchasing power of the dollar) may remain constant provided that the specific price increases on certain goods and services are offset by specific price decreases on other goods and services. Whenever such is the case, current cost adjustments like those we have just made will be sufficient in and of themselves.

For the most part, however, the recent experience in the United States (and in many other countries) has been that *both* specific prices and the general price level fluctuate. Since more of the specific prices have tended to rise rather than fall, the general price level has risen (i.e., we have had inflation rather than deflation). As a consequence, the dollar buys less today than it did before—its command over goods and services has fallen over time. Because a dollar of a few years ago had a greater purchasing power than does a dollar of today, the two dollars cannot be realistically compared with each other, nor can they be added to or subtracted from one another and produce a meaningful result. It is as if one were an apple and the other, an orange. Thus, in an inflationary economy such as ours, another set of adjustments beyond our current cost adjustments is required—this to convert all dollars to ones of equal purchasing power.

General Principles of Adjustment

In order to convert all dollars to ones of equal purchasing power, it will be helpful to use the concept of the *dated dollar*. Each dollar input to the accounting period has a date attached to it; similarly, each dollar output from the accounting period also has a date attached to it. These dollars and their related dates provide the raw materials for the conversion. All else that is needed is an objective general price level index for each date associated with either a dollar input or dollar output. Given dollars of any date, then, the index serves as a vehicle for their conversion to dollars of any other date.

An objective basis for making such conversions is provided by the various price indices published periodically by the federal government. While many of these indices deal with particular classes of goods and services, the ones germane to our needs are those that relate to the overall prices of goods and services throughout the economy. In particular, the Consumer Price Index appears to be the most appropriate for our task. One of the primary purposes of business firms is to generate spendable funds for the people who provided capital to the firms. For these people, the relevant index is one that indicates command over goods and services as consumers. Accordingly, all future references to a general price level index will be taken to mean the Consumer Price Index.

Given a general price level index, we are able to convert a dollar of one date to its equivalent purchasing power at another date. However, the question remains as to which date the conversion should be made, i.e., which date should be used as the standard for purposes of financial statement presentation. Should everything be converted to dollars as

of the date that the firm was organized? Should the conversion be
to dollars at the beginning, middle, or end of the current year? Or
should some other, perhaps arbitrary, date be used? We shall opt for
conversion to dollars at the end of the current period for two reasons:
(1) These dollars are the most familiar as they are "today's dollars,"
and (2) they permit ready comparison of the firm's present status with
those of previous periods. .

One final note must be made before we move on to the Leavenworth
example. None of these conversions are made directly in the accounts
of the entity; rather, all accounts are left in terms of "raw dollars,"
but each amount is "dated." Given these "dated raw dollars," we apply
the general price level index to those amounts only at statement
preparation time. Thus, the conversions are made when we *transfer
the data from the accounts to the financial statements.* The task is really
quite straight-forward and simple, particularly when the entity's accounts
are maintained on a computer. All that need be done is to program
the computer to convert "dated raw dollars" into year-end dollars and
then to feed general price level index information into the computer.
The converted amounts are then simply printed out from the computer.

The Leavenworth Example: Some Additional Assumptions

In order to convert the current cost data we generated earlier with
respect to the Leavenworth Corporation into dollars of comparable
purchasing power at the end of 19X8, some additional assumptions
will be necessary. They are as follows:

(1) Sales were made on account and were evenly distributed throughout the year.

(2) Purchases of merchandise were made on account and evenly
distributed throughout the year.

(3) Leavenworth's other expenses were incurred evenly over the
course of the year and required the use of net current monetary assets.

(4) Receivables were collected and payables paid evenly throughout
the year.

(5) All of Leavenworth's other payables are monetary liabilities.

(6) Common dividends were declared and paid on December 31,
19X8.

These assumptions are made so as to simplify matters; the even
distributions of activities over the year need not have been made, but
had the patterns been otherwise the conversions might have become
sufficiently cumbersome as to require the use of a computer. The general
procedure would be the same, however, regardless of the pattern of
activities.

We also will need some data with respect to general price level indices. Let us assume the following:

	General Price Level Index
January 1, 19X8	100
Average for period from January 1 through June 30, 19X8	102.5
Mid-year 19X8 and average for the year	105
Average for the period from July 1 through December 31, 19X8	107.5
December 31, 19X8	110

Thus, to convert $100 dated January 1, 19X8 to dollars as of December 31, 19X8, we simply multiply by 110/100, thereby yielding $110. Similarly, to convert $100 dated at mid-year to year-end dollars, we multiply by 110/105, yielding $104.76.

Let us turn now to the specifics of the Leavenworth Corporation example.

Position Statement Adjustments

Of all the adjustments to be made, those involving the amounts reported on the comparative position statement are perhaps the simplest and most straight-forward. Given a comparative position statement in current cost terms, such as Leavenworth's current position statement in Table 12-5, only two general conversions are needed to put all amounts in end-of-period dollars: (1) beginning-of-the-year assets and liabilities (year-end amounts are *already* stated in terms of current dollars) and (2) owners' equity at the beginning and end of the year.

To convert beginning-of-the-year amounts for Leavenworth's assets and liabilities to current (year-end) dollars, all that need be done is to multiply each amount by 110/100 (the "conversion factor"), the ratio of the general price level index at year-end to that at the beginning of the year. Because each dollar contained in the January 1, 19X8 column for assets and liabilities represents a *current cost at that date*, those "dated dollars" are simply converted into an equivalent amount of purchasing power at year-end. The dollar amounts for assets and liabilities in the December 31, 19X8 column represent *current costs at that date*, hence, those "dated dollars" require no conversion whatever because December 31, 19X8 dollars are what everything else is to be converted to.

The general procedure for converting owners' equity at the beginning and end of the year into current dollars is somewhat different from that for assets and liabilities. Consider first the dollar amount for capital directly invested by owners (in Leavenworth's case, its common stock). This amount is converted to current dollars by multiplying it by the ratio of the general price level index at year-end to that *at the date the dollars were originally invested.* The result then represents the *real* investment made by owners and is reported in both the January 1, 19X8 *and* the December 31, 19X8 columns. In Leavenworth's case, that investment was made at the beginning of the current year, thus the conversion factor is 110/100. In preparing Leavenworth's current real position statements in all *subsequent* years, the conversion factors' denominator will remain at 100 for those dollars originally invested. If, in later years, Leavenworth's stockholders directly invest additional capital, those newer dollars will be dated at the time the new investments are made, and the denominator of the conversion factor for those increments will be fixed at whatever the general price level index is at that time.

In our discussion of owners' equity conversions, our focus has been limited to *direct* capital investments by owners. But what about the *indirect* capital investments, i.e., earnings retained? To determine a conversion factor for these amounts, it should be expected that we need to know more about the components of the income statements, the sources from whence emerged retained earnings. However, since we already know the amounts for assets, liabilities, and direct owner investments, retained earnings must be equal to the amount required to balance the others. Thus, for now we can simply treat retained earnings as a "plug" figure. Because Leavenworth only began business on the first of the year, its retained earnings balance on January 1, 19X8 must necessarily be zero; at December 31, 19X8, the "plug" figure required to balance the statement is $54,030.

Given the conversions we have made for Leavenworth's assets, liabilities, and owners' equity at both the beginning and end of 19X8, we can then prepare a *comparative current real position statement* in terms of December 31, 19X8 dollars. That statement appears in Table 12-7.

Income Statement Adjustments

The adjustments required to convert an income statement in current cost terms to one in *real* current cost terms is more complex. This is because the "dated dollars" in an income statement come from a wider array of dates than is the case with a position statement; moreover,

TABLE 12-7

LEAVENWORTH CORPORATION

COMPARATIVE CURRENT REAL POSITION STATEMENT

As of January 1 and December 31, 19X8

(in December 31, 19X8 dollars)

	December 31, 19X8			January 1, 19X8		
ASSETS:						
Current:						
Cash		$ 72,000			$ 93,500	
Accounts Receivable		120,000			-0-	
Merchandise Inventory		135,000	$327,000		55,000	$148,500
Plant:						
Land		$ 52,000			$ 44,000	
Building	$230,000			$220,000		
Less: Allowance for Depreciation	11,500	218,500		-0-	220,000	
Equipment	$126,500			$121,000		
Less: Allowance for Depreciation	37,950	88,550	359,050	-0-	121,000	385,000
			$686,050			$533,500
EQUITIES:						
Current Liabilities:						
Accounts Payable		$100,000			$ 38,500	
Other Payables		40,000	$140,000		-0-	$ 38,500
Long-Term Liabilities:						
Bonds Payable		107,020	$247,020		110,000	$148,500
Common Stockholders' Equity						
Common Stock		$385,000			$385,000	
Retained Earnings		54,030	439,030		-0-	385,000
			$686,050			$533,500

the translation of a current *real* income statement typically involves the addition of a new line item, the purchasing power gain or loss that stems from holding net current monetary assets during a period of deflation or inflation. To see how a current real income statement is prepared, let us consider the amounts contained in Leavenworth's current income statement in Table 12-6, item by item.

Sales revenues. Each sales dollar is a "dated dollar." Ideally, these dollars each should be multiplied by a conversion factor consisting of the ratio of the general price level index at year-end over the index *at the date the sale was made.* For entities having irregular sales patterns over the accounting period, this procedure would almost of necessity require the use of computers. For firms (such as Leavenworth) having steady sales patterns, however, the conversion process is much simpler. All that need be done is to multiply sales for the year by a conversion factor made up of the ratio of the general price level index at year-end over the average index for the year. In Leavenworth's case, then, "raw" sales of $1,000,000 are multiplied by 110/105, yielding $1,047,619.

Cost of goods sold expense. The general approach here is to find the current cost of each item *on the date it was sold* and to multiply that amount by the ratio of the year-end general price level index over the index at the date of sale. For firms having irregular sales patterns over the accounting period, this conversion would best be accomplished through the use of computers. However, since Leavenworth's sales were spread evenly throughout the year, its cost of goods sold expense must have been similarly distributed. All that need be done, therefore, is to multiply Leavenworth's *current* cost of goods sold (as reported in Table 12-6) by a conversion factor identical to that used in converting sales revenue into year-end dollars. Accordingly, $720,000 is multiplied by 110/105 to yield $754,286—the current cost of goods sold stated in terms of December 31, 19X8 dollars.

Depreciation expense. The process for converting current cost depreciation into year-end dollars is the same as that for cost of goods sold expense, i.e., multiply the dollar amount of current cost depreciation on each day the assets were consumed by the ratio of the year-end index over the index on the date of consumption. Because in Leavenworth's case consumption of the assets occurred steadily over the course of the year, Leavenworth's current cost depreciation of $46,225 is simply multiplied by 110/105 to yield $48,426. Had depreciation occurred irregularly during the year, however, then current cost depreciation would better have been computed quarterly, monthly, or perhaps even daily and then multiplied by the ratio of the year-end index over the index for the quarter, month, or day.

Other expenses. These are treated in the same fashion as cost of goods sold expense and depreciation expense. Because Leavenworth's other expenses of $200,000 were incurred evenly over the year, that amount is multiplied by the conversion factor of 110/105, yielding $209,524.

Current real operating income. Once sales revenue, cost of goods sold expense, depreciation expense, and other expenses have all been converted into year-end dollars, the expenses are subtracted from revenues to produce current *real* operating income. In Leavenworth's case, this is $35, 383. This same amount could also have been determined simply by multiplying Leavenworth's current operating income of $33,775 (from Table 12-6) by 110/105. It should be noted that this short-cut procedure will work *only* when every revenue and every expense is multiplied by the *same* conversion factor, which was the case with Leavenworth. If *any* factor differed from the others, however, this short-cut procedure would be rendered invalid.

Realizable real holding gain (loss) on net current monetary assets. This first item in the holding gains category is a new one, emerging *only* when financial statements are converted into dollars of common purchasing power. In a period of general inflation, holding an excess of current monetary assets over current monetary liabilities will cause a decrease in a firm's purchasing power; in a deflationary period, the firm's purchasing power will increase. Therefore, for a firm to gain from inflation, its current monetary liabilities must exceed its current monetary assets; the converse is true during a period of deflation. This is because both current monetary assets and liabilities are *fixed* in dollar amount. Thus, if a firm maintains, say, $10,000 in a checking account during a period in which the general price level rises by ten per cent, the $10,000 in the checking account at year-end will buy goods and services that would have cost only $9,091 at the beginning of the year ($10,000 × 100/110); stated alternatively, it would take $11,000 at year-end to buy what $10,000 would buy at the beginning of the year ($10,000 × 110/100). Being fixed in amount, the checking account balance cannot compensate for changes in general prices.

To determine the realizable real holding gain or loss that arises from holding net current monetary assets during an accounting period, we must return to the input/output analysis we used earlier in the chapter. In particular, the following equation is used to measure the gain or loss in purchasing power:

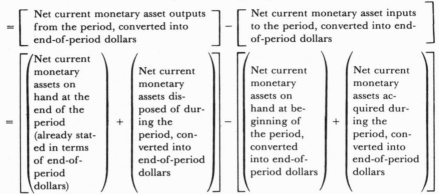

$$\text{Holding gain (loss) on net current} \atop \text{monetary assets during the period} =$$

Thus, when the outputs exceed the inputs, the firm has gained purchasing power; when the opposite occurs, the firm has lost.

To see how this works, let us consider the data with respect to the Leavenworth Corporation. The input and output components of the equation can be reduced to a schedule such as the following:

Outputs of Net Current Monetary Assets from the Period,
  Converted into Year-End Dollars:
  Balance at end of the period:
     ($192,000 − $140,000) × 110/110   = $ 52,000
  Disposals during the period for:
     Merchandise purchases
        $780,000 × 110/105   = $817,143
     Other expenses incurred
        $200,000 × 110/105   =   209,524
     Interest incurred
        $8,000 × 110/105   =   8,381
     Common dividends declared
        $10,000 × 110/110   =   10,000 $1,045,048 $1,097,048

Less: Inputs of Net Current Monetary Assets to the Period,
  Converted into Year-End Dollars
  Balance at beginning of the period:
     ($85,000 − $35,000) × 110/100   = $ 55,000
  Acquisitions during the period from:
     Sales revenues
        $1,000,000 × 110/105   =   1,047,619   1,102,619

Realizable Real Holding Gain (Loss) on Net Current
  Monetary Assets During the Period, Converted
  Into Year-End Dollars   ($5,571)

Each of the disposal outputs from the period entailed either a decrease in a current monetary asset or an increase in a current monetary liability. A purchase of merchandise, for example, will generally cause either a decrease in cash or an increase in accounts payable. The same is basically true for other expenses. When these are added to the ending balance of net current monetary assets, the result is the total of outputs from the period.

On the other side of the coin, with the exception of the beginning balance, the inputs to the period either increased a current monetary asset or decreased a current monetary liability. In Leavenworth's case, sales revenue either increased cash or accounts receivable or decreased advances from customers. When added to the beginning balance of net current monetary assets, the total of inputs to the period emerges.

Alternatively, we can reason that Leavenworth needed an ending balance of $57,571 (its inputs of $1,102,619 less disposal outputs of $1,045,048 in end-of-period dollars) to be as well off as it was at the beginning of the period. It had only $52,000. Hence, there was a real loss on net current monetary assets of $5,571.

Realizable real holding gain (loss) on merchandise inventory. In the absence of general inflation or deflation, no holding gain or loss can arise on net current monetary assets. Such is not the case, however, with any item falling outside the net current monetary category. Even when the general price level remains constant, prices of specific goods and services such as merchandise may rise or fall. We found earlier that in the case of its merchandise inventory, Leavenworth gained $25,000 by holding merchandise during a period in which its price rose. During that same period, however, there was also a rise in the prices of goods and services *in general*. Thus, the question arises as to whether or not Leavenworth beat the general inflation by owning inventories and, if so, by how much? In other words, how much of Leavenworth's $25,000 gain was *real* rather than *fictional*?

We can determine how much of the gain was real by recourse to the original formula for determining the holding gain on merchandise, i.e.,

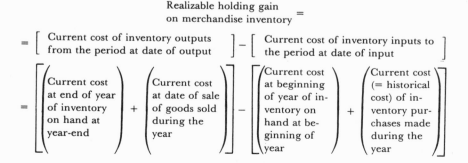

All that need be done is to convert each dated dollar amount contained in the equation to its year-end equivalent. This is accomplished as follows:

$$\text{Realizable } \textit{real} \text{ holding gain on merchandise inventory} =$$

$$= \left[\left(\begin{array}{c} \$135,000 \\ \times \\ 110/110 \end{array} \right) + \left(\begin{array}{c} \$720,000 \\ \times \\ 110/105 \end{array} \right) \right] - \left[\left(\begin{array}{c} \$50,000 \\ \times \\ 110/100 \end{array} \right) + \left(\begin{array}{c} \$780,000 \\ \times \\ 110/105 \end{array} \right) \right]$$

$$= [\ (\$135,000) + (\$754,286) \ ] - [\ (\$55,000) + (\$817,143) \ ]$$

$$= \quad \$889,286 \qquad\qquad - \qquad \$872,143$$

$$= \quad \underline{\underline{\$ \ 17,143}}$$

Thus, of Leavenworth's $25,000 gain, $17,143 was *real* and the remainder, $7,857, *fictional*; by investing in inventories rather than goods and services in general, Leavenworth beat inflation to the tune of $17,143.

Realizable real holding gain (loss) on land. In the absence of inflation or deflation, Leavenworth's gain from holding land was $12,000. How much of this gain was real and how much fictional? The answer is arrived at in the same fashion as it was with merchandise inventory, by recourse to the original formula:

$$\text{Realizable holding gain on land} =$$

$$= \left[\begin{array}{c} \text{Current cost of land} \\ \text{outputs from the period} \\ \text{at date of output} \end{array} \right] - \left[\begin{array}{c} \text{Current cost of land} \\ \text{inputs to the period at} \\ \text{date of input} \end{array} \right]$$

$$= \left[\begin{array}{c} \text{Current cost at year-end} \\ \text{of land on hand at} \\ \text{year-end} \end{array} \right] - \left[\begin{array}{c} \text{Current cost at} \\ \text{beginning of year of} \\ \text{land on hand at} \\ \text{beginning of year} \end{array} \right]$$

These amounts are converted to year-end dollars in the following manner.

$$\text{Realizable real holding gain on land} =$$

$$= [\$52,000 \times 110/110] - [\$40,000 \times 110/100]$$

$$= \quad \$52,000 \qquad\qquad - \quad \$44,000$$

$$= \quad \underline{\underline{\$ \ 8,000}}$$

Again, Leavenworth bettered general inflation by investing in land rather than in goods and services in general. In this case, its real holding gain was $8,000 and its fictional holding gain (the amount necessary just to keep up with general inflation), $4,000.

Realizable real holding gain (loss) on building. Earlier in the chapter, we determined the realizable holding gain on Leavenworth's building by means of this formula:

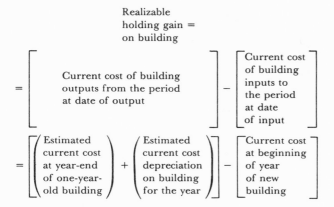

If we convert the data contained in the formula into year-end dollars, we then can find the real holding gain:

$$\text{Realizable real holding gain on building} =$$

$$= [(\$218,500 \times 110/110) + (\$10,750 \times 110/105)] - [\$200,000 \times 110/100]$$

$$= (\$218,500) + (\$11,262) - \$220,000$$

$$= \$229,762 - \$220,000$$

$$= \$ \underline{\underline{9,762}}$$

Of the $29,250 realizable holding gain, $19,488 was fictional (an amount necessary just to keep up with general inflation) and $9,762, real (the amount by which Leavenworth was able to beat inflation with its investment in the building during the year).

Realizable real holding gain (loss) on equipment. The real holding gain on equipment is computed in essentially the same fashion as with Leavenworth's building. We simply take the data from the original formula for the computation of the holding gain and convert to year-end dollars. The gain as originally computed was:

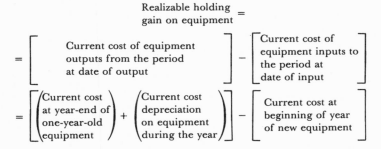

$$\text{Realizable holding gain on equipment} =$$

$$= \left[\begin{array}{c} \text{Current cost of equipment} \\ \text{outputs from the period} \\ \text{at date of output} \end{array} \right] - \left[\begin{array}{c} \text{Current cost of} \\ \text{equipment inputs to} \\ \text{the period at} \\ \text{date of input} \end{array} \right]$$

$$= \left[\left(\begin{array}{c} \text{Current cost} \\ \text{at year-end of} \\ \text{one-year-old} \\ \text{equipment} \end{array} \right) + \left(\begin{array}{c} \text{Current cost} \\ \text{depreciation} \\ \text{on equipment} \\ \text{during the year} \end{array} \right) \right] - \left[\begin{array}{c} \text{Current cost at} \\ \text{beginning of year} \\ \text{of new equipment} \end{array} \right]$$

Converting into year-end dollars yields the following real gain:

$$\text{Realizable real holding gain on} = \text{equipment}$$

= [($88,550 × 110/110) + ($35,475 × 110/105)] − [$110,000 × 110/100]

= [($ 88,550   ) + ($37,164   )] − [$121,000   ]

= $125,714   − $121,000

= $ 4,714

Thus, the majority of the nominal gain of $14,025 was fictional ($9,311); Leavenworth was able to do better than general inflation by its investment in equipment only to the extent of $4,714.

Current real entity income. When the current real operating income of $35,383 is added to the sum of realizable real holding gains on assets of $33,857, the result is current *real* entity income of $69,240. When this amount is compared to the "raw dollar" current entity income contained in Table 12-6, we find that in real terms Leavenworth's entity income is significantly smaller than it was before taking into account general inflation. While current real operating income differs little from its "raw dollar" counterpart ($35,383 versus $33,775), a dramatic difference is apparent between realizable real holding gains on assets and its "raw dollar" counterpart ($33,857 versus $80,275). Inflation has cut Leavenworth's asset holding gains in half.

Interest charges. We determined earlier in the chapter that Leavenworth's 19X8 interest charges on a current cost basis amounted to $7,234. Of this amount, $4,000 was incurred in the first half of the year and $3,234 in the second half. To convert these interest charges from raw dollars to year-end dollars, we simply multiply $4,000 by the ratio of the year-end index over the average index for the first half of the year, then multiply $3,234 by the ratio of the year-end index over the average index for the second half of the year, and then sum the two. The computations are as follows:

$$\$4,000 \times 110/102.5 = \$4,293$$
$$\$3,234 \times 110/107.5 = \$3,309$$
$$\underline{\underline{\$7,602}}$$

Realizable real holding gain (loss) on bonds payable. The process of determining the real gain on bonds is basically the same as with assets with one important exception—since bonds are liabilities and the opposite of assets, we deduct *outputs* from *inputs* rather than the reverse. The raw dollar holding loss on bonds, as computed earlier in the chapter, was as follows:

Realizable holding gain (loss) on bonds payable =

$$= \left[\begin{array}{c} \text{Current cost of bonds} \\ \text{inputs to the period} \\ \text{at date of input} \end{array} \right] - \left[\begin{array}{c} \text{Current cost of bonds} \\ \text{outputs from the period} \\ \text{at date of output} \end{array} \right]$$

$$= \left[\left(\begin{array}{c} \text{Current cost} \\ \text{of bonds at} \\ \text{beginning} \\ \text{of year} \end{array} \right) + \left(\begin{array}{c} \text{Current cost} \\ \text{interest} \\ \text{charges} \\ \text{during} \\ \text{the year} \end{array} \right) \right] - \left[\left(\begin{array}{c} \text{Current cost} \\ \text{of bonds at} \\ \text{year-end} \end{array} \right) + \left(\begin{array}{c} \text{Cash paid} \\ \text{for interest} \\ \text{during} \\ \text{the year} \end{array} \right) \right]$$

Converting each component to year-end dollars, we find:

Realizable real holding gain (loss) on bonds payable =

$$= \left[\left(\begin{array}{c} \$100,000 \\ \times \\ 110/100 \end{array} \right) + \left(\begin{array}{cc} \$4,000 & \$3,234 \\ \times & + & \times \\ 110/102.5 & 110/107.5 \end{array} \right) \right] - \left[\left(\begin{array}{c} \$107,020 \\ \times \\ 110/110 \end{array} \right) + \left(\begin{array}{c} \$8,000 \\ \times \\ 110/105 \end{array} \right) \right]$$

$$= [(\$110,000) + (\$7,602)] - [(\$107,020) + (\$8,381)]$$
$$= \$117,602 - \$115,401$$
$$= \underline{\underline{\$\ 2,201}}$$

Note that, while Leavenworth had a holding *loss* of $7,786 in terms of raw dollars, when these are converted into year-end dollars, a $2,201 *gain* emerged. The effect of inflation simply overrode the price change in the bonds as a result of interest rate changes. As a debtor, Leavenworth has benefited from having bonds outstanding during a period of inflation.

Current real ownership income. The difference between current real entity income and current real ownership income stems from the financial leverage employed by the firm. In Leavenworth's case, this difference is a negative $5,401 in year-end dollars. Because the value of Leavenworth's bonds declined by $2,201 in terms of real dollars, this partially offset interest of $7,602, also in real dollars. When compared with the corresponding data in Table 12-6, a significant difference is apparent. Before converting to year-end dollars, the effect of Leavenworth's financial leverage had a negative impact on income of $15,020; after converting, this was reduced to only $5,401. Thus, in terms of real dollars, Leavenworth did much better than in raw dollars primarily because the principal amount of the bonds remained fixed while the purchasing power of the dollar declined, enabling Leavenworth to pay off its debt (if it so desired) by means of cheaper dollars. What had been a $7,786 holding loss on bonds was converted into a $2,201 holding gain when changes in the purchasing power of the dollar were considered.

Common dividend charges. Because Leavenworth declared and paid its dividends on December 31, 19X8, the dollar amount of dividends was already stated in year-end dollars and no conversion was required (alternatively stated, the conversion factor was 110/110). While in this case the date of declaration and payments were one and the same, this coincidence does not always hold—indeed, the declaration date usually precedes the payment date. What is of importance in the conversion of dividend charges into year-end dollars is the date of declaration, not the date of payment. If the date of declaration occurs before year-end, then the amount of the dividend is converted into year-end dollars by means of a conversion factor having as its numerator the year-end index and as its denominator, the index at the date of declaration. As soon as the dividend is declared, the company becomes a debtor, hence, will benefit from any general inflation that occurs between the dates of declaration and payment.

Increase in retained earnings. Once common dividend charges have been deducted from current real ownership income, the residual that remains is the increase (or decrease) in retained earnings for the period. At this point the current real income statement has been completed; the finished statement appears in Table 12-8. Note that Leavenworth's

TABLE 12-8

LEAVENWORTH CORPORATION
CURRENT REAL INCOME STATEMENT
For the Year Ended December 31, 19X8
(in December 31, 19X8 dollars)

REVENUES:		
Sales		$1,047,619
EXPENSES:		
Cost of Goods Sold	$754,286	
Depreciation	48,426	
Other	209,524	1,012,236
CURRENT REAL OPERATING INCOME		$ 35,383
REALIZABLE REAL HOLDING GAINS (LOSSES) ON ASSETS:		
On Net Current Monetary Assets	($ 5,571)	
On Merchandise Inventory	17,143	
On Land	8,000	
On Building	9,762	
On Equipment	4,714	34,048
CURRENT REAL ENTITY INCOME		$ 69,431
Interest Charges		7,602
		$ 61,829
Realizable Real Holding Gain (Loss) on Bonds Payable		2,201
CURRENT REAL OWNERSHIP INCOME		$ 64,030
Common Dividend Charges		10,000
INCREASE IN REAL RETAINED EARNINGS		$ 54,030

increase in real retained earnings of $54,030 corresponds with the change in its retained earnings balances from beginning to end of the year as in Table 12-7, the comparative current real position statement.

CONCLUSIONS

Our assumptions as to price changes in the exercise have not been at all unrealistic. A general level of inflation on the order of ten per cent has been common in recent years, and prices of inventories and plant assets for a particular firm can easily change by 10 to 15 percentage points more or less than general inflation (in other words, not change at all or rise by 20 to 25 per cent). As can be seen in Table 12-9, since 1967 the prices of plant assets in general (as indicated by the Department of Commerce's GNP deflator series for nonresidential

TABLE 12-9

PRICE-LEVEL INDEXES

| | | | | Implicit Price Deflators | | |
| | | | | FIXED INVESTMENT | | |
YEAR	Consumer Price Index (1972=100)	Wholesale Price Index (1972=100)	Personal Consumption Goods (1972=100)	Nonresidential Structures (1972=100)	Producers' Durable Equipment (1972=100)	Gross National Product (1972=100)
1929	40.9	41.2	35.8	24.1	33.4	32.9
1933	31.0	28.5	26.8	19.1	26.2	25.1
1939	33.2	33.4	30.4	22.8	32.0	28.4
1940	33.5	34.0	30.8	23.1	32.8	29.1
1941	35.2	37.9	33.1	24.7	34.9	31.5
1942	38.9	42.7	36.7	28.1	37.3	34.8
1943	41.3	44.3	40.0	32.0	37.3	36.4
1944	42.1	45.0	42.3	33.4	38.0	37.1
1945	43.0	45.8	44.0	33.6	37.9	38.0
1946	46.7	52.3	47.7	36.3	42.8	43.9
1947	53.4	64.2	52.8	43.7	48.5	49.7
1948	57.5	69.5	55.9	48.4	52.9	53.1
1949	57.0	66.1	55.7	48.0	55.9	52.6
1950	57.5	68.7	56.8	48.8	57.6	53.6
1951	62.1	76.5	60.5	54.7	61.6	57.3
1952	63.4	74.4	61.9	55.8	62.5	58.0
1953	63.9	73.4	63.1	56.8	63.7	58.9
1954	64.2	73.6	63.6	55.9	65.4	59.7
1955	64.0	73.7	64.2	57.0	66.5	61.0
1956	65.0	76.2	65.5	61.8	71.0	62.9
1957	67.3	78.3	67.6	64.4	75.4	65.0
1958	69.1	79.4	69.1	63.3	76.5	66.1
1959	69.7	79.6	70.4	63.6	78.2	67.5
1960	70.8	79.3	71.7	63.1	79.3	68.7
1961	71.5	79.4	72.5	62.7	79.2	69.3
1962	72.3	79.6	73.6	63.0	79.4	70.6
1963	73.2	79.3	74.7	63.5	79.6	71.6
1964	74.1	79.5	75.7	64.4	80.1	72.7
1965	75.4	81.1	77.1	65.9	80.6	74.3
1966	77.6	83.8	79.3	68.8	82.1	76.8
1967	79.8	84.0	81.3	71.8	84.3	79.0
1968	83.2	86.1	84.6	75.3	87.3	82.6
1969	87.6	89.4	88.5	81.1	90.0	86.7
1970	92.8	92.7	92.5	88.0	93.4	91.4
1971	96.8	95.7	96.6	94.4	97.6	96.0
1972	100.0	100.0	100.0	100.0	100.0	100.0
1973	100.0	113.1	105.5	107.8	101.7	105.8
1974	117.9	134.4	116.9	128.7	110.0	116.4
1975	128.7	146.9	126.3	141.6	127.4	127.3
P1976	135.8	153.6	132.7	145.5	134.7	133.8

SOURCE: *Economic Report of the President (1977)*

TABLE 12-10

	Under Historical Cost Income	Under Current Income	Under Current Real Income
Ownership income for 19X8 / Average common stockholders' equity during 19X8	$\dfrac{\$60,000}{1/2\,(\$350,000 + \$400,000)} = 16.0\%$	$\dfrac{\$99,030}{1/2\,(\$350,000 + \$439,030)} = 25.1\%$	$\dfrac{\$64,030}{1/2\,(\$385,000 + \$439,030)} = 15.5\%$
Entity income for 19X8 / Average total assets during 19X8	$\dfrac{\$68,000}{1/2\,(\$485,000 + \$640,000)} = 12.1\%$	$\dfrac{\$114,050}{1/2\,(\$485,000 + \$686,050)} = 19.5\%$	$\dfrac{\$69,431}{1/2\,(\$533,500 + \$686,050)} = 11.4\%$
Operating income for 19X8 / Average total assets during 19X8	$\dfrac{\$68,000}{1/2\,(\$485,000 + \$640,000)} = 12.1\%$	$\dfrac{\$33,775}{1/2\,(\$485,000 + \$686,050)} = 5.8\%$	$\dfrac{\$35,383}{1/2\,(\$533,500 + \$686,050)} = 5.8\%$

structures and machinery and equipment) have typically risen by more than—and often by twice—the increase in the Consumer Price Index.

A comparison of Tables 12-3 (conventional historical cost income), 12-6 (current income), and 12-8 (current real income) suggests that even moderate price changes in the economy have a significant impact on reported income. Adjusting or not adjusting the data for the effects of such price changes makes a marked difference in the reported primary measure of a firm's performance. Current ownership income in Table 12-6 is nearly twice the ownership income reported in terms of historical costs shown in Table 12-3. On the other hand, current real ownership income in Leavenworth's case falls between these two—only slightly more than the latter but over one-third less than the former. If our individual price changes (with respect to specific assets and liabilities of the firm) had deviated more markedly from the general price level change, as may often be the case, current real ownership income would have differed more substantially from traditional historical cost owner- ship income. Position statements show similar striking differences, as seen in Tables 12-2, 12-5, and 12-7.

It is also instructive to compare various rates of return between the three approaches to income measurement and asset valuation. Some of the more commonly used are given in Table 12-10.

First, compare the returns computed in columns one and two. When specific price changes are incorporated into the financial statements, both the rate of return to owners and to the entity are increased by more than 50 per cent (from 16.0 per cent to 25.1 per cent and from 12.1 per cent to 19.5 per cent), but the rate of return on operations is more than halved (from 12.1 per cent to 5.8 per cent). Thus, even though Leavenworth was only in its first year of business, a dramatic difference in rates of return occurs. In later years, it is quite likely that these differences would become even greater.

When we further refine our adjustments to include changes in the purchasing power of the dollar, dramatic differences occur once again. Consider the data in columns two and three. The rates of return to owners and to the entity are cut by nearly 40 per cent (from 25.1 per cent to 15.5 per cent and from 19.5 per cent to 11.4 per cent). Only the rate of return on operations remains unchanged. All this suggests that *both* adjustments—for specific price changes *and* for changes in the general price level—should be made if accounting information is to be of greater utility.

Given our relatively modest assumptions about price changes affecting Leavenworth in a single year (and its first year at that)—assumptions that are generally realistic in terms of those experienced all the time by firms in the economy these days—it is difficult to see how the performance of business firms can be adequately analyzed without considering such price changes. Clearly, the objectives of accounting we set forth in Chapter 1 and extended early in Chapter 11 cannot be adequately served *unless* data are put in terms of current values, indeed, in terms of current *real* values. If there has been a significant rise in the general price level, two firms that might report the same current income could have substantially different current *real* incomes. This is because one firm's current income might be comprised primarily of current operating income (a figure affected only minimally by changes in the general price level) while the other firm's current income might be largely made up of realizable holding gains (which may be heavily affected by changes in the general price level).

Many accountants, both in academia and in practice, agree with our conclusion that the problem is a serious one with which the profession must come to grips and resolve. However, there are differences of opinion about how best to resolve the issue, many of which are at odds with the solution we have proffered in Chapters 11 and 12. It is to these differences of opinion that we now turn in our concluding chapter.

Appendix

Accounting Real Income: Restating Historical Costs for Changes in the General Price Level

While the current cost approach to the problem of accounting for changing relative prices and for inflation (as outlined in the chapter) has received considerable attention and support both within the United States and elsewhere, it is not the only approach that has been proffered. In terms of support from the community of practicing accounting professionals, the primary competitor to the current cost approach is one we shall term the "accounting real income" approach. This method involves converting conventional historical cost-based accounting data into dollars of common purchasing power by means of a general price level index such as the Consumer Price Index or the GNP Implicit Price Deflator. As such, the method is also known as "common dollar accounting," "general price level accounting," "price level-adjusted historical cost accounting," or "historical cost/constant dollar accounting."

The accounting real income approach may be compared to and contrasted with other approaches to income in terms of the traditional accounting conventions accepted and rejected. (These conventions, initially introduced in Chapter 1, are discussed in greater detail in Chapter 13.) In contrast to the accounting income and current income methods, the accounting real income approach rejects the assumption of a stable measuring unit contained in the money convention; in this respect, accounting real income is similar to the current real income approach. On the other hand, the realization convention indigenous to the accounting income approach is retained, but it is modified to include the recognition of purchasing power gains and losses from holding monetary items during a period of inflation or deflation. (This modification is necessitated by the rejection of the money convention.) As a result, the accounting real income approach is *not* a current value accounting method as are the current income and current real income approaches, although many accounting practitioners mistakenly believe that it is. Current values do not enter into the calculus any more than they do in historical cost accounting. We shall return to this issue later; in the meantime, let us consider the workings of the accounting real income approach.

General Principles of Adjustment

In the chapter, we explained the conversion of current cost data on holding gains into real terms by means of an input/output analysis. There, our focus was upon the current accounting period and the resource inputs to and outputs from that period. The *inputs to the accounting period* consisted of the items on hand at the beginning of the period (as listed on the beginning-of-the-period position statement) and those items acquired during the period; all of these inputs were stated in terms of their current cost at the date of their input into the period. The *outputs from the period* were composed of those items disposed of during the period and those items still on hand at the end of the period (as listed in the end-of-the-period position statement); these outputs were all stated in terms of their current cost at the date of their output from the period. All of the inputs and outputs were then restated in terms of end-of-period dollars by multiplying them by the ratio of the end-of-period general price level index to the index at the date of input to or output from the period. Taking the difference between the restated inputs and outputs yielded the *realizable real holding gain or loss* for the period, one of the two primary components of current real income.

The other component of current real income, *current operating income*, resulted from the sale of goods and services during the period. These goods and services were the items disposed of by the firm during the period, and as such, constituted one of the two output categories. Current operating income, of course, is the excess of the sales value of the goods and services disposed of during the year over their current cost. The sales value of the goods and services is generally established by the current value of the items received in exchange (usually current monetary assets such as cash or accounts receivable) and is recorded as *revenue.* The raw dollar amount of revenue is then converted into end-of-period dollars by multiplying it by the ratio of the end-of-period index to that at the date the item received in exchange was received. The corresponding *expense*, stated in terms of current cost at the date of output, is converted into end-of-period dollars by multiplying by the ratio of the end-of-period index to that at the date of output. Thus, usually both the revenue and expense will be converted using the same conversion ratio.[1] The excess of the former over the latter, then, is current operating income for the period stated in end-of-period dollars.

Current real income differs from accounting real income, however, in much the same fashion as current income differs from accounting income. Stated generally, current income stems from two sources: (1) income that is recognized upon the disposal of a firm's assets or liabilities during the period and (2) income that is recognized as a result of changes in the specific prices of a firm's assets and liabilities during a period. In contrast, accounting income arises only from the disposal during the period of assets and liabilities, changes in their specific prices being ignored until date of disposition.

---

1. The primary exception here arises when the customer makes payment in advance of receipt of goods and/or services, thereby giving rise to "advances from customers," a current nonmonetary liability on the books of the firm. In this case, the revenue is converted to real terms by multiplying it by the ratio of the end-of-period index to the index at the date the nonmonetary liability was established.

Once changes in the general price level are recognized in the context of accounting income (now accounting real income), however, the concept of realization must also be redefined. Under general price level-adjusted historical cost accounting, realization may occur in two ways:

(1) realization from the disposal of an item by the firm during the accounting period (as before), and
(2) realization from holding monetary items during the period when the general price level rises or falls.

As a result, we must divide inputs and outputs into three categories—current monetary items, noncurrent monetary items, and nonmonetary items—because the realization convention, as adhered to in historical cost/constant dollar accounting, is applied differently to each of these three categories. Let us now examine in greater detail how each of these is treated.

Current monetary items. The treatment of items in this category (such as cash, accounts receivable, accounts payable, and so on) is conditioned by the fact that while each item is nominally stated at its historical cost, the dollar amounts recorded in these accounts are *also* stated in terms of current cost or current value. In other words, for this unique class of assets and liabilities, it is always necessarily true that

$$\frac{\text{Historical}}{\text{cost}} = \frac{\text{Current}}{\text{cost}} = \frac{\text{Current}}{\text{value}}$$

As such, the treatment of current monetary items under accounting real income is precisely the same as that under current real income. Thus, purchasing power changes in the dollar during the accounting period—our second means of realization—are regarded as having caused a realization of gains (losses) during the period, and these gains (losses) are reported in the income statement. Realization upon disposal is not possible, however, so our first means of realization is irrelevant for current monetary items. The gain or loss on current monetary items under historical cost/constant dollar accounting is measured by subtracting price level-adjusted inputs from price level-adjusted outputs (as was done in the chapter). Similarly, for purposes of the comparative real position statement, current monetary items at the beginning of the period must be converted into end-of-period dollars; no conversion is necessary for end-of-period current monetary items as they are already stated in end-of-period dollars.

Noncurrent monetary items. At first blush, it would appear that noncurrent monetary items (such as long-term notes or bonds receivable and long-term notes or bonds payable) should be treated in the same fashion as current monetary items in the determination of accounting real income. And such would be the case if the historical cost balances of noncurrent monetary items were always equal to their current cost or current value, as is the case for current monetary items. The current cost or value of noncurrent monetary items, however, is frequently not the same as the balance carried on the book because of changing market interest rates in the economy or changing assessments of risk. When, for example, the market rate of interest on bonds of comparable terms and quality rises subsequent to date of issuance, the current value of the bonds in the market place will fall; conversely, when interest rates decline, the current value of the bonds will climb. As a result, the book value of the bonds will differ from their current market value. This difference will not be recognized on the accounting records under the modified realization convention, however, until the bonds are extinguished (disposed of) by the firm.

Under historical cost accounting, the historical cost balance of an item is equal to its current cost or value only if *either* of two conditions are satisfied: (1) the market rate of interest for notes of similar terms and quality remains unchanged from the date of the note's issuance, or (2) the book balance of the note is callable on demand by the lender or repayable at any time by the borrower without prepayment penalty. In the real world, of course, neither condition is likely to be satisfied. Market rates of interest do fluctuate widely over time; lenders typically cannot call a note on demand unless the borrower defaults in some fashion, and borrowers are rarely offered the privilege of early debt extinguishment without paying substantial prepayment penalties.

When converting historical cost-based data into terms of dollars of constant purchasing power, however, accountants proceed as if one or the other of the two conditions had been met and that, therefore, the book balances of assets and liabilities held represent current values. A holding gain or loss to reflect purchasing power changes in the dollar is computed in a fashion analogous to that used for current monetary items, i.e., taking the difference between price level-adjusted noncurrent monetary inputs to the period and outputs from the period. For noncurrent monetary assets, the computation is as follows:

Holding gain (loss) on noncurrent =
monetary assets for the period

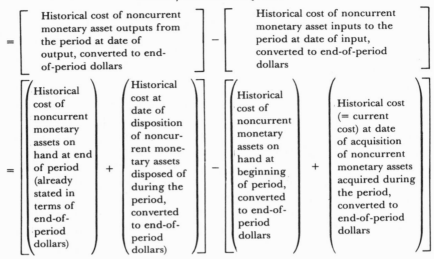

For noncurrent monetary liabilities, the computation is made in the following manner:

Holding gain (loss) on noncurrent =
monetary liabilities for the period

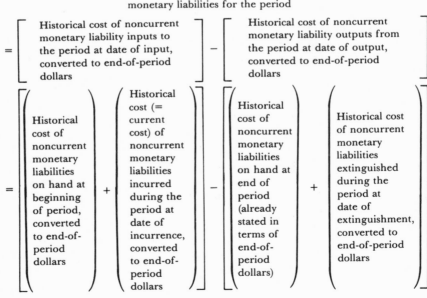

Note that, in both of the equations above, inputs and outputs are stated in terms of *historical costs* rather than *current costs*. Only in the case of inputs acquired or incurred during the period do current costs or values enter the picture and only there because they are equal to historical costs. Because the other input and output components will only be equal to current costs or values when one of the two unlikely conditions are met, the resulting holding gain or loss on noncurrent monetary items is an accounting artifact and devoid of meaning. The result cannot be otherwise since the assumption by accountants that the historical cost of noncurrent monetary items equals current cost is generally counterfactual.

But the accounting for gains and losses on noncurrent monetary items in accordance with price-level-adjusted historical cost accounting does not end with purchasing power gains or losses. If a noncurrent monetary asset is disposed of or a noncurrent monetary liability is extinguished during the period, quite possibly a gain or loss on the disposal or extinguishment will have to be recognized. Hence, in the case of noncurrent monetary items, unlike current monetary items, gains (losses) can be realized through disposal; and these gains (losses), as well as gains (losses) realized through changes in purchasing power, must be recorded. Noncurrent monetary items are the only ones in which *both* types of realization may occur. Such recognition will have to be made whenever a noncurrent monetary asset is collected or a noncurrent monetary liability repaid prior to maturity *and* either of the above-mentioned conditions is not met. If either market interest rates for comparable notes have shifted since date of issuance or a prepayment penalty is involved, the amount collected for a noncurrent monetary asset or the amount repaid for a noncurrent monetary liability will differ from the book balance for the asset or liability. This difference is a realized gain or loss on disposition. (Such gains or losses would be recognized regardless of whether or not historical cost-based accounting data is converted to reflect changes in the general price level.) To restate such a gain or loss into "real" terms, the amount received or paid is converted into end-of-period dollars by multiplying by the ratio of the end-of-period index to that at the date of receipt or payment. The book balance is similarly converted into "real" terms by multiplying it by the same ratio. The difference between these two price level-adjusted amounts, then, is the gain or loss on disposition as restated in terms of end-of-period dollars.

All of the foregoing have to do with historical cost-based income statements restated in terms of end-of-period dollars. In the comparative real position statement, historical cost balances for noncurrent monetary items must also be restated. The book balance for any noncurrent monetary item on hand at the beginning of the period is converted into end-of-period dollars by multiplying it by the ratio of the end-of-period index to the index at the beginning of the period, under the oftimes erroneous assumption that the book balance represents current value on that date. The same assumption is made for the balances on hand at the end of the period; hence, no conversion of these balances is deemed necessary as they are presumably stated in end-of-period dollars. Note, however, that unless the book balances at either date are equal to current values on that same date, the resulting amount will be no more than an accounting artifact and devoid of meaning.

Nonmonetary items. Compared with noncurrent monetary items where two types of realization are possible under historical cost/constant dollar accounting, only one kind of realization occurs with nonmonetary items—realization upon disposal. For the most part, such realizations involve the recognition of revenues and expenses when the nonmonetary item disposed of is a good or service that the firm typically deals in. Realization will also occur, however, when the firm disposes of a nonmonetary item that it does not usually deal in; but this is reflected in a gain or loss rather than a revenue and expense. Until disposal, nonmonetary items are carried at values reflecting historical cost restated in current dollars, that is, the number of today's dollars that has the same purchasing power now as the number originally spent for the item. Hence, any gain realized from disposal is measured from adjusted historical cost.

In the typical revenue/expense situation, the goods or services provided by the firm to its customers involve the outgo of one or more nonmonetary assets. The profit or loss that is realized on such transactions is measured by the difference between the historical cost balances of the nonmonetary assets at the date the assets are output from the firm (the expense component) and their sales value at date of output (the revenue component). The sales value of the nonmonetary asset output is, in turn, generally measured by the current value of the items received in exchange, usually monetary items and, in particular, current monetary assets.[2] When current monetary assets are received in exchange, the sales value of the output is restated in terms of

___

2. Exceptions may occur when nonmonetary items are received in exchange. The exception most likely to occur is when the customer pays for the goods or services in advance of receiving, thereby giving rise to "advances from customers," a current nonmonetary liability. In this case, the sales value of the outputs is set equal to the amount of the "advances from customers" that is extinguished by delivery of the goods or services to the customer.

end-of-period dollars by multiplying it by the ratio of the end-of-period general price level index to the index at the date of the sale. The corresponding expense is converted to end-of-period dollars by multiplying it by the ratio of the end-of-period index to the index at the date of *input* of the nonmonetary assets given up. The difference between these amounts, then, represents operating income as restated in terms of end-of-period dollars.

When the firm disposes of a nonmonetary item that it does not usually deal in, a gain or loss on the disposal is realized rather than a revenue and expense. However, such gain or loss is nothing more than a revenue "netted" against an expense and, as such, is determined in precisely the same manner as is operating income. Since the measurement of operating income in "real" terms has just been discussed, no further discussion is warranted at this point.

Under the accounting income approach, the balances displayed on the comparative position statement are stated in terms of historical cost. So, too, under the accounting real income approach, except that these balances must be restated in terms of end-of-period dollars. The appropriate conversion ratio for all nonmonetary items, therefore, has as its numerator the end-of-period general price level index and, as its denominator, the index at the date the nonmonetary item was input into the firm. This *same* conversion ratio is then applied to *both* the beginning of the period and end of period balance for any nonmonetary item held throughout the period. Moreover, it also applies to nonmonetary items on hand at the beginning of the period that were disposed of during the period (but were, therefore, in the beginning position statement) *and* to nonmonetary items acquired during the period and on hand at the end of the period. The amounts reported for nonmonetary assets on a comparative real position statement under the accounting real income approach are nothing more than historical costs restated for changes in the purchasing power of the dollar. They do *not* represent current values, except by chance.

A final note. In converting historical cost data into real terms—just as with current cost data—the accounts themselves remain undisturbed, the raw dollar data from the accounts being converted only when the data are transferred to the financial statements. If the accounts are maintained on a computer, the computer can be programmed to make the conversions once the general price level index data and input dates are fed into it; thus, the computer will simply print out the converted data needed to prepare the financial statements. Let us now put these principles into practice using the Leavenworth Corporation data from the chapter.

The Leavenworth Example

The conversion of Leavenworth Corporation's historical cost-based accounting data into "real" terms is a relatively simple process because Leavenworth has been in operation for but a single year. Had Leavenworth been in business for a number of years, the conversion process would be a bit more complex, even though the same general principles would still be applicable. Were that the case, we would need, in addition to general price level indexes for the current year, indexes at the date of input to the firm of every noncurrent monetary item and every nonmonetary item on hand at the beginning of the current year (something not needed under the current real income approach). As a note of caution, therefore, it should be recognized that in this simple example the same conversion ratio may be applied to a variety of disparate items, but for *different reasons.* Had Leavenworth been in business for a number of years, a wider array of conversion ratios would be used, and these different ratios would highlight the different reasons. But since Leavenworth has been in business for only a year, many ratios that would otherwise be different will be the same.

Virtually all of the data required to convert Leavenworth Corporation's historical cost/raw dollar financial statements into "real" terms are contained in the chapter. The only missing piece of information is the general price level index at the date Leavenworth's ending merchandise inventory was purchased, which we shall assume to be 108. With this added bit of information, we can commence with the conversion process, starting with Leavenworth's comparative position statement.

Comparative accounting real position statement. The raw dollar data needed to prepare a comparative real position statement as of January 1 and December 31, 19X8 in terms of December 31, 19X8 dollars are contained in Table 12-2 in the chapter. The conversion is made into year-end dollars on the assumption that these, more current, purchasing power units will be more familiar to the users of the financial statements. As explained earlier, inputs and outputs must be divided into three categories—current monetary items, noncurrent monetary items, and nonmonetary items—in order to undertake the conversion process. Accordingly, we shall divide Leavenworth's position statement accounts in these three categories in order to convert their historical cost-based balances into "real" terms.

1. **Current Monetary Items.** Leavenworth's current monetary items consist of the assets, cash and accounts receivable, and the liabilities, accounts payable and other payables. The balances in these accounts at the beginning of the year are inputs into the period, and their

nominal dollar amount is their historical cost. (It is also their current cost or current value at that date, but current values do not concern the accountant following historical cost/constant dollar accounting principles.) These input amounts are converted into year-end dollars by multiplying them by the ratio of the year-end index to that at the beginning of the year (their date of input), or by 110/100.

The balances in these accounts at the end of the year represent outputs from the period. The nominal dollar amounts on that date are again historical cost amounts, and since these amounts are already stated in terms of year-end dollars, they need no conversion. (That these amounts for current monetary assets and liabilities are also current values at the end of the period is again of no concern to the historical cost/constant dollar accountant.)

2. **Noncurrent Monetary Items.** Leavenworth has only one noncurrent monetary item—the liability, bonds payable. The balance in the bonds payable account at the beginning of the year is the input into the period. This balance is always stated in terms of historical cost, which may or may not be equal to current cost on that date (in contrast to current monetary items where historical cost is always equal to current cost). In Leavenworth's case, they are equal at the beginning of the year since the bonds were issued just the day before. Regardless of whether or not they are equal, however, under historical cost/constant dollar accounting they are *assumed* to be equal. Accordingly, the historical cost of this noncurrent monetary input into the period is converted into year-end dollars by means of the ratio 110/100, the year-end index over the index at the beginning of the year. Multiplying the $100,000 historical cost by 110/100, then, yields $110,000, the beginning balance restated in terms of year-end dollars.

The balance in the bonds payable account at year-end is the output from the period. This balance, too, is stated in terms of historical cost. Again this may or may not be equal to current cost at year-end. In Leavenworth's case it is not, since the decline in market interest rates during the year drove the price of these bonds up. Such changes in current value are, however, of no concern under historical cost/constant dollar accounting. Because, presumably, the "cost" or "price" of this bond is assumed to be fixed in nominal dollar terms, like the "cost" or "price" of current monetary assets and liabilities, no conversion is made of the year-end account balance in historical cost/constant dollar accounting. A general inflation is assumed to produce holding losses on noncurrent monetary assets just as in the case of current monetary assets, and holding gains on noncurrent monetary liabilities just as in the case of current monetary liabilities, because the "price" of noncurrent monetary assets and liabilities, like the "price" of current monetary assets and liabilities, is *assumed* not to change while these assets and liabilities are held by the firm. (If this bond had been disposed of during the period, of course, the gain or loss to Leavenworth's shareholders resulting from difference between the *current* value of the bond and its historical cost balance would have been recognized.)

3. **Nonmonetary Items.** The Leavenworth asset accounts in this category are: merchandise inventory, land, building (including the related allowance for depreciation), and equipment (also including the depreciation allowance). The ownership equity accounts of common stock and retained earnings comprise the remainder of Leavenworth's nonmonetary items. The balance in these accounts at the beginning of the year are all inputs into the period and, as such, are each multiplied by 110/100, the ratio of the year-end index to the index at the date they were input into the firm (which in Leavenworth's case happens to be at the beginning of the year) in order to express these historical costs in end-of-year dollars.

The balances in these same accounts at year-end are outputs from the period, all of which are also stated in terms of historical cost. With the exception of the merchandise inventory and retained earnings accounts (to be discussed below), each of these outputs is now multiplied by the same conversion ratio as the inputs, since each item is held throughout the year and must be restated in the number of end-of-period dollars which has the same general purchasing power as the number assigned to the item at the beginning of the period. Unlike current and noncurrent *monetary* items, the nominal dollar amount which expresses historical cost at the end of the period in the case of *nonmonetary* items is not assumed to be already in end-of-period dollars but rather is in "historical cost dollars" representing dollars of the date the asset was purchased. (The assumptions of historical cost/constant dollar accounting are that there is *no change* in the current value of *noncurrent monetary items* over the period under consideration, but the current value of *nonmonetary items changes in equal proportion* to the *change in the general price level*.)

Such are our general rules with respect to items carried over the entire period by Leavenworth. In considering inventory, however, the merchandise inventory on hand at year-end was not on hand at the beginning of the year but rather was acquired during the year under Leavenworth's FIFO assumptions. As a consequence, the balance in that account at year-end is converted by means of the ratio 110/108, the year-end index over the index at the date the ending inventory of merchandise was acquired.

TABLE 12-A-1
LEAVENWORTH CORPORATION
COMPARATIVE ACCOUNTING REAL POSITION STATEMENT
As of January 1 and December 31, 19X8
(in December 31, 19X8 dollars)

	December 31, 19X8			January 1, 19X8		
ASSETS:						
Current:						
Cash		$ 72,000			$ 93,500	
Accounts Receivable		120,000			-0-	
Merchandise Inventory		132,407	$324,407		55,000	$148,500
Plant:						
Land		$ 44,000			$ 44,000	
Building	$220,000			$220,000		
Less: Allowance for Depreciation	11,000	209,000		-0-	220,000	
Equipment	$121,000			$121,000		
Less: Allowance for Depreciation	24,200	96,800	349,800	-0-	121,000	385,000
			$674,207			$533,500
EQUITIES:						
Current Liabilities:						
Accounts Payable	$100,000			$ 38,500		
Other Payables	40,000	$140,000		-0-	$ 38,500	
Long-Term Liabilities:						
Bonds Payable		100,000	$240,000		110,000	$148,500
Common Stockholders' Equity:						
Common Stock		$385,000			$385,000	
Retained Earnings		49,207	434,207		-0-	385,000
			$674,207			$533,500

This leaves the retained earnings account as the only nonmonetary item not yet converted. As we shall soon see, the converted amount falls out of Leavenworth's accounting real income statement for 19X8. It is sufficient for our purposes at this stage, therefore, to simply "plug" the amount for retained earnings at year-end with the amount necessary to make the total of Leavenworth's equities at year-end equal to its assets total at the same date. The required "plug" figure, $49,207, appears then in Table 12-A-1, along with the other restated assets and equities to form Leavenworth's comparative accounting real position statement.

Accounting real income statement. The raw dollar data needed to prepare Leavenworth's real accounting income statement for the year ended December 31, 19X8 in terms of year-end dollars are contained in Table 12-3 in the chapter. In the income statement, of course, the focus is upon realization that occurred during the period. As we noted earlier, realization under the accounting real income approach has two facets: (1) realization of nonmonetary and noncurrent monetary items disposed of during the period and (2) realization of current and noncurrent monetary items as a result of changes in the general price level during the period. Accordingly, we shall divide our discussion of the conversion into year-end dollars of Leavenworth's income statement accounts into these two categories.

1. **Realization Upon Disposal.** In Leavenworth's case, the only items disposed of during the year were the goods and services rendered to its customers, all of which involved the consumption of nonmonetary items. The excess of the sales value of these outputs over their historical cost as inputs is Leavenworth's operating income for the year. The sales value of outputs is recorded as sales revenue, and their historical cost as inputs is recorded as cost of goods sold expense, depreciation expense, and other expenses.

It should be recalled that Leavenworth's sales revenue was assumed to have been evenly distributed over the year; moreover, all sales were made either for cash or on account. Accordingly, we can use the short-cut procedure for converting sales revenue into "real" terms, the appropriate conversion ratio being 110/105, the ratio of the general price level index at year-end over the average index for the year. When "raw dollar" sales of $1,000,000 are multiplied by 110/105, the result is $1,047,619, the amount displayed in Table 12-A-2, Leavenworth's accounting real income statement for 19X8.

The conversion of cost of goods sold expense into real terms is somewhat more complex, since the goods output from the firm were acquired at different input dates. However, we do know the historical costs of merchandise inputs to the period (beginning inventory and purchases during the year) and, given Leavenworth's FIFO cost flow assumption, the historical cost of one of the two outputs from the period (ending inventory). If we convert each of these into end-of-period dollars and subtract the one known output from the two known inputs, we will find the remaining output (cost of goods sold expense) in year-end dollars. Because the beginning inventory was acquired the day before the opening of the current period, the conversion ratio appropriate to it is 110/100, the year-end index over that at date of acquisition.

FIGURE 12-A-2

LEAVENWORTH CORPORATION
ACCOUNTING REAL INCOME STATEMENT
For the Year Ended December 31, 19X8
(in December 31, 19X8 dollars)

REVENUES:		
Sales		$1,047,619
EXPENSES:		
Cost of Goods Sold	$739,736	
Depreciation	35,200	
Other	209,524	984,460
OPERATING INCOME		$ 63,159
HOLDING GAINS (LOSSES) ON ASSETS:		
On Net Current Monetary Assets		(5,571)
ENTITY INCOME		$ 57,588
Interest Charges		8,381
Holding Gain (Loss) on Bonds Payable		10,000
OWNERSHIP INCOME		$ 59,207
Common Dividend Charges		10,000
INCREASE IN RETAINED EARNINGS		$ 49,207

Purchases of merchandise were all assumed to have been made on account and distributed evenly over the year, thereby permitting us to use the short-cut procedure; their conversion ratio is 110/105, the year-end index over the average index for the year. The conversion ratio appropriate to the ending inventory is 110/108, the year-end index over that at the date the goods were acquired. Combining these items, we have:

Beginning inventory	
$50,000 × 110/100 =	$ 55,000
Add: Purchases	
$780,000 × 110/105 =	817,143
Cost of Goods Available for Sale	$872,143
Less: Ending Inventory	
$130,000 × 110/108 =	132,407
Cost of Goods Sold Expense	$739,736

This, then, is the amount that appears in Table 12-A-2.

Converting depreciation expense into year-end dollars is a fairly straight-forward task since all of Leavenworth's depreciable assets were acquired on the same date, the day before the opening of business on January 1, 19X8. The conversion ratio is the year-end index over that at the date the depreciable assets were acquired, or 110/100. Multiplying this by the historical cost depreciation expense of $32,000 yields $35,200, the amount reported in Table 12-A-2.

The process of translating other expenses into year-end dollars is similarly straight-forward. Leavenworth's other expenses were assumed to have been incurred evenly throughout the year and each was paid for in cash. As a result, the short-cut procedure is applicable here, with the conversion ratio being 110/105, the ratio of the year-end index over the average index for the year. Multiplying other expenses of $200,000 by this conversion ratio yields $209,524, and this is the amount reported in Table 12-A-2.

When the price level-adjusted expenses are summed and subtracted from price level-adjusted revenues, the result is Leavenworth's operating income as stated in terms of year-end dollars, or $63,159, as shown in Table 12-A-2. Since Leavenworth disposed of no other nonmonetary items during the year, nor of any noncurrent monetary items, the next step is to deal with the realizations that stemmed from inflation during the year.

2. **Realization from Changes in the General Price Level.** As pointed out earlier, both current monetary items and noncurrent monetary items are subject to gains and losses during a period of inflation or deflation. Because Leavenworth held both current monetary items and noncurrent monetary items during 19X8, it was subject to purchasing power gains and losses in both categories.

The gain or loss on current monetary items is determined in exactly the same fashion as in the chapter under the current real income approach. Rather than repeat that discussion here, we shall simply pick up the purchasing power loss on net current monetary assets of $5,571 as reported in Table 12-8 and place it in Table 12-A-2. Once this amount is subtracted from operating income, "real" entity income of $57,588 appears.

The only noncurrent monetary item that Leavenworth had was bonds payable, which remained outstanding throughout the year. Because this is a monetary item, a purchasing power gain or loss must be determined, using the formula for noncurrent monetary liabilities as outlined earlier in the appendix, i.e.,

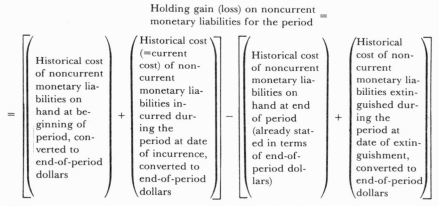

Using the data from the Leavenworth example in the formula, we have:

$$= \left[\left(\begin{array}{c} \$100,000 \\ \times \\ 110/100 \end{array} \right) + \left(\begin{array}{c} \text{NONE} \\ \text{(in Leaven-} \\ \text{worth's case)} \end{array} \right) \right] - \left[\left(\begin{array}{c} \$100,000 \\ \\ \end{array} \right) + \left(\begin{array}{c} \text{NONE} \\ \text{(in Leaven-} \\ \text{worth's case)} \end{array} \right) \right]$$

$$= \quad \$110,000 \quad\quad\quad - \quad\quad \$100,000$$

$$= \quad \underline{\underline{\$\ 10,000}}$$

This, then, is the gain reported in Table 12-A-2. Recall that, unless the historical cost balances in the bonds payable account at both the beginning and end of the year are equal to current values on those respective dates, the amount reported as a gain or loss is meaningless.

3. **Interest and Dividend Charges.** The final items that need to be stated in terms of year-end dollars to complete Leavenworth's accounting real income statement are interest and dividend charges, both of which are fairly straight-forward.

Leavenworth's historical cost interest charges of $8,000 related to the bonds payable that were outstanding throughout the year and, accordingly, were accrued evenly throughout the year. To convert them into year-end dollars, therefore, we may use the short-cut procedure of multiplying them by 110/105, the ratio of the year-end index over the average index for the year. This yields $8,381, the "real" interest charges for 19X8 as reported in Table 12-A-2. When these interest charges, together with the holding gain on bonds payable, are subtracted from entity income, we have ownership income, as stated in year-end dollars.

Leavenworth's common dividend charges may be dealt with even more simply than its interest charges. This is because Leavenworth's dividends of $10,000 were declared and paid on December 31. As a consequence, no conversion need be made of this amount as it is already stated in terms of year-end dollars. Once this amount is subtracted from ownership income, the increase in "real" retained earnings is obtained. That increase, $49,207, of course, is precisely the difference between the beginning-of-year and end-of-year balances in retained earnings in Table 12-A-1, Leavenworth's comparative position statement under the accounting real income approach, and is the amount that we "plugged" earlier in order to complete that statement.

Conclusions

Converting raw dollar historical cost-based financial statements into "real" terms may be an improvement—albeit a very limited one—over the conventional statements that are found in practice today. The major advantage lies in overcoming the shortcomings of the money convention that assumes the purchasing power of the dollar remains constant over time. Statements in terms of dollars of constant purchasing power *do* permit more meaningful comparisons of revenue figures over time and among firms. They also recognize the gains and losses that stem from holding current monetary items during a period when the dollar's purchasing power is changing and, as such, permit meaningful comparisons of stocks of current monetary items over time and among firms.

Other advantages *may* be attributed to price level-adjusted financial statements, but *only* if certain very specific conditions are met. If, for example, the specific prices of a firm's nonmonetary assets always move in direct proportion to changes in the general price level, then amounts reported for those assets in "real" position statements will represent current costs, and the related depreciation expenses on those assets will equal current cost depreciation. Such coordinated price movements are highly unlikely, however. In a similar vein, if the historical cost balances of a firm's noncurrent monetary items are equal to their current values on these same dates, then both the "real" position statement amounts and the related gains or losses in the "real" income statement will have meaning. Such occurrences, however, are dependent on very specific and unlikely conditions as outlined earlier.

Beyond these advantages, there is little to be said in favor of price level-adjusted historical cost financial statements. Such statements still suffer from the limitations of the realization convention which precludes the recognition of changes in *specific* prices of assets and liabilities held by the firm. As a consequence, current costs or current values cannot be reported even though they are the significant factors in the making and evaluation of decisions and of the decision-making process as a whole. Only an approach such as that outlined in the chapter can overcome this serious shortcoming.

DISCUSSION QUESTIONS

1. Consider the adjustment posited in the text to bring the Leavenworth Corporation accounts to *current* (entry, or purchase) *values*, i.e., to adjust for the effects of specific price changes (ignoring interest) which occurred during a period on the firm's particular asset and liability items but to *ignore* at this point any effects on the firm's accounts that might have resulted from a change in the general price level.

   a. Suppose Leavenworth had marketable securities, valued at the end of year 1 in Leavenworth's books at $17,000 original (historical) cost and at $15,000 current market value, and that these had risen in value to be worth $20,000 at market at the end of year 2 when one-half of these securities had been sold for $10,000, the other half being carried over to year 3. The carry-over ledger from year 1 is:

   Marketable Securities—Current Cost Increment (Decrement)

	Dec. 31, 19X8 Balance $2,000

   Record all the journal entries for year 2 related to Leavenworth's marketable securities consistent with current value (specific price change) accounting. Post these to appropriate ledgers. Explain the relationship between the realizable holding gain on securities accruing in year 2; the gain on sale of securities realized in year 2; and the change and new balance in the Marketable Securities— Current Cost Increment accounts, the last representing cumulative unrealized gains in marketable securities at the end of year 2 which may or may not be realized in future years. [Hint: The

   new balance at the end of year 2 in the Marketable Securities—
   Current Cost Increment ledger account should be a debit of
   $1,500.]

b. Suppose, alternatively, that Leavenworth's marketable securities
   had risen in value *during the first half of year 2* to be worth $20,000
   at market, that one-half of these securities had then been sold
   for $10,000, and that the remaining securities were held to the
   end of the period when their market value had fallen to $7,000.
   Record the journal entries for these events and post to appropriate
   ledgers so as to account fully for the mid-year sale and end-of-year
   adjustments with respect to Leavenworth's marketable securities.
   [Hint: The total realizable holding gain on securities in year 2
   amounts to a $2,000 gain (credit balance); the total cumulative
   unrealized holding loss left as a new credit balance in the Marketable Securities—Current Cost Increment account at the end of
   year 2 is $1,500.]

2. While current values at any point in time should be fairly readily
   obtainable in the case of inventory items, as well as in the case
   of marketable securities, and averages can be used for cost of goods
   sold figures based on these readily obtainable current values at
   beginning- and end-of-periods, the same cannot always be said for
   noncurrent assets, in particular, buildings and equipment. Inventory
   items are normally purchased new, and there should be a continuing
   market for such items, just as there is, by definition, for marketable
   securities, albeit they may be "old" securities. Buildings and equipment
   are used up, however, over time. We are here considering the value
   of a used asset where a functioning used-asset market may not exist
   and where even the most nearly comparable asset new may differ
   substantially from that which you bought and are using because
   of technological change. Let us consider the Leavenworth Corporation
   faced with somewhat more realistic measurement difficulties than
   those rather glibly posited in Chapter 12.

a. Leavenworth was established at the beginning of 19X8 on projections that it could earn entity income on its operations equal
   to about 22 per cent of its initial investment of $340,000 in plant
   assets, i.e., it expected to earn entity income of about $75,000
   in its first year, which is 15 per cent of total initial assets of
   $500,000. Further, Leavenworth planners expected earnings (in-
   come plus depreciation) to decline at about $7,500 a year there-
   after, or about at ρD per year, where ρ (= 25%) is the expected
   rate of return on *depreciable* assets (of $300,000) and D is deprecia-
   tion. Earnings, or income plus depreciation (initially expected

to be $105,000), will decline *after year 1* because of growing repairs and losses due to temporary breakdowns. Our work of Chapter 6 would suggest, then, that straight-line depreciation *overall* on depreciable assets was appropriate, although this would admittedly not necessarily apply to each asset. A breakdown of the plant assets, their purchase prices, and original depreciation schedules is given in Table 12-11 (with straight-line depreciation assumed for all assets). The current value of the land is separately appraised by real estate consultants at the end of 19X8. There is at least a once-and-for-all used-asset market for land plus building; a plant contiguous to Leavenworth wants to expand and makes an offer, good for six months, of $280,000 for Leavenworth's land and building, with the building to be left clean ("broom swept"). You estimate that it would cost $25,000 to remove all equipment to another plant which might be built elsewhere. The index of construction costs put out by the U.S. Department of Commerce show that these have risen over the year from an index of 100.00 to an index of 127.78. A general index of machinery prices (electrical and mechanical) shows exactly the same rise in prices over the year, and a spot check of the purchase price on used-asset markets of one-year-old small machines of Leavenworth's type M machines corroborates that this is about the right current purchase price for the type M machines Leavenworth owns. There is no used-asset market, however, for Leavenworth's large machine. A check with the manufacturer indicates that he is now turning out a machine which yields 25 per cent more output as compared with yours for a sale price, installed, of $162,500. Fill in, as best you can, the missing current value amounts in Table 12-11, and explain briefly how and why you arrived at the figures you did. (Be careful about latching on too quickly to the offer from the contiguous manufacturer in order to establish a current value for land and building. Leavenworth managers like their current location and do not expect to sell their land and building at the present time. Perhaps a footnote indicating confirmed net realizable value is in order.)

b. Indicate and explain the *journal entries* that would put Leavenworth's *individual* plant asset accounts into current value accounting terms at the end of 19X8. Why, specifically, is the realizable holding gain on machinery only 95 per cent of the total increase in the market value of the machinery assets new from beginning to end of year, and why is current cost depreciation based on assumed middle-of-the-year current value of the assets new? [You

TABLE 12-11

	Original Cost	Estimated Length of Life	Historical Cost Depreciation (straight-line)	Estimated Current Cost New (end-of-year)	Current Cost Depreciation for the Year (straight-line)
A. Land	$ 40,000	∞	. .	$52,000	. .
B. Building	$144,000	24 yrs.	$ 6,000		
C. Large Machine	120,000	10	12,000		
D. Small Machines	36,000	3	12,000		
Total	$300,000		$30,000		

should understand these adjustments, which seem "tricky" at first, thoroughly.]

c. Practicing accountants are very uneasy about making the type of adjustments you just made in (a) and (b) above. They feel that the current value figure to be used in depreciation (if no used-asset market exists) is too susceptible to interpretation and, therefore, to manipulation. Leavenworth's use of current value accounting for depreciable assets tended to *lower* current operating income by $3,000 (the current cost depreciation increment) but *raise* reported entity income overall by $54,000, or by 70 per cent (realizable holding gains on buildings and equipment of $57,000 less the $3,000 current cost depreciation increment). If they had decided to use double-declining-balance depreciation based on historical costs instead of straight-line depreciation based on historical costs, they would have *lowered* reported entity income by $30,000, or by 39 per cent. Given facts such as those presented in (a) above, do you think that you can justify current value accounting and the sometimes lack of precision in the data used to accomplish this, given perhaps the degree of manipulation already allowed under what are today "generally accepted accounting principles" applying to depreciable assets?

3. If current value accounting is controversial for depreciable assets (indeed, for inventories and other assets as well), many people can see little or no merit at all in adjusting long-term liabilities to current values if current value income and position statements *are* to be formulated. The arguments *against* making such adjustments with respect to long-term liabilities might run as follows:

a. The adjustments effect only ownership income, not entity income, and therefore have no significance for "the entity."

b. *Nor* are the adjustments of any significance even to creditors since a firm pays a creditor a fixed nominal amount of interest over the life of, say, a bond payable, as committed to at time of issuance of the bond, and a fixed nominal principal amount at maturity, or at time of liquidation or bankruptcy of the firm. If creditors are interested in trading their bond, they will most certainly look to current prices in the bond market, which should show the bond's current value, not to the books of the company. And this current value will normally not be very significantly different than maturity value anyway—the differential is only seven per cent in the Leavenworth illustration, for example.

c. *Even owners* are for the most part unaffected by changes in the current value of a firm's bonds payable—much *less interested* in that value surely than in the current value of their stock as might be quoted on the stock exchanges. Why doesn't the position statement show that?

d. Current value·*equity* adjustments are just too complicated anyway, especially if they are not worth making in the first place.

An answer to these arguments by a proponent of reporting current values for long-run liabilities might run along the following lines:

a. We agree that current value adjustments for long-run liabilities do not affect *entity income*, but that does not mean that such adjustments necessarily do not affect *entity decisions*. Indeed, the reporting of such values may bring out clearly long-run financing options open to the firm—options now shown by maintaining only maturity values, plus premium or minus discount values determined at time of issue and adjusted over the life of the bond by amortization. The current long-run liability values that we wish the firm to show on its books (*along with* the maturity value obligation—we think both should be shown, much as a firm shows the current value of a machine new as well as its current value used) reflect the *current book value* of claims of different equity holders on the current value of the firm's assets. True, the claim of long-term bondholders may not be exercised until maturity, in which case the current value is the principal or maturity value. But if the firm chooses to recall the bond or purchase it in the market and eliminate long-run creditor claims on the enterprise's assets or refinance the bond at current rates of interest, *then* surely current values are highly relevant. Everyone should know that such contingencies exist and how much might be at stake. (The current value/principal value differential is not always "insignificant"—try a 20-year bond of $100,000 for Leavenworth and a drop in interest rates from 11 per cent to 7 per cent in the first year, for example.)

b. We would have no objection to, indeed, would strongly approve of a firm reporting *separately* the current value and changes in the current value of its stock outstanding as reported on stock exchanges. But such values do not bear the same relationship to claims on assets as the current values of bonds payable outstanding. Shareholder claims involve a *residual* claim. If shares of stock are recalled or purchased by the firm at their current market value, the action cannot be such as to threaten or diminish current bondholder claims, whereas if this is done for bonds it may be such as to diminish shareholder claims.

c. Once you get used to them, current value adjustments for long-term liabilities are not unduly complicated and there is normally no difficulty in determining objectively the current value figure to be employed.

Consider these questions:

(1) Is it true that changes in current value of long-term liabilities have no effect on current entity income? How so?

(2) How big must a change in interest rates in the market be to have a "significant" (say, more than ten per cent) effect on the current value of a $100,000 bond in the case, say, of a bond with 5, 10, 20, and 40 years to maturity? Explain.

(3) Is there a fundamental difference, no difference, or perhaps some difference—to the firm and to interested outsiders, including creditors and owners—in the current value of a firm's long-term liabilities, on the one hand, and the current value of a firm's ownership equities, on the other? Explain your position.

(4) To ascertain how difficult it is to effect and understand the current value adjustment for bonds payable, assume that Leavenworth's bonds payable consists of a $100,000 maturity value, 20-year-life bonds paying semi-annual interest of four per cent, and that the bond is now at the beginning of the fourth year of its 20-year life. Interest rates in the market for such a bond rise gradually over the year from eight per cent per annum to twelve per cent per annum in 19X8. Record the journal entries necessary to account for the rise in interest rates in the market on the firm's books for the year 19X8, *explaining* briefly the nature and meaning of the current cost increment to interest charges and the realizable holding gain on bonds payable that would accrue to Leavenworth, and to Leavenworth's shareholders, in 19X8 under these assumptions (instead of the assumptions made in Chapter 12).

PROBLEMS

12-1. *Stewart Company*

The Stewart Company acquired a new building on January 1, 19X1 for $400,000 cash. The building was expected to have a 40-year useful life with no salvage at the end of that time. Because of the building's expected use and earnings pattern, the company elected to depreciate it on a straight-line basis.

Because the building was a unique one, no current market values were available for similar used buildings. However, a study of current construction costs at the end of 19X1 and again at the end of 19X2 revealed that to build a new one would cost approximately $500,000 at the end of 19X1 and $550,000 at the end of 19X2.

INSTRUCTIONS:

(a) Assuming that the general price level remained constant throughout 19X1 and 19X2, (1) prepare journal entries on Stewart's books to record the acquisition of the building and its depreciation on a historical cost basis for 19X1 and 19X2, and (2) prepare appropriate adjusting journal entries as of December 31, 19X1 and December 31, 19X2 as the basis for the preparation for current value income and position statements for Stewart Company.

(b) Assume the following general price-level indexes:

January 1, 19X1	100.0
Average for 19X1	107.0
December 31, 19X1	114.5
Average for 19X2	123.7
December 31, 19X2	133.6

(1) Determine the amount of current cost depreciation and realizable holding gains or losses that would appear in Stewart's current real income statements for 19X1 (in December 31, 19X1 dollars) and 19X2 (in December 31, 19X2 dollars).

(2) If, on December 31, 19X2 Stewart Company prepared a comparative current real position statement (in December 31, 19X2 dollars), what amounts would appear for the building and related allowance for depreciation?

12-2. Willis Company

The Willis Company purchased a new machine for $10,000 cash on January 1, 19X6 for use in its manufacturing process. The company expected the machine to have a useful life of five years, at the end of which time its net salvage value would be $1,000. For historical cost accounting purposes, the company elected to depreciate the machine on a straight-line basis.

Because the machine is a fairly common one and has a wide variety of uses, an active market exists for both new and used units identical to this one. Current market price data are available as of the following dates:

| | Current Price to Purchase on December 31 | | |
	19X5	19X6	19X7
New	$10,000	$11,000	$12,000
One-year-old	7,000	7,700	8,400
Two-years-old	4,500	4,950	5,400

INSTRUCTIONS:

(a) Prepare journal entries on Willis' books to record the acquisition of the machine and its depreciation on a historical cost basis for 19X6 and 19X7.

(b) Prepare the appropriate adjusting journal entries on Willis' books as of December 31, 19X6 and December 31, 19X7 as a basis for the preparation of current value income and position statements for Willis.

12-3. *Evanston Corporation*

The Evanston Corporation was organized on January 1, 19X6, on which date it purchased a tract of land for $40,000 as a building site. During the first three months of 19X6, it had a building constructed on that site. The building was completed on March 31 and Evanston paid the contracted price of $200,000 on that date. Also on that date, Evanston purchased for $60,000 certain equipment for use in the building. The building and equipment were put into service immediately.

Evanston expected that the building's useful life would be 40 years, at the end of which time its net salvage value would be negligible. Because the passage of time was thought to be the primary determinant of the building's decline in usefulness, Evanston elected to depreciate it on a straight-line basis.

The equipment's expected useful life was set at five years with no net salvage value. As wear and tear was thought to be the primary factor in determining the equipment's decline in utility and since Evanston planned to use it evenly over its life (as do most firms owning such equipment), the straight-line method of depreciation was adopted for it.

An examination of real estate transactions involving nearby land similar to Evanston's indicates that land prices rose during the year by approximately 15 per cent. In addition, a qualified appraiser called in by Evanston at year-end estimated the current market value of Evanston's land to be $46,000.

Because Evanston's building is rather unique, no market prices were available on it at year-end. However, a construction cost index published by the government at year-end indicates that the cost to construct an identical building at year-end would be approximately $222,000.

A published government index regarding the prices of durable equipment of the general group to which Evanston's belongs indicated that the prices of such equipment rose over the year 19X6 by about eight per cent. There also exists a wide market for equipment identical to Evanston's, both new and used. On December 31, the prices of such equipment were as follows:

	Current Price to Purchase
New	$66,000
One-year-old (in average condition)	46,200
Two-years-old (in average condition)	34,650

Evanston closes its books annually on December 31.

INSTRUCTIONS:

(a) Assuming there has been no change in the general price level during the year, determine the following amounts that would appear in Evanston's current income statement for 19X6 and on its current position statement as of December 31, 19X6:
   (1) Depreciation expense
   (2) Realizable holding gain or loss on land
   (3) Realizable holding gain or loss on building
   (4) Realizable holding gain or loss on equipment
   (5) Land as of December 31, 19X6
   (6) Building (net) as of December 31, 19X6
   (7) Equipment (net) as of December 31, 19X6

(b) Assume the general price level rose during 19X6 as follows:

January 1	100
April 1	102
July 1	104
October 1	106
December 31	108

Determine the amounts (1) through (7) requested under (a) above that would appear on Evanston's current real income statement for 19X6 and its current real position statement as of December 31, 19X6.

12-4. Exetron Corporation

Finding itself with a temporary surplus of cash, Exetron Corporation purchased three blocks of marketable securities on October 1, 19X0. The securities so obtained and their costs were as follows:

$$\begin{array}{llll}
\text{Security A:} & 1,000 \ @ \ \$54 = & \$ \ 54,000 \\
\text{Security B:} & 500 \ @ \ \$62 = & 31,000 \\
\text{Security C:} & 500 \ @ \ \$30 = & \underline{15,000} \\
& & \$100,000
\end{array}$$

On December 31, 19X0, Exetron sold all of its holdings of Security C for $18,000 and used the proceeds of the sale to purchase 400 more of Security A.

On March 31, 19X1, Exetron sold all of its holdings of Security B, receiving $35,000 which it then used to acquire 700 more of Security A.

On November 1, 19X1, Exetron sold 500 of Security A for $24,500. The remainder of Security A was still held on December 31, 19X1.

The current market prices of the securities held by Exetron were as follows at the end of each year:

	Current Market Prices Per Unit As of December 31	
	19X0	*19X1*
Security A	$45	$52
Security B	64	70
Security C	36	35

INSTRUCTIONS:

(a) Determine the impact of marketable securities on Exetron's income (ignoring interest) for 19X0 and 19X1 and the amount to be reported for marketable securities on Exetron's position statements as of December 31, 19X0 and December 31, 19X1 under each of the following cost flow assumptions:
   (1) FIFO
   (2) FIFO, constrained by lower of cost or market applied to each class of security
   (3) Average cost
   (4) Specific identification, assuming that the sale of 500 of Security A was composed of the 400 purchased on December 31, 19X0 and 100 from the March 31, 19X1 purchase

(b) Assuming that Exetron accounts for its marketable securities on a current cost basis, determine the impact of marketable securities on Exetron's current income for 19X0 and 19X1 and the amount to be reported for marketable securities on Exetron's current position statements as of December 31, 19X0 and December 31, 19X1.

12-5. *Loos Corporation*

Loos Corporation issued $1,000,000 of ten-year, ten per cent convertible bonds at face amount on January 1, 19X2. Interest on these bonds is payable semi-annually on June 30 and December 31.

By December 31, 19X6, bonds of similar quality and maturity were being actively traded at a price to yield eight per cent compounded semi-annually. The market rate of interest dropped suddenly on July 1, 19X7 from eight per cent to six per cent and remained there through December 31, 19X7.

Loos closes its books annually on December 31.

INSTRUCTIONS:

(a) Assume that the general price level has remained constant since the date the bonds were issued. Determine the following with respect to Loos Corporation's current income statement for 19X7 and its related comparative current position statement:
   (1) Current interest charges.
   (2) Realizable holding gain or loss on bonds.
   (3) Amount to be reported for the bonds December 31, 19X6 and December 31, 19X7.
   (4) Current entity income and current ownership income, assuming that Loos' current operating income was $580,000 and that there were no realizable holding gains and losses other than with respect to the bonds.

(b) Assume that the general price-level index has risen as follows:

January 1, 19X2	80
December 31, 19X6	100
Average for period from January 1 to June 30, 19X7	105
Average for period from July 1 to December 31, 19X7	115
Mid-year 19X7 and average for 19X7	110
December 31, 19X7	120

Determine the following with respect to Loos Corporation's current real income statement for 19X7 and its related comparative current real position statement, all in terms of December 31, 19X7 dollars:
(1) Current interest charges
(2) Realizable real holding gain or loss on bonds
(3) Amount to be reported for the bonds on December 31, 19X6 and December 31, 19X7.

12-6. Debtron Company

On July 1, 19X7, Debtron Company issued $1,000,000 of five-year, six per cent debenture bonds at a price to yield eight per cent compounded semi-annually. Interest on the bonds is payable semi-annually on December 31 and June 30.

The market rate of interest for bonds of similar quality and maturity remained at eight per cent until January 1, 19X9 when it rose to ten per cent where it remained throughout 19X9.

Debtron closes its books annually on June 30.

INSTRUCTIONS:
(a) Assume that the general price level has remained constant since the date the bonds were issued. Determine the following with respect to Debtron's current income statement for the fiscal year ended June 30, 19X9 and its related comparative current position statement:
(1) Current interest charges
(2) Realizable holding gain or loss on the bonds
(3) Amount to be reported for the bonds on June 30, 19X8 and June 30, 19X9
(4) Current entity income and current ownership income, assuming that Debtron's current operating income was $660,000 and that there were no realizable holding gains and losses other than with respect to the bonds
(b) Assume that the general price-level index has declined as follows:

July 1, 19X7	105
June 30, 19X8	100
Average for period from July 1 to December 31, 19X8	95
Average for period from January 1 to June 30, 19X9	85
Average for fiscal year ended June 30, 19X9	90
January 1, 19X9	90
June 30, 19X9	80

Determine the following with respect to Debtron's current real income statement for the fiscal year ended June 30, 19X9 and its related comparative current real position statement, all in terms of June 30, 19X9 dollars:

(1) Current interest charges
(2) Realizable real holding gain or loss on the bonds
(3) Amount to be reported for the bonds on June 30, 19X8 and June 30, 19X9 on the current position statement

12-7. Freland Corporation

At the beginning of 19X1, Freland Corporation purchased equipment for $135,000. The equipment is expected to have a useful life of five years with no net salvage value. For income tax purposes, the equipment is being depreciated on a sum-of-the-years' digits basis.

In each of the years 19X1 through 19X5, inclusive, Freland had sales revenues of $500,000 per year and expenses other than depreciation and income taxes of $420,000, all of which were taxable or tax deductible in the year incurred. Freland is subject to a corporate income tax rate of 40 per cent. Income taxes are payable at year-end.

Over the five-year period, purchase prices of new equipment identical to Freland's remained constant at $135,000. Although the market for similar used equipment is only sporadic, indications are that a straight-line method of depreciation applied to the cost of new equipment will provide a reasonable approximation of its market value used. Accordingly, Freland has been depreciating its equipment on this basis for financial reporting purposes.

INSTRUCTIONS:

(a) Assume that the general price level index has been rising steadily over the five-year period. The price-level index at the end of each period was as follows:

Year	Index at end-of-period
19X1	100
19X2	105
19X3	110
19X4	115
19X5	120

Prepare a schedule showing income tax expense, income taxes paid, and the change in deferred income taxes payable over the five-year period. Based on this data, determine the total purchasing power gain or loss that has accrued to Freland Corporation (in terms of December 31, 19X5 dollars) as a result of adopting sum-of-the-years' digits depreciation for tax purposes rather than straight-line.

(b) Same as (a) above, except assume that the general price level has been declining steadily over the five-year period, in accordance with the schedule below:

Year	Index at end-of-period
19X1	100
19X2	95
19X3	90
19X4	85
19X5	80

12-8. *Abacus Company*

The Abacus Company began business on January 1, 19X3. At the end of 19X3, its income and comparative position statements on a historical cost basis were as follows:

Abacus Company
Comparative Position Statement
As of January 1 and December 31, 19X3

	December 31, 19X3			January 1, 19X3		
ASSETS:						
Current:						
Cash		$ 20,000			$ 60,000	
Accounts Receivable		70,000			-0-	
Merchandise Inventory		60,000	$150,000		30,000	$ 90,000
Plant:						
Land		$ 10,000			$ 10,000	
Buildings & Equipment	$200,000			$200,000		
Less: Allowance for						
Depreciation	20,000	180,000	190,000	-0-	200,000	210,000
			$340,000			$300,000
EQUITIES:						
Current Liabilities:						
Accounts Payable		$ 40,000			$ 50,000	
Other Payables		20,000	$ 60,000		-0-	$ 50,000
Common Stockholders' Equity:						
Common Stock		$250,000			$250,000	
Retained Earnings		30,000	280,000		-0-	250,000
			$340,000			$300,000

Abacus Company
Income Statement
For the Year Ended December 31, 19X3

REVENUES:		
Sales		$400,000
EXPENSES:		
Cost of Goods Sold	$240,000	
Wages	80,000	
Depreciation	20,000	
Other	10,000	350,000
ENTITY AND OWNERSHIP INCOME:		$ 50,000
Common Dividend Charges		20,000
INCREASE IN RETAINED EARNINGS:		$ 30,000

Additional Information:
(1) Common dividends were declared and paid half on June 30 and half on December 31.
(2) General price-level indexes during the year were as follows:

	General Price-Level Index
January 1, 19X3	100
Mid-year 19X3 and average for 19X3	110
December 31, 19X3	121
At acquisition date of ending inventory	118

(3) Sales, collections of receivables, purchases of merchandise, payment of payables, and incurrence of wages and other expenses occurred evenly throughout the year.
(4) Other payables are all monetary liabilities.

INSTRUCTIONS:
Prepare, in good form, a schedule of purchasing-power gains or losses on net current monetary assets for Abacus Company for the year ended December 31, 19X3.

12-9. Wilkinson Company

The Wilkinson Company, a retailing firm, commenced operations on January 1, 19X3. Wilkinson's comparative position statement for

January 1 and December 31, 19X3 is presented below together with its income statement for the year ended December 31, 19X3, both in terms of historical costs.

Wilkinson Company
Comparative Position Statement
As of January 1 and December 31, 19X3

		December 31, 19X3			January 1, 19X3	
ASSETS:						
Current:						
Cash		$ 80,000			$160,000	
Accounts Receivable		180,000			-0-	
Merchandise Inventory		140,000	$400,000		130,000	$290,000
Plant:						
Land		$ 50,000			$ 50,000	
Buildings & Equipment	$300,000			$300,000		
Less: Allowance for						
Depreciation	30,000	270,000	320,000	-0-	300,000	350,000
			$720,000			$640,000
EQUITIES:						
Current Liabilities:						
Accounts Payable		$140,000			$110,000	
Other Payables		20,000	$160,000		30,000	$140,000
Common Stockholders' Equity:						
Common Stock		$500,000			$500,000	
Retained Earnings		60,000	560,000		-0-	500,000
			$720,000			$640,000

Wilkinson Company
Income Statement
For the Year Ended December 31, 19X3

REVENUES:		
Sales		$600,000
EXPENSES:		
Cost of Goods Sold	$350,000	
Depreciation	30,000	
Other	140,000	520,000
ENTITY AND OWNERSHIP INCOME		$ 80,000
Common Dividend Charges		20,000
INCREASE IN RETAINED EARNINGS		$ 60,000

Additional Information:

(1) The buildings and equipment are being depreciated on a straight-line basis with an expected service life of ten years and no salvage.

(2) The beginning merchandise inventory consisted of 13,000 units which had been acquired at $10 each. During 19X3, 30,000 units were purchased at an average cost of $12 per unit. The ending inventory consists of 10,000 units acquired at a price of $14 each.

(3) Sales, collections of receivables, merchandise purchases, payment of payables, and other expenses occurred evenly throughout the year.

(4) Common dividends of $10,000 were paid on June 30, 19X3 and another $10,000 on December 31, 19X3.

(5) Other payables are all monetary liabilities.

INSTRUCTIONS:

(a) Assume that there have been no changes in the general price level during 19X3 but that the following current costs exist at year-end:

Merchandise Inventory	$155,000
Land	65,000
Buildings and Equipment (new)	370,000

Determine the following amounts that would appear on Wilkinson's *current* income statement for 19X3:
(1) Current cost of goods sold
(2) Realizable holding gain on merchandise inventory
(3) Realizable holding gain on land
(4) Current cost depreciation
(5) Realizable holding gain on buildings and equipment

(b) Assume the same data as in (a) above, except that the following information regarding general price levels is available:

January 1, 19X3	100
Mid-year 19X3 and average for 19X3	110
December 31, 19X3	121
At acquisition date of ending inventory	117

Determine the following amounts that would appear on Wilkinson's *current real* income statement for 19X3, expressed in end-of-year dollars:
(1) Current cost of goods sold
(2) Realizable real holding gain on merchandise inventory
(3) Realizable real holding gain on land
(4) Current cost depreciation
(5) Realizable real holding gain on buildings and equipment

12-10. *Key Corporation (I)*

The Key Corporation was organized and began operations on January 1, 19X8. The first year's operations were successful as reflected by the income statement and comparative position statement (both in terms of historical costs) presented below:

Key Corporation
Comparative Position Statement
As of January 1 and December 31, 19X8

	December 31, 19X8			January 1, 19X8		
ASSETS:						
Current:						
Cash		$ 20,000			$ 65,000	
Accounts Receivable		90,000			-0-	
Merchandise Inventory		80,000	$190,000		55,000	$120,000
Plant:						
Land		$ 50,000			$ 50,000	
Buildings and Equipment	$150,000			$150,000		
Less: Allowance for						
Depreciation	15,000	135,000	185,000	-0-	150,000	200,000
			$375,000			$320,000
EQUITIES:						
Current Liabilities:						
Accounts Payable		$ 35,000			$ 20,000	
Other Payables		15,000	$ 50,000		-0-	$ 20,000
Common Stockholder's Equity:						
Common Stock		$300,000			$300,000	
Retained Earnings		25,000	325,000		-0-	300,000
			$375,000			$320,000

Key Corporation
Income Statement
For the Year Ended December 31, 19X8

REVENUES:		
Sales		$300,000
EXPENSES:		
Cost of Goods Sold	$185,000	
Depreciation	15,000	
Other	55,000	255,000
ENTITY AND OWNERSHIP INCOME:		$ 45,000
Common Dividend Charges		20,000
INCREASE IN RETAINED EARNINGS:		$ 25,000

Additional Information:

(1) Key Corporation accounts for inventories on a FIFO basis. Cost of goods sold was accounted for as follows:

Beginning Inventory	
10,000 units @ $5.50	$ 55,000
Purchases	
35,000 units @ $6.00 (average)	210,000
Goods Available for Sale	$265,000
Less: Ending Inventory	
12,800 units @ $6.25	80,000
Cost of Goods Sold	$185,000

(2) Half of common dividends were declared and paid on June 30 and the remainder on December 31.
(3) Depreciation is being taken on a straight-line basis under the expectation of a ten-year life with no salvage.
(4) Sales, collections of receivables, merchandise purchases, payment of payables, and other expenses occurred evenly throughout the year.
(5) There has been no change in the general price level during 19X8.
(6) The following are current costs at year-end:

Merchandise Inventory ($6.50/unit)	$ 83,200
Land	65,000
Buildings and Equipment (new)	180,000

(7) Other payables are all monetary liabilities.

INSTRUCTIONS:

Prepare Key Corporation's current income statement for the year ended December 31, 19X8 and its related comparative current position statement as of January 1 and December 31, 19X8.

12-11. Key Corporation (II)

Assume the same data as in Problem 12-10 except that the general price level, rather than remaining unchanged, has risen as follows:

	General Price-Level Index
January 1, 19X8	130
Mid-year 19X8 and average for 19X8	140

| | December 31, 19X8 | 150 |
| At aquisition date of ending inventory | | 147 |

INSTRUCTIONS:

Prepare Key Corporation's current real income statement for the year ended December 31, 19X8 and its related comparative current real position statement as of January 1 and December 31, 19X8, all in terms of December 31, 19X8 dollars.

12-12. Santa Cruz Corporation (I)

The Santa Cruz Corporation began business on January 1, 19X2. Given below is the position statement as of January 1 and December 31, 19X2, together with the 19X2 income statement, all in terms of historical costs:

Santa Cruz Corporation
Comparative Position Statement
As of January 1 and December 31, 19X2

	December 31, 19X2		January 1, 19X2	
ASSETS:				
Current:				
Cash	$ 15,000		$ 20,000	
Accounts Receivable (net)	35,000		-0-	
Merchandise Inventory	80,000	$130,000	50,000	$ 70,000
Plant:				
Equipment	$ 40,000		$ 40,000	
Less: Allowance for				
Depreciation	5,000	35,000	-0-	40,000
		$165,000		$110,000
EQUITIES:				
Current Liabilities:				
Accounts Payable		$ 40,000		$ 10,000
Common Stockholders' Equity:				
Common Stock, $10 par	$100,000		$100,000	
Retained Earnings	25,000	125,000	-0-	100,000
		$165,000		$110,000

Santa Cruz Corporation
Income Statement
For the Year Ended December 31, 19X2

REVENUES:

Sales		$200,000
EXPENSES:		
Cost of Goods Sold	$120,000	
Depreciation	5,000	
Other	35,000	160,000
ENTITY AND OWNERSHIP INCOME		$ 40,000
Common Dividend Charges		15,000
INCREASE IN RETAINED EARNINGS		$ 25,000

Additional Information:

(1) Santa Cruz accounts for its merchandise inventory on a FIFO basis. The beginning inventory consisted of 6,000 units, which was augmented by two purchases during the year, one of $100,000 for 10,000 units and the other of $50,000 for 4,000 units.

(2) The equipment was purchased on January 1, 19X2 and is being depreciated over an expected useful life of eight years on a straight-line basis with no net salvage value anticipated.

(3) Sales occurred evenly throughout the year, as did collections of receivables and payments of payables and other expenses.

(4) Common dividends were declared and paid on December 31.

(5) The books have not yet been closed for the year.

(6) There have been no changes in the general price level during 19X2.

(7) Purchase prices of merchandise rose steadily throughout the year and by year-end stood at $13 per unit. The average price at which a unit of merchandise was offered to Santa Cruz during the year was $11.

(8) Because the type of equipment owned by Santa Cruz is adaptable to a wide variety of uses, numerous units, both new and used, are regularly traded. Market price data are readily available, as follows:

	Current Price to Purchase on December 31	
	19X1	*19X2*
New	$40,000	$44,000
One-year-old	30,000	33,000
Two years-old	22,000	24,200

INSTRUCTIONS:

On the basis of the foregoing information, prepare the necessary year-end adjusting journal entries, opening additional accounts as necessary, to convert Santa Cruz's records to a current value basis and prepare a current income statement for the year ended December 31, 19X2 and comparative current position statement as of January 1, 19X2 and December 31, 19X2.

12-13. Santa Cruz Corporation (II)

Assume the same data as in Problem 12-12 except that the general price level, rather than remaining unchanged, has risen as follows:

	General Price-Level Index
January 1, 19X2	100
At date of first merchandise purchase	107
Mid-year 19X2 and average for the year	110
At date of second merchandise purchase	118
December 31, 19X2	120

INSTRUCTIONS:

Prepare Santa Cruz Corporation's current real income statement for the year ended December 31, 19X2 and its related comparative current real position statement as of January 1 and December 31, 19X2, all in terms of December 31, 19X2 dollars.

12-14. Winn Company (I)

The Winn Company was organized on January 1, 19X0 by a group of investors who bought its common stock for $300,000 cash. The firm also commenced its business activities on that date.

The company has been successful from the outset, generating income in each year of operations. Given below are Winn's December 31, 19X3 *post*-closing trial balance and its December 31, 19X4 *pre*-closing trial balance:

	December 31, 19X4 Dr	December 31, 19X4 Cr	December 31, 19X3 Dr	December 31, 19X3 Cr
Cash	$ 15,000		$ 50,000	
Accounts Receivable	280,000		260,000	
Merchandise Inventory	329,000		310,000	
Land	80,000		80,000	
Building	400,000		400,000	
Building—Allowance for Depreciation		$ 30,000		$ 20,000
Equipment	150,000		150,000	
Equipment—Allowance for Depreciation		90,000		60,000
Accounts Payable		170,000		220,000
Other Payables		40,000		30,000
6% Bonds Payable		500,000		500,000
Common Stock		300,000		300,000
Retained Earnings		120,000		120,000
Sales Revenue		2,000,000		
Cost of Goods Sold Expense	1,826,000			
Depreciation Expense	40,000			
Other Expenses	75,000			
Interest Charges	30,000			
Common Dividend Charges	25,000			
	$3,250,000	$3,250,000	$1,250,000	$1,250,000

Additional Information:

(1) The December 31, 19X3 inventory consisted of 7,750 units which had been purchased at a price of $40 per unit. During 19X2, 41,000 units were purchased for a total price of $1,845,000. At the end of the year, 7,000 units remained on hand. Winn Company uses the FIFO basis of accounting for its inventories.

(2) Both the building and the equipment were purchased on January 1, 19X2 and are being depreciated over their expected useful lives of 40 years and 5 years, respectively, on a straight-line basis. Neither is expected to have a net salvage value at the end of its life.

(3) The six per cent bonds were issued on January 1, 19X2 at their face amount and mature ten years from date of issuance. Interest on the bonds is payable semi-annually on June 30 and December 31.

(4) All sales, collections of receivables, purchases of merchandise, payments of payables, and incurrences of other expenses are made evenly throughout the year.

(5) The other payables are monetary liabilities.

(6) Common dividends were declared and paid on December 31, 19X4.

(7) There have been no changes in the general price level during the period from January 1, 19X0 to December 31, 19X4.
(8) An examination of price lists made available from suppliers indicates that, if the December 31, 19X3 merchandise inventory had been purchased on that date, it would have cost Winn $325,500. Similarly, if Winn had bought its December 31, 19X4 inventory on that date, it would have cost $336,000.
(9) A study of real estate records concerning recent purchases and sales of nearby property indicates that the purchase prices of tracts of land similar to Winn's approximated $95,000 at the end of 19X3 and $100,000 at the end of 19X4.
(10) No current price data is available regarding Winn's building, as similar ones are not regularly bought and sold. However, examination of current construction cost data indicates that to have built an identical building would have cost approximately $450,000 on December 31, 19X3 and $480,000 on December 31, 19X4. Straight-line depreciation with no expected salvage value on a 40-year expected life, when applied to current construction costs, is thought to produce a reasonable approximation of market value of the used building.
(11) The type of equipment that Winn owns is widely used and has a variety of different applications. As such, an active market exists for such equipment, both new and used, price data from which follows:

| | Current Price to Purchase on December 31 | |
	19X3	19X4
New	$180,000	$200,000
One-year-old	126,000	140,000
Two-years-old	81,000	90,000
Three-years-old	45,000	50,000

(12) On December 31, 19X3, bonds of similar maturity and quality as Winn's were being actively traded at prices to yield eight per cent compounded semi-annually. During 19X4, interest rates on such bonds rose steadily such that by year-end they were yielding ten per cent compounded semi-annually.

INSTRUCTIONS:

On the basis of the foregoing information, prepare the necessary adjusting journal entries, opening additional accounts as necessary, to convert Winn's records to a current value basis and prepare Winn's current income statement for the year ended December 31, 19X4 and its related comparative current position statement as of December 31, 19X3 and December 31, 19X4.

12-15. Winn Company (II)

Assume the same data as in Problem 12-14, except that the general price level, rather than remaining unchanged, has risen as follows:

	General Price-Level Index
January 1, 19X0	85
January 1, 19X2	90
December 31, 19X3	100
Average for period from January 1 to June 30, 19X4	105
Mid-year 19X4 and average for 19X4	110
Average for period from July 1 to December 31, 19X4	115.5
December 31, 19X4	121
At date of acquisition of merchandise inventory on hand at:	
December 31, 19X3	98
December 31, 19X4	117

INSTRUCTIONS:

Prepare Winn Company's current real income statement for the year ended December 31, 19X4 and its related comparative current real position statement as of December 31, 19X3 and December 31, 19X4, all in terms of December 31, 19X4 dollars.

12-16. Goostree Company (I)

The Goostree Company was organized on January 1, 19X5 by a group of investors who bought its common stock for $250,000 cash. The firm is a distributor of radios and televisions, buying directly from manufacturers and selling to retailers. Goostree's income statement for 19X9 and its comparative position statement as of December 31, 19X8 and 19X9, all on a historical cost basis, appear on following page:

Goostree Company
Comparative Position Statement
As of December 31, 19X8 and 19X9

	December 31, 19X9			December 31, 19X8		
ASSETS:						
Current Assets:						
Cash		$ 50,000			$ 40,000	
Accounts Receivable		60,000			55,000	
Merchandise Inventory		175,000	$285,000		160,000	$255,000
Plant Assets:						
Land		$ 15,000			$ 15,000	
Building	$160,000			$160,000		
Less: Allowance for						
Depreciation	20,000	140,000		16,000	144,000	
Equipment	$ 50,000			$ 50,000		
Less: Allowance for						
Depreciation	25,000	25,000	180,000	20,000	30,000	189,000
TOTAL ASSETS			$465,000			$444,000
EQUITIES:						
Current Liabilities:						
Accounts Payable	$ 45,000			$ 40,000		
Other Payables	42,000	$ 87,000		36,000	$ 76,000	
Long-Term Liabilities:						
8% Bonds Payable		100,000	$187,000		100,000	$176,000
Common Stockholder's Equity:						
Common Stock		$250,000			$250,000	
Retained Earnings		28,000	278,000		18,000	268,000
TOTAL EQUITIES			$465,000			$444,000

Goostree Company
Income Statement
For the Year Ended December 31, 19X9

REVENUES:		
Sales		$400,000
EXPENSES:		
Cost of Goods Sold	$262,000	
Depreciation	9,000	
Other	97,000	368,000
OPERATING AND ENTITY INCOME		$ 32,000
Interest Charges		8,000

OWNERSHIP INCOME	$ 24,000
Common Dividend Charges	14,000
INCREASE IN RETAINED EARNINGS	$ 10,000

Additional Information:

(1) Goostree uses the FIFO method of accounting for its inventories. Its merchandise inventory is comprised of two general categories: radios and televisions. Within each category, there are three different types: low-priced, medium-priced, and high-priced. Thus, Goostree's inventory is made up of six different goods (low-priced radios, high-priced televisions, and so forth). Although the proportion of radios to televisions may vary during the year, within each category Goostree maintains the same relative "mix," i.e., one-quarter low-priced, one-half medium-priced, and one-quarter high-priced. Goostree's cost of goods sold for 19X9 was determined as follows:

Beginning Inventory		
Televisions: 800 at an average purchase price of $175	$140,000	
Radios: 1,000 at an average purchase price of $20	20,000	$160,000
Purchases:		
Televisions: 1,200 at an average purchase price of $190	$228,000	
Radios: 1,750 at an average purchase price of $28	49,000	277,000
Cost of Goods Available for Sale		$437,000
Ending Inventory:		
Televisions: 740 at an average purchase price of $200	$148,000	
Radios: 900 at an average purchase price of $30	27,000	175,000
Cost of Goods Sold		$262,000

(2) The land, building, and equipment were all acquired in early January, 19X5. Neither the building nor the equipment are expected to have any net salvage value upon their retirement. Both are being depreciated on a straight-line basis since their decline in utility is expected to be a function of the passage of time rather than wear and tear or obsolescence. The building's expected life is 40 years and the equipment's, 10 years.

(3) The eight per cent bonds were issued on June 30, 19X7 at their face amount and mature ten years from date of issuance. Interest on the bonds is payable semi-annually on June 30 and December 31.

(4) All sales, collections of receivables, purchases of merchandise, payments of payables, and incurrences of other expenses were made evenly throughout the year.

(5) Common dividends were declared and paid on December 31, 19X9.

(6) The other payables are monetary liabilities.

INSTRUCTIONS:

(a) Assume that there have been no changes in the general price level but that the prices of certain specific items have fluctuated as follows:

(1) An examination of price lists made available from the manufacturers of radios and televisions indicates that the average prices to purchase them on December 31, 19X8 and December 31, 19X9 were as follows:

	Average Price to Purchase in the "Mix" Maintained by Goostree on December 31	
	19X8	19X9
Radios	$ 24	$ 31
Televisions	$178	$202

(2) A study of real estate records concerning purchases and sales of nearby property indicates that the purchase prices of tracts of land similar to Goostree's approximated $29,000 at the end of 19X8 and $34,000 at the end of 19X9.

(3) Because buildings such as Goostree's are not regularly bought and sold, no current market prices are available. However, published government construction indexes indicate that for Goostree to have built the same type of building it now owns would have cost approximately $205,000 at the end of 19X8 and $215,000 at the end of 19X9. Straight-line depreciation with no expected salvage value on a 40-year expected life, when applied to current construction costs, is thought to provide a reasonable approximation of market value of the used building.

(4) The equipment that Goostree owns consists of regular store and office furnishings and, as such, is regularly bought and sold both new and used. Price lists available from dealers in such furnishings indicate the following data with respect to Goostree's specific equipment.

	Current Price to Purchase on December 31	
	19X8	19X9
New	$70,000	$75,000
One-year-old	60,900	65,250
Two-years-old	52,500	56,250
Three-years-old	44,800	48,000
Four-years-old	37,800	40,500
Five-years-old	31,500	33,750

(5) Bonds of similar quality and having similar maturity dates to Goostree's were being actively traded at prices to yield ten per cent compounded semi-annually at the end of 19X8 and twelve per cent at the end of 19X9. The rise in effective interest rates from ten per cent to twelve per cent occurred at mid-year.

On the basis of the foregoing information, prepare the necessary adjusting journal entries (opening additional accounts as necessary) to convert Goostree's records to a current value basis and prepare a current income statement for 19X9 and related comparative position statement.

12-17. Goostree Company (II)

Assume the same data as in Problem 12-16, except that the general price level, rather than remaining unchanged, has risen as follows:

	General Price-Level Index
January 1, 19X5	80
June 30, 19X7	90
December 31, 19X8	100
Average for period from January 1 to June 30, 19X9	105
Mid-year 19X9 and average for 19X9	110
Average for period from July 1 to December 31, 19X9	115
December 31, 19X9	120
At date of acquisition of merchandise inventory on hand at:	
December 31, 19X8	97
December 31, 19X9	118

INSTRUCTIONS:

Prepare Goostree Company's current real income statement for the year ended December 31, 19X9 and its related comparative current real position statement as of December 31, 19X8 and December 31, 19X9, all in terms of December 31, 19X9 dollars.

CHAPTER 13

EPILOGUE: DIVERGENT VIEWS IN THE ACCOUNTING PROFESSION

WE HAVE ARGUED THE CASE for current value accounting in Chapters 11 and 12. Full current value accounting, which takes into account the effects on the enterprise of both individual price changes and changes in the general price level, is vital for two reasons. First, in a current real income statement, we get an accurate picture of *when changes occurred* in ownership equity—*all* the events of a period are included, and *only* the events of that period are included, in terms of the conditions (price and quantities) prevailing in that period. Second, a current real income statement is designed to classify the changes which occurred—into operating and holding gains and losses—in such a way as to make clear *why the change occurred.*

We have tried to show that these two features are vital if there is to be proper (1) *evaluation of decisions* which have been made and are in the process of being carried out, so that these decisions can be altered if need be and/or a new plan devised; (2) *pinpointing of problems* (the purchasing problem in our inventory illustration in Chapter 11); and (3) *evaluation of performance* in an appropriate comparative manner, over time, and in comparison with other firms by both insiders and interested outsiders. The current real income statement, finally, is consistent with a comparative current real position statement, which reports current costs of assets, liabilities, and ownership in terms of dollars of constant purchasing power.

In recent years, world-wide inflation and uneven but sharp price advances for particular assets have brought the problem of accounting for individual and general price level changes to the fore and stimulated protracted discussion within the business and accounting professions. Practicing accountants—perhaps American practicing accountants, in particular—have tended to be reluctant to alter existing principles and practices, inflation or no inflation. European, Canadian, and Australian accountants have been somewhat more flexible; but when they have moved toward possible acceptance of some form of current value accounting, it has tended to be either a somewhat different approach from that which is set forth in Chapters 11–12 or only a partial adjustment to what is indicated there. Indeed, the world-wide accounting profession seems to be somewhat at sea at present, with many different approaches being espoused by different groups. In this chapter we shall try to analyze and compare some of the principal proposals supported by one or another group, starting with traditional practice and historical costs, and the principal conventions which underlie and support these positions. We can then show how each of the various alternatives being considered involves giving up and/or modifying and reinterpreting one or more of these conventions.

CONVENTIONAL ASSUMPTIONS AND GUIDING PRINCIPLES OF TRADITIONAL ACCOUNTING

Basic Conventions

There are four basic conventions that underlie traditional accounting practices, but one is so generally accepted (and used uniformly in all the various proposals we are to consider below) that we do not need to dwell on it here. There is no quarrel about the *period convention,* which stipulates the need for periodic reports over fairly short periods of time (usually one year) on progress of the enterprise, whether it is a going concern or a concern put together for a limited life, with respect to income over that period and position at the beginning and end of the period. Exactly what goes into these periodic statements is the point at issue; and much depends, as we will show, on the nature and degree of acceptance of the other three, more controversial conventions underlying traditional accounting practices.

1. *The realization convention.* The realization convention holds that no revenue or gain should be recognized until an asset is sold or a service is rendered for an agreed price. Production is not considered to yield revenue, unless sold, nor is appreciation in the value of assets previously acquired, unless they are sold.

There are thus two dimensions to the realization convention: (1) a purchase/production/sale dimension which may be termed an "operating" dimension and (2) a holding dimension. The first concerns when income is to be recognized on the primary operations of the firm, i.e., on assets which increase in value because of the physical transformation of the asset through production or the transforming of the asset from a wholesale to a retail good. The second (or holding) dimension concerns when to recognize gains from holding activities because of changes in prices of assets as a consequence of the passage of time rather than the use of the assets. As we will see, one can give up one dimension of the realization convention without giving up the other—and, indeed, we, and most other current value proponents, do just that.

Closely allied with the realization convention is the "cost principle" which holds that the value of the assets of a firm should be measured by the unexpired portion of the cash or cash equivalent given to secure them, irrespective of their current value; and expenses should be measured as the expiration of those asset values, i.e., in terms of the cash or cash equivalent originally given to acquire the asset services now used up. This approach to asset and income measurement, based as it is on historic costs, is defended as being the only method which can be relied upon as being completely unambiguous and objective.

2. *The money convention.* The money convention presently practiced in accounting can be stated as follows: The accountant employs money as a unit of measurement (the dollar in the United States); he accounts only for changes that can be measured in money terms; and he keeps records and prepares financial statements as though the unit of measurement were absolutely unchanging in value over time. It should be noted that the money convention does not deny the existence of what is known to be true—that the value of money is subject to change, as we argued in Chapter 11. Rather it holds that it is not a proper function of accounting to account for changes in the value of the monetary unit itself. This position is defended on basically the same ground as the defense of the realization convention above, viz., that financial statements prepared in compliance with the money convention are based on verifiable, objective evidence and contain a minimum of subjective speculation, whereas any effort to correct for changes in the value of the dollar will inevitably involve some use of indices which may not be entirely suitable for the task at hand and which depend on surveys and averaging which the accountant cannot accept as entirely objective in the way that dollars paid for an asset are an objective fact.

3. *The going concern convention.* Acceptance of the going concern convention in accounting means that accounting records should be kept on the assumption that the business entity has an indefinite life. Continuity rather than liquidation is the reasonable expectation. *Nonac-*

ceptance of this convention means that the business entity is treated as if it were to liquidate at the end of each period. It may liquidate or it may not, but accounts are to be kept in terms of liquidation values (exit values), with these immediately realizable values then compared with alternative possible investments each period—maintaining the asset and using it, or selling it and investing the proceeds in some alternative asset, or distributing them. We will consider such an approach below. But what does the assumption of continuity imply? An entity may grow, decline, or remain stable and still continue. But there must, then, be some benchmark against which to measure growth, decline, or stability; and this benchmark is usually "maintenance of capital" interpreted in one of three ways:

a. maintenance of the *historical cost of assets;*
b. maintenance of the *current market value of assets;*
c. maintenance of the *existing physical assets currently held by the firm.*

A going concern will not continue to be a going concern very long if it continually dissipates capital. But which of the three versions of "capital maintenance" is adopted—and whether it is expressed in money or "real" terms—essentially determines the concept of income to be employed, for entity income is the increase in the value of assets held by the firm independent of any change due to new commitments (by creditors or owners) or new disbursements (to creditors or owners).

Guiding Principles

All of the various concepts of income supported by different groups today and the various position statements that go with each concept can be cast in terms of acceptance or rejection of these three accounting conventions, with acceptance of the third involving one of the alternatives (a), (b), or (c). Before going on to consider these, however, let us set forth briefly six guiding principles, sometimes in conflict with one another, which greatly influence accountants and their decisions about the basic conventions:[1]

1. *Objectivity.* Accounts should be capable of independent verification so that all "reasonably-minded" accountants might agree on the fact being considered, i.e., accounts should *not* be based on *subjective* judgments of a particular party.

2. *Consistency.* Accounting procedures should be applied consistently

---

1. These guiding principles are essentially those suggested in the Sandilands Report in the United Kingdom. See *Inflation Accounting. Report of the Inflation Accounting Committee* (Sandilands Report, after the Chairman) (United Kingdom: HMSO, 1976—Cmd. 6225). [Hereafter referred to as Sandilands]

to different events and over time as far as possible.

3. *Intelligibility*. Accounting reports should be capable of being readily understood by intelligent (although not necessarily expert) legitimate users of the data, outside as well as inside the firm.

4. *Usefulness*. Accounting data should provide legitimate users with the information they need in order to make the judgments they must make with respect to the performance of the firm.

5. *Realism*. Accounting reports should show a "realistic" view of a company's position and performance akin to the sometimes stated legal view (for example, in Great Britain) that they should show a "true and fair view."

6. *Comparability*. Accounting reports should be prepared in such a way that meaningful comparisons can be made among firms at a moment of time and for a single firm and/or among firms over time so that when there are identical events there are identical reports of those events and when events differ accounting reports show the differences in a meaningful way.

The first three of these guiding principles have traditionally been deemed to be of paramount importance by the accounting profession. But for reasons in part illustrated in Chapter 11, principles 4, 5, and 6 are taking on increasing importance among many accountants. The rub is that they may sometimes seem to conflict with one or more of the first three principles, in particular with "objectivity."

Let us now consider, in the light of the conventions and principles set forth above, the various alternative approaches for the measurement of income and position being considered by accountants around the world.

MAINTAINING ALL THREE CONVENTIONS—TRADITIONAL ACCOUNTING INCOME AND REALIZED INCOME

Traditional Accounting Income and its Reliance on the Three Conventions

At the core of present-day accounting practice is the realization convention and the reliance on historical costs in accounting records which inevitably follows if the realization convention is rigidly adhered to.[2] In fact, while present accounting practice *in general* follows the

2. Accounting literature is full of defenses of the realization convention and of the importance of adhering to historical costs in accounting records. The issues, both pro and con, with respect to adherence to the realization convention are ably summarized, in the concept of a historical background, in Sidney Davidson, "The Realization Concept," in Morton Backer (Ed.), *Modern Accounting Theory, op. cit.,* pp. 99–116, which is a summary

realization convention, occasional deviations from the principle of historical costs are permitted, sometimes required. Property acquired without cost, through donation or bequest, is recorded in the accounts at its "implied cash cost" (usually its appraised value); resources discovered or developed which have immediate economic significance far in excess of the actual outlay required for their acquisition may be written up to establish formally a new point of departure on the basis of implied cash cost—the amount of money which would unquestionably be necessary to acquire the resource in its established commercial status—in lieu of an actual bargained price. To maintain balance in the accounting equation, such a write-up of asset value must be reflected also in some equity account, although it is usually not treated as income.

Not entirely consistent with the realization convention is the doctrine of "conservatism" that pervades accounting practice. The essence of this doctrine is that while a disregard for asset appreciation is not only proper but essential to objective reporting, unrealized reductions in asset values must be recognized promptly in the accounts. Thus, it is usual to carry inventories and temporary investments at the lower of their cost or fair market value on the position statement. In general, this doctrine is not applied to noncurrent assets, such as plant and equipment, and long-term investments, where "temporary" reductions in value are ignored. If it is felt that there has been a permanent and substantial loss of value in respect of such assets, however, write-downs to "true value" prior to realization through sale or abandonment are in order. Such write-downs must be matched by reductions in appropriate equity accounts.

But it is not so much our purpose here to quibble about deviations from the convention as it is to point out its weaknesses when it is followed faithfully. These weaknesses can be summarized as follows:

> 1. Strict adherence to historical cost as the proper basis for asset valuation means that cost savings or holding gains and losses are not recorded as they arise, i.e., as individual prices change, which in turn has three undesirable manifestations:
>   a. Holding gains and losses taking place during a period are excluded from the accounts of the period unless the

---

of a report on the subject of the American Accounting Association Concepts and Standards Research Study Committee which appeared in *The Accounting Review* XL (April 1965), pp. 321–322. A brief but adamant defense of historical costs is given in Yuji Ijiri, "A Defense for Historical Cost Accounting," in Robert R. Sterling (Ed.), *Asset Valuation* (Lawrence, Kansas: Scholars Book Co., 1971), pp. 1–14. (See also the response by James H. MacNeill which follows Ijiri's chapter.)

asset whose value has changed is sold during that period or used in the production of goods or services which are sold during that period (in the case of inventories, is deemed to have been sold through some artificial flow assumption such as FIFO or LIFO).

b. Holding gains and losses taking place during prior periods may be recognized as gains or losses of this period when assets whose value has increased or decreased over an extended period of time are sold or consumed in this period.

c. Position statement values may bear so little relationship to current values as to be almost meaningless.

2. Holding gains or losses which are realized through sale or use of a product whose cost includes the using up of assets whose prices have changed since acquisition are included as part of normal operating profit. In fact, the profit results from simply holding the asset rather than from operations. This difficulty, too, stems from keeping records at historical cost.

3. There is no recognition of the effects of changes in the general price level and thus no separation of the "real" and "fictional" elements in reported net income as well as no statement of "real" ownership on the position statement.

As we have tried to show in Chapter 11, these weaknesses severely limit the usefulness of accounting reports as presently compiled. Traditional accounting income fails to meet any of the four tests set out at the beginning of Chapter 11 (see p. 457)—tests which we feel must be met if the data provided are to be useful for both management and interested outsiders. Before considering the traditional accountant's defense of accounting income, let us see how accounting income might be modified slightly, yet all three conventions be retained, so as to make it a little more useful.

Realized Income and Maintenance of the Three Conventions

The second defect listed above, the confusion of holding gains realized through use (cost savings) with operating income, can be corrected without abandoning either the realization convention, the money convention, or the going concern convention. We simply substitute the concept of realized income for traditional accounting income.[3] Realized

3. See Edwards and Bell, *op. cit.*, Chapter 4 and elsewhere.

income reports the same *total* income as traditional accounting income and the same historical costs on the position statement. It differs only in separating realized cost savings from operating income. This reclassification serves, however, to identify current operating income as a separate and distinct figure on the income statement, just as current income does.

If A is current operating income, C is realized holding gains through sale of assets, and D is realized holding gains through use of assets (the excess of current costs over and above historical costs as in Chapter 11, pp. 471–72), realized income compares with traditional accounting income as follows:

	Income elements included	
	As operating income	As holding gains
Traditional Accounting Income	$A + D$	C
Realized Income	A	$C + D$

This is an improvement, one which can be accomplished without giving up the essentials of the realization convention in that gains are still reported only as and when realized. We have shown in Chapter 11 that current operating income is in itself a useful figure in measuring performance (although to be more useful it must be compared with the *current* value of assets, which realized income and its position statement values do not provide). Realized income classifies change better than traditional accounting income but, like traditional accounting income, fails to include all gains which occurred in a period and does include some gains which occurred (were earned) in previous periods as gains of this period (because they were realized in this period). It is a *partial* adjustment, revealing data on current operating performance but not on overall performance and, indeed, in this respect is just as weak as traditional accounting income. It necessitates *some* measurement of current values, albeit only to divide accounting income more realistically into two components—income from operations and realized holding gains—and as such is not acceptable to the strict historical cost accountant. We must try to understand that case.

A Defense of Historical Costs and the Critic's Reply

Essentially, the case for maintenance of the realization convention and strict historical costs in accounting records rests on a belief that the principle of objectivity in accounting records must take precedence over all else, that any deviations from the objective facts of historical

acquisition costs and the using up of those values over time is going
to be subject to abuse. The strict historical cost advocate might argue
as follows:

> We may not meet your four tests, but we meet the one
> test (and you do not) that we think is the most important
> test of all—the objectivity test: No income is recognized unless
> actually consummated by the sale of an asset or a service
> rendered for an agreed price. We may report "wrong"
> incomes, but our "wrongness" is at least safeguarded by certain
> objective checks. Your method would enable you to report
> any income figure desired.

A current income advocate (of one or another variety) might answer
as follows:

> First, we recognize that original acquisition costs are objective
> facts, but how objective are your cost figures which involve
> future subjective forecasts of the life of a plant asset, allocation
> of these original acquisition costs through time by often
> arbitrary depreciation methods to measure the using up of
> that asset, and artificial flow assumptions for the using up
> of inventories? In the case of inventories, even the acquisition
> cost, after the first period, i.e., the beginning inventory figure,
> is based on the arbitrary flow assumption being employed.
> Second, on our supposed freedom to report any income
> figure we desire, surely auditors can and should keep us
> honest. That is their function! The current market value
> of inventories, securities (both owned and owed), and many
> plant assets can be readily checked. Consistent use of the
> most appropriate price index on those plant assets not having
> a readily available market value can give, in this day and
> age of sharply changing prices, a much more reliable indica-
> tion of market value than historical costs.

If neither side can convince the other, then we suggest that two
income concepts can be reported, current income and realized income
(it certainly does not do any *harm* to report traditional accounting income
in more realistic component parts), which can be done by simple
end-of-period adjustments in the accounts, and be placed side-by-side
in a comprehensive income statement. And a current value and historical
cost comparative position statement can similarly be placed side-by-side,

with the user able to take his or her choice.[4] We do not believe there is any informational content in statements based on historical costs when current values are reported. But it can be done.

This, in effect, is what the Securities and Exchange Commission in this country, and the Sandilands Committee in the United Kingdom, argued for in the mid-1970s. Sandilands argued for basic statements in current value terms, with footnotes to indicate historical costs. The SEC decreed in *Accounting Series Release No. 190* that present accounting practices were to be followed in the body of reported statements but "replacement costs," i.e., current costs, of all assets and liabilities were to be reported in footnotes, from the end of 1976 forward, for all companies with assets over $100 million.[5] We applaud this SEC breakthrough of 1976 in forcing firms to supply the data so much needed for purposes of evaluation of decisions and performance and the making of new decisions—needed by outsiders (the SEC is primarily concerned with the needs of investors) *and* by the firms themselves! We have qualms about some of the specific directives employed to define "replacement costs.[6] *And* we have serious qualms about the manner in which the SEC seems to be interpreting the objective of the exercise, specifically that it seems to be interpreting the objective as the reporting of "replacement cost income." We will turn to this subject a little further on.

A much more substantial break with tradition came on December 28, 1978 with the publication of the Financial Accounting Standard Board's Exposure Draft on *Financial Reporting and Changing Prices*—a document that appeared after the manuscript for this book went to press. For all intents and purposes, the FASB proposes in this draft that all firms in the United States over a certain size publish, as supplementary information in their financial statements, basically the *current real income* information, properly dichotomized, that we have set forth and urged in Chapters 11 and 12—calling the proposed framework *current cost/constant dollar* accounting. As this book goes into page proofs, we cannot be certain what, if any, amendments may be made in any final FASB edict. We hope that they might amend the exposure draft so as to (1) incorporate marketable securities and long-term liabilities (treatment of both of which escaped the exposure

4. See Edwards and Bell, *op. cit.*, Statements 1 and 2, pp. 218–219.
5. Securities and Exchange Commission, *Accounting Series Release No. 190*, March 23, 1976.
6. See L. Todd Johnson and Philip W. Bell, "Current Replacement Costs: A Qualified Opinion," *Journal of Accountancy* (November 1976), pp. 63–70.

draft); (2) provide for a more meaningful reconciliation between current real income and traditional historical cost accounting income; and (3) provide general-price-level-adjusted data for their suggested five-year summaries of current real income as they do in the case of historical cost information (rather than simply suggesting publication of the Consumer Price Index and leaving it to the user to make the correction himself). As the accepted setter of standards for accounting in this country, the Financial Accounting Standards Board carries great weight. We believe that there is now real reason to hope that a student who has worked through the material of Chapters 11 and 12 will have not merely engaged in an "academic exercise" (the term "academic" unfortunately connoting to many irrelevance) but in fact will find the material an essential exercise if he or she is going to engage in actual accounting work or in interpretation of accounting reports from 1979 onwards. Still, many in the profession disagree with the FASB and with us, and we must continue to try to understand their reasoning in this last chapter.

MAINTAINING THE REALIZATION AND GOING CONCERN CONVENTIONS BUT GIVING UP THE MONEY CONVENTION

Price-Level-Adjusted Historical Costs

Under pressure to do something about the effects of inflation on accounting records and reluctant to give up the realization convention, practicing accountants' professional bodies in both the United States and the United Kingdom have put forward proposals in recent years aimed at correcting existing historical costs for changes in the general price level, i.e., the exercise we have performed in the Appendix to Chapter 12.[7] The American group has proposed using the most general price index to be found to do this (the GNP deflator series), while

7. American Institute of Certified Public Accountants, Statement of Accounting Principles Board No. 3, *Financial Statements Restated for General Price-Level Changes* (New York: American Institute of Certified Public Accountants, 1969). [Hereafter referred to as APB#3]. This was followed by an Exposure Draft of the AICPA's Financial Accounting Standards Board, *Financial Reporting in Units of General Purchasing Power* (December 31, 1974), which proposed that all U.S. companies adopt the purchasing power method of accounting for inflation for fiscal years after January 1, 1976, using the general GNP price deflator index—a proposal which was largely not accepted, or at least has not been put into practice, by U.S. corporations. The main professional accounting bodies in the United Kingdom (Institute of Chartered Accountants in England and Wales, the Institute of Chartered Accountants in Scotland, the Institute of Chartered Accountants in Ireland, the Association of Certified Accountants, and the Institute of Cost and Management Accountants) produced a very similar proposal in May 1974

the British groups have proposed using the British equivalent of the Consumer Price Index.

The effect of these proposals, variously dubbed CPP (for current purchasing power), PLAHC (for price-level-adjusted historical costs), and, perhaps irreverently, PuPU (for purchasing power unit), can be seen by reference back to our five basic equations employed in Chapter 11 to illustrate current value adjustments for price level changes (p. 487). Again, let M denote net current monetary assets, N nonmonetary assets, L long-term liabilities, and R residual equity. Further, ARI is accounting real income, S sales revenue, C operating costs other than depreciation, and D_H is historical cost depreciation adjusted to last period's dollars but not for price level changes of the current period. Again, GI is gross investment during the period and B is new borrowing, both assumed to occur at the end of the period. And again, subscripts 1 and 2 denote periods 1 and 2, respectively, and the subscript H denotes historical cost in terms of dollars of the subscript period, i.e., N_{H1} is the historical cost of assets, purchased at different points back in time adjusted for the change in the value of the dollar from date of acquisition to period 1. Finally, p is the percentage change in the general price level which occurs in one jump at the beginning of period 2. Then to adjust historical costs for changes in the general price level, we have:

$$M_2 - M_1(1 + p) + N_{H2} - N_{H1}(1 + p) - [L_{H2} - L_{H1}(1 + p)]$$

$$= R_{H2} - R_{H1}(1 + p) = ARI_2, \tag{13.1}$$

$$M_2 - M_1 = S_2 - C_2 - GI_{H2} + B_{H2}, \tag{13.2}$$

$$N_{H2} = (1 + p) N_{H1} - (1 + p) D_{H2} + GI_{H2}, \tag{13.3}$$

$$L_{H2} = L_{H1} + B_{H2}, \tag{13.4}$$

and substituting (13.2), (13.3), and (13.4) into the left-hand side of (13.1) we obtain:

$$ARI_2 = [S_2 - C_2 - (1 + p) D_{H2}] + L_{H1} p - M_1 p. \tag{13.5}$$

These, of course, are *very* different results from those obtained for current real income using a similar set of equations in Chapter 11.

---

in their Provisional Statement of Standard Accounting Practice No. 7 (hereafter referred to as SSAP 7), but they proposed using the British equivalent of the consumer price index (RPI) for use in correcting historical costs.

There our comparative current real position statement (given by the first equation) was in current value terms both for period 1 and period 2, and our current real income was given by:

$$CRI_2 = [S_2 - C_2 - D_{C2}] + N_{C1}(q - p) - L_{C1}(r - p) - M_1 p, \quad (11.5)$$

where the subscript C denotes current value and q and r are price increases on nonmonetary assets and liabilities, respectively, which occur at the beginning of period 2. It is not just that these period 2 individual price changes are accounted for in the current real income approach, but not in the accounting real income approach, and current cost depreciation rather than price-level-adjusted historical cost depreciation is subtracted from earnings to arrive at operating income. Of even greater significance is the fact that N_1 and L_1 values are current values (in period 1) rather than historical costs. If all asset prices move together (*and have moved steadily together from the date assets were acquired*) and if there are no interest rate changes and therefore no changes in the current value of long-term liabilities ($r = 0$), then since $D_{C2} = D_{H2}(1 + p)$, the two approaches come to the same thing, for with $p = q$ there are no real holding gains on nonmonetary assets and liabilities. But since specific prices and the general price level may diverge extensively one from another over long periods, the two "real" income statements and comparative position statements are as different as night from day. Price level adjustments applied to historical costs cannot even be said to remedy limitation 3 above of present-day accounting income, much less limitations 1 and 2, which the proposals do not touch (see pp. 613–14). The "real" values on income and position statements are not "real" values at all because they are based on outdated price-level-adjusted historical costs.

> But (supporters of price-level-adjusted historical costs assert) at least it is a step in the right direction to adjust for the effects of inflation, and one that can be taken with only a minimum deviation from "objectivity" if all can agree on the price level index to be employed in the adjustment.

> No, (opponents argue) not only does it not do most of what needs to be done, it may actually be a step in the *wrong* direction.

Consider our basic example used to illustrate current real income in Table 11-3, reproduced here for convenience. With a 5 per cent general price level change in period 1 and a 15 per cent change in period 2, we applied equation (11.5) and determined current real income as follows:

	Period 1		Period 2
	(in period 1 dollars)	(in period 2 dollars)	(in period 2 dollars)
Current Real Income	$2,450	$2,817	$1,120

If we apply equation (13.5) to obtain accounting real income, we obtain:

$$[(S - C) \quad - (i + p)D_H \qquad\qquad] + L_{H_p} - Mp \qquad = ARI$$

Period 1
(in period 1 dollars) $[(\$\ 7,700) - (1.05)(\$5,000)$ $\qquad\qquad\qquad] + \ 0 \ - (\$5,000)(.05) = \$2,200.00$
$\times\ 1.15 =$ period 2
dollars $\qquad\qquad\qquad\qquad\qquad\qquad\qquad\qquad\qquad\qquad\qquad\qquad\qquad\qquad\ = \$2,530.00$
Period 2
(in period 2 dollars) $[(\$14,520) - (1.15)(1.05)(\$5,000) - (1.15)(\$5,500)] + \ 0 \ - (\$5,000)(.15) = \$1,407.50$

Since accounting income (unadjusted for price level changes) is $2,700 in period 1 and $4,020 in period 2, it does seem as though we have at least gone part way in the right direction, overcorrecting in period

TABLE 11-3

	Period					
	0	*1*			*2*	
		Before dividends and rein-vestment	*After dividends and rein-vestment*		*Before dividends and rein-vestment*	*After dividends and rein-vestment*
Cash	$ 5,000		$12,700	$ 5,000	$19,520	$ 5,000
Machine(s)	10,000	$11,000			$12,100	
Less: Current cost depreciation	0	5,500			12,100	
Net value	$10,000		5,500	5,500	0	
Reinvestment	0			5,500		12,100
Total assets (= ownership equity)	$15,000		$18,200	$16,000	$19,520	$17,100

	Period	
	1	*2*
Earnings before depreciation	$7,700	$14,520
Current Cost Depreciation	5,500	12,100
Current Operating Income	$2,200	$ 2,420
Realizable Holding Gains	1,000	1,100
Current Income	$3,200	$ 3,520
Dividends (= Current Operating Income)	2,200	2,420
Change in Retained Earnings	$1,000	$ 1,100

1 and undercorrecting in period 2. But suppose the general price level rose by only 3.33 per cent in period 1. Then current real income would be $2,700 while accounting real income would be $2,366. Accounting income (unadjusted) exactly equals current real income, and the adjustment of historical costs for changes in the general price level moves *away* from that current real income figure. An eight per cent (rather than 15 per cent) rise in the general price level in period 2, following our 3.33 per cent increase in period 1, would then show current real income falling sharply as compared with current real income in period 1 (i.e., current real income in period 2 would be $2,240), whereas accounting real income would report an increase in real income in period 2 as compared with period 1 (i.e., accounting real income in period 2 would be $2,600). Adjusting accounting income and historical costs for changes in the general price level may well report events as changing in the opposite direction to events as reported by current real income because accounting real income does nothing to correct limitations 1 and 2 of (unadjusted) accounting income—specifically, some holding gains go unreported and other holding gains are reported in the wrong period (i.e., when realized rather than when earned), not to mention that holding gains realized through use (some earned perhaps long ago) are still reported as operating income.

The adjustment of historical costs for price level changes is at best intended to be a partial adjustment, but it is misguided and misleading because the basic data, historical costs, are not appropriate for the adjustment being applied.

Realized Real Income

Correcting realized income (rather than traditional accounting income) for price level changes does not help much. In effect, all that is involved is adding and subtracting current cost depreciation on the right-hand side of equation (13.5), so that we have:

$$RRI_2 = [S_2 - C_2 - D_{C2}] + [D_{C2} - (1 + p) D_{H2}]$$
$$+ L_{H1}p - M_1 p. \qquad (13.5')$$

Realized holding gains are taken out of operating income and reported separately (current operating income is then the bracketed figure), but the total of realized real income is exactly the same as the total of accounting real income and the related position statement still reflects historical costs (adjusted for price level changes). Realized real income is a slight improvement, but it still has basically the same defects as accounting real income. To remedy those defects, we must give up the realization convention, at least in its holding dimension.

GIVING UP THE REALIZATION CONVENTION BUT MAINTAINING THE MONEY AND GOING CONCERN CONVENTIONS

There are two basic approaches (and many variants) in the existing literature which abandon the holding dimension of the realization convention, i.e., its historical cost base, and report current *entry* values. Both retain the money and going concern conventions. One approach would report current income (unadjusted for general price level changes) and its components on an income statement and current values on the position statement. This is our Chapter 11 concept before adjusting for price level changes.

Another approach, "current replacement value accounting" (CRVA), is widely practiced in the Netherlands and seems to be gaining acceptance on other parts of the European Continent and in Australia.[8] Probably the most widely accepted variant of this approach is to report only current operating income as income on the income statement. Current values for assets and (sometimes) liabilities are reported on the position statement by crediting realizable holding gains directly to a "reserve" or "equity" account without carrying them through an income statement. In this approach, such gains are clearly not regarded as income. A variant of the CRVA approach is that adopted by the Sandilands Committee. Like CRVA, the committee would exclude all cost savings or holding gains in the computation of "income"—their income figure is essentially current operating income—and they would report current values on the comparative position statement. Sandilands, however, would "reconcile" these two statements by adding a third "total gains and losses statement" wherein they would add realizable cost savings or holding gains to current operating income to yield a figure of "total

---

8. The Sandilands Report, *op. cit.,* gives an extensive survey of replacement cost value accounting principles (pp. 139–151) and practice, particularly in the Netherlands (pp. 228–229). Another very good summary can be found in Jan Klassen, "Current Replacement Cost Value Accounting in Western Europe," *A Symposium Presented by the Department of Accounting,* College of Business Administration, Oklahoma State University, Stillwater, Oklahoma (197?). Early expounders of the position were R. S. Gynther in *Accounting for Price-Level Changes—Theory and Procedures* (Oxford: Pergamon Press, 1966), pp. 141–142 and elsewhere; and Edward Stamp, "Income and Value Determination and Changing Price-Levels: An Essay Toward a Theory," *The Accountant's Magazine* 75 (June 1971), pp. 277–292 (reprinted in Stephen A. Zeff and Thomas F. K. Keller, *Financial Accounting Theory I* (New York: McGraw-Hill, 1973), pp. 552–579. Support in Australia is given in The Institute of Chartered Accountants in Australia at the Australian Society of Accountants (preliminary exposure draft), "A Method of Current Value Accounting," June 1975. See also R. L. Mathews, "Income, Price Changes and the Valuation Controversy in Accounting," *Accounting Review* (July 1968), pp. 509–516. For a sharp critique of replacement cost value accounting (by a price-level-adjusted historic costs advocate), see Paul Rosenfeld, "Current Replacement Cost Accounting—a Dead End," *The Journal of Accountancy* (September 1975), pp. 63–73.

gain" which was consistent with the increase in ownership equity (retained earnings) on the comparative position statement. But as realizable holding gains are not income in the committee's view, they would not be subject to income-type taxes.[9]

The two approaches reflect fundamentally different assumptions with respect to maintenance of capital (hence, gains over and above that which is necessary to maintain capital). In the first case above, a firm is considered to have gained over a period if there is an *increase in the market value of its assets minus liabilities.* In the case of replacement cost value accounting, a firm is considered to have gained only if the market value of its net assets has *increased by more than that necessary to replace existing (physical) assets currently held by the firm.* A rise in the value of assets due to an increase in asset prices simply means higher replacement costs and so such a gain is not recognized as income for the firm or for its shareholders. Let us consider each of these approaches in turn.

Are Realizable Holding Gains "Income"?

We arrived at our concept of current income as the most relevant concept for accounting in the absence of price level changes in Chapter 11 by analyzing the objectives of the firm and the planning process. A firm tries to "outguess the market" and establishes a plan to turn initial subjective goodwill into market value, i.e., into excess current income (increases in market value over and above what could be earned by interest on risk-free securities over the life of the plan). Changes in the price level aside, a firm could be considered "better off" in an objective sense only when the market value of its net assets increased.

It follows, then, that the firm *could* distribute all of its current income as dividends and just maintain its capital, i.e., the market value of its assets. As we argued in Chapter 11, the firm may be prepared to do this or it may wish to distribute more or less than its current income in any period for any of a number of reasons. For example, it may wish to stabilize dividends over time; or the firm may believe that to distribute all of current income, including holding gains, would put the firm into a liquidity bind in the near future; or the firm may retain all of its current income in order to expand in profitable directions. How much to distribute as dividends is a *policy* decision; and while it may be in part dependent upon how much is generated, i.e., on

9. In early sections Sandilands clearly *rejects* the CRVA approach (pp. 139–151), but then the committee, in effect, *adopts* the CRVA approach in its essentials—lock, stock, and barrel. Sandilands, *op. cit.*

current income, the outcome of the dividend decision should in no way affect the definition of income. Income is the increase in the market value of the firm's net assets; how to *dispose* of current income is another matter.

The Sandilands Committee has perhaps taken the strongest stance in favor of making the distributability of income an integral part of the *definition* of income. It redefined income (its term is "profit") for the year as "the amount of the total gains arising in the year that *may prudently be regarded as distributable*" (italics ours).[10] The committee then argued that while all realizable holding gains should indeed be regarded as part of "total gains arising in the year," they are not income because they cannot "prudently be regarded as distributable."

Why distributability should be an essential characteristic of income is not clear. Distribution should depend on *liquidity* and on *relative profitability* of investment options open to the firm. If the firm is highly liquid and has no attractive prospects for investment, distribution would appear to be in order even if (and perhaps more so if) current income is negative. As Professor William Baxter has said in criticizing the committee on this point:

> Cash distributions may be imprudent for all manner of reasons; where do we draw the line in deciding on whether imprudence changes income? If I commit myself to buying a car, the budgetary strain may be agonizing; but does it cut down my salary?[11]

Replacement Cost Income

While the Sandilands Committee considers realizable holding gains to be gains (but not distributable gains) for the enterprise, current replacement value accounting does not see such holding gains to be gains at all. Higher asset prices mean higher replacement costs which do not result in any increase in the firm's command over the physical goods that *it* consumes.

More generally, of course, an increase in the prices of the firm's assets has two effects—the current cost of the asset services used to

10. Sandilands, *op. cit.*, p. 28. Their choice, then, from among five alternative profit concepts—none of which includes holding gains—is current operating income, i.e., concept no. 5: "Profit for the year is regarded as any gains arising during the year which may be distributed after charging for the 'value' of the company's assets consumed during the year. Capital is regarded as the 'value to the business' of the company's assets." (p. 37).

11. William T. Baxter, "The Sandilands Report," *Journal of Business Finance and Accounting* 3, 1 (1976), p. 120.

generate income in the current period is higher, and the assets themselves are worth more in the market place. The CRVA school focuses attention exclusively on the first (cost) effect and its consequences for current operating income; it pays no attention to the second (value) effect and its consequences for the wealth of the firm and its owners.

The argument is that the appropriate concept of capital to be maintained is capital of the company (i.e., an "entity view") rather than of the shareholders (a "proprietary view"). The company is considered to have a more limited set of options from which to choose the forms in which to invest its capital than the shareholders. There is an element of truth in this statement, but the CRVA case rests on a much narrower view than this one, namely, that the firm is *irretrievably* tied to its present forms of capital investment and income should be measured as though the firm *must* replace its assets with like assets, i.e., it has no other options. In other words, the rise in the value of the firm's assets cannot be counted as an increase in wealth because those assets cannot be exchanged for or converted into any other form available in the market place. There is no increase in the firm's purchasing power because the price index of the only assets the firm is permitted to purchase is identical to the price index of the assets the firm already has.

The argument rests on this rigid constraint of options, and the CRVA approach is valid for such cases. For example, if a firm bought a piece of real estate and the government then decreed that if it is ever sold, the proceeds can only be used for its repurchase, the appropriate price level index for determining if any increases in value of the property are real increases is the price of the property itself. But in such a situation, the CRVA approach is a very special (and strange) case of the current income approach; there are, and can be, no realizable real holding gains.

Consider another example. Two families buy two identical homes in different but equally convenient locations for the same price. There are many such homes in both locations. Over the next decade the value of Family A's home triples because, say, employment opportunities outstrip land in Family A's living area, while the value of Family B's home stays the same (as does the general price level). If both families are *prohibited* from ever selling, one could argue that Family A is no better off in real terms than Family B because the options open to both families are the same, namely, nil. (More properly, the market values cannot, in this case, give us any guidance on this question.) If the constraint is removed, however, the argument loses its validity, whether either actually sells or not. If Family A chooses not to sell, it is because the subjective value of the house exceeds its (tripled) market value. Family A has the option (whether exercised or not does not matter) of selling its house and buying three houses in Family B's neighborhood (which may be just as suitable to Family A in terms of its commuting needs, and so forth, as its own house). Family A then clearly has options that are not open to Family B—for example, renting two houses or selling two and using the proceeds for other purposes. On what ground can it be argued that Family A is not three times as wealthy as Family B?

The real issue is not an entity versus a proprietary view of capital but rather the array of options open to management. In general, firms are not seriously constrained in their opportunities and can modify, in directions that are most promising, the scale and the composition of their activities as time passes. Viewed in this more realistic way, replacement of present assets with like assets is only one option among many and merits no preferential treatment.

Consider, for example, the following case.[12] On December 31, 19X0, the Acme Taxi Company purchased 20 new taxis at $5,000 apiece, expecting each to generate net cash inflows of $3,500 and $3,000, respectively, during a two-year service life, at the end of which time each taxi will be worthless. Taxi prices are not expected to change during the next two years (one-year-old taxis are presently priced at $2,500). Thus, if Acme's expectations are correct, the taxis will generate a 20 per cent rate of return over cost over their service lives and the firm's assets at the end of the first year (before any distributions to owners) will consist of $70,000 cash (20 taxis having generated net cash inflows of $3,500 apiece) and 20 taxis worth $50,000 (20 used taxis valued at $2,500 apiece).

Suppose, however, that events do not unfold exactly as Acme anticipated. In particular, suppose that prices of taxis, new and one-year-old, increase on January 1, 19X1, to $6,000 and $3,000, respectively, for reasons external to the taxi business (i.e., expected net cash inflows from operating the cars as taxis remain unchanged). CRVA advocates would argue that Acme's income for 19X1 would be $10,000, the difference between $70,000 net cash inflows from operations and current cost depreciation of $60,000 (depreciation is equal to the decline in price of 20 taxis from $6,000 to $3,000). Assuming that projected cash flows for 19X2 remain unchanged at $3,000 per taxi, it would

12. Our example is adapted from Philip W. Bell and L. Todd Johnson, "Current Value Accounting and the Simple Production Case: Edbejo and Other Companies in the Taxi Business," in Robert R. Sterling and Arthur L. Thomas (Eds.), *Accounting for a Simplified Firm* (Houston: Scholars Book Co., 1979).

be apparent that continuation in the taxi business could not be justified as the rate of return for 19X2 would be zero. Thus, Acme might well decide to sell its 20 used taxis for the going market price of $3,000 each and distribute all cash to its stockholders. If Acme did this, however, it would pay its stockholders $130,000 ($70,000 from 19X1's operations and $60,000 from sale of used taxis), $30,000 more than the stockholders had invested originally. But since the only income reported to date was $10,000, as there have been no new contributions by shareholders, one must ask where Acme got the extra $20,000 to distribute to its owners.

At least some CRVA advocates say, "Oh, well, if you liquidate, we will count any holding gain that is realized by sale as part of income, of course." But let us suppose two alternative cases where Acme does *not* liquidate. Under one assumption, taxi prices rise in period 1 as above, but replacement is undertaken because projections for period 2 suggest that the cash flow from a used taxi will be $3,600 rather than $3,000 (and $4,200 rather than $3,500) for a new taxi. To maintain its physical capital, Acme can sell its 20 used cabs for $60,000 and use $60,000 of its $70,000 period 1 cash flows to buy 20 new cabs for $120,000. It then pays out all that CRVA advocates argue it earned as income in period 1, i.e., its "distributable income" of $10,000, as dividends. Alternatively, it can spend the $60,000 of its period 1 earnings available after dividends to buy 20 used taxis, thereby having a fleet of 40 used taxis, which economically is equivalent to 20 new taxis. (With 20 new cabs Acme would earn $84,000 in period 2, could reinvest $60,000 of this in 20 used cabs and pay out $24,000 in dividends, and then earn $144,000 cash in period 3; with 40 used cabs Acme would earn $144,000 in period 2, could reinvest $120,000 of this in 40 more used cabs and pay out the same $24,000 in dividends, and then again earn $144,000 cash in period 3.) Let us assume that Acme chooses the latter option and starts period 2 with 40 used taxis. "Income" and "Dividends" under the CRVA approach and under our Current Income approach can be compared as follows:

	CRVA		Current Income	
	19X1	19X2	19X1	19X2
Cash flows or Earnings	$70,000	$144,000	$70,000	$144,000
Current Cost Depreciation	60,000	120,000	60,000	120,000
Current Operating Income			$10,000	$ 24,000
(=CRVA Income)	$10,000	$ 24,000		
Realizable Holding Gains			20,000	0
Current Income			$30,000	$ 24,000
less Net Current Contributions				
(Withdrawals)			20,000	(120,000)
equals Dividends	$10,000	$144,000	$10,000	$144,000

Under our second assumption, replacement is undertaken because projections of cash flows for period 2 rise slightly (to $3,272.73 per used taxi rather than the $3,600 posited above) and then on the first day of period 2 the prices of new and used taxis suddenly drop back to their original level of $5,000 and $2,500, respectively. Again, $10,000 of "distributable income" is paid out at the end of period 1 and $60,000 is now reinvested in used taxis *after* the price drop (only then is it profitable to do so), hence, *24* used taxis can be purchased. We can compare the CRVA and Current Income approaches under this second assumption about events as follows:

	CRVA		Current Income	
	19X1	19X2	19X1	19X2
Cash flows or Earnings	$70,000	$144,000	$70,000	$144,000
Current Cost Depreciation	60,000	110,000	60,000	110,000
Current Operating Income			$10,000	$ 34,000
(=CRVA Income)	$10,000	$ 34,000		
Realizable Holding Gains			20,000	(10,000)
Current Income			$30,000	$ 24,000
less Net Current Contributions				
(Withdrawals)			20,000	(120,000)
equals Dividends	$10,000	$144,000	$10,000	$144,000

Having more taxis and a slightly increased cash flow per taxi leads to a higher reported income figure in period 2 with the CRVA approach whereas clearly, from the dividends row, shareholders are equally well off under either assumption. Our Current Income data correctly report the identity of the two situations. *Whatever* the price of taxis at the beginning of period 3, the firm and its shareholders are in absolutely identical positions under the two assumptions to face decisions looking ahead to period 3 and beyond. And again, thinking back to Chapter 11, the Subjective Goodwill that the firm and its shareholders wish to maximize and turn into market value is the present value of cash inflows (the top line of the table) less cash outlfows (the initial investment plus the $60,000 reinvestment). *Or* it is the present value of the Dividends row minus the initial $100,000 outlay, where "Dividends" are Current Income less Net Current Contributions (new investment plus Realizable Holding Gains less Current Cost Depreciation). *Or*, as a third alternative, it is the present value of the Excess Current Income stream. In all three approaches, Subjective Goodwill (G_o) for both alternatives turns out to be $28,099.

Cash flows:
$$G_o = -\$100,000 + \frac{\$70,000}{1.1} - \frac{\$60,000}{1.1} + \frac{\$144,000}{1.21}$$
$$= \underline{\$28,099}$$

Current Income
less Net Current G_o = $-\$100,000 + \dfrac{\$10,000}{1.1} + \dfrac{\$144,000}{1.21}$
Contributions =
Dividends:
= $\underline{\$28,099}$

Excess Current
Income: $G_o = \dfrac{\$20,000}{1.1} + \dfrac{\$12,000}{1.21}$
= $\underline{\$28,099}$

Subjective Goodwill relates to Current Income (which includes holding gains) and to Excess Current Income, *not* just to Current Operating Income. Our firm gains equally in the above illustration from (a) higher asset prices and substantially improved cash flows, and (b) no change in the reinvestment price of assets, hence, a larger physical quantity of assets, and only slightly improved cash flows. CRVA advocates argue that a firm is "better off" if the physical volume of their assets increase but not if the value of a fixed physical volume of their assets increases. Although cash flows per taxi increased by more in the first case than in the second, since the physical volume of assets increased in the second, CRVA income is higher in that case. In fact, as we have shown, the two situations have identical outcomes. Our illustration, we feel, proves the point of Professor Baxter's argument:

> Surely the right criterion of asset expansion is that the outlay
> is expected to improve the cash flow. Dearer units are just
> as likely as more units to do this (unless the firm is queerly
> placed). Both types of outlay are investment in extra resources,
> and so bring expansion in the economic sense.[13]

Because the "replacement cost income" concept does not include realizable holding gains, the income statement with this approach, like traditional accounting income based on historical costs and the realization convention, fails each of the four tests we have established if measured and reported income is to be useful in the making of decisions and evaluation of performance by insiders and outsiders. It, too, is only a partial adjustment. It does not classify change into its basic two components but gives us only one. It does not tell us all of the income events that occurred in the period but only part of them—those dealing with operations. It, thus, cannot be used appropriately to compare events of two periods, for the missing element may have occurred in one period but not another. Our first concept of current income,

---

13. William T. Baxter, *op. cit.*, p. 120.

on the other hand, meets the first two of our tests set forth at the outset of Chapter 11—it appropriately classifies changes that have occurred and reports *all* the events of a period and *only* the events of that period. It thus remedies defects 1 and 2 of traditional accounting income set forth earlier in this chapter (pp. 613–14). But because it takes no account of changes in the general price level in the economy (defect 3 of traditional accounting income), it does not adequately meet our third test (comparability among firms) nor certainly our fourth test (comparability over time). To this matter, and why the Sandilands Committee strongly opposes taking this last step of giving up the money convention, we must now turn.

Giving Up the Realization and Money Conventions but Retaining the Going Concern Convention

Current Real Income and Its Critics

In Chapter 11 we argued that data on current income on the income statement and current values on the position statement had to be adjusted for general price level changes in the economy:

> 1. to compensate for the changing value of our unit of measurement, the dollar, over time so that meaningful comparisons of performance and of position statement values can be made over time for a given firm and among firms, i.e., so the fourth test for accounting data to be useful may be met;
> 2. to show the real gains of shareholders in a given firm for any given period as opposed to their nominal dollar gains—real gains will normally be somewhat less than nominal dollar gains if there has been a rise in the general price level;
> 3. to make meaningful real comparisons of owner gains among firms in a given period—two firms, for example, may report the same current income, but for one this may consist entirely of current operating income while for the other it may consist heavily of cost savings or holding gains so that current real income may differ for the two firms for that period although their current incomes are identical.

A very different position on adjustments for general price level changes is taken by current replacement value accounting adherents. The Sandilands Committee is representative of this viewpoint:

In our opinion Current Cost Accounting is a fully comprehensive method of accounting for inflation, and we do not
consider any useful purpose would be served by combining
it with the current purchasing power method.[14]

In this view once current operating income has been determined, no
more need be done to determine current income *or* current real income.

The rationale for this position stems from the assumption that the
firm must continually replace its assets with more of the same and
in the same mix as before. Thus, the firm may not alter its line of
business or go out of business. As such, the firm and its stockholders
are thought not to benefit (or lose) because of any differential between
the changes in prices of the firm's assets and the changes in price
of goods and services *in general;* the firm is prohibited from buying
goods and services *in general.* In these circumstances there can be no
real gains—all nominal increases in asset values are fictional. Hence,
adjusting for price level changes in order to identify real realizable
gains is a meaningless exercise; we know in advance that there can
be none. Income comparisons among firms are limited to current
operating incomes and these are already stated in comparable terms
for the *same* period.

Even in this interpretation a price level adjustment should, however,
be required to restate in dollars of the same vintage the COI's of
different periods for the same firm so that one can judge their relative
magnitudes. The appropriate index for this adjustment for changes
in the purchasing power of the dollar would be—for CRVA advocates—
an index specific to the firm's own basket of assets. Sandilands regards
even this adjustment as having little practical effect. It is certainly true
that if each firm uses its own index to deflate current operating income
of different periods, the income which is revealed for different firms
cannot be directly compared.

In reality, of course, most firms are neither rigidly constrained to
continue in the same line of business nor limited to the purchase of
the same types of assets. Firms can and often do alter the focus of
their endeavors. What is more, firms can and do liquidate. Thus, when
not constrained as to options available, firms may gain or lose relative
to others when the prices of their assets change at a rate different
from prices in general.

When this wider (and more realistic) view is taken of the firm's options,
the index of purchasing power must be widened accordingly to reflect

14. Sandilands, *op. cit.,* p. 4.

the choices open to the firm. It will now be highly unlikely that percentage changes in the value of the firm's assets will match precisely percentage changes in the purchasing power index. Real holding gains and losses will need to be measured and considered in comparing the relative success and standing of business firms and the real increase in the wealth of owners. And once real holding gains have been identified and current real income determined for each period, comparisons over time will require a further adjustment to dollars whose common value reflects the broader index.

The fundamental issue in all of this is the appropriate breadth of an index of general purchasing power. Two considerations weigh heavily in deliberations on the matter. First, if firms use different indices, comparisons among firms may be made more difficult; certainly comparisons of how incomes have changed over time for different firms would, as noted above, be virtually impossible. Hence, we conclude that all firms should employ the *same* index in adjusting for changes in general purchasing power.

Second, one of the options open to all firms is to pay dividends, whether out of income or capital, to owners. What the owners regard to be an appropriate index of *their* purchasing power is, therefore, an essential factor in the decisions of any conscientious management. Indeed, the ultimate purpose of all production is consumption. Hence, as we suggested in Chapter 11, we would favor the use of a *broad* index of purchasing power, in particular, either the Consumer Price Index or the GNP deflator for consumption goods, as an appropriate index of purchasing power to be used by all business entities in measuring real holding gains and reporting the results of their activities for a given period and over time. Only then can real gains of owners (presumably the maximization of which comprises the end-objective of all firm activity) be appropriately compared for a single period (where the current income components differ in that period) and for a single firm and among different firms over time.

GIVING UP ALL THREE CONVENTIONS: EXIT VALUE ACCOUNTING AND REALIZABLE INCOME

In developing our plan for the firm in Chapter 11, the subjective value which a firm's managers attach to the assets the firm purchases and owns proved to be a significant variable in the firm's initial choice among investment alternatives and in general in the firm's maximizing decisions over the life of the plan. The difference between this subjective value the firm attached to its assets (which in Chapter 11 we termed V_O, V_1, and so on, but which we will now term SV) and the assets' market value (there termed C_0 or M_0) is "subjective goodwill." It is subjective goodwill that the firm tries to maximize, turning this subjective goodwill—what the firm believes it can earn by "outguessing the market"—into increases in market value over the life of the plan. The projected increases in market value attached to the firm's assets over the life of the plan, over and above normal interest that owners could derive from investing their funds in risk-free securities, is the excess current income stream; and it turns out that the present value initially of this excess current income stream exactly equals the initial subjective goodwill—that which the firm is trying to maximize. Current income and excess current income become key elements in the evaluation process in determining whether or not the firm is in fact turning the subjective goodwill *it* envisages into appropriate market values as the plan unfolds.

In Chapter 11, and up to now in Chapter 13, the "market value" of the firm's assets at any point in time has been assumed to be a single, unique value. We have assumed that the current entry (purchase or produced cost) price of an asset is identical to its current exit price (that which could be derived from its immediate sale in the event of liquidation). This might be true if the following conditions hold: (1) there exist a large number of identical assets in each of various age and use categories, assets which are traded on one market so that market prices are known for both new and used assets; (2) the firm has nondiscriminatory access to both the selling and buying sides of that market; (3) there are no transportation or installation costs involved in either the purchase or the sale of the particular asset involved. These conditions, of course, normally do not hold in practice. In the case of plant assets there are usually transportation and installation costs, and used-asset markets may be imperfect. For such assets, current *entry* (purchase) cost, including all transportation and installation charges and any profit accruing to the seller (call this CC for current cost) will normally exceed current *exit* value (net proceeds that could be derived from the immediate "crash" sale of the asset—call this net realizable value to the firm RV). In the case of inventory assets, RV might normally (but would not necessarily) exceed CC often because, as in trading operations, a firm's customers cannot buy directly from the firm's suppliers.

Where they diverge one from another, should we use CC or RV in measuring the market value of a firm's assets and liabilities, and the change in CC or RV over a period in measuring current income? Uncertainty and disagreement on this matter have produced a major schism among current value accounting adherents.

The issue is perhaps best put in perspective by considering the configuration of possible orderings of SV, CC, and RV values a firm may be faced with. We have six possibilities as follows:

(1)	(2)	(3)		(4)	(5)	(6)
SV	CC	CC		SV	RV	RV
$>$	$>$	$>$		$>$	$>$	$>$
CC	SV	RV		RV	SV	CC
$>$	$>$	$>$		$>$	$>$	$>$
RV	RV	SV		CC	CC	SV

The three possible configurations on the left might normally be associated with a firm's plant assets, while the three on the right might normally be associated with its inventory assets.

In considering these three possible valuation choices and these six possible configurations, we have already shown (in Chapter 11) that SV, in either its *ex ante* or *ex post* sense, while often potentially useful in plan projections, cannot be made to be useful in *evaluating* the plan as events unfold. It inevitably involves *subjective* elements—what the managers of the firm *think* their assets are worth, based on anticipations of future revenues less expenses other than depreciation. Actual events in the market place must be used to evaluate the plan.[15]

As between the other two choices, CC and RV, which *are* market value concepts, while treating them as being interchangeable up to now we have couched our approach essentially in entry value clothing. In terms of our three fundamental accounting conventions, we have suggested that our current real income measure involves giving up the realization convention in its *holding dimension only* (retaining it in its production/sale dimension, i.e., not recognizing revenue until inventory items are sold); giving up the money convention; but retaining the going concern convention (albeit not in the extreme form implied by the replacement cost income concept—using entry values implies

15. While subjective estimates of future cash flows *may* be useful in the planning exercise, and do prove to be useful given our assumptions in Chapter 11, in fact, projections of future excess current incomes (the present value of which also equals subjective goodwill, like $V_0 - C_0$ in Chapter 11) or of future current incomes less new current commitments (the present value of which again equals subjective goodwill) are, we believe, a preferred way of expressing plan objectives. The latter will *always* prove to be appropriate, whereas cash flows are appropriate only when asset lives coincide with the plan period *and* no holding gains are projected—assumptions which have allowed us to use the discounted cash flow approach here, an approach which is almost universally employed in the existing literature. Under these assumptions the two approaches come to the same thing. Use of projected current income and/or excess current income rather than cash flows in planning, further, ties planned objectives directly with the evaluation process. See Edgar O. Edwards, "The Primacy of Accounting Income in Expansion: An Exercise in Arithmetic," in Cees van Dam (Ed.), *Trends in Managerial and Financial Accounting* (Leiden: Martinus Nijhoff, 1978), pp. 45–62.

that the firm must continue in order to transform entry values into exit values, but it does not necessarily imply that the firm must continue to do in the future precisely what it is doing now, as implied by the replacement cost income concept).

In contrast to an entry value approach, an exit value approach involves *giving up all three conventions completely*, including the realization convention in both its dimensions. Assets are valued at what may be considered their immediate objective external *opportunity cost*, i.e., the cash given up by not selling them. The income concept advocated by exit value proponents—what we shall term realizable income—is then the difference between a firm's cash equivalents at the beginning of the period and its cash equivalents at the end of the period. While some exit value adherents argue that the cash equivalents used in this measure should be the cash that could be generated, net, by an orderly liquidation over some limited time period, it would seem that that approach would inevitably involve subjective estimates about the future. If we are to keep within the realm of strictly objective market values, we must use the cash (or cash equivalents) that could be obtained immediately in a liquidation "fire sale" today.[16]

Let us consider an exit-value version of accounting for our Chapter 11 problem in its simplest form and compare this with an entry-value approach. Exit-value proponents differ somewhat in their handling of income statements, if indeed they believe an income statement should be published at all. To the best of our knowledge, Sterling has never indicated what, if any, income statement he would evolve for either a production or a trading enterprise. He centers on the comparative position statement in exit-value terms, i.e., simply the change in cash equivalents as between beginning- and end-of-period. Chambers, on the other hand, has recently been fashioning an income statement in some of his work, subtracting, in the case of fixed assets, the exit

16. The two principal advocates of exit value accounting are Raymond J. Chambers, *Accounting, Evaluation and Economic Behavior* (Englewood Cliffs, N.J.: Prentice-Hall, 1966), and his many other writings on the subject; and Robert R. Sterling, *Theory of the Measurement of Enterprise Income* (Laurance, Kansas: University Press of Kansas, 1970), and his many other writings on the subject. Chambers tends to lean toward "orderly liquidation" and argue for short-run maximization of changes in "cash equivalents" period-by-period, believing that such behavior will inevitably maximize the long-run gain in "cash equivalents," calling his framework "Continuously Contemporary Accounting" (CoCoA). Sterling, on the other hand, argues, we believe correctly, that if exit values are to be used in income measurement in accounting, "cash equivalents" are the cash that could be derived from an immediate liquidation sale and that it is the long-run increase in cash equivalents, over the life of the plan, that must be maximized. For a criticism of Chambers on this issue, see Philip W. Bell and L. Todd Johnson, "Current Value Accounting and the Simple Production Case: Edbejo and Other Companies in the Taxi Business," in Robert R. Sterling and Arthur L. Thomas (Eds.), *op. cit.*, especially Appendix A and footnote 15.

TABLE 13-1

Exit-Value Income Statement—Chambers Version

	0	Period 1			Period 2		
		Expected	*Actual*	*Variance*	*Originally Expected*	*Expected at end of Period 1*	*Variance*
1. Earnings		$7,000	$7,000	$ 0	$6,000	$6,000	$ 0
2. Depreciation		5,250	4,585	(665)	4,750	5,415	665
3. Net Income		$1,750	$2,415	$665	$1,250	$ 585	($665)
4. End-of-Period Asset Value	$10,000	$4,750	$5,415	$665	$ 0	$ 0	$ 0
5. Rate of Return (3 ÷ 4, end of previous period)		17.5%	24.2%		26.3%	10.8%	

TABLE 13-2
Exit-Value Income Statement—Friedman Version

	0	1			2		
		Expected	Actual	Variance	Originally Expected	Expected at end of Period 1	Variance
1. Earnings		$7,000	$7,000	$ 0	$6,000	$6,000	$ 0
2. Current Cost (Entry Value) Depreciation		5,000	5,700	700	5,000	5,700	700
3. Net Operating Income*		$2,000	$1,300	($ 700)	$1,000	$ 300	($700)
4. Holding Gains on Fixed Assets (Entry Value)**		0	1,400	1,400	0	0	0
5. Gain on Opportunity Cost		250	215	(35)	250	285	35
6. Acquisition Gain (Loss)		(500)	(500)	0	0	0	0
7. Net Income		$1,750	$2,415	$ 665	$1,250	$ 585	($665)
8. End-of-Period Asset Value†	$10,000	$4,750	$5,415	$ 570	0	0	0
9. Rate of Return							
(3 + 8, end of previous period)		20.0%	13.0%		21.1%	5.5%	
(7 + 8, end of previous period)		17.5%	24.2%		26.3%	10.8%	

*(= Current Operating Income)
**(= Realizable Cost Savings or Holding Gains)
†(Acquisition Cost or Exit Value)

value of an asset at the end of the period (1) from the purchase cost
in the period the asset was acquired or (2) from the asset's exit value
at the end of the previous period in subsequent periods, and calling
the result "depreciation," which is then subtracted from revenues less
other expenses to arrive at "net income."[17] In a recent article Laurence
Friedman has attempted to separate Chambers' polyglot "net income"
figure into relevant component parts by using entry values as a primary
measure and then grafting onto that framework separate adjustments
to change these entry-value figures to exit values and so provide an
income statement consistent with that of Chambers and consistent with
an exit-value comparative position statement.[18]

Consider once again a firm purchasing a two-period-life asset at the
end of period 0 for $10,000 expected to produce revenues less expenses
other than depreciation of $7,000 in period 1 and $6,000 in period
2. Exit value is a fixed 95 per cent of entry value on both new and
used assets. At the beginning of period 1, the purchase price of the
asset new jumps by 14 per cent, to $11,400 (and the exit price new
jumps to $10,830). At the end of period 1, the entry (purchase) price
of a one-period-old asset is $5,700, its exit price $5,415, whereas these
values were initially expected to be $5,000 and $4,750, respectively.
Table 13-1, using Chambers' exit-value income statement, shows the
results at the end of period 1.

The Friedman approach, on the other hand, using entry values and
then grafting onto these entry-value income calculations adjustments
to express the final "net income" figure in terms identical to Chambers,
may be seen in Table 13-2. (Friedman actually applies his approach
only to a trading enterprise; we adapt it, we believe accurately, to

17. See Raymond J. Chambers, "Accounting for Inflation. Exposure Draft" (Sydney:
The University of Sydney, 1975) and "The Taxi Company under CoCoA," in Robert
R. Sterling and Arthur L. Thomas (Eds.), *op. cit.*

18. See Laurence A. Friedman, "An Exit-Price Income Statement," *The Accounting
Review* LIII (January 1978), pp. 18–30. Like so many other writers, Friedman (p. 24)
quite wrongly argues that Edwards and Bell favored normal depreciation methods and
allocating not historical but current costs. But Edwards and Bell argued that there should
be resort to *internal rate depreciation* (not traditional methods) *only when viable used-asset
markets do not exist.* Throughout Chapters 2 and 3 on the theoretical base for the system,
used-asset market values were clearly assumed to exist. When they came to the problem
of practical application in Chapter 6, they had to recognize that in many cases viable
used-asset markets might not exist. See pp. 175–180 and particularly p. 179 ["It is
market values, then, that measure the value of resources used in the firm and it is
the relationships among them that reveal the depreciation pattern to be applied to
either the historic cost or current cost base. The estimation of such a pattern may
require recourse to various approximations *in the absence of second-hand markets*" (italics
ours)] and p. 284 ["We do not feel, however, that objectivity is a major point at issue
in our proposal. Current costs are in most instances as objectively verifiable as are
historic costs. And in instances in which current costs *must* be estimated on the basis
of index numbers . . ." (italics ours)].

show how it would apply to a production enterprise.) Friedman subtracts the decline in the asset's value on purchase as it moves from entry to exit value as an "acquisition loss" (the entry value of our asset is $10,000, the exit value $9,500). He then transforms all exit values on the position statement *temporarily* into entry values by debiting the appropriate asset account and crediting a "gain on opportunity cost" account (i.e., he moves the fixed asset value *back* to $10,000 at time of purchase). At the end of the period, *after* computing "net operating income" (which equals our current operating income) and "holding gains on fixed assets" (which equals our realizable cost savings or holding gains), both measured in entry value terms, he transforms all entry values *back* to exit values by debiting the "gain on opportunity cost" account and crediting the appropriate asset account by the difference in entry and exit value of the asset at the end of the period (i.e., by $5,700 − $5,415 = $285 at the end of period 1 in the example). The net credit of $215 in the "gain in opportunity cost" account plus the net debit of $500 in the "acquisition gain (loss)" account can then be added to the credits in the "net operating income" plus "holding gains on fixed assets" [which together equal our (entry value) current income] accounts. The residual then yields an exit-value "net income" which is consistent with Chambers' figure and with the change in exit values of assets minus liabilities on the comparative position statement.

The Friedman exercise in formulating an exit-value income statement is essential, he feels, as we certainly do, if meaningful exit value data are to be provided management and interested outsiders for evaluative purposes. The Chambers income statement, intertwining true long-run income from operations (bearing significantly on replacement decisions and whether or not to continue in the firm's present line of activity) with holding gains (in entry and/or exit value terms) and with changes in the method of valuation (from entry to exit value at time of acquisition)—rolling these three quite different phenomena into one simple "net income" figure (equal to the change in "cash equivalents")—is inevitably misleading. The Chambers approach will *always* signal to the managers of the firm and to interested outsiders that the firm is doing better than expected in its chosen activity when exit values rise unexpectedly, *ceteris paribus* (as in our illustration), for the Chambers polyglot depreciation figure will then inevitably be smaller than expected. As clearly depicted in the entry-value approach, however, and in Friedman's version of the exit-value approach which employs entry values, our firm is doing *worse* than expected in its chosen activity and perhaps should be casting about for new uses for its fixed asset, for a completely new line of activity, or possibly for liquidation, distributing to owners the firm's net assets.

The entry-exit-value controversy in current value accounting can be resolved (or, if not resolved, at least understood better), we believe, by casting our current value difficulties in terms of "deprival value"—a valuation concept developed in 1937 by Bonbright, revived in 1965 by David Solomons, and endorsed by many others since then.[19] If present (subjective) value (SV) (of expected future earnings) exceeds current (purchase) cost, current cost (CC) should be used for valuation. This presumably would be the most usual case. There is positive subjective goodwill in use and, if "deprived" of the asset, you could replace it at current cost and earn that subjective goodwill. This is not to suggest that if *actually* deprived of the asset you would necessarily replace it with an identical asset. You might, or you might not. Hence, the term "replacement costs" can be misleading if it connotes the idea of *necessary* replacement.

The use of current (purchase) cost to value assets under these circumstances—assets which you hold at the end of a period—presumes that you are going to *continue to use* these assets (that is why you hold them) in accordance with the going concern convention. This, we feel, should be the normal presumption. If, on the other hand, present (subjective) value falls below current (purchase) cost, the "value to the business" (VB) of the asset is no longer current cost. "Value to the business" becomes what it is worth by use [present (subjective) value] versus what it is worth by sale [net realizable value (RV)], and you would choose the higher of the two. Since the former depends upon subjective anticipation about the future, presumably an independent appraisal (perhaps using present value methodology) would be necessary; but this measure would then be objective so far as the firm were concerned.

An asset's "value to the business" (VB), then, can be viewed in either of two ways. It can be thought of as the amount the firm would be willing to pay to recover an asset if (hypothetically) "deprived" of it, which in no case would be more than the firm has to pay to repurchase it, i.e., CC, and would be less than this, the higher of SV and RV, if both these values are less than CC. Alternatively, since "hypothetical deprival" might appear to be a rather artificial concept to some, we can, as Edward Stamp suggests, think of an asset's "value to the business"

19. See J. C. Bonbright, *The Valuation of Property* (New York: McGraw-Hill, 1937); David Solomons, "Economic and Accounting Concepts of Cost and Value," in M. Backer (Ed.), *Modern Accounting Theory* (Englewood Cliffs, N.J.: Prentice-Hall, 1966); R. H. Parker and G. C. Harcourt (Eds.), *Readings in the Concept and Measurement of Income* (Cambridge: Cambridge University Press, 1969), esp. pp. 17–19; Sandilands, *op. cit.*, p. 58; and Philip W. Bell and L. Todd Johnson, in Robert R. Sterling and Arthur L. Thomas (Eds.), *op. cit.*

as *"the least costly sacrifice avoided by owning the asset,"* the sacrifice
(opportunity cost) being the cash that would have to be given up to
acquire the higher of SV or RV, either directly or through purchase
of the asset if CC were less than this higher value so as to achieve
SV or RV indirectly.[20] The two alternative ways of viewing "deprival
value" or "value to the business" come to the same thing.

"Value to the business" of an asset, then, in terms of the six possible
valuation orderings considered earlier in this section, would be as follows:

(1)	(2)	(3)	(4)	(5)	(6)
SV	CC	CC	SV	RV	RV
$>$	$>$	$>$	$>$	$>$	$>$
$CC(=VB)$	$SV(=VB)$	$RV(=VB)$	RV	SV	$CC(=VB)$
$>$	$>$	$>$	$>$	$>$	$>$
RV	RV	SV	$CC(=VB)$	$CC(=VB)$	SV

An entrepreneur acting rationally would replace the asset, perhaps
when it is worn out, and use it to generate SV in cases (1) and (4).
He would immediately sell it (and immediately buy as many more as
he could get and resell them) in cases (5) and (6). He would not replace
it when worn out but would continue to use it until the end of its
life (assuming his alternative rate of return is given by the discount
rate—in our case, interest on risk-free securities) in case (2). And he
would immediately *sell* it, whatever its remaining life, in case (3) (and
not buy any more like assets).

Our "deprival value" configuration of asset value possibilities leads
us to a comprehensive set of "decision rules" which managers, owners,
and other interested outsiders might adopt in evaluating past decisions
and using these evaluations to draw up new plans involving new decisions.
Inevitably these "decision rules," in part involving evaluation of decisions
previously undertaken, suggest the accounting data necessary for the
exercise.

Let us assume that our firm has, as its next-best available alternative
at the end of period 1, the earning of risk-free interest at 10 per
cent. (We might well assume that its next-best available option was
earning 15 per cent on funds invested—its "target rate of interest"
for undertakings of equal risk to that currently embarked on, the
additional 5 per cent over risk-free interest being the reward for the
risk involved.) Two different rates of return are involved, one for
entry-value formulations, and one for exit-value formulations, viz.:

20. See Edward Stamp, "Financial Reports on an Entity: Ex Uno Plures," in Robert
R. Sterling and Arthur L. Thomas (Eds.), *op. cit.*

$$\rho = \frac{\text{Current Operating Income}}{\text{Current Entry Value}},$$

(on current entry value basis)

$$\rho' = \frac{\text{Net Income}}{\text{Current Exit Value}}.$$

(on current exit value basis)

We assume that any holding gains due to changes in prices of assets held by the firm involved unexpected windfalls in period 1 and that no further such windfalls are expected in period 2. Any actual holding gains or losses in period 1 which were expected should be added to the numerator of ρ in evaluating the actual rate of return in that period and comparing it with the initial planned rate of return; the objective was then holding gains as well as operating income.

Clearly the actual events of period 1 and new expectations about events in period 2 depicted in the Friedman exit-value table (Table 13-2) (which provides us with needed entry-value data) suggests that our firm is in deprival value situation (2). Our rate of return ρ is considerably less than anticipated in period 1 and is expected to fall below the risk-free interest rate of 10 per cent in period 2. We are tipped off by our entry-value measures of period 1 that we are in trouble. A reassessment, then, of an overall two-year rate of return on this type of asset, at a current market purchase price (new) of $11,400 and existing earnings that can be derived from use of the asset (at least as we are presently employing it) of $7,000 and $6,000, indicates that $\rho < 10$ percent, the risk-free market rate of interest.[21] Our ρ' value is considerably higher than expected in period 1. If we used only exit values and an exit-value rate of return (expected and actual), as Chambers might, the accounting data for period 1 would suggest absolutely no cause for concern. We did better than expected. While using ρ' alone, then, can be highly misleading, this measure is useful to use *with* ρ once the latter tells us we are in trouble and should be considering new alternatives. For if $\rho' > 10$ percent (our best rate of return on an alternative investment), we should continue to *use* the asset rather than sell it (ρ' represents the return from *not liquidating*, i.e., earnings from using the asset relative to its current "cash equivalent" or exit value, while the 10 percent represents the return as a result of liquidating and investing the proceeds in the

21. Solving for ρ in $-\$11,400 + \dfrac{7,000}{1 + \rho} + \dfrac{6,000}{(1 + \rho)^2}$ indicates that $\rho = 9.48\%$.

only alternative available—risk-free securities).

Given our alternative investment rate of return of 10 per cent, then, our analysis using ρ and ρ' yields the following decision rules which can be stated in terms of traffic signals as follows:[22]

(1) $\rho > 0.10 = $ *Green Light.* (Reinvestment in our asset is still profitable.)

(2) $\rho \leq 0.10$ but $\rho' > 0.10 = $ *Yellow Light.* (Reinvestment in our asset is no longer profitable, but use of our existing asset is preferable to its liquidation; consideration should be given, however, to alternative means of using the asset more effectively.)

(3) $\rho' \leq 0.10 = $ *Red Light.* (Neither reinvestment in our asset nor continued use is preferable to liquidation.)

More generally, if ρ_B is our next-best investment alternative, while ρ_A and ρ'_A are the entry- and exit-value rates of return on our existing investment, we have:

(1)$'$ $\rho_A > \rho_B$ *Replace*

and if $\rho_A < \rho_B$ and

(2)$'$ $\rho'_A > \rho_B$ *Use But Do Not Replace*

(3)$'$ $\rho'_A < \rho_B$ *Liquidate*

The trouble with this simple set of decision rules is that two different rates of return are involved, only one rate of return (ρ) being consistent with the initial rate of return that might be posited as an expected rate at the time of the acquisition of the existing asset. This same ρ is the only rate of return which is relevant to use with respect to a new, alternative investment when comparing it with our existing investment, for you have to purchase the new asset, i.e., entry value is inevitably involved). If, however, we use a common numerator in our two rates of return—(a) Friedman's "Net Operating Income" (equals entry value Current Operating Income) or (b) either total Current Income (entry value basis) or Realizable Income (exit value basis), the two usually not being very different one from another—multiply both sides of (2)$'$ and (3)$'$ by RV_A, and multiply and divide the left-hand side of each by CC_A, we have:

(1)$''$ $\rho_A > \rho_B$ *Replace*

and if $\rho_A < \rho_B$ and

(2)$''$ $\rho_A \times CC_A > \rho_B \times RV_A$ *Use But Do Not Replace*

---

22. See Bell and Johnson in Sterling and Thomas (Eds.), *op. cit.,* where these rules were first set forth, drawing on Edwards and Bell as cited therein.

$$(3)'' \; \rho_A \times CC_A < \rho_B \times RV_A \qquad \textit{Liquidate}$$

Entry values and entry-value rates of return are always important in evaluating decisions and in formulating new decisions. Replacement decisions cannot be made without them. Exit values become significant only if and when liquidation becomes an issue. It may always be an issue; clearly liquidation is one alternative a firm should always consider. But we suggest that this latter way of taking exit values into account [using (1)″, (2)″, and (3)″] is preferable to the former means of doing this [using (1)′, (2)′, and (3)′], although, as we have shown, they come to the same thing.[23] Because of the desirability of comparing actual rates of return as the asset is employed with expected rates of return formulated at time of acquisition, *in comparable terms*, we believe that *entry values* should be continuously employed in the primary records of the firm, with *exit values* employed in supplementary records so that the possibilities of asset liquidations can be continuously evaluated. Entry values are needed to evaluate what the firm set out to do and actually did do in the period under consideration; exit values are needed to evaluate an alternative that the firm might choose in preference to what it is currently doing.

CONCLUSIONS

We have argued in this chapter that among the various alternative concepts of income presently being proposed by one school of thought or another it is the current real income concept, properly divided into current operating income and realizable real holding gains—the concept using primarily entry values along lines developed in Chapters 11 and 12—that best serves the needs of interested insiders and outsiders. These are the people who must evaluate the decisions of management and measure the performance of a business firm, often comparing the performance of that firm with the performance during the same period of other firms or with performance of the firm in question or other firms at different times in the past.

Let us compare entity income (and its components), ownership income, and return on invested capital as these would be reported using (1) simple historical cost accounting; (2) historical cost/constant dollar accounting; (3) replacement cost accounting; (4) current income (uncorrected for changes in the value of the dollar); and (5) current real income as detailed in Chapter 12.

---

23. One of the authors is especially indebted to talks with one of his former students, Catherine Harrison (now Reed), who recognized the identity of the two sets of decision rules before he did and helped him to see the issue more clearly.

If one looked only at the last column of Table 13-3, detailing the rates of return to the owners of the Leavenworth Corporation on their invested capital given the price changes assumed in the text for 19X8, one might think that there is little difference between the two primary options to traditional historical cost accounting, viz., alternatives 2 and 5. More to the point, *under these price assumptions,* not only are the rates of return for alternatives 2 and 5 approximately the same, but neither alters the basic picture given by traditional historical cost accounting *unadjusted* for price changes (alternative 1).

First, we must stress that the fact of roughly equal rates of return of ownership income on invested capital for the Leavenworth Corporation under the three alternative approaches, 1, 2, and 5, stems from two factors—(1) the particular set of price changes assumed in the problem and (2) the equality at the beginning of the period between historical and current costs because Leavenworth's history began at that time. If we had chosen changes in specific prices that deviated more from changes in the general price level, we would have come up with much more divergent overall results. Moreover, as Leavenworth's activities extend into the future, the difference between historical and current costs will widen even if price changes continued at the same rates. But the important point is what the rest of the table shows *in spite of* the overall similarity in rates of return as given by approaches 1, 2, and 5. In particular, the *component parts* of entity and ownership income differ one from another in the five approaches, which in turn helps to explain why the rates of return under approaches 3 and 4 differ so markedly from the rates of return under approaches 1, 2, and 5.

The key difference in the table is the reporting of current operating income as an independent element in approaches 3, 4, and 5, but not in approaches 1 and 2. The rate of return on ongoing operations, based on using an income figure which subtracts current costs from current revenues, is less than half the rate of return that would be reported using "income from operations" as measured under traditional historical cost accounting *or* price-level-adjusted historical cost accounting (even in this starting-up period with quite normal price changes occurring, all in the same direction). Let us assume that Leavenworth initially projected a rate of return from operations of, say, 20 per cent in 19X8 and beyond. That rate of return turned out to be only 7.4 per cent in 19X8. If the risk-free rate of interest is 10 per cent, Leavenworth should not now plan to replace its assets *unless* it can expect future real holding gains to be large enough to compensate for any squeeze on current operating income, so that total current real income represents a rate of return on capital in excess of 10 per

TABLE 13-3*

	Entity Income			Less	Equals		
	Reported as Operating Income	Reported as Holding Gains	Total	Interest Charges and Loss (Gain) on Bonds Payable	Total Ownership Income	Invested Capital at Beginning of Period Per End-of-Period Comparative Position Statement	Ownership Income as Percentage of Invested Capital
1. Historical Cost Income (Accounting Income)	$68,000	-0-	$ 68,000	$ 8,000	$60,000	$350,000	17.1%
2. Historical Cost Real Income	63,159	$(5,571)	57,588	(1,619)	59,207	385,000	15.4
3. Replacement Cost Income	33,775	-0-	33,775	8,000	25,775	350,000	7.4
4. Current Income	33,775	80,275	114,050	15,020	99,030	350,000	28.3
5. Current Real Income	35,383	34,048	69,431	5,401	64,030	385,000	16.6

*Data in respective rows are from: row 1, Tables 12-2 and 12-3; row 2, Tables 12-A-1 and 12-A-2; rows 3 and 4, Tables 12-5 and 12-6; row 5, Tables 12-7 and 12-8.

cent. In other words, the very important element of "holding gains" or "cost savings," separately shown in approaches 4 and 5, is significant in decision evaluation and in the making of new decisions just as is current operating income. The shareholder should be told of the existence of these holding gains or cost savings. Under the replacement cost income approach, he is not told of their existence, at least on the income statement. In approaches 1 and 2, he is told only of gains which were realized in 19X8 through use and sale, regardless of when these gains were earned.

Even without consideration of the interest, and gains or losses, on bonds payable, the treatment of which can be seen to differ markedly under the five approaches, only approaches 4 and 5 provide the two crucial components of "income" we deem essential for both management and interested outsider decision-making and evaluation purposes. Which to choose? Clearly, at least to us, approach 4 *overstates* the real gain to shareholders just as approach 3 *understates* it. Approach 5 seems to us to provide the most meaningful picture of events of the present and immediate past—events which must be weighed against expectations of the past in making new decisions about the future.

Regardless of where the reader ends up in terms of his or her preference among approaches, Table 13-3 makes one thing clear. If such different results are obtained for a very simple starting-up case with such reasonable assumptions about price changes as those imposed on the Leavenworth Corporation, one can hardly remain neutral among approaches on the grounds that "it does not matter." Clearly the issues facing the accounting profession on how to deal with the changing prices in the economy—changes in both specific prices and the general price level—are important issues, and not ones that can continue to be swept under the rug.

DISCUSSION QUESTIONS

1. In order to sort out the various alternative income concepts discussed in Chapter 13, fill in Table 13-4 with a + (plus) indicating the convention is adhered to by the income concept on that line, a − (minus) indicating the convention is not adhered to by the income concept on that line, or a 0 (zero) indicating that the convention is neither specifically adhered to nor specifically given up, i.e., it is, in effect, ignored.

2. The following is taken from "Note 23—Replacement Cost Information (Unaudited)," pp. 41–42 of the 1976 *Annual Report* of the Gulf Oil Corporation:

TABLE 13-4

	Realization Convention in its			Going
	Production / Sale Dimension	Holding Dimension*	Money Convention	Concern Convention
Traditional Accounting Income (historical costs)				
Accounting Real Income (price-level-adjusted historical costs)				
Realized Income				
Realized Real Income				
Replacement Cost Income				
Current Income				
Current Real Income				
Realizable (Exit Value) Real Income (Continuously Contemporary Accounting)				

*Note: If holding gains are recognized in some way before realization through sale of the asset being valued, thus affecting the reporting of operating income but not total income, put $+/-$. If holding gains are recognized in some way before realization through sale of the asset being valued, thus affecting the reporting of operating income, but are *not included* in total income either as they are realized through use or as they become realizable, put $-/-$.

While the calculations assume a one-time replacement actual replacement will occur over future periods when decisions concerning replacement will be made in light of the economic, regulatory and competitive conditions at that time, and most probably will differ substantially from the assumptions on which the data included herein are based.

In addition, the replacement cost data required by the SEC does not consider several factors, the absence of which makes the information incomplete. No consideration is given to the effects which would result in times of inflation from holding gains experienced by a borrower and holding losses resulting from the possession of monetary assets, such as cash, receivables, etc. Further, no recognition is given to operating efficiencies, such as a reduction in the labor force, or for the substantial investment tax credit which would result from the replacement of total productive capacity.

a. The authors of this text feel that the most serious error the SEC made in introducing *mandatory current value information* into the published financial reports of almost all major American corporations in 1976 was to term such data "replacement costs." Inevitably this term, and use of the data, is interpreted as having to do with "replacement" of existing assets, now or in the future, as the concept and its use have obviously been interpreted by Gulf Oil executives. The Gulf Oil report seems to suggest that general *price-level effects on net monetary assets and perhaps long-term liabilities* should be taken account of in inflationary times *in addition to the effects of specific price changes on a company's replacement needs with respect to inventories and plant assets.* How exactly does this interpretation, and this approach, differ from that espoused by the authors in Chapters 11 and 13?

b. Some businessmen, emphasizing the need for replacement of assets which are rising in price, have suggested that the replacement cost income concept does not go far enough in taking account of the effects of inflation on the business firm and of the firm's replacement needs stemming into the future, that adhering to the replacement cost income concept does not fully provide for replacement when the time comes to replace.

    (1) Do you think that the Gulf Oil statement is suggesting this?
    (2) Do you think that it is suggesting a need for "backlog depreciation"?
    (3) What does this mean, and what would it imply?
    (4) Does the taking of "backlog depreciation" just ensure retaining within the firm sufficient earnings to replace assets as they wear out, or does this depend often on whether the firm is growing, declining, or remaining in a steady state? Explain.
    (5) Does "backlog depreciation" in any way ensure having the liquidity needed, at the time it may be needed, to replace existing assets?
    (6) Is replacement of existing assets, now or in the future, an appropriate guideline which should be used in the determination of a firm's income? What are the arguments for and against on this issue?

3. All through the 1960s and to some extent into the 1970s, most practicing accountants and many academic accountants argued that *if* one is to adjust accounts for the effects of inflation, one has a choice between two options: adjusting asset (and perhaps liability) values for *specific price changes* occurring with respect to these assets (and perhaps liabilities); *or* adjusting asset and liability historical cost values for changes in the *general price level.* Most practicing accountants, and their professional bodies here and in England, given what they conceived as a choice between two alternatives, tended to choose the latter option principally because they felt it could be accomplished with greater "objectivity," using either the well-established Consumer Price Index or the general GNP deflator.

a. Discuss the relative virtues and drawbacks of the two approaches, one yielding current income and one price-level-adjusted historical cost income.

b. *Can* the two approaches be considered in any way *alternatives?* Will they necessarily yield corrections in accounts which are at least in the same direction, if not in the same magnitude? Why do the authors of this text insist that correcting for specific price changes and for the change in the general price level are *complements* rather than *substitutes?* What do you think?

c. Would the choice of a price index to be used to make a correction in accounts for changes in the general price level, say, between the general GNP deflator (which has been favored by the AICPA), on the one hand, and the Consumer Price Index (which has been favored by its British counterpart, the Institute of Chartered Accountants), on the other, depend to some extent on whether you interpreted adjustment for specific price changes and for the general price level as substitutes or complements? Explain.

4. A survey by the "Big Eight" accounting firm Arthur Young and Company of current cost information on inventories and plant assets as provided in 1976 *Annual Reports* of some 175 major companies suggests that raising cost of goods sold from a historical (FIFO or LIFO) base to a current cost base would have raised the value of cost of goods sold by only one or two per cent on the average. Suppose cost of sales or cost of goods sold for a company were equal to seventy per cent of the value of sales and net income were equal to five per cent of the value of sales (as the report points out this was the average for the *Fortune* 500 largest industrial corporations in 1976). By what percentage and in what direction would reported net income be changed as a result of adjusting cost of goods sold from historical to current costs? Does the adjustment have a significant or insignificant effect on reported *current operating income* in your judgment? How would this adjustment have to be amended to compare (total) current income with what the corporation reported in accordance with traditional accounting practices?

5. The same Arthur Young and Company study cited in Question 4 suggested that raising historical cost depreciation expenses to a current cost basis would have increased reported depreciation expenses in 1976 by 67 per cent on the average. If depreciation expense reported on the basis of historical costs were 15 per cent of the value of sales on the average for our company whose reported net income was 5 per cent of the value of sales, what would the current cost adjustment do to the reported net income figure, i.e., current operating income in accordance with the amended deprecia-

tion expense figure? Can you say much about a comparison between total current income and the reported historical cost net income figure? Are holding gains included in either of these latter two measures, and, if so, what kind of holding gains? Will it solve (perhaps help solve?) our problem of comparing total current income with reported historical cost net income data when we have 1977 current cost data to go with 1976 current cost data? Explain.

6. Of the six possible sets of relative values for PV, RC, and NRV, three sets might ordinarily apply to *use-assets*—e.g., plant and equipment of a manufacturer—and three to final-goods inventories—e.g., for a wholesale or resale trader. Which three might ordinarily apply to each type of case? Why? Explain.

APPENDIX

INTEREST AND ANNUITY TABLES

TABLE A1

Compound Interest: the Future Value of $1 with Continuous Reinvestment at interest i to Period n

$$a_{\overline{n}|i} = (1 + i)^n$$

n	1/4%	1/2%	3/4%	1%	2%	3%	4%	5%	6%	7%	8%	10%	12%	15%	20%	25%
1	1.00250	1.00500	1.00750	1.01000	1.02000	1.03000	1.04000	1.05000	1.06000	1.07000	1.08000	1.10000	1.12000	1.15000	1.20000	1.25000
2	1.00501	1.01002	1.01506	1.02010	1.04040	1.06090	1.08160	1.10250	1.12360	1.14490	1.16640	1.21000	1.25440	1.32250	1.44000	1.56250
3	1.00752	1.01508	1.02267	1.03030	1.06121	1.09273	1.12486	1.15762	1.19102	1.22504	1.25971	1.33100	1.40493	1.52087	1.72800	1.95313
4	1.01004	1.02015	1.03034	1.04060	1.08243	1.12551	1.16986	1.21551	1.26248	1.31080	1.36049	1.46410	1.57352	1.74901	2.07360	2.4141
5	1.01256	1.02525	1.03807	1.05101	1.10408	1.15927	1.21665	1.27628	1.33823	1.40255	1.46933	1.61051	1.76234	2.01136	2.48832	3.05176
6	1.01509	1.03038	1.04585	1.06152	1.12616	1.19405	1.26532	1.34010	1.41852	1.50073	1.58687	1.77156	1.97382	2.31306	2.98598	3.81470
7	1.01763	1.03553	1.05370	1.07214	1.14869	1.22987	1.31593	1.40710	1.50363	1.60578	1.71382	1.94872	2.21068	2.66002	3.58318	4.76837
8	1.02018	1.04071	1.06160	1.08286	1.17166	1.26677	1.36857	1.47746	1.59385	1.71819	1.85093	2.14359	2.47596	3.05902	4.29982	5.96046
9	1.02273	1.04591	1.06956	1.09369	1.19509	1.30477	1.42331	1.55133	1.68948	1.83846	1.99900	2.35795	2.77308	3.51788	5.15978	7.45058
10	1.02528	1.05114	1.07758	1.10462	1.21899	1.34392	1.48024	1.62889	1.79085	1.96715	2.15892	2.59374	3.10585	4.04556	6.19174	9.31323
11	1.02785	1.05640	1.08566	1.11567	1.24337	1.38423	1.53945	1.71034	1.89830	2.10485	2.33164	2.85312	3.47855	4.65239	7.43008	11.6415
12	1.03042	1.06168	1.09381	1.12683	1.26824	1.42576	1.60103	1.79586	2.01220	2.25219	2.51817	3.13843	3.89598	5.35025	8.91610	14.5519
13	1.03299	1.06699	1.10201	1.13809	1.29361	1.46853	1.66507	1.88565	2.13293	2.40985	2.71962	3.45227	4.36349	6.15279	10.6993	18.1899
14	1.03557	1.07232	1.11028	1.14947	1.31948	1.51259	1.73168	1.97993	2.26090	2.57853	2.93719	3.79750	4.88711	7.07571	12.8392	22.7374
15	1.03816	1.07768	1.11860	1.16097	1.34587	1.55797	1.80094	2.07893	2.39656	2.75903	3.17217	4.17725	5.47357	8.13706	15.4070	28.4217

16	1.04076	1.08307	1.12699	1.17258	1.37279	1.60471	1.87298	2.18287	2.54035	2.95216	3.42594	4.59497	6.13039	9.35762	18.4884	35.5271
17	1.04336	1.08849	1.13544	1.18430	1.40024	1.65285	1.94790	2.29202	2.69277	3.15882	3.70002	5.05447	6.86604	10.7613	22.1861	44.4089
18	1.04597	1.09393	1.14396	1.19615	1.42825	1.70243	2.02582	2.40662	2.85434	3.37993	3.99602	5.55992	7.68997	12.3755	26.6233	55.5112
19	1.04858	1.09940	1.15254	1.20811	1.45681	1.75351	2.10685	2.52695	3.02560	3.61653	4.31570	6.11591	8.61276	14.2318	31.9480	69.3889
20	1.05121	1.10490	1.16118	1.22019	1.48595	1.80611	2.19112	2.65330	3.20714	3.86968	4.66096	6.72750	9.64629	16.3665	38.3376	86.7362
22	1.05647	1.11597	1.17867	1.24472	1.54598	1.91610	2.36992	2.92526	3.60354	4.43040	5.43654	8.14027	12.1003	21.6447	55.2061	135.525
24	1.06176	1.12716	1.19641	1.26973	1.60844	2.03279	2.56330	3.22510	4.04893	5.07237	6.34118	9.84973	15.1786	28.6252	79.4968	211.758
26	1.06707	1.13846	1.21443	1.29526	1.67342	2.15659	2.77247	3.55567	4.54938	5.80735	7.39635	11.9182	19.0401	37.8568	114.475	330.872
28	1.07241	1.14987	1.23271	1.32129	1.74102	2.28793	2.99870	3.92013	5.11169	6.64884	8.62711	14.4210	23.8839	50.0656	164.845	516.988
30	1.07778	1.16140	1.25127	1.34785	1.81136	2.42726	3.24340	4.32194	5.74349	7.61226	10.0627	17.4494	29.9599	66.2118	237.376	807.794
32	1.08318	1.17304	1.27011	1.37494	1.88454	2.57508	3.50806	4.76494	6.45339	8.71321	11.7371	21.1138	37.5817	87.5651	341.822	1262.18
34	1.08860	1.18480	1.28923	1.40258	1.96068	2.73191	3.79432	5.25335	7.25103	9.97811	13.6901	25.5477	47.1425	115.805	492.224	1972.15
36	1.09405	1.19668	1.30865	1.43077	2.03989	2.89828	4.10393	5.79182	8.14725	11.4239	15.9682	30.9127	59.1356	153.152	708.802	3081.49
38	1.09953	1.20868	1.32835	1.45953	2.12230	3.07478	4.43881	6.38548	9.15425	13.0793	18.6253	37.4043	74.1797	202.543	1020.67	4814.82
40	1.10503	1.22079	1.34835	1.48886	2.20804	3.26204	4.80102	7.03999	10.2857	14.9745	21.7245	45.2593	93.0510	267.864	1469.77	7523.16
42	1.11057	1.23303	1.36865	1.51879	2.29724	3.46070	5.19278	7.76159	11.5570	17.1143	25.3395	54.7637	116.723	354.250	2116.47	11754.9
44	1.11612	1.24539	1.38926	1.54932	2.39005	3.67145	5.61652	8.55715	12.9855	19.6285	29.5560	66.2641	146.418	468.495	3047.72	18367.1
46	1.12171	1.25788	1.41017	1.58046	2.48661	3.89504	6.07482	9.43426	14.5905	22.4726	34.4741	80.1795	183.666	619.585	4388.71	28698.6
48	1.12733	1.27049	1.43141	1.61223	2.58707	4.13225	6.57053	10.4013	16.3939	25.7289	40.2106	97.0172	230.391	819.401	6319.75	44841.6
50	1.13297	1.28323	1.45296	1.64463	2.69159	4.38391	7.10668	11.4674	18.4202	29.4570	46.9016	117.391	289.002	1083.66	9100.44	70064.9

TABLE A2

The Present Value of a Single Receipt of $1 in Period n with Interest Rate i

$$p_{\overline{n}|i} = \frac{1}{(1+i)^n}$$

n	1/4%	1/2%	3/4%	1%	2%	3%	4%	5%	6%	7%	8%	10%	12%	15%	20%	25%
1	0.99751	0.99502	0.99256	0.99010	0.98039	0.97087	0.96154	0.95238	0.94340	0.93458	0.92593	0.90909	0.89286	0.86957	0.83333	0.80000
2	0.99502	0.99007	0.98517	0.98030	0.96117	0.94260	0.92456	0.90703	0.89000	0.87344	0.85734	0.82645	0.79719	0.75614	0.69444	0.64000
3	0.99254	0.98515	0.97783	0.97059	0.94232	0.91514	0.88900	0.86384	0.83962	0.81630	0.79383	0.75131	0.71178	0.65752	0.57870	0.51200
4	0.99006	0.98025	0.97055	0.96098	0.92385	0.88849	0.85480	0.82270	0.79209	0.76290	0.73503	0.68301	0.63552	0.57175	0.48225	0.40960
5	0.98759	0.97537	0.96333	0.95147	0.90573	0.86261	0.82193	0.78353	0.74726	0.71299	0.68058	0.62092	0.56743	0.49718	0.40188	0.32768
6	0.98513	0.97052	0.95616	0.94205	0.88797	0.83748	0.79031	0.74622	0.70496	0.66634	0.63017	0.56447	0.50663	0.43233	0.33490	0.26214
7	0.98267	0.96569	0.94904	0.93272	0.87056	0.81309	0.75992	0.71068	0.66506	0.62275	0.58349	0.51316	0.45235	0.37594	0.27908	0.20972
8	0.98022	0.96089	0.94198	0.92348	0.85349	0.78941	0.73069	0.67684	0.62741	0.58201	0.54027	0.46651	0.40388	0.32690	0.23257	0.16777
9	0.97778	0.95610	0.93496	0.91434	0.83676	0.76642	0.70259	0.64461	0.59190	0.54393	0.50025	0.42410	0.36061	0.28426	0.19381	0.13422
10	0.97534	0.95135	0.92800	0.90529	0.82035	0.74409	0.67556	0.61391	0.55839	0.50835	0.46319	0.38554	0.32197	0.24718	0.16151	0.10737
11	0.97291	0.94661	0.92109	0.89632	0.80426	0.72242	0.64958	0.58468	0.52679	0.47509	0.42888	0.35049	0.28748	0.21494	0.13459	0.08590
12	0.97048	0.94191	0.91424	0.88745	0.78849	0.70138	0.62460	0.55684	0.49697	0.44401	0.39711	0.31863	0.25668	0.18691	0.11216	0.06872
13	0.96806	0.93722	0.90743	0.87866	0.77303	0.68095	0.60057	0.53032	0.46884	0.41496	0.36770	0.28966	0.22917	0.16253	0.09346	0.05498
14	0.96565	0.93256	0.90068	0.86996	0.75788	0.66112	0.57748	0.50507	0.44230	0.38782	0.34046	0.26333	0.20462	0.14133	0.07789	0.04398
15	0.96324	0.92792	0.89397	0.86135	0.74301	0.64186	0.55526	0.48102	0.41727	0.36245	0.31524	0.23939	0.18270	0.12289	0.06491	0.03518

n																
16	0.02815	0.05409	0.10686	0.16312	0.21763	0.29189	0.33873	0.39965	0.45811	0.53391	0.62317	0.72845	0.85282	0.88732	0.92330	0.96084
17	0.02252	0.04507	0.09293	0.14564	0.19784	0.27027	0.31657	0.37136	0.43630	0.51337	0.60502	0.71416	0.84438	0.88071	0.91871	0.95844
18	0.01801	0.03756	0.08081	0.13004	0.17986	0.25025	0.29586	0.35034	0.41552	0.49363	0.58739	0.70016	0.83602	0.87416	0.91414	0.95605
19	0.01441	0.03130	0.07027	0.11611	0.16351	0.23171	0.27651	0.33051	0.39573	0.47464	0.57029	0.68643	0.82774	0.86765	0.90959	0.95367
20	0.01153	0.02608	0.06110	0.10367	0.14864	0.21455	0.25842	0.31180	0.37689	0.45639	0.55368	0.67297	0.81954	0.86119	0.90506	0.95129
22	0.00738	0.01811	0.04620	0.08264	0.12285	0.18394	0.22571	0.27751	0.34185	0.42196	0.52189	0.64684	0.80340	0.84842	0.89608	0.94655
24	0.00472	0.01258	0.03493	0.06588	0.10153	0.15770	0.19715	0.24698	0.31007	0.39012	0.49193	0.62172	0.78757	0.83583	0.88719	0.94184
26	0.00302	0.00874	0.02642	0.05252	0.08391	0.13520	0.17220	0.21981	0.28124	0.36069	0.46369	0.59758	0.77205	0.82343	0.87838	0.93714
28	0.00193	0.00607	0.01997	0.04187	0.06934	0.11591	0.15040	0.19563	0.25509	0.33348	0.43708	0.57437	0.75684	0.81122	0.86966	0.93248
30	0.00124	0.00421	0.01510	0.03338	0.05731	0.09938	0.13137	0.17411	0.23138	0.30832	0.41199	0.55207	0.74192	0.79919	0.86103	0.92783
32	0.00079	0.00293	0.01142	0.02661	0.04736	0.08520	0.11474	0.15496	0.20987	0.28506	0.38834	0.53063	0.72730	0.78733	0.85248	0.92321
34	0.00051	0.00203	0.00864	0.02121	0.03914	0.07305	0.10022	0.13791	0.19035	0.26355	0.36604	0.51003	0.71297	0.77565	0.84402	0.91861
36	0.00032	0.00141	0.00653	0.01691	0.03235	0.06262	0.08754	0.12274	0.17266	0.24367	0.34503	0.49022	0.69892	0.76415	0.83564	0.91403
38	0.00021	0.00098	0.00494	0.01348	0.02673	0.05369	0.07646	0.10924	0.15661	0.22592	0.32523	0.47119	0.68515	0.75281	0.82735	0.90948
40	0.00013	0.00068	0.00373	0.01075	0.02209	0.04603	0.06678	0.09722	0.14205	0.20829	0.30656	0.45289	0.67165	0.74165	0.81914	0.90495
42	0.00009	0.00047	0.00282	0.00857	0.01826	0.03946	0.05833	0.08653	0.12884	0.19257	0.28896	0.43530	0.65842	0.73065	0.81101	0.90044
44	0.00005	0.00033	0.00213	0.00683	0.01509	0.03383	0.05095	0.07701	0.11686	0.17805	0.27237	0.41840	0.64545	0.71981	0.80296	0.89596
46	0.00003	0.00023	0.00161	0.00544	0.01247	0.02901	0.04450	0.06854	0.10600	0.16461	0.25674	0.40215	0.63273	0.70913	0.79499	0.89149
48	0.00002	0.00016	0.00122	0.00434	0.01031	0.02487	0.03887	0.06100	0.09614	0.15219	0.24200	0.38654	0.62026	0.69861	0.78710	0.88705
50	0.00001	0.00011	0.00092	0.00346	0.00852	0.02132	0.03395	0.05429	0.08720	0.14071	0.22811	0.37153	0.60804	0.68825	0.77929	0.88263

TABLE A3

The Future Value of an Annuity of $1 for n Periods with Interest Rate i

$$A_{\overline{n}|i} = \frac{(1+i)^n - 1}{i}$$

n	1/4%	1/2%	3/4%	1%	2%	3%	4%	5%	6%	7%	8%	10%	12%	15%	20%	25%
1	1.00000	1.00000	1.00000	1.00000	1.00000	1.00000	1.00000	1.00000	1.00000	1.00000	1.00000	1.00000	1.00000	1.00000	1.00000	1.00000
2	2.00250	2.00500	2.00750	2.01000	2.02000	2.03000	2.04000	2.05000	2.06000	2.07000	2.08000	2.10000	2.12000	2.15000	2.20000	2.25000
3	3.00751	3.01502	3.02256	3.03010	3.06040	3.09090	3.12160	3.15250	3.18360	3.21490	3.24640	3.31000	3.37440	3.47250	3.64000	3.81250
4	4.01503	4.03010	4.04523	4.06040	4.12161	4.18363	4.24646	4.31012	4.37462	4.43994	4.50611	4.64100	4.77933	4.99337	5.36800	5.76563
5	5.02506	5.05025	5.07556	5.10101	5.20404	5.30914	5.41632	5.52563	5.63709	5.75074	5.86660	6.10510	6.35285	6.74238	7.44160	8.20703
6	6.03763	6.07550	6.11363	6.15202	6.30812	6.46841	6.63298	6.80191	6.97532	7.15329	7.33593	7.71561	8.11519	8.75374	9.92992	11.2588
7	7.05272	7.10588	7.15948	7.21354	7.43428	7.66246	7.89829	8.14201	8.39384	8.65402	8.92280	9.48717	10.0890	11.0668	12.9159	15.0735
8	8.07035	8.14141	8.21318	8.28567	8.58297	8.89234	9.21423	9.54911	9.89747	10.2598	10.6366	11.4359	12.2997	13.7268	16.4991	19.8419
9	9.09053	9.18212	9.27478	9.36853	9.75463	10.1591	10.5828	11.0266	11.4913	11.9780	12.4876	13.5795	14.7757	16.7858	20.7989	25.8023
10	10.1133	10.2280	10.3443	10.4622	10.9497	11.4639	12.0061	12.5779	13.1808	13.8164	14.4866	15.9374	17.5487	20.3037	25.9587	33.2529
11	11.1385	11.2792	11.4219	11.5668	12.1687	12.8078	13.4864	14.2068	14.9716	15.7836	16.6455	18.5312	20.6546	24.3493	32.1504	42.5661
12	12.1664	12.3356	12.5076	12.6825	13.4121	14.1920	15.0258	15.9171	16.8699	17.8885	18.9771	21.3843	24.1331	29.0017	39.5805	54.2077
13	13.1968	13.3972	13.6014	13.8093	14.6803	15.6178	16.6268	17.7130	18.8821	20.1406	21.4953	24.5227	28.0291	34.3519	48.4966	68.7596
14	14.2298	14.4642	14.7034	14.9474	15.9739	17.0863	18.2919	19.5986	21.0151	22.5505	24.2149	27.9750	32.3926	40.5047	59.1959	86.9495
15	15.2654	15.5365	15.8137	16.0969	17.2934	18.5989	20.0236	21.5786	23.2760	25.1290	27.1521	31.7725	37.2797	47.5804	72.0351	109.687

n																
16	16.3035	16.6142	16.9323	17.2579	18.6393	20.1569	21.8245	23.6575	25.6725	27.8881	30.3243	35.9497	42.7533	55.7175	87.4421	138.109
17	17.3443	17.6973	18.0593	18.4304	20.0121	21.7616	23.6975	25.8404	28.2129	30.8402	33.7502	40.5447	48.8837	65.0751	105.931	173.636
18	18.3876	18.7858	19.1947	19.6147	21.4123	23.4144	25.6454	28.1324	30.9057	33.9990	37.4502	45.5992	55.7497	75.8364	128.117	218.045
19	19.4336	19.8797	20.3387	20.8109	22.8406	25.1169	27.6712	30.5390	33.7600	37.3790	41.4463	51.1591	63.4397	88.2118	154.740	273.556
20	20.4822	20.9791	21.4912	22.0190	24.2974	26.8704	29.7781	33.0660	36.7856	40.9955	45.7620	57.2250	72.0524	102.444	186.688	342.945
22	22.5872	23.1944	23.8223	24.4716	27.2990	30.5368	34.2480	38.5052	43.3923	49.0057	55.4568	71.4027	92.5026	137.632	271.031	538.101
24	24.7028	25.4320	26.1885	26.9735	30.4219	34.4265	39.0826	44.5020	50.8156	58.1767	66.7648	88.4973	118.155	184.168	392.484	843.033
26	26.8290	27.6919	28.5903	29.5256	33.6709	38.5530	44.3117	51.1135	59.1564	68.6765	79.9544	109.182	150.334	245.712	567.377	1319.49
28	28.9658	29.9745	31.0282	32.1291	37.0512	42.9309	49.9676	58.4026	68.5281	80.6977	95.3388	134.210	190.699	327.104	819.223	2063.95
30	31.1133	32.2800	33.5029	34.7849	40.5681	47.5754	56.0849	66.4388	79.0582	94.4608	113.283	164.494	241.333	434.745	1181.88	3227.17
32	33.2716	34.6086	36.0148	37.4941	44.2270	52.5028	62.7015	75.2988	90.8898	110.218	134.214	201.138	304.848	577.100	1704.11	5044.71
34	35.4406	36.9606	38.5646	40.2577	48.0338	57.7302	69.8579	85.0670	104.184	128.259	158.627	245.477	384.521	765.365	2456.12	7884.61
36	37.6206	39.3361	41.1527	43.0769	51.9994	63.2759	77.5983	95.8363	119.121	148.913	187.102	299.127	484.463	1014.35	3539.01	12322.0
38	39.8114	41.7354	43.7798	45.9527	56.1149	69.1594	85.9703	107.710	135.904	172.561	220.316	364.043	609.831	1343.62	5098.37	19255.3
40	42.0132	44.1588	46.4465	48.8864	60.4020	75.4013	95.0255	120.800	154.762	199.635	259.057	442.593	767.091	1779.09	7343.86	30088.7
42	44.2260	46.6065	49.1533	51.8790	64.8622	82.0232	104.820	135.232	175.951	230.632	304.244	537.637	964.359	2355.00	10577.4	47015.8
44	46.4499	49.0788	51.9909	54.9318	69.5027	89.0484	115.413	151.143	199.758	266.121	356.950	652.641	1211.81	3116.63	15233.6	73464.4
46	48.6850	51.5758	54.6898	58.0459	74.3306	96.5015	126.871	168.685	226.508	306.752	418.426	791.795	1522.22	4123.90	21938.6	114790
48	50.9312	54.0978	57.5207	61.2226	79.3535	104.408	139.263	188.025	256.565	353.270	490.132	960.172	1911.59	5456.00	31593.7	179362
50	53.1887	56.6452	60.3943	64.4632	84.5794	112.797	152.667	209.348	290.336	406.529	573.770	1163.91	2400.02	7217.72	45497.2	280256

TABLE A4

The Present Value of an Annuity of \$1 for n Periods with Interest Rate i

$$P_{\overline{n}|i} = \frac{1 - (1 + i)^{-n}}{i}$$

n	1/4%	1/2%	3/4%	1%	2%	3%	4%	5%	6%	7%	8%	10%	12%	15%	20%	25%
1	0.99751	0.99502	0.99256	0.99010	0.98039	0.97087	0.96154	0.95238	0.94340	0.93458	0.92593	0.90909	0.89286	0.86957	0.83333	0.80000
2	1.99252	1.98510	1.97772	1.97040	1.94156	1.91347	1.88609	1.85941	1.83339	1.80802	1.78326	1.73554	1.69005	1.62571	1.52778	1.44000
3	2.98506	2.97025	2.95556	2.94099	2.88388	2.82861	2.77509	2.72325	2.67301	2.62432	2.57710	2.48685	2.40183	2.28323	2.10646	1.95200
4	3.97512	3.95050	3.92611	3.90197	3.80773	3.71710	3.62990	3.54595	3.46511	3.38721	3.31213	3.16987	3.03735	2.85498	2.58873	2.36160
5	4.96272	4.92587	4.88944	4.85343	4.71346	4.57971	4.45182	4.32948	4.21236	4.10020	3.99271	3.79079	3.60478	3.35216	2.99061	2.68028
6	5.94785	5.89638	5.84560	5.79548	5.60143	5.41719	5.24214	5.07569	4.91732	4.76654	4.62288	4.35526	4.11141	3.78448	3.32551	2.95142
7	6.93052	6.86207	6.79464	6.72819	6.47199	6.23028	6.00205	5.78637	5.58238	5.38929	5.20637	4.86842	4.56376	4.16042	3.60459	3.16114
8	7.91074	7.82296	7.73661	7.65168	7.32548	7.01969	6.73274	6.46321	6.20979	5.97130	5.74664	5.33493	4.96764	4.48732	3.83716	3.32891
9	8.88852	8.77906	8.67158	8.56602	8.16224	7.78611	7.43533	7.10782	6.80169	6.51523	6.24689	5.75902	5.32825	4.77158	4.03097	3.46313
10	9.86386	9.73041	9.59958	9.47130	8.98259	8.53020	8.11090	7.72173	7.36009	7.02358	6.71008	6.14457	5.65022	5.01877	4.19247	3.57050
11	10.8368	10.6770	10.5207	10.3676	9.78685	9.25262	8.76048	8.30641	7.88687	7.49867	7.13896	6.49506	5.93770	5.23371	4.32706	3.65640
12	11.8073	11.6189	11.4349	11.2551	10.5753	9.95400	9.38507	8.86325	8.38384	7.94269	7.53608	6.81369	6.19437	5.42062	4.43922	3.72512
13	12.7753	12.5562	12.3423	12.1337	11.3484	10.6350	9.98565	9.39357	8.85268	8.35765	7.90378	7.10336	6.42355	5.58315	4.53268	3.78010
14	13.7410	13.4887	13.2430	13.0037	12.1062	11.2961	10.5631	9.89864	9.29498	8.74547	8.24424	7.36669	6.62817	5.72448	4.61057	3.82408
15	14.7042	14.4166	14.1370	13.8651	12.8493	11.9379	11.1184	10.3797	9.71225	9.10791	8.55948	7.60608	6.81086	5.84737	4.67547	3.85926

n →	16	17	18	19	20	22	24	26	28	30	32	34	36	38	40	42	44	46	48	50
	3.88741	3.90993	3.92794	3.94235	3.95388	3.97049	3.98111	3.98791	3.99226	3.99509	3.99683	3.99797	3.99870	3.99917	3.99947	3.99966	3.99978	3.99986	3.99991	3.99994
	4.72956	4.77463	4.81219	4.84350	4.86958	4.90943	4.93710	4.95632	4.96967	4.97894	4.98537	4.98984	4.99295	4.99510	4.99660	4.99764	4.99836	4.99886	4.99921	4.99945
	5.95423	6.04716	6.12797	6.19823	6.25933	6.35866	6.43377	6.49056	6.53351	6.56598	6.59053	6.60910	6.62314	6.63375	6.64178	6.64785	6.65244	6.65591	6.65853	6.66051
	6.97399	7.11963	7.24967	7.36578	7.46944	7.64465	7.78432	7.89566	7.98442	8.05518	8.11159	8.15656	8.19241	8.22099	8.24378	8.26194	8.27642	8.28796	8.29716	8.30450
	7.82371	8.02155	8.20141	8.36492	8.51356	8.77154	8.98474	9.16095	9.30657	9.42691	9.52638	9.60857	9.67651	9.73265	9.77905	9.81740	9.84909	9.87528	9.89693	9.91481
	8.85137	9.12164	9.37189	9.60360	9.81815	10.2007	10.5288	10.8100	11.0511	11.2578	11.4350	11.4569	11.7172	11.8289	11.9246	12.0067	12.0771	12.1374	12.1891	12.2335
	9.44665	9.76322	10.0591	10.3356	10.5940	11.0612	11.4693	11.8258	12.1371	12.4090	12.6466	12.8540	13.0352	13.1935	13.3317	13.4524	13.5579	13.6400	13.7305	13.8007
	10.1059	10.4773	10.8276	11.1581	11.4699	12.0416	12.5504	13.0032	13.4062	13.7648	14.0840	14.3681	14.6210	14.8460	15.0463	15.2245	15.3832	15.5244	15.6500	15.7619
	10.8378	11.2741	11.6896	12.0853	12.4622	13.1630	13.7986	14.3752	14.8981	15.3725	15.8027	16.1929	16.5469	16.8679	17.1591	17.4234	17.6628	17.8801	18.0772	18.2559
	11.6523	12.1657	12.6593	13.1339	13.5903	14.4511	15.2470	15.9828	16.6631	17.2920	17.8736	18.4112	18.9083	19.3679	19.7928	20.1856	20.5488	20.8847	21.1951	21.4822
	12.5611	13.1661	13.7535	14.3238	14.8775	15.9369	16.9355	17.8768	18.7641	19.6004	20.3888	21.1318	21.8323	22.4925	23.1148	23.7014	24.2543	24.7754	25.2667	25.7298
	13.5777	14.2919	14.9920	15.6785	16.3514	17.6580	18.9139	20.1210	21.2813	22.3965	23.4683	24.4986	25.4888	26.4406	27.3555	28.2348	29.0800	29.8923	30.6731	31.4236
	14.7179	15.5623	16.3983	17.2260	18.0456	19.6604	21.2434	22.7952	24.3164	25.8077	27.2696	28.7027	30.1075	31.4847	32.8347	34.1581	35.4555	36.7272	37.9740	39.1961
	15.0243	15.9050	16.7792	17.6468	18.5080	20.2112	21.8891	23.5422	25.1707	26.7751	28.3557	29.9128	31.4468	32.9581	34.4469	35.9137	37.3587	38.7823	40.1848	41.5664
	15.3399	16.2586	17.1728	18.0824	18.9874	20.7841	22.5629	24.3240	26.0677	27.7941	29.5033	31.1955	32.8710	34.5299	36.1722	37.7983	39.4082	41.0022	42.5803	44.1428
	15.6650	16.6235	17.5795	18.5332	19.4845	21.3800	23.2660	25.1426	27.0099	28.8679	30.7166	32.5561	34.3865	36.2077	38.0199	39.8230	41.6172	43.4024	45.1787	46.9462

INDEX

and "nearness-to-cash," 69–70
noncurrent, 70–72
realizable holding gains (or losses) on, 522–523
recorded as expenses, 123
plant, 70–71, 214–241
on position statement, 67–72
tangible/intangible, 69
types of, listed, 68
values of, 68–69
wasting, 71
Average cost method of valuation, 192–196

Bad debt problem, 125–127
Balance sheet, 29. *See also* Position statements
Balances, book, 593–595
"Basket" purchases, 217–218
Baxter, William, 625
Beneficiaries of accounting data, 22–25
Bonbright, J. C., 641
Bond contracts, 281
Bonds, 280–287
    book balances of, 563–565
    call price, 286–287, 329
    corporate, 280–281
    current cost adjustments on, 534–536
    at discount, 282–284
    gains and losses on, 287
    at par, 281–282
    premium, 284–285
    realizable holding gain on, 534–536
    realizable real holding gain on, 553–554
    refunding of, 286
    repayment of, 280–281, 286
    reserves for retirement of, 338–339
    retirement at maturity, 285
    retirement prior to maturity, 285–287
Book balances, 563–565
Book value
    compared with salvage value, 233–236
    of stocks in acquisitions, 431–433
Buildings
    current cost adjustments for, 528–532
    as plant assets, 216
    realizable holding gain on, 528–532
    realizable real holding gain on, 551
Business accounting, 10–18